Volume 4

A STUDY OF
THE LOGBARA (MA'DI) LANGUAGE

T0389275

A STUDY OF
THE LOGBARA (MA'DI) LANGUAGE
Grammar and Vocabulary

J. P. CRAZZOLARA

Routledge
Taylor & Francis Group

LONDON AND NEW YORK

First published in 1960 by Oxford University Press

This edition first published in 2018
by Routledge
2 Park Square, Milton Park, Abingdon, Oxon OX14 4RN

and by Routledge
711 Third Avenue, New York, NY 10017

Routledge is an imprint of the Taylor & Francis Group, an informa business

© 1960 International African Institute

British Library Cataloguing in Publication Data
A catalogue record for this book is available from the British Library

ISBN: 978-1-138-08975-4 (Set)
ISBN: 978-1-315-10381-5 (Set) (ebk)
ISBN: 978-1-138-09303-4 (Volume 4) (hbk)
ISBN: 978-1-138-09309-6 (Volume 4) (pbk)
ISBN: 978-1-315-10708-0 (Volume 4) (ebk)

Publisher's Note
The publisher has gone to great lengths to ensure the quality of this reprint but points out that some imperfections in the original copies may be apparent.

Disclaimer
The publisher has made every effort to trace copyright holders and would welcome correspondence from those they have been unable to trace.

A STUDY OF THE
LOGBARA (MA'DI)
LANGUAGE

Grammar and Vocabulary

BY

J. P. CRAZZOLARA, F.S.C.J.

(VERONA FATHERS)

Published for the

INTERNATIONAL AFRICAN INSTITUTE

by the

OXFORD UNIVERSITY PRESS

LONDON NEW YORK TORONTO

1960

Oxford University Press, Amen House, London E.C.4

GLASGOW NEW YORK TORONTO MELBOURNE WELLINGTON
BOMBAY CALCUTTA MADRAS KARACHI KUALA LUMPUR
CAPE TOWN IBADAN NAIROBI ACCRA

PRINTED IN GREAT BRITAIN

INTRODUCTION

In introducing this Grammar and Vocabulary a few preliminary notes on the linguistic and ethnological relationship between the Logbara and their nearer and remoter neighbours may be of some interest.

1. First of all then: The Logbara people live between, roughly, 2° 30′ N. 30° 30′ E. and 3° 30′ N. 31° 30′ E. extending from the west bank of the Nile, about 50 miles north of Lake Albert, inland and westwards across the political boundary into the Belgian Congo. They number about 250,000 to 280,000.

2. The Logbara language belongs to the Ma'di[1] group of languages, just as, say, Acooli belongs to the Lwoo[2] group. The name 'Logbara' was introduced into general use by the white colonizers, probably first by the Belgians. How this term originated cannot be definitely determined. There is in the Aringa area a tribal group called Lógbàrà as well as a clan group called Lògbáarà—quite small groups. The name may have come to the ears of some early traveller or government official in the area, who probably took it to comprise the whole tribe; the name has since remained as the collective name for this division. All Logbara agree, however, that they are of the Ma'di nation, that they are Mà'dí. They are called Ma'di by the Aluur of Okööro, their immediate neighbours, in Bunyoro and Buganda.

3. The Ma'di and Lwoo peoples: their age and relationship are pertinent matters. The Ma'di are entitled to lay claim to the title of 'ancestors' of at least a considerable section of the Lwoo. The dissociation of the two peoples takes us back to a period not much later than A.D. 1000 when, we must infer, the Lwoo partly, or possibly wholly, came into being, i.e. started their separate existence.[3] The Ma'di appear to be infinitely older than the Lwoo.

The important historic fact in this regard is that the large Ma'di nation, up to about A.D. 1000, were the occupants of the territories

---

[1] Or, to be more exact, Mà'dí.

[2] Lwoo is a branch of the Jii group of languages.

[3] The manner of this separation and the origin of the Lwoo has been touched upon in *The Lwoo*, Part III, published by the Missioni Africane, Verona, 1954.

on the east and west of the Nile, from about the Mongalla area
in the north to about Lake Albert in the south. The greater part
of the people, however, lived towards the north and west, while
in the vicinity of Lake Albert, if they reached it at all in those early
times, the Ma'di population was less dense. To the east of the Ma'di
lived, almost in their entirety, the even larger Laŋo nation. The
'Western Laŋo' occupied almost the whole of present-day Acooli
country, reaching the Nile only at about Wadelai (Wod-Lei) and
to the south as far as Lake Albert, and from that longitude on,
occupying present Aluur country also. But in this region the Laŋo
and Ma'di lived side by side, more or less intermixed, from very
early times. This was the state of things up to about A.D. 1000.

4. At that period, or not much later, the Mongalla region of the
Ma'di country experienced a forceful invasion by strong 'Eastern-
Laŋo' tribal groups. The first wave of invasion appears to have been
by the Pàdzùlú. These were later followed by the Lowi or Looi
(commonly nicknamed Kakoá), who fought the aboriginal Ma'di
and the previous Pàdzùlú invaders (the latter apparently even more
savagely) and occupied part of the country. Then a third wave
arrived, another Eastern-Laŋo division, nowadays known as the
Bari.[1] It was probably the Lowi who ravished the country the more
violently and before whom various Ma'di groups, mixed with fragments of Pàdzùlú, chose to retire in practically every direction to
remoter regions. We may conclude from various traditional sources
that the removal to new areas apparently did not take place all at
one time, but probably continued over the centuries. The whole
movement was, overall, a withdrawal to the nearer or farther periphery of former Ma'di-occupied territories as well as a considerable
extension of the periphery in various directions, in particular at
the expense largely of the 'Western-Laŋo'. The invaders—the
Eastern-Laŋo—thus came to form a large wedge-shaped enclave
in Ma'di-land, remaining almost completely surrounded by Ma'di
divisions, such as the Mörö, Àvòkàyá, Kàlìko, Lògò, Lógbàrà,
Mà'dí-Móyo, and Mà'dí-Opari (Nilotic Sudan). The Mìsá-
Mondǒ and Màkàràká appear as larger groups among the Lògò.

Thus it appears that the Ma'di have lived on the Nile from
immemorial times.

5. Now to come back to our Logbara in particular: the origin
of their present-day existence as a distinct, separate, and independent people, goes back to that time of invasion, shifting, and migra-

---

[1] This was not their original name.

tion. It is important to appreciate the fact that the routes by which they came to their present country followed no single pattern. The Logbara of today, as a whole, came from three different main directions:

(*a*) It would seem, though there is no real evidence to support it, that a first and large group came from, broadly speaking, the region of Yei via modern Aba, roughly along the present Belgian Congo border, and entered the West Nile district of Uganda, penetrating in an easterly direction for about 10 miles. These were the 'South-eastern Ma'di' group of the West-Ma'di.

(*b*) Large groups of Ma'di, coming from the north to the east or west of the Nile, had left to invade Western-Laŋo territories, or modern Acooli-land. One gets the impression that the refugee Ma'di who reached the area of the upper Onyama and Ayugi plateau (modern Patiko) were so numerous that they themselves considered the territory too narrow to contain them all comfortably. Hence various groups at different times set out in a westerly direction towards the Nile. One such group, a large one (from modern Acooli-land, so the people themselves insist), probably the first in this region, reached the Nile, crossed it at about Rhino Camp, and moved inland for a distance of 30 to 40 miles to 'Bɛ́ Étí[1] in the region of Tɛrɛgo. By separating and spreading from here (Tɛrɛgo) the greater part of modern Logbara country was occupied as far south as Ófákà, Lɔ́gîrr, and the Belgian Congo as far as Aŋal. These belonged to the Eastern-Ma'di group.

(*c*) A third group came from the north, passed Lomule (Nimule) and, south of Rhino Camp, crossed the Nile to the west and occupied the mainly flat land of Olepi, Okɔlɔ, and, most probably, a considerable part of present-day Aluur-land, extending even into Bunyoro. These were the Mà'dí-Ñdrí or, as they are called in Aluur—the Ma'di-Dyel (lit. 'Goat-Ma'di') and, in Bunyoro—the Abatembuzi (supported by the Nyoro 'aristocracy'). These were the southern section of the Eastern-Ma'di.

6. What are nowadays called the Logbara were thus, on arrival in their present country, a motley collection of groups fleeing from different parts of the country and having different social and political affiliations—refugees in search of a new home. They were far from being 'one' nation and, apparently, never felt themselves to be a united people: they hardly do so even now. The two last

---

[1] Arabic *Jebel Woti*.

mentioned (those who came to Tɛrɛgo and Olepi) were possibly two separate tribes, and to some extent, even now, feel themselves to be (and with reason, it would appear) each a distinct tribal unit. The remaining Logbara (those from the Yei region) probably represent quite a number of fragments—disparate groups, coming only roughly from one direction (the north-west) but as distinct, detached groups fleeing towards the unknown, in search of a new home: in the end they met by chance in what is now Logbara country.

The main tribal groups of present-day Logbara country are: in the north (West-Nile, Uganda)—the Ramogi, O'dupi, Odravo, Ariŋga, A'upi, Omugo, Rigbɔ (these are Lowi), Ulivu, Iyi'ba, Iyiidu; in the centre—the Tɛrɛgo, Maratsa, Ofɔdɛ, Mundru, Olovo, Kidzɔmɔrɔ, Ewadri, Ɔrɛdzini, Ɔtsɔdri, Ɔrɛɛkɔ, Ɔleevo, Aivu, Oluko, Adziia, Aripi, Pàdzùlú, Mitsu, Adömi, Vura, Otsɔkɔ, Arivu; in the south—the Ma'di-Ndri, Ofaka, Lɔgirr; in the Belgian Congo—the Awozak, Aluuru, Kaliko, Luu, Ɔtsɔ, Ɗïïo.

The number and variety of dialects in the different parts of the country serve but to reflect the very nature of the origin of the people.

7. Existing conditions, resulting from the past history of Logbara, have made it difficult to decide which dialect of the language to choose for purposes of this analysis. In deciding upon the dialect spoken around Arua, the district headquarters of the West Nile (Northern Province), i.e. the dialect of the Aivu and Pàdzùlú, as a basis for this Grammar and Vocabulary, the author has allowed considerations of practicability alone to influence his choice and has disregarded such criteria as—which is the 'authentic' or 'proper' or 'best type of' Logbara, since such claims are, in his opinion, untenable when applied to any one of the existing dialects.

The Grammar as a whole, in its general features, details or rules, is common to all parts of the country. The Vocabulary, however, differs considerably from one part to another. The region of the Tɛrɛgo-Omugo forms a major language-group having a more or less uniform, distinctive dialect; whereas the larger, further distant areas, such as Lɔgirr, Adömi, &c., have, in their turn, their own distinctive peculiarities. The most distant dialect is apparently that of the Ma'di-Ndri (also called Màdé) of the Olepi-Okɔlɔ area. The Vocabulary here given, as a rule, registers not only Aivu-Pàdzùlú words, but numerous terms from other dialects have also been included for purposes of comparison; only in exceptional cases, however, are Ma'di-Ñdri terms given, otherwise we might be led too far afield. Many terms belonging to individual dialects may in time become general, since intercommunication between the different groups nowadays is unhampered. Several of these 'special' terms are not in common use at present, but by and large are understood by everybody. To include these words, while it might serve to expand the Vocabulary, would, at this stage, probably only confuse the student.

8. Another important factor, connected with the Ma'di, is formed by the linguistic traces of Ma'di found in the Jii languages generally, and more particularly in those of the Lwoo. History seems to give plain hints as to how the two peoples came into contact, or how Ma'di elements came to be introduced into the Jii (Nueer, Denka, Lwoo) languages.

When the Ma'di as a whole had to abandon their home and the movement of dispersion started, one larger group, or possibly a number of groups, moved north-west along the Nile and eventually reached and settled in modern Atwot country or thereabouts, which was the home of the Lwoo, and where the Ma'di at that time were incorporated with them. These Ma'di groups joined the Lwoo as well as the Denka and the Nueer.

Ma'di influences in the Jii languages though not numerous are evident. The manner, period, and degree of this influence has yet to be investigated in detail; such a study may eventually lead to very interesting results. The traces of Ma'di found in LuNyoro, Lu-Ganda, &c., go back, essentially, to the same early period of migratory movement.

9. Particular Ma'di traces in the Aluur, Acooli, &c., languages go back to a more recent past. As mentioned above, when the Lwoo arrived they found the respective countries largely in the hands of Ma'di tribal groups, side by side, perhaps, with no less considerable Laŋo groups. It was probably the rather unsettled state of affairs under such entangled conditions that favoured, or rather, was responsible for, the arrival of the neutral Lwoo and their installation as unprejudiced rulers in the country, and the adoption of the Lwoo language and customs by both the Ma'di and Laŋo tribal groups. It is not difficult to understand how numbers of useful Ma'di and Laŋo words came to be retained in the new language—evidence of old times and events.

10. *The Logbara language.* The present Grammar and Vocabulary.

Logbara, as has been shown, is one of the Ma'di languages. It differs considerably from the Ma'di spoken in the neighbouring north-eastern regions by the Moyo and Opari and from that of its western neighbours, the Lɔgɔ and Kaliko, with all of whom contact is easy. Only a short time, say about a month, is necessary in the neighbouring region to pick up, more or less, the other's language without much difficulty. The languages of the Avokaya and the Mörö, in the farther north-west Nilotic Sudan, no doubt have less in common with Logbara.

The following features are characteristic of Logbara and, to a great extent, of the other Ma'di languages:

1. *Tone* plays an extremely important part in the composition and the distinguishing of words.

2. The large number of *monosyllabic* root-words, especially verbs. They consist of an open syllable, i.e. consonant (or consonant combination) plus vowel: C+V. A few consist of a single vowel only, or a vowel preceded by a glottal stop.

3. Among the consonant sounds, the velar-labials **gb, kp, ŋgb**; the labio-velar-labial **mŋgb,** and the 'glottal' sounds ' before vowels and in **'b, 'd, 'w, 'y** are characteristic.

4. There is *no grammatical gender*.

5. There are *no* true *articles*.

6. There is *no declension* for *cases*; 'case' relationship is shown by position of words in the sentence, or else by means of postpositions.

7. In the *genitive construction* the Possessor (genitive or nomen rectum) with the postposition **mà** (expressed or implicit) precedes the Possessed (nomen regens); with the other postpositions the Possessor follows the Possessed.

8. The *adjective* as *attribute* follows its noun.

9. There is *no conjugation* of any form: the verb is invariable except for intonation. The personal pronoun or any other subject is simply placed in front of the verb; some change occasionally takes place in the tone-pattern of the verb.

10. There is *no passive voice*; the third person plural of the verb is often used in an impersonal passive sense.

11. The prefixes **a-, e-, o-** appear as *Verb Formatives* to express special meanings.

12. There is a *general tendency* to place constructional particles (such as relative pronouns, prepositions or postpositions, con-

junctions, &c.) *after* the term they refer to, or towards the end of the sentence.

13. The terms for the different parts of the body are used as postpositions or, more especially, as a kind of *auxiliary noun* in colloquial phraseology.

Note: Of the above features, Nos. 1, 4, 5, 6, (7), 8, 10, 13 are common to the Logbara and Acooli (or Lwoo); Nos. 2, 3, (7), 9, 11, 12, are peculiar to the Logbara (or Ma'di).

Orthography: The orthography adopted in this book, which has been worked out by the author as a result of his own field researches, differs in some respects from that recently adopted for schools and official publications. Forms used in the present study are listed first, those used by schools, &c., follow in brackets: a or ä (a); ɛ or e (e); ë or ï (i); i (i); ɔ or o (o); ö or u (u); dz (j); ts (c); ġb or mġb (ġb); kp (kp); ŋg (ng); double vowels (not used).

J. P. C.

Catholic Mission
Lira, Uganda
28th September, 1953

ACKNOWLEDGEMENTS

AFTER two unsuccessful attempts, in 1937 and 1939, to make a study of the Logbara language, in 1950 I was charged by the diocesan authorities of Gulu with the task of providing a book on the language. The credit for this last definitive enterprise must go to the persistence of the Rev. Fr. C. Tupone, Diocesan Secretary of Education.

I enjoyed my study of the language, but my health often failed, and I am afraid the work suffered because of this. I was especially conscious of the need for a thorough revision of the English text of the book, and I am very much obliged to the International African Institute for having undertaken this very necessary work on the manuscript.

I gratefully acknowledge the part of the Uganda Government in providing the necessary funds for this publication, through the kind interest of Mr. R. M. Bere and Mr. E. C. Powell-Cotton, Provincial Commissioners, Northern Province. I should also like to thank the Secretary of the Languages Board, Mr. J. D. Chesswas, for his assistance throughout, and all those others who have helped me in any way.

J. P. C.

C.C. Lira
16th November, 1958

CONTENTS

CONTENTS

CHAPTER 1

SOUNDS

I. Alphabet

Orthography

1. The orthography adopted in this book follows that of the Rejaf Language Conference (1928) and its suggestions; and also the explanations contained in D. Westermann and Ida C. Ward, *Practical Phonetics for Students of African Languages*, London, 1933.

The 'central' type of vowel for the o-sound considered at the Rejaf conference is represented by the symbol ŏ, and, by analogy, for the marking of other vowels of the same type, the diacritical mark ¨ (diaeresis) is employed, thus avoiding special symbols.

1. *Vowels*

2. *General notes.* (1) Special vowels, as distinct from the ordinary ones, are represented by special symbols (ɛ, ə) or the diacritical mark ¨; in addition, the mark of nasalization ˜ (tilde) is occasionally used. All other signs, above the vowels or consonants, serve to indicate intonation.

(2) All vowels may be short or long or of intermediate length. Long vowels are shown by doubling the symbol, and similarly with long consonants.

It is often very difficult to determine the length of a sound or even the quality of a vowel; for the Logbara, in running together the words of a perhaps rather complicated sentence, elide many of the vowels. This gives the impression that Logbara speech is careless or slipshod. Furthermore, the influence and variety of dialects, strongly felt everywhere, encourages vagueness on questions of pronunciation. Even natives themselves are often found discussing the pronunciation of a word or its vowels. Sometimes these discussions end in unanimity; at other times they refrain from committing themselves, agreeing that various districts have different pronunciations. As a result of such vagueness, the present book will sometimes show up differences in transcribing a word; this reflects the actual state of things rather than a lack of consistency. The student should not forget this circumstance.

(3) The ordinary vowels have the Italian values.

3. *The single vowels.* (A) i and ï: respectively cardinal i and central ï, roughly as in Engl. 'see' and 'bit'. Many words, in Logbara, are distinguished only by these two different types of i-sound. Central ï is apparently more frequent, and Logbara pronunciation seems to tend instinctively towards it. In a good number of words the ĭ is quite clear, in other cases it is not; in cases where no difference of meaning results, it may not matter if no distinction in writing is made.

4. Examples:

bì *to bend down*	bĭ *to catch*
bbí *ear, leaf*	'bĭ(kə) *feather*
dzì *to bring*	dzĭ *to sharpen*
sí *tooth, point*	sĭ *hailstone*
sì *to fit*	sĭ *to tear;* with
tí *cow*	tĭ *in vain*

5. (B) **ɛ, e, ë.** Logbara has three distinct e-sounds. The close or central ë is very marked, it tends towards ĭ; these two are often difficult to distinguish. In the case of gềrì or gĭrì (*way*) both pronunciations are actually in use, ë = ĭ. The general tendency is ë = ĭ, as 'alëá or 'alĭá (*in*). The open ɛ largely prevails in Logbara. A medium quality between ɛ and ë does also exist, as in the personal pronouns é *thou*, è *you*, èì *they*, but generally the fluctuating character of the language often makes it difficult to decide which is correct, ɛ or e. Apparently, however, the difference of ɛ and e does not serve to distinguish words. One might well adopt the convention that, with the exception of ë, the Logbara e-sound can be pronounced as ɛ, as a rule, and, with this understanding, the symbol ɛ could be abolished.

Future practice might decide in favour of these three symbols: i, ĭ (= ë), e (= ɛ). The present book keeps to the distinction: i, ĭ/ë, e, ɛ.

6. Examples:

bbí èdo *lobe of ear*	èdrè *to set upright*	
fè *to give*	lè *to like*	nè *to see*
kĕnà *all*	kènì *says that*	èdú *dense*
àmvé *outside*	mëërì *the Nile*	èdzí *left*
kérĕá *small calabash*	mbèlè *quickly*	ŋgèyèŋgéyè *Nile pike*
ꞥárĕkì *target*	meenóa *a termite*	

7. (C) **a, ä.** Open a, as in Engl. 'path', and dull ä with a tendency towards ɛ. This ä is quite distinct from the former a in ordinary pronunciation. However, what is pronounced in one district with ä may be pronounced with a in another area, though this is not usual.

ma, á *I, me*		à, àma *we, us*
màarí *gourd-blowing instrument*		määrí *loan, debt*
kàméè *spoon*	kàmì *lion*	pätí àgài *side of tree*
gáráma *branch*	gári *rainbow*	däälì *depressed* (ground)

8. (D) **ə, o, ö.** We have here almost a parallel to the above-mentioned three e-sounds. The open ə (cf. *aw* in 'law') is the most frequent of the o-sounds and next to this in frequency is the close ö. The middle or normal o is less frequent and on account of its unstable nature (in Logbara speech) is often difficult to delineate. The symbols o (= ə), ö might suffice.

9. Examples:

əlófɛ *bridge*	ósǒ *bean*	ə̀sə̀ *to pierce*
ə̀do *oil, fat*	óní *stone, rock*	óbíró or ábíó *rhinoceros*
ősu *bow*	fǒ *to go out*	fə̀ *to itch*
ɛ̀ndzə̀ *lie*	ɛndzó *a shrub*	ə̀ndzí *bad*
ópí *chief, king*	ə̀kó *woman, wife*	òku *old* (of the past)

10. (E) u, as in Engl. 'food'.

mu *to go*	mvu *to drink*	òmvu *nose*
ŋgúrú *wild beast* (of prey)	rú *name*	
àvù *to bow down*	àvə̀ *a corpse*	

Special symbols

11. (1) *Nasalization.* Nasalization is not a common feature in Logbara. When it occurs it is found in the diminutive suffix -a, and marked in this book with the sign ˜: -ã. The vowel preceding this suffix takes over nasalization too. It seems, however, that many people do not trouble about nasalization in this case; this may be due to the influence of foreigners who, in most cases, do not even bother about its existence. Examples:

èvǒ *a basket* èvə̃̌ə̃́ (or simply èvǒöá) *a tiny little basket*

2. Diphthongs

12. (1) Of the ordinary type of rising diphthongs (or union of vowels forming a single syllable) consisting of semi-vowel plus vowel, the common forms with w and y do exist. Thus: if to w and y (and, for that matter, to any consonant) any of the vowel sounds used in Logbara is added, a full-formed verb is obtained, or, to a lesser extent, a noun.

Combinations of consonant +w or y do not exist with the unimportant exceptions of hwe, hwi.

(2) Examples:

waa vn. *to swim; be clean, be fresh* (milk); *to jump; to stop* (raining)
wɛ *to swim; to sweep*
wi (wï) vn. *to grow; to pinch off, to skin; to ripen; to dry; to split*
    N.B. Wi very often has the alternate form uu/wu (cf. vocabulary).
wuu vt. *to collect; to skin, to bark*
ya vt./vn. *to move, tremble; to knock; to besprinkle, to till*
yɛ vt. *to do, make*
yï *to throw away*
yo/yə *to bask; to assuage; to speak; there is not*
yuu av. *lukewarm*

(3) To root words of this kind prefixes (a, e, ə) or other syllables may be added to form other words.

Vowel plus **w** or **y** combinations are practically non-existent.

13. As to pronunciation, **w** and **y** of Logbara correspond roughly to English *w* in 'will', or *y* in 'yes'.

(1) **W** is a weak **o**-glide rather than an **u**-glide.

(2) **Y** is generally difficult to perceive before **i**. In some districts the y-glide before **i** is definitely perceptible, in others not. Natives have taken to writing **yi** in place of double **ii**, e.g. **ìyí-ìyí** in place of **ǐí-ǐí** (*leisurely*), or **ìyí** for **ií** (*water*): it may be more practical. As far as pronunciation goes this can be interpreted either as a prolonged **i** or as a very soft y-glide plus **i**; it is not the strong **y** of Engl. 'year'.

14. Ordinary vowel combinations, giving the impression of diphthongs, do occur in Logbara, but they must be considered as separate syllables. Examples:

    ai *to scatter*　　**ɔ́ó** *to cry*　　**à'bòà** *banana*　　**rúá** *body*

3. *Consonants*

15. While the Logbara and their south-eastern Lwoo neighbours have an approximately identical system of vowels, the former have, however, a distinctive system of consonants, by which it at once becomes evident that the Ma'di and Lwoo represent two distinct types of language. Logbara has a greater variety of consonants and consonant combinations.

16. *Vowel-consonant pronunciation.* While in Logbara, as has been mentioned already, vowels are, one might almost say, generally pronounced in a leisurely or vague way, eventually with complete suppression (as is short **i** among consonants), the consonants are commonly pronounced with considerable force, thus creating the impression of being doubled. (In this book they are occasionally written doubled.)

17. The consonants and consonant-combinations of Logbara are these:
    b, 'b, d, 'd, dr, dz, f, pf, g, gb, ', h, k, kp, l, m, mb-mv, mŋgb, n, nd, ndr, ndz, ŋg, ṇ, p, r, s, t, tr, ts, v, w, 'w, y, 'y, z

18. The following consonant symbols have the English sound values:
    b, f, p, v　e.g. **báká** *rope*; **pá** *leg*; **fàlá(kó)** *bone*; **vàá** *on the ground*
    g, h, k　e.g. **ga** *to fill, to cut*; **hwèɛ** *to burst*; **ka** *to shine*
    m, n　e.g. **má** *I*; **àma** *we*; **nna** *three*; **nè** *to see*
    s, z　e.g. **só** *barb*; **z** (as in Engl. 'zeal') **zá** *meat*
    ŋg (=**ng** as in Engl. 'finger')　e.g. **ŋga** *to rise*
    ṇ (= **ny**) (as -**gn** in French 'Boulogne')　e.g. **éṇá** *polenta*; **àṇá** *corn*

The Tɛrɛgo group uses **n** for **ṇ** regularly; **ŋ** (= *ng* as in Engl. 'sing') is not in use. **pf** (bilabial) is occasionally heard in place of **f**, as **pföröpförö** *easily crumbled*.

19. *Special consonants*: **d** and **t** are dentals (or almost interdentals) as in English 'this' and 'thick'. Examples:

dì *to forge*   **tíbí** *savoury*

20. **'**, the glottal stop, i.e. a momentary stopping of the breath-current bringing the vocal chords together, an analogy to the guttural stop for **g** or **k**.

(*a*) It is used as an ordinary consonant and may occur before any vowel and before the consonants **b**, **d** : **'b**, **'d**; or before the semi-vowels **w** and **y** : **'w**, **'y**. Examples:

'alɛ̀ *inside*	**'ɛ́** (= **'yɛ́**) *arrow*	
'ípì *proprietor*	**'ɔ** (= **'yɛ**) *to do*	
'bá 'dà *that man*	**'bà** *to put*	**'bɛ** *to throw*
'dǒ *eleusine*	**'dɛ** *to die*	**dɛ** *to finish*
dà *to pour*	**'da** *to insult*	**'wï** *to dry*
wï *to pinch off, skin*	**'yɔ** *to speak*	**yɔ** *there is not*

(*b*) This glottal stop often serves to distinguish words otherwise alike, cf. the examples above and the Vocabulary. Consonants preceded by a glottal stop have also been called 'implosive' consonants. To the author in the two sounds *'ba* and *gba* we have two essentially equal 'explosives': the one being preceded by a glottal stop (*'ba*) the other by a guttural or velar stop (*gba*).

(*c*) Verbs consisting of a simple vowel only, e.g. **'a** and **'ì**, but with a variety of shades and meanings, are mostly preceded by the glottal plosive **'**.

21. As this **'** is a consonant, it functions, of course, as such in the following ways:

(*a*) It obviates a hiatus and, because of it vowels which would otherwise meet, are never contracted: e.g. **dzɔ́ 'aléa** *in the hut*.

(*b*) Before verbs composed of **'** plus a vowel, the shortened forms of personal pronouns (**e**, **a**) are used, as is the case before other consonants, instead of the full-form ones which have to be used before a vowel. Cf. :

é 'ì ǹdrí áséa ! *fasten the goat* (to something) *in the grass*
mí ɔ̀'ì tí lítsóa ! *fasten the cows in the pen* (**ɔ̀'ì** pl. form of **'ì**).

22. Here as elsewhere the glottal plosive is not always clearly perceptible. It is often almost absorbed, one might say, in a 'careless' chain of speech although, when otherwise similarly spelled words—with and without such a glottal plosive—are put side by side natives will insist stubbornly on the particular difference. Their way of pronouncing this plosive is mostly very delicate or light, but their sense of perception is very sharp; this is, of course, the effect of natural training since earliest youth. For foreigners who are not familiar with this peculiarity, at least not with so pronounced a variety, it requires a conscious effort to imitate the native. With a few exceptions, this practice has not been observed among foreign educationalists—to the detriment of the language. Even official advisers

on general orthography, who have visited Arua more than once, have
failed to make themselves heard on this point as on others.

23. l is, as a rule, a flapped consonant in Logbara, sometimes strong,
as before **i**, e.g. **lï** *to cut*, sometimes less so. The tip of the tongue is turned
backward (behind the alveoli) and pressed lightly against the front part
of the palate to stop the current of breath; on releasing the breath suddenly
the tip of the tongue flaps back, e.g. **alazà** *crosswise*; **lè** *to like*; **òlí** *the wind*.

24. r in Logbara is strongly rolled, with a number of taps so that it
suggests a double or triple **r**. This is especially so in the **dr** or **tr** combinations or when between vowels, as in **ïrrï** *two*; **drà** *to die*; **tra** *to gather*;
dri *to warm*; **tri** *to anoint*; **dría** *all*; **tré** *full*; **drò** *to pile up*; **trò** *to undo*.

25. *Combination of consonants* is an important feature of Logbara.
dr and **tr** are frequent and ordinary (see § 24).

26. dz, ts, and ndz are likewise of frequent occurrence. **ts** is the
equivalent of German *z* as in 'Zeit'; **dz** being the voiced counterpart of
it.[1] Lwoo have **c** and **j** (with the English pronunciation as in 'chair' and
'jealousy'), but the Ma'di and Logbara have **dz** and **ts**. A Logbara speaks
of **Atsooli** and **PaDzule** for Acooli and PaJule, and vice versa. **-dz** preceded by **n**, i.e. **ndz** (not **nj**) is a frequent sound in Logbara. Examples:

dzɛ *to buy*	**edzí** *to bring*	**àdzú** *spear*	**tsa** *to reach*
tsé *truly*	**tsí** *is*	**tsúrú 'dò** *now*	**ndzɛ** *to take out*
andzi *children*	**èndzò** *lie*		

27. nd, ndr: nd as in 'kind', and ndr with strongly rolled **rrr** are
common and present no difficulty. Note that **n** of **ndr** forms an independent syllable and often has a distinct tone. Examples:

ndà *to seek*	**ndè** *to surpass*	**àndè** *to be tired*
ǹdrí *goat*	**ándrâ** or **ńdrâ** *of old*	**ándrìi** *mother*

28. ɡb, kp labio-velar plosives; the breath current is simultaneously
obstructed by closed lips and the tongue pressed against the soft palate;
the stops are also simultaneously released, thus producing the peculiar
voiced or unvoiced sound of **ɡb** or **kp**. It needs some practice. Examples:

ɡbà *to blow*	**ɡbέ** *egg*	**ɡbï** *to shoot*	**ègbè** *cold*
kpà *to snatch*	**kpɛrɛ** *as far as*	**kpii** *straight*	**kpò** *to hide*

29. mŋɡb. By adding **m** before **ɡb** we obtain **mɡb** or, actually,
mŋɡb, not easy to pronounce. Note initial lip-closing of **m**. It may be

---

[1] Competent phoneticists have repeatedly stressed the existence of the two
sound combinations *dz* and *tz* in Logbara, as Dr. A. N. Tucker in *Eastern
Sudanic Languages*, p. 104. Unfortunately *ts* and *dz* exist as initial consonants
neither in English nor in Italian; English and Italian educationists have, therefore,
with Dr. Tucker as linguist adviser, combined to introduce *c* (instead of *ts*) as
represented in Engl. *c*hair or Ital. *c*inque and *j* (instead of *dz*) as represented in
Engl. '*j*ealousy' or Ital. *g*iorno, in Logbara literature, and English and Italians
generally pronounce it in their own (not the Logbara's) way.

easier to try to pronounce simultaneously mgb, which would automatically become mŋgb. Examples:

àmŋgbakà *hyena* ɛ̀mŋgbɛ̀lɛ̀kɛ̀ *chimpanzee* mŋgbí *in line*

N.B. ŋ does not occur alone in Logbara, but is frequent in the combinations ŋg, ŋgb, or, to be more exact, m(ŋ)gb. Examples:

ŋgɔ́á yà? *where?* mŋgbàrï *real, true*
mŋgbú *all* bɔ̀ŋgɔ́ *cloth*

30. mb and mv are common combinations; lip-closing points to initial m: thus no nb or nv spelling can replace them. Examples:

mbá *month* ɛmbá *to teach* mbɛ̀lɛ̀ *quickly* mbo *to jump*
mvá *child* ámvïí *sister* mvi *to go back* mvu *to drink*

31. The letters c, j, q, x do not occur in Logbara.

32. *Consonants occurring in Logbara.*

	Bi-labial	Labio-dental	(Inter-)dental	Alveolar	Palatal	Velar	Labio-velar	Laryngeal
Explosive	p, b	..	t, d	..	..	k, ǵ	kp, ǵb	'
Affricate	..	..	..	ts, dz	..	..	..	..
Nasal	m, mb	mv	..	n, ndz	n̠	ŋǵ	mŋgb	..
Rolled, flapped	..	..	tr, dr	r, l	..	..	..	..
Fricative	pf	f, v	..	s, z	..	..	..	h
Semi-vowel	w	..	..	..	y	..	..	..

Tone Marks

33. The tone of a syllable will be shown on vowels (or consonants) by means of the conventional marks given below. The tone of a syllable may be simple (level) or combined (kinetic). (See also § 53.)

(*a*) Marks for simple tones:

high tone (h.t.) ´; tí *cow*; ɛ́wá *beer*; tí mvá *cow calf*
mid tone (m.t.) ¹; ɔzɔ́ɔ́ *rain*; ɛ̄'dà *to show*; tı̄ *mouth*
low tone (l.t.) `; lɛ̀ *to like*; sı̀ *with*

(*b*) Marks for combined tones (unbroken ascent or descent from one level to another by combination of the simple tones):

high-low tone ^; tı̂ zá *beef*; ɔpî nı̂ *the chief's*
high-mid tone ⌐; ádrı̄í (or ádrı̄) *brother*; átı̄ *father*
mid-high tone ˅; ɔzɔ̌ or ɔzɔ̌ɔ́ *rain*
mid-low tone ˄; tsɔ̂-tsɔ *to strike*
low-mid tone ˅; fɛ̌ *he gives*
low-high tone ˇ; lǎ *they read* (past)
intermediate tones: see § 53, p. ii.

34. *General notes.* (1) A double vowel or vowel combination with level tone is marked with a single tone mark on the first vowel, as **'dáalɛ́** *there*, **'álɛ̆a** *in.*

(2) No mark on a syllable, whether simple or composite vowel, indicates mid-level tone: e.g. **əvö** *to be*; if another tone is added to a middle tone, both tones must, of course, be marked: e.g. **əzɔ́ɔ́** *rain.*

For further details see *Intonation*, § 43 sqq.

II. Sound Changes

35. In Logbara (unlike some of the other languages, such as Jii), word-linking does not, generally speaking, postulate change of sounds. The two following cases, however, are slight exceptions to this statement.

36. (1) Before the locative suffix **-á,** and to some extent before **-ti,** open vowel-sounds (**ɛ** and **ə**) tend to become close. A typical, one might almost say unique, instance is **'alɛ́** (*inside*): **'alɛ́-á** (*in the inside*) becomes **'alɛ́a** or **'alɛ̆a** or even **'alía.** **Dzɔ́-á** becomes **dzɔ́a** (*in the hut*). Similarly, **dzɔ́-ti** (*hut's opening, door*) is generally pronounced **dzɔ́ti** or, more commonly, **dzɔ́tilɛ́.**

37. (2) The adjectival formative suffix **-rö** tends to be **-ru** after **i, o** or **u** in a preceding syllable.

N.B. Both these 'exceptions' to the general simple rule may be disregarded without danger of inconvenience or ambiguity, though in speaking the Logbara keep to them. This book will mostly reflect them.

38. A more widespread sound-change—consisting of vowel-elision— is an important feature of spoken Logbara. This is important in the sense that its use permeates the language, so much so that it requires some ability and experience for a foreigner to understand Logbara people when they speak naturally. Logbara is unusual in respect of the marked degree to which words are contracted in speech, at the expense of vowels.

In writing and in literature, on the other hand, the educated native is familiar only with the language based on etymology and writes it in full, quite unaware of the ways of current speech: for this reason this book will ignore the contracted forms of the spoken language.

39. In the spoken language, the following is normal usage:

When an end vowel of a word meets with the initial vowel of a following word, their connexion is an extremely close one in speech, i.e. there is no pause between one word and the next. Example:

> **àma ɛ'da ɛ̀rï-nï ɛ́'dá** becomes **àmɛ'dɛ̀rïnïï'dá** *we showed him a picture*

40. Elision takes place, especially in colloquial speech, when even an utterly 'mutilated' word is immediately recognized in context. In some cases, in a word consisting of **v–c–v**, both initial and terminal vowel may be dropped leaving only the consonant.

As a consequence of the catenation, either one of two meeting vowels is dropped, resulting in the following:

(a) The tone of a disappearing vowel, whether it vanish by assimilation or elision (whichever way one looks at it), is always retained and added to the tone of the remaining vowel.

(b) When the two meeting vowels are identical, they become, for all practical purposes, one long vowel.

(c) When one vowel is dropped, the one retained is generally relatively long.

41. *Dropped vowels*

(a) An initial a- is normally not dropped as it generally conveys some special shade of meaning, and ambiguity might otherwise arise.

(b) i(ï), o(ö, ǝ), and u are strong vowels; they are never dropped.

(c) The end vowel -a is dropped before any other vowel.

(d) The vowel -e or e- is dropped in contact with any other vowel except a-; a and e are weak vowels.

42. Examples:

maa -'á bïïrï yà ? (ma a'á ...) *have I delayed much?*

mí adri 'dé mî z-óósí (=zá osí) ! *do stay where you are to fry the meat!*

èdzò 'î p-èèdzò-dzò (for pá è-) *he stretched his leg(s)*

m- èèdzò m- èèdzò -dzò *I am stretching myself*

CHAPTER 2

INTONATION

43. If one compares these three commonplace expressions—mâ drí *my hand*, mâ drì *my head*, mádrí *my, mine*—it appears evident that the musical tone or pitch with which a word is pronounced is an essential part of it, since, in numerous cases, tone alone distinguishes one word from another, for example, dri may mean either *head* (drì), *hand* (drí), or *to warm* (drï). Compare also: tí (*cow*), ti (*mouth, to give birth*), tì (*rise*—of a river), or sí (*tooth*), sí (*hail*), si (*to knock*), sì (*with*), si (*to build*). Such instances are extremely common in Logbara. The importance of tones must thus become clear to everybody. If a person speaks without regard to tones, it will mean that the native hearers will have to be more ingenious than the speaker and discover from the circumstances or context or from his gestures what he is trying to say; the native will have to learn the Logbara of the foreigner: a poor expedient which must lead to impoverishment of the language.

Apart from the etymologically distinct tones (see Vocabulary), intonation is governed by an ample body of regulations, especially in relation to verbs.

Intonation and Verbs

44. *Preliminary notes.* Verbs in Logbara have the following forms. (1) A *simple verb* represents a root in its simplest form, i.e. C(onsonant) + V(owel)—a simple open syllable, e.g. **fɛ**. A closed syllable, i.e. V + C, does not occur. (2) As a rule any consonant, or ordinary consonant-combination, may combine with any vowel and thus form a full verb. Thus **fa, fɛ, fï, fo, fɔ, fu** are all important verbs in Logbara.

45. The said simple or primary verbs may take one of the following prefixes: **a-, ɛ(e)-, ɔ(o)-.** The prefixes imply a particular modification in the meaning of the simple verb; they are, therefore, annexed according to fairly fixed rules, not arbitrarily. Examples:

mvi *to go back*	**fɛ̀** *to give*
ɛmvi *to come back*	**ɛ̀fɛ̀** *to give hither*
ɔmvi *to give back*	**ɔ̀fɛ̀** *to give much or to many*

N.B. **Tɛrɛgo**, &c., commonly uses **a-** where others use **e-**.

46. The following are the rules governing the tone-patterns of verbs: (1) Simple verbs have either *low* or *mid tone*, never high. Examples:

fɛ̀ *to give*   **ga** *to cut*   **'di** *to kill*   **drɔ̀** *to pile up*

N.B. There are a few exceptions (generally indicated in the Vocabulary) when a verb may have both forms, one with low and one with mid tone. Generally, however, a difference in tone indicates a difference in meaning.

47. (2) When a *low*-toned simple verb takes a prefix (§ 45), both verbal root and prefix keep to low tone. Examples:

ɛ̀fɛ̀, ɔ̀fɔ̀, ɔ̀drɔ̀, ɔ̀'bà, &c.

48. (3) If a *mid*-tone simple verb takes a prefix, the prefix will have mid tone only. The mid-toned verbal root (of a simple verb), however, may keep its mid tone or may, possibly, exchange mid tone for high tone; it is common usage which is the deciding factor, not one's own preference.

In some cases a verb composed in this way (root with prefix) may have either mid-level or mid-high tone. Usually the difference in intonation indicates a difference in meaning. Examples:

  ɛtsí *to deceive*   **ɛtsi** *to close*, &c.

49. The following change—or rather, slight addition—in the tone pattern of verbs takes place regularly. Changes here refer to the *end-syllable* only.

In sentences with the Construction of Incomplete Action (CIA) the following tone additions are made:

50. (1) A *low*-toned verb adds to its low tone a slightly raised tone-tail, a 2/5 tone. Examples:

    fè *to give,*   but: àfa fĕ *to give something*

51. (2) A *high*-toned verbal root, e.g. ɛmbá, takes an additional slightly falling tone-tail, a 4/5 tone. Examples:

    ɛmbá *to teach*   èri andzi ɛmbâ *he is teaching the children*

52. (3) A *mid*-toned verb sometimes adds a slightly rising tone-tail, from 3/5 to 4/5. Examples:

    mvu *to drink*   ɛ́wâ mvǔ *to drink beer*

Number of Tones

53. Certain rules, of general application in Logbara, are given here for those interested. They will not be referred to again in this book. In this book only three tones are marked (no mark means mid-tone): *low* or 1/5, *mid* or 3/5, *high* or 5/5, and their combinations (see § 12). But what is marked in this book with mid-tone in fact comprises three tones marked: ˇ or 2/5, ' or 3/5, ˝ or 4/5, which all come between low and high tones. There are thus actually five distinct tone levels; and an ordinary high tone may sometimes be surpassed by a higher syllable.

54. I have abstained from more minute investigation or collection of evidence in the matter of intonation in view of the fact that 95 per cent., probably, of the readers of this book will not appreciate it and may find it annoying, to say the least.

55. The *intermediate tones* (2/5 and 4/5) may be determined by general rules to a certain extent; these have been set out tentatively here for the benefit of students interested in them.

The *low intermediate* (2/5) tone is employed in the following cases:

(*a*) All dissyllabic personal pronouns have a low-tone first syllable and a slightly higher (2/5) second one, ˇ

    èrĭ *he* . . .   àmă *we* . . .   èmĭ *you* . . .   èĭ *they, them*

(*b*) On the relative element -rĭ, when suffixed to low-tone syllables, as in the case of the demonstrative pronouns:

    'dĭ-rĭ / 'dĭĭ *this*   'dàrĭ / 'dàĭ *that*

(*c*) On the second syllable of àlŏ *one*

(*d*) As an addition to low-toned verbs in CIA sentences (cf. § 50).

56. The *third* or *real middle tone* is the tone of many verbs (cf. § 46); and it is the tone of the vowel prefixes added to mid-tone verbs (cf. § 48).

57. The *high-intermediate* or *raised mid* tone ˝ (4/5) is found mainly in the following cases:

(*a*) In the full-form personal pronouns (1st and 2nd pers. sg.), i.e. the monosyllables mă *I*, mĭ *thou*, 'ĭ *he, she, him-* or *her-self.*

(*b*) A good proportion of nouns of kinship (and a few others) end in a high plus an additional raised mid- (4/5) toned syllable. The latter is

apparently the result of a shortening of an end syllable -pǐ to -ǐ, or -ípǐ
to -íǐ. Examples:

ándríǐ *mother*	átíǐ *father*	ádríǐ *brother*
ámvíǐ *sister*	ágúǐ or ágíǐ *friend*	'ípǐ or 'íǐ *owner*

(*c*) There are a number of dissyllabic nouns which in some parts of the
country are pronounced with level high tone, while in other parts their
first syllable has a high intermediate (4/5) tone. This latter feature is,
however, apparently on the point of giving way to the former or high-level
tone pronunciation. Examples:

pătí *tree*　**ătíǐ** *father*　**ɛ́mvó** *pot*
cf. **pătí mà pátí** *stem of a tree*

Inter-tonic Reaction

58. In many cases a low-toned syllable is required before certain words.
This means that whenever the syllable preceding such a word has other
than a low tone, the low tone has to be added to it. This phenomenon
occurs, of course, in connected speech, i.e. when words—maybe just
two—are grammatically connected. Thus **pătí**, if followed by the verb
ga, becomes **pătî**, e.g. **pătî ga** *to cut wood* (or a tree).

There are two categories of words which come under this heading; the
one follows simple rules, the other requires every single word to be
checked separately.

59. The first category refers to *verbs with mid tone*. Only a *simple verb*,
consisting of a simple root, has the property of postulating a low tone
before it. If any of the verbal prefixes (see § 45) is annexed, it loses this
property.

Before a *simple mid-tone verb* a word has to have a low tone:

(*a*) If the preceding syllable has a low tone, no change occurs.

(*b*) If the preceding syllable has a high tone, a low tone has to be added
to it: e.g. **ɛ̀ri dzó 'alɛ̂ wɛ** *she is sweeping the hut's inside* ('alɛ́).

(*c*) If the preceding syllable has mid or low-mid tone, this tone is
replaced by the low tone. **'yɛ** *to do*, **mu** *to go*, are two mid-toned verbs
which also serve as auxiliaries to form the future tense. Examples:
ɛ̀rì 'yɛ̀ mu rá *he will go*　　**ɛ̀rì mù 'yɛ rá** *she will do it*
N.B. In each of these examples the first (auxiliary) verb has low tone
as it is followed by a mid-tone verb. The pronoun subject **ɛ̀ri** has become
ɛ̀rì because it precedes a verb with etymologic mid tone, although in
these particular cases the verbs themselves had already taken a low tone
in consequence of the rule.

(*d*) In the case of a 4/5 or raised mid-tone syllable preceding a mid-tone
verb two alternatives are possible: either a low tone is added to the original
tone or, as with mid-tone syllables, the etymologic tone is replaced by
the low tone. Example:

mâ 'yè mu rá or **mà 'yè mu rá** *I shall go*

60. -rö. The predicative adjective formative suffix **-rö** (with mid tone) requires an *additional low tone* whenever the preceding syllable has not a low tone already. Examples:

ɛka *red* ɛmvɛ *white*

ɛka-rì and ɛmvɛ-rì (attributive), but ɛkà-rö, ɛmvɛ̀-rö (predicative)

N.B. The **rö** of reflexive verbs has no such property.

61. Second category: nouns postulating a low tone to precede them. A typical instance is **zá** *flesh.* It makes **tî zá** *ox-meat*, **ǹdrî zá** *meat of goat.* This word **zá** is **èzá** in the north of the country (Ariŋga). Here the clue to the explanation of this particular phenomenon seems plain: namely, that the low tone required is the remnant of a dropped low tone syllable.

In the case of **ǹdrí** *goat*, the low tone of the syllabic **ǹ** is residual, it would seem, of the original low-tone prefix of **èndrí.**

CHAPTER 3

MORPHOLOGICAL NOTES: A SUMMARY

62. Since the principle of 'postposition' is a universal feature of Logbara, 'suffixes' play an important part in it. I refer here only to such suffixes as are employed mainly in the formation of nouns, but also of other words. They are not numerous but frequent.

63. Some of the formative suffixes are purely factual ones; they do occur, though often optionally, but contribute nothing to the meaning and have no grammatical function. In origin they were, in all probability, dialectal peculiarities of some districts and, owing to easier communications, have become more widely known and, to some extent, been accepted in other districts. Thus for *neck* one may say əmbɛ or əmbɛ-lɛ́ or əmbɛlɛ́kɔ̀; all of these are in use.

64. On the other hand, the suffix **-kà** as in **àtsí-kà** *smoke*, (**àtsí** *fire*), or **ètú-kà** *sunshine*, (**ètú** *sun*), functions as an essential part of some words.

65. -k- is often interfixed to avoid a hiatus in the case of reduplicated adjectives beginning and ending with a vowel. Some of these formations have become fixed, others are used with or without this **-k-**: e.g. **èpɛ́-k-èpɛ́** *light*; but cf. **ɛŋaŋa** or **ɛŋa-k-ɛŋa** *poison.*

66. There are other formative suffixes with a *grammatical* function: these are annexed to verbs or other words for a definite purpose: e.g. **-pi**, **-rì, -rö, tá** (see below).

In the following paragraphs a short alphabetic summary of the common formative suffixes is given.

67. -ắ is used to form the diminutive of anything (cf. § 18). Examples:
mvá *child*   **mvããắ** *small child*   **èvŏ** *basket*   **èvŏ-ắ** *small basket*

68. -fí (lit. *grain*) is added to terms for ordinary substances to express single particles or pieces, or a small piece of the substance. Examples:
    érà-fí or **óní-fí** (or **érà-mvá**) *a (small) stone; a piece of gravel*

69. -kà, see § 64.

70. -kɔ (1) Often added to nouns, or omitted, according to dialect:
Examples:
    gìrì or **gìrìkó** *way, path*
    évéré-kó, i.e. **àŋgŏ vĕpi vɛ-rì'ï** *site where grass has been burned out*
(2) Added to a verb which is dependent upon **gà . . . sì** *to refuse.*
Examples:
    gà mu-kɔ sì *he refused to go*
    gà àfa fè-kɔ sì *he refused to give something*
    gà fŏ-kɔ sì *he refused to go out*

71. -lé is a very frequently occurring suffix; it pin-points a noun, &c., as a direct (or prepositional) object. It often appears to serve as a purely formal addition to a monosyllabic noun or adverb, &c., to give to the latter, as it were, a more formal consistency, to stress it. It is found in all areas, in some districts more than in others. Examples:
    'a or preferably stressed **'alé** *inside*; hence **'a-lĕ-á** *in, in the inside*
    'dà or **'dá** *that, there*; stressed **'dá-lé** *over there, that there*; **'dò** or **'dó**
    this here; **'dó-lé** *towards . . . here.*

72. -ó is often (though not in all districts) added to a proper noun to denote an individual or a member of some collective group or concept, as **ma Pàdzùlú-ó** *I am a member of the Padzulu tribal group.*

73. -pi. (1) Is a purely (mostly optional) formative suffix for most terms of kinship (cf. Noun, § 85) and a few other terms. Examples:
    átá or **átíí** or **átí-pi** *father*
    ándríí or **ándrí-pi** *mother*
    'dì ma átíí mà ádrí-pi *this is my father's brother*
    'í-pi or **'íí** *owner*
    cf. **àfa-nï** pl. **àfa-pi** *so-and-so*

(2) Is a grammatical suffix by means of which a relative clause is turned into a substantive expression—Noun Agent (cf. Verb, § 434; Relative Pronoun, § 257). The relative suffix or element **-rì** is generally added too.
Examples:
    Cf. **ámvú àgăí tĕ** *to guard* (the side of) *a field*; and
    ámvú àgăí tĕ-pi-rì *who guards a field*; hence
    'bá ámvú àgăí tĕ-pi-rì *one who guards a field, a field-guard*

'bá drapi (-rì) *one who died*, i.e. *a dead person*
'bá émvó sí-pi (-rì) *a potter*
'bá gbándzá fĕ- (or ŋ̶ă-) pi-rì *a creditor* (*debtor*) (*loan, give/take*)
è'bí bǐ (or kŏ or pĕ) -pi (-rì) *fisherman*
'bá tà (or ŋaatá) a'dípi *cook* (lit. *one cooking food*)
('bá) mvá (mà) tà mbǎ (= ətsĕ or èzŏ) pi-rì *child's nurse, guardian*
ɛmbá-pi *teacher*

74. -rì, -rö are grammatical suffixes for which see Adjectives, §§ 133 sq., and Relative Pronoun, § 257.

75. -tá is, as a rule, the suffix by which the Verbal Noun is made from a verb (cf. Verb, § 435). Examples:

ɛmbá *to teach*   ɛmbá-tá *teaching, instruction, doctrine*

76. -zà is largely used as an Adjective formative (cf. Verb, § 596).

77. -ma is, apparently, sometimes, though rarely, used in place of -tá to form a Verbal Noun, as in **drì ri-ma** *punishment, repression.*

PART I: GRAMMAR
GENERAL RULES FOR LOGBARA

78. 1. In Logbara there is *no* distinction of *grammatical gender*.

2. In Logbara there are *no articles*.

For grammatical and practical purposes, however, when required:

(a) The *definite article* is rendered either by the suffix **-nï** or by a corresponding *demonstrative pronoun*.

(b) The *indefinite article* may be rendered by the *indefinite pronoun* **àzḯ-nï** (*another, some, an*).

CHAPTER 4
NOUN

79. In Logbara, as in other languages, nouns may be grouped into different categories: proper, common, collective, material, abstract; but they are all governed by the same general grammatical rules, and these only are considered here.

I. Number

80. In Logbara only nouns indicating kinship have distinctive forms for the plural, and these are fairly regularly used in practice.

81. (a) Of these, only the following two or three nouns have, one might say, irregular plurals, but they are the most generally used and therefore the best-known plural forms:

mvá, intimately: **mvíi** *child*	pl. andzi or **andzií**
záa (**záã**), záamvá; ziï *girl, daughter*	„ ɛ́zó-andzi, ɛ́zó-pi (**ï**)
also: **kɔ̀dzáã**, kàdzoa *calf*	„ kɔ̀-andzi, kàdzo-andzi

82. (b) For the remaining kinship terms there is a standardized plural form of a fairly regular type consisting essentially in applying a tone-pattern quite distinct from that of the singular. The plural suffix **-ï** (a contraction of **-èï**, which may also be used) is often added optionally (as seen in the above examples). This plural tone-pattern must, consequently, be well noted.

Tone-pattern of singular: ´ ´ (´), i.e. high, high, (higher-mid)

„ „ plural: ` (`) ˇ (-**ï**), i.e. low, (low), mid, (high-mid)

Examples:

ándríi or **ándrápi** *mother* pl. **àndrapï** (-**ï**)

83. Both singular and plural may vary from dialect to dialect. Thus the first syllable of the singular, as well as the last, may have a higher-mid

C

tone ʼʼ, thus ʽ-, as in ăúpi *aunt* (paternal). The formative element -**pi**, often met with in kinship terms, frequently becomes simply -**i** (dropping the -**p**-), before which another vowel may also have to give way or be assimilated. Here again it depends on dialectal usage. The composite end-syllable -**íi**, e.g. ándríi for ándrápi, is, in fact, composed of two syllables with two distinct tones, resulting in a semi-long **í** (íi) with two tones.

In the plural, the uncontracted forms often reappear, of course with the corresponding plural intonation, as in ándríi pl. àndrapí. The (short) **í** (with composite tone) may or need not be added. Some dialects have the suffix -**pìrö** for the singular, which regularly becomes -**pìrúka** in the plural.

84. Whether a high-mid tone (see § 57) or the high tone is used on the first syllable of these kinship terms depends on the dialect concerned, as does the use or not of the suffixes -**pi** (very frequent in general), -**pìrö** (rare), and **í**- (optional). -**àzí** is likewise sometimes added instead of -**pi**. Apparently a change of such final syllables in no way interferes with the meaning; -**pìrö**, however, is a necessary part in some expressions.

These fairly regular plural forms of kinship terms are possibly survivals of old ones and therefore of interest.

85. A fairly complete list of kinship terms is given below.

For the purpose of addressing each other within a family, special forms of intimacy are used; they generally end in -**íi**. In several cases the form in -**íi** (as átíi) is the ordinary term and remains: e.g. **má átíi!** or **bàbá!** *my father!*

Often, though not always, a term such as 'uncle' differs according to whether a paternal or a maternal relationship is implied: f.s. (father's side) or m.s. (mother's side) after a word indicates this difference.

	Singular	*Plural*
1. *grandfather, ancestor*	á'bíi; má á'bíi! (*my grandfather*)	à'bipi
2. *grandmother*	dèdè, èdíi, díi, dèdèá! dápi	diipi
3. *father*	átá(-pi), átíi! bàbá!	àtapi (-í, -ka)
4. *mother*	andré, ándríi (!), àyíïà! áyằ!	àndrɛpi
5. *uncle* (f.s.)	átápìrö, átáàógú	àtapi-ógúrí
6. *aunt* (f.s.)	àúpi, á'wíizí, wáatsò	àupi, wáatsòí
7. *aunt's husband*	átíïá, átápìrö	àtapièi
8. *uncle's* (f.s.) or *father's other wives*	ándría	àndrapií
9. *uncle* (m.s.); *sister's child*	àdrò, ádrúi, ádrói, ádrópi	àdropi

10. *aunt* (m.s.)	ándrápìrö	àndrapi-ì or -rúka
11. *uncle's* (m.s.) *wife*	ó'díi	ò'dapi
12. *man* (homo)	ágú ; 'bá	àgu ; 'báì
13. *man, husband* (vir)	ágúpí	àgùpi
14. *woman, wife*	ɔ̀kó ; okíi, má okíi !	ɔ̀kóì, ɔ̀kupíì
15. *baby, child*	mváã ; mvá ; mvíi !	andzi ; andzipi
16. *boy, son*	ágúpi-(é)mvá	àgùpi-andzi
17. *girl, daughter*	záã ; záa (-mvá) ; mâ zíi̯ !	ézó-andzi ; ézópi
18. *brother*	ádríi ; ádrípi	àdripi
19. *sister*	ámvíã, ámví, -àzí, -pi	àmvipìèì
20. (woman calls) *brother's wife; husband's sister*	a'wíi or a'wíìzí *sister- in law (of woman)*	
21. (man calls) *bro- ther's wife; wife's sister; sister's husband; hus- band's brother*	ɔn̯ere ; ɔn̯ìi(ìzì) ! *sis- ter-in-law (of man); brother-in-law (of wo- man)*	ɔ̀n̯ipììzi
22. *wife's brother, sis- ter's man*	ɔ̀tíi, ɔ̀túpi (T.)	ɔ̀tupíì
23. *brother's child*	mvápi ; záãpi ; má ázíi !	andzipi ; zaapíì
24. *father-in-law*	án̯íi	àn̯ipíì
25. *mother-in-law*	èɛdrá, èɛdríi	èɛdripíì
26. *wives of a man* or *of brothers* call each other	a'íi, a'ípi	a'ipi-àzi

86. These special plural forms are regularly used, and qualifying adjectives have also to conform in number. Examples:

 má àdrɔ̀èì wɛrɛ 'dìi *my little nephews* or *nieces*

87. There are a few other nouns which have plurals of the above pattern. Examples:

friend	ágúi or ágíi	pl. àgui or àgii
owner, proprietor	ɛ'ípi	pl. è'ipi or 'ípi

88. With the great majority of nouns the plural is formed, or rather indicated, by adding the suffix -ì (correctly, èì) without further change. This -ì is nothing but the personal pronoun third person plural èì or ìì in a 'slurred' form. Both ìì and èì may be quite clearly heard, but are very short, always, however, retaining the tone-pattern `ˊ, low plus low-mid. This plural suffix can be added to any noun, even to the specific plural forms given above (see § 83). This suffix is felt to be something almost foreign to the word. It is, therefore, dropped whenever plurality is expressed either through an adjective with a plural suffix, or èì preceding the verb, or a special form of the verb itself, or a corresponding numeral. In short

the Logbara have many ways of expressing the plural which they use in preference to the symbolic plural suffix -ĭ. Examples:

'bá àzíni̇̀ 'yə nĭ *somebody* (sg.) *said*
'bá àzíni̇̀ 'yɔ́ nĭ *some people* (pl.) *said* (N.B. tone of 'yɔ́)
ɔ̀kó kèni̇̀: 'ïmà andzi tsĭ *the woman says that her children are all right*
ɔ̀kó kéni̇̀: èimà andzi tsĭ *the women say that their* . . . (note tone of kéni̇̀)

89. The plural of all other nouns is formed by adding the suffix -èĭ or the contracted or assimilated forms -ìĭ or -ĭ. Examples:

tí *cow*	pl. tíĭ;		kàbìlɔ̀ *sheep*	pl. kàbìlòĭ;
ǹdrí *goat*	„ ǹdríĭ;		a'ú *fowl*	„ a'úèĭ;
dzɔ́ *hut*	„ dzɔ́èĭ;		lítsɔ́ *cow-pen*	„ lítsɔ́èĭ, &c.

II. Case

90. Nouns are not inflected for purposes of indicating case. The case of a noun is indicated either by its position in the sentence or by means of postpositions, which are fairly numerous.

91. A noun in the *nominative* case, i.e. the subject, is indicated by its position at the head of a sentence, as a rule, and by the suffix -nĭ added to it in sentences of CIA (see Verb, § 337). For examples see below.

92. A noun in the *accusative*, i.e. the direct object, precedes the verb in sentences with CIA; it follows the verb in sentences with CCA.

N.B. Noun or pronoun, as subject or object, follow the same rules.

The Genitive or Possessive Case

93. The *genitive* case is of particular importance in Logbara on account of the various forms it may assume, and the choice that has to be made among them.

A noun is added to another noun in the genitive case for the purpose of qualifying and thus restricting its meaning; a noun in the genitive case has the function of an adjective.

A noun in the genitive case usually denotes the possessor, the owner of a thing; the whole related to its part; the source related to its product or, maybe, social relationship, e.g. the child of the chief; the roof of a hut; the egg of the fowl; a man of Padzulu.

94. The *genitive* case can be expressed in four different ways, i.e. by means of four different postpositions, mà, vélé, drí, nĭ or nĭ.

A *postposition* in Logbara corresponds to a preposition in the classical languages; the term 'postposition' is here used because it is regularly placed after its object, while in other languages it precedes it. Example:

on the table mɛza drìá (lit. *table on*)

95. The case of the postposition mà is peculiar: an object with mà precedes the noun it qualifies, very much like the Engl. *the chief's child*, in Logb. ɔ́pí mà mvá.

96. In the case of **vélé**, the noun with its postposition may precede or follow the noun it qualifies. Example:

(1) 'dὶ má átíí vélé dzó-rὶ'ï *this is my father's hut,* or 'dὶ dzó má átíí vélé (-rὶ'ï).

97. In the case of the two other postpositions, **drí** and **nï**, the noun in the genitive with the postposition follows the noun it qualifies. Examples:

(2) ṅdrí 'dὶ má átíí drí (-rὶ'ï) *this goat is my father's*
(3) dzó 'dà má ó'díí nï (-rὶ'ï) *that hut is my aunt's*

98. *Use* of the different forms.

As a rule, any one of the different forms may be used in any particular case; no difference of meaning is implied.

99. (1) **Mà.** The **mà**-form is the normal form commonly used for ordinary speech: it is the unstressed form of narrative.

100. (*a*) In ordinary compound colloquial expressions, even the use of **mà** would be felt to be cumbersome and pedantic. **Mà** is, therefore, dropped in many such expressions which, as a result, consist simply of two terms (nouns), the noun in the genitive preceding, as in:

a'ú g̔bé (for a'ú mà g̔bé) *a fowl's egg*
kàbìlò mvá (or kàbìlò mà mvá) *young of sheep* (i.e. a lamb)

(*b*) If any qualifier is added to the noun in the genitive, the **mà** is normally added before the governed noun, as in:

(4) ṅdrí ɛmvɛ-rὶ mà mvá *the kid of the white goat*
(5) 'bá àlío-rὶ mà àfa yɔ *a pauper has no property* (i.e. to marry)
(lit. *a poor man's things are non-existent*)

101. In order to emphasize an expression or to avoid ambiguity, **mà** must, of course, be used, unless one of the other three postpositions be preferred for the sake of clarity.

In made-up, less common combinations, the **mà** may not be dropped.

102. Detailed illustration of the use of the *form without* **mà.**

This shortened form (called **g̔èrì àlí**) is used especially:

103. (1) To indicate *parts of the body*:

Combine two words, one from the first line followed by one from the second line below:

Nomen regens / genitive

'bá	mvá	ṅdrí	tí
man	*child*	*goat*	*cow*

Nomen rectum / noun to be qualified

rúá	ti	drì	àrὶ	óɲófí	zá	mìlé	drí, &c.
body	*mouth*	*head*	*blood*	*nail*	*flesh*	*eye*	*hand*

thus:

'bá rúá *man's body*   tî zá *beef*
mvá drí (or drì) *child's hand (head)*

104. In such close combinations there is a tendency for open vowels to become closer: a>ä, ɔ>o, ɛ>e(ë).

'bǎ drí *man's hand*   dzó ti (-lé) *hut's (dzó) opening* or *door of hut*

105. (2) To indicate *parts of a whole* in general, as in:

dzó drì / 'alé / (mà) àbì *hut's roof / inside / wall*

Observe dzó mà àbì (apparently more often with mà) as it is not a very common expression:

àdzú drìlé / sí *a spear's point / edge*
pätí mà páti *trunk of a tree* (clearness requires mà; unusual term)

106. (3) To indicate *natural products*:

tí	kàbìlɔ̀	ǹdrí	mvá	lé(-sú)	ɔ̀do
cow's	*sheep's*	*goat's*	*young*	*milk*	*fat*, &c.

107. (4) For *descriptive expressions in general*, as:

à'í sú, = zá à'í sú *broth* (lit. *salt juice*)
andrálé 'bá *lowland people*
ányú ɔ̀do *sesame oil*
ànyú ɔ́sɔ̀ *bee's fat = honey*
ásé bbí *grass leaf, blade of grass*
dzó àgǎí (-á) (on) *the side of a hut*
kómárá ɔ̀do *shea butter*
ɔ̀ndó ɛ́wá *beer from durra*
àtsí sí *glowing embers (fire tooth)*
'bá yíia *highland people*
'bá orú or orúlé 'bá *highland people*
'bílé 'alé *inside of a hole*
drí (á)mvá *finger (hand's child)*
drì bbí *head hair, hair of the head*
ámvú 'ípi *a field's owner, owner of a field*
orúlé 'bá ti *highlanders' language*
pätí ètí *place under a tree*

108. Miscellaneous examples:

(6) ma àmbó mà gǎrì dzi, *I am taking the cycle of the big man*
(7) Térégo mà ti ndó *Terego's language is different*
(8) ɔ̀'dónï 'bá àrî mvu *a leopard laps up* (lit. *drinks*) *human blood*
(9) andzi emú màákɔ̀ mà èlï sï *the boys came for longing of pota-toes* (i.e. because they were hungry)
(10) ǹdrí 'dɔ̀ï mà 'ípi ŋgólé yà? *where is the owner of these goats?*
(11) ma tíbí mà àdzi 'bï *I am tasting the savoury*
(12) má ándríi mà ádríi-nï ma adrúi *my mother's brother is my uncle*
(13) ágú 'dà èri mvá 'dï mà átá *that man is this child's father*

109. The *genitive* expressed by any of the postpositions **drí, ní,** or **vélé** implies, on the whole, more emphasis than the above.

The construction required by these postpositions is that the genitive, i.e. the noun with its postposition, be placed after the noun to be governed, as in English. Example:

the cloth of this child **bòŋgó** ('dǐ) **mvá 'dǐ ní** (= **drí,** = **vélé**)

110. Vélé with its noun may, however, be placed before the noun to be governed, as in the case of **mà** :

'dǐ mvá 'dǐ vélé bòŋgó *this is this child's cloth*

111. Note that the genitive postposition **ní** requires a low tone on the preceding syllable, which eventually has to be added to an original higher tone of the noun, as **ágú : ágû ní** *of a man.*

112. The use of any of the three postpositions is left to choice; the meaning remains the same. This applies to **mà** also. Although this is what educated Logbara will readily assert (without much reflection), yet the present writer feels that **'bâ ní** seems to imply the idea of *'for* a person' rather than *'of* a person', while **'bá vélé** implies rather *'at* a person's', suggesting the place or home of a person.

113. Formally and theoretically the forms given above (§ 109) are all correct, but actually they are not much used in their simple form. Usually the above simple genitive is converted into a kind of adjectival clause or phrase by adding, at the end, the relative pronoun -**rǐ** or, for greater emphasis, -**rǐ 'ï.** This represents the emphatic, possessive, form of the genitive. Examples:

(14) **a'ú má ándríí véléri'ï** *the fowl of (belonging to) my mother*
(15) **tí ma ádríí vélérǐ** *the cow of (that belongs to) my brother*
(16) **dzó 'dǐ ágúpí 'dǐ vélé òkó àzírǐ vélérǐ 'ï** *this is the hut of one of the wives of this man*
(17) **'dǐ ma átíí vélé ámvú rǐ 'ï** *this is my father's field*
(18) **á lè ágú 'dà vélé dzó 'dàrǐ tò** *I like that man's hut very much*
(19) **émvó ìyí drí-rǐ 'dò** *this is a water pot*
(20) **àfa 'dǐrï sàfarǐ drí kìɛ? dí kìɛ** *is this a thing for safari? so it is*
(21) **andzi 'dǐǐ tí drírǐ 'ï** *these* (young) *are cow calves*
(22) **kànì 'du àfa 'bá àzǐnï drí rá, mu èì bɛ rá** *if some one has taken away somebody's things, he has gone off with them*
(23) **ma ɛnïrïkə ńdrí ùúa 'dǐrï ùú** *I am stripping the skin from the foreleg of this goat*

(For further examples see under Postpositions.)

The Dative Case or Indirect Object

114. The *dative case,* or the *indirect object,* is indicated by either of the postpositions **drí** or **ní,** and sometimes by **vǒ** or **vélé.** The indirect object or the postpositional object are hardly distinguishable in practice. Any of these postpositions may generally be used indiscriminately in any one case, although each, at bottom, conveys some particular shade of meaning.

115. The postposition **nǐ** of the dative does not require a low tone in the preceding syllable as does the genitive or possessive **nǐ**. **Nǐ** is used to indicate that a thing is given . . . with the intention of leaving it in the possession of a person, or for consumption.

(24) **fè má-nǐ àfa 'dǐrǐ 'ǐ** *he has given me this thing* (for me)

116. The pstp. **drǐ** of the dative indicates, mainly, that a thing is given to a person for use, temporary keeping only (not for possession).

(25) **fè má drǐ (tà nǐ mba)** *he gave it to me* (for guarding, to look after)

117. The postpositions **vǒ** and **vélé** indicate that something is 'conveyed, carried', &c., 'to the site of', 'towards . . .' (cf. Postpositions).

N.B. An indiscriminate use of these various postpositions does not, apparently, impair the meaning substantially.

118. If the indirect or dative (postpositional) object happens to be qualified by a genitive following it, the dative postposition follows the genitive expression.

119. Examples:

(26) **é fè kàlámò 'dǐǐ 'bá 'dà nǐ** (or drǐ) *give the pencils to that man !*
(27) **dzi èri ándrǐǐ nǐ ìyǐ** *she brought water to her mother*
(28) **èri ɲaaká a'dǐ andzi ópí drǐ 'dǐǐ nǐ** *she is cooking food for the children* (people) *of the chief*
(29) **òkó edzǐ àɲá 'ǐmà andzi nǐ** *the woman brought food for her children*
(30) **á drɔ tǐ záa átǐǐ nǐ** (or vǒ) *I drove cattle to the girl's father* (e.g. bride-wealth)
(31) **ópí li ǹdrǐ òmú drǐ** *the chief has killed a goat for the guest*
(32) **èri éɲâ 'ǐ má-nǐ** *she prepares polenta for me*
(33) **àgu rǒ mánǐ tǐ nǐ** *people have bewitched my cow*
(34) **à'di rɔ mǐnǐ nǐ?** *who has bewitched you?* (i.e. *your cows*)

III. Gender

120. In Logbara, as in English, there is no grammatical distinction of gender. Difference of gender coincides with difference of sex.

There are a number of distinct nouns for beings of each sex. Apart from these, nouns for living beings are of common gender, and, where the sex needs to be specified, appropriate words (nouns) denoting 'male' and 'female' are added as if in apposition or adjectivally, as:

a'ú *fowl* **a'ú ándrǐǐ** *hen* (lit *mother fowl*).

Nouns denoting Human Beings: (v. §85)

121. (1) Distinct words for each sex:

Masculine

Singular		Plural
ágúpía	boy	àgùpìà
ágúpía 'wàrà	big boy	àgùpìà 'wàrà
kàrílè	youth, lad	kàrílèì
kàrílè 'wàrà	grown youth	kàrílèì 'wàrà
ágúpí	man, husband (Lat. vir)	àgùpi
ɔ́dzɔ́lɔ́	bachelor[1]	ɔ́dzɔ́lɔ́ì
mbàzà	old man	mbàzàò

Feminine

Singular		Plural
záa	} girl, lass, maid,	{ ɛ́zó-andzì
záa-mvá	} daughter	{ ɛ́zópi
ɔ̀kó	woman, wife	ɔ̀kóì
àwízyó	widow[1]	àwizyo (àùzio)
ɔ̀kó-àmbó	old woman	ɔkambo (ɔkombo)

122. (2) Nouns of common gender:

Singular		Plural
ɔ̀dɛ́kolɛ́	baby	ɔ̀dɛ́kolɛ́èì
mvá	child	andzì
ágú }	man, human	{ àgu
'bá }	person (Lat. homo)	{ 'báèì

123. If the sex of the common personal nouns requires to be specified then the appropriate masculine or feminine noun must be added. Examples:

(35) ɔ̀dɛ́kolɛ́ 'dìrï ágúpíá nï   *this baby is a boy*
      "   "   záa-mvá nï   "   "   *girl*
(36) mvá 'dì mba àrɔ̀kpà-rö 'bɔ *this child (infant) has grown strong*

Nouns denoting Animals

124. Of the nouns for animals, all but three are generic terms, therefore, of common gender and require special words (nouns) to be added when the sex is to be specified.

(1) Animals of *common gender*:

a'ú *fowl*	tí *neat, cattle*
kàbìlɔ̀ *sheep*	ǹdrí *goat* (often comprising *sheep*)
kằmì *lion*	ɔ̀tsɔ́ *dog*

(2) Animals of *masculine gender*:

With regard to animals, there are apparently only three distinct nouns

---

[1] Also *widower* in some dialects.

which do not require additional terms to specify sex. They are all masculine:

lɔɔlɔɔ *cock*   mǒníö or múnío *bull*   ráao or ráṇá *castrated animal*

Of these, the first two have alternatives which are formed by use of the term for male (see below).

125. To specify the sex of animals special terms for 'male' and 'female' are added after the common noun.

The terms for *male* are:

(*a*) ágɔ́ or átá and dim. ágóā or átáā

Examples:

a'ú átá or lɔ̀ɔ́ átá *cock*	lɔ̀ɔ́ átáā *small cock*
tí átá or tí mǒnío *bull*	tí átáā or tí mǒníóā *small bull*
ǹdrí ágɔ́ *he-goat*	ǹdrí ágóā́ *male kid*
kàbìlɔ̀ ágɔ́ or kàbìlɔ̀ átá *ram*, &c.	

126. (*b*) The term ráṇá or ráao *gelding*, added to the common nouns for animals, indicates a castrated male, as:

tí ráṇá *ox*   kàbìlɔ̀ ráṇá *gelded ram*, &c.

127. The terms for *female* are:

kǎrì for young ones, dim. kǎrìá for small young ones
ándrí for adult females

Examples:

tí kǎrì *heifer*	tí kǎrìá *small heifer*	tí ándrí *cow*
kàbìlɔ̀ ándrí *ewe*	ɔ̀tsé ándrí *bitch*, &c.	

128. The term mvá (*child, young one*) pl. andzì is added after a noun as a kind of diminutive (with mà expressed or implied) to indicate the young offspring of a human or animal. Examples:

záa-mvá *girl, daughter*	ágúpi-mvá *boy, son*
a'ú mvá *chicken*	pl. a'ú andzì
[1]tí (mà) mvá *cow-calf*	„ tí (ma) andzì
kǎmì mvá *lion cub*	„ ɔ̀tsɔ́ andzì *puppies*, &c.

129. The diminutive suffix -ā́ may be added to the nouns, human and animal, to indicate *little* or *small and young ones*. Sometimes both -ā́ and mvá are used together—a kind of double diminutive. Examples:

tí mǒníóā́ *small bull*	tí kǎrìā́ *small heifer*
ágúpíā́-mvá *little boy*	záā-mvá *little girl*

(See §§ 125, 127).

130. The term àrɔ́ (lit. *immature, unripe, green*) may be added after a common noun to indicate *older young ones, not yet physically mature*. àrɔ́ is used for either sex; it is of common gender. Examples:

ɔ̀tsɔ́ àrɔ́ *young dog*   ǹdri àrɔ́ *young goat*

[1] Commonly kɔ̀dzáā.

CHAPTER 5
ADJECTIVES

131. In Logbara there are a large number of adjectives, i.e. words used to qualify nouns. A number of them are primary or original adjectives, i.e. words used exclusively as adjectives, while a large number are derived from nouns, adverbs, or verbs.

GENERAL RULES FOR ADJECTIVES

132. An adjective is used either (*a*) as an *epithet* or *attribute*, or (*b*) as the *predicative*.

> *Epithet*: a good child **mvá mŏkɛ́-rì**,
> *Predicate*: the child is good **mvá mŏkɛ̂-rö.**

The adjective always follows the noun it qualifies.

I. Epithet or Attributive Use

133. General rules:

An *adjective* when used *attributively* has the suffix **-rì** added. This suffix is essentially the *relative pronoun* suffix **-rì** (cf. § 253). Its tone may be considered low, for practical purposes. But when the preceding syllable has a low tone, the suffix **-rì** regularly takes a low-intermediate tone (cf. § 55), as in **'dìrì** (more correctly) **'dìrì**) *this*.

N.B. This suffix **-rì** corresponds to the Acooli prefix **mà-**.

134. Sometimes the common (-)**nï** is used in place of **-rì**.

135. If the suffix **-rö** has come to be regarded as part and parcel of an adjective, the epithetic **-rì** is added to **-rö**, as in **ɔ̀ndî-rö-rì** *dirty*. In a similar way **-rì** may even occasionally be added after **nï**. Generally, however, **-rö** or **nï** are dropped before **-rì** or **'dìì**. However, as a rule it makes no difference whether or not this **-rö** is inserted before **-rì**.

136. The plural of nouns is generally formed (except those mentioned in § 81) by suffixing **-ì**, that of adjectives by adding **'dìì** after them. Note the low-mid tone of these plural suffixes **-ì** or **'dìì**. The former is the 3rd person plural pronoun (§ 82), the latter is the demonstrative plural pronoun **'dì-èì** *these* (often functioning as a definite article).

137. It is interesting to observe that, while the plural form of an adjective can, and indeed must, remain when used epithetically with a plural noun, as in **andzi mŏké 'dìì** *good children*, the conventional plural noun suffix **-ì** is dropped when an adjective with **'dìì** follows, as in **ɔ̀kó mŏké 'dìì** *the good women*; one cannot say **ɔ̀kóì mŏké 'dìì** or **ɔ̀kóì mŏké.** The reason for this is that the adjectival plural form is sufficient to indicate that the noun is in the plural, so that the plural noun suffix **-ì** is unnecessary. The same rule holds when the 3rd person plural pronoun **èì** functions as the copula in a sentence, as in

> **ɔ̀kó èì mŏké** *the women are good*; **-ì** and **'dìì** are here dropped.

138. The *plural suffixes* are simply a convenient symbol for indicating plurality, used only when no other sign of plurality occurs in the sentence.

II. Predicative Use

139. An adjective used in a predicative way sometimes has no suffix; generally, however, the predicative adjective takes the suffix -rö immediately after its root. If the preceding syllable contains a **u**, -rö commonly becomes -**ru**. If the preceding syllable has anything but a low tone, a low tone must be added to it: this is an important characteristic of all adjectival -rö forms. Verbal adjectives ending in -zà take -rö after -zà. Example: **ambí-zà-rö** *cold*.

Here, again, -**nǐ** may be used in place of -rö (cf. § 134).

The above rules hold good for adjectives of the common type; but they require some modification when applied to other types of adjectives (cf. §§ 140 ff.).

CLASSIFICATION OF ADJECTIVES

140. Adjectives may be grouped into the two following classes:

(1) *Primary* or *original* adjectives, i.e. words or roots used only as adjectives. These are either (*a*) *simple* or *ordinary* ones; (*b*) *compound* ones; or (*c*) *reduplicated* adjectives.

(2) *Derived* adjectives from nouns, adverbs, verbs.

It is difficult, if not impossible, to draw a rigid line of demarcation between the different groups; only for the last class do a few special rules hold.

1. Primary or Original Adjectives

141. The rules as set out above apply regularly to this group. The following is a list of (*a*) *simple* or *ordinary* adjectives:

àlá *clean, pure; regulated; holy*	fòrò *light-brown, khaki*
àlí *short*	'bara *broad—flat—thin*
àlío *poor, needy*	kpàrà *flat* (of low thick object)
àmbó *big, great; important*	kùlù *thick* (of long round object)
àmorè *raw, uncooked* (of food)	lúrú *narrow* (of space)
àndzì *thick, strong* (of make)	mòké *good, nice*
à'ói = à'wí *dry, ripe; dense*	ó'dí *new*
àró *green, unripe*	òku *old, worn*
èbì *green—soft, tender, raw* (of food)	òndzì *bad, ugly*
èdú *thick, dense*	òdúrú *deaf*
ɛka *red, brown*	òré *thin, fluid*
ɛmvɛ *white*	mŋgbàa *true, real*
ëni *dark, black*	mŋgbə *open, empty*
èzíí, èzöö *long* (*thin—thick*)	wàlà *broad, spacious* (room)
	wătá *unripe, sour*

N.B. It is difficult to say which of the above are in reality verbs.

142. Examples:

(1) ma àŋgò ëni-rì sì òrì-rö (= òrì bɛ) *I am afraid on a dark night*

(2) á gà búkù òkurì sì ; á lɛ̀ ó'dírì'ï *I refuse an old book, I want new ones*

(3) gìrì 'dìrï pirì-rö *this path is straight*

(4) àfa 'dìrï àfa ó'dínï nòsì àfa òkunï yà? *is this thing something new or something old?*

(5) tí ópî nì ɛmverì drà rá *the white cow of the chief died*

(6) àma esú ɛ'yó águ 'dì bɛ àmbórì ; ɛ'yónï dɛ àŋgà 'ï kö *I have (found/got) an important question for this man; it is not yet settled*

(7) á lɛ̀ tsúpà ɛríkòrì kö *I do not want a cracked bottle*

(8) mí edzí mání kàbìlò mókérì, á lɛ̀ òndzínï kö *bring me a nice sheep, I do not want a bad one*

(9) á 'bà à'bòà wátárì àmvé ásɛ́ tálá 'dàá *I have put the green banana outside among the grass there*

(10) nì ǹdrí ɛmvɛ 'dïï kö, nì ëni 'dïï 'ï *he does not know the white goats, but he knows the black ones*

(11) nì òbí andzi móké 'dïï nï kö *they do not know the habits of good children*

143. (b) *Compound adjectives.* These adjectives are often formed in a peculiar way, and there are many of them.

àndzì'bìrìtì or àndzírítítí *thick, strong*

áŋgírí = àmbó (see above)

bálákándí *thin* (as an iron rod)

'barakala = 'bara (see above)

kəkətɛ = kòŋgòlòrö *rigid, stiff*

kú(kú)rùlúkù = kúkúrú, *pitch-dark*

kúkúté = kúŋgúté *thick-flat*

lúurúmbé *variegated*

ŋgörölö = ŋgörökö'dö *elevated*

ɲiŋgíríkí *small, minute and numerous*

ɲírí(á) (similar to former)

ɲírïɲïɲï = ɲïkìrìkìrì *restless*

òdíríkpà = àdárákpàlá *wrinkled*

òká/òkáŋgálí(ká) *sour/very sour*

òkpólò(kò) *old (and worn)*

tìlìkpa *sticky, tenacious*

yéŋgérékɛ̀ *rough* (of surface)

144. Examples:

(12) kóbi ɛ̀ri 'barakalàrö *the* (round) *winnowing basket is* (almost) *flat*

(13) ódrá mà rùá òlíŋgólòrö *the* (stem of the) *bamboo is round*

(14) bòŋgó 'dìrï kəŋgələkòrö *this cloth is strong/stiff*

145. (c) *Reduplicated adjectives* are numerous and mostly used predicatively; but they can conveniently be used as epithets with -rì or -rö-rì suffixes. The consonant **k** is commonly inserted when otherwise reduplication would bring two vowels together.

ằrì-k-ằrì *pleasant, agreeable* (taste)

dìnà-dìnà *adhesive, sticky, elastic*

'dŏrŏ'dŏrŏ *even, level, plane* (ground)

eníkèni *small and fine* (grain); *soft*

ɛ̀pɛ́-(k-)ɛ̀pɛ́ *thin* (of make), *threadbare*

fɔ̀ŋ̣ì-fɔ̀ŋ̣ì, fŏŋ̣ì-fŏŋ̣ì *grey—dirty*

fútú-fútû-rö *foamy*

ɡə'də-ɡə'də, ɡ̀lí-ɡ̀lí *crooked, curved, tortuous*

hào-hào = lằu-lằu, hɔ́rə-hɔ́rə *light*

kàlí-kàlí *sweet*

kárákàràrö = kákáó *many*

kɛmè-kɛmè *lithe, supple, pliant*

kɔ̀ŋ̣í-kɔ̀ŋ̣í, kɔ̀rí-kɔ̀rí, ndzǐ-ndzǐ *variegated, mottled*

n̲ào-n̲ào *loose, crumbling*

mɛ̀nɛ̀-mɛ̀nɛ̀ *soft, supple*

ndzɔ̀(là)ndzɔ̀là *smooth, slippery*

ŋgörö-ŋgörö, tùlútulu *uneven, hilly* (area)

òbikòbi = ònikòni *dark ash-grey, dark*

òlíŋgóló = òlóŋgólóŋgo, ŋgŏlŏŋgŏlŏ *round(ish)*

òndràkòndrà, òkàlàkòkàlà *light yellow, darker yellow*

òŋgbàkòŋgbà *reddish-brown* (complexion)

pfŏrŏpfŏrŏ *decaying, crumbling*

ràö-ràö *thin—weak*

rutsurutsuru *light, unsteady*

sìrösurúlé, surú-surú *green* (as **surú**)

tàlàtàlà or talakpa = takpala *insipid, flat*

tékètékè *fine/delicately* (done)

trikítríki *heavy*

wàrà-wàrà, ɔ̀kà-ɔ̀kà *yellow* (-reddish)

N.B. The meanings given above are often tentative only.

146. Examples:

(15) óní pföröpförŏ-rö i.e. óní mbắpí kö rì̀'ï: óní àndǐ-rö-pi àndì-rì̀'ï *the stone is easily crumbled, is not hard: is crumbling*

(16) bɔ̀ŋgó ɛ̀ri ëníkëní (= akázàrö) *the cloth is soft*

(17) a'ú 'bíkə mɛ̀nɛ̀mɛ̀nɛ̀rö *the feathers of a fowl are supple*

(18) kàni bɔ̀ŋgó mâ rùá-rìlé háòháòrö, ndzì mâ rùá kö *if material is light on me (if I wear light clothing), it does not oppress me*

(19) súrú Nŏnŏ pi Àdŏmí bɛ èi ɛ̀ŋ̣ï-ɛ̀ŋ̣ï *the groups (clans) of Nönö and Adömi are close to each other*

2. Derived Adjectives

147. There are an unlimited number of *derived adjectives*. These adjectives are derived from nouns, adverbs, or verbs.

(a) Adjectives derived from nouns.

Nouns used as *adjectives* sometimes take the suffix **-rì** (and thus appear as primary), where usage sanctions it, in which case they are used as epithets. More commonly the suffix -rö is added for the predicate (cf. § 139); and -rĭ is then added to this -rö for the attribute. This rule is apparently always correct; in many cases this method (i.e. -rö-rĭ) is the only correct one.

The qualification of a noun by a noun-adjective may also be effected by means of the postposition bɛ (meaning *to be with*, i.e. *to have a given quality*) instead of the suffixes. This latter construction is obviously not admissible in every case; the exceptions do not seem to be numerous, which means that the bɛ construction is very common. -rĭ is suffixed to this bɛ when the construction of the sentence requires it, for instance in a relative Clause. Just as -rĭ may occasionally be replaced by nĭ (§ 134), so also may this -rö.

148. In the following examples the suffix -rĭ is only shown in those cases which have been checked; usage probably differs from area to area. The other constructions mentioned above are regular and common.

An end vowel before bɛ tends to become longer.

> àdzí *taste*: àdzí-nĭ, àdzî-rö-rĭ, àdzíi bɛ (-rĭ) *tasty, delicious*
> àyìkɔ̀ *joy*: àyìkɔ̀ bɛ . . . *pleased, glad, happy*
> àrí *blood*: àrî-rö, àrí bɛ, &c., *to the point of shedding blood, bloody*
> àtsí *fire*: àtsí-rĭ . . . *warm, hot*
> àvŏ *corpse*: àvŏ-rö (one cannot say àvŏ bɛ !) *sick, feeble, weak*
> aya *iron*: ayâ-rö, aya-nĭ (not aya bɛ) . . . *of iron, ironlike*
> à'yà *jealousy*: à'yàa bɛ (-rĭ), à'yà-rö . . . *jealous*
> àzɔ́ *disease*: àzɔ́-rĭ, àzɔ́-nĭ, àzɔ̂-rö, àzɔ́ bɛ *sick, ill*
> édri *life*: édri-nĭ, édrî-rö-rĭ, édri bɛ *still living, alive, brisk*
> èndzà = ɔ̀vŏ *laziness*: èndzà-rö (-rĭ), èndzà bɛ/ɔ̀vŏ-rö, &c., *lazy, indolent*
> èndzɔ̀ *lie*: èndzɔ̀-rö-rĭ, &c., 'bá èndzɔ̀ bɛ *liar*
> èwá *elephant*: èwâ-rö-rĭ, èwá bɛ . . . *strong; difficult*
> mvá *child*: mvâ-rö-rĭ . . . *childlike, while a child.*
> ògù *steal, theft*: ògù-ru-rĭ *thievish*; 'bá ògùrurĭ *one stealing/thief*
> ɔ̀kpɔ̀ *strength*: ɔ̀kpɔ̀-rö, ɔ̀kpɔ̀-nĭ or bɛ (= èwâ-rö) . . . *strong, difficult*
> ɔ̀ndí *dirt*: ɔ̀ndî-rö-rĭ, ɔ̀ndí-nĭ, ɔ̀ndí bɛ . . . *dirty, unclean*
> ɔ̀drí *clay*: ɔ̀drí nĭ, -rö . . . *clayey, earthen*
> ɔ́vá *duiker*: ɔ́vâ-rö . . . ɔ́vá-lɛ́ *grey* (as a duiker)

All nouns may be used in this way.

149. Examples:

> (20) ɔ̀tsɛ́ ndzĭndzírĭ má ádríi nĭ *the spotted, piebald dog is my brother's*
> (21) èimà milɛ́ édrî-rö *their eyes are sharp* (very much alive)
> (22) ɔ̀línĭ fĭ ma òmvu àzɔ́rĭ mà 'a fĭfĭ *the wind* (blows and) *enters my sore nose*
> (23) 'bá àvŏrĭ ɛtsɔ́ nĭ àzî ŋgazŏ kö *a feeble person cannot do work*

(24) ɛ̠ɲá ga ìyî-rö (ὲri tsàzàrö) *the polenta is too watery*

(25) 'bá 'dàrï ògùru ; kànì efï dzóa, ὲri àfa àzînî 'du rá *that man is thievish; if he goes into a hut, he will carry off something*

(26) zá ɔ́sɔ̀rörî : áɲ̠ú ɔ̀donï (one speaks of) *fat meat; sesame oil*

(27) ὲri mînî ὲwâ-rö yà? *is it* (the language) *difficult for you?*

(28) Yosefu mà rùá àzɔ̂rö *Joseph is sick* (lit. *Joseph's body is sick*)

(29) ëlï 'dïrï ayâ-rö *this knife is of iron*

(30) mvá ὲri ŋgà ɛ́drî-rö *the child is still alive*

(31) àdzíkɔ̀ ὲri ɔ̀drí-nï : ὲl sîsi *the pot is earthen: they mould it*

(32) ma ádríi drà mvâ-rö *my brother died as a child* (*when he was a child*)

(33) àŋgɔ̀ drìɔ ὲri ndrá à'dî-rö *old times were once warlike*

(34) ma ágúpí ɔ̀kpɔ̂-rörî ndâ, ma àzîŋga-zɔ̂ (or ma àzî-nï) *I am looking for a strong man to do my work* (or *for my work*)

150. (b) *Adjectives derived from adverbs.* These adjectives are formed by adding the suffix -rï/'dïi alone to the adverb. In this way any adverb may be made into an epithet. No other forms are used.

Note the occasional insertion of **ká** before -rï.

ádzê *yesterday* : ádzê-rï *of yesterday, yesterday's*

àndrò *today* : àndrò-rï *of today, today's*

té *time ago* : té-rï or té-ká-rï ; 'ɛ'yó tékárï *the previous question*

ándrâ *in the past* : ɛ'yó ándrâká-rï *the past matter*

ńdrá-drìɔ *of old* : 'bá ndrádrìɔrï *the ancients*

tsúrú'dɔ̀ *now* : 'bá tsúrú'dɔ̀rï *people of the present day; moderns*

vàálé and vàá ὲlὲ *on the ground* : àfa vàálé-rï *things on the ground*, or *things hereabout*

151. Examples :

(35) ɲ̠aaká ádzê-rï ὲri ɲ̠aaká ɔ̀kpɔ́-nï *food* (*left over*) *from yesterday is the breakfast*

(36) 'dïi ná àfa àlörî mà rú *these are all names for the one thing*

(37) é ŋga àzí térî rá yà? *have you done the work mentioned before?*

(38) ɛ'yó térî àvὲ mánî rá *I have forgotten the recent matter* (*of a moment ago*)

(39) andzi ndé 'dïi mu rá *the boys we spoke about have gone*

(40) súrú àmadrí àkúarï Àlívò *our home clan-group is Alivo*

(41) àlíbɔ àrîa ásɛarî ; ὲri kìlé a'ú lɛ́ *a partridge is a bird of the bush; it is like a fowl*

(42) ὲtú àndrò 'dɔ̀ sî *on this day*; or *nowadays*

(43) mï àfa tákárî sî yà? *are you writing of that earlier matter?*

(44) ɛ'yó ndɛ́rî mà ɔ̀ɲ̠i yɔ *that* (*aforesaid*) *question does not look favourable*

(45) mî edzí vélé(= ὲtïa)-rï'ï ! *bring me the last* (*bottom*) *one !*

(46) 'bá 'dòá-rï *people of the place*

(47) àfa agáá-rì (or ètí'alɛ́-rì)'ï *a thing from the middle* (or *underneath*)

(48) mí edzí vǒnï vǒsì-rì'ï! *bring me the one next* (to it)!

152. (c) *Adjectives derived from verbs—verbal adjectives.* In Logbara this type of adjective appears in a great variety of forms, each used according to the interpretation required.

Neuter or intransitive verbs of state or condition can be used as adjectives without much change; in fact it is sometimes difficult to decide whether a given word is an adjective or a verb.

Below is set out a full list of the forms in use as verbal adjectives. Note that here as elsewhere **-rö** indicates the predicate and **-rì** the attribute.

List of adjectival forms from the verb **bì** or the reduplicated form **bìbì**, inf. *to be dark, dirty.*

(a) **bì-zà-rö** or **bì** or **bìbì** are the predicative forms.

(b) **bì-zà**
(c) **bì-zà-rì** or **bì-zà-nï** } are all used epithetically, as attributes,
(d) **bì-zà-rö-rì** or **bìzàrö-nï** { to qualify a noun
(e) **bì-pi-bìbì-rì**

(f) **bì-pi-'bə-rì** (relative clause) *that is/has become dirty*

N.B. The emphasizing element **'ï** may always be added after **-rì**.

153. Examples of very common verbal adjectives:

alu, alu-alu *pleasant, agreeable*
aká, aká-aká *soft, supple*
ambí (-ambí) *to be* (*-come*) *cold, cool*
atsí (-atsí) *to be rust-eaten*
drà (drà) *to die, be dead*
drǎ (-dra) *to be sour, bitter*
drì (drï) *to be warm, hot*
fì (-fï) *to be cold, fresh* (milk)
mbǎ (-mba) *to be hard, strong*
ndrì (-ndrì) *nice; gentle*

ndzì (-ndzì) *to be heavy*
ndzὸ (-ndzὸ) *to be slippery*
o'bí (-o'bí) *to be worm-eaten, crumby*
ədi (-ədi) *to be wrinkled, shrivelled*
əka (-əka) *to be yellowish brown*
ὸmvὲ (-ὸmvὲ) *to be convalescent*
əse (-əse) *to be fat, stout*
'wì (-'wï) *to be dry, ripe*

154. Examples:

(49) má edzí mǐní ìyî drïzàrörì'ï yà? *should I bring you* (some) *hot water?*

(50) yə; á lὲ ìyí ambízàrì'ï; á gà ìyî drïzàrì sì *no; I want cold water; I refuse warm water*

(51) cf. àndrò àŋgὸ ambí-ambí *it is cold today*

(52) óní ɛtsó ədzá rö drïzàrö ètú sì rá *a stone can become hot by means of the sun*

(53) lὲ àfa àrìkàrì-rì mbɛzàrö *they like something delicate to eat* (nibble)

(54) Àdróà-nï mu emû 'bá ɛ́driȓ pi 'bá dràzàrȉ bɛ ɛ'yónȉ li
God will (come and) *judge the living and the dead*

(55) emúpi ó'díȓ mà rú à'di 'ï yà? *what is the newly arrived's name?*

(56) 'dȉ àfa mbắpi mbằmbarȉ'ï *this is something really hard*

(57) ògúo lɛ̀ àŋgò bȉzàrȉ *a thief likes darkness*

(58) 'bȉ'bíiə ɛ̀ri ndrȉndrȉrö *the star is bright*

155. *Diminutive form of adjectives.* In Logbara there is a peculiar formative particle—the suffix -ắ or -ắā. It itself is nasalized and when added to an adjective the final vowel of the adjective generally becomes nasalized too. To the meaning implicit in the adjective it gives a *diminutive* aspect, as of something *small, tender, delicate.* It can be added to any adjective whose meaning admits of a 'diminutive' in this sense. Examples:

wɛrɛ or ga make wɛrɛ́ắ, gáắā or gáắkắā or gáắkáɳắā, and mbíɳắā, mbítắā, ɳȉríắ, ŋgölöắā *very small, tiny, delicate*
àlí *short,* àlíắā *short, dwarfish* . . .
ɛzȉ *long* (and thin), ɛzȉắā *tiny long thing* (as a needle)
ɛzö́ *long* (rather stout, thick), ɛzö́ắā *something small long and thick*

The suffix -rȉ or -rö (§§ 133, 139) is added, in keeping with normal requirements, after this suffix -ắā.

COMPARISON

1. Comparison of Similarity and Equality

156. *Similarity* or *equality*, two terms often taken as identical, is expressed in the following ways, either of which may as a rule be used for the other indiscriminately.

(*a*) *Similarity* is very commonly expressed by placing lɛ́ after the term of reference, as in àfa 'dȉ ndzi óní lɛ́ *this thing is as heavy as a stone.*

kìlɛ́ (or ɛ́kìlɛ́) used especially in a simple independent sentence, is the correlative of the above lɛ́ and is placed before the term of reference: kìlɛ́ . . . lɛ́ (*like, as*): e.g. 'dȉrȉ àmbô-rö kìlɛ́ 'dà lɛ́ *this is as big as that.*
This kìlɛ́ is, however, often omitted in ordinary sentences.
The *negation* of similarity is expressed by yə or kö placed after lɛ́.

157. Examples:

(59) ǹdrí àmbô-rö kìlɛ́ tí lɛ́ yə *a goat is not as big as a cow*

(60) é mu ndắ mání àfa 'dȉ lɛ́! *go and look for a thing like this for me!*

(61) òví ɛ̀ri oɳúkoɳú àmbórȉ-lɛ́ or òví àmbórȉ kìlɛ́ oɳúkoɳú lɛ́ *a horsefly is as big as a* (common) *fly*

(62) mï aza kìlɛ́ mï ádriìnï azarȉ lɛ́ *you are as stupid as your* (stupid) *brother*

(63) kàlamò 'dȉ mà sí ɛkằ-rö àtsȉ lɛ́ or kìlɛ́ àtsȉ lɛ́ or sì (*resembling*) àtsȉ lɛ́ *the point of this pencil is as red as fire*

(64) àŋgǒ àndròrì (èri) ambízàrö kìlé ádzé-rì lé (kö) (àtsízàrö warm) *today it is (not) as cold as yesterday*

(65) 'bá 'dàrï wɛɛrɛáà-rö ɛ́kìlé mváa lé *that man is as small as a boy*

(66) Kàlía mà èndzà Mà'dírá mà èndzà lé *Kalia's laziness resembles Ma'dira's (Kalia is as lazy as Ma'dira)*

(67) ɛ́kìlé tí lé ɛkà-rö *it is as brown as a cow*

158. (b) Another way of expressing similarity or equality is by using either the adverb **trótrò** *alike* or the reduplicated verb **òsì-rö-òsì** (cf. **sì** ex. 63) *is the same* or *are equal to, resembles,* preceded by the postposition **bɛ,** placed after the term of comparison. Examples:

(68) lóá èri àn̩àpá ɔvǒpi tí bɛ trótrò nï *the hartebeest is an animal of the size of a cow*

(69) àma trótrò or àma èri bɛ trótrò *we (two) are equal*

(70) òví pi on̩úkon̩ú àmbórì bɛ trótrò or òví àmbórì sì on̩úkon̩ú àmbórì lé *a horsefly and a fly are equal* (cf. ex. 61)

(71) 'dì pi 'dàì bɛ trótrò, 'dì pi sì rö 'dà bɛ *these are the same as those there, this is equal to that*

(72) 'dì lé = sì 'dì lé = 'dì bɛ trótrò *like this,* or *the same as this*

(73) é 'yɔ ɛ'yó ɛ'yó 'dì mà àzí lé! or é 'yɔ àzïnï 'dì lé! *say another word like this!*

(74) bòŋgó 'dì pi èi 'dì bɛ òsì-rö-òsì *these cloths and these there are alike*

(75) sì má lé = èri má bɛ trótrò *he is equal to me,* or *he is my equal.*

2. Comparison of Inferiority

159. (a) Comparison of *inferiority* is commonly expressed by the *negative* form of the comparative of equality. See example 59.

(76) mvá 'dì ɔvö mǒkɛ́ kìlé mvá 'dà lé kö *this child is not as good/ nice as that one*

(77) àndrò àŋgǒ ambí àdzérì lé kö *today it is not as cold as yesterday*

(b) Inferiority is also expressed by *contrast* between or *antithesis* of two qualities or statements.

(78) àndrò àŋgǒ òn̩irö, ádzê (àŋgǒ) òndzí tǒ *today it (the weather) is pleasant, yesterday it was very bad*

(79) mvá 'dìrï mǒkɛ́, mvá 'dàrï òndzí *this boy is good that one bad*

(80) mànìà èri ënìrö, án̩ú ɛmvɛ̀rö also án̩ú ɛmvɛ̀rö mànìànï ndɛ́ nì *mania grains are darker than sesame, sesame is white surpassing mania*

3. Comparison of Superiority

160. (a) *Superiority* also is expressed by stressing the quality of one term with reference to others; the latter term of reference is in genitive relationship as in English. Example:

(81) **Mòndóa-nï andzi 'dàǐ mà àmbó** or . . . **mà drìlé** lit. *Mondoa is the big one of those children* (i.e. is bigger/the biggest).

161. (*b*) Superiority may also be expressed by using the postpositional phrase **àgàíá** *on the side, beside,* or *among,* instead of the genitive to introduce the term of reference. Example:

(82) **à'dinï èmï àgàía àmbô-rö nǐ yà?** *who is the biggest of* (among) *you?*

Comparative and Superiority Superlative

162. (*a*) The verb **aga** *to surpass* or the verbal expression **nděnǐ** or **nděpi** *that exceeds, exceedingly,* are frequently used to express, in the first place, relative superiority and only indirectly the superlative. **Aga** is simply construed as a verb and so is **ndè** sometimes. Examples:

(83) **àfa 'dǐ aga 'dàrï rá** *this thing is better than* (*surpasses*) *that one*
(84) **kòlíkòlí aga àkufi-àkufíä àmbó sǐ wεrε** *a wagtail is slightly bigger than a sparrow*

163. (*b*) The postposition **nï** and **nděnǐ**, placed after the reference term, expresses superiority over (or inferiority to) the first term. Examples:

(85) **tí mávélérǐ àmbôrö tí mǐvélérǐ nï nděnï nǐ** *my cow is bigger than* (*big exceeding*) *yours*
(86) **àŋgǒ àndrò ambǐzàrö àdzérǐ nï nděnǐ** *today it is colder than yesterday*
(87) **ma adríïnï ɔndòârö má-nï ndě nǐ, ndè ma ɔndòá sǐ rá** *my brother is cleverer than I* (*he surpasses me with cleverness*)
(88) **ma adríï mà milé-mba má-nï ndě nǐ** *my brother is cleverer than I*
(89) **dzó 'dǐrï àmbôrö dzó 'dà-nï ndě nǐ** *this hut is larger than that*
(90) **lóà mà zánǐ mu adri tí vélérǐ nï ndě nǐ** *hartebeest meat will be superior to cow meat* (in quantity; as the former swells on cooking)
(91) **éŋá alu ndè sùkarì** *polenta is* (*sometimes*) *more delicious than sugar*

Superlative

164. **Tǒ** *very much;* or the terms **nděnǐ, ndě wǒrɔ́, aga drìlé** are used to express the superlative degree. Examples:

(92) **'bá 'dǐ èri ɔkpɔ̂rö nděnǐ** (= **tǒ**) *this man is very strong*
(93) **tí 'dǐrï mǒké tǒ, ndè àfa àzíïnï pírǐ rá** *this cow is very fine, it surpasses all*
(94) **'bǐ'bía ndrǐ tǒ** *the star is very bright*

(95) é ndrǐ kö, á ndrǐ nděnǐ ma 'ǐ, é kà mu ɔ̀ndí edzɪ́ mâ rúá kö, nděnǐ á ndrǐ má 'ǐ *you are not handsome, I am exceedingly handsome; unless you bring dirt on me, I am the most beautiful one* (in fun)

165. Numerous adverbs (see Adverb) are also employed to express a superlative degree in either direction. Given here are a few adjectives with the corresponding adverbs used, for comparisons.

ga *little* kaṇàrö (tɔ̌ may be added) *very small, little*
ɔ̀ndzí kàṇàrö *very bad, very ugly*
mŏkɛ́ ṇàrö (seldom heard) *very good, nice*
bǐ (or ëni) kúkúrùlukù *very dark, pitch-black* (of night)
bǐ, ëni, or bǐ ëni tsúbìli *very dark, jet-black* (of objects)
àmbó tíirí or kukutɛ *extraordinarily thick, voluminous*
dra òkáŋgálí *very sour, bitter*
ënìrö àtsǐ-pèlèŋgú lɛ́ *black as charcoal*
ɛkàrö àtsǐ-óló lɛ́ *red as glowing charcoal* (at night)

166. Further examples illustrating the superlative:

(96) ìyí ëni kúkúru or ìyí ɔ̀ndíi berǐ *the water is very dirty*
(97) ìyí 'dǐrǐ ɔ̀ndzí kàṇàrö, mà dǎ vàá! *this water is very bad, pour it away!*
(98) fɛ̀ máні ǹdrí ga kaṇàrö *he gave me a very small goat*
(99) 'bá 'bá 'dàǐ mà drìléárǐ èi ɔmvɛ àmbó *the man ahead of those people (leader) is called ambo (big man or elder)*
(100) ɛmví ɛ̀ri ɛmvɛ̀rö bɔ̀ŋgó lɛ́ (or kɔ́ɔ̌ lɛ́) *chalk is as white as linen* (or *an egret*)
(101) ó'dîrö ndrǐndrǐ *brand-new*
(102) mǐ àmbòo tɔ̌ *you are an absolute rascal*
(103) kànì àŋgö bǐ ëni tsǐtsí, ɔ̀vǐnì ṇǐ lɛ́ɛlɛ́ɛ, 'dǐ 'bá ɔmvɛ 'àŋgö bǐ kúkúrùlukù' *when it has become quite dark (before) it (then) lightens, that is what they call pitch-black* (bǐ kú . . .)

CHAPTER 6

NUMERALS

I. Cardinal Numbers

167. The *cardinal* numbers are the following:

one	àlö	*six*	azia
two	ìrrì	*seven*	ázíǐrrì
three	nna	*eight*	àarɔ̀
four	ssu	*nine*	ɔ́ɔrɔ̀mì
five	tääú or tääwí	*ten*	möödrí

11 möödrí drì-nï àlö (lit. *ten on-it one*)
12   „   „   ìrrì
15   „   „   tääwí, &c.
20 kàlí ìrrì (lit. *sticks two*)
21   „ ìrrì drì-nï àlö
30   „ nna
39   „ nna drìnï ɔ́ərɔ̀mì
40   „ ssu
50   „ tääwí
60   „ azia
70   „ ázî̀rrì
80   „ àarɔ̀
90   „ ɔ́ərɔ̀mì
100 tŏörŏ̌ àlö
105 tŏörŏ̌ àlö drì-nï tääú
111 tŏörŏ̌ àlö drì-nï möödrí drì-nï àlö, &c. (quite regular)
1000 álìf(ù) àlö
1953 álìfù àlö tŏörŏ̌ ɔ́rɔ̀mì kàlí tåú drìnï nna

168. Syntactic and other notes.

(1) In Logbara, as in the Ma'di languages generally, the cardinal numbers are unusual, in that the first *ten* numerals appear to be simple and original, whereas in many other languages (such as Jii and Laŋo) only the first *five* are.

kàlí *ten* (also *stick*) and tŏrŏ̌ *hundred* are also simple and original terms. All other numbers are compound terms of a very regular kind, presenting no difficulty.

169. (2) (*a*) The cardinal numbers as such never take suffixes, as other adjectives may do.

When used attributively, they follow the noun as adjectives do, but remain unchanged. If the noun be qualified by some other determinative, this latter is placed before the numeral. Examples:

(1) á lè tí àrɔ̀ *I want eight cows*
(2) andzi nna ; ézó andzi tåú *three children; five girls*
(3) ǹdrí àlö àvè̀ áséa ádzê *one goat went astray yesterday in the bush*
(4) á nè andzi ŋ̩ɩ́rɩ́ŋ̩ɩ́rɩ́ azia *I saw six small children*

170. (*b*) When the numeral is used predicatively, it is preceded by the 3rd person pronoun, i.e. èri or èl, but it takes no suffixes. When used substantively the numeral may be followed by a postposition. Examples:

(5) águ 'dà mà tí èri àlö *that man's cow is one/he has one cow*
(6) ma águí mà ǹdrí èl möödrí drìnï azia *my friend's goats are sixteen*
(7) sawà tsa (= ga) sí yà? sawà tsa ázî̀rrì *what is the time? it is 7 o'clock*

(8) 'bá padri mà àndró ɛrípi kàlí ssu *the people who listened to the sermon of the father were forty*

(9) àma ɛmbá, m̀bá Februari mà 'aléa, o'dú möödrí drìnï ìrrì sì *in the month of February we taught on twelve days*

(10) àgu nna 'dàì sɔ̆ drì sɔ̀sɔ̀ *those three men walked in single file*

(11) andzi ssu 'dàì òtìkí èì òtìòtì *those four boys walked abreast*

(12) á kènì: ádzê nï é ŋga èmbá o'dú sí yà? *I say, by yesterday you had worked how many days of the month?*

(13) 'bá pätí àzïnï 'bǎ àlö a'á-zɔ̆ ; èì a'á pätí 'dà mà ndúa o'dú azia nɔ̀sì ázïrrì pärí àlö ɔ̀gɔ̀gɔ̀ (at teeth extraction) *they are determined to stay at one tree; they will stay under that tree six or seven days continuously in one place*

1. Modifiers of Cardinal Numbers

171. 'About' is expressed by **tsa** (*to reach*) . . . **'dïpi**, as in

(14) **tsa 'bá möödrí 'dïpi** *there are about ten persons*

'Exactly' is expressed by **'yékɛ́** or **kílílí** as in

(15) **atsɛ o'dú kàlí nna 'yékɛ́** *exactly thirty days remain*

'More' is expressed by **ddíká** (*again*) after the numeral, as in

(16) **lè ǹdrí ázïrrì ddíká** *he wants seven more goats*

'Only' or 'alone' is expressed by any of the following adverbs: **lɔ̆** placed before the word; or **a'dúlɛ** *alone*, **tɔ̀ɔkɔ́** *only*, **àyákáká** *only* (after plurals), placed after the word or numeral; **a'dúlɛ** = **a'dú sì** = **a'dúkúlɛ**.

(17) **ma 'í ma a'dúlɛ** *I myself alone*

(18) **mvá 'dìrï mà ɛlí täwí tɔ̀ɔkɔ́** *this child('s years are) is only five*

(19) **á ndrɛ̀ lɔ̆ andzi tsǎpi azia 'dïpi** *I have seen only about six children*

(20) **èì andzi àyákáká** *they are exclusively children* (no grown-ups)

(21) **'dìrï lɔ̆ a'dúkúlɛ nï** or **káanï àlö 'dìrï** *this is possibly the only one*

(22) **ɛrimà àfa tsí, àmadrí àlö nï yɔ** *he has some things, we have not one (none)*

(23) **ma esú àlö nï yɔ** *I did not find one/any one*: cf. **ma esú àlö-rì yɔ** *I did not find one of them*

2. Arithmetical Terms or Expressions

172.

+ **emó** or **ɔ̀'bà** *to put more*

— **ndzɛ** *to remove*

× **ezózà** *to be increased* or **pá'alɛ́** *times*

÷ **awazà** *to be divided*

(24) **é sì alá mà emózà (ndzɛzà . . .) drírì!** *write the sign of addition (subtraction)!*

(25) **ssu pi èì nna bɛ** or **ssu mï ezó (emó, ɛdrì) nna bɛ** (**ɛndzɛ** = **trɔ́trɔ̀** = **fɔ̀**) **ázïrrì** $4+3 = 7$/*four plus three make seven*

(26) ázîïrrì é ndzε ssu atsε (or ko rö) nna $7-4 = 3$/*seven minus four leaves three*

(27) ssu mï ezó nna sì (or ssu pá'alé nna), èri möödrí drìnï ìrri $4 \times 3 = 12$/*four times three make twelve*

(28) möödrí drìnï azia mï awa ssu sì, fï ('alénìá) ssu $16 \div 4 = 4$/ *sixteen divided by four make four*

Fractions:

half = àlí or agavŏ or dzólókó *a rest*

$\frac{1}{2}$, *one-half* = àlö ìrrì-nï; $1\frac{1}{2}$, *one-and-a-half* = àlö àlí bε

$3/7$ = nna ázîïrrì-nï or nna ázîïrrì driá (lit. *three above seven*).

II. Ordinal Numbers

173. Ordinal numbers in Logbara are formed by suffixing -rì or -zŏrì, or -rö to the cardinal numbers. -rì or -zŏrì are employed when the numbers are used epithetically; both are equally correct, but some areas may prefer one to the other. The form with -zŏrì (full form) is preferable to that with -rì where ambiguity might otherwise arise.

-rö is used when the ordinals are used predicatively.

The ordinal numbers are thus:

1st àlö-rì or àlö-zŏrì; àlŏ-rö (cf. '*first*', '*last*', below)
2nd ìrrì-rì or ìrrì-zŏrì; ìrrì-rö
5th tääú-rì or tääú-zŏrì; tääû-rö
10th möödrí-rì or möödrí-zŏrì; möödrî-rö; &c.

174. The plural of these forms, if required, is formed by replacing -rì by 'dìï (one time 'dìrï).

'The first', 'the next', 'the last'

175. 'The first' has various forms, each of which often has a different shade of meaning.

'The first', ðkð-rì or kààórì.

mvá kààórì 'dì'ï *the first child*
drì-tsɛ́pirì *who goes ahead, first(-born), (ring-)leader*
ε'dó-pi-rì *the beginner*; ε'dó-zŏrì *the first*
mvá drìtsépirì = mvá ðkð-yìià-rì *the first-born child*
ndrí mívélérì sí-zŏ-rì 'ï yà? *which goat (of a series) is yours?*
ndrí mávélérì tääú-zŏrì 'ï *my goat is the fifth*
andzi kààó 'dìì emú má vŏ nì *these are the first children who came to me*
'bá ðkð-yìiàrì or 'bá kà-yìiàórì emúzŏ Àrúwárì *the first man to come to Arua*
'bá àzî-ŋgá-pi ε'dópirì *the starter of work—who began to work*

andzi 'dǐǐ tääwí etsá má vǒ ǝkǝ (-rǐ sǐ) ò 'búti sǐ *these five children
arrived first in the morning (and stood) beside me*
emú kàáↄ nǐ (= ǝkǝ nǐ) = ǝkǝrè sǐ emú nǐ *he came first*

176. 'The next', vúti-á-rǐ or vútinǐ-sǐ-rǐ.

mvá èrimà vúti-á-rǐ èri 'dǐ *the next (-born) child after him is this one*
'bá mâ vúti sǐ ɛ'dↄ-zↄ́rǐ (or ɛ'dↄpirǐ or drǐ-ɛtsépirǐ) 'ǐ *the man
who came next to (after) me*
'bá àzǐ-rǐ ŋgↄá yà? 'bá àzǐrǐ vélé *where is the other? the other is
behind*
'bá aga-rǐ'ǐ *the one born in between* or *man in the middle*
mǐ efǐ dzótilé kálá-á 'dà sǐ! *enter by the next/side door there!*

177. 'The last' is also expressed in various ways, as:

vélé-rǐ/'dǐǐ, 'bá ǝkↄ-pi vélé-rǐ *one who finished the last*
àsì-zↄ́-rǐ/'dǐǐ, 'bá atsɛ́-pi vélé-rǐ *one who remained behind*
ǝkↄ-zↄ́-rǐ/'dǐǐ, 'bá awǐ-pi vélé-rǐ *one who left behind*
dɛ-zↄ́-rǐ/'dǐǐ, &c.
mvá vélérǐ'ǐ or mvá àsìzↄ́rǐ'ǐ *the last-born child*
(29) Kàlía-nǐ andzi ndé'dǐǐ mà nna-rö *Kalia is the third of
the aforeseen boys*
(30) 'bá póstá ǝdzípirǐ èri èimà ssûrö *the mail-bearer is the fourth
of them*
(31) 'bá èmbá o'dú ŋgǎpi àlözↄ́rǐá-rǐ (= àlörǐárǐ) *the man who
worked on the first day of the month*

III. Distributive Numbers

178. Distributive numbers are expressed simply by reduplication of
the cardinal numbers.

singly = àlö-àlö; by twos = ǐrrì-ǐrrì; by threes = nna-nna; &c.
(32) gǐrì 'dǐrǐ lúrúa, 'bá mà atsí ànǐ àlö-àlö *this path is narrow,
people have to march single file (singly) on it*
(33) èì mu àzî ŋgarïá sí sí yà? èì mu tääwí-tääwí *how many at
a time do they go to work? they go five at a time*
(34) andzi mà emú ssu-ssu *let the boys come on by fours*
(35) èmï pǐrǐ èmï mà 'du ǐrrì-ǐrrì *let each of you take two at a time*

IV. Multiplicative Numbers

179. These numbers are formed, as in English, by having the cardinal
numbers preceded by the term which corresponds to 'times' in English.
In Logbara there are several alternatives which are all equal in meaning,
although some are preferred in particular districts. These terms all
signify 'how many times'.

(a) vǒ sí yà? or vǒsì sí yà? *how many times?* vǒ postposition (Latin
apud) *at, with*; sí? *how many?*

(b) =pá'alέ sí yà? or pá'alέ vŏsĭ sí yà? pá 'alέ means *sole of foot*; used for *times*

(c) = pá milέkɔ sí yà? or pá milέkɔ vŏsĭ sí yà? pá-milέkɔ = *point of foot* or *tiptoe* = *times*

(36) é mu a'á 'dálέ (pá 'alέ) vŏsĭ sí yà? *how many times have you gone to stay there?*

(37) é dzi 'bá 'dĭĭ àzî ŋga-zŏ (pá milέkɔ) vŏ sí yà? *how many times have you taken these people to work?*

(38) á dzi èi àzî ŋgazŏ pá'alέ azia *I have taken them to work six times*

CHAPTER 7

PRONOUNS

I. PERSONAL PRONOUNS

180. In Logbara there are two forms of *personal pronouns*, they are (a) the *absolute* or full form, and (b) the *short* form.

(a) Absolute form	(b) Short form	
ma (áma)	á	*I, me, to me*
mï (émï)	é	*thou, thee, to thee*
èri, 'ï, -nï	—	*he, she, it; him, her, to him,* &c.
àma	à	*we, us, to us*
èmï	è	*you*
èi, ii, è(i)kí	—	*they, them, to them*

A. The Absolute or Full-form Personal Pronouns

181. (1) The singular pronouns ma and mï, as can be seen, do not correspond entirely with the plural àma, èmï; the latter are fuller. The fuller forms of the singular—áma, émï—are actually still in use in the northern districts of the country (Aringa); but on the whole, they have sunk into oblivion.

182. Ma and mï have high-intermediate tone, which occasionally assimilates to a following mid or high tone. The second syllable of àma and èmï has low-intermediate tone which occasionally changes to low or mid.

183. (2) The *3rd person* is more complicated.

(a) The ordinary full-form is èri and plural èi (ii) and, in the north and east, èkï or, less frequently, èikí.

184. (b) The Logbara distinguishes two kinds of 3rd person pronoun, analogous to Latin *eius* and *suus*. If a person be introduced as the speaker or doer, i.e. as the subject of a sentence, all references to him are expressed by the special form 'ï (with high-intermediate tone). The plural has no corresponding special form, but has a distinct construction

185. (c) **-nï** *him, her, it,/his, hers, its.*

Logbara makes profuse use of the pronoun suffix **-nï** to refer back to a noun in the sentence or to an object in view or in the mind of the speaker, especially when it is the object of some postposition. The locative postposition **-á** is often added to it. This **-nï**, and especially the corresponding absolute form, the adverb **ànï**, is a form analogous to French *en* or *y*, or Italian *vi*. Examples:

(1) **mï adzí kəme, é rï drì-nï-á** *bring a stool and sit on it*
(2) **ɛmbápi 'dɔ̀, é zi ti-nï-á** *here is the teacher, ask him*
(3) **mvá 'dì ɛ́dri ŋgà rúa-nï-á tsí** *this child is still alive* (lit. *life is still in his body*)
(4) **sö pätí lɔ̀kìrï-nï-á tsí** *he planted sticks/plants on its boundary*
(5) **é tu drì-nï-á 'dì sì** *climb over it from this side*
(6) **ɔ̀lɛ̀ fï rúa-nï-á tsí** *a charm/disease took possession of him* (lit. *his body*)
(7) **é mu ámví-nï əmvɛ** *go and call his sister*
(8) **tí ɛ̀ví ɛ̀rì gbɛ̂ sö 'a-nï-á** *the gadfly deposits her eggs in it* (*cow's body*)

186. In connexion with personal pronouns the student is especially reminded of the following observations or rules, which are part and parcel of the general rules for sound- and tone-change in connected speech (see §§ 39–42).

(a) If the meeting vowels of two words are identical, they become one long vowel, as in **fèɛrinï rá** (**fè ɛrì nï rá**) *he gave it to him*.

(b) The strong vowels **i o u** are never suppressed. The weak vowels **a e** are suppressed on meeting with the strong ones; also **a** gives way to **e**. The remaining vowel is, normally, lengthened and takes over the tones of the combined syllables. Example:

(9) **mïidzí mánï** = **mï edzí mánï** *bring to me*; **méèdzí rá** (= **má e—**) *I brought it*

(c) The initial vowels of the personal pronouns are treated as if they were preceded by a potential glottal stop (in **'ï** the glottal stop is real), which prevents their ever being suppressed. The following sentence, therefore, is pronounced without elision:

(10) **ɛri ɛ̀rimà ti rá** *he heard* (obeyed) *his* (her) *words* (command)

187. For tonal reaction in connected speech, see §§ 59 ff.

(a) The tone of **ma, mï, 'ï, -nï** occasionally becomes high when preceded or followed by a high-tone syllable, as in **má vélɛ́** or **má vɔ̌** *to me*.

(b) When followed by a word or syllable requiring a preceding low tone (see § 59), the pronouns **ɛ̀ri, àma, èmï, èi** change their mid-tone to low.

(11) **àmà 'yè mu rá** *we shall go*

(c) In the conditions mentioned under b, the pronouns ma, mï, 'ï, -nï either take an additional low tone or change to a low tone. Example:

(12) mã̀ (or mà) ŋga emú drùsì rá *I shall come tomorrow*

Use of the Absolute Personal Pronouns

188. The *absolute personal pronouns* are used to a much larger extent than the short ones.

These absolute pronouns must be used in the following cases:

(1) When the *subject* is represented by a personal pronoun.

189. (a) In a sentence with a nominal predicate. Examples:

(13) èmï andzi ə̀ndzí 'dì (or -rì, -nï) *you are bad children*
(14) èì mǒké tò *they are very good* (or *nice*)
(15) àma ópí andzi (-nï or 'ï) *we are children of the chief*

190. (b) In sentences with the Construction of Incomplete Action (CIA, cf. Verb, § 339), when the verb is preceded by the direct object, and this by the *subject*, as in:

(i) Sentences in the *present indicative*:

(16) ma ǹdrí dzi 'bà àkúa *I am taking the goat home*
(17) èì dzó mà àŋgò sì-sì *they are drawing the ground-plan of a hut*
(18) èrì éꞑá gà èkpéré sì *he refuses polenta out of stinginess*

191. (ii) Sentences in the future tense.

(19) (àfa àzínï) èrì ŋgà mu nyò rö rá (something) *it will break*
(20) mì 'yè mvi àkúa ('bùrú) drùsì *you will return home tomorrow*

192. In sentences with the Construction of Completed Action (CCA) the full-form pronouns must be used before verbs beginning with a vowel. Compare the following sentences:

é mu 'dálé! *go there!* but mí emú má vǒ! *come to me!*

(2) Whenever the direct or indirect *object* is represented by a personal pronoun.

193. (a) Examples for *direct* or accusative *object*.

(21) mvá 'dì lè ma tò *this child loves me very much*
(22) gbà ma kàlí sì *he struck me with a stick*
(23) mï emó èì wóró àlö *you have pressed them all together (assembled)*
(24) mï mã̀ tsə tòəkó-tòəkó à'do sì yà? *why do you beat me without reason?*

194. (b) Examples for *indirect*, dative, *postpositional* object. This is expressed by means of **drí, nǐ** . . . and as a rule precedes the direct object.

(25) ma ándríi ɛ̀fɛ̀ mánǐ ɛ́n̯á *my mother gave me polenta*

(26) ɛ'dá ɛ̀rinǐ kàlí *she showed him a stick*

(27) é lɔ̀ mánǐ ɛ'yɔ́ ! *tell me the matter!/do inform me!*

(28) mǐ atri mánǐ ɛ̀tú kɔ̈ ! *do not keep (obstruct) the sun (light) from me!*

(29) ɛ̀ri dzɔ̂ si 'ǐ drí *he is building a hut for himself*

(30) ɛ̀mǐ àma drí àŋgɔ̈ ɛmvɛ atri *you are obstructing the light from us*

195. The 3rd person pronoun *object*, be it direct or indirect, tends to be omitted in Logbara whenever it can easily be implied from the context. This phenomenon is specially noticeable in their fables. Example:

(31) é fɛ̀ ɛ̀inï rá or simply é fɛ̀ rá ! *give 'it' to them!*

196. The cumulative conjunction 'and' and the personal pronouns.

When connecting a personal pronoun with another personal pronoun or a noun, the corresponding plural pronoun is anticipated and connected with the other. For example, 'I and thou' is commonly rendered by 'we and thou' **àma mï bɛ**. If this results in there being two subjects to a simple sentence, the plural personal pronoun precedes the verb, and the connected part-subject follows. Examples:

(32) à mvi mï bɛ Gùlùá *I went back to Gulu with thee*

(33) è mú àkúa ɛ̀ri bɛ ! *go home with him!*

(34) àma ə'yɔ́ mvá 'dà bɛ *I was talking to (with) that boy*

(35) àma emví ɛ̀i bɛ o'dú àlö sǐ *I came back with them the same day*

(36) àma má amvíi piɛ *I and my sister*
      ɛ̀i Lúidzì bɛ *he and Luidzi.*

197. The last two examples exhibit the simple connexion of two nouns. In place of **piɛ**, the postposition **bɛ** can be used(cf. §§ 440 ff.).

B. The Short-form Personal Pronouns (see § 180 (b))

198. The short personal pronouns each consist simply of a short vowel **a** for the 1st person and **e** for the 2nd person. There is no short form for the 3rd person pronouns. The vowels **a** and **e** have a *high tone* in the *singular*, and a *low tone* in the *plural*.

á *I,* **à** *we;* and **é** *thou,* **è** *you*

These pronouns never undergo changes of any sort.

199. As to their *origin*, these pronouns represent simply the first vowels of the corresponding full-form as mentioned above, § 181.

200. The 2nd person singular é is not always of fixed quality; any shade of vowel between é (or even ɛ́) and i may occasionally be heard. This unstable quality is possibly due to Aluur influence, where i is the corresponding pronoun. Though the great majority of Logbara use plain é, its origin, together with the other analogous forms, should certainly exclude any, even slight, doubt in the matter.

The pronoun 'ï (cf. § 184) bears no relation to the short personal pronouns here in question.

Use of the Short-form Personal Pronouns

201. These short forms are used regularly and only as subject in sentences with CCA (cf. Verb, § 372).

These pronouns are used and placed immediately before the verb, but only when this begins with a consonant (cf. § 192).

202. For the 3rd persons (singular and plural) a short form is lacking, so the verb used alone (i.e. without pronoun) automatically expresses the third persons in sentences with CCA (cf. Verb, § 372).

These short pronouns are used in the following cases:

203. (a) In the past tense:

(37) á nɛ̀ òdrú rá *I have seen a buffalo*
(38) nɛ̀ andzi ádzɛ́ rá *she saw the children yesterday*
(38a) è mvi té àkúa à'do sǐ yà? *why did you* (pl.) *go back home a moment ago?*

204. (b) In the *imperative* mood:

(39) é rï vàá! pl. è rï vàá! (*go*) *sit down!*
(40) é fò àmvé! pl. è fò àmvé! *go outside!* or *go away!*
(41) é tɛ̀ ŋgà wɛrɛ! *wait a moment!*

205. In cases as described in § 184 the special pronoun 'ï pl. èi has to be used in sentences of both CIA and CCA, i.e. whether it is, say, in the present or past tense. Examples:

(42) ma ádríi kènì: ándrâ 'ï nɛ̀ mï rá *my brother says, that he saw you once before*
(43) ópí kéni: ándrâ èi nɛ̀ ma rá *the chiefs say that they saw me before*
(44) ópí kéni: ándrâ nɛ̌ ma rá *the chiefs say that they (somebody else) saw me before*
(45) ɔ̀kó kènì: 'ï gà sǐ *the woman says that she (herself) refuses*
(46) ɔ̀kó kènì: gà sǐ *the woman says that he/she (a person in question) refuses*

II. REFLEXIVE PRONOUNS—EMPHASIZING PARTICLES

206. In Logbara there are (*a*) quite distinct *particles* of *emphasis* or *stressing*, on the one hand, and (*b*) on the other hand, plain forms of *reflexive pronouns*. The former have nothing to do with the latter.

A. Emphasizing Particles

207. These particles are treated here as they are used in the first place with personal pronouns. Moreover, they bear a striking resemblance to personal pronouns.

These emphasizing particles are used with much more frequency in Logbara than similar particles in classical languages. This point must not be forgotten.

We may translate the particles simply by light stressing of the appropriate word or, when feasible, with a '-self' compound.

There are two main emphasizing particles: 'ï and nï.

1. The Emphasizing Particle 'ï or áyò

208. 'ï is the more commonly used particle. Its tone fluctuates between mid and high. It is placed immediately after the word to be stressed. It may be used with any part of speech. The particle áyò may be used in its place but is not often heard.

209. (*a*) This 'ï is very frequently added to personal pronouns.
Actually it is connected only with the *absolute* (full form) personal pronouns.

(47) 'dï à'dï 'ï yà? 'dò ma'ï *who is this there? it is I*
(48) mï à'dï 'ï yà? ma ma'ï *who art thou? I am myself!* (common answer)
(49) á 'yɔ má'ï *I myself said it*
(50) èmï 'ï èmï ɔvòrö *you, you are lazy*
(51) kànì àfa àvè rá, á bï mï'ï *if anything gets lost* (i.e. in your presence), *I will catch you*

210. (*b*) If the *short* personal pronoun (subject) has to be stressed, the short form as subject, naturally, precedes the verb, but at the end of the sentence the pronoun is repeated in its full form and 'ï is added to it. Example 52 below shows an instance of a multiple stressing of interest.

(52) é sï mï àfa-nï mï 'ï *you have written it* (the matter) *yourself*
(53) à'dï ɔmve manï yà? *who called 'me'?*
ma ɔmve mï (-nï) ma'ï *it is I who called you, or, I myself . . .*

211. (*c*) When a postpositional object is to be stressed 'ï is placed after the postposition, as in:

(54) táarì ɔdo 'dàrï é fè dï má-nï 'ï kö à-sï yà? *why do you not give that kerosene oil to me?*

212. (*d*) 'ï is used after other pronouns and adjectives:

(55) é 'ï àɲá 'dìrï 'ï! *do grind this corn here!*

(56) éfínï mŋgbà ŋgà 'ï mŋgbà kö *the grains are not yet formed*

(57) mǐ a'í àfa mávélé 'dìrï 'ï! *accept this here from me!*

(58) á 'bà à'bǒà àzǐnï ɔ̀kpɔ́rɔ́a *I have put some bananas in the pocket*
   á mbɛ àzǐnï 'ï *I have eaten the others*

213. (*e*) 'ï is used after *nouns*. It is typical of the Logbara use of this emphasizing 'ï that, on asking for somebody's name, he uses 'ï after the interrogative pronoun and, again, in answering, after the proper name.

(59) mǐ rú à'dì 'ï yà? *what is your name?*
   mâ rú Àŋgòdɔ̀rɔ̀ 'ï *my name is Aŋgodoro*

(60) 'bá 'dìrï ópí 'ï yà? *is this the chief?*
   'dà ópí'ï *that is the chief*

(61) mï wárágà 'dì mà 'ípi 'ï yà? *are you the owner of this book?*

(62) á nɛ̀ mótòkà 'ï, á nɛ̀ àfa 'alénǐárǐ kö *I have seen the motor-car itself; I did not see what was in it*

(63) á lɛ̀ kɔ̀dzáǟ kö, á lɛ̀ tí (àmbórǐ) or ándrií 'ï *I do not want a calf, I want a (big one) or cow*

214. (*f*) 'ï used after verbs.

(64) 'bá 'dà ògù 'ï rá *that man has 'stolen'*

(65) 'dǐ 'dǒ 'ápi 'bɔ-rǐ 'ï *this is eleusine that is already developing*

(66) á lɛ̀ mânï à'bǒà mbɛ 'ï *I want to eat a banana*

2. The Emphasizing Particle 'nǐ or 'nï

215. 'nǐ, postulating a preceding low tone, is another particle used for stressing. It is always combined with a full-form personal pronoun corresponding to the subject. We have thus the following reflexive-emphasizing forms: mâ-nǐ mǐ-nǐ 'ǐ-nǐ àmâ-nǐ èmǐ-nǐ èǐ-nǐ. This kind of emphasis is employed (apparently) only with the subject; it implies the idea of contrast. It conveys the meaning of 'with regard to . . .', 'as for . . .', '. . . for . . . part', '. . . for . . . self'.

This form functions, grammatically, as a reflexive direct object; as such it precedes or follows the verb in accordance with the construction of the sentence.

If the subject to be stressed is a noun (introduced as acting and explaining), its corresponding reflexive-emphasizing object is 'ǐnǐ.

In some particular cases nǐ may be replaced by drí.

216.

(67) mï mǐnǐ à'dò 'yɛ yà? *what will you in particular be doing?*
   ma mânï mvìmvi *as for me, I return*

(68) á lɛ̀ káanï mânǐ 'dìrï 'ï *I for my part prefer this*

(69) 'ĭ 'ĭní èrì ŋa a'dúlɛ (*he says*) *he will eat alone, as far as he is concerned*

(70) 'ĭ tsa 'ĭní mbèlè (*he said*) *he, on his part, arrived early*

(71) lè 'ĭní àfa 'dĭrĭ kö *as for her* (*she says*) *she does not like this*

(72) é tu mĭní pätí sía 'ĭ (or 'dɛ́); ma 'dɔ̀ mâní mùmu, á tu mâní kö *you, you may climb the tree; as for me I go on, I will not climb the tree*

(73) èrì ànï mâ drì ɛndzâ; 'ĭ kɔ 'ĭní (= 'ĭdrí) bàtisìmù 'bɔ *he shames* (*taunts*) *me with it, because he himself has already been christened*

Cf. Nï §. 561.

B. Reflexive Pronouns

217. The Logbara make great use of *reflexive verbs*, even in cases where other languages do not. The *reflexive pronoun* proper is expressed in two ways according to the double form the reflexive object of a verb may take; both ways are identical in meaning, and may be used indiscriminately.

The reflexive pronouns are direct objects and as such precede or follow the verb according to rules (cf. Verb, §§ 377, 421 ff.).

1. The Reflexive Pronoun (Full-form Personal Pronoun)

218. The reflexive pronoun object may be expressed by the plain full-form personal pronoun corresponding to the subject of the sentence. Subject and object are thus in many cases identical. The reflexive pronoun (-object) for a 3rd person pronoun or noun can in this case obviously only be 'ĭ or èi. Examples:

(74) é 'dà (= sɛ, kɔ) mĭ rá! *withdraw* (lit. *move yourself back*)!

(75) dzó asó̌ 'ĭ 'bɔ *the hut has collapsed*

(76) àfa 'dà ŋɔ 'ĭ rá *that thing broke* (itself)

(77) ma ma àtĭ àbì rúaa I *am leaning* (myself) *against the wall*

(78) mvá 'dĭ, mĭ rúá ɔndĭrö; é lè mĭ ɔdzĭ kö? *child, you are dirty; you do not like to wash/bath?*

2. Reflexive Pronoun Particle rö

219. Instead of the full-form personal pronouns the particle **rö** may be employed. It is invariable for all persons, singular and plural. Its position in a sentence is that of a direct object. Examples:

(79) mvá 'dà mà 'dàa rö rá *that boy ought to withdraw*

(80) ma rö àtì-àtì I *am leaning* (against something)

(81) dzó mà pätí ŋɔ rö rá; èì té àrì-àrì: èì té ó'dĭnĭ sö 'ĭ ká *a pole of the hut has broken; they have just propped it up* (with a new one)

III. POSSESSIVE PRONOUNS

220. The *possessive form* of personal pronouns is made up in complete conformity with the genitive or possessive construction of nouns (cf. §§ 94 ff.), i.e. the genitive or possessive of personal pronouns is formed by adding the same postpositions after the full-form personal pronouns. There are, therefore, *four forms* of the possessive pronoun according to the four postpositions used for the purpose: they are **mà, drí, nï, vélé.** To a certain extent a fifth form with the postposition **-rï** may be added.

221. The *four/five forms* of the *possessive pronoun* are:

	my/mine	thy/thine	her, hers, its	our(s)	your(s)	their(s)
(a) **mà:**	má-mà	mï-mà	èri-mà/ '¨ï-mà	àma-mà	èmï-mà	èl-mà
contracted:	mâ	mî	../'ï	àmà	èmï	..
(b) **drí:**	má-drí	mï-drí	èri-drí/ 'ï-drí	àma-drí	èmï-drí	èl-drí
(c) **vélé:**	má-vélé	mï-vélé	èri-vélé/ 'ï-vélé	àma-vélé	èmï-vélé	èl-vélé
(d) '**nï**	mâ-nï	mî-nï	èri-nï/ '¨ï-nï	àmà-nï	èmï-nï	èl-nï
(e) **-rï**	ma-rï	mï-rï	èri-rï/ 'ï-rï	àma-rï	èmï-rï	èl-rï

222. The forms (a), (b), (c), (d) above are, for all practical purposes, identical in meaning. Formally, therefore, it is immaterial which of them one chooses to use. Slight differences in their use, however, seem to exist. It may be a question of finding out by experience which one is more in use in a particular area.

223. There is the tendency to lengthen the vowel of the pronoun before the postpositions.

Observations about the Various Forms

(a) The form with **mà** *(cf. §§ 95, 99 ff.)*

224. (i) The 'mà-form' is the easy short form of everyday speech. With **ma** and **mï** the contracted form is the ordinary one. *Contraction* in this case means that the postposition **mà** is dropped, but in such a way that its low tone is retained and, in this case, regularly added to the higher tone of **ma** and **mï**: má-mà > mâ; mï-mà > mî.

The *uncontracted* form is occasionally found—though rarely, especially for the purpose of explanation or stressing. The forms '¨ï or 'ïmà are used about equally.

225. (ii) The other pronouns, i.e. èrì, àma, èmï, èì are only rarely used in the contracted form; their usual form is èrimà, àmamà, èmïmà, and èìmà.

226. (iii) This mà-form is used only as an adjective, i.e. in connexion with a noun; it never stands alone as a possessive pronoun proper. Neither has this form any further special form for emphasis. If stressing be required the other forms have to be used.

227. (iv) This mà possessive form is peculiar in that it always precedes the noun it qualifies. Example:

mâ dzó *my hut*   àmà (mà) àŋgò-á *in our country*

228. Examples:

Translate: mâ sí; mî drí; 'î drì; 'dà èrimà mvá; èì àmà andzi; mî tí tsí yà? èɛ, 'ïmà kàbìlò tsí; á nè èmïmà andzi; é sö mààkò mî ti lèa; òkó lè èrimà mvá tò; bì bàtisìmù 'î drì sì; sì ma èrì drí sì; èrimà dzó yò; é dà ìyí èìmà rùá kö! ġbà ma èrimà kàlí sì; mvá 'dì kènì: é sì 'î rű; kènì: edzí 'ïmà è'bí, ɔlè dí bòŋgó ànï.

Translation: *my tooth/teeth; thy hand; his head; that is his child; they are our children; have you got (any) cows? yes, he has sheep; I saw your children; put the potato in your mouth! the woman loves her baby very much; he accepted baptism of his own (free) will; he knocked me with his hand; he has no hut; do not sprinkle them with water! he struck me with his stick; the child says that you have written his name; he says he brought his fish and purchased a cloth with it.*

229. A partial exception. Just as the particle mà is fairly regularly dropped in the genitive relationship of nouns, leaving no trace (cf. § 100), so too there are instances, though few, when it is dropped after personal pronouns, without its low tone being retained (cf. § 224). This seems, however, to refer exclusively to the more common kinship terms (as accepted through usage). As:

ma (or mï, àma) átíì (or ándríì, ámvíì, ádríì), a'wíì, ágíì... *my (or thy, our, &c.) father (or mother, sister, brother), sister-in-law, friend...*

'dà ma átíì mà tí *that is my father's cow*
but: mâ mvá or mâ mvíì *my child*

(b) *Forms with* drí, 'ní, vélé (cf. § 221 (b)–(d)).

230. (i) The possessive forms with drí and 'ní are placed after the noun they determine. This ní requires an additional low tone on the preceding syllable or pronoun (cf. § 111).

231. The form with vélé may precede its noun or follow it. We have thus these forms for, say, *my goat*:

ndrí mádrí or ndrí mânï or ndrí mávélé and mávélé ndrí.

232. Again and again the following idea was expressed to the author, while others seem to deny it (cf. § 111): **Nǐ** would imply some idea of ownership or the intention of giving something as such. **Drí** does not imply anything of the kind. **Vélé** generally suggests the idea of connexion with one's home; actually the two following phrases are taken to be identical: **èi-vélé** and **èi-rǐ** (cf. §§ 237 ff.), *their*, i.e. *something of their home*.

233. (ii) The simple possessive forms are regularly used when the stress of the sentence lies on the noun to be determined by them or on some other part of the sentence, rather than on the possessive itself.

234. (iii) The relative or adjectival suffix **-rǐ** or **-rǐ'ï** is, however, added to these possessive forms when they are stressed or emphasized.

(82) **ɛmbátá àmavélé-rǐ ǝkǝ ádzê** *our instruction finished yesterday*

(83) **sǝ̀ ma àdzú ɛri-vélé-rǐ sǐ** *he stabbed me with his own spear*

235. (iv) The three above forms are found more commonly after nouns, i.e. as *adjectives* or *epithets*. But the identical forms are also used alone or as *pronouns* proper, as predicate or subject complement, as in

(84) **ǹdrí 'dàrǐ mádrí-rǐ 'ï** *that goat is mine*

236. (v) Miscellaneous examples: For the following examples note that any one postposition may be replaced by the other.

(85) **'dǐ àfa à'dɩ drí yà?** *whose thing (property) is this?*

(86) **mvá 'dǐ ògù àfa àma-drí rá** *the boy has stolen our thing*

(87) **ǝvï sǝ̀ dzǝ́ má-drí rá** *the lightning has struck my hut*

(88) **lǝ̌dè mǒká tí vélé-rǐ 'du kéré mà ǝndí 'alénïárǐ wǝ́rǝ́** *stale cow urine removed all the dirt from the inside of the calabash*

(89) **gárǐ 'dà ɛrïnǐ kö, ɛri 'bá àzïnǐ-rǐ (= 'bá àzïnǐ-nǐ)** *that cycle is not his, but somebody else's*

(90) **bǝ̀ŋgǝ́ ɛmǐ-nǐ-rǐ mà ti mba kö** *your cloth('s make) is not strong*

(91) **á lè ǹdrí mádrírǐ'ï** *I want my own goat*

(92) **é sǐ ti àmadrí-rǐ'ï!** *write (in) our language!*

(93) **ágú ɛri ǝkó 'ï-vélérǐ ǝmvɛ rú ɛri-drí-rǐ sǐ** *a man calls his wife by her name* (i.e. no title, &c.)

(94) **ɛwá vélé ǝ́ŋa ɛ'dǝ́ rá ɛ̀tǝ́ drí-rǐ ɛ'dǝ́ vïnï rá** *the termites on the side of the elephant started* (swarming), *the hare's started also* (fable)

(95) **ǹdrí 'dǐ mávélérǐ'ï** *the goat is mine*
    = **'dǐ ǹdrí mávélérǐ'ï** *this is my goat*

(96) **tí 'dǐ mâ-nǐ-rǐ'ï (= mádrírǐ'ï)** *this cow is mine*

(97) **ǝ́drá 'dǐ ɛri-drí-rǐ, é ko dzà!** *the bamboo is his, let it be!*

(c) **-rǐ** *at, to, from the place of . . .* (cf. § 221 (e))

237. -rǐ is a pronominal suffix of a locative-adverbial nature. It stands for 'to —, at —, from the home (village, place of event) of . . .'. In the Lɔgiri region -rǐ is replaced by -awa: àma-awa, èì-awa, &c. In other areas they use -drí or -vélé or vǒ in the same sense.

This suffix is largely used in Logbara as a very convenient method of making speech terse. A foreign student must note carefully the difference between this suffix -rǐ with high tone, and the relative element -rǐ with low or low-intermediate tone. The position of the combination with -rǐ is, naturally, the end of the sentence: it has the value of an adverb.

238. *Use.* (i) It may be freely suffixed to any noun or pronoun referring to persons and their homes, as

ópí-rǐ *at the chief's village, residence* . . .   also ópí vélé
àma-rǐ *to,* or *at our home*   also àma vélé

Note: -rǐ is used exclusively in a locative sense, while drí, vélé, vǒ are used with this meaning, too, as well as in their wider sense (as shown elsewhere).

239. (ii) We may say, however, that it is more commonly used combined with the full-form plural personal pronouns as in:

àma-rǐ *to, at . . . our* (comprising 'my') *home, village*
èmï-rǐ *to, at . . . your* (comprising 'thy') *home* . . .
èì-rǐ *to, at . . . their* (comprising 'his, her') *home* . . .

This form is analogous to the Acooli **tuu-wa, tuu-wu, tuu-ǵï.** But while in Acooli we have only these four forms (including **tuu-ru**), in Logbara the use of the corresponding form is much more extensive.

(98) é mvi èmï-rǐ; é rï àŋgǒ àmànírìá (= àmavélérìá) kö!
    go back home (to your country), *do not sit* (*delay*) *in our country!*

(99) mï ɔvö ŋgɔá yà? ma ɔvö àmarǐ *where have you been? I have been at our village*

240. (iii) -rǐ is, however, though not very frequently, also used with the singular personal pronouns, and with other pronouns, in the same sense. Examples:

(100) águ ǹdérì mvi 'í-rǐ *the said person returned to his village*
(101) á la ma márí *I slept at* (my) *home*
(102) mu à'di-rǐ yà? *to whose village did he go?*
(103) ɔkó mvi 'í átíi-rǐ (= átíi vǒ) *the woman returned to her father's*

(d) *The dative of personal pronouns*

241. The dative case of personal pronouns is expressed by the postpositions drí or ní, as in the case of nouns (cf. § 114 ff.). Examples:

(104) mǐ ɛ'dá má ní mǐ drí! *show me your hand!*

(105) ándríinï èri drí màákò a'dï nï or ándríinï màákò a'dï
èri drí nï *it is his mother who cooks potatoes for him*

(106) má ámvíinï iyí edzï má nï mvu-zà-rö *my sister brings me
water to drink*

(107) má mï ndrí əmvi vélé *I am returning/your goat/you the goat*

(108) má ándríinï a'ú a'dï-a'dï má nï ŋaa-zàrö *my mother is
cooking a fowl for me to eat*

IV. DEMONSTRATIVE PRONOUNS

242. The *demonstrative pronoun*, adjective and substantive, is based on
the monosyllables 'dò, 'dï, 'dà, which correspond to the local adverbs
'dó, 'dé, 'dá *here, there.*

Cf. èri 'dò 'dò *he is* (this way) *here* (on the side of the speaker).

Here again the Logbara use various forms according to the degree of
stressing required.

243. (*a*) In a simple casual descriptive statement, intended simply to
draw attention to the subject itself (which happens to be in sight), the
simplest form is used, namely,

'dï pl. 'dïï *this/these*   'dò pl. 'dòï *this* (nearer at hand)
'dà pl. 'dàï *that/those*   'dï pl. 'dïï *this* (just beyond 'dò)

N.B. 'dï or 'dò also serves to express our definite article.

244. (*b*) In ordinary speech 'this' is translated by 'dï, not by 'dò
(although 'dò would do also). Where, however, a distinction has to be
made between two near-at-hand objects, say, between two objects on my
table, I indicate the one nearer to me, possibly in my hand, by using 'dò;
that just a little beyond the former, by 'dï. This distinction is very
common in languages of eastern Central Africa.

245. (*c*) This simple form of demonstrative is commonly used as an
adjective after a noun. If the noun be modified by a further adjective,
the latter follows the noun and is in its turn followed by the demonstrative.

(109) mvá wɛrɛ 'dï mu ádzê èri átïl-rï *this small child went to his
father's village yesterday*

246. (*d*) Not seldom this simple form stands alone at the beginning
of a sentence, as the formal subject, followed by a subjective complement
as predicate.

(110) 'dï má ándríi *this is my mother*

Cf. Examples 47, 65, 85.

If a sentence is expressed, as it were, with more ease and completeness,
some appropriate word (such as àfa, ágú, 'bá . . .) has to be added before
the simple demonstrative. Example:

(111) á lè àfa 'dï kö (instead of á lè 'dï kö) *I do not want this* (thing)

247. The *allusion demonstrative.* As in other east Central African languages, we find in Logbara a particular demonstrative form used for the purpose of hinting at 'the (person or thing) just mentioned . . ., or seen . . ., or in sight', without naming it: ndé-rì/ndé-'dìì or, in its simple form, ndéè alone. It is used as the other demonstratives are. Examples:

(112) έwá ndéè alu tŏ *the beer* (we drank . . .) *was delicious*

(113) ópí ndéè mà dzó mŏkέ tŏ *the hut of that chief is very nice*

(114) ágú ndéè mà rúá àzôrö *that man is sick*

(115) andzi ndéè (-'dìì) òndzí *the aforeseen boys are bad*

(116) ε'yó ndé-rì á lὲ kö, á gà sὶ = ε'yó kàò mà òŋì yə *the proposal (made) I do not like, I refuse it—it has no attraction*

248. The full(er) demonstrative form is used when more or less stressing of the demonstrative determinative is intended.

For ordinary light stressing the (adjectival-relative) suffix -rì pl. -ìì is added to the basic demonstrative element (cf. § 242).

For a more marked stressing, implying special emphasis or selection 'ï (cf. §§ 208 ff.) is added to the former. We have thus the forms:

'dì-rï (-'ï) pl. 'dì-ì (-'ï) } *this/these*
'dò-rï (-'ï) „ 'dò-ì (-'ï) }
'dà-rï (-'ï) „ 'dà-ì (-'ï) *that/those*
ndé-rì „ ndé-'dìì *the aforementioned, aforeseen . . .*

249. The plural suffix -ì or -ìì is a short vowel with a double tone, low and low-intermediate/mid, and, on account of this very marked double tone, is often written with a double vowel (-ìì), which is rather misleading.

250. These full forms are used either adjectivally and placed after the noun, or alone as proper pronouns.

251. *Note:* 'dò, 'dì, 'dà or 'dò'ï, 'dì'ï, 'dà'ï are fairly frequently used in an *adverbial-demonstrative* way, especially where we should expect a proper demonstrative pronoun, and even more so at the end of a sentence as predicate or subject complement: with the meaning *it is* (or *happens to be*) *here, present.* Examples:

má 'dò *I am here, I am present*
'dò 'ï (it is) *this one here !*

252. Miscellaneous examples illustrating the demonstratives.

(117) mâ pá 'dì pìpì *my foot here is swollen*

(118) andzi 'dòì ògúuo nï *these boys are thieves*

(119) έzó-andzi ndé'dì àŋgà ɲíríârö *the girls (who were here a moment ago) are still very small*

(120) 'bá ŋgà 'yə kènì: 'ε'yó 'dìrï 'dínï áda (or yə)' *they will say: 'this question is really (or not) like that'*

(121) é mu mvá 'dàrï əmve ! *go and call that boy/child!*

(122) é 'yɛ òku àfa 'dìrï kö yà? *have you never done this before?*
(123) é 'i àn̩á 'dìrï 'ï! *do grind this corn here !*
(124) 'bá 'dàï àzî ŋga òvò sì *those people work lazily*
(125) mâ 'yè mu lǒ 'bá 'dàï nï rá *I shall tell those people*
(126) é 'bà ndrâ sìndánì 'dòï, èinï orízǒ 'dónï, à'dóá yà?
　　　　wherever did you put these needles, to get rusty like this? (*to
　　　　get so rusty*)
(127) ɛ'yó 'dìrï 'délé àdzîrö, mï ogú ànï 'dì *this matter with you
　　　　is pleasant* (pleases you), *since you* (there) *are laughing at it*
(128) èri 'dà 'ï mà àfadzó ègà *he is sewing that man's calabash*
(129) mâ mvá èri 'dì'ï *my child is this one here*
(130) kàikə ǹdrâ mïnï ndàlé (= ndàá) 'dà 'ï *the beans you were
　　　　asking for some time ago, there they are*
(131) mvá ǹdérì áó àkúa àzôrö *the aforementioned child is staying
　　　　at home sick*
(132) andzi ndé'dìï mvï àkúa *the boys of* (who were here) *the
　　　　other day went back home*
(133) á lè mvá 'dàrï kö, èri ògù 'ï bɛ *I do not want that boy, because
　　　　he is a thief* (lit. *is with thieving*)

V. RELATIVE PRONOUNS

253. The *relative clause,* and so too the *relative pronoun,* is characterized
by the particle -rï (sometimes -rë) with low-mid tone, plural 'dìi (or
'dǐi) with the same end tone. These suffixes -rï/'dǐ are among those
little words which occur so frequently in Logbara (as the pages up to this
point have shown). Familiarity with its use is, therefore, a necessity for
the student of this language. As most foreigners in Logbara country, who
are interested in its language, are more or less familiar with Acooli or
Aluur, it will be useful for them to keep in mind that the use of this -rï/-'dǐ
corresponds, more or less completely, with the use of the relative particle
mà of Acooli, with the essential difference in position: while mà always
begins an adjective or a clause, -rï/'dǐ terminates it—a general Logbara
characteristic.

The emphasizing particle 'ï is often added.

254. Instead of -rï/'dǐ, on the other hand, the demonstrative 'dì
(-rï)/'dì-ì, 'dò (-rï)/'dòï, 'dà (-rï)/'dàï may often be found, especially
when it follows the verb immediately. In this case the demonstrative
pronoun is employed in place of -pi . . . rì.

The use of pi and lé in relative clauses will be explained below.

255. *Use.* -rï is properly the relative pronoun particle of the relative
clause. Its use as such, however, like Acooli mà, is wider than, say, the
English relative pronoun, and will necessarily be met with under several
headings in this grammar. (Cf. Adjective, § 133; Numerals, § 169; Pronouns, §§ 234, 248.)

The Relative Clause

256. The relative clause may represent various syntactic forms with corresponding constructions. In order to render the use of the relative pronoun easier and more familiar, the various forms will be treated separately.

A. Clauses with Relative Pronoun as Subject

257. The subjective form of the relative pronoun, i.e. its full form, is ... ′pi ... rǐ/′dǐǐ. Pi follows the verb immediately, and is conveniently annexed to it. Pi has mid tone, and requires that a high tone be added to the last syllable of the verb preceding, if its tone is not high already. In cases where the reflexive particle rö is interposed between the verb and pi, as is the rule, rö keeps its mid tone, but the preceding verb must end in a high tone. A high tone is added to a low tone but it apparently *replaces* a mid tone.

258. (1) Relative clauses in which the *verb* is represented by a copula—*implied* but not expressed: in contracted sentences of this kind pi is missing, only -rǐ/′dǐǐ remains.

> (134) mï əmvó àfa 'alénǐá 'dǐrï wóró rá *you have snatched up everything that was in it (this)*

Note: The relative expression follows its noun **àfa**, but is followed by a further adjective (**wóró**) referring to **àfa** also:

> (135) èì ásέ ìyía-rǐ tsɛ 'ì *they are pulling up grass* (that is) *in the river*
> (136) á lǐ ìyí mâ rùárǐ bòŋgó sǐ *I wiped off the water which was on me with a cloth*
> (137) òzǒ ìyía-rǐ *reedstalks which are in the water*
> (138) andzì tέ àzí-á 'dǐǐ ɛŋgá nǐ *the boys who were at work are coming back*
> (139) kànì mï ədzì drí bésènìá, mï ìyí 'alénǐárǐ dǎ vàá: mï tìnï ɛlǒ vàálé, ìyí 'alénǐárǐ oŋgú (= ərá) ànï *when you have washed your hands in a basin, you pour out the water in it: thus you turn its brim downwards, that the water in it may run out*

259. (2) If the *verb* is *expressed*, it is followed by pi or, in the case of a reflexive verb, by röpi and, towards the end of the sentence, by rǐ/′dǐǐ. Note the high tone before pi or röpi (§ 257).

260. If the relative clause includes a *direct* (accusative) *object*, this precedes the verb (see CIA). Any *indirect* or *postpositional object* or adverbial complement is, as a rule, placed between pi and rǐ.

261. This kind of clause is much in use for the purpose of rendering simple English terms by descriptive *noun-agent* expressions.

262. Various examples illustrating these rules:

(140) 'bá əvǒ-pi dzó àlǒá-rì *persons who live in one hut* (family)

(141) éṇá dzólókó atsé (pi rì) 'dò ; mí emû ṇaa kìá! *the remnants of polenta which were left over here; come and eat, please!*

(142) á lè 'dǒ 'àá-pi 'bə-rì'ï *I want eleusine that has developed grains*

(143) ma e'dú àfà 'dɛ́pi vàárï *I took up what fell to the ground*

(144) àtsífǒrá vɛ́pi 'bərì, èi əmvɛ əfota nï *embers that have burned out, they are called ashes*

(145) 'bá ɛŋgá-pi à'bí àlǒá-rì èi əmvɛ ádríi àzínï *persons descended from one ancestor they call 'brothers'* (lit. *other-brother*)

(146) iyí egápi àŋgǒ àlǒárì, àma əmvɛ iyí à'di *water that gushes forth from the earth at one point, we call a* (*water-*)*spring*

(147) ɛlírígà atsípi orí-lɛ́ 'dɛ́ rì'ï *a millipede that walks there like a snake*

(148) ópí emúpi ó'dírì mvi 'bə yà? *has the chief who came recently already gone back?*

(149) fɛ̌ mání éṇá tsǎpirì sì *they gave me polenta that sufficed*

(150) 'bá bùrúdzi vǒpirì *a bugler* (lit. *a person who blows a bugle*)

(151) 'bá àfa ògǔpi 'dà'ï *that is a thief* (one stealing things)

(152) àŋgbakà 'bâ ṇáápirì, sǒ èri àdzú sì ádzê *the hyena which eats man was speared* (*stabbed with a spear*) *yesterday*

(153) 'bá àfà ṇáápi tòrì, èri àŋgbáláo nï *one who eats much is a glutton*

(154) 'bá mǎärî ṇáápi tǒ 'dìi, mà mvi èi-rí *the persons who have taken much on loan* (debtors), *let them go home!*

(155) àfa líröpi 'dìi, èi tra 'bǎ sàndúkùá *the things that remained over, they collect and put them in a trunk*

(156) ǝtse pätí trǎröpi àngǒ àlǒrìàrì (or àŋgǒ àlǒárì'ï) *trees which are gathered together in one place are a forest*

(157) but cf. mvá àmalì èrinï átïi mà ti à'ï rì sì *a well-bred child—when he heeds his father's words/commands*

B. Clauses with Relative Pronoun as Direct Object

263. In clauses where the relative pronoun represents the direct or *accusative object* of the sentence, the *subject*, be it a noun or a pronoun, is invariably marked by the postposition **nï** (with high-mid tone), which may be called the *subject particle* of CIA sentences and subordinate clauses.

264. The verb immediately follows the subject. The verb in its turn is followed by the *object indicator* **lɛ́**. In everyday speech, however, this **lɛ́** is often omitted, while over a large part of the country it is almost never used.

265. -rì/'dìi or, preferably, a demonstrative pronoun (if something obvious is in question) is added after lɛ́ or, if this is absent, after the verb or some further modification.

266. The relative clause is inserted in the sentence after the words to which it refers and which is the *real direct object* of the clause, and the rest of the main sentence comes after the clause. This general rule is confirmed in the following examples:

(158) mvá èinï tsə (= tsəlɛ́) rì, ɔ́ó rá *the boy they are beating is crying*

(159) andzï èinï edzílɛ́ (= edzî) ádzê rì (or 'dì) apáa rá *the boys they brought yesterday have run away*

(160) á lè wárágà mïnï sìlɛ́ (= sì) 'dì nˇɛ *I want to see the paper which you have written*

(161) ma mòémbè èrinï tì (or tìlɛ́) èrimà dríá 'dì ɛpa rá *I am snatching from his hand the mango he has plucked*

(162) ɛ̈lï èinï fˇɛ (fèlɛ́) mánï ádzê 'dà àvˇɛ rá *the knife which they gave me yesterday is lost*

(163) bèŋgɔ́ òku mïnï sǔ (= sùlɛ́) 'dà mà milɛ́fï èri ndó *the cloth which you were wearing before looked different(ly)*

(164) á lè ti 'bánï 'yɔ́ (= 'yəlɛ́) àkúá-rì'ï *I want the selfsame language which people speak at home*

(165) mïnï sì (= sìlɛ́) 'dì tsa rá *what you have written is correct*

(166) ɛ'yɔ́ àmanï tê 'yɔ́ (= 'yəlɛ́) 'dé èri ɔndzí *what we said here a moment ago is incorrect*

(167) mvá 'dì ɛri ɛ'yɔ́ mïnï 'yɔ́ (= 'yəlɛ́) rì kö *the boy did not understand the words/what you said*

(168) 'bá àŋgbakànì tsï (-lɛ́) ádzê rì, drà rá *the man whom the hyena mauled yesterday has died*

(169) ɛ'yɔ́ tɛ́ lòlɛ́ lò (= lòlò) rì ɔndzí *what he said before was wrong*

(170) ɛ'yɔ́ manì ndzɛ rì 'dínï *what I said is this*

(171) ɛ́'dá ǹdrâ àmanï gbǎ (= gbàlɛ́) bàrádzàá 'dàrï ɛdɛ́ 'ï rá yà? *the picture we took some time ago under the veranda, did it succeed?*

C. Relative Clauses with Relative Pronoun as Indirect Object

267. When the *relative pronoun* is in a *dative* relationship or dependent on some *postposition*, we have the same construction as that explained above (§§ 263 ff.), with the one essential difference that lɛ́ is replaced by the conjunction zö, meaning *for the purpose of, in order that . . . .* zö cannot be dropped; it is sometimes replaced by ànï or -rìá (which convey the same meaning).

The subject of the clause may be missing, and in place of a sentence proper we get a phrase describing some object by its purpose, origin, &c. The verb in this case represents a kind of *gerundial infinitive.*

268. Examples of relative clauses, or phrases, with zǒ.

(a) *Dative*:

(172) 'bá ɔ́pínï tí fὲ-zǒrï̀ 'dà *that is the man to whom the chief gave a cow*

(173) 'bá ádzê mïnï à'bǒà fὲ-zǒ drínïá 'dàï̀, emú àndrò kö yà ? *the men to whom yesterday you gave bananas* (in their hands), *did they not come today?*

(b) *Receptacle*:

(174) ὲrɔ́ 'bánï à̤ɑ́ dà-zǒ 'anï-á-rï̀'ï *a granary into which people pour corn*

(175) ɡbɔ́lɔ́ laa-zǒ-rï̀'ï: ὲri bǎò Lógbàrànï εdέ rï̀ *a plank to lie on* (it): *it is a plank the Logbara make*

(c) *Instrument*:

(176) ε'bǒ mïnï ámvú 'à-zǒrï̀ mï̈ ògù-ògù *the hoe with which you till the field you have stolen* (it)

(177) kàmέ̀ὲ̀ ὲ̤â ̤aa-zǒrï̀ *a spoon to eat polenta with*

(178) àdzú ὲrinï àŋgbakà sò-zǒrï̀ (ὲri) mádrí *the spear with which he stabbed the hyena is mine*

(179) ɡbɔ́lɔ́ lítsɔ́ mà tílέ ɔ̀pì-zǒrï̀'ï *planks with which to shut* (block) *the cattle pen*

(180) dzɔ́ (è)tálá ɔzɔ́ɔ́nï ra-zǒrï̀'ï *ditch/passage near hut* (or *on roof*) *by which rain water may run off* (or *trickle into hut*) (*a gutter*)

(d) *Origin*:

(181) àŋgò-milέ ɔzɔ́ɔ́nï 'di-zǒrï̀'ï *clouds from which rain drops/falls*

(e) *Reason*:

(182) ε'yɔ́ manï̀ muzǒ Árúwá rï̀ tsḯ *there is a reason for my going to Aruwa*

(f) *Destination*:

(183) àŋgò ǹdrâ manï̀ muzǒrï̀ mókέ *the place where I once went was nice*

(184) à mú atsí mï̈ bε àŋgò tέ mïnï̀ mu-zǒ 'dà! *let us walk together with thee to that place where you went before !*

(185) ndzìlá έràfí dàzǒ 'dàrï *that road on which they spread gravel*

VI. INTERROGATIVE PRONOUNS

269. There exist a fairly large variety of interrogative pronouns and adverbs in Logbara; not all of them are simple or easy of application, at least for a beginner. The following explanations and illustrations by examples should prove helpful in studying them.

270. The interrogative pronoun is seldom found alone in a sentence; as a rule the interrogative particle yà is added at the end. The *asserting*

nǐ (meaning *it is*), quite distinct from nï, is often found to precede yà
... nǐ yà? *is it* ... ? Even more common is ... nï ya?

After the particle nǐ, as after end vowels generally, yà tends to become
à, as in nǐ-à? or sǐ-à?

271. The basic interrogative pronouns, or adverbs, are:

à'dï? *who?*   à'do? *what?*   ŋgɔ̀? *which?*

These pronouns are used alone and in various combinations.

272. I. À'dï? *who?* Used only as a noun, *never* as an adjective.

(1) As *Subject*, à'dï, also à'dï-pi, is placed at the beginning of the
sentence. Examples:

(a) *As the subject proper*:

(186) à'dï etsá 'dǐ nǐ yà? *who (is it who) arrived here?*
(187) à'dï tsà èvǒ 'dǐrï nǐ yà? *who made (plaited) this basket?*
(188) à'dïpi 'da mǐ rú 'dǐnï nǐ yà? *who gave you such a name?*
(189) à'dï (pi) nì ɛ'yɔ́ 'dǐrï kö nǐ yà? *who does not know this
(matter)?*

273. (b) *As subjective complement*—à'dï'ï placed towards the end:

(190) 'bâ mǔpi 'dà à'dï 'ï yà? *the man walking there, who is he?*
(191) mǐ ɔ́pǐ à'dï'ï yà? *your chief, who is he?*
(192) mvá 'dǐ mà rú à'dï'ï yà? mvá 'dǐ mà rú Árɔ̀ɔmǎ lit. *this
boy's name what is it? this boy is called Arooma*

274. (2) As *object*. (a) As *direct object* à'dï takes the place of a common
accusative object. Either 'ï or nï is added after it, for emphasis.

(193) mï ǝmvɛ à'dï'ï yà? *whom did you call?*
(194) mï à'dï-nï ndǎ yà? *whom do you seek?*
(195) tsǝ à'dï'ï yà? *whom did he beat?*

275. (b) À'dï as *genitive, dative*, i.e. as *postpositional object*, is placed
as an ordinary postpositional object generally.

(196) 'dà à'dï mà tí yà? *whose cow is that there?*
(197) mvá 'dàrï à'dǐ nǐ yà? *whose is that child?*
(198) ṅdrí 'dɔ̀ǐ à'dïpǐ nǐ (or à'dï vélé) yà? *whose are these goats?*
(199) é 'yǝ à'dï nǐ yà? *to whom did you speak?*
(200) fɛ̀ ɛ̀'bí ádzêrǐ à'dï drí yà? *to whom did he give the yesterday's
fish?*
(201) mï emú 'dɔ̀á à'dï sǐ yà? *on whose behalf did you come here?*
(202) mï ɛ'bí té emú à'dï-rí yà? má emú mvá 'dǐ-rí 'dálɛ *from
whose village have you come? I've come from the home of this boy*
(203) mu à'dï-rí kö *he did not go to anybody's*
(204) mu nï à'dǐ (= àfa àzǐnï) 'yɛ kö *he did not go to do anything*

276. II. À'do? *what?* is used as a noun; rarely (if ever) as an adjective. (*a*) Its position is, like à'dï, the usual one for nouns. (*b*) As subjective complement it is emphasized by adding nï after it.

277. (*a*) As *subject* and subjective complement:

(205) à'dồ 'yɛ mínï yà? *what has affected (happened to) you?*
      pätí sồ mâ pá nï *a piece of wood has pierced my foot*
(206) 'dà à'do nï yà? 'dà tí nï *what is that? that is a cow*
(207) ɛ'yó 'dï éfïnï à'do (= ŋgó)-nï yà? *what is the meaning of this word?*

278. (*b*) À'do as *direct or indirect object*.

(208) èrì à'dồ 'yɛ yà? *what is he doing?*
      èrì ámvú 'ầ *he is tilling the field*
(209) emú 'dòá à'dồ 'yɛ yà? *what did he come here for/to do?*
(210) é mvi àkúa à'do (or à'do ɛ'yó) sï yà? or ... à-sï-(y)à? *why did you go back home?*
(211) é 'bà 'dáanï à'do mà drïá yà? *upon what will you possibly put it?*
(212) tí 'dà drà à'do mà ɛ'yó sï? *what did that cow die of?*
(213) 'dï à'do mà ɛ́'dá yà? *this is the picture (photo) of what?*

279. (*c*) À'do used *adjectivally*: it is placed before its noun.
(214) é ŋga à'do àzí yà? *what kind of work did you do?*

280. (*d*) À'do used *predicatively*: à'dò-rö? *for what purpose?*

(215) 'dï àɲá à'dò-rö nï yà? *this is corn for what purpose?*
      'dï àɲâ 'i-zà *this is corn for grinding*
(216) 'bá èrì 'yɛ à'dò-rö yà? *what do people use it for?*
      èi 'i éɲâ-rö *they grind it for polenta*

281. III. À'dokồ or à'dokồó? (of) *which tribe* or *clan group?* This is used for questions about nationality, tribal or subtribal membership, or the respective languages.
(*a*) À'dokồ ... is used only substantively or as a pronoun proper.
(*b*) It is commonly used in the form of a subjective complement (with nï), rarely as subject, with various postpositions.

282. (*a*) À'dokồ ... as *subject*:

(217) à'dokồ emú ámvú 'ầ 'dòá nï yà? *which tribe's (or village's) men have come to till the field here?*

283. (*b*) À'dokồ as *subjective complement*:

(218) mï à'dokồ-nï yà? *of which tribal group are you (a member)?*
      ma Òmbàtsí (-ó)-nï *I am of the Ombatsi (a member)*

(219) súrú èmïdrírì à'dokò nï yà? *which ıs your tribal or clan group?*

súrú àmadrírì/=àma Pàdzùlúnï/Ìyívù nï *we are Padzulu, Iyivu*

(220) èrimà súrú à'dokò nï yà? *of which tribal group is he? (to which tribe does he belong?)*

(221) súrú èmïdrí àkúarì à'dokò nï yà? *which is your clan group at home?*

(222) á'dïá-nï à'dokò nï yà? *so-and-so is of which tribe?*

284. (c) À'dokò in *indirect* or *postpositional relationship*:

(223) 'dì à'dokò ti sì yà? *in which (tribe's) language is this?*

(224) á sì 'dì Pàdzùlú ti sì *I have written this in the Padzulu dialect*

(225) é sì 'dì ti à'dokò drí sì yà? or é sì 'dì à'dokò mà ti sì yà? *you have written it in which language/dialect?*

(226) mvá à'dokò-árì'ï yà? = mvá 'dìrï à'dokò mvá nï yà? èri mvá à'dokò drí yà? = mvá 'dìrï à'dokòó nï yà? *he is a child from which tribe?*

èri Pàdzùlú mvánï = èrì mvá Pàdzùlúárì *he is from the Padzulu*

(227) mî mu à'dokò-á yà? *to which district do you go?*

(227a) Òlúkɔ 'di rö (= à'dî 'di) à'dokò bɛ yà? *with whom (which tribe) did Oluko fight (make war)?*

285. IV. Ŋgò pl. ŋgòì? *which? what kind of . . .?* is the interrogative pronoun of selection from among a larger number of . . .

It is used both substantively and adjectivally.

286. It is used *substantively* only as a subjective complement; the emphasizing particle 'ï is generally added after it:

(228) ndrí mídrírì ŋgò 'ï yà? *which is your goat?*

ndrí mádrírì 'dò'ï/ɛmvɛrì'ï *my goat is this here/the white one*

(229) gìrì muzǒ Àrìŋgà-á-rì ŋgò'ï yà? *which is the way to Aringa?*

(230) 'dì drírì mà ti èrì ŋgò yà? *which is the lid of this one (pot)?*

(231) mì kàlámù 'dìì mà 'aléa ŋgòrì ya (= ama, ɛpě) 'ï yà? *which of these pencils do you choose? (from among these pencils)*

(232) mì andzi 'dìì mà 'aléa(rì) ŋgòì ya 'ï yà? *which of these children do you choose? (from among these children)*

287. It is more commonly used as an adjective and placed after its noun:

(233) 'bá ŋgò 'yɔ ɛ'yó 'dínï nì yà? *which man spoke like this?*

(234) 'dì tí ŋgò'ï yà? *what kind of ox is this?*

'dì tí má vélé ráaô-rörì 'ï *this is my ox*

(235) é lè mîní àfa ŋgò 'ï yà? *which thing do you want for yourself?*

(236) 'dì àŋgò ŋgò mà é'dá yà? *this is the picture of which country?*

(237) mï mvá àŋgò̤ ŋgò̤ (= à'dokò̤) drí yà? *you are a child of which country (place, district)?*

(238) mï àtsí 'bǎ gìrì ŋgò̤ sǐ? *in which manner do you light a fire?*

(239) εŋgá gìrì ŋgò̤ sǐ? *how did it happen?*

(240) mï ε'yô ndzε ti ŋgò̤ sǐa? *in which language do you speak?*

288. *Dates:*

(241) èì emvï o'dú ŋgò̤ (or sí) sǐ yà? = èì emvíŋgò̤á (= à'doŋgá)-rè yà? *on which day/date will they come back?*

　　èì emvî o'dú nna sǐ/nna nï èì emvî *they will return on Wednesday*

In which year? εlí ŋgò̤ sǐ yà? = εlí sí sǐ yà?

(242) mï ε'dó a'á 'dòá εlí ŋgò̤ (= sí) sǐ yà? (ŋgò̤ = ŋgò̤pi) *since which year have you been here/or when did you start being here?*

Language:

'In which language did you write this?' may be translated:

(243) é sǐ 'dǐ 'bá ŋgò̤ì mà ti sǐ? = é sǐ 'dǐ ti ŋgò̤ sǐ? é sǐ 'dǐ à'dokò̤ (or súrú ŋgò̤ mà) ti sǐ yà? (cf. ex. 226 ff.)

289. Ŋgò̤pi? *of which size?* ... 'dǐpi *like this* (indicating *by gesture*).

(244) kàarî mí-vélérǐ ŋgò̤pi yà? *how big is your heifer?*

(245) mâ dǐ fὲ mǐnǐ ŋgò̤pi ká yà? *how much ought I to give you?*

(246) mï ə'á àkúa wàŋgì (= εlí) ŋgò̤pi (= sí) yà? *how many years have you been at home?*

(247) é ɲa éɲá ŋgò̤pi? *how much polenta have you eaten?*

(248) é lὲ dǐ á fὲ mǐnǐ ŋgò̤pi káa yà? é lὲ dǐ àmbórǐ ɲaa 'ï yà *how much do you ask me to give you?* (angry rebuke to an insatiable exactor) (cf. ex. 245)

290. V. Ŋgó and its compounds. They are really *adverbs.*

(1) Ŋgò̤-á? ŋgó(á)lέ or ŋgóə? *where? whereto? whence?*

(249) èmï-rǐ (§ 237) àŋgò̤ ŋgóá yà? *where is your country (district)?*

(250) mǐ mvi ŋgóa yà? mǎ mvi àmarǐ *whither do you return? I return home*

(251) mï àfa èri ŋgóə yà? *where are your belongings?*

(252) mï ε'bí εŋgá ŋgólέ yà? *whence do you come?*

291. (2) Ŋgəárè? à'do-ŋgárè? à'dóárè? *when? at what time, season?*

(253) èrì ŋgà mvi ŋgəárè yà? *when will he go back?*

(254) ópí drà à'doárè yà? *when did the chief die?*

292. (3) Ŋgónï-ŋgónï yà? ŋgó-ŋgónï yà? or ŋgónï yà? *how?*

(255) èì dǐ ε'yórǐ 'yə ŋgò̤ŋgónï yà? *how do they pronounce this word?*

(256) mvá 'dǐ mà àzó èri ŋgóənï yà? *how is the boy's illness/how does he feel?*

(257) é 'yɛ ŋgóníŋgóní yà? *how did you do it?*

(258) bòŋgó mî rúárï ŋgó yà? *what is the matter with the cloth you have on?*

(259) kànì èrì 'yɛ adri ŋgóníŋgóní áàni, á nì àŋgà kö; 'yɛ̀ 'yɛ̀ paa rö kö áàni *how he may (one day) behave, I do not yet know; he may possibly not escape*

VII. INDEFINITE PRONOUNS AND ADJECTIVES

293. (1) The following expressions are used as *adjectives* as well as *pronouns*. Syntactically they follow the general rules for adjectives or nouns respectively.

àzï mostly àzíní or àzírï *another; some more*
àlö-àlö *some, a few; singly, one by one*
àmbóòrö *much, in great quantity*
gáã, wɛɛrɛ *little; few*
kárákàràrö, kákàò *many, numerous*
dríìa, ná, pírí, wóəró, &c., *everybody, all*

Other terms of a similar kind will be found under *Adverbs.*

294. (2) Apart from their primary use, the following nouns are used, alone or in various combinations, in an indefinite sense.

á'dïá pl. á'dïápïï ⎰ *what's his name, so-and-so, the individual* (used
àfa'ï pl. àfa-pïï ⎱ for a person whose name is unknown or secret . . .)

'bá pl. 'báï *man; one; people; he, she, they* (when undetermined)
ágú pl. àgu *person, individual* (when used in a general sense or of unknown persons; used rather more than 'bá)
àfa *thing, something; it* (indefinite)

295. (3) Common combinations of the above expressions:

'bá àzíní . . . *somebody; some more; one more* . . .
'bá àlö *a single individual; a person*
'bá àlö-àlö *one or the other; every single individual; a few*
'bá àlö kö, 'bá àzíní kö *nobody, none; not one; nobody else*
àfa àzíní *another thing, something more; something; anything*
àfa àzí-nï (or -rï) kö *nothing; nothing else; no more*
àfa àlö-àlö *one or the other thing; a few things*
àfa bàdà(kàrö) *useless, unprofitable things; trash, rubbish* . . .

Examples illustrating the three sections above:

296. (1)

(260) fɛ̀ mání éɳá wɛɛrɛ *she gave me very little polenta*
(261) mï òfò tí wóəró ! *drive out all the cattle* (from lítsó *pen*) !

(262) andzi mu àzía wɛrɛ *few boys went to work*

(263) èri wɔ́ərɔ́ 'dǐ *that is all* (completed, finished)

(264) àtsǐ vɛ mǎ dzɔ́ kěnàkěnà rá ; atsɛ àtsǐfúlɔ̀rö *fire burned down my hut completely* (to the ground); *there remained glowing remnants*

297. (2)

(265) ágú 'dǐ lǒ ɔ̀ndzí *this fellow pronounced it badly*

(266) é fè àfa ágú 'dà drí 'dálé! *give that person there something!*

(267) á'dǐá ɛ'dɔ́ àndrò emú 'ǐmà èwá 'dǐ bɛ 'dǐ yɛ! *here comes what's his name again to start trouble* (*elephant!*) *today* (angry exclamation)

(268) àfapǐǐ èì ŋgɔ́lé yà? *where are the fellows . . . ?*

(269) á nè á'dǐá-nǐ ámvúá 'dà *I saw so-and-so there in the field*

(270) pádrè àfanǐ ŋgɔ́ə yà? *where is father so-and-so?*

298. (3)

(271) mǐ èfè mání àfa àzǐnǐ! *give me something* (more)!

(272) 'bá àlö-àlö emú té rá *a few persons came a moment ago*

(273) á nè 'bá àzǐnǐ kö *I have not seen anybody*

(274) mǐ èfè mání àfa bàdà *you have given me rubbish*

(275) fè ǹdrí 'bá àzǐnǐ kö *he did not give a goat to anybody*

(276) mvá àzǐ àlö Àlúrù ti nǐpi emǐ 'a 'dǐá tsǐ yà? *is there any boy among you who knows the Aluur language?*

(277) pätǐ a'bó 'bá àzǐrǐ tsǐ *a tree hides somebody*

(278) á mu 'bá àzǐ-rǐ kö *I did not go to anybody's village*

(279) éfǐnǐ àzǐ àlörǐ pè rö rá or àvě mâ drǐá rá *another meaning* (of the word) *escaped* or *I forgot*

(280) pè àŋgà kàlámò àzǐrǐ mà sí kö *he has not yet sharpened/ pointed any pencil*

CHAPTER 8

THE COPULA

299. The *copula* is that part of a nominal predicate that merely joins the qualifying adjective, noun, or noun-equivalent to the subject of the sentence.

In Logbara copular function may be expressed in various ways, i.e. (*a*) by mere juxtaposition, (*b*) by means of the personal pronoun èri pl. èì, (*c*) by using one of the copular verbs a'á, əvö, adri.

In this connexion the verbs tsǐ and yə and the structural combinations for the English 'to have' must also be referred to.

I. The Predicate: an Adjective or a Noun

300. When the predicate is an adjective, a noun, a noun-equivalent, or an adverbial postpositional expression, it is joined to the subject:

(a) As a general rule the corresponding 3rd person pronoun èri or èl is placed before the predicate. This way of expressing the copula is always correct, e.g. mvá èri mŏké *the child is good*.

301. (b) *Juxtaposition.* In actual colloquial speech, however, the Logbara omit the expected personal pronoun and the predicate is simply placed immediately after the subject or its adjuncts: we thus have simple juxtaposition. As in mvá mŏké instead of mvá èri mŏké *the child is good.* The last sentence is quite correct, but would in ordinary speech sound clumsy or pedantic to the native.

302. The simplified construction of juxtaposition is used:

(a) In simple everyday sentences with an adjective as predicate. The suffix -rö (cf. § 139) indicates the predicative adjective:

(1) 'bá 'dà mà bòŋgó ɛkàrö (ɛmvèrö) *that man's cloth is red (white)*
(2) àŋgò ënîrö *it (the world) is dark*
(3) ópí àmavéléri ndrâ mŏké *our chief of old was kind*
(4) dzó 'alé wàalàrö *the hut ('s interior) is wide/spacious*

303. (b) Numerals or nouns (often with predicative suffix -rö) or postpositional expressions are joined to the subject in the same way:

(5) ǹdrí mádrí àarò *my goats are eight/I have eight goats*
(6) èrivélé bòŋgó ndrâ òndîrö *his cloth was dirty*
(7) ɛ'yó 'dì ɛ'yó àkání (or àmbôrö) *this question is an important one*
(8) àma àkú Áivùá *my home (-village) is in Aivu*
(9) mvá mŏkéri 'ï átíi-nï òrïpi trátrári 'ï *a good child is one who always fears/obeys his father*

304. (c) When the subject is particularized by the addition of the emphasizing -nï or the demonstrative pronoun 'dìrï, &c., or the relative -rï, the èri or èl is even easier to dispense with.

(10) òkó 'dì mà ádríi-nï ópí-nï *the brother of this woman is chief*
(11) záä 'dàrï má ámvíi àzí *that girl is my step-sister*
(12) 'dì má ádríi mà záä *this is my brother's daughter*
(13) pätí 'dì mà rú ódrá-nï *the name of this tree is bamboo*
(14) Árúwá-nï ògògò *Arua is near*, &c.

305. (d) The copular personal pronoun èri or èl is used, however, whenever the nominal predicate is stressed in some way, or when the complexity of the sentence requires it for the sake of clarity.

The addition of the suffix -nï to the predicative noun, &c. (as in examples 10, 13) serves to stress this noun also.

(15) 'ï ádríinï àŋgò 'dï mà ópí *his brother is the chief of this country*

(16) èrì òndó-nï *it is durra*

(17) èrì dí 'dé tí-nï yà !? *is he now a cow?*
èrì 'bá áda-nï *he is a real human*

(18) ágú 'dà mà mvá èrì ŋgà wɛrɛ *that man's child is still small*

(19) kórékɛ èri ɛnìrö, ɔmbɛ-nï ɛmvɛ̀rö *the crow is black, its neck is white*

(20) milénï (i.e. bélɛ́) èrì dí ɛkàrö, dza ŋgà kö *the scar (of a sore) is still red, it is not yet healed*

(21) òkó 'dï èrì òkó ɔmvɪzà-nï *this wife is an inherited one*

(22) kànì tí èrì tìbí-nï, mï èrì lì rá, mï èrì ɳàɳa *if a cow is (for consumption) a dish you slaughter and eat it*

(23) ɳaká èrì àfà ɳaazà-nï *food is something for eating*

(24) è mǔ tá 'dálɛ́ ìrrì ; mï àzí èri ŋgà ŋgóɔ yà? ma àzí èrì ŋgà vélɛ́ *you went there as a pair; your companion is where? my companion is still behind*

(25) ósò èrì tí mà 'aléa *fat is found in a cow*

N.B. Even in the above cases **èrì** can generally be omitted. In 'it is a child' **èrì mvá**, or similar phrases, **èrì** is, of course, essential. If an *imperative* or *hortative* has to be expressed, as 'be clean!', the auxiliary verbs **adri, ɔvö,** or some similar verb has to be used.

II. The Auxiliary Verbs *a'á* (or *ɔ'á*), *ɔvö, adri* as copula: *a'á, ɔvö, adri* 'to be'

306. The two verbs **a'á** (in some areas **ɔ'á**) and **ɔvö** and—to some extent—**adri,** are identical in meaning, use, and construction; as a rule, either may be used. Sometimes they are even combined, **a'á-ɔvö.**

They are commonly used as a kind of auxiliary verb—a copula, and followed by a verb in the infinitive, hence in CIA sentences.

Sentences with these verbs as copula commonly refer to the *past;* they serve (*a*) to describe actions in progress, (*b*) to describe a psychological or physical state.

307. (*a*) Action in progress:

(26) àma ɔvö wárágà sǐ, àma ɔvö à'bòà mbɛ *we were writing, we were eating bananas*
mvá 'dïrï ɔvö ɛɳâ ɳa *this boy was eating polenta*

(27) mï ádzê ɔ'á ŋgólɛ́ yà? *where were you yesterday?*
ma ádzê a'á bòŋgó òdzì *yesterday I was washing clothes*

(28) 'bá 'dàì èì tá a'á ɔmbî kɔ *those people were collecting locusts a moment ago*

(29) má əvö mùtsùŋgùà ètǐ mberïá *I have been picking and eating mandarins*

(30) à'dïnï ə'ǎ mvá 'dǐ tsə nǐ yà? *who has been beating this child?* ma (ə'ǎ) tsə ma'ï *I was beating him*

(31) èri ádzê ə'ǎ gbándà ǹdú əfô *he was loosening the soil under the manioc yesterday*

308. (b) Describing mental state, physical behaviour, manners, &c.:

(32) èri a'ǎ kòmú sǐ *he was kneeling*

(33) ma ásínï əvö èmvò (= ètsáandí) bɛ *I am heart-broken/sorely grieved*

(34) óŋófïnï a'ǎ ò'dó óŋófílɛ́ *its claws are like leopard's claws*

(35) dzó 'alɛ́ òndzí; kànì kó èri 'bə, èri əvö àlârö *the hut is dirty; when they have swept it, it will be clean*

(36) èmï əvö (= adri) è'yɛrɛ, ma fɛ̂ rá *be quiet, I shall give* (you)

(37) mvá 'dǐ èri əvö àfa nǐ kókòrö *this boy is ignorant* (without knowing things)

(38) ɛmbá mvíìnï əvözó (= mà əvö) mǒkêrö *he exhorted his son to behave properly*

(39) èri əvö àvìàvì kókòrö *he is/was breathless*

309. (c) Living, staying . . . in . . ., . . . with . . .

(40) èi kànì əvö àkúalɛ́ áánì *they are possibly staying at home*

(41) édró ə'ápi ásɛ́ 'aléarǐ èri àlótsókónï *the mouse which lives in the grass is a field-mouse*

(42) mǎ mu àzí mávélɛ́-rǐ dɛ o'dú nna sǐ; o'dú ssu sǐ mǎ ŋga a'ǎ àkúa *I will go to finish my work on Wednesday; on Thursday I shall stay at home*

(43) àma a'ǎ òku èi bɛ kö *I have not been with them before*

(44) mǐ əvö 'dòà andzi ìrrì 'dǐ bɛ! *stay here with the two boys!*

(45) é kà té 'dò mu a'ǎ andzi vǒ láìnǐá, é nì té 'dò àfa dɛ 'bə *if you had gone before to stay in the compound with the boys, you would by now have known things*

(46) o'dú manï əvözó kaunsilá, mǎ véléa ma esú ɛ'bó sùkúlù drí àlö àvɛ̀ rá *the day I was at the council, I found that after* (my) *leaving a hoe of the school was missing*

(47) èri əvö ə'ǎ bòŋgó òdzì (= òdzìrǐá) *he was washing clothes*

III. *Adri* (or *a'á, əvö*)

310. This auxiliary is, in part, identical with **a'á** or **əvö**. Where it differs is that it, apparently, refers rather to a particular state or condition at a given moment, while the others, as a rule, refer to a relatively continuing state or action. We find it used in sentences of unreal condition, or such as express an imperative or hortative mood of a simple copular nature (cf. § 305, N.B.). **Adri** is more nearly a real copula than an auxiliary verb. Adri answers to: 'to be how' or 'in what state'.

(48) á lè á'dĭá mà adri ópîrö *I wish so-and-so to be chief*

(49) é fŏ mu adri dzó'bélékò ǹdúa! *go and stay (wait) under the veranda!*

(50) mà kə àŋgŏ rá, àŋgŏ mà adri àlârö! *have the ground swept, that the floor be clean!*

(51) 'bá àzínï mà adri mâ drìléa (or gĭrĭá) kö! *may nobody stand in front of me* (obstructing my view, movements)!

(52) mĭ adri (= əvö) àma àŋgŏá àŋgŏ nè-zŏ! *remain in our country to observe it!*

(53) mĭ adri tsĭrĭ! or mĭ əvù ndì! *be silent!*

(54) mĭ adri àyìkò bɛ! mĭ adri ásí bɛ àlârö! *be happy! be pure of heart!*

(55) á kà té adri mĭ 'ï, mâ té mvì àkúa! *if I had been you, I should have gone home!*

(56) é ko (or fè) mà adri 'dáanï! *let it be like that!*

(57) èri adri àtsĭ bɛ ká, mâ ŋaa ndò! *let it first be warm, then I shall eat*

(58) 'dĭrĭ mu adri èndzòrö áánï *this may possibly be wrong*

(59) àfa mïnï adrizŏ èi berĭ, 'bá èi əmvɛ dzòfó *things you have on you, they call them trinkets*

(60) mâ gárĭ àzínï kà té adri tsĭ, ma té əndzo ànï *if I had had some bicycle, I should have hurried along with it*

IV. *Tsĭ—Yɔ*

311. **Tsĭ** *to be*, in the sense of *to exist, to be present, ready*. **Yɔ**, the negative of the former, i.e. *not to exist, not to be present*, &c., *to be absent*; often, simply, *not*.

In themselves they are *indicative present* forms; they are unchangeable. These two defective verbs are never used as copulas. They may be found in sentences of past and future tense.

(61) sùkarì mĭvélé dzóa tsĭ *there is sugar in your hut*

(62) é kènì té: ò'bu èrimà pá tsĭ *you said that there is a jigger in his foot*

(63) é ko àzínï tsĭ *you have left some over*

(64) átíinï tsĭ, kə bàtisìmù 'bə *his father still lives; he was christened*

In sentences like the above, **yɔ** in place of **tsĭ** expresses the opposite, the negative form.

(65) 'bá mà ə'yó yɔ *man's horns do not exist*, i.e. *a man has no horns*

(66) á mu 'dálé, ma esú mĭ yɔ *I went there but found you absent*

(67) 'dŏ 'dĭ mà 'aléa àŋgà éfĭ yɔ *this eleusine has not yet formed grain*

(68) maaɲà mà 'yò yɔ *the monitor lizard has no poison/is not poisonous*

(69) èri tá (ɛmbátáa) yɔ *he was absent* (from instruction)

(70) èri 'dá yɔ, èri 'dòá *he is not there, he is here (present)*

(71) Índì èri 'bá àmadrí yɔ *an Indian is not of our people*

(72) àzí mâ drìléá yɔ *there is no work incumbent upon me/I am not occupied*

V. 'To have', and how is it rendered in Logbara

312. Logbara, like many other African languages, has no verb corresponding to 'to have'. What we have to note is the way in which Logbara expresses our idea of 'to have'.

'To have' is rendered in Logbara by means of the *possessive pronouns* or the *possessive case* and 'to be' or the 'copula': in a variety of ways. Yɔ or kö added to the positive forms produces 'not to have'.

313. (1) 'bá mà àfa tsí, i.e. *a man's things exist*, thus, *he has.*

(73) èrimà tí möödrí *his cows are ten*, i.e. *he has ten cows*

(74) mâ ṅdrí ndrâ täáú *I once had five goats* (lit. *my goats once were . . .*)

(75) mâ tíní mu adri nna, kà ti rá *I shall have three cows, when (the one) she has calved*

(76) 'bá 'dà mà tí kàlí-ìrrì *that man('s are) has twenty cows*

(77) mâ bɔŋgó ɔdzìzàrö tsí *I have clothes to be washed*

(78) mï andzì èl sí yà? *how many children have you?*

ma andzi (èl) ìrrì *I have two*

314. (2) 'bá àfa bɛ *a man is with; is accompanied by, provided with.*

(79) èri tí bɛ möödrí drìnï täáú *he is with (has) fifteen cows*

(80) ma ìyí bɛ bɔŋgɔ̂ di-zɔ́ *I am with*, i.e. *have water to wash my clothes*

315. (3) àfa . . . drí (=vélé, ˀní) . . .*'s things are.*

(81) kàbìlɔ̀ mádrí (mâní, mávélé) azìa *my sheep are six = I have six sheep*

(82) 'bá àlö-àlö èri tsérè ˀîní bɛ *everybody has his own cry*

(83) dzó 'bá 'dì-ní nna *this man has three huts* (thus, *wives*)

(84) sìlíŋgì drínîá àarɔ̀ *he has eight shillings (eight shillings are in his hand)*

(85) tí 'î-vélé ázì'ìrì *he has seven cows*

316. (4) 'to belong' is expressed in a manner analogous to the above.

(86) ṅdrí 'dìrï 'bá àzî-ní (or àzíní ní) *this goat belongs to somebody else*

(87) = 'dǐ 'bá àzǐ mà n̄drí = 'dǐ n̄drí 'bá àzǐ drírǐ *this goat belongs to somebody else*

(88) tí mávélɛ́ yɔ = ma tí bɛ yɔ *I have no cow*

ɛ̀ri à'di vǒ? à'di ɔvö ɛ̀ri bɛ nǐ (yà)? *who has it?*

ɛ̀ri má-vǒ yɔ *I have it not* (*I don't have it*) (*I haven't got it*)

CHAPTER 9
VERB

317. *Verb* is a word used for saying something about a person or a thing.

The verb in Logbara has certain peculiarities. At first sight a verb differs in nothing from other parts of speech; only the meaning and construction of the sentence show which is the verb. The verb, as far as its spelling goes, remains unchanged throughout its so-called 'conjugation'. There are no distinctions of voice, tense, mood, or person expressed by the verb itself.

On the other hand, some distinctions are expressed by the verb by means of tone changes—a field regrettably neglected by most students of the language.

318. In connexion with verbs, we are accustomed to speak of a *conjugation*—a simple matter in Logbara: take a verb, say **fɛ̀** *to give*, and place before this unchangeable stem successively the six personal pronouns, and we have the conjugation. But this is not the whole story, as foreigners are inclined to think. As a matter of fact the 'conjugation' is not quite so simple: for certain distinctions, inherent in the general nature of Ma'di languages, need to be observed.

319. (*a*) One cannot, as a matter of fact, separate the verb in Logbara from the framework of the sentence, as will appear very clearly from what follows. In Logbara we have, in the first place, to distinguish two types of sentence according to their *construction*. We shall have to speak of (*a*) the *Construction of Incompleted Action* (CIA), and (*b*) the *Construction of Completed Action* (CCA).

(*b*) As to these terms, they are here given for want of something better. They have this merit, however, that they are, to a certain extent, self-explanatory, in that the CCA is the construction used in sentences denoting the past—its main function, no doubt, but not the sole one. The name CIA is more nearly adequate, as it is the construction used for sentences denoting the present and future.

N.B. The meaning of the terms CIA and CCA should be kept clearly in mind.

320. Now these constructions, which comprise the whole syntactic structure of sentences, also affect the 'conjugation' of the isolated verb. It is only through appreciation of these two types of sentence that we are able to give some sort of *scheme* of *conjugation*. Thus we append two short tables of conjugation, leaving out of account the usual paradigms of the various tenses, moods, and voice. The difference of the two tables lies chiefly in the different forms of personal pronoun employed in each, and also in the differences of tone.

SCHEME OF CONJUGATION

I. Conjugation of a Verb in the CIA

321. (*a*) The *absolute* or full-form personal pronouns (§ 180 (*a*)) are used in CIA. These pronouns may undergo changes of (i) *tone*, and (ii) *end-vowel* (in speech). These changes do not apply in the following table, as the verbs chosen for the paradigm have an etymological low tone, and begin with a consonant.

322. (*b*) Low-toned verbs add a mid tone after the existing low one: fè becomes fě, for instance. The verbs nè *to see*, bǐ *to seize*, 'bà *to put*, fò *to go out*, and numerous others are all of the same category.

323. (*c*)

ma	fě	*I* (*shall*) *give*, &c.
mï	ně	*thou seest, or wilt see* . . .
èri, 'ï	bǐ	*he, she, it catches, or will catch* . . .
àma	fǒ	*we* (*shall*) *go out* . . .
èmï	'bǎ	*you* (*will*) *put*, &c. . . .
èi, èki	'bǐ	*they* (*will*) *taste*, &c. . . .

Full details are given later.

II. Conjugation of a Verb in the CCA

324. (*a*) The short personal pronouns (§ 180 (*b*)) are used in CCA. They never undergo any change. They can only be used, however, before a consonant.

325. (*b*) When the subject of the sentence is a 3rd person pronoun, it is implied but seldom expressed. Further details below.

326. (*c*) Verbs with etymological low or mid tones. In the 3rd person plural, if the etymological tone of the verb is *low*, a *high* tone is added to it; if it is *mid*, it is replaced by a high tone.

327. (*d*)

á	mu	*I went, brought, went out* . . .
é	dzi, ga	*thou broughtst, cutst*
—	fò	*he, she, it went out* . . .
à	lè	*we wanted, liked, loved*
è	fï	*you went in* . . .
—	mú, fě, lě, fǐ . . .	*they went, gave, liked, went in* . . .

Coalescence of vowels in the Conjugation

328. A conjugational scheme is given below to show how a hiatus is avoided in speech, when a verb begins with a vowel and is immediately preceded by a personal pronoun, which, as we know, always ends in a vowel.

The way in which one vowel prevails over another when two vowels meet, and also the tone-changes, have been described in §§ 40 ff.

329. Verbs may begin with a-, e-, or ɔ-. Such verbs are: **emvi** *to come back*, **edzi** *to bring here*, **ɛri** *to hear*, **ɛmbá** *to teach*, **ɛfɵ̀** *to come out*, **ɔfɵ̀** *to drive out*, **ɔfï** *to drive in*, **ɔmvɛ** *to call*, &c.

ma *I*	m-ɛɛri, m-ɛɛmbá, m-èèfɵ̀, m-ɔɔmvɛ, m-ɔ̀ɔ̀'bì (I examine) . . .
mï *thou*	mïï-ri, mïï-mbá, mï̃ï̃-fɵ̀, mï ɔfï, mï ànà (thou art confused) . . .
èri *he*	èrii-ri, èrii-dzí . . . as with mï
'ï *he*	'ïi-fɵ̀, 'ïï-mbá, 'ï ɔfï, 'ï a'á, &c., as with mï
àma *we*	àm-ɛɛri, àm-ɛɛmbá, àm-ɔ̀ɔ̀bì (compress), àm-ɔɔmvɛ, &c.
èmï *you*	èmïï-dzí, èmïï-mví, èmï ɔfɵ̀, èmï alú (to curse), &c.
èï *they*	èïi-mví, èïi-ri, èï ɔmvɛ, èï alú, &c.

330. The above examples will give the beginner some idea of the technique used to counter a hiatus. The coalescence of vowels is a regular feature of Logbara speech and occurs in almost every sentence. The student should keep it well in mind.

THE LOGBARA SYSTEM OF SENTENCE STRUCTURE

To form sentences for everyday use, a knowledge of the peculiarities and difficulties of the Logbara system of sentence structure is absolutely essential.

331. (1) In speaking of the different kinds of sentence, let it be clear that we are not here concerned in distinguishing co-ordinate and sub-ordinate clauses, &c., as is done in classical grammars, but rather in differentiating two main types of sentence according to their internal structure. The Logbara avails himself of two distinct systems in disposing the parts of a sentence in order to differentiate, to a certain extent, tenses and moods. By ignoring these differences, the meaning of a sentence may easily be changed and confusion result.

332. (2) In this twofold system of syntax, the parts of the sentence fall into three main categories:

(a) *principal parts*, viz. Subject (S), Verb (V), Accusative or Direct Object (DO), whose relative positions are fixed by rules;

(b) *subsidiary parts*, such as the Dative or Indirect Object (IO), post-positional object, adverbs, whose positions may vary;

(c) *the other essential parts or elements* (*accidence*) which characterize one system, while they are lacking or different in the other, such as (i) the particle indicating the Noun-Subject, (ii) the Pronoun-Subject, (iii) the Tonal features.

Thus in treating each of the two types of sentence it will be necessary to set out in detail the factors governing the use of these parts and their position in the sentence.

333. (3) The criteria governing the application of the systems in the *extensional field*, i.e. to express the various tenses, moods, and types of clause, are important and peculiar (cf. §§ 352 ff.).

As already mentioned the two systems are here called:

I. *Construction of Incompleted Action* (abbr. CIA), and
II. *Construction of Completed Action* (abbr. CCA).

I. Construction of Incompleted Action (CIA)

1. Characteristics of the CIA

A. *Principal Parts of this Type of Sentences*

334. Their *essential order* is: S–DO–V.

B. *Other Essential (accidental) Elements*

335. These are:

(1) A noun-subject requires the particle -nï after it, or some regular equivalent.

(2) A personal pronoun-subject requires the full-form of the pronoun.

(3) Certain tones have to be added to the verb, as shown below.

336. (1) *The subject.* The subject always precedes the direct object, if any, and the verb. The subject is either a noun or a pronoun.

337. (a) *The subject a noun.* If the subject of a sentence be a noun (i) it must be followed by the *particle* -nï (§ 335 (1)) or, after plural nouns, ïi (or èi). If determinatives are added to the noun-subject, nï is added after them. Examples:

(1) àrïïa-nï ɔ́ɔ́-ɔ́ɔ́ *the bird sings* (lit. *cries*)
(2) 'bá èi dzô si *people build a hut*

338. (ii) This -nï can be replaced either by the personal pronoun èri/èi or, where the context admits or requires it, by the demonstrative determinatives 'dɔ̀rï/'dɔ̀ǐ, 'dìrï/'dìǐ, 'dàrï/'dàǐ, after none of which can -nï be used (cf. § 339 (b)). Examples:

(3) 'bá 'dàrï tî dzi 'dálɛ́ *that man is taking a cow yonder there*
(4) àgu 'dàǐ dzɔ́ bǐ-bǐ ɔ̀drí sǐ *those men are daubing the hut with clay*

339. (b) *The subject a pronoun.* (i) If the subject be a personal pronoun, its *full form* must be used; the subject pronoun is *expressed* (not just implied), in all six persons. (ii) It should be observed that the term 'bá used in a generic sense, is a pronoun (*one, somebody*) (cf. § 294), and takes no nï after it. Examples:

(5) èǐ ólǐ lï *they are whistling*
(6) mâ mu àdrɔ̀-á *I am going to my brother-in-law's* (m.s.)
(7) mâ 'yɛ ɛ'dá rá *I shall show it*
(8) 'bá tinï bǐ ɔ̀drí sǐ *they smooth its opening* (of mǒdà *pot*) *with clay*

340. (2) *The accusative* or *direct object.* The direct object is placed before the verb. Cf. examples 2, 3, 4, 5, 8, 9, 11.

For the purpose of emphasizing it, the direct object may be placed before the subject. Cf. example 10.

(9) ɔ̀ndɛrɛkɔ́-nï 'bâ rùá ɳà̀-ɳa *small-pox affects/consumes one's body*
(10) sàndúkù 'dǐ 'bá èǐ èwá ɛni (or ɛnirikɔ) ɛdɛ 'ǐ yà? *this trunk, do they make it from elephant's skin?*
(11) mâ mu màákò ɠa *I am going to dig potatoes*

341. (3) *Rules of Intonation of the CIA.*

Rules regulating tonic changes in CIA sentences are dependent on the verb and its etymologic tone. Tonic reaction varies according to whether the verb has an etymologic low, mid, or high tone. We must, therefore, consider the various cases.

N.B. The play of tone also serves as a means of identifying the etymologic tone of a verb in doubtful cases.

342. (a) *Verbs with etymologic low tone.* A verb with low (end) tone regularly adds a mid tone after the low in CIA: fɛ̀>fɛ̌; bǐ>bǐ.

In cases of reduplicated verbs only the first part takes this additional mid tone. fɛ̌fɛ̀, bǐbǐ, &c.

(12) má átíìnï tí fɛ̌ àmbónï *my father gives a cow to the Bigman*
(13) kàbìlɔ̀nï 'bá sǐsì *the ram knocks against the man*
(14) mǐ búkù mà 'alénï lǎ dɛ rá yà? *will you finish reading the book*('s content)?
(15) mvánï tí ɔ̀fǒ 'dɛ́ *the boy drives out the cattle all right*

343. (b) *Verbs with etymologic mid tone.* Here various possibilities have to be considered. (i) Verbs with *mid* tone do not generally undergo any change of tone themselves. (ii) Verbs with *mid* tone, which begin with a consonant, postulate that a *low tone* be added to that of a preceding word or syllable which has other than a low tone.

(16) èri tî tsə kàlí sì *he strikes the cow with a stick*
(17) èri ɛ'yɔ̂ 'yə è'yɛrɛ sì *he speaks calmly* (with calm)

344. It is the application of this rule which explains the *mid-low* tone in the first part of a reduplicated verb of this class, as dzî-dzi (from dzi *to bring*); the additional *low* tone in the first part is conditioned by the *mid* tone of the second part.

345. (*c*) The requirement of a preceding *low* tone applies whether the preceding word is object or subject or any particle which may happen to precede the verb. It is especially as subject that we find everyday words take on a *low* tone *in place* of their etymologic *mid* tone (which in these cases seems to disappear). This happens especially where there are auxiliary verbs (mu, ŋga, 'yɛ) in the future. In the same way àma, èmï, èì, èri become àmà, èmï, èì, èri. Even ma, mï, nï tend to become mà, mï, nï before the same auxiliary verbs, although they may also be found with their original *mid* tone plus a *low* one—mà, mï, nï.

(18) ètú àzïnï sì èì emû dzɔ̂ si mádrí *some day they will build me a hut*
(19) mà mu èri nè̌ (or nèrïá) *I shall* (go to) *see him*
(20) àmà mu andzì dzi 'dálɛ *we shall take the boys there*
   Cf. àmà mu andzi andrî *we shall visit the boys*

346. (*d*) When the common prefixes a-, e-, ə- (cf. § 59) are added to *mid*-toned verbs, they take a mid tone and the root-words very often a high tone. These mid-tone prefixes, however, no longer have the property of postulating a preceding low tone. See example 20 and the following:

(21) àmà mu andzi edzí 'dólé *we shall bring the children hither*
(22) mvánï tï əfï lítsóa *the boy drives cattle into the enclosure*
(23) mà̌ mu àfa ɔlɛ tsûwá *I shall buy something on the market*

347. (*e*) A verb with *high-toned root-syllable* adds *mid* (actually a *high-mid*) tone after its own high tone. Verbs with high tone on the stem are, apparently, all verbs with mid-tone prefixes (cf. § 346). Examples:

(24) èri mu atsî drùsì *he will journey tomorrow*
(25) èì emû rá (cf. mvá emú 'bə) *they will come* (*the boy has come*)
(26) èri emû mâ tsə *he is coming to beat me*
(27) èri mu tï edzî drùsì *he will bring cows tomorrow*
(28) èri mu tî dzi drùsì ɔkóa *he will deliver cows for the bride tomorrow*

C. Subsidiary Parts of a CIA Sentence

348. The *subsidiary parts* of a sentence are: (*a*) the *indirect* or *dative object*, (*b*) the *postpositional object*, (*c*) the *adverb*. Their relative positions in a sentence are not rigidly fixed, as the sentences already given and the following show.

349. (*a*) *The Dative Object* is (*a*) commonly placed immediately after the verb, or (*b*) it may be placed ahead of the DO or the V. Examples:

(29) ópínï ɛ'dɔ̌ ṅdrí fɛ̌ mí-ní rá *the chief will give you a goat*
(30) é mu má-nï pằrí ndằ dzɔ̂ si-zɔ̌ *go and look for a place to build a hut for me*
(31) mí emú má-nï drì-bbí fằ! *come* (to) *and cut my* (head-) *hair!*

350. (*b*) *The postpositional object* is mostly placed after the V and, commonly, after the dative object (IO), if any. However, it may even be found before the DO. Examples:

(32) ma emû ɔ̀l�̌ mí-nï mí-vélé dzóa *I shall tell you in your room*
(33) ɛ̀ri ɛ'bô sö àbɛ́ sía *he fixes the hoe to the end of the handle*
(34) 'bâ ndzo kằmì sì *people flee from a lion*
(35) èi ɲaŋgì-ɲaŋgí sì fòŋgóà sǔ *they carry a key on a chain*

351. (*c*) The *adverb* is very often placed after the V and after the IO, if any. Quite frequently it is found at the head of a sentence, before the subject, or after the subject and before the DO. Thus an adverb may occasionally be found almost anywhere in a sentence. Examples:

(36) ma emú mï andrí drùsì 'dólé *I will come to visit you tomorrow*
(37) ma drùsì mâ zâ ɲa or o'dú àzínï sì ma mằ zâ ɲa *tomorrow I shall eat my meat* or *some day I shall eat my meat*
(38) 'ï ándríinï tsɛ́ òku ('ínï) éɲá edzí rá (he says) *his mother for a long time has been bringing him polenta* (regularly)
(39) wárágà òku mïnï 'bằ ìí 'aléa 'dàrï, ɛ̀ri å̌ ìí driá ('bùá) *the paper which you put in the water before, is floating* (on top of) *on the water*

2. The Extensional Use of the CIA

352. The CIA is used to express the (*a*) *infinitive*, (*b*) *present indicative*, and (*c*) the *future* tense.

The present indicative, future, and infinitive have, in the main, the same construction. The infinitive is singled out here for illustration of the CIA sentence.

A. The Infinitve

The infinitive may be represented in the following forms:

353. (1) *The isolated verb.*

(a) *The simple and the reduplicated form*:

to see nĕ or nĕ-nĕ   to bring dzi or dzì-dzi
to wash ɔ̀dzí or ɔ̀dzì-ɔ̀dzì   to cheat ɛtsí or ɛtsí-ɛtsí

(b) *The isolated V plus the conjunction zŏ.*

N.B. Before zŏ the tonic inflection of the V is omitted:

to see nĕ-zŏ   to wash ɔ̀dzì-zŏ   to bring dzi-zŏ   to cheat ɛtsí-zŏ

354. (2) Usually the infinitive is given as an absolute phrase, accompanied by the DO it governs. For this purpose some general term such as 'bá *somebody*, àfa *something*, is commonly employed.

(a) Here again the phrase may stand alone or be introduced by the conjunction zŏ. Examples:

to see something àfa nĕ or àfa nèzŏ
to call somebody 'bá ɔmve or 'bá ɔmvɛzŏ
to wash a cloth bɔ̀ŋgɔ́ ɔ̀dzí or ɔ̀dzìzŏ
to cheat a person 'bá ɛtsí or ɛtsí-zŏ

N.B. In place of the conjunction zŏ, the particle -zà is used in special phrases (cf. §§ 596 ff.):

iyí bɔ̀ŋgɔ́ ɔ̀dzì-zŏ *water for washing clothes*
bɔ̀ŋgɔ́ ɔ̀dzì-zà *cloth to be washed*

355. (b) This second form of the *infinitive*: DO–V (-zŏ), often applies even to *intransitive verbs*, which, due to the Logbara technique of adding some logically convenient verb-integrating noun or auxiliary, appear outwardly to be transitive, as:

to forget drì (*head*)-àvĕ (*to loose*) or drì àvĕ zŏ
to lie down rɵ̀ laa vàá or rɵ̀ laa-zŏ vàá
to sleep o'dû (*sleep*)-kɔ (*to catch*) or o'dû-kɔ zŏ

356. *Use.* (a) The *infinitive* is very commonly used as an English gerundial or qualifying infinitive. Examples:

(40) à'dï-nï emû ma ekâ nì yà? *who will come (to) and help me?*
(41) mâ mu 'dálɛ́ àfa edzí *I am going there to bring something (here)* (to fetch something)
(42) à mu arî tsɔ ... mvá ndâ *we have gone to beat the drum, ...* to seek a boy
(43) ma àvù àfa e'dû *I stooped to collect something*
(44) é mu záa 'dà mà ádríi nï ɔmvĕ! or edzí! *go (to) and call (or bring) the brother of that girl!*

357. (*b*) When the *gerundial infinitive* is used for the purpose of qualifying a noun, either of the postpositions zà or zŏ is added after the verb, according to the meaning. Examples:

(45) kàrtásì ɔlɛ-zà yɔ *there is no paper for selling* (*for sale; to sell*)

(46) àfà ŋa-zà mívŏ tsí yà? *have you anything to eat* (*for eating; to be eaten*)?

(47) Ɔmbâ zíìnì záă dzɛ-zà nï *the daughter of Omba is a marriageable girl*

(48) èré èró-tì zì-zŏ *a pole to open* (*prop up*) *the granary* (with)

358. The *infinitive* is commonly met with in the future, as this tense is formed by means of auxiliary verbs (cf. Future, § 362).

Mu, emú, ŋga, 'yɛ (= 'ɔ), ɛ'dɔ́ . . . are all auxiliary verbs used in combination with the infinitive. Example:

(49) ɛ'dɔ́ 'ïmà òmvu ɔlŏ (amvî), esú àzô-rö *he began rubbing* (*to rub*) *his nose and discovered it was hurt*

B. *The Present Indicative*

359. (1) The *present indicative* is used to state that an action is in progress (present progressive or continuous).

360. (2) One and the same sentence may, however, under certain circumstances, also express the idea of an action 'about to take place', 'soon', or 'in the near future'. The adverb tsúrú'dɔ̀ (*just now*) or a similar one, when added, confirms this idea. Examples:

(50) èrì tí mvâ dzi ópí vŏ *he is taking a calf to the chief*

(51) ma ádríìnï èrì tsɔ kàlí sì *my brother is beating him with a stick*

(52) ɔzɔ́ónï ǹdrî fu 'dà ; mà mu ètrŏ *rain is striking* (*beating down on*) *the goat there* (in the grass); *I am going to remove the rope from its neck* (that it may run to shelter)

(53) ma àyíríbe vĭ *I am scratching myself* (*my itching*)

(54) à'dï mà mvánì mu 'dà nì yà? *whose child is going there?*

(55) ɔ̀línï érífŏrâ 'du ooru *the wind carries dust high up*

(56) ɔzɔ́ónì 'dì'di *it is raining*

(57) èri èfĕ má nï rá *he will* (*no doubt*) *give it to me*

(58) èì efĭ 'dĭ *they are entering there*

361. (3) It is also used to express the habitual or customary present. Examples:

(59) ma tí ɔtsĕ o'dú zù, ma àndè dí 'bɔ *I daily guard the cows, I am now tired*

(60) àrí'bó-nï ɔndzî àma drà sì *an enemy takes delight in our death*

(61) èì mŏnió fĕ ǹdrí tääwí sì *they give an ox for five goats*

(62) èì a'ú mà rùá trǒ ìyí àtsí sì *they dress a fowl* ('s body) *with hot water*

(63) èì kaaká mà ǹdú əfǒ ɛ'bó sì *they break the ground under maize with a hoe*

(64) èì ɔ́mbî kə tsíkí sì *they catch locusts with tsiki baskets*

C. The Future Tense

362. For practical purposes we distinguish (*a*) a *nearer*, and (*b*) a *farther* future, either of which may be *definite* or *indefinite*.
The common future auxiliary verbs are **mu** *to go*, **emú** *to come*.

363. (1) The *nearer future* does not extend beyond the day.
(*a*) If an action is 'about to take place' (immediate future), it is expressed by the present indicative form (cf. § 360).

364. (*b*) To express a *definite future*, i.e. that an action will take place 'afterwards', 'later in the day', 'sooner or later within the day' some particle such as ɛ'dɔ́ *to start*, (ɛ́)'díə̀, ńdrí, (ɛ́)ndrɔ̂, (ɛ́)ndríə̀, is added after the subject or, in the case of a noun, after the noun particle **nì** or **èrì**; otherwise the sentence is identical in form with the present indicative. (E)mu is sometimes added after the particle.
These particles do not seem to have any basic meaning in themselves. They are a kind of *tense symbol* which render what we might translate with 'soon', 'very soon', 'later (during the day)', or the like. Examples:

(65) əzɔ́ɔ́-nï ńdrî 'di rá *it will rain later on*

(66) Árəma èrì ńdrí emví sáwà àarɔ̀ mí ní Lógbàrà ti ɛmbárïá *Arɔma will come back afterwards, at about 2 p.m., to teach you Logbara*

(67) ma ńdrɔ̂ (= ɛ́ndríə̀) dzɔ́ 'álé ɛwɛ rá *I shall sweep the room later*

(68) ma ɛ'dɔ́ emú 'dɔ́lé sáwà ázîrrì *I shall come here later, about 1 p.m.*

(69) ma ɛ'dɔ̂ mu sìlíŋgì a'î ma átíì vǒ *later on I shall go to my father to ask for shillings*

(70) èì ńdrí emú mî vǒ *they will come to you afterwards*

(71) èì ńdrî ŋga emú ndɔ̀ *then (afterwards) they will come here*

(72) á kà ɛ'dɔ́ àzî ŋga kö, á ɳa éndrí(ɔ̀) kö *if I do not work afterwards, I shall not eat later*

(73) əzɔ́ɔ́nï (ɛ́)'díə̀ mù 'di rá *it will soon rain (it's going to rain)*

365. (2) The *indefinite future*: *farther future*.
(*a*) By using one of the *auxiliary verbs* 'yɛ *to do*, ŋga *to rise, start*, also mu and emú (§ 362), or a combination of them, as 'yè mu, ŋgà mu, mu emú, 'yè 'yɛ, . . . after the subject, a tense is obtained which may refer to any time to come, from today to a far future.

366. (*b*) These auxiliary verbs are used in sentences/phrases with an infinitive. Note that mu, ŋga, 'yɛ have mid tone and are governed by the rules explained earlier (§§ 344 ff.). Examples:

(74) əzɔ́ɔ́ ɛ̀rì mù 'dì rá or əzɔ́ɔ́nǐ 'yɛ̀ mù 'dì rá *it will rain (sooner or later)*

(75) 'bá 'dàrǐ emú ǹdrí (fɛ̀) mǐ nǐ fɛ̀fɛ̀ or ɔ́pínǐ mu mvá nǐ ǹdrí fɛ̀ *that man will give you a goat, the chief will give the child a goat*

(76) 'bá pǐrǐpǐrí ɛ̀ì 'yɛ ɔ̀drä̀ rá *all men will die*

(77) mä̀ ŋgà mu fɛ̀ mǐ nǐ ndɔ̀ *I will give it to you in the end*

(78) mǐ 'yɛ àfa 'dǐ mà rú nǐ rá *you will know its name one day*

(79) ɛ̀rì mu emǘ 'dɔ́lɛ́ rá *he will come here* (some day)

(80) 'bá 'dìrǐ 'yɛ drä̀drà *this man will die* (from it).

367. (c) In order to indicate a nearer or farther future with more precision, any pertinent adverb can be added. A sentence with adverbs indicating futurity may remain in the present indicative, or use the future with auxiliary verbs. Examples:

(81) mǐ mu drùsǐ ɛ̀ri vɔ̌ rá yà? *will you go to him tomorrow?*
cf. mä̀ mu ɛ̀ri vɔ̌ drùsǐ 'dɔ́lɛ́ 'dǐ *I will go there to him tomorrow*

(82) drùsǐ mä̀ ŋga àfa ndä̀ *tomorrow I shall look for (seek) it*

(83) mǐ ŋga emǘ esǘ o'dú àzǐ sǐ *you will get it some day*

(84) o'dú àzǐ sǐ mä̀ ŋgà mu mààkò sa or mààkò ga; or . . . mu emú rá *some day I shall plant potatoes; dig potatoes; . . . come*

(85) àma àfa 'dìrǐ ɛdɛ̌ drùsǐ *we shall accomplish this tomorrow*

368. The *adverb* ŋgà or àŋgà (low tone) must not be confused with the common future auxiliary verb ŋga (mid tone). It is used in the following ways:

(a) Meaning *still, first of all*:

(86) ɛ̀ri ŋgà bbà ndrɔ̃ndrö *it (or he) is still sucking* (the breast)

(87) àma ŋgà ɔ̀rä̀ àfa 'dǐ mà rú ndä̀ *we are still trying (thinking) to find out the name of this thing*

(88) àma ŋgà àzǐnï ɔ̀rä̀ *we are still thinking about another*

(89) ma àŋgà mu mvá 'dà əmvɛ *I am first of all going to call that boy*

(90) ɛ̀ri àŋgà fɔ̌ ò'bu ɛndzɛ̌ àmvɛ́ *he is first of all going out to remove a jigger*

(b) Meaning *yet, only just, still.*

(91) ɛ̀ri àŋgà òmú-nï *he is still a guest*

(92) é tɛ̀ ŋgà wɛrɛ! *wait a little longer!* (yet)

(93) drà àŋgà ɔ́'dí *he died only recently*

(94) àfa 'dìï ɛtsá (àŋgà) ádzɛ̂ *these things arrived only yesterday*

(c) ŋgà . . . kö *not yet.*

(95) mǐ əkə ŋgà ɛ'yɔ́ 'dà dɛ kö yà? *have you not yet finished that word?*

(96) mvi ŋgà kö *he hasn't yet returned (gone back)*

II. Construction of Completed Action (CCA)

369. The other main type of sentence construction is the CCA. The features of this construction are simpler and present hardly any serious difficulty; its extensional use is wider than that of the CIA.

The difference between the two constructions is mainly connected with the principal parts of the sentence (cf. § 332). It is, therefore, necessary to treat (a) the *principal parts*, and (b) the *subsidiary parts* of the sentence and their relationship to other parts.

1. Characteristics of the CCA

A. *Principal Parts of this Type of Sentence*

370. Their order is: S–V–DO.

N.B. There are no other *essential* elements (cf. § 332 (c)) to be considered in connexion with the CCA.

371. (1) The *subject* is either a *noun* or a *pronoun*.

(a) *The subject a noun.* If the subject of the sentence be a noun, this is placed at the head of the sentence, and it is not followed by any subjective recapitulating pronoun such as **nǐ, èri** (cf. § 337). Examples:

(97) **àmbó mu 'dálé** *the Bigman has gone there*
(98) **àtsǐ drà dɛ 'bə** or **drà rá** *the fire has gone out* (*died*)

372. (b) *The subject a pronoun.* (i) When the subject is a *personal pronoun*, as a rule the short-form is used (cf. § 327). Examples:

(99) **á dzi wárágà 'dàrï ópí vǒ** *I have taken that letter to the chief*
(100) **é sǐ wárágà dɛ rá yà?** *have you finished writing the letter?*

Note: As there are no short-forms for the ordinary 3rd persons singular or plural, 'he', 'she', 'it', or 'they' is *implied* in the verb not *expressed*. Example:

fɛ̀ dɛ 'bə *he has already given it*

Eri/èi are, however, employed, if the 3rd person is stressed or in some way singled out, as when it is in sight, &c.

373. (ii) The *full-form* 1st and 2nd personal *pronouns*, however, must be resorted to (in place of the short ones) in the following two cases: (a) when the verb following the personal pronoun begins with a vowel. N.B. The glottal stop before a vowel functions as a consonant. Examples:

(101) **mǐ əsǒ iyí bésèn 'dǐ mà 'aléa!** *pour water into this basin!*
(102) **mǐ emví à'do-ŋgárè yà?** *when did you come back?*
(103) **ma ɛ'bí ŋgà emví ádzɛ̂** *I came back yesterday*
(104) **é 'i ɛɲá!** *prepare the polenta!*

(b) When the pronoun-subject is separated from the verb. Example:

(105) mï ádzê mu ŋg̣ó yà? *where did you go yesterday?*

374. (iii) Any other pronoun may be the subject in the 3rd person. Example:

(106) 'dì dɛ 'ï 'bɔ *this is now finished*

375. (2) *The verb.* The verb follows the subject; it retains its etymological form and tone, in general, unchanged.

376. Important exception: (a) For the 3rd person plural a high tone is added to the end syllable of the verb if it has no high tone already. Examples:

fǒ rá *they went out*   mǔ 'bɔ *they have already gone*

N.B. Mid-high tone often gives place to a simple high tone, mú 'bɔ.

(b) In the *imperative* or *hortative* a high tone is added for the 1st and 2nd in the same way as for the 3rd person plural. Examples:

(107) mǐ emú à fǒ àmvé! *come (thou) let us go out !*
(108) èmï emú à fǒ àmvé! *come (ye) let us go out !*

377. (3) *The direct object* (DO). The direct or accusative object follows the verb plainly, i.e. without any particle added. In exceptional cases the DO may be found at the head of the sentence (see example 111). Examples:

(109) ma okú 'dǒ dɛ 'bɔ *I have now finished weeding the eleusine*
(110) ŋg̣ǎ àzí wóró 'bɔ yà? *have they finished the whole work ?*
(111) ámvú mídrí kànì é vɔ̀ rá, vɛ rá, mï 'yɔ kènì: ma drùsì fǒ ma ámvú 'ǎ *when you have cleaned the field and burned (the stubble), you say: tomorrow I will go out (to start) to till my field*

B. Subsidiary Parts of the CCA (cf. § 332)

These Parts are the Dative and the Postpositional Objects and Adverbs

378. (1) *Dative object.* The dative or indirect object is generally placed after the verb and after the direct object; but it may equally well be placed before the direct object or, occasionally, even before the verb. Examples:

(112) kànì mvá 'dì etsá 'bɔ, é fɛ̌ èri nï ɛ́ɲá rá! *if the boy has arrived, give him polenta !*
(113) è fɛ̌ àfa dì 'bá àzî ŋg̣ǎpi 'dì nï! *give this to the workmen !*
(114) ɛ́zó-andzi mà kǒ édzá àzí àma nï! *the girls ought to leave some fuel for us*; cf. example 99

379. (2) *Postpositional object*; *adverbs*. Generally, their usual position is after the verb, and after the DO; but they may also be found before the verb, or even before the subject. Their different positions generally imply a shifting of emphasis to different parts of the sentence. Examples:

(115) è ɳà zá ŋgɔ̀áre yà? — à ɳà zá ádzê = à ɳa á — zá = á —
à ɳà zá *when did you eat meat? we ate meat yesterday* (what did you eat yesterday?)

(116) é là ètú àndrò sì dɛ rá yà? *did you finish reading it today?*

(117) **mu andzi vǒ fúnòá andrá** *he went down to the boys in the pignuts*

2. Extensional Use of the CCA

380. The CCA is used to express (*a*) the *past tense*, (*b*) the *imperative*, (*c*) the *hortative* mood, and also found in (*d*) particular sentences.

A. The Past Tense

Introductory remarks. Among the innumerable adverbial particles of Logbara there are a few which frequently occur in the past tense, and which require some explanation.

381. Of these, **'bə** is the most frequently used; it is an exclusively past tense particle. It is normally placed at the very end of a sentence. It stresses the circumstance of an action, event, &c., 'already' finished. Example:

(118) **tí 'dà drà 'bə** *that cow has now died* (= *finished dying*)

It is very common in subordinate clauses of 'time before', expressing the earlier of two consecutive periods, i.e. when the completion of one action is the starting-point of another, as in:

(119) **kàní mvá 'dì emú 'bə, mằ mu òbélɛ́** *as soon as the boy has come, I will go quickly*

N.B. While **'bə** emphasizes the completing of an action, **rá** stresses the fact that something is to be done or not done. **'bə** is used in the past tense exclusively; **rá** in all tenses and moods.

382. **Dɛ** (with *higher intermediate* tone) is another very frequent particle which is found towards the end of a sentence, as, for instance, before **'bə** or **rá**. It is actually an additional verb meaning 'finish', 'complete', and stresses the fact that the action or event has been exhaustively or conclusively carried out. It is rather one of the pleonastic elements so much in use in Logbara. Example:

(120) **fɛ̀ dɛ 'bə** *he has now given it* (definitely)

383. Té (tá), a very common adverb of time referring to the near past, commonly within the day: 'a moment ago', 'a minute ago', 'just now', or the like. It is placed immediately after the verb or, if no verb is expressed (copula), after the subject. Examples:

(121) é fὲ té ὲrï nἱ dε 'bǝ, mï ὲfὲ dἱ 'dἱrï má nἱ! *you have just given him* (something), *now give this to me!*

(122) à mu té à'dἱrἱ kö, àma té vàá 'dέ *we did not go anywhere* (just now), *we were just here*

(123) ma emú té mï tὲ̀ 'dɔ́ rá *I did come here to wait for you a moment ago*

(124) mvá 'dἱ tsǝ té ma rá *this child has just struck me*

(125) ǝlíkà té tö, tsúrú 'dɔ̀ ǝlíkà yǝ *it was very windy a moment ago, there is no wind now*

(126) á ŋa té àfa kö, è ŋa té àfa rá *I have eaten nothing, you have just eaten*

(127) àma emú té èi bε *we have just come with them*

384. ˈdἱ, requiring an additional low tone on a preceding syllable, is the commonest of particles to be found in a sentence (of any tense or mood). It indicates a simple hint of sequel in ordinary daily life: 'then', 'so then', 'now' (German *nun*) or the like. (As with té above, it needs no translation in most cases.) Examples:

(128) Greetings: mî dî mu 'dἱ yà? mî dἱ ὲrì zìzì! —mâ dἱ mâ mu 'dɔ̀! *are you going now?/good-bye* (then)! *give him my regards!* —*I am going/good-bye!*

(129) esû dἱ 'bá àzἱnï 'bǝ *he has now found somebody*

(130) mâ dἱ εdέ ŋgɔ́nï yà? *what ought I to do next?*

(131) àmà dἱ àmà mvi àkúa 'dɔ̀! é mu dἱ ἳ! *now let's go home! good-bye!*

385. For the *past tense*, keep in mind the essential distinguishing points (cf. §§ 370–7: S–V–DO); most of the rest is optional. Examples:

(132) 'bá àzἱnï kὲnì: 'ἱ fu έdrɔ́ 'bǝ *somebody said that he had just killed the mouse*

(133) mu nɔ̀sì ŋgɔ́ǝ áánï!? *where can he have gone?*

(134) ɔ̀kó dzi a'ú àmbó nἱ (= vɔ̌) *the woman has taken a fowl to the Bigman*

(135) àma etsá emú mï eká 'bǝ *we have arrived to help you* (cf. § 354)

(136) a'dἱ εmbá mínἱ nἱ yà? *who taught you?*

(137) ɔ́pí fὲ 'ἱ ádrἱi nἱ ǹdrí rá = ɔ́pí fὲ ǹdrí 'ἱ ád— . . . *the chief gave his brother a goat*

386. The past tense may, of course, be expressed in various ways by

adding appropriate adverbs (see §§ 379, 383; Adverbs of Time, &c.).
Examples:

(138) ágú 'dà kènì, ándrâ mu sùkúlùá rá, but ... kènì, ándrâ
        ḯ mu sùkúlùá kö *that man (speaking of somebody else) said
        he had once been at school; but he himself had not been* ...

(139) ɔzɔ́ɔ́ 'dì ádzɛ́ kö *it did not rain yesterday*

B. The Imperative

387. (a) The *imperative* mood is identical in form and construction
with the 2nd persons of the past tense. For the 2nd person plural, however,
the verb takes an additional high tone on its last syllable (cf. § 376). For
the rest, additional particles, stressing or context, &c., show the difference
in meaning.
Compare é fè ! pl. è fɛ̌ ! *give (it)* ! Examples:

(140) é 'bà kàlamù búkù ètïa ! *put the pencil under the book* !
(141) andzi ! è kó bbïlé-àkɔ 'dínï 'dì dzà ! *boys! leave off* (from)
        this kind of deafness (i.e. stubbornness) ! *stop being so stubborn*
(142) é ŋga kö ; mï̌ adri 'dɛ́ ! *do not rise; remain as you are* !
(143) mï̌ ɛmvɛ́ ma ŋakú sï̌ kö ! *do not soil me with earth* !
(144) è zï̌ dzótílɛ́ rá ! 'bá mu 'bɔ *do open the door! the people have
        gone*
(145) mï̌ ɔmvɛ mvá àzínï àlö ! *call another boy* !
(146) é 'bà àfa 'dìrï 'bǎ'bà ! *put this thing aside* (or *in its place*) !

388. (b) While the form of the imperative itself presents no difficulties,
it will, however, be useful to become acquainted with various grammatical
and syntactical combinations which have some connexion with this mood.
What is said of the *imperative* is mostly true also of the *hortative*, which is,
broadly speaking, the term applied to the first and third persons, corresponding to the *imperative* for 2nd persons.

389. The imperative may be found in the following combinations:

(a) The imperative may be followed by a gerundial infinitive (cf. § 357):

(147) è mú màákɔ̀ ga/or ga-rïá ! *go and (to) dig potatoes* ! cf.
        example 44)

390. (b) The imperative may also be followed by the hortative of a
subordinate clause of purpose:

(148) é ko 'dì mà ɔvö a'dúlɛ ! *let it (be) alone* !
(149) é zì kàáti mà fò ànï ! *open the door so that one may go out* !

391. (c) The imperative may be followed by another imperative in
a co-ordinate clause, if a double injunction is directed to the same person:
the commands together being in the relation of cause and effect, or of

purpose, or mere succession. By omitting the personal pronoun before the 2nd imperative it becomes the infinitive (with corresponding tonal alterations). Examples:

(150) mǐ ayu báká rá, é 'ǐ n̄drí ànï! *unfasten the rope and tie the goat with it !*

(151) é 'du pätí wɛrɛ 'dǐ̧ (é 'bà or) 'bǎ ètǐnǐá! *take the piece of wood and put it underneath !*

(152) é dzi n̄drí ɔ̀'ǐ ɛ̆ríbía, èi mà n̖aakí ɛ̆ríbí! *take the goats and fasten them to the green grass so that they may eat !*

N.B. dzi imp., ɔ̀'ǐ inf., n̖aakí hort.

(153) mǐ ètrɞ̀ bɔ̀ŋgɔ́ edzǐ 'dɔ́lé! *take off the cloth and bring it here !*

392. (*d*) When the command or request is expressed with a tone of familiarity or intimacy, either of the particles kǐ(y)à or ǐǐ is added at the end of the imperative sentence. Fɔ̂ !, added likewise at the end, corresponds more or less to our 'please'. Examples:

(154) è mú ǐǐ! or è mû dǐ ǐǐ! *you may now go (or you had better go now) !*

(155) é mu ɔ̀dzǐ kǐa! *now you had better go and (to) take a bath !*

(156) é mu drùsǐ ǐǐ; ma drùsǐ mï tɛ̆ àkúa 'dà *do go tomorrow; I shall wait for you at home tomorrow*

(157) cf. ma emú ɔ̀kɔ̀, é mu vélé ǐǐ *I came first, you went later on*

(158) mǐ edzí má nǐ ɔ̀gɞ̆ä, fɔ̂! *bring me a chair, please !*

(159) mǐ ɛ̀fɛ̀ má nǐ, fɔ̂! *give it to me, please !*

393. (*e*) The imperative or hortative expression ending in ká or, more commonly, in rá-ká, implies the meaning 'first of all', 'in the meantime', 'for the moment'; when a consequential clause is added, the latter commonly ends in ndɔ̀ *then*. Examples:

(160) é fà mádrí" rá-ká, má ŋgà mǐdrí" fǎ ndɔ̀ *do cut mine (my hair) first, I will then cut yours*

(161) má ŋgà rï vàá rá-ká! *let me sit down for the time being !*

(162) má ŋgà iyî mvu ráká! *let me first drink water !*
mà mvu ŋgà 'ǐnǐ 'dǐrï ráká! *let him first drink of it !*

(163) é mvu mǐnǐ 'dǐrï ráká! *you yourself do drink of it first !*

(164) má ŋgà esǐ ɛ'yɔ́ ɛri èn̖ǐ ká! *let me draw near to hear the words !*

C. The Hortative Mood

1. The Form of the Hortative

394. The common characteristic particle of the *hortative* is mà; its low tone never changes.

Mà may be rendered by 'may', 'let', 'ought', 'should', 'have to', 'must', &c.

395. As a rule **mà** follows the subject (when expressed) to whom or to which the injunction or imprecation is directed, and is immediately followed by the verb; the rest of the sentence follows the rules for CCA.

(165) **àzó mà bì mï tsí!** (alú imprecation) *may illness overcome/ catch you!*

The particle **(à)ŋgà** is often used in addition to **mà**, but not necessarily immediately after it. (Cf. Ex. 160 ff.)

396. If the *subject* is a *noun*, the simple rule given above holds.

397. If the *subject* is a *personal pronoun*, the following possibilities apply:
(1) For the 1st and 2nd persons the following forms are found:

(*a*) Both the *full* and the *contracted* forms are in use in everyday speech. The *full* form consists of the full-form personal pronoun plus **mà**. The *contraction* consists in omitting **mà**, while adding its low tone to the preceding pronoun's; for the plural pronouns this low tone replaces their normal mid tone. Thus we have the following forms:

Full form	Contracted form
má mà	mâ *I may, should, . . .*
mï mà	mî *thou mayest, shouldst, . . .*
àma mà	àmà *we ought, may, . . .*
èmï mà	èmì *you ought, may, should, . . .*

398. The *full* form is fairly frequent in everyday usage; it is apparently always correct and may, for clearness' sake, in some cases be preferable. The *contracted* form is doubtless the more usual one among natives. Examples:

(166) **má átíi kènì: má mà (= mâ) mvi àkúa!** *my father said: I must go home*

(167) **àmà fŏ àmvé!** *let us go outside!*

399. (*b*) The 1st and 2nd persons, singular and plural, are frequently expressed by the short-form personal pronouns immediately preceding the verb, *without* the hortative particle **mà-**. This construction coincides with the imperative and is, in turn, identical in the singular with the corresponding forms of the past tense.

400. (*c*) Characteristic *high tone*. If the subject, whether a *noun* or *personal pronoun*, is in the *plural*, the last syllable of the verb takes *high tone*, which is added to an etymologic low tone, or replaces an etymologic mid tone. This holds for both the hortative and the imperative. Examples:

(168) **má átíi kènì: á mvi àkúa drùsì!** *my father said that I should go home tomorrow!*

(169) **àma átíi kènì: àma mà (= àmà) or à mú ǹdrí ətsέ!** *our fathers ask of us that we (should) guard the goats!*

(170) **andzi mà mví àkúa** *let the children go home !*

(171) **à wùú ə̀góa dzi 'bǎ dzóa orú 'dálé !** (past tense **à wùù ə̀góa** . . .) *let us transfer the chairs to the room above !* (past tense *we have transferred* . . .)

(172) Past: **à zì (té) dzótílé rá** *we have opened the door*
Hort.: **à zǐ dzótílé rá !** *let us open the door!*

(173) Past: **è mu té màákò ́garǐá** *you went to dig potatoes*
Hort.: **è mú màákò ́garǐá !** *go (ye) to dig potatoes !*

401. (2) For the 3rd persons these are the rules:

(*a*). If the subject, to whom the injunction is directed, is a *noun*, that noun is placed at the head of the sentence (cf. § 395) and is followed by **mà** and the simple verb. If the noun is in the plural, the verb takes a high tone (cf. § 400). Examples:

(174) **'ètóə mà èfè 'ǐmà ròbíà !'** *the hare should give him his pay !'* (fable)

(175) **'ə̀kó 'ǐdrírǐ mà 'i ɛ̨á !'** *his wife will prepare the polenta !* (fable)

402. (*b*) If the subject denotes a 3rd person singular or plural pronoun, the pronoun is not expressed and **mà** only is placed before the verb. This particular form of hortative sentence, i.e. the verb preceded by simple **mà**, is very often met with. The persons in question (whether present or absent), when entreated, are generally addressed in this manner: **mà** + verb *let him (them)* . . . *!* The subject has to be conjectured from the circumstances or from the context. The plural is indicated by a high tone (§ 400). Examples:

(176) **mà ndzɛ́ ɛ'yɔ́ 'dǐ mà ètǐ kílílí !** *let the meaning of this word be expressed clearly (by them or you) !*

(177) **mà ə̀fǒ tí àmvé !** *have the cattle driven out* (of the pen) *!*

2. *Use and Constructional Forms of the Hortative*

403. (1) The hortative is employed: (*a*) to express a wish, desire, or request, or even a curse; (*b*) to notify, quote (generally indirectly) a command, request, . . . by somebody; (*c*) to express the idea of convenience, necessity, duty.

The hortative corresponds to the imperative for 2nd persons; 2nd person commands are often also rendered by the hortative mood.

404. (2) The hortative mood may be found in the following types of sentence or combination of sentences:

(*a*) Single independent sentences:

(178) **drà mà sə̀ mï rá !** *may death come upon you !* (curse)

(179) **mǐ emú à mú 'áálé !** (come) *let us go over there !*

(180) èmï emú à fí dzóa kì̀a ! (come) *let us go into the hut/room !*
(181) mvá 'dì̀ mà ɛŋgá örú ! *let this boy stand up ! = boy, stand up !*
(182) andzi 'dàì̀ mà dă èi rá ! *those boys must withdraw !*
(183) mǐ mà tὲ ma tsí ! = é tὲ àŋgà ma tsí ! *(do) wait for me !*
(184) mǐ mà ko dzɔ́'alé, mïnï̀ lὲ-lérì̀ lé ! *leave the hut, as you wish !*
(185) èmï mà fŏ, nɔ̀sì è lὲ rá è lὲ kö ! *go out! whether you like it or not*

405. (*b*) Mostly, of course, a hortative sentence is subjoined to some introductory verb or verb-equivalent of 'saying', 'commanding', &c., such as 'yɔ *to say* or the very common (verb equivalent) conjunction kὲnì/pl. kénì (*he/they say that . . .*) by which an intimation of any kind is notified, in which case the person giving the command is generally implied, seldom expressed. Examples:

(186) é 'yɔ andzi nǐ, andzi mà emú su-su ! *tell the boys to come by fours!*
(187) é 'yɔ mà ὲfὲ má nǐ sέntὲ tääό ! *tell him to give me five cents !*
(188) àmbó kὲnì: andzi mà mú 'í vŏ ! *the headman wants the boys to go to him*

406. (*c*) To express 'convenience', 'duty', or the like, the following expressions are used:

(*a*) mŏké-nï̈, dὲko-nï̈, drì̀ga'dì̀ *had better . . ., should . . .*
(*b*) kànì'dǐnï̈, kà adri 'dǐnï̈, kà dɔ́ adri 'dǐnï̈ *if things . . . are like this . . .; under these conditions . . . ought . . .*
(*c*) lὲ or lὲ káanì̀ *it is necessary, convenient, . . . that . . .*
bὲlénï̈ lὲ té . . . *should, ought . . .*

Most of these expressions are practically identical:

(189) mŏké-nï̈ andzi àzínï̈ mà mú 'bílé ɔ̀lö̀rì́á fúnɔ̀ sa-zŏ *some children should go and dig holes for planting groundnuts*
(190) dὲkonï̈ èmï (mà) ogá andzi kö ! *you had better not hinder the boys !*
(191) kànì 'dǐnï̈ á mu 'dálé kö ! *in that case I will not go there !*
(192) kà adri 'dǐnï̈ mvá 'dì̀ mà mvi àkúa ! *if so, the boy may go home !*
(193) dὲkonï̈ mǐ mà adri ὲndzɔ̀ bɛ kö ! *you ought not to tell lies !*
(194) lὲ mà ɛdé tí 'dà ɳaazàrö ! *that cow ought to be turned over for eating*

407. (*d*) Analogously with § 391, a sentence with a hortative is often connected with another clause (co-ordinate or subordinate) in the same mood to explain or expand it. Examples:

(195) é bì̀ mŏkémŏké mà 'dɛ kö ! *hold/catch it carefully lest it fall !*
(196) é ko á li ápípì̀á 'dì̀, ὲvìnï̈ mà fŏ ànì ! *let me cut this sore (swelling), so that the pus may drain out !*

(197) è ndzέ ódrəkə mà ólá pírípírí àmvέ, mà ko àzíní ŋaakúa
kö ! *remove all the roots of the* ódrəkə *weeds, so that none
remains in the ground !*

(198) kànì 'bá àzíní ɛza àfa, mà tsə èri, mà drə èri rá ! *if somebody has spoiled things, let him be beaten and driven away !*

(199) ìyí kòrɛ fu ma kái ; mí edzí má ní ìyí mà mvûmvu ! *I am
extremely thirsty; bring me water to drink !*

(200) é 'bà àtsí (tinïá), mà nè àŋgǒ ànï ! *light a fire* (or *it* (lamp)),
so that one may see (the ground—world . . .) *!*

(201) é zì dzótilέ, òlí àlárǐ mà efí ànï ! *open the door, so that fresh
air may come in !*

(202) andzi mà adri tsírí, 'bá mà ɛri ɛ'yó ànï ! *let the boys keep
silent, so that one may hear/understand the speech !*

(203) é tsə arí, andzi mà fí (= andziní fï-zǒ) ɛmbátáa dzóa ! *
beat the drum, that the children may enter the room for instruction !*

D. Special Cases

408. (1) There are certain actions and states whose very nature, according to Logbara feeling, exclude the concept of a present (progressive)
tense. These actions or states are either existent or non-existent. If they
are existent, then they are also *ipso facto* completed and require the CCA,
viz. the *past* tense. If they are not, they may become existent in the future,
and the CIA may be found in the future tense.

409. (2) Verbs of this category are: lè *to like, wish,* &c.; nè *to see*;
nì *to know, understand, see*; à'ǐ *to believe, agree*; tsa . . . zǒ *to be able*;
ga . . . sǐ *to refuse,* &c. Examples:

(204) é lè à'do yà ? *what do you want ?*
lè àfa kö *he does not want anything*

(205) à nì Àlúùr ti rá *we know the Aluur language*

(206) ètú àzí sǐ mã mu Bääri mà ti nì ndǒ *some day I shall know
the Aluur language* (in the end)

(207) o'dú àzí sǐ mã ŋgà mu lè mu-zǒ ìyíiá rá *some day I may
well wish to go beyond the Lake* (Albert, i.e. to Bunyoro,
Buganda, i.e. for work.)

(208) mã mù tsa emú-zǒ drùsǐ *I shall be able to come tomorrow*

The Negative Sentence

410. (1) The negative sentence is peculiar in Logbara; essentially it is
expressed by the CCA. A negative sentence corresponding to a positive one
in the present tense appears in the form of a past tense, with CCA; it corresponds to the above (§ 408) conception. Kö *not* is put at the end. Examples :

(209) kàmì ŋaa ásέ kö, èrì zâ ŋaa 'ï . . . *a lion does not eat grass,
it eats flesh*

(210) **yə, dzi tí-mvá àmbó vǒ kö, ɛ̀rì dzi tsûwá** *no, he is not taking
the calf to the headman, he is taking it to the market*

(211) **ma drùsǐ mu mǐ tsə rá** *I shall beat you tomorrow*
é tsə drù ma 'dɛ́ kö *thou wilt not beat me tomorrow*

(212) **drùsǐ mâ zâ ɲaa rá** *I shall eat meat tomorrow*
drùsǐ á ɲaa zá kö *tomorrow I will not eat meat*

(213) **é mu ńdrí Árúwá kö yà?** *wilt thou not go to Arua afterwards?*
mâ̰ 'yɛ̀ mu rá *I shall go*

(214) **kànì mǐ ɛ̀tsɛ̀ àzí sǐ trátrá, á fɛ̀ mǐ nǐ sìlíŋgì kö** or **á mu mǐ
nǐ sìlíŋgì fɛ̀ kö** *if you continually abstain from work, I shall not
give you (any) money* (i.e. construction either of past or
future tense (not present))

411. (2) For the further indefinite future a restricted CIA is in use.
Peculiarity: the noun-subject takes no **nï**, and for the personal pronoun-
subject the short-form is used. Examples:

(215) Positive: **əzɔ́ɔ́-nǐ 'yɛ èsǒ rá** *it will rain*
Negative: **əzɔ̀ɔ̂ 'yɛ nï èsǒ 'dɛ́ kö** *there will be no rain(ing)*

(216) **àmbó ŋga nǐ mu mǐ nǐ sìlíŋgì fɛ̀ 'dɛ́ kö** *the headman will
not give you money*

(217) **mvá 'dà 'yɛ̀ 'yɛ̀ pa rö àzɔ́ 'dà sǐ kö áàni?** *won't that boy
possibly recover (escape with his life) from that disease?*

REDUPLICATION OF VERBS

412. In the preceding examples a verb has more than once occurred
in a reduplicated form; here follow some explanations on this point.

(1) *Meaning.* The reduplicated form is used for the purpose of emphasizing the inherent nature or meaning of the verb. It may be found in
any tense or mood. It gives a plastic descriptive effect to the sentence.

413. (a) There are cases when the emphasis in a sentence lies precisely
on the specific action, thus indirectly implying the exclusion of any other
purpose which might be connected or suggested in given circumstances.
This latter is often expressed by means of a co-ordinate or subordinate
clause indicating cause and effect, purpose, &c. Examples:

(218) **ma atsí-atsí** (i.e. **á mu à'dò 'yɛ-rï-á kö**) *I am just taking
a walk* (i.e. *I am not going to do anything*)

(219) **'bǎ lɛ́sú kǒkò** *they have put milk aside so that it may coagulate*

(220) **ayébbí sǔsù ŋgókó-á-rǐ** *the leaves the women wear as clothes*

(221) **mǐ ɛ̀fɛ̀ mánǐ wárágà mâ sǐ-sǐ** *give me paper that I may write!*

414. (b) The reduplicated forms in some cases serve to point to slight
differences in verbs of a similar meaning, such as '**zɔ̀** and **mba'**. (According to some these are identical in meaning.) (cf. example 236):

(222) **'bánï zɔ̀zɔ̀** *a man grows* (**zɔ̀** is used for *a man growing*)

(223) **tínï mbàmba** *a cow grows* (**mba** is used for *animals*)

415. (*c*) In other instances the reduplicated verb relates to some particular happening in special circumstances:

(224) Éɲáónï tìtì əzɔ́ɔ́ sì = Éɲáónï emú əzɔ́ɔ́ sì emúemú *the Enyao river is rising due to rain*

(225) Éɲáó-nï ndzû-ndzu *the Enyao river is receding*

(226) mí òtì andzì òtì-òtì! *put the children in line!*

416. (2) *Form.* (*a*) A verb is reduplicated, in Logbara, by repeating jointly the same verb twice, as fɛ̀ *to give*; fɛ̀-fɛ̀.

(*b*) In effecting reduplication, modifications are made only in conformity with general rules; they are insignificant. (i) In speech vowels in juxtaposition are freely assimilated (cf. § 41), as əmvɛ *to call* əmv-əmvɛ; (ii) intonation changes follow general rules (cf. §§ 342, 344).

417. N.B. When a term is defined and/or stressed by special particles, such as 'bə, rá, tsí, &c., reduplication does not, evidently, take place as well, since emphasis of the verb is already expressed in some way by the said adverbs, &c.

418. (3) *Use.* (*a*) The reduplicated form is used in two ways. In the first place it stands for the ordinary verb of the sentence of CIA (cf. §§ 413 ff.). Examples:

(227) èri fúnò əpi-əpi *he is husking groundnuts*

(228) ètú drï àmbôrö; èri mâ rùá vɛ̀-vɛ *the sun is very hot; it burns me*

(229) ɛgbɛ-nï mâ fû-fu *I am very cold* (lit. *cold kills me*)

(230) əzɔ́ èri egbí-egbí ìyí 'aléa *reeds (stalks) germinate in water*

(231) kànì é lɛ̀ əmb·-əmbǎ 'bá àzínï bɛ, Lógbàrà èì əmvɛ: 'bá èì àwà-àwà: = èì àwà-rö-àwà = èì əmb·-əmbà *if you want to quarrel with somebody, the Logbara say: they are quarrelling* (thus əmbà = àwà)

419. (*b*) In sentences with CCA, in which a verb is placed at or towards the beginning of the sentence, with various complements following it, the verb proper commonly keeps its simple form, while a reduplicated form of the same verb is added at the end of the sentence as a kind of cognate object. Examples:

(232) fɛ̀ mánì ǹdrí fɛ̀-fɛ̀ *he gave me a goat* (gratis)

(233) ma agɔ́ pätí agɔ́-agɔ́ *I have bent the wood* (or *tree*)

(234) 'bá èì ər̀ vàálé sì ər̀-ər̀ *people are stiff from sitting on the ground* (CIA; cf. example 227)

(235) embó mótókà mà drià embó-embó *he jumped from the motor-car*

(236) má əlɛ àfa 'dìri əlɛ-əlɛ kö, fɛ̀ mani fɛ̀fɛ̀ (cf. § 414) *I did not buy this thing, they gave it to me*

THE REFLEXIVE VERB

420. When the action of a transitive verb is directed upon the subject itself, we speak of *reflexive verbs*. As the verb or verbal root is unchangeable in Logbara, it would be more appropriate to speak of a *reflexive construction*. The reflexive construction is very common in Logbara, even in cases where a reflexive action is not evident. It has the following forms.

421. (1) The full-form personal pronoun, corresponding to the personal-pronoun-subject of the verb, is generally used as direct object (3rd person singular 'ï), and as such takes its regular position in a sentence according to whether the construction is CIA or CCA. Examples:

(237) é sɛ mï rá ; mï asé g̀ìrì kö ! *withdraw ; do not obstruct the way !*

(238) mï ɛsé mï 'dólé má vǒ ɛ̀ɲ̣ï ! *move hither near me !*

(239) ma ɔ̀dzì ma iyí 'dìá rá *I have washed myself (bathed) in this water*

(240) pätí agɔ́ 'ï rá *the tree has bent*

(241) émvó àndì (= àsì, aga) 'ï rá *the pot has cracked*

(242) 'di (= fu) 'ï tsé nì̀ *he killed himself*

(243) dè̀ dï 'ï 'bə or dɛ àŋgà 'ï kö *it is finished or it is not yet finished*

(244) mï mï àtì mvá 'dà mà rúá à-sìyà ? *why are you leaning against that boy ?*

(245) mà̀ mu ma tì báká sì̀ mï àl̂ìrö *I am going to hang myself with a rope because of your hostility*

422. (2) What might be called the reflexive construction proper uses the unchangeable particle **rö** *self* as direct object in place of the above-mentioned absolute personal pronouns, no matter what the subject, whether noun or pronoun, singular or plural, may be. **Rö** is, in all probability, simply a shortened form of **rùá** *body* and is in this construction treated as a noun. This **rö** requires *no* preceding low tone (as the adjectival **rö** does).

N.B. In every case it is immaterial whether one uses the above personal pronouns or this particle **rö** as object. Examples:

(246) ma rö dǎ vélé rá ; *I do withdraw ;*
àmà rö dǎ vélé rá ! *let us withdraw !*

(247) èrì 'yɛ rö ŋ̣ə̂ rá *it will break some day*

(248) ma rö ayu báká sía rá *I am freeing myself from my fetters* (lit. *from the rope's teeth*)

(249) mï àtì rö rùánìá kö ! *do not lean against it !*

(250) é la rö dzùl̂ûrö ! *do lie on your back !*

(251) ma andzo rö èri bɛ rá ; *I separated from him ;*
andzo rö (= 'ï) ma bɛ rá *he separated from me*

(252) ǹdrí ɛré rö má nì̀ kínàkínà, aísé ǹdúa 'délé 'dï ; ma 'dò mu mâ ǹdrí ndǎ *the goats have completely dispersed (from*

me) *among this grass here* (in front); *I am now going to seek my goats*

(253) mǐ ombɛ rö 'dǐnǐ à'do sǐ yà? *why do you cross your arms (in that way)?*

(254) ma ombɛ rö ombɛ ɛgbɛ sǐ *I hugged myself on account of the cold*

(255) mǐ ayu rö (= mǐ) rá! *relax* (yourself)!

423. (3) Synecdoche: in place of a personal pronoun or rö, the word for a particular part of the body is used for the whole, and the appropriate reference particle or pronoun is added. The word rǔá *body*, defined by the appropriate possessive pronoun, is often used for 'man'. This method is of limited use. Examples:

(256) kànì mǐ ədzì mǐ rǔá iyí 'dǐá rá, mǐ emví àkúa *when you have washed yourself* (lit. *your body*) *in this water, come home!*

(257) é sɛ mǐ rǔá 'dálɛ́ (or vɛ́lɛ́)! *withdraw separately!*

(258) Cf. mǐ ədza rö! *turn round*

mǐ ədza mǐ 'dálɛ́! *turn (your face) that way!*

mǐ ədza mǐ ti vɛ́lɛ́ (or 'dɔ́lɛ́)! *turn your face this way!*

mǐ ədza mǐ ŋgókó (= ǹdú) vɛ́lɛ́ (or 'dɔ́lɛ́)! *turn your back hither!*

424. *Reduplication* in *reflexive sentences.* (a) In cases of CIA the direct object precedes the reduplicated verb. Examples:

(259) ma rö àtì-àtì àzɔ́ sǐ *I am leaning because I am ill (on account of sickness)*

(260) èrì 'yɛ rö ŋɔ̀-ŋɔ̀ (cf. example 247) *it will break*

(261) èrì 'ï tǐtǐ: èrì mu 'ï tǐtǐ *he is hanging himself; he will hang himself*

425. (b) In cases of CCA the direct object follows the simple verb and, often, is followed again by the simple form of verb (or by the reduplicated form). Example:

(262) tǐ 'ï tǐ *he hanged himself* (cf. example 254).

STRESSING OF VERBS

426. Reduplication of the verb, a fairly common feature of Logbara, serves to emphasize a verb in a particular way, generally in simple sentences, as we have seen (cf. §§ 412 ff.).

For the purpose of stressing individual verbs, however, the Logbara make use of a very considerable number of special adverbs.[1]

---

[1] A similar grammatical feature has developed in Acooli, and we may justifiably assume that on this point the influence of the *Ma'di* aboriginals on the supervening Lwoo and the Acooli language (which they introduced), was strong.

427. It should here be noted, at the outset, that normally no two methods of stressing verbs can be combined. For instance, the above-mentioned special adverbs, like **rá**, cannot be used in addition to reduplication, nor may one of these adverbs be used with another.

These adverbs are placed at the end of a sentence; they are found in all tenses or moods. They are, logically, not employed in *negative* sentences, save for a few special ones.

428. Rá is the particle (rather than adverb) commonly used for stressing; it is universally employed in all parts of the country; it can occur with any verb. It expresses definiteness or determination, the idea that an action has actually taken place, or that a state, &c., really exists or will have to take place. It is in use for all tenses or moods.

429. Besides this particle **rá** there are numerous adverbs which have not merely a grammatical value (as has **'bə**), but a real etymological meaning of their own.

These adverbs seem to have originated to a large extent from onomatopoeia, as the Logbara hear and conceive it, of course. They are profusely used in daily conversation. To translate them is often very difficult, to say the least, as they often express psychological aspects of things or actions not commonly conceived or expressed in an analogous way in classic languages.

430. The proper place in a grammar to treat these adverbs is, of course, under the heading of 'Adverbs'. Just a few instances are given here to illustrate this kind of verb-stressing feature. Examples:

(263) **'du búkù àyïï** (= ndïïrï) *he took the book away* openly
(264) **mu ɔtséa esú ɛwá, nɛ̀ ɛri bïrïbïrï** (= ï̆-ï̆), **ɛrinï ɛri nɛ̆ drìɔ kö-rì sì** *he went to the forest and found an elephant; he stared (looked* steadily) *at it, as he had never before seen one*
(265) **àŋgɔ̆ ɛ'dá Árúwá fɔ̀ɔ(r)** *the place of Arua looks* hazy—bright
(266) **ɔ́ɔ́kɔ́nï ɛrì ŋa kái** *he is furious* (lit. *anger corrodes him* exceedingly)
(267) **é mvi** (= gɔ̀ dri) **kátrà** (= hwérɛ)! *go back immediately !*
(268) **é sɔ̆ pá kìlílí! é rï k—!** *stand upright! sit straight !*
(269) **ɛná kìlílí** *it is* clearly *visible*
(270) **gìrì 'dà mu kílílí** (= kpii) *that way goes* straight
(271) **é bì mvá 'dìrï kírikíri** (= trítrí)! *catch* (or *hold*) *the boy* firmly *!*
(272) **mĭ ɔmbé kírikíri, kà mú ayu rö zɔ̆ kö!** *tie them* (things) firmly, *lest they untie !*
(273) **ɛri 'ɔ** (= 'yɛ) **òrì sĭ kpɔ̀lɔ́kpɔ̀lɔ́** *he proceeds* excitedly *from fear*
(274) **'yɔ ɛ'yɔ́ ɛrimà ti-á ndii** (= mù) *he spoke to him* secretly
(275) **ɛtɔ̀ dzɔ́ mà ti píipí** *he went* straight *on to the door of the hut*

(276) mǐ ɛ'bɛ́ mǐ pàlà, mïnï drì àdàzǒ go (*fling yourself*) quickly,
in order to come back
(277) nì àfa 'dǐ pùú (= tsɛ́) he really *knows the thing*
(278) mâ drì-nï ga (= lǐ)rrrï *my head is swimming* (dizzily)

SPECIAL VERBAL FORMS

Participle, Gerund, &c., Verbal Noun

431. As has already been stated, Logbara, unlike the classical languages, has no specific verb inflexions, as we are accustomed to think of such, to indicate Tenses, Moods, Gerunds, &c. Only the grammatical function of a word within the sentence tells us which part of speech it is, or, with regard to verbs, which tense or mood they are in.

Faced with the task of translating Logbara texts, the student will, of course, come upon a variety of constructions (not word-*forms !*) where he will find it convenient to use the classical grammatical terminology, such as 'gerund', 'gerundial infinitive', 'participle', &c., for constructions corresponding with those in his own language.

Verbal Derivations. A Brief Sketch

432. There are a few instances of verbal derivatives which have special *formative* elements. Mostly these 'forms' are mainly parts of a CIA sentence or forms of words obtained by adding a suffix: all in conformity with the general trend of the language = absence of 'inflexion'.

Here are set out the few 'formatives' for rendering *verbal adjectives* and *verbal nouns* commonly in use in Logbara.

433. (1) We have the *adjective-forming* suffix **-zà**, which is added to the simple verb; the suffixes **-rǐ** and **-rö** are eventually added after **zà**. Further explanations have been given in § 147, and examples, § 155. cf. §§ 596 ff.   Examples:

ámvú 'à-zà *a tilled field*
èì 'dǒ rï ámvú 'àzà mà 'aléa *they sow eleusine in a tilled field*

434. (2) The ordinary *noun-agent* is rendered by a relative phrase or clause, as explained in detail in §§ 258 ff. Examples:

Inf. àzî ŋga-zǒ *to work*
'bá àzî ŋgápirǐ *worker* (lit. *man who works*)
andzi laá (rö)-pi àkúalɛ́ *day-school* (lit. *boys who sleep at home*)
'bá tà a'dǐ-pi-rǐ *cook* (lit. *man who cooks food*)
'bá ɛ̀ndzɔ̀ bɛ or 'bá ɛ̀ndzɔ̀ lí-pi-rǐ *liar* (lit. *man with lies* or *man who tells lies*)

435. (3) The *verbal noun*, abstract or concrete, is commonly formed by adding the suffix -tá to the simple (unchanged) verb. Examples:

ámvú 'à-tá *field-tilling*
drì àvĕ-tá *forgetfulness*
ètúkà èri drïtá 'ídrí-rì bɛ *the sunshine has its own heat*

In many cases (of very common words) the simple infinitive alone is used as a verbal noun. Examples:

(279) ma ɛdé kö drì-àvĕ sì (= drì-àvĕtá sì) *I did not accomplish it by forgetfulness*
(280) é mu Árúwá mí emví pâ-tö kɔ́kɔ̀rö! *go to Arua and come back immediately* (lit. *without stopping;* pâ tö *to stop*)!

436. (4) A kind of *verbal adverb* of time or place, of frequent occurrence in Logbara, is obtained by adding the suffix -rìá to the plain verb. Examples:

(281) bǐ èri àzî ŋga-rìá rá *they caught him (while) (being) at work*
(282) à mu àrïïá ndà-rìá *we went in search of birds*
(283) èri ə'á əŋgɔ̀ tö-rìá *he/she is at a dance*

For further details see §§ 584 ff.

CHAPTER 10

CONJUNCTIONS

437. The number of distinct conjunctions or conjunctional elements is small in Logbara; various combinations of those there are make up for their lack in number. This does not mean, however, that they present no difficulties; they require a close study and a good deal of practice.

A list of conjunctions or conjunctional elements is given below. As to their usage, it is hardly possible to treat them otherwise than under the headings of the various clauses to which they belong and in connexion with the corresponding constructions.

List of conjunctions

kà *pl.* ká; kànì; kànì áanï *if; provided that; when,* ...
kà/ká mu ... zɔ̌ kö *lest; in order that* ... *not*
There are several combinations with kà or kànl.
... rá ká, ... ndɔ̀ *first, then* or *afterwards*
... ɔ̀kɔ̀, esú ... *happened, before* ...
mà; mà ànï ... *that* ... *not; lest*
nɔ̀ or nɔ̀sì; nɔ̀sì ... nɔ̀sì *perhaps; whether perhaps*
pi ... bɛ; piɛ *and; and also; together*

pia sì . . . pia sì *whether . . . or*
. . . -rìá *while; as*
. . . sì, -(zŏ-) rì sì *because*
vínï, vínï èndì *also; again*
. . . -zŏ *for; for the purpose of; that . . .*

438. *Note*: As a rule (*a*) Logbara does not favour the use of conjunctions; (*b*) it prefers putting sentences side by side, leaving the context to suggest the connexions or logical interrelations (see § 444); (*c*) at times co-ordinate sentences are turned into corresponding subordinate sentences, for example, *either you go away or you will be beaten* is expressed thus:

(1) *if you do not go, they will beat you,* i.e. é kà mu kö, èì mu mî tsə rá

Co-ordinating Conjunctions

439. The few *co-ordinate conjunctions* in use are: pi . . . bɛ; . . . bɛ; pie *and*; pia . . . pia (rare) *or*; nò ; nòsì *or*; nòsì . . . nòsì *either (whether)* . . . *or*; vínï *also, again*

440. The word for 'and' is frequently found in Logbara speech to connect words; but it is *not* used for linking sentences together.

Whenever two or more terms are joined by a conjunction, an occurring personal pronoun is, as a rule, put into the plural, in view of the plurality of the combination. Thus in the case of personal pronouns the corresponding plural pronoun is used for the singular one; 'I and thou' is translated by àma mï bɛ *we with thou.* See § 196.

441. (*a*) Bɛ is not often found by itself except in phrases similar to the one above, or in connexion with numerals. Examples:

(2) mbá àmadrí ìrrì nùsù bɛ *our months* (for a job) *are two and a half*
(3) má əlɛ kàbìlò àlö ǹdrí ssu bɛ *I have bought a sheep and four goats*
See ex. 21, 22.

442. (*b*) Pie placed after the two terms to be joined is used mainly in cases where a personal pronoun is connected with a noun; it may, however, be used as a general link. The 'plural' personal pronoun precedes. Examples:

(4) à mu èri pie àkúa *I* (lit. *we*) *went home with him* (lit. *we with him went home*)
(5) mú té Ezatí pie ámvúa *he* (lit. *they*) *and Ezati went to the field*
(6) àma má ámví pie àkúa *I* (*we*) *and my sister are at home* (lit. *we with my sister*)

(7) èÍ káíkɔ̀ rrï mànÍà pie tú àlö *they sow beans and sesame together*

(8) àma àkú Ràimóndò pie pÍ àlö *my (our) and Raimondo's village is (all) one*

(9) à fu drì èri pie gÍrÏá 'dà *I (we) met with him on the way there*

443. (c) If the words connected with 'and' are nouns or proper nouns, pÍ (from pi-Í), the equivalent of a plural suffix, is added to the first noun and bɛ to the second. A proper noun with the suffix pÍ means that the person named is accompanied by others (his suite); the term with this suffix may also be used alone, to express something like 'and Co.'.

Note: (1) The verb referring to a double subject, joined by -pÍ . . . bɛ, is often placed after the first part-subject and pÍ, as in example 14.

(2) If the two nouns together are the object of a postposition, the postpositional element is placed only after the first part after pÍ, as below example 15. Examples:

(10) mànÍà pÍ áɳ̟ú bɛ àlö *mania and anyu are the same* (two kinds of simsim)

(11) eníkinìrö pÍ onókònòrö bɛ òsï rö òsï-òsï (the words) *enikini and onokono are identical in meaning* ('soft') *and use*

(12) ma ándríí pÍ mâ ámvíí bɛ àkúa *my mother and my sister are at home*

(13) 'dÏ̀ mà ándríí pÍ 'dàÍ mà átíí bɛ àÏ̀à àlö *this (boy)'s mother and that one's father have (are of) the same mother*

(14) ètɔ́ə pÍ mù̀ dÍ a'úá́ bɛ *the hare and a small fowl went together* (fable)

(15) 'bókɔ́ èri gÍrÏ̀kɔ̀ 'bá ádaa pÍ nÍ tÍ bɛ *'bɔkɔ is a road/path for people as well as for cattle*

(16) súrú Nŏnò pÍ Àdómí bɛ èÍ èɳ̟ïɳ̟ï *the Nono and the Adomi tribal groups are situated close to each other*

(17) Òmbàtía-pÍ tsa 'dɔ̀ ŋgɔ́ áání?! *where can Ombatia and his companions have arrived by now?*

444. Compare the Logbara rendering of co-ordinate sentences:

(18) mvá 'dà mu àkúa; emví 'dÏá ɔ̀ndrè sÏ̀ *the child went home and came back here in the evening*

(19) à ŋga àzí de (= à de àzí) rá; à mu àkúa *we finished work and went home*

(20) 'bá tsə èri rá, drə èri àkúa *he was beaten and driven home* (from school)

(21) mu sùkúlùá ágúi bɛ *he went to school, and his friend also*

(22) fè tÍ má nÍ má ádrípi bɛ *he gave a cow to me and my brother*

(23) á mu ɔ́pí bɛ (or vŏ̌), nè ma 'dé kö (or gà ma nè-kə sÏ̀) *I went to the chief, but he would not (refused to) see (receive) me*

(24) èri àzɔ̂-rö, drà 'dé kö *he was ill, but he did not die*

445. Nɔ̀ ; nɔ̀sï; nɔ̀ . . . nɔ̀ or nɔ̀sï . . . nɔ̀sï *or; whether . . . or.* This conjunction is frequently used. Nɔ̀sï alone is often used for *perhaps, maybe;* nɔ̀sï áánï *possibly;* káanï nɔ̀sï . . . áánï *who knows . . . possibly.* Examples:

(25) nɔ̀sï èri àzɔ̀-rö, nɔ̀sï èri èndzà bɛ emú zɔ̋ 'dïá áánï, á nì kö
whether he is sick or possibly too lazy to come here, I do not know

(26) ndà éwá kö ; éwá káanï nɔ̀sï 'bánï èrivélé áánï *he was not looking for beer; beer is* (who knows) *possibly* (to be) *found at this man's*

446. The particles . . . bɛ trɔ́trɔ̀ *as well as, equally as*; and vínï bɛ *as well as, and also;* are also often met with. Examples:

(27) èri ɔ̀ndzí mï bɛ trɔ́trɔ̀ *he is equally as bad as you*

(28) èri milé mbà̀-rö mï bɛ trɔ́trɔ̀ *he is as clever as you*

(29) èri ɔ̀kpɔ̀-rö vínï milé mba bɛ *he is strong as well as clever*

(30) tí-mvá drà rá, tí ti mvá drà vínï rá *the calf died and the calving cow also*

(31) mu ópí vélé vínï rá *he also went to the chief's*

SUBORDINATE CLAUSES IN LOGBARA

447. In Logbara we have four main types of Subordinate Clause which correspond to the various subordinate clauses of classic grammars, i.e. of (*a*) Condition, (*b*) Purpose, (*c*) Reason, (*d*) Concession–Contrast. These clauses are shown to be subordinate mainly by construction, and to a lesser extent by conjunctions, which may be regarded as typical of the construction.

Adverbial clauses of time present some variety of their own.

1. *Adverbial Clause of Time (-condition)*

448. Clauses of time may express a variety of aspects of time to which, in Logbara, correspond various special constructions and particles. (*a*) time 'before . . . then (after) . . .', 'first, then . . .'. Example:

(32) à'bɔ̀à mà mba rá ká, 'bá èì ŋgà ɳa ndɔ̀ *let the bananas first be well developed, then they will eat them = when the bananas are quite ripe* (then) *they will eat them*

The full form of this type of sentence consists of a subordinate clause ending in rá ká, generally preceding the main clause which ends in ndɔ̀.

Rá has been mentioned in § 428.

Ká, which may be doubled or trebled, is an additional stressing element; its meaning is *positively, absolutely, by all means and,* hence, *in the first place.* It is also used in single, simple sentences, as

mà̀ ŋga fè rá kákáká *I will give/consign it by all means*

449. Either of these particles **rá** and **ká**, or even both, are sometimes omitted; the end **ndɔ̀** of the main clause is, however, kept and indicates the nature of the complex sentence. Example:

(33) **é zi gĕr̈ mu-zŏ Àdómíalé-r̈ zi̇zi (ká), é mu ndɔ̀!** (first) *inquire about the road (going) to Adomi and then go! = After inquiring about the road to Adomi, go!*

450. According to the meaning and use of **rá-ká** sentences, the mood of the verb is often the imperative or hortative with **mà**. This particle **mà** may, however, be missing in a sentence with an essentially hortative meaning, a fairly common feature, demonstrating the elasticity of the Logbara language.

However, a sentence with **rá-ká** need not always express an injunction, it may be used in a statement of fact, say in the future, and the verb will thus be in the indicative mood.

451. The particle **ŋgà** *still, for the moment, in the meantime* is also frequently used in the same sentence as **mà**, or alone as if to replace **mà**. The future particle, **ŋga**, enters into its own, of course, in future subordinate clauses and, more often even, in the main clause. (Cf. § 369)

452. Illustrating examples:

(34) **mà emví rá-ká, mï emû mu ndɔ̀** *let him first come back* (= *when he comes back*), *then you will go*

(35) **ɔzɔ́ɔ́-nï (mà) àtï rá-ká, ma ɛ'dɔ̂ mu ndɔ̀** *once the rain has ceased* (= *let the rain first cease*), *I shall start going* (= *then I shall go*)

(36) **àn̩á mà 'wï rá-ká, ma lɔ́ɔ́ ndɔ̀** *let the corn be ripe first, or, once the corn is ripe, (then) I will harvest (cut) it*

(37) **Ònítálá mà emú rá-ká, Àndèrè mà ŋgà mu àkúa ndɔ̀!** *let Onita come back first then Andere may go home* (= *when Onita returns, Andere can go home*)!

(38) **èmï adri ŋgà 'dɛ́; àmà ŋga emví Árúwárï sï rá-ká, àmà ŋgà mu àkúa ndɔ̀** *remain where you are for the moment; after we (have) come back from Arua we will go home*

(39) **è tĕɛ́ ŋgà mvá mà etsá rá-ká; èri emú 'dà** *wait until the boy arrives back; he is coming there*

(40) **ărï té àfa 'dïrï ká, ŋgà asŏ (rö) ndɔ̀** *they had first propped this thing up, still it collapsed in the end* (= *even though they propped this thing up, it collapsed (in the end)*)

(41) **ma ŋgà emú mà sókà sï rá-ká, ma ásí-nï rï ndɔ̀** *I am coming first of all to secure (by work) my cloth, then I shall feel comfortable*

453. (*b*) Time 'before . . .', 'ere . . .', 'sooner than . . .'; usage similar to the above, i.e. a complex sentence to express one event occurring before another has been completed.

These conjunctional ideas are rendered in Logbara by two clauses, the first ending in **ɔ̀kɔ̀** *first, before* . . .; the second beginning with the verb **esú** *it was, he, they found*, which may be followed by **dèrè** *regretfully, surprisingly*. Examples:

(42) **ɔzɔ́ɔ́-nï ɛ'dɔ̌ èsɔ̌ ɔ̀kɔ̀, esú (dèrè) á tsa àkúalé kö** *it will start raining before (unfortunately) I have reached home*

(43) **ópí etsá ɔ̀kɔ̀, esú dèrè mâ ándrïí etsá ŋgà kö** *the chief arrived before my mother* (lit. *he found (that) my mother had not yet arrived*)

454. (*c*) 'Afterwards', 'after' is rendered either by a postpositional gerundial phrase . . . **-zɔ̌-(rá-)rï̀-sï̀** or by **vélérï̀ sï̀**.

The main clause in this case precedes the subordinate one. Examples:

(44) **mvi àkúa, àzɔ́-nï àtï̀-zɔ̌ rá rï̀ sï̀** *he went home after the subsiding of his illness*

(45) **ma ŋgà wárágà sï̀; vélérï̀ sï̀ mâ ŋgà mu mḯ-vɔ̌** *I am still writing a letter, afterwards I shall come to you*

455. (*d*) 'Since . . .' is rendered by **ɛŋgá o'dú . . . zɔ̌ sï̀; ɛ'bí ṅdrâ . . .** (lit. *starting from the day . . .; since old . . .*). Examples:

(46) **ɛŋgá o'dú mánï emvḯ-zɔ̌ Gùlúa 'dà sï̀, mâ rùá trátrá àzɔ̂rö** *ever since the day I came back from Gulu, I have been sick*

456. (*e*) 'As soon as . . .', 'directly . . .' is rendered by **kà** or **ká** with CIA. Examples:

(47) **kà mu efḯ dzóa 'bɔ, 'bá pïrḯ ŋgá (or sɔ̀ pá) öru** *as soon as he entered the room, everybody rose (to their feet)*

(48) **é kà té ɔ̀kó mà rú adzí tsḯ, ma té ɛrì rá** *directly you mentioned the name of the woman, I understood*

457. (*f*) 'While . . .' to denote that actions are simultaneous. The subordinate clause is a CIA sentence with **-rï̈á** added to the verb or at the end of the sentence: a frequent Logbara construction. Examples:

(49) **é 'yɔ ɛ'yó ɛrinï̈ ɔŋgɔ́-ɔŋgɔ́-rï̈á kö!** *do not talk while he is singing!*

(50) **ɛrinï̈ efḯ dzóa-rï̈á, 'bá pïrḯ sɔ̀ pá öru** same as example 47.

2. Ka, kànì .., Adverbial Clause of Condition.

458. The two conjunctions **kà** pl. **ká** and **kànì** introduce *clauses of condition*. It should be noted, however, that this section deals with the mentioned conjunctions, and with clauses of classic grammars only in so far as they coincide.

459. There are, in Logbara, three categories of *conditional clauses*, introduced by one or other of the two conjunctions, seemingly at the discretion of the writer or speaker, which differ in construction, but not in meaning.

460. (*a*) The *temporal condition*; in English introduced by the adverbial conjunctions 'when', 'whenever'; e.g. *when the sun rises, it becomes day*.

(*b*) The *real condition* in the case of interdependent events; e.g. *if you work, you will be paid*.

Sentences of *temporal* or of *real* condition are not distinguished in Logbara construction.

(*c*) The *unreal condition*; an event is merely assumed but not expected to happen; e.g. *if he were a bird, he would fly*.

461. Both the conjunctions are placed at or towards the beginning of a sentence and each requires a different construction.

462. (1) **Kà** (or **ká** when the subject is a 3rd person plural) requires the subject, be it a noun or a pronoun, normally to precede it. The sentence has the form of CIA.

463. *Note*: A sentence with CIA, introduced by **kà** or **ká**, has the following special exceptions:

(*a*) The **nĭ** after a noun subject is missing (cf. § 335 (1)).

(*b*) If the subject be represented by a personal pronoun, its short-form has to be used instead of the full one (§ 339); a 3rd person pronoun-subject is in this case omitted. See ex. 47.

464. Examples:

(51) 'bá àzĭ kà Àlúrù ti nĭ, dèrè nì Àtsóli ti 'bɔ *if a man knows the Aluru language, he (happily) also knows (the) Acooli (language)*

(52) é kà ɛtsɔ̂ rá, mĭ aɡa ma rá! *if you can, do pass (beat) me (in running)!*

(53) Ònítálá kèni: à kà ɛ'dɔ̂ mu mĭ ɛmbâ 'ĭ, àmanï séntè yɔ *Onitala said that if we came to teach you, there would be no money*

(54) á kà ɛ'dɔ̂ àzĭ ŋɡa kö, á n̩a ńdrí kö *if I do not go (= set) to work, I shall not eat afterwards*

(55) é kà 'dĭ ɡbâ rá, èrì mu ɔvö mö̌ké tŏ *if you strike this (type-writer key), it (script) will come out very nicely*

(56) mǎ mu àfa 'dĭ ɛdɛ̂, ká mǎ ko rá *I shall do it, if they allow me*

(57) mǎ mu ɛ'yɔ́ 'dĭ à'ĭ, mĭ kà drí tĭ rá *I shall agree to these terms, if you put your hand to (i.e. sign) it*

(58) á kà drì fu kǎmì bɛ, ma apá rá *if I meet a lion, I run away*

(59) é kà 'bà zá əzə àtsía, mï pätí e'dû zá əpè ànï (or zǒ) *if you
put meat for roasting into the fire, you take a piece of wood to
recover it with*

465. **(2) Kànì.** The conjunction **kànì**, unlike the conjunction **kà**,
introduces a sentence with the CCA.

Kànì commonly precedes the subject of the sentence.

Kànì appears to be preferred for introducing clauses of time, and
kà/ká clauses of real condition.

466. As has been mentioned already, subordinate clauses, introduced
by **kà, kànì,** &c., usually precede the main clause. Examples:

(60) kànì ěríti yə, ètû drï rá *when there are no clouds, the sun shines
warmly*

(61) kànì 'bá àzî 'du àfa mídrírï rá, èri àfa mídrírï mà àriótí
əfě *when somebody has taken something of yours (your thing),
he should compensate you for it*

(62) kànì é sɛ tábà kö, mï ɔlɛ à'do-nï ? ma tábà ɔlɛ 'bá àzïnï
*if you do not smoke tobacco, what do you buy it for? I buy
tobacco for others*

(63) kànì é di bəŋgó 'bə, é 'yə kènì: é dzi edza ètúa *when you have
washed a cloth, you say: go (take) and spread it in the sun*

(64) kànì 'bá drà rá, èi əmvɛ àvǒ *when a man is dead, they speak
of a corpse*

(65) kànì efï dzóa, èri àfa àzïnï 'du rá *when (if) he enters one's hut,
he will take something*

(66) kànì drùsï mï esú èri rá, é 'yə èri nï: mà mu ɔpí vǒ *when
you meet (find) him tomorrow, tell him to go to the chief*

(67) éŋá kànì a'dï àtsï driá 'bə, 'bá əva àgúrú driá *when they
have cooked the polenta on thɛ fire, they serve it on wooden
plates*

(68) kànì ɔkó àzïnï mà águpi drà rá, èi èri əmvɛ àwízyó ; kànì
ɔkóni drà rá, èi èri əmvɛ ɔdzóló *when a woman's husband
has died, they (will) call her widow (àw—); when the woman
dies, they (will) call him ɔdz— (; also àw—)*

(69) ká éwá zə áŋûba sï 'bə, ó'búrúsɔ̀-nï etú fúu(t)rú *when
they pour beer through a strainer, foam will rise sparklingly*

(70) èri ámvú mà 'alé fǎ àŋá sï ; kànì fǎ 'bə, 'dǒ 'aléníárï kà
ɛŋgá kö, èi 'yə kènì: 'dǒ afï rá *he rakes the field for the corn ;
if, after raking, eleusine fails to come forth, they (will) say: it
is stunted*

467. Beside the above conjunctions, a clause of condition (of time)
may be introduced by the general conjunctional phrase . . .zǒ-(rï)sï;
cf. § 454, and below. Examples:

(71) əzɔ́ɔ́-nǐ'yɛ-zɔ̌ emú-zɔ̌ 'di-zɔ̌ áyi sǐ ndə̀rǐ sǐ, mǎ ŋga ámvú 'ǎ
when eventually rain falls during the rainy season, I shall till the field

(72) ètú drà mádrírǐ-nï etsá-zɔ̌-rǐ sǐ, mǎ ŋgà 'yɛ ŋgɔ́-nï yà?
when my day of death arrives, what shall I do/what will happen to me?

3. Clause of Unreal Condition

Kà tɛ́ (pl. ká tɛ́) . . . rá, tɛ́ . . . rá̌ (CIA)

468. (1) The subordinate clause of unreal condition is introduced by the conjunction **kà** or **ká** preceded by the subject, seldom **kànì**, to which the particle **tɛ́** is added; the particle **rá** or **'bə** (negative **kö**) terminates the clause.

469. (2) The main clause is likewise marked by the particle **tɛ́** after the subject and **rá** at the end, where the meaning demands it.

470. Examples:

(73) àzí kà tɛ́ ma ndě rá, ma tɛ̂ 'yɛ yà? *if the work had been too much for me, would I have done it?*

(74) tí kà tɛ́ ma ndě rá, ma tɛ́ kàbìlò əlɛ 'ï *if a cow had been too expensive (much) for me (my money), I would have bought a sheep*

(75) é kà tɛ́ lɔ̂ má nï drìə, ma tɛ̂ mu ma àzía rá *if you had told me before, I should have gone to (my) work*

(76) mvá kà tɛ́ nǐ kö, èri tɛ́ əlɔ̂ mǐ nï rá yà? *if the boy had not known it, would he have told you?*

(77) kà tɛ́ ɛtsɔ̂ rá, èri tɛ́ kǎmì fu rá *if he could, he would have killed the lion*

(78) ǹdrí ssu 'dǐǐ kà tɛ́ (or ǹdrí tɛ́ ssu kà . . .) ədrǎ kö, mâ ǹdríǐ tɛ́ adri möödrí *if four goats had not died, I would by now have ten goats*

(79) kànì tɛ́ ma ámvíí (= ma ámvíǐ kà tɛ́) drà kö, tɛ́ 'də̀ əlé èri rá *if my sister had not died, they would by now have married (her)*

(80) à kà ndrâ èndzɔ̀ ndzɛ, drɔ́ tɛ́ 'də̀ àma kírí kö yɛ̀à? *if we had told lies in the past, would they not by now have driven us away?*

(81) kànì tɛ́ bǐ ágú ndɛrǐ kö, èri àma əfu dría *if they had not arrested that individual, he would/might have killed us all*

(82) kànì tɛ́ mùsorò 'bɛ-zɔ̌ ndě mǐ rá, mǐ emú àzî ŋga míssìòná *if you were unable to pay the taxes, you would come to the mission to work*

(83) Ándróa kà tɛ́ ɛ'bɔ̂ 'du kö, àma tɛ́ emú mǐ ɛmbá rá *had not Androa (started) taken up the hoe, we would have come to teach you*

471. (3) An *unreal* or *unrealized supposition* is expressed by . . . **kènì té** . . . (had thought that), as:

(84) **á kènì té 'dǐ əzɔ́ɔ́nǐ 'yè 'di rá** . . . *I thought it would have rained* . . .

(85) **á kènì té mï 'dǐ àlö-rǐ gba 'ï, dèrè mǐ gba ìrrì trɔ́** *I thought you were typing one (copy), whereas you typed two*

4. Adverbial Clause of Concession or Contrast

472. The English conjunctions 'although', 'even if . . .' may be expressed in the following ways:

(*a*) The more usual method of expressing concession or contrast is again based on **kànì** or **kà/ká** *though, although, even if* with their respective constructions (cf. §§ 463, 465); thus we have:

using **kànì**: **kànì trɔ́ S–V–DO tǐ** . . .⎱ *although, even if, though*
using **kà/ká**: **S kà trɔ́ V–DO tǐ** . . . ⎰

473. Examples:

(86) **kànì trɔ́ é drə tí möödrí tǐ, á fè mâ zìi mǐ nǐ kö** *even if you brought ten cows, I will/would not give you my daughter*

(87) **á kà trɔ́ lè kö tǐ, mâ ŋgà mu rá** *although I do not like it, I shall go*

(88) **kà trɔ́ èri àlǐonǐ tǐ, èri 'bá áda-nǐ** *even if/though he is wretched, he is an honest man*

(89) **kànì trɔ́ andzi ssu ká etsâ mávǒ rá tǐ, á fè èi nǐ àfa 'dǐrï kö** *even if four boys were to come to me, I would not give them this*

(90) **kà trɔ́ má nǐ ńdrí fè thöörǒ àlö tǐ, á mu èri nǐ tí ɛmvɛ 'dǐrï trɔ́ fè kö** *even if he gave me a hundred goats, I would not give him this (the) white cow*

474. (*b*) Apparently, **kànì vínï S–V–DO** . . . is also occasionally used.

(91) **kànì vínï èri yə, mâ mu a'dúlɛ** *even if he be absent, I will go alone*

475. (*c*) The following form is used especially where the main clause is negative: **S té DO–V (rá) 'bə** . . . (*negation*). Examples:

(92) **èri té ɛtsə̂ gbï-zǒ rá 'bə, gbï kö** *although he could have shot, he did not (shoot)*

(93) **ma té'yè mu mǐ vǒ 'délé 'bə, à fǔ dǐ drì mï bɛ rá** *I would have come there to you, but then I met you*

(94) **èri té emú rá 'bə, gà sǐ** *in spite of the fact that he was about to come, he refused then*

5. Correlative Conjunction kànì . . . áánï; nəsì . . .

476. There is another combination with **kànì** (not **kà**) used to introduce clauses: **kànì áánï** . . ., **'dǐnï áánï** may be used instead of **áánï**.

Kànì . . . áánï may be used in correlation with nòsï in the same clause. Thus we have the forms:

kànì . . . áánï, or also nòsï . . . áánï ⎫ *whether perhaps, whether*
kànì . . . 'dïnï (or bïnï) áánï, (nòsï . . .)⎭ *possibly . . . or*

(95) kànì fĕ lïfú kö áánï, èi nòsï fĕ rá áda áánï, á nì kö lit. *whether they will perhaps not give holidays or actually give them, I do not know* (= *whether or not they might give holidays, I don't know*)

(96) kànì éfïnï 'dïnï áánï, á nì ŋgà kö *whether this is possibly its meaning, I do not yet know* (= *whether this might be its meaning or whether it might mean this, . . .*)
Cf. Example 26.

477. Another simpler, and rather frequent, form of this correlative relationship is nòsï . . . nòsï . . . *whether . . . or . . .; either . . . or. . . .*
Examples:

(97) nòsï èri emú rá, nòsï emú kö, á nì kö *whether he will come or not, I do not know*
(98) nòsï èri àzô-rö, nòsï èri èndzà bɛ *he is either sick or lazy*

6. *The General or Introductory Conjunction* kènì/kénì

478. Kènì is a very frequent term in Logbara conversation or narrative. It introduces statements made by anybody, or thoughts or opinions. It is equivalent to the verb 'to say' 'to think', 'to be of opinion'. It generally introduces indirect speech.

It has a past tense form, thus the CCA is used; hence the short-form personal pronouns a, e for the first two persons, while third person pronouns are not expressed. But note: kènì *he (she) says*; kénì *they say*. A noun subject takes no nï after it: all in accordance with the rules for CCA (q.v.).

(99) 'dà ma kènì: 'mï ti dzúlû-ru a'ú ti lɛ́' *he insulted me, saying: 'your mouth is pointed (protruding) like a fowl's'*
(100) 'dò kènì: 'yɔ' lit. *this here says that there is none*/or *he says (he is) 'absent'*
(101) andzi kénì: 'èi gà mukɔ́ sï' *the children say that they refuse to go*
Cf. examples 84, 85.

7. *Subordinate Clause of Reason* : . . . rì sì

479. A complex sentence indicating the reason for some happening is expressed in the following ways:

(*a*) The two clauses are very often given as two co-ordinate ones:

without any connecting particle they are placed side by side. This method is always correct and ought to be familiar to the student. Examples:

(102) ávánï tsúrú'dɔ̀ yɔ, é sɔ̀ ává-nï mŏ́ké ! *it* (i.e. *the bicycle*) *is deflated* (*has no air*) *now, pump it up* (*its air properly*) *!*

(103) mà zì dìrísà ŋgbɔ, àŋgŏ̀ bì dzóa bìbì *let the window be opened* (wide), *because it is dark in the room*

(104) ɔ̀mbí mbɛ àɲá èìdrí wɔ́rɔ́, mvá 'dà mà mvì màákɔ̀ sa 'ï *as the locusts have eaten all their corn, that boy has to go back to plant potatoes*

(105) á mu Árúwá, á dzi ɔ́sŏ̌ *I went to Arua to carry beans* (*there*)

(106) ɛŋgá ŋgà mìlé wɛrɛ, tsa ŋgà àzî ŋga-zŏ̌ kö *he has still only partly* (*slightly*) *recovered, therefore he cannot yet* (do) *work*

(107) ma aǧa rá ; mà mu 'aléñìá *as I have passed* (exam.) *I will enter . . .*

480. (*b*) A special method of expressing a clause of reason consists in using a sentence with CIA, terminated by the conjunction sì, often rì sì.

(108) ɔ̀kó 'dì fŏ̀ à'yàrö, èìnï ámvú 'à-zŏ̌ èri vélé kö rì sì *the woman became jealous, as they* (her man) *did not till her field*

(109) ndrâ mïnì mu-zŏ̌ Dzúbà-á-rì sì, é 'yɔ ŋgɔ́ nï yà? *of yore, when you were about to go to Juba, what did you say ?*

(110) té 'ï ándríì-nï èri ɔmvɛ-zŏ̌ 'dà sì, mà mu 'ï vŏ̌ *as his mother has called him* (there), *he has to go to her*

(111) èri-nï àzî ŋgalé ɔ̀kpɔ́-rì sì, èri mu ɔ̀rɔ̀táa esú tŏ̀ *because he has worked hard, he will get/find a reward*

(112) fɛ̌ má nï sìlíŋgì àzî ŋga andzi bɛ rì sì *they gave me a shilling for having worked with the children*

(113) ma 'dì mù 'yɛɛ, mïnï lɛ̀-lɛ́ rì sì *I shall do this, because you want it*

(114) ma-nï àzî ŋgalé kö rì sì, má ma ándríì nï mǎ ɛɲá sì *since I do not work, I am relying on my mother for* (daily) *polenta*

(115) èri-nï ɔ'yɔ́-lɛ́ (= ɔtrɛ) tŏ̀ rì sì, ɔ́líkɔ-nï asé tsì *because he talked/cried so much, he* (his voice) *became hoarse*

(116) à mú o'dû kɔ àŋgɔ̀-nï bì rì sì *let us go to sleep as it is now dark/late*

(117) èì lúlû ga, 'bá-nï drà sì *they shout a signal as a man has died*

8. *Subordinate Clause of Purpose* : . . . zŏ̌ (-rì)

481. The *subordinate clause of purpose* is a very common construction in Logbara. Logbara has at hand convenient expressions to describe the purpose or use of any object. These phrases or clauses require the 'conjunction' zŏ̌ *for*. -rì, added after zŏ̌, indicates that the noun concerned is restricted or qualified adjectivally.

The expression of purpose has the form of either a *phrase* or an *adjectival clause*. In both cases the word-order is that of CIA with the verb (retaining its simple etymologic tone unaltered) followed by zŏ̌ (or zŏ̌-rì).

482. (a) The use of the *phrase of purpose* corresponds to an English gerundial or qualifying infinitive or to an adjectival noun or a gerund, according to how one prefers to translate the phrase concerned. Examples:

(118) tǎǎrí sénté 'bà zǒ *a money-box*, i.e. lit. *a box to put in/keep money* or *a box for keeping money in*

(119) tídzó ìí kə-zǒ-rì̀ *a water-pot, the* (particular) *pot for fetching water*

(120) tsúpà lέsú ədzí-zǒ-rì̀ *a milk-bottle, a bottle to carry milk* (to market)

(121) ɡbóló 'bá àzô-rö-rì̀ dzì-zǒ *a plank on which to carry a sick person*

(122) á lὲ wáráɡà sì̀-zǒ *I want some writing-paper* (*paper to write on*)

(123) έsέ àrï̈a ə̀'bà-zǒ *glue for catching birds*

(124) àzí ŋaaká a'dí̌-zǒ-rì̀'ï sì ɔ̀kóèì *cooking*, i.e. *the work of cooking food is suitable for women*

(125) é 'bà tábà 'dì̀ à'dì̀ 'yεε zǒ yà? *for what purpose have you brought these cigarettes?*

(126) mì̀ edzí má nì̀ ìí bɔ̀ŋɡó ɔ̀dzì-zǒ! *bring me water for washing clothes!*
cf. if . . . ɔ̀dzì-zǒ-rì̀ meaning: *the water set aside only for washing clothes*

(127) é mu má nì̀ àŋɡò nὲ̌, dzô si-zǒ! *go and look for a place for me to build a hut in!*

(128) ma e'dú àtsí̀ tà a'dí̌-zǒ *I carried fire* (to go) *to cook*

(129) 'bá èì àzî̀ ŋɡa εdrí-zǒ *people work for a living*

483. (b) At other times, a full (relative) sentence, with subject and verb, &c., following a noun indicates purpose.

(130) è ndǎ pǎrí manì̂ laa-zǒ *look for a place that I may lie down* (*for me to lie down in*)

(131) tɔ̀rő̀ ὲri àfa àŋú-nì̂ fï̈-zǒ-rì̀ *a hive is a thing where bees enter*

(132) yófέ Àvùdrì-nï̈ àŋɡò wεε-zǒ-rì̀ *a broom with which Avudri sweeps the ground*

(133) mvu áaró rùá-nï̈ nì̀ àtì-zǒ-rì̀ *he drank medicine so that he may recover*

(134) ὲri 'dő̌-pá àŋá-nï̈ lɔ̀-zǒ-'bə-rì̀ 'ï *it is an eleusine stalk, from which the corn has already been cut/harvested*

484. (c) Where more than one interrelated clauses of purpose succeed each other, each verb is generally (though not necessarily) followed by zǒ. Similarly also with auxiliary verbs in a single sentence: zǒ may, or need not, be repeated after each 'verb'. Examples:

(135) mì̀ edzí ásé àtsí̀ əvo-zǒ, έŋâ 'ï-zǒ *bring* (dry) *grass to fan the fire for cooking polenta*

(136) èbìyó mu ètɔ́ ándríi-nï ɔbɛ́ (or ɔbɛ́-zɔ̌), ŋaa-zɔ̌ *the cannibal*
went to tempt the mother of the hare and to eat her
Cf. examples 71, 137

485. (*d*) When postpositional compliments are added to the qualifying
expression or sentence, they are placed after zɔ̌. The same is true of the
negative particle kö. Examples:

(137) 'mâ ŋgà mu àkúa ?' — manï emú-zɔ̂ zi-zɔ̌ mî tiá '*may I go*
home ?' ('*I am going home*') (*I say*—) *when I come to ask your*
permission (i.e. *to go home*)
(138) àtiliko èri àfa 'bánï ɛmvó 'bà-zɔ̌ drìniá-rì *fireside-lumps*
(*of earth*) *are things on which to put a pot* (*for cooking*)
(139) à mú atsí mî bɛ àŋgɔ̌ té mï nï ɔvö-zɔ̌-rìá (or . . . -rì mà
'aléa) *let us walk together to the place you were living in*
(140) ma kàlá e'dú 'bǎ àmvɛ́, ɔzɔ́ɔ-ìi a'í-zɔ̌ or ɔzɔ́ɔ ìi-nï tì-zɔ̌
I am taking the tub outside to collect rain-water|or rain-water
to drop in (DO–V*!*)
(141) èi arî tsɔ andzi-nï fɔ̀-zɔ̌ àmvɛ́ *they beat the drum, for* (that)
the boys to (may) *go out* (*school-break*)

486. (*e*) Zɔ̌ must regularly be added after verbs dependant on such
'auxiliaries' as tsa, etsá, ɛtsɔ́ *can, to be able to.* Examples:

(142) é tsa vínï 'yɔ-zɔ̌ 'dínï rá *you* (or *one*) *can also say this*
(143) á tsa (or ma ɛtsɔ́) arî tsɔ-zɔ̌ rá *I am able to beat a drum*
(= *I can play the drum*)
(144) à tsa àfa 'dì 'yɛ-zɔ̌ kö *we are unable to do this*
(145) è tsa àma ɛmbá-zɔ̌ rá yà ? *can you teach us ?*
(146) á tsa emú-zɔ̌ Árúwá andzi bɛ mbá 'dì mà o'dú sí yà ?
on which day of the month may I come to Arua with the
children ?
(147) ma etsá mî nï àfa 'dì 'du-zɔ̌ kö *I am unable to lift this for you*
(148) ti 'bánï ɛ'yɔ̂ ndzɛ-zɔ̌, vínï ɛ́ŋâ ŋaa-zɔ̌ *the mouth with which*
man speaks, or eats polenta

487. The negative *clause of purpose*, English 'lest', 'that not'. This is
expressed by a sentence in the future tense with the following word-order:
S (without nï)–kà mu–DO–V–zɔ̌ kö. Examples:

(149) é tè mvá tsí, mvá kà mu ɛ'dé-zɔ̌ kö ! (= mvá mà ɛ'dé kö)
guard the baby well lest it fall ! (= *that the babe may not fall*)
(150) mvá fúnò àgǎí tĕpirì èri a'ú tè, kà mǔ ŋaa-zɔ̌ kö (= mà
ŋaa kö bɛɛnì) *the boy looking after the pignuts attends to*
the fowls lest they eat . . .
(151) mî akú kóbí mî drìá tsí (= mî akú mî dri kóbí sǐ tsǐ) !
ɔzɔ́ɔ kà mu-zɔ̌ mî tsɔ-zɔ̌ kö *cover your head with the*
basket, so that the rain doesn't drench you !

(152) 'bá fè 'bá àzǐ (-nï) nǐ àɳá, 'bá kà mu dràa-zǒ kö *they give a person food, lest he (should) die*

(153) é ko dzà, kà mu mǐ sí ɛza-zǒ (à'dȍ-rö) kö *leave off (scratching (your) teeth with metal) lest your teeth are spoiled*

(154) lukú èìnï mvá drì sö-zǒ-rǐ, mvá kà mu ȍó-zǒ kö *luku basket with which they cover (for covering) a baby's head, so that it might not cry*

(155) é sȍ pá, é kà mu-zǒ àtì-rö-zǒ àfa 'dà mà rùá o'dû kə-zǒ kö! *stand up, lest you lean against that thing and fall asleep!*

CHAPTER 11

POSTPOSITIONS

488. A preposition in English, in so far as it serves to express the relationship in which one person or thing stands to another, corresponds to a Logbara *postposition*. While normally the *pre*position (as the name implies) is placed before a noun or noun-equivalent, in Logbara it is regularly placed after (*post-*) it. So it is right and proper in this chapter to use the term *post*position, in order to avoid a contradiction in terms.

Engl.: *The book is* on *the table.* Lgb.: **búkù èri médzà drìá** (*table on*) The rule is therefore: *all postpositions are placed* after *the word of reference.*

489. (1) There are, in Logbara, *proper* postpositions which are used only as such, as:

-**á** (amplified -**lǐ-á**) *in; to; at; from*
ànï *with it; through it; from it,* &c.
bɛ (rare **ébɛ**) *with* (company; possession)
drí *of; to; for*
kȍkə-rǐ, kȍkȍ-rö *without*
lɛ́ or **kìlɛ́** ... **lɛ́** *like, in accordance with*
mà *of*
nï, nǐ *to; for; of* ...
pál(i)á (rare) *under*
sǐ *with* (instrument); *on account of,* &c.
vélɛ́ *of; to(-wards); at; from* ...; *behind; after*
vǒ *to; with* (i.e. *at somebody's side,* or *village,* &c.)
vútìá *behind; after*

490. (2) Probably the majority of postpositions are really postpositional expressions with a noun basis. In most cases this kind of postposition represents a noun in the *locative*, as indicated by the locative postpositional suffix -**á**; and this compound term governs another noun or noun-equivalent in the genitive with **mà** *of*, either expressed or, frequently, only implied. This locative suffix -á is sometimes used also in combination with the above-given proper postpositions, as will be seen from the examples below.

491. The object element lɛ́ often occurs before this locative -á for euphony, as an extra formative element (without any particular meaning). Lɛ́ in these cases is regularly weakened to lé, lɛ̆ or líᵢ -á.

492. (3) The principal, more commonly used *postpositional* terms are:
'a-lé-á; 'a-lé-nï-á (lit. *in the inside* (of)), *in*; *in it*
àgắí-á or àgắí sǐ, àgắpí-á (lit. *on the side*), *beside; with* (company); *in the presence* (of), (near)
andrati-á (closely) *in front, before*
àsalá(á), àsákàlé-á, àsalíᵢ-á, ɛ̀sɛlɛ̆-á *between, among*
drì-á, drì-nï-á *on, upon* (it)
drì-líᵢ-á *before, in front* (*of it* drìlé-nǐ-à) (ːandrati-á)
ɛ̀dzɛ̀-kò-á, ɛ̀dzɛ̀-lé-kò-á *on the side/flank, beside*
ɛɲï *in*: bɛ ɛɲï or vǒ ɛɲï = bɛ (or vǒ) ɔgɔ̀gɔ̀ *near*
ɛtíᵢ-á, ǹdú-á *under, underneath, beneath*
ŋgókó-á *on the back; behind, after* (= vélɛ́) (locally, temporally)
pằrí-á, pằrí-tà-á *in place, instead* (of)
sí-á *on, up* (a tree, pole), *at the top*
tálá(-á), ètálá(-á) *among, within* (folds, thicket); *in/through* (a fabric)
ti-á *on* (or *along*) *the side of* (river, valley, field, &c.)
rùá *on* (the body of)/ *against*

493. *Observations.* (1) The nouns, on which the above postpositions are based, are: 'a *inside*; àgắí *surroundings*; andrati *face, front*; àsalá *space between, boundary*; drì *head*; ɛ̀dzɛ̀ *flank*; ɛtíᵢ = ǹdú *lower part*; ŋgókó *back*; pằrí *place*; sí *tooth, point*; tálá *fold, peep-through* (*fissure*), *net-* or *mesh-work of fabric*, &c.; ti *mouth*; rùá *body*.

(2) Locative -á after a noun ending in -á is generally imperceptible; an expected doubling of the vowel does not occur.

Use of Postpositions illustrated by Examples

494. (1) -á the *locative* suffix. It is the most frequently used postposition in the Logbara language. It is used alone or as as additional element for forming other postpositions. It is always the locative indicator. It is found enlarged to -léa (-líᵢa) after 'a, ti. Its meaning: *in, to, at* (*on*), *from.*

The vowel of a syllable tends to become closer before this -á.
(1) ma ándrii mu àkú-á; ɛ̀ri dzó-á *my mother went home ; she is in the hut*
(2) ɔ'ï ǹdrí átsí-á *they tied the goats in their enclosure/hut*
(3) é ŋga mâ pằrí-á! *move away from my place !*
(4) é fï rrï dzó-á! *go into the hut* (*room*) *and sit down !*

(5) ètú drï tȍ ; mà ŋgà fï éndri-á ! *the sun is very hot; let us go into the shade !*

(6) àmà mu àma-rï̀ àŋgò-á Pàdzùlú-á *we are going home to Padzulu*

(7) ŋàmparà drȍ àma àzí-á nǐ *it is the headman who drove us to work*

(8) drȍ tïèi ȍkó-á *he drove cattle for his bride('s)* (price)

(9) ma drî sö ȍkpȍȍrȍ-á, bȍ̀ŋgȍ́ ɛndzɛ́-zȍ̆ *I am pushing my hand into my pocket, to take out the cloth (handkerchief)*

(10) é bǐ·drí-á ! *hold it in your hand !*

(11) é 'bà drì-á (cf. dri-nï-á) ! *put it on your head (. . . on it) !*

(12) ȍzȍ̆-nǐ gbï (= zȍ) iǐ-á *reeds grow in the water*

(13) é dà mï dzó-ti-lǐ-á rá ! *withdraw from the door !*

(14) é sö mî ti-lǐ-á ! *put it in your mouth !*

(15) mvá àzí sȍ̀ pá dzó-ti-lǐ-á *a child/(boy) is standing at the door*

(16) èi ŋgȍ̈lȍ̆-rö pǎrí àlȍ̆-á *they are together in one (the same) place*

495. (2) 'Alé-á or 'alí-á (from 'a or 'alé *interior, belly*); meaning: *in the interior; in; within;* 'alé-nï-á *in it.*

(17) ɛŋgá dzȍ́ 'alïá *he came from the hut* (inside the hut)

(18) 'bá àŋgȍ̀ 'dà mà 'alïa 'dǐ drïia gbándà 'àà *all the people of that area cultivate manioc*

(19) èrì zá osí-osí émvó 'aléa *he is frying meat in a pot*

(20) lésú 'dǐ mà 'aléa ȍ'bu tsǐ, drà-dra *there is an insect in this milk, it has become sour*

(21) é fï dzóa/or dzȍ́ 'alé-nï-á ! *go into the hut (house, room) !*

(22) ȍlè, édrȍ́-nǐ ndzo 'alé-nǐ-á sǐ or édrȍ́-nǐ ndzo ȍlè 'alïa sǐ *a hidden path, in which mice run* or *mice run in hidden paths*

(23) é sö 'alé-nï-á ! *fix it in it !*

496. (3) Àgǎí-á, àgäpí-á, àgǎí(-á) sǐ (from àgǎí *neighbourhood*); meaning: *beside, by the side of, next to, with (company); in the presence of.*

(24) ȍtsé atsí mvá 'dà mà àgǎí(á) sǐ *the dog is walking beside that boy*

(25) mǐ emú ȍvȍ̆ àma àgǎía ! *come and stay with us !*

(26) é dà mï ma àgǎía rá ! *get away from me (my side) !*

(27) mvá 'dǐ ndzo dzȍ́ 'dà m'àgǎía sǐ *the boy runs round the hut*

(28) drà ma àgǎía sǐ (mâ vútí sǐ) *he died in my presence (my absence)*

(29) ma ágúi osi ma àgǎí sǐ *my friend was born 'on my side' (i.e. when I was already born, after me)*

497. (4) Andrati-á *before, in front of (close by).*

(30) é tö pá ma andrati-á (= mǎ milí-á) ! *stand in front of me !*

(31) mvá rrï 'ï ándríi mà andratiá *the child sits in front of his mother*

498. (5) Ànï *with it, by* or *through it, in such a way,* &c. This appears to be a postpositional phrase; it is really an adverb (see Adverbs).

499. (6) Àsalá(-á), àsalí-á, àsamvú-á (fr. àsalá or àsakala *space between*); meaning: *among, amongst; amidst; with (mingled with); between.*

  (32) mvá èri àma àsaláa *the boy is with (amongst) us*

  (33) mvá mu 'bá 'dǐ mà àsalíá *a boy went/walked amongst the people*

  (34) dzó —, àkú àsaláa *between the huts, — the villages*

  (35) mbí èri àŋgò lí-röpi ǐ mà àsaláa-rǐ'ï *an island is land/earth which is surrounded by (cut off amidst) water*

  (36) tí èri pätí ìrrì 'dàǐ mà àsaláa *there is a cow between those two trees*

500. (7) Bɛ (sometimes ɛbɛ), is a frequent term; meaning: *(endowed) with (qualities); (to be) with (possession)* = *to have; with (company), through.* In describing qualities bɛ is interchangeable with the suffix -rö.

  (37) mvá 'dǐ èri èndzò bɛ = èndzò-rö *the child/boy (is with) lies/a liar*

  (38) èri òrì bɛ/èri òrì-rö *he (she) is afraid (frightened, timid . . .)*

  (39) 'bá 'dǐrï tí bɛ kákàò-rö *this man has many heads of cattle*

  (40) 'bá àlö èri tsérè 'ǐnǐ bɛ *every man has his own particular call*

  (41) èri 'bá ndìì àzó bɛ = àzò-rö *he pinches one hard (painfully)*

  (42) ndzo mòémbè bɛ sùkúlù-á 'dálé *he ran away to school with a mango*

  (43) èri mvá drì-òkpó-ɛbɛ nǐ, lè ɛmbátɛmbá kö *he is a hard-headed boy, he does not like to learn*

  (44) lè òmbà-òmbǎ ma bɛ *he wants to quarrel with me*

  (45) èri òkó mvá ɛbɛ 'dǐǐ bɛ *she lives (together) with these women and children*

  (46) èríbí tí-nǐ ɲaalé ǹdrí bɛ-rǐ'ï *green grass which cows and also goats eat*

  (47) ɛlímákɔroa pǐ etsá wìtsí bɛ ɛ́lǐ sǐ ndrò *the swallows and the yellow wagtails arrive together in the dry season (winter)*

  (48) mbàzà atsî ɡbɛléfe bɛ *the old man walked with a stick*

  (49) tí èri mvá bɛ 'ïmà 'alǐa *the cow is with calf (pregnant)*

  (50) èì mu ábélésó 'bǎ zè ɛbɛ *they will excrete intestinal worms together with the excrement*

  (51) èri 'bá èkpéré bɛ-rǐ/= èkpérê-rö *he is a miser (i.e. man with stinginess)*

  (52) àŋgò èbì-rö ǐ bɛ *the ground is soft from (through) water*

  (53) mvá 'dǐ mà 'ï ándríi nǐ ɛ́ɲá ɛbɛ/or 'ï ándríi nǐ ɛɲâ 'i *this child relies on his mother for polenta/that she will prepare polenta*

  (54) èmï ɔvö àzî ŋga à'dï bɛ yà? *with whom were you working?*

  (55) à'ǐ 'dò alu tíbí bɛ tò *this salt is very palatable in a savoury*

(56) ndzɛ ɛ'yó ɔndzírɨ̀ 'bá àzɨ́ bɛ rá *he uttered bad words to somebody*
(57) 'dɨ̀ à gbà ndrâ ɛ̀ri bɛ mákìnà sɨ̀ *we have written this with him on the typewriter some time ago*
(58) Kariɔ tsɨ́ ; à kɔ àŋgɔ̀ ɛ̀ri bɛ *Kario is here; I swept the ground with him*

501. (8) **Drí** is the genitive and dative postposition: *of; to; through, from.* **Drí** (cf. §§ 109 and 114) may often be interchanged with either **nï**, **vélé** or **vɔ̌**.

(59) dzɔ́ 'dàrï ópí drí (-rɨ̀) *that hut is the chief's* (for use)
(60) ma wárágà 'dɨ̀rɨ̀ dzi ópí drí (= vɔ̌) *I am taking this letter to the chief*
(61) á fɛ̀ àfa àzɨ̀nï ma átïi drí *I gave something to my father*
(62) kàlámò 'dɨ̀ eza 'ï à'dï drí yà? *the pencil was spoiled by whom?*
(63) mâ lɛ̀dzó ŋɔ̀ rö mɨ̌ drí 'bə *my finger was broken* (through) *by you*
(64) ágú 'dà drà ándrâ à'dï drí yà? *that man was killed* (lit. *died*) *some time ago by whom?*
(65) ma ɔlɛ-ɔlɛ 'bá àzɨ̀ drí (= vɔ̌) *I bought it from somebody*
(66) ɛ̀ri ɛ̀ri ɔmvɛ rú bàtízìmù drí-rɨ̀ sɨ̀ *he calls him by his Christian name (name taken on Baptism)*
(67) 'bá-rɨ̀-mà-dɨ́-'dɔ̀ 'yɛ àbírí drí ŋgɔ́ nï yà? *however is it possible to do such a thing when hungry?*

502. (9) **Drì-á** (fr. **drì** *head*) *on, upon; about, on account ot* . . . ; **drì-nï-á** *on it (him, her);* **drì-á 'bùá sɨ̀** *over, above* . . . ; *across.*

(68) àrïïá ɛ̀ri dzɔ́ drìá *the bird is on the hut*
(69) é 'du 'bɨ̀lɨ́ é rrï drìnɨ̌á! *take a stool and sit (take place) on it!*
(70) é mu búkù ɛ'dú bǎò ètïa ɛ̀lɛ̀, é 'bà médzà drìá! or é 'du 'bǎ médzà mà drìá! *go and fetch (take up) the book from under the plank and put it on the table* or *fetch (take) and put it on the table!*
(71) li ɛ̀rimà drìá à do yà? *what did he condemn him to?* (lit. *cut on him?*)
(72) àtsífɛ sɔ̀ 'Bílía mà drìá tsɨ́ *the magic stick stuck fast on 'Bilia* (indicating his guilt)
(73) gûgúã ɛ̀i 'ɔ'á ïi mà drìá 'bùá sɨ̀ *midges are found over the water* Cf. 'bǎ drì-nï ra ɔndó-bí sɨ̀ *they cover it over with durra leaves*

503. (10) **Drì-lé** is used for place and time, meaning: *before, in advance, ahead, in front* (any distance); *beforehand, previously.* **Drìlé** is, generally, equal to **ɔ̀kɔ̀**. Both these postpositions are preceded by a postpositional expression with **nï**, when the term of reference—ahead of whom?—is expressed. **Drìlé sɨ̀** *away over.*

(74) é mu drìlé (= é tsɛ drì)! *go ahead (first)!*
(75) drà átápi nï drìlé *she died before/previous to her father*

(76) mvá 'dà etsá átíi-nï drìlé (= ɔ̀kɔ̀) *that boy arrived before his father*
(77) é fɔ̀ má-nï drìlé! *go out before me* (first)!
(78) aga íi drìlé sì *he stepped away over the brook*
(79) kằmì mbo pätí mà drìlé sì *the lion jumped away over the trunk*
(80) àrï̈ä ŋga dzó drìlɛ sì *the bird flew away over the hut*
(81) é mu drìlé, mằ ŋgà mu ndɔ̀/= mằ ŋgà 'dɛ ànï *go first, I shall follow*

504. (11) Drì-lí-á (related to the former), meaning: *(closely) before, in front of*; equal to andrati-á or mìlí-á. Drìlé-nï-á *in front of him* (or *it, her*).

(82) èrì mu ópí mà drìlíá *he walks in front of the chief*
(83) èrì rrï ándríi mà drìlíá *she sits in front of her mother*
(84) é 'ï̀ àfa 'dìrï drìlénìá! *hang this thing up in front of him (her, it)!*
(85) àndrò àzí àma drìlía tsí (or àma drìlía àzí tsí) *today we are busy*
(86) é ŋga àzí mî̀ drìlía 'dìì̀, é ko àzí 'dà dzà! *do this work before you (your duty); leave that work there!*
(87) é 'du àfa mî̀ drìlía 'dì̀ ráká, é ŋgà mu ndɔ̀ *first pick up these things in front of you, then you may go*

505. (12) Èŋï = ɔ̀gɔ̀gɔ̀, two adjectives, both are preceded by either of the postpositions bɛ or vɔ̌, to form a postpositional expression. The forms èŋï̈a or èŋïïrö are used as adverbs. Meaning: *near, close to*.

(88) mí ɔvö èri bɛ èŋï (= ɔ̀gɔ̀gɔ̀)! *stay near her!*
(89) lítsó èri àkú bɛ èŋï *the cattle-pen is near/close to the village*
(90) èri ma-nï (or má-vɔ̌) ɔ̀gɔ̀gɔ̀ *he is near me*

506. (13) Ètí-á (= ǹdú-á) (*posterior; lower part of anything*); meaning: *under, underneath, below* . . .

(91) é 'bà wárágà búkù ètía! *put the paper under the book!*
(92) èi médzà ètía èlè *they are down under the table*
(93) tí èrì pätí ètía *the cow is under the tree*
(94) ódrúkódrú fípi íi ǹdúa *a frog which goes (enters) under water*
(95) mvá mì édzá àtsí ètía *the child pushed fuel into (under) the fire*

507. (14) Kìlé (= èkìlé) . . . (lé); . . . lé; meaning: *like, similar to, according to*. (È)kìlé (before the word) and lé (after the word) may be used together, or either one or other of them.

(96) sì kìlé 'dì̀lé (or èri kìlé...) yà? *is it like this?* (is it equal? = sì)
(97) 'dì̀ kìlé ɔbí èridrí (lé) *it (this) is in keeping with his character*
(98) ɛdé ɔbí 'ïdrí lé *he acted according to his custom*
(99) èri kìlé pätí lé wɛrɛ 'dìpi *it is thin/small as a stick*

508. (15) Kókɔ-rì̀, kókɔ̌-rö a postposition with the form of an adjective; meaning: *without.*

(100) 'bá milé (or bbílé, andra) kɔ́kɔ̀rö lit. *a man without eyes* (blind), *ears* (deaf), *tongue* (dumb)

(101) 'bá milé kɔ́kərì nὲ àŋgὸ kö *a blind man does not see* (the world)

(102) 'bá ὲndrà kɔ́kərì ὲri 'bá àfa fἔpi 'bá-nɪ́-rì'ï *a man without stinginess* (i.e. *generous*) *is one who gives people things*

(103) ὲri atsí tɔ̀əkɔ́, bɔ̀ŋgɔ́ kɔ́kɔ̀rö *he walks naked, without clothes*

509. (16) Kpɛrɛ or tröa . . . (vɔ̆, vélé); kpɛrɛ or tröa precedes its noun; vɔ̆ or vélé . . ., when added, follows it; meaning: *as far as, till, up to* (*the place or time of*).

(104) ndzílá mu kpɛrɛ Éɲ̜ɑ́ó tǐá *the road goes as far as the Enyao river-bank*

(105) é ndzo tröa dzɔ́ 'dà vɔ̆! *run up to that hut!*

(106) . . . kpɛrɛ ὲtú manï drà-zɔ̆-rï-á *up to the hour of my death*

510. (17) Mà is much used for the genitive, see §§ 95, 99 ff.

(18) Ñdú-á (identical with ὲtǐa, q.v.), *under*(*neath*), *below* . . .

(107) laa rö pätí 'dà ṅdúa *he is lying under that tree*

(108) màȧkò fï ɲ̜aakú ṅdúa *potatoes grow down below the ground*

(109) ὲ'bí ὲi 'ə'á ïí ṅdúa (= ὲtǐa) *fishes live under water*

511. (19) Nï, a ubiquitous particle, is not an easy postposition to define in all its various uses. As a postposition proper (see §§ 555 ff.) it is used in the following two ways:

(*a*) Nɪ́, with a preceding low tone, expresses the idea of *possession* or *destination*; it is, therefore, the postposition of the genitive, as in:

(110) zɑ́ɑ̃ mvá 'dà ɔ̀kó 'dɪ̀ nɪ́ *that girl is this woman's*

(111) tí mvá 'dɪ̀ mâ-nɪ́ *this calf is mine*

(112) àfa 'dɪ̀ à'dɪ̀ nɪ́ yà? ὲri ὲìnɪ́ *whose is this* (thing)? *it is theirs*
Cf. §§ 109 ff.

(*b*) Nɪ́, irrespective of preceding tone, is much used for the dative case, as also is drí (cf. §§ 114 ff.). The difference between the two is that nɪ́, apparently, indicates possession proper, drí does not. Often, however (probably depending on the district), the two are used indiscriminately. Meaning: *to, for.*

(113) mɪ̆ ὲfὲ má-nɪ́ (= má-drí) ïí! *give me water!*

(114) é dzi ɔ́sɔ̆ ɔ̀kó 'dà nɪ́! *take beans to that woman!*

(115) mɪ̆ ɛ'da ὲri-nɪ́ pɔ́stà mà dzɔ́, fɔ̀! *please show him the Post Office!*

(116) əŋgə 'dɪ̀ ndrì má-nɪ́ tɔ̀ *this song is very pleasant to me*

512. (20) Ŋgɔ́kɔ́-á (ŋgɔ́kɔ́ *back*), generally = vélé-á, vútiá; meaning: *at the back, behind.*

(117) òmú ὲri mɑ̃̀ ṅgɔ́kóa (= vútiá) *the guest is behind me*

513. (21) ɔ̀kɔ̀ (= drìlɛ́), preceded by the reference term with nï; when used alone it is an adverb; meaning: *in advance, ahead, before, at first.*

(118) etsá 'dɔ̀á ɔ̀kɔ̀ (or má-nï ɔ̀kɔ̀) *he arrived here first* (or *before me*)
(119) ma emú èrinï ɔ̀kɔ̀ *I have come before him*
(120) é fï ópí-nï ɔ̀kɔ̀ *you entered before the chief*

514. (22) Pálá (rarely used), identical with ètïa, ǹdúa: *under* ...

(121) tí èri pätí 'dà mà páláa *a cow is under that tree*

515. (23) Pàrí-á or pàrítà-á (pàrí *place*); meaning: *in place of, instead.*

(122) emú átápi mà pàría *he came in place of his father*

516. (24) Rùá-á (rùá *body*), the locative -á is generally not heard. It refers to somebody, something as a whole (its body); it is very much used; meaning: *on to; of* or *about; with; against* ...

(123) é li ti (è)ndzɔ̀ mɑ̀ rùá *you have slandered* (lit. *told lies about*) *me*
(124) èì tí 'ï áló rùá *they are tying a cow to a stake*
(125) é 'ï (= 'bà, ɔvö) àtsí aíssé rùá! *set fire to the grass!*
(126) ma ɔ̀rà 'bá àzí-nï mà rùá *I thought of/about somebody*
(127) ma a'bɔ̌ ma pätí rùá *I hid* (myself) *behind a tree*
(128) mí àtì mï mɑ̀ rùá kö! *do not lean against me!*

517. (25) Sï, apart from -á and nï, is the postposition met with most frequently in Logbara: it is used in many adverbial expressions (cf. also conjunctions). In some cases a translation seems difficult. In some cases it points to the means instrumental in producing a certain effect. Sï may thus indicate:

(*a*) *Instrument*: 'with'.

(129) tsɔ mvá kàlí sï *he beat the boy with a stick*
(130) ádzê á 'di ŋgúrú àdzú sï *yesterday I killed a wild beast with the spear*
(131) ma ezí ròsali sï *I told my beads* (*prayed with my rosary*)
(132) lukú sï èi mvá mà drì sö ètú sï *they cover a baby's head with a special basket against* (*to shade it from*) *the sun*
(133) é sï ti èmïdrí sï tsí *you have written it all in your language*
(134) èri mɑ̀ sí sï pätí sï *he is knocking out my teeth with a stick* (*wood*)
(135) èi lésû zɔ gɛlɛkúa sï *they milk with a ball-gourd*

(*b*) *Cause, reason*: 'from', 'on account of', 'through', 'because'.

(136) ma ɔ̀ri ŋgúrú sï *I am afraid of wild beasts*
(137) á 'yɛ ɔ̀ri sï kö *I did not do it out of fear*
(138) àma emú pìkìpìkì ɛ'yɔ́ sï *we have come on account of the motor-cycle*

(139) ə'yətáa sǐ o'dúkə̀-nǐ ədzáa 'ǐ arí-zà-rö *from so much talking his voice became hoarse* (= *he became hoarse through talking a lot*)

(140) 'bá èi ə̀rə̀ vàálέ sǐ ə̀rə̀-ə̀rə̀; àmà àma èdzǒ! *people ('s legs) have become stiff from* (sitting on) *the ground; let us stretch ourselves!*

(141) ézó andzi èi ə́ó-ə́ó ègbè sǐ *the girls are crying with cold*

(142) èi tí əfǐ kàlâá əzə́ə́ sǐ *they are driving the cattle into the pen because of the rain*

(143) èri apa ópí sǐ apa-apa *he ran away from the chief*

(144) ģu àyìkə̀ sǐ *he laughed for joy*

(*c*) *Motion* away from: 'from' (one's position). The construction requires the locative -á (-rǐ) sǐ; rǐ may be inserted before sǐ. Both rǐ and sǐ may be omitted, say before rá.

(145) é sε mï εmvεlétiá (rǐ) sǐ rá! *withdraw from the light* (opening)!

(146) é ko rö ģìrì-á rǐ sǐ rá! *withdraw from the way* (make way)!

(147) mï èfờ dzóa-rǐ sǐ 'dǐ yà? ma èfờ dzóa (rǐ sǐ) rá *did you come from this hut? I came out of the hut*

(148) etsá lífò-á rǐ sǐ ádzê *they came back from leave yesterday*

(149) mï emú ə́ə̀kə̀ 'də̀ sǐ! *come out/along* (by) *this way here!*

(150) ma emú ģìrì 'dà sǐ *I came* (by) *that way*

(151) è'bí fờ ìi-á (rǐ sǐ) kö *a fish did not come out of the water*

(*d*) *Various*:

(152) sàbitì dría sǐ mǐ emú drì atri emú-zǒ sindanì esú-zǒ! *come back every week for* (to get) *an injection!*

(153) lə́ə̀ndrè èri atsí pätí sí-á sǐ *the colobus* (monkey) *walks on trees*

(154) èi dǐ əzə́ə́ nễ Éɲáó sǐ *they* (downriver) *will know of the rain by the* (state of the) *Enyao* (say in Terego)

518. (26) Sí-á (lit. *on the tooth*), *up on* (high object, as a tree, hut, rock); *on the point; from* (on high).

(155) èri dzó síá *it* (bird . . .) *is on the hut*

(156) àrïïá rrï pätí sía *a bird perches on a tree*

(157) ε'dέ pätí sía, ŋə̀ 'ǐ ùú rá *he fell from a tree and broke his arm*

(158) èi tờrờ 'bǎ pätí sía, àɲú-nǐ fï ànï (or zǒ) *they put* (basket-) *hives on trees so that bees may enter* (and settle in) *it*

(159) èi kờlû sö έú sía *they are fixing a hayhopper on to* (the top of) *a hook*

519. (27) Tálá (-á) (tálá *folds, inside of fabric or anything*); meaning: *in between, among, in the folds.* . . .

(160) ờrí bə̀ŋgó táláa tsǐ; èi mǎ ɲàɲa, ờrí drì-bbí tálá tsǐ *there are lice in the cloth; they are biting* (eat) *me; there are lice in head hair*

(161) ŋgúrú èl pätí táláa *there are wild beasts among the trees* (= *in the forest*)

(162) ma bákâ sö sìndanì mà tálá *I am fixing thread in the* (eye of) *a needle* (= *I am threading the needle*)

(163) 'bí'bí èri 'ɔ'á à'bɔ̀à-bbí tálá *the bat lives among the leaves of bananas*

(164) Cf. áyìpi mà àsalá ɛ́lí bɛ *between the rainy and the dry season*

520. (28) Tí-á (ti *mouth; edge of space*); meaning: *at, on the side of, along; from; in place of.*

(165) á'dǐá atsí ǐí tìá sǐ *s.-s. is walking along the river*

(166) tö pá 'àá ǐí tìá *he is standing over there on the bank of the river*

(167) ma ǹdrí ɔ̀'ǐ áló ti-á *I am tying the goats to stakes*

(168) ma a'í mǐ tìá (= mǐ vɔ̌) sàbúnì 'dàrï *I am asking you for that soap*

(169) ma àkú á'bu tìá *my home-village is on the slopes of the valley*

(170) fè ǹdrí kàbìlɔ̀ mà tìá *he gave a goat for a sheep*

521. (29) Vélé is used in a variety of forms and meanings.

(*a*) Vélé the possessive postposition—genitive (cf. §§ 110, 112). It commonly implies a local relationship to the object referred to. This genitive expression (noun followed by postposition) may precede or follow the noun it qualifies. While vélé suggests 'to the site of', it expresses possession in general, like the postpositions drí and nï; from this point of view, the three postpositions (often also vɔ̌, which corresponds more nearly to a suggestion of 'place') may be used indiscriminately as a rule.

(171) 'dà tí má-vélérǐ'ï/= 'dà mávélé tí-rǐ'ï *that is my cow*

(172) ópí vélé àkú-rǐ 'dà *that is the chief's residence*

(173) dzɔ́ 'dà Lógbàrà vélé (= nǐ) nǐ yà? *is that a Logbara* (country) *hut?*

'dà Lógbàrà vélé dzɔ́ *that is a Logbara hut*

(174) dzɔ́ 'dà Lógbàrà drí-nï, kǐ *yes, that is a Logbara hut*

(175) 'yé òku ágú 'dà vélé dzɔ́-rǐ-á tsí *once arrows used to be found in that man's hut*

N.B. Note that where the genitive expression precedes its noun, the adjectival particle -rǐ is added after the noun (separated from vélé to which it refers).

522. (*b*) It is further used, apparently in the same way as drí or vɔ̌, to indicate the *place of an object, towards, where, whence one goes*. Thus its meaning is *to, at, with, from.*

(176) à mú àndrò ɛ́ɳâ ɳa má vélé! *today let us go to my home and have polenta!*

(177) á mu ópí vélé (or vɔ̌) or á mu ópí drí àŋgɔ̀-á *I went to the chief's*

(178) ma etsá èi vélé *I arrived at their site/village*
(179) é kà mvi èmï vélé àŋgò-á-lé, é dzi ma èndì! *when you go home* (to your's), *take me* (with you) *too!*

523. (c) Vélé is much used as adverb also; it refers to place and time; meaning: *behind, afterwards, later* . . .

(180) ma ágíi nï àŋgà vélé *my companion is still behind*
(181) èri əvö vélé *he is behind*
(182) ma vélé, mï drìlé *I am behind, you are first/in front*
(183) èri má-nï vélé, mï èri-nï òkò *he is inferior to me* (in quality, age), *you are superior to him* (in quality, age)

524. (d) Vélé-á vis-à-vis vélé. Vélé, used absolutely, is a pure adverb. If a reference noun is added, and vélé has thus the function of a postposition, while at the same time it has to serve as an adverb, the adverbial function has to be expressed by adding the postpositions -á or sï to vélé, and we thus have vélé-á = vélé sï, which is, again, identical with vúti-á or vúti sï (see next).

525. (30) Vúti-á, is probably a compound, a kind of locative to the postposition vǒ. Vúti-á or vúti sï is identical with vélé-á or vélé sï; meaning (both local and temporal): *at the back of, in the rear of; behind, after departure of*, i.e. *in the absence of* . . .

(184) èri dzó 'dà mà véléá *it* (he, she) *is behind that hut*
(185) ma etsá èrimà véléá (= vútiá) *I arrived after him/or in his absence*
(186) mï əvö mà vútiá!— ma mï vútiá *stay behind me! — I am behind you*
(187) emú mï vúti sï (= véléa) *he came after you*
(188) drà èrimà véléá (= vúti sï) *he died after* (him), i.e. *after he had left, thus, in his absence*
(189) 'dà mà vútiá á sï wárágà dzi 'bǎ postà-á *afterwards I wrote a letter and took it to the Post Office*

526. (31) Vǒ and vǒ sï, a versatile postposition; meaning: *to, with* (*company*); *at, to, from the side of* . . .

(190) ma edzí mï vǒ *I have brought it to you*
(191) à'dïəvö èri bɛ nï?/= èri à'dï vǒ yà? *who has it* (lit. *is with it*)?
(192) èri má vǒ yə *I haven't* (got) *it*
(193) èri 'ə'á à'dï vǒ yà? *with whom was he staying?*
(194) é rrï àma vǒ sï! *sit with us!*
(195) mï emú má vǒ sï! *come and follow me!* (. . . má vǒ *to me*)
(196) é ŋga (= si) má vǒ 'dì-á rá! *get away from me!*
(197) èri ǹdrí 'í vǒ 'dìǐ drə *he is driving the goats to his site*
(198) mu tíí vǒ *he went to* (see) *the cows*
(199) Dràvǒro, mï emú má vǒ 'dòá! *Dravoro, come here to me!*

CHAPTER 12
ADVERBS

527. There are quite a number of what may be called *proper adverbs,* though, in any single case, it may prove difficult to decide which is which. In Logbara, what at first sight appears to be an adverb may, if convenience or circumstances so require, be used as an adjective or something else, by adding the ordinary formative suffixes. Similarly the elasticity of Logbara may turn a Noun or an Adjective into an Adverb; a noun is made an adverb by means of the suffixes or postpositions **-rö, -á,** or **sì** or by a combination of these; an adjective is turned into an adverb by dropping the suffix **-rì** or **-rö.** Quite frequently both techniques may be found combined and, seemingly, confused in one expression or phrase to act in sundry ways. This essentially Ma'di/Logbara linguistic characteristic must always be kept in mind. Compare the following examples which use **vélé**:

Postp./Noun: **mu èì vélé** *he went home* (to their site)
Adverb: **ǹdri ŋgà vélé 'dà** *the goat is still there behind*
Noun/Adv.:   **etsá èrimà vélé-á** *he arrived in his absence/after he had left*
Noun/Adv.:   **tí èri dzó 'dà (mà) vélèa** *the cow is behind that hut*
Postp./Adj.:   **dzó àma-vélé-rì** *our hut/room, our house*
Adj./Adv.:   **ágú vélérì** (= **véléarì, véléalérì**) **'dà** *that man who remained behind*
Adverb: **vélérì sì mǎ ŋgà mu rá** *afterwards I shall go*

528. There are also a few auxiliary-like verbs or verb combinations which are more easily translated by an adverb. But to know how to translate the great variety of adverbs of manner is no easy task.

The following catalogue of a large number of the more common adverbs or adverbial phrases, with numerous illustrating examples, will guide the student in the syntactical use of Logbara adverbs. Fixed rules can hardly be established. As a whole, adverbs may be placed, though with slight differences of meaning, in any position in a sentence.

1. *Adverbs of Time*

529. (*a*) *Questions.*

à'do ŋgárè yà? or **ŋgɔ̀árè yà?** *when? at what time?*

N.B. **Sí yà?** *how many?* **sì** *in, for . . .,* **sí sì?** *in which . . .?* **ŋgɔ̀pi sì?** or **ŋgɔ̀ sì?** may commonly be used instead of . . . **sí sì?**

ɛlí (o'dú . . .) sí sì? *in which year (or day)?* **o'dú sí yà?** *how many days?*

N.B. **ɛlí** or **wàŋgì** = *year;* **o'dú** or **ètú** *sun* = *day.*

vǒ (= **vǒ-sì, pálé, pá'alé, pá-milɛ́kɔ́**) **sí yà?** also **vǒ ŋgɔ̀pi yà?** *how many times? how often?*

(1) mǐ etsá ètú ŋgɔ̀pi yà ? *at what time of day did you arrive, come ?*
(2) mǐ etsá àkúa o'dú sí yà ? *on which day did you reach home ?*

530. (b)

ɔ̀kɔ̀-rǐ sǐ, kàɔ́ɔ̀-rǐ sǐ, kàíɔ̀-rǐ sǐ *first of all, in the beginning*
drìɔ̀, drìɔ-drìɔ, té = tá, té drìɔ *early, betimes, in good time*
ńdrâ, ndrá-drìɔ, drìɔ̀ú (= drìɔ̀wǐ) sǐ *days ago, long ago, in the past,
   in days past, once*
òku, òku drìɔ, té-òku, tsé-òku *of old, formerly, in the past, in past
   times, in days of yore, long ago, for a long time*
N.B. These various terms have a relative value; they may refer to a
near or a far past; the expressions are often combined. Té or tá, cf. § 383.

(3) mǐ tsé òku 'dɔ̀á drìɔ *you have been here for a long time*
tsé òku ... kö ; té-òku ŋgà kö ; ŋgà dè kö *not/never before, not
      yet, without ever*
ŋgà *still, yet* ; ŋgà kö *not yet*

(4) èri ŋgà àkúa, eŋgá ŋgà kö *he is still at home, he has not yet
   left for (to come) here*
(5) ŋgà dè andzi etsá kö *the children have not yet arrived, strangely
   enough*
(6) etsá té má vǒ drìɔ *he came to me early (today)*
(7) emú òku ŋgà kö *he has not come here before*
(8) Èré'bɔnǐ ndrâ drìɔ̀ú sǐ lè zɔ̀ kö *ever since Ereboni would not
   grow (remained stunted)*

531. (c)

ètú-zù, zù-zù, drù-drù, táa or táatá, trátrá, o'dú pírǐ ; *always,
   everyday, regularly, constantly* : etselɔ̀(wà) kö *unfailingly*
ètú 'dǐ mà 'aléa *during (in the course of) these days*
ɛlǐ/wàŋgì 'dǐ sǐ or ɛlǐ vàá 'dǐ sǐ *during/in the course of this year*
ɛlǐ aga-rǐ sǐ or ɛlǐ ádzê-rǐ sǐ *during ... the last year*
ɛlǐ ndrâ agápi 'dà sǐ *in past years*
ɛlǐ (or wàŋgì) vǒ ... ɛlǐ (/wàŋgì) vǒ, àsì kɔ́kɔ̀rö *always, without
   ceasing, perpetually, on and on, eternally*
(ɛlǐ or) o'dú ... àzǐ (nǐ) sǐ, tǎrótǐ *another time, sometime in the future*
atsɛ wɛrɛ *very soon, in short (lit. there remains little over)*
tsú(tsú)rú 'dɔ̀, é'díò *now, just now*
tsötí, kpérékpéré, ɔ̀bɛlɛ, mbèlèmbèlè *immediately, instantly, quickly*
vélé, vélérǐ sǐ *behind, afterwards*

(9) ma emú ètú ìrrǐ nda-rǐ sǐ *I came last Monday*

532. (d)

ádzê *yesterday* ; ándrâ *the day before yesterday*
àndrò *today* ; drù or drù-sǐ *tomorrow*
drózí *the day after tomorrow*

drózí 'dà sǐ or drózí àzírǐ (sǐ) *the day(s) afterwards*

(10) àmà ŋga emú drù (sǐ) *we shall come tomorrow*

ètú-sǐ *by day, during the day*

ètú líitrì, ètú trá (or mŋgbílǐ or nǎmù), ètú 'dǐ *all day long*

(11) mï 'ə'á àŋgǒ àlǒá ètúzzù *you always stay in one place*

íní-sǐ, íní-nï *at night, in/during the night*

íníïǎ-ii *at midnight*

ràa or íní (-sǐ) ràa *all night long*

ètú 'yépi emúpi vélé 'dǐ sǐ = ètú 'dà ŋgárè *some day or other*

(12) ètú 'dà ŋgárè àmà ŋga rǒ fu mï bɛ rá *one fine day I shall have a fight with you* (threat, challenge)

533. (*e*)

drùsǐ drìə a'ú-átá tsérè sǐ orᶣlǒlǒ-nï tsérè berǐá or lǒlǒnï ɛ'dǒ tsérè ə'bɛzǒ 'bə 'dǐ(rï) or àŋgǒ trà nï or ò'búti drìə-drìə = ò'búti kúlàkúlà *early in the morning, at cock crow* (*about 4 a.m.*)

àŋgǒ sàrà (or trà or mǎnìmǎnì) or óú (v.) *at dawn, at first light, at daybreak*

àŋgǒ óû dí 'bə, atsɛ̀ dí wɛrɛ *day (dawn) is breaking, the sun will soon rise*

ò'búti drìə; ò'bíti sǐ; 'bùundúnï àmvérǐá *at dawn . . .* (these three expressions are all used often indiscriminately for the time about an hour or half an hour before sunrise and after)

òdzíə sǐ, à'íə sǐ *at an advanced morning hour* (up to about 9 a.m.)

ètú-nï-íialí ò'bìrǐá or sáwà azia *at midday*

ètú ala sǐ *at about 4–5 p.m.* (alias *2–6 p.m.*) (? *any time in the afternoon*)

ɔ̀ndré sǐ *in the evening*

àŋgǒ-nï bǐ-zǒ wɛrɛrǐ sǐ *at dusk* (*evening darkness*), *twilight* (about 20 minutes after sunset)

'òmú-nì-rö-tí-sǐ' *in complete darkness* (lit. *when an arriving guest cannot be readily recognized*)

534. *Notes on use. Examples.*

(1) Usually adverbs or adverbial phrases are placed after the verb, towards the end of the sentence; for purposes of emphasis, however, they may be placed at the beginning or in other positions in the sentence.

(2) Some adverbs have been referred to, according to their particular functions, under Verb (cf. § 364; 'bə, § 381; té (tá), § 383, &c.), Conjunction, &c.

(13) ma ɛdé 'dìrï ɔ̀kɔ̀rǐ sǐ, tsúrú'dò ma àzǐ-rǐ ɛdé *I did this first, now I shall do something else*

(14) mï ɛ'dǒ wárágà lǎ, ma lǎ vélé *you (begin to) read the paper first, I shall read it afterwards*

(15) mï etsá à'doŋgárè yà? ma etsá drìə *when did you arrive? I arrived early* (or possibly, *long ago*)

(16) àndrò mbá o'dú sí yà? *which day of the month is it today?*

(17) Àndèré mu àndrò àkúa; èri emví àndrò rá *Andere has gone home today and he will come back today*

(18) á tsə mï ádzê rá *I beat you yesterday*

(19) ádzê á mu ámvú 'ǎ *yesterday I went to till the field*

(20) ágú 'dà ɛdɛ ádzê ma rá *that man fooled me yesterday*

(21) è mú tsòrónïá driərö (= òkòrö)! *go to the W.C. first!*

(22) mï etsá ádzê-ádzê 'dò, é nì ŋgà àŋgò 'dòárï kö (mïnï a'á-zǒ mïdrí àkúa o'dú wɛrɛrï 'dï sï) *you arrived* (so to speak) *only yesterday, you do not yet know the country here* (*as you have been in your village only a few days*)

(23) óŋa-nï ŋga ïnï sï *termites* (some of them) *swarm at night*

(24) (èri) 'yə ma bɛ, mâ mvi tsúrú'dò àkúa *he told me, I ought to go back home immediately*

(25) mï 'ə'á ŋgó yà? ma etsá tá 'dó (or 'dòá) ò'búti sï *where have you been? I arrived here in the morning*

(26) té ò'bútisï á fò àzía rá; ma vínï fò àzía ètú ala sï à'dò 'yɛ yà? *I went to work this morning; why should I go to work again in the afternoon?*

(27) o'dú nna mï etsá 'dòá kö; á nè mï àzía 'dïá tï *you haven't been here for three days; I looked in vain for you here at work*

(28) á sɛ té tábà driòú sï *I smoked a good while ago* (today)

(29) àma emû mu Àriŋgàá, kànì mï èfǒ drùsï driə a'ú-átá tsérè sï *we shall go to Aringa, if you get up early, at cock crow, tomorrow*

(30) mï etsá té tsútsúrúá'dò yà; mï àndè ŋgónï yà! é ŋga té àzí kö, á ŋga té rá *you arrived here just a moment ago; how is it you are tired!* (*how can you be tired!*) *you have done no work, I have* (worked)

(31) drùdrù èmï èfǒ emú àwà rö ágú 'dï bɛ! *you always start quarrelling with this man!*

(32) èri àzô ta ïnï bɛ ràa *he groans all night* (a sick person)

(33) 'bá àzôrö óó àndrò ràa *the sick person cried all night*

(34) á mu ràa Vǒrà-á *I went to Vörra even by night*

(35) dzó vɛ ádzê òndré sï 'dálé; dzó kə ti tsénï *the hut burned down yesterday evening; it caught fire* (by itself)

(36) àvǒ-nï èri ńdrí 'yɛ (-rö) èbï rö rá áánï; kǒko àvǒ dzóa *the seriously ill man will probably soon be dead; he is left dying* (alone) *in the hut*

(37) ɛ'bí ńdrâ'ï ndzɛ 'dó, 'ï asi emví 'dólé kö *since he left here long ago, he has never come back* (hither)

(38) é ŋa tɛ-òku ògárá'bá mà tà rá yà? *have you ever before eaten the food of a White Man?*

(39) 'dï mâ mvá ńdrâ sïpi ïí-á driərï 'ï *this is my boy who once went down 'beyond the lake'* (i.e. to Bunyoro)

(40) ádzêrï sï àma emví sáwà azia *we came back at noon yesterday*

(41) àŋgŏ sàrà èrinï ŋgà óú-zŏ mŋgbàa körï̀ (=óú ŋgà dɛ kö)
    at dawn, when day has not yet quite dawned (broken)

(42) atsɛ wɛrɛ mà mvi àkúa *very soon I shall go back home*

(43) ósŏ 'bánï fǎ ìíá ɛlḯ sìrì̀'ï̈, èì əmvɛ tsïkïrḯ *they plant beans on
    the riverside during the dry season* (October . . .) *they call them
    'tsïkïrï'*

(44) 'bá kə drìə ókŏroŋà 'dìrï̈ àmvé kö, fŏ dï àní àmbôrö *for
    a long time they have not swept away the dirt; it has thus
    accumulated*

(45) ágú 'dìrï̈ òdúrûrö, vínï 'yə ɛ'yó kö o'dú drïia *this person is
    deaf and neither has he ever spoken a word all his days (is
    dumb)*

(46) ma etsá té 'dòá ò'bíti sì̀ *I arrived here early in the morning*

(47) etsa té ədzíə sì̀ *he arrived later in the morning*

(48) ágú 'dà 'ə'á àma vŏ ètú-zù *that person is with us every day*

(49) 'ǎ ámvú ètú-ddìì *they tilled the field every day*

(50) ma drùsì̀ (or dr—ma) mǐ tsə rá (or ma mǐ tsə dr—rá) *I'll
    beat you tomorrow*

(51) Àndèrë́ ədzì àndrò 'ïmà rùá rá *Andere took a bath today*

(52) té drìə mï̈ əvö ŋgòá yà? *where have you been earlier?*

(53) mǐ emú té drìə kö àsìa? *why did you not come earlier?*

(54) é lŏ té ŋgà àmaní kö *you did not tell us before*

2. Adverbs of Place

535. The chief *adverbs* or *adverbial phrases* of *place* are:

(*a*) **-á**, the ubiquitous locative suffix: = *in*; **-lɛ́**, complementary
formative, often implying 'direction'; it has no particular meaning.
Questions: **ŋgòá yà? ŋgólɛ́ yà?** *where? whereto? whence?*

(*b*) **'dò, 'dòá; 'dó, 'dólɛ́;** *here, on this (my) side,* } seemingly used
    'dì̀, 'dìá *here (on your side)* } indiscriminately
    'dà, 'dá, 'dálɛ́ *there (any distance), yonder*
    'dɛ́, 'dɛ́lɛ́ *there* (near or at known or mentioned place without
    further pointing it out): slight reference to an event or statement
    in question.

536. The simple term **'dò, 'dó; 'dì̀; 'dà,** &c., is, so to speak, an
incidental indication (without so much as looking in the direction); the
same term with the suffixes **-á** or **-lɛ́** is used for the stressed indication or
in pointing out a place. It may be doubled for emphasis, as **'dálɛ́-'dálɛ́**
there yonder there. Similarly:

    ə́ókó (or gèrì̀) 'dì̀ (or 'dà) sì̀ or 'dólɛ̂-rörì̀ sì̀ *in this* (or *that*) *way or
    direction* or *manner* or *on this (that) side . . .*

537. 'áá, a'á, 'àá 'dálɛ́ *over/yonder there; beyond the vale or river.*

('a, 'alé) 'aléa/'alía, 'anía, 'alénía (inside) in (-side) it
àmvé outside, away
vàá (properly vă), vàálé on the ground; èlè lower down
ètí(ní)á, ndú(ní)á below, beneath (it); ètíníá èlè down underneath (it)
öru, 'bùá on high, aloft, overhead, high up; örulé sì upwards
N.B. örú, örúlé upland, highland
     andrá (-lé) down country, lowland

(1) àmavélé àkú èri örú 'dálé our village is up country there
aga in the middle; agà-dua in the centre; dzó mà agàdua in the centre
of the hut
drílé, adv. and pstp. (cf. § 503) ahead, before

(2) é mu drílé, ma emú mî véléa go ahead, I shall come after you
drilía = andratíá adv. and pstp. (see §§ 497, 504) before, in front of . . .

(3) èri mâ drilía he is in front/ahead of me
vélé and véléá (see §§ 523 f.) behind, at the back; late

(4) Bìanò etsá vélé Biano arrived late
ngókóa at the back, behind (lit. on the back)
èdzè(-lé)kò-á on the side/flank
ògògò (a) = ènï; 'bá vő (or bɛ) ò—near a person
     (b) still, up to the moment (say, staying in . . .)
ènï (-á) near
rèrè, rè 'dálé; tsèrè far (away), distant; èri ngà rèrè he is still far off
á(í)séa in the grass (bush, veldt, wilderness); at large (Ac. i tim)
àngò (or pàrí) píría (or dríia) or pírí driá, órò-drì(-á)-kúrù,
ùú-dri-kúrù, ròkò-dri-kúrù, àngò-driá wórò (or mngbú) everywhere, in every place, in all places, all over the world

538. *Use and examples.*
Rule: Adverbs of place or adverbial phrases are, as a rule, placed towards
the end of a sentence or after the word they determine.

(5) mï engá àngò ngòá yà? where did you come from?
     ma engá Térégòá I came from Tɛrɛgo
(6) mî mu ngólé yà? èri ngòá yà? where are you going?
     where is he?
(7) èrimà ádríi-nî mu 'áá yà? is his brother going beyond there?
(8) àmà ndrâ ngà 'dò yo at that time we were not yet here
(9) òdò de 'dò 'ï 'bɔ the oil (kerosene) is apparently (doubt) finished
    cf. affirm. òdò de 'ï 'bɔ the kerosene is finished
(10) mâ ngà mu vélérï sì Gùlúa later I shall go to Gulu
(11) ògògò vàá 'dòá it is near here/this place here
(12) é 'bà 'dïá ògògò! put it here near!
(13) à mú àmvé 'dálé! let us go outside (there)!
(14) mï esú 'dï yà? have you found it?
(15) mvá 'dàrï 'dé tsí yà? is that boy (there) present?

(16) èrì mu rǔ pa rö rá = èrì mù pa rö rá *he will/may run off*

(17) mú té 'dálɛ́ ; 'bá èìrí àzɔ̂rö *they went there; a man at home is ill*

(18) mï emú gèrì̀ (or ɔ̀ókɔ̀) 'dà sǐ! *do come that way!*

(19) é fï dzɔ́ mà 'aléalɛ́! = é fï dzóalɛ́! *do go into (inside) the hut/room!*

(20) andzi 'dàì̀ mvi àkúalɛ́ mvî̀mvi *those children have gone back home*

(21) è zɔ té àndrò 'áálɛ́ à'dò 'yɛ yà? *why did you pass yonder today?*

(22) mâ mu dzóa vǎ 'dì̀! *let us go into this hut!*

(23) àtsí̀kà èrì̀ ŋga öru *the smoke rises in the height*

(24) tö pá örulɛ́ sǐ *he stands upright*

(25) ɔ̀ŋgɔ̀rɔ̀kɔ̀ n̞a màákò 'dì̀ rá, mà 'bɛ vàá! *worms have eaten these potatoes, have them (potatoes) thrown away!*

(26) ìì-à'di ɛ'bí eɡa ɛ̀lɛ̀ 'dálɛ́ *a spring rises (comes forth) down there*

(27) èrì mání drìlénï or mâ drìlɛ́ (= . . . lía) *he is above me (situation, or birth . . .)*

(28) àŋgǒ mádrí rɛ̀rɛ̀ ; á lɛ̀ pǎrí ɔ̀gɔ̀gɔ̀ dzô si-zǒ *my place (country) is far away; I want a place nearby to build a hut*

(29) èrì 'bá ámvú 'ǎpi vàálɛ́ sǐrì̀'ï *he is the man who works the field (sitting or kneeling) on the ground*

(30) é pi (= mï, dza) kìfúŋgà 'délêrö! *turn the key that way!*

(31) ma e'dú àfa 'dìrì̀ 'ï̀ öru (= 'bùá) *I took the thing and hung it up*

(32) èì tî drɔ 'alénì̀á (i.e. àkúa or áséa) *they drive the cattle in (home or on to the pasture)*

(33) á zi 'dì̀ zì̀zi *I am* (here) *just asking*

(34) àmà mu Térégòá 'dálɛ́ gèrì̀ ŋgɔ̀ sǐ yà? *by which route shall we go to Tɛrɛgo?*

(35) 'bá tra èì órɔ̀drìkúrù *people are gathering from everywhere/all sides*

3. Adverbs of Manner

539. The *adverbs of manner* represent a special feature in Logbara, because of their profusion and, one might say, because of their oddness of form (onomatopoeic). For convenience' sake a good number are listed here.

It should be noted that particular verbs are commonly found with particular adverbs, which is only logical as the adverbs have a cognate meaning.

Adverbs of manner are commonly placed at the end of a sentence.

Questions: ŋgó-nï yà? ŋgɔ̀-ŋgó-nï yà? *how? in which manner?*
gèrì̀ ŋgɔ̀ sǐ? *in which way? in which manner?*
ŋgónï áánï? *in what possible way?*

540.

(1) àbálá sǐ *vying with* (or *emulating*) *each other, racing for a wager*

(2) agaa = kpɔ̀yɔ̀ *half full (about)*

   (1) ïí ndɔ̂ 'a agaa (= kpɔ̀yɔ̀) *water in the pail is half full* (sic !
   Note the particular Logbara construction.)

(3) ándá = dərɔ̀ *by mere accident, by good luck (to one's surprise), by
chance*

   (2) mu ándá tsa mí vǒ rù or mǔ rǔ tsa mívǒ ándá *by good luck
   he came upon you suddenly !*

   (3) á mu ma ágúi nï esú ándá èrï-vélé *I went and quite accidentally
   found my friend at home*

   (4) mï ádrïï etsá àma-vélé àkúa dərɔ̀ *your brother arrived at
   my (or our) village by chance*

(4) ámútí = adetí = yǒkö *by turn(s), alternately* (cf. Vocabulary)

(5) àyï̈ = ǹdï̈rï̈ *frankly, openly, publicly, under one's very eyes (nose)*

   (5) 'yə ɛ'yó 'bâ drìá àyï̈ *he spoke openly about people*
   (6) lǒ 'bání ɛ'yó ǹdï̈rï̈ *he spoke plainly to the people*

(6) bïrïbïrï = ïï-ïï = èrï-èrï *delaying; leisurely; detailed*

   (7) lǒ lǒ mání (or mâ tiá) vǒsï àlö, lǒ mání ïï-ïï kö *he spoke to
   me only once (incidentally), he did not speak to me at length*

   (8) ma ɛɳâ ɳa b-b-, àbíríní mà fu kái sï *I am eating polenta
   (protractedly) slowly as I am very hungry*

(7) dàa-rö-dà (cf. verb) *obliquely, slanting(ly), sloping(ly)*

(8) dìi = mù (q.v.) *secretly, unobserved, without being seen . . .*

(9) dìi-dìi *swingingly, by balancing*

   (9) èi ɔ̀láɳgî sɛ dìidìi *they ring the bell by a swinging movement*

(10) dərɔ̀ see ándá

541.

(11) dzùlû-ru = tɔ̀líàrö, agara-lì-rö, *on one's back*
   cf. ɔ̀'búkùru or à'búkùru *on one's face*

(12) èdzèdrì, èdzè-sí-drì *on one's side*

   (10) 'bá la 'ï èdzèdrì (or dzùlûru) *one lies on one's side (or back)*

(13) èdzèdzè sï̀, èdzè-sí sï̀, lɔ́mà-lɔ́mà sï̀ *sideways, side-long*

   (11) atsí èdzè-èdzè sï̀ (cf. ǹgókó-ǹgókó sï̀) *he walks sideways
   (backwards)*

(14) èrïi sï̀ = ɔ̀kpó sï̀ *strongly, vigorously; aloud* (see Vocabulary)

(15) ɛ'yéré, ɛ'yéré-ɛ'yéré *slowly; carefully, with attention*

(16) fɔ̀ər *hazily-whitish-brightly* (see Vocabulary)

(17) góní-góní = gɔ̀lí-gɔ̀lí (see kíllílí)

(18) hwɛ́rɛ = kátrà (q.v.)

(19) hwèrè *trailingly, dragging along*

   (12) mï rǒ sɛ ɳaakúa sï̀ hwèrè *you move along dragging yourself
   on the ground*

(13) kànì ǹdrí lὲ mu pá sì̀ kö, mï̈ ὲrì sɛ vàá sì̀ hwὲrὲ *if a goat does not want to walk* (on its legs) *you pull dragging it along on the ground*

(20) ìyàa = ndii, ɛ'yέrέ *calmly, unconcernedly; happily, peacefully*

(14) ὲrì mu Árúwá ìyàa *he is going to Arua quite unconcernedly*

542.

(21) ìyìi = ndró (q.v.)

(22) ìyìò *without stopping* or *delaying (anywhere)*

(15) è mú ìyìò! (i.e. mà mukí 'dálέ mà tökí pá kö) *go without stopping!*

(23) kái *very much, exceedingly, utterly, to excess*

(16) má tέ 'dò ἑwâ mvu 'ì̈ ká, kòrέ-nì̀ fu ma kái *let me in the first place drink beer, I had a great longing for it*

(17) tsə ὲrì kái, lὲ drà̀-drà *he beat him excessively, he nearly died*

(18) àbírí (or ì̀ kòrέ) fu ὲrì kái *he is extremely hungry (thirsty)*

(24) kátrà = hwέrɛ, mbὲlὲ, pàlà, oru-oru *at once, forthwith, without delay, immediately; briskly, unflinchingly . . .;* (opposite: ì̀ì̀-ì̀ì̀, ὲrí-ὲrí . . . trìkítríkí *allowing ease/delay*)

(19) mì̀ èdà drì (vélέ) kátrà! *come back—from your walk—instantly!*

(20) é mvì (= gò̀ drì) kátrà! *turn back* (home) *at once!*

(21) mì̀ ɛ'bέ mì̈ pàlà, mï̈nï̈ drì àdà-zỏ̆! *be quick, so that you might get (come) back!*

(22) mì̀ e'dú àfa hwέrɛ (àfa ndzï̈pi körì̀)! *pick the* (light) *thing up briskly!*

(25) kíllílí = kpii, kpikpi, piri, áda-áda, mŋgbà *straight (any direction); clear, distinct, plain, lucid (to eye, ear);* (opposite: gónígóní, gòlígòlí *crooked, tortuous; confused, obscure . . .*)

(23) é lò̀ ɛ'yó kíllílí (= ádarö . . .), ὲrì rö ɛrì mânì̀ mỏ̆kέ ndò̀! é lò̀ mânì̀ ɛ'yó gónígóní kö! *speak plainly, so that it may be intelligible to me at last! do not speak to me confusedly!*

(24) 'bá drăpi 'bə-rì̀ ὲrì laa rö (or 'bá ὲrì 'bà̆) 'bílía kpii *a dead person lies (or is laid) stretched out straight in the grave*

(25) ètò̀ má piri/= emú má vỏ̆ sì̀ kpikpi *he came straight up to me*

(26) ètò̀ ὲrì 'yέ sì̀ kpikpi *he aimed straight at him with the arrow*

(27) ètò̀ dzó 'dà mà ti kpikpi *he went straight on to the door of that hut*

(28) nὲ ὲrì piri *he looked straight at him*

(26) kírí = ríiti, durù (a) (placed after subject) *still, even now*

(29) mï̈ kírí àfa ədzí (= ò̀lì̀) yà? *are you still transporting things?*

(30) mï̈ ŋgà ríiti a'á 'dálέ yà? *are you still staying there?*

(b) (placed at the end) *for good, for ever, indefinitely*

(31) K.A.R. emví àkúa ríiti *the soldier came home for good*

(32) é mvì èmïrí (= èmï̈-vélέ) 'dà sì̀ ríiti! *go home for ever!*

(27) kírrikírri = títí, trítrí, rírí *firmly, tightly, properly*

   (33) mí epá kəmɛ kírrikírri! *fix the chair firmly!*

   (34) é 'ĭ ndrí títí, kà mu ètrö-zǒ kö! *tie the goats fast (to stakes), lest they break away (disengage) (and go off)!*

   (35) é sö kírrikírri, kà mu ɛ'dé (-zǒ) drà-zǒ kö! *place it well| firmly lest it fall and break!*

   (36) bǎò ɛ̀kpà búkù kírrikírri *the board (-press) holds the book firmly!*

(28) kpɔ̀kpɔ̀ = kpɔ̀lókpɔ̀ló *fussily, excitedly, restlessly*

   (37) èrì (or èrimà rùá-nĭ) yà (or 'yɛ) kpɔ̀kpɔ̀ òrì drí *he is trembling| moving restlessly with fear*

   (38) lɛ̀ mu 'bá 'dà bɛ, èrì dí àzî ŋga rùá kpɔ̀kpɔ̀ sĭ *he wants to take a walk with that man, he is, therefore, working with verve*

   (39) mĭ mu Árúwá kpɔ̀kpɔ̀ à'do 'ə yà? *what are you in such a flurry about going to Arua?*

   (40) èrì 'bá kpɔ̀lókpɔ̀ló bɛ-rĭ *he is a busybody*

   (41) èì dí ɛ'yô ndzɛ 'bá àzínĭ ándrâ 'ə-zǒ kpɔ̀kpɔ̀ rá 'dĭ mà drìá *they are discussing a man who, some days ago, acted in a fussy way*

   (42) èì dí ɛ'yô ndzɛ kpɔ̀kpɔ̀ drìá *they are discussing (the word) 'kpɔ̀kpɔ̀'.*

(29) lí *in drops, drop by drop*

   (43) ìí (or ɔzɔ́ó; à'í)-nĭ tĭ lí, lésú 'dɛ lí *water (or rain, lye) trickles drop by drop, milk falls in drops*

(30) lìi = tsipa, lipa *at a standstill, immovable; completely*

   (44) ìí sɔ̀ pá lìi, èrinĭ ra-zǒ kö-rĭ sĭ *the water is stagnant (stands quite still) when it does not (run) flow*

   (45) drìnĭ àvɛ̀ lìi *he has completely forgotten*

   (46) Gàlìlèo àbà lìi, èrì ɔ̀vù tsírí *Galileo looks dumbfounded; he keeps silent*

543.

(31) mǎänì *dimly, vaguely, indistinctly*

   (47) ɔ'dó ali mǎ drìlĭa sĭ mǎänì-mǎänì *a leopard crossed|passed in front of me phantom-like*

   (48) á nɛ̀ 'bá àzínĭ mǎänì 'dáa *I saw somebody there indistinctly (at night)*

(32) mù(u) = dìi, ndìi, tsírí, ɔtsízàrö, (ə'yó kɔ́kɔ̀rö) *unobserved, unnoticed, leaving no trace, spirited away, out of sight, dissolved into thin air; secretly, confidentially*

   (49) 'bí'bíə àtĭ (= àvɛ̀) mági-nĭ mù *the star stopped, disappeared for the magi as if into thin air*

   (50) é zì ma àfa 'dĭ mùu! *hide this thing of mine out of sight!*

   (51) etsá mùu; ndzo áséa dìi *he arrived unnoticed and ran into the bush and was lost*

   (52) àvɛ̀ mùu; ma awí esú kö yɛ́ *it got lost; I have not found it again*

(53) mvá 'dà òlǒ mánǐ ɛ'yó 'dìi ndii *that boy told me the matter clandestinely*

(54) àfa 'dǐ àvě dìi, á ndà tǐ *the thing was completely lost, I searched in vain*

(55) é 'bà àfa àŋgǒ dìi-á! *put the thing in a secret place!*

(56) lǒ mánǐ ɛ'yó ǝtsízàrö *he spoke to me privately/to have a private talk*

(57) á 'bà búkù 'dà dìi: ɛná kö *I put the book out of sight; it is invisible*

(33) ndrǐ (cf. Vocabulary) *fine, nicely, delightfully; brightly*

(58) kàíkǝ ka ndrǐ; tsa tsúrú'dǝ ɳaa-zàrö 'bǝ *the beans have developed splendidly; they are now ready for eating*

(59) ètú èfǒ/ɛ'dá ndrǐ/= ètú nï ɡu ndrǐ *the sun is shining brilliantly*

(34) ǹdró = ìyǐi (a) *remaining empty, vacant, evacuated, unoccupied*
    (b) = rû *suddenly, unexpectedly, unnoticed*

(60) àŋgǒ fǒ (pàrítinǐá) ǹdró *the place (area) became vacant*

(61) mú kó pàrǐ ndró 'bǝ *they went/left the place without occupants*
    etsá ndró (= rû) 'bǝ *he has arrived unexpectedly*

(35) ńdzǐ = ándzíríkáandzi, ndzíkǝrǝ *away over something* (without even touching)

(62) wa/mbo drìnǐá sǐ ńdzǐ *he jumped high over it*

(63) 'bɛ óní dzó drìlé (or -á) sǐ ńdzǐ *he threw a stone high over the hut*

(64) áɡú 'dà wǐ tùsú ńdzǐ *that man spat (arch-like) a long distance*

(36) mŋgbàa (-rǐ) = kíllílí, q.v.

(37) mŋgbí (*quite empty*) *off, out, to the last bit* (or *drop, morsel*)

(65) ɳaa ɛ́ɳá mŋgbí *he ate the polenta to the last bit (he polished off the polenta)*

(66) 'du mòémbɛ dzóIókǝ mŋgbí *he took the last remaining bit of mango*

(38) ɳáaɳaa *flashing up all over an area*

(67) ǝ'bà (or ò'ǐ) àtsí ásétiá ɳáaɳaa *he lit grass fires all over the place*

(68) àtsí ǝvö ɳáaɳaa óɳa tè-zǒrǐ *fires for collecting termites were flaring everywhere*

(69) èbìɳá-nï ŋga ɳáaɳaa *glow-worms fly flashing up everywhere*

(39) ɳǐrǐɳǐrǐ *minutely; into/by (small) bits* and *pieces*

(70) ǝndì (or ǝli) zá nï ɳǐrǐɳǐrǐ *they pulled the meat off bit by bit*

(40) oru-oru = kátrà, q.v. *without delay* or *without stopping, immediately*

(71) mǐ emú oru-oru (or tsítsí)! *come back (from errand) without stopping!*

(72) mǐ emví oru-oru! mà 'yǝ lǒ ɛ'yó tá 'bánï èri-ti pèzǒrǐ *return hither immediately! he must say (do) only what he has been sent for* (without stopping anywhere)

544.

(41) óyέ *one-sidedly, unilaterally*

  (73) tsɔ ma óyέ *he has beaten me onesidedly* (i.e. *I did not beat him*)

(42) pí *hitting (shooting successfully)*

  (74) á gbï àrïa 'yέ sï pí *I shot a bird with an arrow* (scoring a hit)

(43) pùù *in fact, in reality*

  (75) á lŏ ε'yó pùù 'bɔ *I have actually already said it/the word*

  (76) tsa 'dálέ pùù rá *he has really arrived there*

  (77) à tsa pùù dùkánïá rá *we did in fact arrive at the shop*

(44) pírïnï *empty, empty-handed*

  (78) mï mu emví drí bε pírïnï *you will come back empty-handed* (from an enterprise)

(45) tàyà *scattering about*

  (79) à'í ε'dέ tàyà, εrέ 'ï ndóndó *the salt* (-packet) *fell scattering, it spread about*

(46) tràí *straight towards, in the direction of* . . .

  (80) fï (or aga) tràí má vŏ 'dò sï *he came in and straight up to me*

(47) trέ = lïà-lïà, mmbói, tsŏkùtsŏkù, zŏrŏ *completely full* (! construction)

  (81) 'bá ga dzó sï trέ/tsŏkùtsŏkù *people fill the hut completely* (for the hut is full of people)

  (82) àn̦á ga èró-á (= èró sï) mmbói/zŏrŏ *corn fills the granary completely*

  (83) ïï ga émvó 'a trέ (! only) *water fills the pot* ('s inside) *completely* = *the pot is full of water*

  (84) é 'bà àn̦á 'alénïá trέ (= mmbói)/ or aga (= kpòyò) *put corn in it full/half, fill it with corn; half-fill it*

  (85) mï edzí ïï mà ko kópò mà tï wεrε! *bring me a glass of water, not quite full!*

(48) tsέ *clearly, plainly, exactly, correctly; in fact, really*

  (86) ε'yó 'dï εga tsέ *the word came correctly to my mind* (= I remember the word well)

  (87) á 'yɔ té mïnï ε'yó tsέ (or rá) é lè té ε'yó à'ï kö *I told you so* (the matter) *plainly; you did not, however, want/refused/to believe*

  (88) nì Ingilízì ti tsέ kïè *he really knows English*

  (89) mvá ε'dá dzó tálá zï tsέ *the child is clearly visible through the fissure of the hut*

(49) tsï *firmly, tightly, closely, properly* . . .

  (90) é bï tsï! é mŏ drí tsï! *catch it firmly! hold your hands together tightly!*

  (91) é sï ti èmïdrí sï tsï *you have written it down in your language*

  (92) à'yà kɔ èri tsï *jealousy took hold of him/her* . . . (*he was consumed with jealousy*)

(93) kànì àfa àzínï àvĕ rá, ma èmï bì tsí *should anything be lost,
I will surely catch you*

545. (50) tsĭrr *making a move/start, jerk*
(94) mằ rúá 'yɛ tsĭrr (e.g. kằmì nè sì) *I started with fright* (at
seeing a lion)
(95) ɔ̀vi-nï fì-rì sì, mằ rúá 'yɛ tsĭrr *when it thunders, I suffer a
shock*

(51) tsírí = tsú, mù, q.v. *quiet, still*

(52) tsŏkùtsŏkù = tré, q.v. *quite (full)*

(53) wằì *without (leaving) a trace*
(96) ɔzɔ́ɔ́ àtì wằì, ɛré 'ï 'bɔ, thus, àŋgŏ wɔ́rɔ́-wɔ́rɔ́ 'a ɔzɔ́ɔ̀ 'di kö
rain completely ceased, clouds dispersing, nowhere does it rain,
i.e. *it is not raining anywhere*

(54) zŏrŏ = tré, q.v.

4. *Other Common Adverbs*

546. (1) *Affirmation* (a):
ɔ̀ɔ, ĕ̆ĕ̆, ɛ̀ɛkĕ̀, ɛ̀ɛ́kɛ̀, and even tsí *yes, so it is*
'yɛ́kɛ̀, mŏkɛ́ *all right, it is right, that 's good, O.K.*
tắändí, tắändí pìru, ádằ-rö, áda-áda *certainly, truly, really*
'dínï, 'dìpì *so it is; like this; in this way/manner*
nì (placed at the end of a sentence) *it is . . ., that . . .* (Ac. àyɛ́)

547. (b)
bɛ ; ɛ̀ndì, ɛ̀trɔ̀ *also, too*
ddíká *again*
tŏ *very, very much*
tööni, ndĕpì *chiefly, mainly; especially*
pá-mvó (or ğɛrì) àlö sì *in the same way* or *manner*
trɔ́trɔ̀ *all the same, identically*
tú (= dríia . . .) àlö = ndrɔ̀ *(all) together*
etsá ndrɔ̀ = etsá tú àlö *they arrived together*
ànï *with; by; from it; in it; in such a way . . .*
Ànï is a relative adverb (similar to French *en, y*) much in use in Logbara;
it functions like a postpositional phrase referring to a noun or statement
previously given. In most cases ànï may be replaced by the conjunction
of purpose zŏ with relative construction. Cf. examples below.

548. (2) *Negation* (a):
á'a *no, not so*; á'a, á lɛ̀ kö; á ɡa sì *no, I do not like it; I refuse* (it)
yɔ ; kö *there is not; no, not*; yɔ̀, á mu 'dálɛ́ kö *no, I did not go there*
ɔ̀ndzí *(that is) bad, wrong*; ɔ̀ndzí kàɳàarö *very bad*

ŋgà kö *not yet*; emú ŋgà kö *he has not yet come*
asi . . . kö *no more* (contrary to habit or intention or expectation in general).

The term asi usually precedes the verb immediately; a direct object or some introductory adverb may, however, intervene. Asi by itself, without kö, is sometimes found and expresses a state arrived at and, for the moment, continuing. Asi/así sometimes = nga, mu, i.e. auxiliary verb of future.

549. (*b*):

pírínï *gratis*; *for nothing*; *empty*
tǝǝkó, bàdàkà (-rö), sákà (³rö), wèèrö *gratuitously, at random, to no purpose, aimlessly*
àkà *unreasonably, preposterously, irresponsibly*
tí *in vain, to no purpose, of no avail*
ló (preceding its object) *only*
àyákáká *only, exclusively*; ézó andzí àyákáká *only girls* (are in)
a'dúlɛ, àlö *alone*; mu àlö a'dúlɛ *he went alone* (only)

550. (3) *Objection, doubt, possibility.*

'dè, 'dèrè *but, whereas*
ŋgà ká, (ŋgà) àká *not at all, not in the least*
dǝbaanï, káanï *it is to be hoped* . . .; *I hope/trust that* . . .
. . . dáanï *still, for all that, all the same, nevertheless*
nǝsï; . . . áánï; nǝsï . . . áánï;
kànì áánï; 'dínï áánï   *perhaps, possibly, maybe* (cf. §§ 476 ff.)
kànï . . . (bínï) áánï
. . . 'dǝ *perhaps*

551. Examples:

(97) mï àlö ɛ'yó tǝǝkó 'ï *you spoke idly/to no purpose*
(98) mà 'yǝ ɛ'yó mbèlèmbèlè, mà sɛ ɛ'yó kö! *one ought to speak more quickly, not so drawlingly (droningly)*
(99) é pa mâ bǝŋgó kǝkǝlǝ-rö kö! *do not take my clothes by force!*
(100) é mu ɛ'yéré-ɛ'yéré! *go slowly!*
(101) mï èfè má drí èɛdrí ma ànï dribbí fǎ/= èɛdrí dribbí fàzǒrï! *give me a razor so that I may cut my hair with it!*
(102) edzí àdzú 'dï ànï tí/= tí sǝzǒrï *he brought a spear to kill an ox*
(103) é ŋa zá nï, mï ǝsɛ ànï/= mïnï ǝsɛzǒ *eat meat so as to become fat!*
(104) kànì li mï rá, àrínï èfö ànï *if it has cut you, blood runs from it = when you are cut, blood flows*
(105) mï èlö éfílénï kílílí, á lö ànï *you have given the meaning correctly, I say the same*
(106) é ko, á sö drí ànï! *leave it (sleeve), I'll push my arm in!*
(107) èrï à'ínï, èì ànï tíbía'dï *it is salt/lye, to (they) prepare a savoury with (it)*

(108) átsí andzi la rö ànï *the hut* (in a pen) *in which boys sleep*

(109) ǒsu èi 'bá tsà ànï/= ǒsu 'bá tsàzǒrï *a bow, they (may) kill a man with* = *a bow to kill a man* (with)

(110) mí edzí mánï kòkɔsì, ma otsí ɛ̀pɛ̀ (= ɛndzɛ) ànï/=manï otsí ɛpɛ̀zǒ, ma ànï otsí ɛ̀pɛ̀ *give me a safety-pin so that I may remove a thorn with it*

(111) mí ɛ̀fɛ̀ mádrí kàlamù, ma ànï wárágà sï ɛmbápi vǒ *give me a pencil, so that I may write a letter to the teacher*

(112) èi 'yɔ gěrï àlö sï *they speak in the same way* (i.e. uniformly)

(113) è 'yɛ/èmï àzî ŋga/àbálá sï *you did it/do work/by competition*

(114) ma ɛri rá (or tsɛ́, kpɛrɛ) *I heard it clearly*

(115) tǒönï ɛ́wá-nï àikɔ̀ edzí nï *it is chiefly beer that produces (conveys) happiness*

(116) mï ɛri éfïnï rá yà? ma ɛri ŋgà kö *have you understood it? = do you understand it? not yet*

(117) é 'yɔ ɛ'yó 'dï ddíká! or é lǒ ŋgà má nï ɛ'yó ddíká! é lǒ té ŋgà má nï kö *tell (it) me (the matter) over again; you did not tell me before*

(118) é lɛ̀ kànì àndrò kö áánï *perhaps you do not like it today*

(119) atsí gěrï múpi Kàmbìafàrì-á-rï sï, tsa kpɛrɛ Òtsódrìá, àsì 'dïpi *he travelled* (on the way) *to Rhino Camp, he reached Otsodri and stopped*

(120) ínkì àfa 'dï mà 'aléa tsí áánï? *is there possibly ink in this thing?* (i.e. bottle)

(121) mï ɛ̀fɛ̀ má nï bɛ! *give me* (some) *also!*

(122) 'bá èi káanï hwïïá sï ïî se *people may drink/draw water through* (straws) *tubes* (i.e. empty grass stems)

(123) é tö àfa 'dï ádzê áánï; 'wï 'bɔ *perhaps you trod it yesterday under your feet, it is dry now*

(124) drà rá áánï *he is probably dead by now*

(125) kà adri ɔ̀ndzí tï, mí ɛdɛ́ dáanï! *even if it is bad, do it all the same!*

(126) é ndà dáanï, mï mu esú sï rá *seek it still* = *go on looking for it, you'll end by finding it*

(127) tíbí 'dɔ̀á yɔ, káanï ɛɲá nï *there is no savoury here, I hope there will be some polenta* (at least)

(128) ǹdrí àyákáká, kàbìlɔ̀ 'alénïá yɔ *there are exclusively goats, no sheep*

(129) fǒ àmvɛ́ 'dálé kírí; asi etsá 'dɔ́ kö *he definitely went off; he came* (continued to come) *here no more*

(130) asi mu Árúwá kö yà? *will he go to Arua no more?* = *won't he go to Arua any more?*

(131) mï asi emú ɛmbátáa kö à'do sï yà? *why do you no longer come to school?*

(132) ma asi dzi ókòroɲà ɛvɛ kö yà? *shall I no longer take the waste and burn it?*

(133) asì 'bá àzǐnï mà àfa ògǔ kö *he will steal other people's goods
no longer*

(134) 'dǐ àfa mádrí, mï asǐ 'du kö ! *this is my property, do not take
it again !*

(135) ma asǐ dǐ tsa mǐ vǒ kö *I shall no longer come to you*

(136) èrì dǐ asi ko dzà ; ǒô dǐ kö *he keeps on leaving it; he no longer
cries*

(137) ma asi 'bá àzǐ mà àfà 'du ddíká kö *I shall no longer take
another person's goods*

(138) lè àfa 'dàrï lǒ'ǐ = èri àfa 'dà mà àvâta ásǐ àlö sǐ *he wants
that thing absolutely*

(139) ma lǒ ɔrà àfa 'dà mà drì-á *I am thinking only of that*

(140) èi asi emú èrì föö ɔ́fótá 'aléa *they will roll him in ashes*

CHAPTER 13

INTERJECTIONS

552. Here is a list of more common interjections or interjectional
expressions:

ɛ̀ɛ'ɛ̀ɛ'ɛ̀ɛ . . .! (expression of pain) *ah me! ay me! woe is me! oo! oh! help!*

(1) ɛ̀ɛ'ɛ̀ɛ'ɛ̀ɛ ! pätí ɛ'dê dǐ mà drìá 'bɔ rá ! *ah me, the wood has
fallen on my head !*

ɛ́ɛ̌'dǐnï ! yé'dǐnï ! ɛɛzí ! á'dàarö ! (approval, assent) *indeed ! so it is !*

(2) ɛ́ɛ̌'dǐnï ! á nè té rá tátsê, èinǐ tsɔ rö zǒ 'dàrï'ï *to be sure ! I
saw it, as they were fighting there*

é-rï pl. è-rï ! (detestation, aversion) *alas ! good gracious ! dear me !*

(3) é-rï ! màdrì etsí 'dǐnï kö ! *how could anyone put me off like that !*

(4) é-rï ! 'bá tsɔ 'dǐnï kö ! *shocking ! one ought not to beat a man thus !*

(5) é-rï ! àfa ògǔ mï ándríi vélé 'dǐnï kö ! *to be sure ! one would
not steal like that in your mother's home !*

érùó ! (surprise) *good heavens !* érùó ! é lè té emú à'dǐ-nǐ 'yɛ yà ! hó !
why ever did you intend to come ?

éyé-wâ-yê ! éyé-wâ-yê ! mâ mvá 'dɔ yê ! *woe is me ! alas, this my child !*
(*mother at death-bed of child*)

há(a)ì ! (disapproval) *fie !* háaì ! mï ma ɔndǐ à'do sǐ yà ? *shame on
you ! why are you pinching me ?*

káaka ! káaka ! or wáàwa ! (disappointment) *pooh ! stuff ! . . . shame !*

(6) káaka ! káaka ! (ma ándríi ma) á ndè tǐ ; àfa lè fǐ mǐ
bbíléa kö ! *shame ! I tried in vain; the matter would not enter
your ear ! (but you would not listen)*

(7) wáàwa ! ɔ̀rì bǐ èri tsǐ ! *ha ! he is afraid (lit. fear caught him) !*

mǎäti ! (?) T. hwàai ! *sorry !*

ùú-ùú-ùú ! (astonished; overwhelmed) cry of alarm, *hi ! oo ! help !*

(8) èri lúlû ga : 'ùú-ùú-ùú ! kằmì-nï mằ ɳa 'dɔ̀ yà !' *he* (attacked by a lion) *sounds an alarm* : '*help ! help! a lion is mauling me here !*'

àwà'dì fɔ̂ ! or àwá'dínï ! àwànìà mí ní ! (satisfaction) *thanks ! thank you !* or also (maliciously) '*it serves you jolly well right !*'

(9) 'bá àzï kà mï pa kằmì mà tíá, mï 'yɔ èri ní : 'àwànìà mí ní !' *if a man has saved you from a lion, you will say to him :* '*my thanks to you !*'

(10) àwànìa mínï ɛɳâ 'ì-zɔ̌-rì ! (after meal) *thank you for the polenta prepared/offered* (host) !

yámà 'dɔ̀ lɛ̂ ! (joy) *welcome !* or *good luck !* (e.g. greeting a friend after long absence, &c.)

drà kátsì ! mï ɛ'dɛ́ kátsì ! *it was right that he died !* ... *that you fell !*

là or la (to call attention) *you there !* ...

(11) mvá là ! é fɛ̀ mà adrì 'dánï ! *boy ! let it be !* or *stop it !*

(12) mvá la ! mằ dï 'yɛ ŋgɔ́nï yà ! *my boy ! what can I do here ?*

(13) Cf. à'do mà èndzà ɔga èinï emú kɔ́kɔ̌rö nï yà ! *what special kind of laziness is it that prevented them from coming !* (angry exclamation)

553. Greeting formulas :

(A) é zi mï tsítsí (yɔ̀) ! (B) é zì mï ɛ̀ndì ! *hail to you ! hail to you too !* mï adrì 'dɛ́lɛ́ tsïò ! mï adrì ɛ̀ndìo ! *how are you at home ! and how at your's !*

Taking leave : á mừ dï ïï yà ! é mừ dï ïï ! *may I go ! all right, go !*

(A) mï atsí ŋgà dí ïyïò ! *are you going, then !* (B) mằ dï atsí 'dɔ̀ ! *yes, I am leaving !*

In the morning : (A) àŋgɔ̀ óú mï drìá 'dìa ! or àŋgɔ̀ àtï mï drìá 'dìa ! or mï èfɔ̀ 'dìa ! *has it dawned for you ! you have come out of the hut !*

(B) ɛ̀ɛ, óú rá ! or ɛ̀ɛ, ma èfɔ̀ 'dɔ̀ ! *it has ! yes, I came out here !*

é rï ŋgà dí vàá 'dɛ́ ; mằ ŋgà fɔ̀ àmvɛ́ ! *do be seated ; I am going outside* ... or *I am leaving*

N.B. Except for the first set of phrases above, on the whole the Logbara have no fixed ones for greetings.

APPENDIX

554. Some of the items in the body of this Grammar have been treated either in their mere essentials only or in a rather perfunctory manner. In this Appendix, therefore, they are discussed in greater detail and summarized.

I. Nï: Its Various Forms and Uses

555. Nï is the particle met with most frequently in Logbara sentences; there is hardly a sentence of any length in which no **nï** is found.

These **nǐ**'s are not all identical, either *morphologically* or *grammatically*.

556. *Morphologically.* (*a*) As far as spelling and pronunciation goes, they appear to be identical; but

(*b*) they differ in regard to the inherent tone: there is:
    (i) the low-toned **nǐ**,
    (ii) the raised mid-toned **nï** (or **ní**), and
    (iii) the high-toned **nǐ**.

(*c*) In one special case, the last **nǐ** (iii) requires a low tone to precede it, and is thus quite distinct from the rest.

557. *Grammatically.* As to grammatical function, four quite distinct categories of **nï** must be distinguished, viz.:
    (*a*) The *asserting* **nǐ**, with low tone (= the Acooli **àyέ**).
    (*b*) The *possessive-reflexive* **nǐ**, requiring a low tone before it.
    (*c*) The *dative* high-toned **nǐ**.
    (*d*) The *emphasizing* **nï**, which has a variety of uses.

558. (1) The *asserting* **nǐ** (cf. § 546)—note its low tone—serves to stress lightly a particular assertion or part of it, perhaps in contrast to a possible or real doubt. It is placed at the end of a sentence, or before the interrogative **yà.** It is analogous with Acooli **àyέ.** It corresponds roughly to, say '*it is so-and-so who . . .*' or '*somebody did do . . .*'. It may generally be so translated, but often vocal stress is sufficient. Examples:

    (1) **ágú àzǐ-nǐ 'yɔ nǐ** *somebody did say it* (the first **nǐ** simply stresses)
    (2) **ɔlí-nǐ ŋga nǐ** *it is the wind blowing*
    (3) **má átíl mba mà tàa nǐ** *it was my father* (who) *protected me*
    (4) **à'dï ŋɔ̀ nǐ yà?** *who* (was it who) *broke it ?*
    (5) **ŋaakú ŋga mâ rúá-nï-á nǐ, á mu ɔdzì-rï-á** *dust settled on me* (lit. *my body*), *therefore I went to take a bath*
    (6) **ɔtsέ ɔ́ó nǐ** *it 's a dog barking* (i.e. *nothing else is happening*)

559. (2) The *possessive-reflexive* **nǐ**, which requires a *low tone* on a preceding syllable (cf. §§ 111, 114 f., 230 ff., 511 (*a*)). This is a special form in Logbara. It expresses possession or a particular relationship or connexion with the object of this postposition. Translation: *of*; *for*; *because of*; *on account of . . .*; *as for . . . part*, &c. Examples:

    (7) **'bà ɛmvɔ̀ átápǐ nǐ** *he went into* (or *put on*) *mourning for his father*
    (8) **èì ɛró e'dí àɳâ** (or **áɳû** or **mâ**) **nǐ** *they are making a granary for corn* (or *simsim, for me,* &c.)
    (9) **ɔ́ɔdrá 'dǐ mâ-nǐ-rǐ'ï** (**àɔɔkɔ́ sǐ**); **é ko dzà!** *this bamboo is mine* (said in anger); *leave it alone !*
    (10) **àfa mǐ-nï ɔ̀gǔ 'bá àzǐ nǐ-rǐ** *what you have stolen is somebody else's*
    (11) **ma bɔ̌rà ɔlɛ έdrɔ̀ nǐ** *I am buying a cat because of the mice*

(12) mvá 'dìrï Karlo pì nǐ Margarita bɛ *this child is Charles's and Margaret's*

560. (3) The *dative case* postposition nǐ (cf. §§ 114 f., 194, 241, 511 (b)) *to, for.* Nǐ can generally be interchanged with drí, véllé (§ 114).

This postposition is, logically, connected with certain verbs, such as fɛ̀ *to give*; lǒ, 'yɔ *tell*; ɔmvi, ɔ̀gɔ̀ *to answer; return something to*; ɔgá *to refuse to*, &c.

(13) ɔ̀kó awa ɛ́ɲá 'bá vàá 'dɨï nǐ *the woman distributed polenta to the people present*

(14) é fɛ̀ ɛ̀ri nǐ àfa rá ! *give him the* (or *some-*) *thing !*

(15) é 'yɔ mvá 'dà nǐ, mà mvi àkúa ! *tell that boy to go home !*

(16) má ágúi, mǐ atri má nǐ ǹdrí 'dɨï mà drì 'dɨ̀ *my friend, do turn back to me the goats* (going off there) *!*

(17) ɛ̀ri ɛ'yɔ́-nǐ lǒ 'í átíi nǐ *he tells/reports the matter to his father*

(18) mǐ ɔmvi má nǐ à'ɨ̀táa-nǐ kö à'do sǐ yà? *why do you not give me an answer ?*

(19) ɔ̀gà ɛ̀ri nǐ mòɛ̀mbɛ̀ ɔ́ɔ̀kɔ́ sǐ *he refused him mangoes out of spite*

561. (4) The *stressing* nǐ. This nǐ is—in origin—essentially an emphasizing particle. But during the course of time it seems to have developed to some extent, i.e. it has taken on certain special grammatical functions in some cases. In these cases it is, of course, no longer optional but compulsory.

Modern Logbara distinguishes the following usages of this nǐ:

562. (1) The *third person singular reference suffix* meaning: *his, her, its* (cf. § 185); the corresponding term for plural is ɛ̀ɨ. Examples:

(20) é 'bɨ ŋgà àdzí-nǐ kö *you have not yet tried its taste, not yet tasted it.*

(21) 'dɛ vúti-nǐ sǐ *he fell in after him,* i.e. *he followed him*

(22) é 'bà drì-nǐ-á ! *put it* (*him . . .*) *on it* (*him . . .*) *! or put it on his head !*

(23) ɛ̀tɔ́ɔ ɔsɔ́ milɛ́-nǐ nǐ (cf. § 558) *the hare did lead him astray* (fable)

(24) 'bá pá-nǐ-nǐ (§ 563) 'ɨ 'bà-zǒ kílílí kö 'dɨ̀, ɛ̀ɨ ɔmvɛ ɔ̀tó'dóá *a person whose foot does not go down properly* (on walking) *is called a cripple*

(25) é sö 'alé-nǐ-á ! *fix it into it !*

(26) ásí-nǐ ɛ̀rì 'yɛ tsulutsulu 'dǐnï *he* (his mind) *is excited/upset*

(27) éwá kérɛ ɛ̀ri zú 'bá-nǐ (§ 563) éwá 'bà-zǒ 'alé-nǐ-á-rɨ̀ *a beer calabash is a calabash in which people put beer*

563. (2) A nǐ with (quasi-)fixed syntactic function appears in two cases:

(A) As *subject indicator* added to a noun (or pronoun) subject in sentences of CIA; after plural nouns nǐ is replaced by ɛ̀ɨ (cf. §§ 337 ff. 263 . . .).

(a) In ordinary CIA sentences present or future indicative. Examples:

(28) mvá-nǐ gû-gu or ... n̄drí ətsɛ̂ *the boy laughs ... herds goats*

(29) mà drì-nǐ gâga *my head aches/I have a headache*

(30) əzɔ́ɔ́-nǐ vǐvi *the rain comes storm-driven*

(31) ə̀kó-nǐ (pl. ə̀kó-èi) ɛŋâ 'i *the woman (women) prepares polenta*

(32) 'bá èi rö̃ 'dǐ'di à'dí sǐ *people kill each other in war*

(33) ɛ́zó-andzi èi əŋgɔ̃ tö *the girls are dancing*

(34) à'dï-nï pätî ga tò-tò-tò 'délé nǐ yà? *who is cutting wood there—tak...?* (i.e. noise of wood being chopped)

564. (b) In sentences with *nominal predicate*, the copula being implied but not expressed; a *noun* or *pronoun*, used as *subject complement*, normally takes **nï** after it (cf. § 305). If, in similar sentences, the subject is a noun and the predicate an adjective or interrogative pronoun, **nï** is also added after the noun-subject, as a rule. Examples:

(35) ágú 'dàrï ópí (-mvá)-nï *that man is a chief (-'s son)*

(36) ágú 'dà mà ádríi-nï ópí-nï *that man's brother is a chief*

(37) òtákà èri aya-nï yə *a pot is not* (made) *of iron*

(38) é kènì: ŋgó-nï yà? *what, do you say, is the matter ?*
    á kènì: ŋgó-nï yə *I reply; nothing* (has happened)

(39) dzó 'dǐ mà 'íi-nï à'dï 'ï yà? *who is the owner of this hut ?*

(40) àfa 'dǐ mà rú-nï à'do-nï yà? *what is the name of this thing or what is this thing called ?*

(41) mï ŋgà òmú-nï *you are still* (only) *a guest.*

565. (c) In *relative clauses* (cf. § 263). Examples:

(42) mvá té mï-nǐ mu nè-lé 'dàrï ò̀lè-nï èri etsandǐ nǐ/ò̀lè fï rúá-nï-á nǐ *that child whom you went to see, a spell is afflicting him* (he is under a spell)

(43) àfa àma-nï ɛdrí-zǒ-rǐ à'do nï yà? *what is it we live on ?*

(44) mu tí 'ǐ ásí-nï lè̀-rǐ amá (= ɛ̀pɛ̀) *he went to chose the cow he likes*

566. (d) *Adjectival suffixes* -rǐ (cf. § 134) and -rö (cf. § 139) are often replaceable by **nï** (cf. above, example 37). **Nï** in these cases has both a syntactic and its own emphasizing function: the latter first, the former as a sequel.

(45) é mvu tò̀rò̀lò̀-nï (= -rö) yà? *have you had a good drink* (i.e. *are you drunk*)?

567. (B) **Nï** as a *mere stressing particle*. For the purpose of emphasis **nï** may be found after any part of a sentence.

(a) **Nï** very frequently occurs after a noun-object.

(46) 'bǎ ma ádríi nï àŋgò̀ 'dǐ mà ópíˀrö *they set up my brother as chief of this country* (*district*)

(47) ə̀pé èri àrǐïä nï áséa *the guinea fowl is a bird of the veldt*

(48) drà ŋgà kö, èri ává nï̀ ndzɛ *he is not yet dead, he is breathing*

(49) mà li màákò àmbó⁻rö, ɔ́drə nï̀ mà ndzɛ pírípírí àmvɛ́ ! *make big heaps of potatoes, and have all the ɔdrə (weed) (roots) removed !*

(50) é mu záā 'dà mà ádríi nï̀ əmvɛ ! *go and call the brother of that girl !*

(51) à'batà ɔbé ètɔ́ə nï̀ dzi (-zǒ) 'ï véllé *the duck tempted the hare to take him to his village* (fable)

(52) mï̀ à'dï̀ nï̀ ndǎ yà ? má má águi nï̀ ndǎ *whom do you seek ? ... I am looking for my friend*

(53) ə̀ndì zá nï̀ ṇírïṇírï *she picked off small pieces of meat*

(54) mvá 'dïrï ɛ̀ndzì(t)áā bɛ, èri-nï̀ (§ 565) 'ï átíi nï̀ ɛ̀ndzï-rï̀ sï̀ *this boy is respectful, as he reveres his father*

(55) nɛ̀ ètɔ́ə-nï̀ bï̀ 'du oru *he saw the hare, he caught and lifted it up*

(56) ètɔ́ə-nï̀ mu ə̀'dó nï̀ 'du rá *the hare went and lifted the leopard* (fable)

568. (b) After attributive adjectives, as:

(57) ə̀kó 'dà lɛ̀ 'ïmà mvá wɛrɛ-rï̀ nï̀ tɔ̀ nï̀ (§ 571) *that woman loves with preference her small child (. . . loves her small child best)*

569. (c) After demonstrative adjectives it should be noted that **nï̀** in this case is placed between the demonstrative itself and its adjectival suffix.

(58) ópí àŋgò̀ 'dï̀ nï̀ rï̀ à'dï̀ 'ï yà ? *who is the chief of this country here ?*

(59) mï̀ edzí má nï̀ Lógbàrà ti á'bii nï̀-rï̀ 'ï ! *bring/i.e. teach me the (real) Logbara language of the ancestors !*

570. (d) After verbs.

(60) èri ɔ́nâ na, 'yɛ́ ɛtsɔ́ nï̀ gbï̀-zǒ kö *he dodges cleverly, (so that) an arrow cannot hit him*

(61) òtùnìá drì nï̀ (§ 562) 'bá nì nï̀ kö *the blind snake—its head one cannot distinguish* (whether head or tail)

(62) 'bá àvò̀(rö)rï̀ ɛtsɔ́ nï̀ àzî ŋga-zǒ kö *a sick man cannot (do) work*

(63) àmbô ŋga nï̀ mu mḯ nï̀ sìlíŋgì fɛ̀(dɛ) kö *the Big man will not give you a shilling*

571. (e) After adverbs.

(64) kànì əzɔ̀ɔ̀ 'di ò̀'bíti nï̀, ɔ́ṇa-nï̀ (§ 563) ŋga ànï̀ ə̀ndré nï̀ *if it rains in the morning, termites will swarm in the evening*

(65) àzi àndrò̀ nï̀ yə, əzɔ̀ɔ́ tsï̀ *today there is no work because it is raining*

(66) 'bá 'wàrà 'dï̀ï ádï̀ ndzɛ tɔ̀ nï̀ nï̀ (§ 558) *it is chiefly old men who remove a spell (they have cast on a person)*

(67) kànì 'bá àzí-nï (§ 563) símítérì-á 'dálé nï èfǒ rá, àma
əmvε èfǒ tálí sì *if somebody from the cemetery there were to
rise, we would say (call it) (he rose by) a miracle*
(68) má emú kö nï kö, má emú rá *I shall not not come, I shall come*

II. –rï

572. -rï as a suffix is found in three different forms in Logbara:

(A) -rí with high tone, is a pronominal locative suffix.
(B) -rï-á, a verbal suffix, corresponding, more or less, to *-ing* forms.
(C) -rì, the commonest of all, with low or low-intermediate tone, is the
relative-adjectival particle.

A. -Rí (see §§ 237–240)

573. -Rí, with high tone, is a pronominal-locative suffix, meaning
to . . ., at . . ., from . . . the home (village, place, site, country) of . . .
-rí was probably originally, and fundamentally still is, a noun, which
reduced, now functions as a suffix; the noun èrî or rî *court-yard*, would
seem to fit this theory.

Surprisingly, in this case, -rí stands for both (*a*) the equivalent of a full
noun (village, place, home = rî), and (*b*) the postpositional suffix -á—
the principal suffix of place, which, though one would expect it here, is
actually never found.

574. This suffix -rí, joined to a noun or pronoun, may stand for any
case, direct or indirect (postpositional), in a sentence.

After the term with -rí, or with the other postpositions (drí, vǒ, vélé,
cf. § 238, *note*), or in place of them, the adverbial term àkú-á *at . . . home*,
may be added at will, especially for the purpose of emphasis or clarity.
Thus má (or àma)-rí or má-rí àkúá or má vǒ (= drí, véllé) (àkúa)
all mean *to, at, from my (our) home . . .*, &c. Examples:

(69) àma-rí 'dálé mǒké, ègbè bε *(at) our home (it) is pleasant and
cool*
(70) mu àmbó-rí, lè èi-rí kö *he went to the Big man's, he does not
like his home*
(71) àlì èi-rí 'dálé tsí *the colobus monkey is found in their country*
(72) é fè àfa 'dìrì dzi 'bǎ (cf. § 659) 'bá 'dà-rí! *give (get) this thing
and take it to that man's village!*
(73) mǎ dí mu àkúá (or má-rí = má-drí = má véllé . . .)
goodbye, I am now going home!
(74) ŋa éŋá ádzê 'ï ándrii-rï *he ate polenta at his mother's yesterday*
(75) èi emú 'bá àzí-rí *they come from somebody's village*
(76) á mu rǒ laa mí águi-rí *I went to sleep/pass night/at your friend's*

B. -Rï-á —*ing* (cf. § 436)

575. (1) -rïá is essentially the same as -rí; the difference lies in the syntactic function which usage—apparently arbitrarily—has allotted to each of them. Thus:

-rí is suffixed to a noun or pronoun, and is the equivalent of *at the home (place, &c.) of* . . . (cf. § 573);

-rïá is suffixed to a verb (infinitive); meaning: *while . . . being . . . or doing* . . . Examples:

(77) 'bá mu àzí ndǎ ópí-rí *a man went to the chief's in search of work*
(78) 'bá mu àzí ndà-rïá *a man went out looking for work*
(79) ɛŋgá ɔŋgɔ̀ tö-rïá *they came from dancing*

576. (2) -rïá is suffixed immediately to the verb of a CIA sentence or phrase, which means that the direct object, if any, precedes the verb, &c. Before -rïá, however, the characteristic *tonic additions* to the verb are omitted.

(80) é li mî drí à'dò li-rïá yà? *you have cut your hand in cutting what ?*
á li mâ drí pätî li-rïá *I cut my hand/finger while cutting wood*

577. (3) *Notes.* (*a*) If the conjunction -ző is required, it is joined immediately to the verb and -rïá follows.

(81) bǐ èri àzî ŋga-ző-rïá *they caught him to do work*

(*b*) If the sentence has more than one verb (auxiliary or other), the suffix is generally added to each of them.

(82) má ágíí, ɔva, á nè èdríká 'dǎ mà-nï ádzê mu-rïá pätî ga-rïá áiséa *my friend, gazelle, I saw mushrooms there, when I went to cut wood in the bush yesterday* (fable)

(*c*) -rïá may be followed by the negative particle kö, but not by any modifying particle such as 'bɔ, rá, dɛ, &c., since -rïá already modifies the verb in its own way.

578. (4) -rïá modifies a verb in the following way: in a sentence or phrase, concluded by -rïá:

(*a*) it indicates a protracted or continuing activity or state, i.e. an activity or state in progress—not a single act—is described;

(*b*) it commonly implies or includes both the idea of locality and time in connexion with activity or state expressed by the verb.

(83) mu ámvú 'à-rïá *he went to engage in field cultivation*
(84) nè ètóɔ-nï mu-rïá dɔɔrïá *he observed the hare going out hunting*

579. (5) *Uses* of the -rïá form.

As with so many constructions in Logbara, this form also allows of a wide range of application. It is a convenient method of expressing a number of everyday locutions, as will appear from the following. The -rïá form is used in two different ways:

(A) In *phrases*, when the **-rǐá** form of a verb *does the work* of:
  (*a*) a *verbal noun* with the value of an infinitive or participle; or
  (*b*) a *verbal adjective*.
(B) In *sentences*, when **-rǐá** does the work of a conjunction.

580. (1) In phrases the *verb* **-rǐá** does the work of a *verbal noun*, i.e.:

(*a*) Of a *noun-infinitive* or of a *gerund*, whichever one may prefer to call it.

(85) mvá 'dǐrï ɛmbá-rǐá ɛ̀ri ɛ̀wá⸋rö *teaching this boy is difficult*
(86) éwá 'dǐrï mvu-rǐá ɛ̀ri ɛ̀wá⸋rö, dra tǒ *to drink this beer is difficult, because it is very/too sour*
(87) wárágà 'dǐrï sǐ-rǐá ɛ̀ri ɛ̀wá⸋rö *to write this letter is difficult*
(88) ǐí 'dǐrï mvu-rǐá (= -zàrö) ɛ̀ri ɔ̀ndzí; ǐí 'dǐrï bɔ̀ŋgɔ́ ɔ̀dzì-zǒ mǒké *this water is bad for drinking; for washing clothes it is all right*

581. (*b*) Of a *gerundial* or *qualifying infinitive* in the sense of 'purpose'.

(89) à mu àrǐã ndà-rǐá *we were going to look for birds*
(90) àmà dǐ mu ɳaakâ ɳaa-rǐá! *let us go to get food!*
(91) kànì drù 'bá mu àzíá, àma emú mǐ ɛmbá-rá (or -rǐá) *tomorrow when people go to work, we shall come to teach you*
(92) mvá kènì: ''ǐ mu àɳá okú-rǐá 'dálé kö'; àyǐià kènì: 'é mu àɳá okú-rǐá kö; ɳaa-rǐá mǐ 'yɛ̀ mu ŋgɔ́lé yà?' *a boy says: 'he would not go out to weed the corn'; the mother says: 'you will not go to weed the corn! where will you go to eat?'*

582. (*c*) Of *verbal-participial adjectives*.

(93) má té ɔvö rùá ɔ̀dzì-rǐá *I have been taking a bath*
(94) bǐ ɛ̀ri àzî ŋga-rǐá rá *they caught him while he was at work*
(95) gbǐ ɔ̀kó éní sǐ ɔ́ɳa tɛ̀-rǐá; ŋga dǐ drà rá *he shot (with arrow) the woman by night while tending termites, and she died*
(96) mvá 'dǐrï apá-rǐá òrì ɔzɔ́ɔ́ kö *the boy, fleeing, was not afraid of rain*

583. (2) In sentences introduced/concluded by **-rǐá**, the CIA rules apply with the exception, as mentioned above, of the characteristic tonic changes to the verb before **-rǐá**. The **-rǐá** clause may be a subordinate noun clause, adjective clause, or adverbial clause. The particle **kö**, relating to the main sentence, as well as other particles, are commonly placed after the subordinate, separated from the main clause.

(97) à nɛ̀ té ɛ̀i-nï mààkò edzí-rǐá kö *we did not see them bringing potatoes*
(98) mání mu-rǐá ófísiá ò'bíti sǐ (= bɛ), ma tsái mvu 'ǐ ká *when I go to the office in the morning, I will first drink tea*
(99) 'bá 'dǐ mǔ tsa pàrí ándrâ ɛ̀tɔ́ɔ-nï drǐkâ ndzɛ-zǒ-rǐá *he went and came to the place where the hare had once pulled up mushrooms*

(100) **mǐnǐ té ɛ'dâ g̣ba-rǐá** . . . *while you were taking a picture*
(*photo*) . . .

(101) **mǐnǐ ŋg̣à ma ətǐ-rǐá, é mvu ŋg̣à dǐ éwá nǐ!** *while you are*
tying me, do drink (some) *beer !*

(102) **'bá 'dǐǐ-nǐ ŋg̣á 'à-rǐá** . . . *while these people were tilling the*
field . . .

(103) **èmǐ emví, èmǐ-nǐ ávâ li-zŏ-rǐá rǐ sǐ, rá yà!** (greeting :)
'*have you come back from* (*your*) *leave* (*rest*) *!*'

C. -Rǐ as an Adjectival or Relative Particle

1. Adjectives; Verbal Derivatives; Relative Clauses

584. Adjectives take the suffix -**rǐ** (cf. § 133) when used attributively.
 „   „   -**rö** (cf. § 139)   „   predicatively.
pätǐ èzŏö-rǐ *a tall tree*; **pätǐ èzŏö̀-rö** *the tree is tall*
From any suitable verb a corresponding adjective may be formed.

585. A *verb* becomes an *adjective* either by adding, i.e. suffixing:
(*a*) the particle -**zà** (-**zàrǐ**, &c., cf. §§ 147, 433), see below; or (*b*) the
relative phrase or form ᷇(**rö**) **pi-rǐ** (cf. §§ 257, 434).

586. The *relative phrase* is the most common form of a phrase met
with in Logbara; it is based on a CIA sentence. The relative phrase is
a subordinate *relative clause* qualifying some noun (see § 257; notice the
rules for tones).
-**nǐ** sometimes replaces -**rǐ** or -**rö** for purposes of emphasis.
'**ǐ** is frequently added after -**rǐ** and -**rö**, for light stressing.

587. An attributive adjective may also be expressed by means of a
reduplicated verb:
'bá drǎ-drà *a dead* (or also *dying*) *person*
àfa aká-aká (= **aká-zà, aká-pi-rǐ**) *something soft*

588. Words like *cook, judge, labourer* or *workman, liar, teacher,*
thatcher, &c., may be grouped as (verbal-) *noun agents.* Logbara seldom
has a corresponding simple single term for such words; it is rendered by
a *relative phrase* (cf. § 434).
Single words for noun agents are very few—e.g. **òg̣úó** *thief,* **àtǐ'bó**
slave, servant.

589. The relative phrase or clause may serve as, i.e. do the work of,
an adjective or a noun.

(104) **'bá 'bá ɛmbá-pi-rǐ** *one/a person teaching people*, i.e. *a teacher*
This phrase, through frequent use in modern life, has become abbrevi-
ated to **ɛmbápi** simply. This kind of development is bound to happen,
by analogy, to phrases of a similar type (i.e. for noun-agents), in the course
of time.

(105) 'bá· dzó drì 'bă-pi-rì *person who thatches a hut's roof* (i.e. *a thatcher*)

(106) ámí èri pätí eŋgá-pi ìí tiá *amï is a tree that grows* (*growing*) *on the banks of rivers*

(107) mvu éwá mŋgbï, atsépi nï yɔ *he drank the beer empty, without leaving a drop*

(108) lí-röpi 'dì èi tra 'bà sàndúkùá *what remains over they gather in a box*

(109) èi 'bá atsífè-ndrípirì zi *they consult* (èi . . . zì) *the stick-rubbing soothsayer*

(110) èrì 'bá a'ú àgáí tèpïrì'ï *she is the guardian* (*waits beside*) (*of*) *the fowls*

2. The Relative Clause

590. Subordinate clauses occur frequently in Logbara; the commonest of these is the *adjectival clause*. They are generally *relative clauses*. As the practice of shortening relative clauses by 'understanding' or 'implying' (but not expressing) the antecedent is unknown in Logbara, the relative clause remains an *adjective clause*.

591. *Noun clause.* For the reason just given noun clauses are very rare. Sentences of the following type are more frequent:

(111) á 'bà ásí, Múŋgù-nì mu má eká rá *I trust* (*that*) *God will help me*

592. *Adjective clause.* The adjective clause is added immediately after the noun it qualifies, so that any further qualifiers of the same noun, together with the rest of the main clause, will come after. If the phrase or clause qualifies a noun in the genitive (*nomen rectum* or possessor), the possessed (*nomen regens*) with mà will thus be separated from the genitive by the intervening adjective clause or phrase.

(112) dzó—ŋaaká a'dí-zŏ-rì—mà rú kǎú = dzó—'bá-nï éŋâ 'i-zŏrì—'bá ɔmve kǎú (or kǎú) *a hut for cooking is called a kitchen;* = *the hut in which they prepare the polenta is called* kǎú/*kitchen*

(113) àŋgŏ anó bɛ—ŋaakánî kazŏ 'anîá kö-rì *soil with* anó *weeds* —*in which grain does not grow*

(114) 'bá mu zǎä, 'bá-nï lě dzɛ rì, mà átíi vŏ *people go to the father of the girl whom they are about to marry*

(115) màákò, ndrâ sá drìɔ-rì, èrì fí ná àká *the potatoes which they planted some time ago, are all growing big*

(116) bádá: dzó 'bánî laa-zŏ-rì, àtsí kóků-rö (edó nï àtsí 'alénîá kö; kà àtsí drï rá, èi 'bǎ àdzíkò drìá) 'bada' *is a hut in which people sleep* (only), *without fire* (i.e. *fire is*

not lighted in; if (in some place) *fire burns in it, they may put potsherds on it—for minor cooking/roastings*)

(117) bɔ̀ŋgɔ́ òku, mï̈-nï̈ sǔ, mà miléfï̈ ndó lit. *the old clothes'—which you have on—appearance/sight is peculiar/strange* (= *the old clothes you have on look peculiar*)

(118) àzí, manï̂ ŋga-lé 'dǐ, mà 'aléa mǎ mu ànï̈ séntè ɛsú sí yà? *for the work* (àzí mà 'aléa) *I am doing here, how much money shall I get?*

(119) àfa mï̂ ti 'aléa-rǐ lè fò rá tsí yà? *have you anything to say?* (lit. *a thing in your mouth which wants to come out, is there?*)

(120) màakò, 'bǎ avö àtsǐá-rǐ, ɛ̀ri nɔ̌ 'dǐ *the potatoes which they put on the fire for stewing are whirling about*

(121) 'bâ múpi édzá əko-rï̈-á-rǐ, ɛmví 'bə *the people (women) who went out to gather wood-fuel, have already come back*

(122) mǎrí, mïnï̂ 'du ágú 'dà vǒ rǐ, mï̈ ɔ̀fè è'yɛrɛ'yɛrɛ; kànì 'dǐ mï̈ ɔ̀fè dɛ 'bə: é pì dǐ mǎrí mà ti 'bə *the loan which you have taken from that man, you return slowly* (in instalments); *when you have returned it all: you will have thus paid off the debt*

593. *Adverbial clauses.* This category has been treated under the different conjunctions (cf. §§ 447 ff.). These clauses, like the others, separate one part of the main clause from the other, as it is placed in where it logically fits. As in:

(123) àfa atsépi áŋ̩ûba 'aléa-rǐ, èinï̈ éwá zərï̈-á 'bə-rǐ, èì əmvɛ éwá-sɔ́rɔ́ *what* (the thing that) *remains back in the strainer, after straining beer, they call beer dregs*

(124) . . . té mánǐ laa rö (-zǒ) vàárǐlé . . . *when I was lying on the ground*

3. Adjectives -rǐ/-'dǐ, 'dǐ̈

594. The adjective and the relative pronoun have the same basic suffix -rǐ pl. 'dǐ (like the Acooli prefix mà-). -rǐ (like mà-) indicates a word, phrase, or clause qualifying a noun.

This -rǐ (like mà-) is added to stress the adjectival relationship that exists between the terms; -rǐ (as has already been noted) is placed at the end of a phrase, whether it be an adjective, a noun, or any other part of speech. Example:

má véllé dzɔ́ or dzɔ́ má véllé (= ɔ̀ət mɛɛrâ) *my hut/house/room*; but stressed dzɔ́ má véllé-rǐ or má véllé dzɔ́-rǐ (=ɔ̀ət mà mɛɛrâ)

595. In certain contexts the noun of such adjectival phrases may be missing, and the adjective then acts as an adjectival substantive—a noun.

(125) má véllé dzɔ́-rǐ əvö nï̈ àmbó²rö kìlé má ádríí véllé-rǐ'ï̈ kö *my hut is not as large as my brother's*

(126) mï e'dú mŏkɛ́ 'dàrï'ï kö à'do sǐ yà? *why did you not take the good* (ones) *there* (say *fruits* ...)?

(127) mǐ edzí drì-lɛ́-rǐ (or ndú-lɛ́-rǐ)! *bring me the upper* (or *lower*) *one!*

(128) 'bá-nǐ 'yə 'dínǐ-rǐ'ï *people talk like this*

(129) ágú dzó-á-rǐ mà èfö àmvɛ́! *the man in the hut may come out!*

(130) mǐ vɛ́llɛ́ dzóa ɛ́dzá 'dǐpi yà? *is the wood/fuel in your hut like this?*

(131) mvá mâ ŋgókóa 'dǐ mà átíi-nï ə̀ndzí lit. *the baby-on-my-back's father is bad,* i.e. *the father of the baby on my back is bad*

(132) Pápá 'du o'dú àmbó òku-drìə àzǐ 'dǐi rá *the Pope has removed/suppressed* ('du) *some* (àzǐ) *feast days* (o'dú àmbó) *of former times* (òku-drìə)

N.B. Here four adjectives are combined (without conjunctions) and the adjective suffix 'dǐi at the end; rá is a concluding particle.

III. The -zà Form of Verbal Adjectives

596. Adjectives formed from a verb by simply suffixing -zà are very frequent in Logbara; they express the state of a thing arrived at or to be arrived at. The attributive -rǐ is added according to general rule.

597. As soon as some other noun or part of speech imparts purpose to the verb, the particle -zà is replaced by the postposition -zǒ (cf. §§ 481 ff.).

bə̀ŋgó ə̀dzì-zà *washed clothes,* or *clothes to be washed*

but ǐi bə̀ŋgó ə̀dzì zǒ *water to wash* (*for washing*) *clothes*

598. The -zà adjective (cf. § 152) can readily be converted into and used as a relative phrase, as will appear from the examples below.

If the state arrived at is (considered to be) the result of development, the past participial particle 'bə may be added (or not) after the *verb* + *pi* of the relative phrase.

599. Verbal adjectives formed from *neutral* or *intransitive* verbs generally correspond to past participles (active); at times a present participle fits better.

A neuter verb indicates the state or condition of a subject, as: **aká** *to be soft,* **drà** *to die,* **'dɛ** *to fall,* **ŋgù** *to smell,* **ɛló** *to be inclined,* **dèɛ** *to be old,* **maa** *to rot,* **əndzu** = **o'ï** *to be lean, meagre.*

(133) ɲ̀áá tí drà-zà (= drăpi ('bə)-rǐ) *they ate a dead cow/ox*

(134) á nè pätí ɛ'dɛ́-zà (= ɛ'dɛ́pi 'bə)-rǐ áséa *I saw a fallen tree in the bush*

(135) á lè àfa ŋgù-zà-rǐ kö *I do not like anything stinking*

(136) si dzɔ́ àŋgö ɛló-zà-rǐ-á or si dzɔ́ àŋgö̀ ɛló-rö-pi ɛló (ɛló) rǐ mà 'aléa *he built his hut on a slope*

(137) dzɔ́ (or 'bá, &c.) dèɛ-zà (= dèɛ́pi rá)-rǐ *an old hut* (*man,* &c.)

(138) é mu bə̀ŋgɔ́ bì-zà (= bĭpi bìbì)-rǐ ə̀dzǐ ïá! *go and wash the dirty cloth in the river!*

but cf. má ɛsú ə̀'dó o'dû kə-rï-á *I have found a sleeping leopard*

(139) é ko dzótílé mà adri òpi-zà-rö! *leave the door* (to be) *closed!*
é ko dzótílé mà adri zi-zà-rö (= mŋgbə̂rö)! *leave the door open!*

N.B. The last examples show verbal adjectives as predicates (. . . -rö !),

600. If the verb be a transitive one, the verbal adjective derived from it corresponds more commonly to the past (seldom present) participle (passive) of classical grammars, indicating an action undergone or (liable) to be undergone. The relative clause/phrase, in this case, does not have -pi rǐ but -lɛ́ rǐ; however this direct object particle lɛ́ is more commonly omitted and a high tone added to the verb in its place.

(140) á gà àfa òɡù-zà-rǐ sǐ = á gà àfa òɡùlé (= òɡŭ) òɡù-rǐ sǐ *I object to/refuse stolen things*

(141) ma à'ǐ àfa ɔlɛ-zà (= ɔlɛlɛ́ ɔlɛ)-rǐ'ï *I agree to/prefer purchased things*

(142) èi tí li-zà (= lilɛ́ = lí)-rǐ mà zá ɔlɛ *they buy the meat of a slaughtered cow*

(143) dzi pätí ga-zà (= galɛ́ = gá)-rǐ àkúa ɔlɛ-zà-rö (= ɔlɛ-ɔlɛ) *he brought/took the wood he had cut home for buying (selling)/to be bought (sold)*

(144) mu pätí ndǎ gaa-zà-rö (or gâga) *he went in search of wood for cutting (to be cut)*

(145) àɲáfǒrá amvi-zà (= amvilɛ́ 'bə = ạmví)-rǐ èri ënîkènǐ-rö *reground flour is fine*

(146) àfa 'dǐǐ àdrə̀-zà-rö (= àdrə̀lɛ́ àdrə̀-rǐ) *these things are heaped up*

(147) andzi láá rö dzóa àdrə̀-zàrö/ə̀drə̀ dzóa *the boys are lying in the hut on top of one another*

(148) gĕrì ala-zà-rǐ/alá-ala-rǐ *a cross-way*

(149) sí pè-zà (= pèlɛ́ = pèɛ́-rǐ) sì èri tò̀ *the extracted teeth-gap suits him very well*

(150) ámvú 'àzà (= 'àlɛ́ = 'ǎ)-rǐ 'dínï 'dǐlɛ́-rǐ à'dï drí yà? *whose is the field tilled in the (bad) manner like this? = whose is this badly-tilled field?*

(151) 'ǐ ádríi-nï ə̀kó əmvi-zà nna bɛ *his brother has three inherited wives*

(152) kàrtásì ozí-zà (= ozílɛ́)-rǐ yə *there is no paper for sale*

(153) ɛ'yɔ́ àma-nï 'yə-zàrö (= 'yəlɛ́rǐ) mï bɛ yə *I have nothing to discuss with thee, lit. there is no question to discuss between us*

(154) àfà ɲaa-zà mǐ vǒ tsǐ yà? *have you anything to eat?*

(155) é ɲaa àfà ɲáá-rǐ 'bə yà? *have you had food already?*

(156) mǐ edzí 'ǐ nǐ ïï/ɛ́wâ mvuzàrǐ/mvulɛ́rǐ! *bring him water/beer to drink!*

(157) zá maazà-rö ; mvá əndzuzàrǐ *the meat is rotten; a thin child*
(158) Òmbǎ zíi-nǐ záà dzɛ-zà nǐ/= dzɛlérǐ *Omba's daughter is a marriageable girl*
cf. drə tí záà dzɛ-zǒ *he drove cows for* (the purpose of) *marrying a girl*
(159) əŋgǒ tö-zà (= tölérǐ = tǒrǐ) va ma rá *dancing enchants me*

601. The same verb may, in certain circumstances, be transitive or intransitive, according to whether a **-zà** phrase or a relative one is used, as the following instances show.

(160) pätí èdrè-zà = èdrě-pirǐ *an erect growing/standing tree*
cf. pätí zɔ̌zɔ̀/zɔ̀ èzɔ̂-rö *the tree grew tall*
(161) pätí èdrè-zà/= èdrè-lérǐ *an upright* (set), *a fixed pole*
cf. èdrě èri rá *they have raised it up*

IV. –rö The Predicative Suffix of Complement

602. -rö, preceded by a low tone, is a predicative suffix, denoting the subject—or, more commonly, object—complement. See §§ 139 ff.
This -rö suffix plays an important part in Logbara.
A *noun* with the suffix -rö serves to indicate (*a*) destination, purpose; (*b*) effect, result; (*c*) a quality.

603. (1) -rö indicating destination, purpose, as in:

(162) mǐ èfè má nǐ silíŋgì òdû-(= gbándzá˅)rö! *lend me a shilling* (on credit)!
(163) ma pätí 'dɔ̀ sǐ ògara sǐ ɛdzá˅rö *I am chopping this wood with an axe for fuel*
(164) edzí má nǐ àɲáfǒrá ɛ́wá (or ɛ́ɲá)˅rö *she brought me flour for beer* (or *polenta*)
(165) á mu áséa ɛdzá òɲɔ̀ àtsí˅rö *I went into the bush to get fuel for fire*
(166) èì ɛ́ndzɔ̂ ga báká˅rö *they cut endzə sticks for* (their) *fibre*
(167) mǐ 'dǐ 'yɛ ɛ'yó˅rö yà? *for what purpose do you do this?*
mǐ 'dǐ 'yɛ ɛdɛ ma (tá-)rá˅rö yà? *do you do this to fool me?*

604. (2) -rö indicating a result intended or reached.

(168) ma àɲâ 'i fǒfǒrá˅rö *I am grinding corn into flour*
(169) èì lésû tsə bòotá˅rö *they churn milk for* (to obtain) *butter*
(170) ɛdrɔ́-nǐ ólè lǒ 'í drí gìrǐkɔ̀-rö, sí sǐ *the mouse cuts out a gallery for itself as a path, with its teeth*
(171) èì pätî sö ɛ́sɛ́˅rö, àríã ɔ̀'bà-zǒ *they spread glue on a tree, to catch birds*
(172) èì òtsɛsíĩa əfà ósú˅rö *they dress otsɛsíĩa sticks to make a bow*
(173) kànì ópí drà rá, èì vínĩ èrìmà mvá 'bǎ ópí˅rö *when a chief has died, they set up* (again) *his son to be chief*

605. (3) -rö also serves to express a quality possessed. In this case -rö may normally be replaced by the postposition bɛ.

(174) águ 'dìrï ɛ̀ndzɔ̀-rö/= ɛ̀ndzɔ̀ bɛ *this fellow is lying or tells lies = is a liar*

(175) àŋgɔ̀ 'dìrï àɲá˙rö/= àɲá ɛbɛ ; àɲá 'a 'a-nï-á tɔ̀ (ámvú˙rö) *this soil is fertile* i.e. *corn grows very well in it* (as in fields)

(176) mvá 'dàrï 'bá òmbà-rö nï/= òmbà bɛ *that boy is quarrelsome*

(177) ɛɲatà-rö èi nì li *for (obtaining) poison they cut up* nì *snakes*

(178) èi ɛ̀dzɛ̀lɛ̀kó˙rö ɛ̀bàrïɔ̀ mà ɔ'yɔ̂ vo *as a whistle they blow a bushbuck's horn*

(179) mï edzí àfa 'dì ozí-ozí kö, mï edzî 'yɛ à'dò-rö yà? *you did not bring this thing for sale, then you brought it to do what (for what purpose)?*

V. Impersonal Constructions: Auxiliary Nouns

606. (1) In everyday speech the use of an 'impersonal construction' is fairly frequently met with in Logbara; it does not, however, correspond to the impersonal 'it' with verbs. Its use is as follows:

(*a*) Where the subject of an action is either unknown or immaterial, as in some more or less explanatory statement, the verb + object is used to render the English indefinite pronoun and passive constructions. Examples:

(180) mvá 'dàrï ɔ́ɔ́ à'do sì yà? *why does that child cry?*
      tsɔ́ ɛ̀ri rá *they have beaten him/he has been beaten by somebody*

607. (*b*) Intimations, orders, or regulations of an impersonal or formal nature are frequently expressed simply by putting the hortative mà before the verb, with the meaning: *one ought* or *must* or *let one* or *it is necessary that*. . . . The context makes it quite clear to whom the order is addressed.

(181) mà ga pätí nna rá! *let three pieces of wood be cut!*

(182) mà rï 'a'á dzóa! *let one* (or people present) *sit down in the hut!*

(183) gìrì 'dìrï lúrúa, 'bá mà atsí ànï àlö-àlö! *the path is narrow, one has* (it is necessary) *to walk singly* (in single file) *on it!*

(184) 'bá mà kɔ 'bá mà àzà tsí! *may one have pity on a man!*

(185) mà (or é) 'du àfa 'déɛpi vàá-rì! = 'bá mà 'du àfa! *take* (pick) *up the thing that fell to the ground!*

(186) mà ɔkonà ɔ́drɔ ŋɔ́lɔ̂-rö, mà dzi èi àmvé! *have the ɔ́drɔ weeds collected together in heaps and moved away!*

608. (2) Phrases, in English, with the impersonal 'it' have no analogous impersonal constructions in Logbara. In this case (as in many others as shown below) the Logbara make use of an appropriate noun-subject (or object) which acts as a kind of *auxiliary noun*.

Thus, speaking of weather the words **àŋgǒ** *earth, world,* **ǝvï** *lightning,* **ǝzǒó** *rain,* are of common occurrence.

(187) **àŋgǒ óú rá** *it has dawned*
(188) **àŋgǒ bìbì, ... ègbɛ̀-rö, ... ndrìndrì** (= **drìdrï**) *it is ... dark, cold, warm*
(189) **àndrò àŋgǒ ètsì-rö, ... dùmù** *today it is cloudy, ... sultry*
(190) **àŋgǒ ǝzà-rì gárí sì** *it is lit up by the rainbow*
(191) **ǝvï** (or **àtsí**) **'ì àŋgǒ** *it is lightning* (lit. *the lightning/fire has flashed/lit up*)
(192) **àŋgǒ-nï lì nì** lit. *the world rolls* ⎫
  ǝvï fì nì lit. *the lightning exploded* ⎬ *it is thundering*
  ǝzǒó-nì nǝ nì lit. *the rain rumbles* ⎭
(193) **ǝvï sǒ** (or **tsǝ, ɡba, asi**) **àŋgö** *lightning has struck* (the earth)
(194) **ǝzǒó-nï lì-lï, ... 'dì'di** *it is drizzling, ... raining*
(195) **ǝzǒó àtì 'bǝ** *rain has ceased/it has stopped raining*
(196) **ǝzǒó ŋga** (or **èsǒ, etsá**) **(vínï) 'bǝ** *it has started raining* (again)
(197) **ǝzǒó-nì 'yɛ èsǒ ... rá** *it will rain*
(198) **lùurú 'dɛ 'dì** *it is foggy/misty* (lit. *fog has fallen*)
(199) **àŋgǒ mà milé ëni꞊rö, ǝzǒó-nì 'yè 'di nì** *the sky is black, it will rain*
  àŋgǒ milé ǝzǒó꞊rö ; á mu kö *it looks rainy; I will, therefore, not go*

VI. The Auxiliary Nouns in Logbara

609. There are a considerable number of common, simple verbs in English to which no similarly simple verbs correspond in Logbara. In many of these cases Logbara renders the English verb by a quite distinct concept: a combination of verb and special *auxiliary noun*.

The particular auxiliary noun required by a verb to render a special meaning, takes the place either of a 'formal' subject, or a direct or post-positional object, according to the Logbara conception in each case. The real subject or object of the sentence is connected with the formal one by the genitive construction. Thus the English sentence: 'a child (boy or girl) guards the field (against birds, &c.)', is rendered in Logbara by:

(200) **mvá èri ámvú (mà) àgǎí tɛ̌** i.e. lit. *a boy waits the field's side* (*beside the field/a boy stands by the side of the field*)

The direct object **ámvú** *field* is added in the genitive case (with following **mà,** which is often missing) to the formal object **àgǎí** *side.*

(201) (*a*) **mǎ drì/= ma tàbì/àvì ɛ'yó rá** or (*b*) **ɛ'yó àvì mǎ drì-á rá** (*c*) **ɛ'yó àvì má nì rá** *I have forgotten the matter ... my head lost the matter/went lost in my head* (lit. *the question was lost to me*)

Instead of 'I' the Logbara says 'my head'; and **drì** functions either as a *formal* subject or as a postpositional object (**drìá** *in the head*) and 'I' appears as possessive pronoun 'my' = **ma**; or . . . 'lost to me' **má nì**. The *main auxiliary nouns* are singled out and illustrated.

A. *Drì* head (cf. above, example 201)

610. (*a*) drì asi, atri or $\left\{\begin{array}{l}\text{dà, èdà}\\\text{gò, ègò}\\\text{pà, èpà}\end{array}\right\}$ -zǒ *to return, to go back, to come back*

    (202) **mu 'dálé rá, atri** (= **èdà**) **(drì) mbèlè** *he went there but came back soon*

    (203) **èrì mu drì èdà rá** *he will come back* (lit. *withdraw his head*)

611. (*b*) **'bá drì (DO) ɛtsí zǒ**, vt. *to delay, detain, put somebody off* . . .

    (204) **mǐ mà̀ drì ɛtsí-ɛtsí à'do sǐ yà?** *why are you detaining me ?* **ma ɛtsí mǐ drì 'dé kö** *I have not delayed you*

612. (*c*) **drì (DO) fu-zǒ 'bá bɛ**, vt. *to meet* (with) *somebody*

    (205) **à fu ádzê drì Bàzílìo bɛ dràá** *yesterday I* (*we !*) *met* (*with*) *Bazilio at a funeral*

    (206) **à fu té drì á'dǐá bɛ rá** *I met* (*with*) *so-and-so a moment ago*

    (207) **drùsǐ àmà mu drì fu èri bɛ rá** *I shall meet him tomorrow*

    (208) **á lè mǐ** (or **'bá àzǐ**) **bɛ drì fu kö** *I do not want to meet you* (*anybody*)

    (209) **kànì è fu drì 'bá àzǐ bɛ, mǐ zi èrimà ti-á 'mǐ mu ŋgó yà?'** **'mà̀ mu àkúa'** *if you meet somebody you say to him 'where are you going ?' 'I am going home'*

613. (*d*) **fu drì** (? related to the former) = **tsa** *to be fit, appropriate, qualified, suitable; to be up to standard/requirement/perfect* . . .

    (210) **é ŋgö fu drì tsǐ** *you are really/quite fat = you are well-fed*

    (211) **é kà sǐ mǐ'ǐ fu drì** (= **tsa**) **rá** *if you write it yourself, it is correct*

614. (*e*) **'bâ drì (DO) tsɛ (ɛtsé)**, vt. *to go ahead, guide, lead*

    (212) **é tsɛ drì (mǐ'ǐ) !** *do lead/go ahead yourself !*

    (213) **é fè á tsɛ drì má'ǐ !** *let me go ahead !*

    (214) **á tsɛ ndrâ drì má'ǐ kö** *I never led before/I did not lead that time*

    (215) **èri andzi mà drì tsɛ** *he leads the boys*

    (216) **mà̀ 'yè mu mǐ nǐ drì tsɛ má'ǐ** = **mà̀ 'ye drì tsɛ mǐ nǐ má'ǐ !** *I myself will lead you on !*

    (217) **má emú èri-nǐ mà̀ drì ɛtsé-lé-rǐ sǐ** *I came under his guidance*

615. (*f*) **'bá mà drì (DO) li-zǒ**, vt. *to go to meet* (lit. *to cut one's head*)

    (218) **mu 'ǐ átǐí mà drì li** (= **tɛ̌**) *he went to meet his father*

(219) ɔpὲ andzi 'wàrà mú drì-nǐ li (= tě) *he sent big children to go to meet him*

(220) kămì-nï ma ɔdrɔ̂ nǐ, li mằ drì lǐli *a lion has driven me to flight, he barred (cut) my way/met me*

616. (g) ὲndzɔ̀ li (or ɛ'yɔ̂ tra = ɔdrɔ̂) 'bâ driá, vt. *to slander, calumniate a person* (lit. *to cut lies on somebody*)

(221) mï ὲndzɔ̀ li (or mï ɛ'yɔ̂ tra or mï ɔdrɔ̂) mằ drì-á tɔ̀ɔkɔ́ *you are slandering me wantonly (mischievously)*

617. (h) drì (DO: refl.) sì-zɔ́ = ti ɛmbɛ *to control one's feelings, to keep one's temper; to refrain* . . . (as ɔmbà 'aléa *in quarrelling*)

(222) é sì mǐ drì tsí/= mí ɛmbɛ mǐ ti tsí! *control your feelings!*

618. (i) 'bâ drì ri-zɔ́, vt. *to correct, punish a person*

(223) ὲri mằ drì ri àzî ŋga sǐ *he punished me with (by giving me) work*

619. (j) 'bá mà drì tsa-zɔ́ or 'bá mà bbílé ɔsɔ̀, vt. *to induce, persuade* . . .

(224) á tsa ὲimà drì (= ma ɔsɔ̀ ὲimà bbílé) má'ǐ, mu-zɔ́ dɔɔri-á; lě ńdrâ mu kö *it was I who induced them to go hunting; they did not want to go*

620. (k) 'bâ drì (subj. refl.) tsi (?= sì), vn. *to be unlucky, hard up*

(225) ὲmï drì tsi, i.e. ὲmï tsàandí esú *you were unlucky : met with trouble*

(226) mằ drì tsi dɔɔri-á, ma ɛsú àɲàpá kö *I was unlucky at the hunt, I did not find any game*

621. (l) 'bá drì-á tsí, vn. *to be claimed, demanded by; to be busy, occupied by.*

(227) àzí mằ drì-lía tsí *there is some business claiming (to claim) me : I am busy*

622. (m) drì (DO refl.) sɔ̀-zɔ́, vt. *to fall (or put) into line (one after the other)*

(228) sɔ̌ drì sɔ̀sɔ̀ *they fell into line*

623. (n) (e)tú-zɔ́ 'bâ drì-á, vn. *to take one unawares, surprise, to come upon suddenly*

(229) tu ágú 'dà mà (or etú mà) drì-á rá *he took that man (or me) by surprise*

624. (o) 'bá mà drì (DO) atri, vt. *to prevent, keep back, hinder from*

(230) atri mằ drì ɲaakâ ɲa *he prevented me from eating*

B. *Ti* 'mouth', 'language', 'side',&c., 'opening'

625. (*a*) ásé ... mà ti 'bǎ (= 'dǒ) àtsí sǐ *to light, set fire to grass*, &c.

626. (*b*) àfa mà ti 'bà-zǒ (àfa sǐ) *to cover something (with something).*
(231) 'bǎ éwá mà ti tsí: èi ti-nï 'bǎ àdzíkò sǐ *they cover the beer (-pot) properly,* i.e. *they put a potsherd on its (pot's) opening (mouth)*

627. (*c*) 'bá mà ti ɛtsí àfa mà 'aléa, vt. *to shut somebody in something.*
(232) ɛtsí èbì mà ti arí mà 'aléa; i.e. e'dú kǎriá 'bà drì-nï-á; 'dǒ ti-nï àtsí sǐ, vɛ arí ɛbɛ rá *he shut the spider in a drum;* i.e. *he turned a roof-frame over it; then they set fire to it, and burned it (spider) together with the drum*

628. (*d*) 'bá mà ti ɛri = 'bá mà ti-á ɛ'yó ɛri-zǒ, vt. *to hear, heed, obey somebody's words, orders.*
(233) mï ɛri mǎ ti kö à'do ɛ'yó sǐ? *why did you not heed my words (orders, exhortation,* &c.)*?*
(234) ɛri átïi mà ti (or ti-á ɛ'yó) kö *he does not obey his father*

629. (*e*) 'bá mà ti-á (ò)lǒ-zǒ *to report to; to inform a person; to denounce to*
(235) mu lǒ átïi mà ti-á *he went and informed his father*
(236) ma emú òlǒ mï ti-á wórò *I have come to tell you everything*
(237) ɛ'dá ǵbɛ éyío ní (= éyío mà ti-á) *he showed the eggs to the crocodile*

630. (*f*) ti (or other part of the body) ɔdza vélé (refl.), vt. *to turn round, about* ...
(238) mï ɔdza mï ti véllé! *turn about* (in any sense)*!*

631. (*g*) ɛsú ti (av.) 'bá ... bɛ, vn. *to meet somebody.*
(239) àma ɛsú ti mvá 'dï bɛ *I met (with) the (this) boy*
(240) Èrúvá pi ɛsú ti Éɲáó bɛ *the Eruva flows into (meets !) the Enyao river*
(241) ïi pi ɛsú ti áǵïi bɛ *one river flows into (meets with) another* ('friend')

632. (*h*) 'bá (DO) 'bá àzï mà ti-á (adv.) sö-zǒ, vt. *to accuse, denounce somebody to*
(242) sö mvá 'dïrï àmbó mà ti-á *he accused/denounced the boy to the Big Man*

633. (*i*) 'bá mà ti (DO) pè-zǒ ... vǒ, vt. *to send a person (messenger) to*
(243) à'dï pè mï ti nï yà? *who sent you?*
ópí pè mǎ ti nï *the chief sent me*

(244) kànì emú rá, é pὲ ὲrimà ti má vǒ! *when he comes, send him to me!*

634. (*j*) zi-zǒ 'bá mà ti-á, vt. *to ask (of) a person.*

(245) á zi mǐ ti-á= á zi mǐ vǒ *I ask(ed) you*

(246) zi ma mǐ ti-á *he asked you about me*

(247) emú mà̰ ti-á ɛ'yə̂ zi *he came to ask me about some matter (question)*

(248) é mu águ 'dà mà ti-á ɛ'yə̂ zi! *go to consult (with) that man!*

(249) cf. á lə̀ ɛ'yə́ (= ma azi) mǐ ti-á rá, mà àvǐ mǐ nǐ kö! *I have informed you, do not forget!*

635. (*k*) àfa mà ɛ'yə̂ zi 'bá mà ti-á, vt. *to beg, request, ask somebody for something* (àfa mà ɛ'yə́).

(250) é zi má nǐ ǹdrí mà ɛ'yə́ ópí mà ti-á! *ask (from) the chief (for) a goat for me!*

(251) mu séntὲ ɛ'yə̂ zi 'ǐ átíi mà ti-á bə̀ŋgə́ ɛ'yə́ sǐ *he went to ask (from) his father (for) money for clothes*

(252) é mu má nǐ ɛ̰ηá mà ɛ'yə̂ zi má ándríi mà ti-á! *go and ask polenta for me from my mother! (= go and ask my mother for polenta for me)*

636. (*l*) àró (or àríó or màrí)-ti ə̀fɛ̌ (or əlɛ) or àfa ə̀fɛ̌ (= əlɛ) àfa mà ti-á, vt. *to pay for, pay back; to compensate, restore.*

(253) ma ə̀fὲ àró-ti-nï᷈rö *I have given it (to make) good*

(254) ma 'dǐrï əlɛ ti-nï-á *I am giving/paying this as compensation*

---

(255) mvá tsɛ drì nǐ, 'bá àmbórǐ 'dɛ vúti-nï sǐ *the boy goes ahead, an old man (elder) follows*

(256) mï ɛsú ti àma vǒ à'dò 'yɛ yà? *for what purpose did you meet us?*

(257) ὲri ti-nï ɛ'də̂ 'à drù sǐ *he will start tilling (a field) tomorrow*

Note: Drì and ti are without doubt the most frequent auxiliary nouns in Logbara. Other instances of this kind of noun (synecdoche) are **ásí, bbílé, milé, rùá,** some examples of which are given below; others will be found in the main body of the Vocabulary.

C. Ásí 'spiritual heart' ('seat of emotions', 'affections'), 'spirit', 'mind', 'temper'

637. Ásí is used as a formal subject or direct object (in a reflexive way).

(*a*) ásí-nï yǎyà (or əmbó-əmbó, òtǐ-òtǐ) *to be afraid, anxious; disheartened, discouraged, daunted, &c.*

(258) é tǐ ásí kö! = mǐ ásí òtǐ kö! *(reflexively) do not be afraid!*

638. (*b*) ásǐ tɛ (= bǐ, ὲkpà, ɛmbá), vn./t. *to take courage*

(259) mǐ ɛté ásí tsǐ ! = mǐ ásí mà tɛ tsǐ ! *pluck up your courage !*
mǐ ɛmbá ásí ! é bǐ (= mǐ ɛ̀kpà) ásí tsǐ ! *be a man ! make an effort !*

639. (*c*) ('bá mà) ásí ándzú bɛ = ásí ambï-zà (lit. *cold*) *to be meek, gentle, friendly*.

'bá ásí bba-rǐ (= àmalǐ, ndrǐ-zà-rǐ) *kind, sociable person*
Cf. lɛ̀ àfa 'dàrï lǒ'ǐ or ɛ̀rì àfa 'dǐ mà ává ta—ásí àlö sǐ *he wishes (desires, longs for) the thing—with his whole heart*

640. (*d*) ásí *principle, spirit of life*.
(260) ásí-nǐ ńdrí ɛ̀bǐ-rö rá, i.e. ává-nǐ atsɛ wɛrɛ *he is about to expire*, i.e. *only little breath remains*

D. Bbílé 'ear'

641. Bbílé is used to express physical or non-physical hearing: docility; intelligence.

(*a*) As *subject*:
(261) mǐ bbílé mà ɛri ɛ'yó ɛ̀ndì ! *do hear/heed/obey orders after all !*
(262) mǐ bbílé yɔ (lit. *you have no ears*) *you do not pay attention/ obey orders*
(263) ɛ̀ri (mà) bbílé mba tǒ (lit. *his ear is strong, well-developed*) *he is intelligent, clever, cunning . . .*
(264) mǐ bbílé-nǐ ɛ'yó ɛri tǒ *you hear* (physically or morally) *extremely well; you are very obedient, respectful; or intelligent, cunning*

642. (*b*) In a *reflexive* way:
(265) á 'bà mâ bbílé 'a-nǐ-á kö = á 'bà ásí drì-nǐ-á kö = á fɛ̀ drì (ʔ-nǐ-á) kö *I did not pay attention; I did not fix my ear/mind on it*

(*c*) As *object*:
(266) ɛ̀tà (or ɔ̀sɔ̀) 'bá àzǐ mà bbílé rá *he has incited, seduced someone*, &c.

E. Milé 'eye'; 'outlook' (of weather); 'surface' (of say 'cloth')

643. (*a*) As *subject*:
(267) àŋgǒ milé ɛ̀ri ɛ̀túkà-rö/or ɔzɔ́ɔ̀-rö *there is sunshine* (*it is sunny*)/*it is rainy*
(268) àŋgǒ mà milé ɔ̀ndzí: ɛ̀tú ka kö, ɛ̀ri ɛ́rítiɔ̀rö *the weather is bad: the sun does not shine, it is cloudy*
(269) mà̀ milé-nǐ à'yǎ/= àndzǎ àfa àmbó mǐ-nǐ fɛ̀-lɛ́ 'bá àzǐ

drí 'dǐ sǐ *I feel jealous because of the big thing you gave to another* (not to me)

(270) édró milé mba bɛ ; èri 'bâ drî n̦a : èri tsǐ wɛrɛ, èri àvìàvì vo 'alé-nï-á tsǐ *the mouse is cunning: it gnaws one's hand* (by night) *biting* (it) *just a bit, then it blows/breathes on* (to smooth) *it*

(b) As *direct object*:

(271) èri milê sö àfa àzǐ mà drì-á *he is glancing at something* (lit. *puts his eyes on it*)

(c) In an *adverbial* way:

(272) mà ɛ'dá 'bá àzǐ mà milǐ-á kö! *it may not appear before anybody!*

F. *Rùá* 'body' (of anything)

644. Rùá is probably related to the *reflexive* rö; it is often used in a similar sense. Rùá, shortened form of rùá-á, is much used as postposition: 'on', 'upon'.

(273) ètú drï àmbó-rö, èri mâ rùá vɛ̀vɛ *the sun is very hot, it burns me*

(274) mâ/or mâ rùá-nǐ/ya òrì (éwá) drí kpòkpò *I am trembling from (with) fear (or from beer)*, &c.

Rùá is often used in a postpositional or adverbial sense:

(275) é dà ìǐ èìmà rùá! *sprinkle them with water!*

(276) andralí-nï 'a ásé rùá *dew is* (found) *on grass*

(277) édri ŋgà rùá-nï-á tsǐ *there is still life in him* (his body)

(278) òlè-nï etsandǐ nǐ, i.e. òlè fǐ rùá-nï-á nǐ *magic* (power, a spell) *troubles him*, i.e. (a spell's) *magic entered his body* = *he is under a spell*

(279) é sö àsǒ mà rùá rá *you have accused/denounced me* (lit. *you have put an accusation against me*)

G. ... *mà tà mba* 'to protect', 'guard', 'look after', 'defend'; 'to favour', 'patronize'

645.

(280) é mba èri (or mvá 'dǐ) mà tà! *guard him/her* (this child)!

(281) Àdrɔ̃ mà mba mǐ tà òkpó-nï'ï! *may God keep* (guard) *you well!* (parent to child)

(282) Àdrɔ̃ mà mba mǐ tà, mǐ adri àmà àŋgò-á, àŋgò nè-zó! *may God keep you, to be in our country and see it!*

(283) 'bá ɛ'yó tà mbápi 'ï ásí-á kö *one who does not bear a grudge* (words) (offence, injury ... *in mind and reproach on occasion*)

(284) **P** ... **mba ɛ'yó**/or **ɔ̀mbà mà tà** ('ï) **ásíá kö** *P* ... *did not take note of an* (unpleasant) *question/quarrel*

(285) **mvá ɛ̀ri 'ï átíi mà ɛ'yó tà mba ásí-á tò** *a child keeps father's words well in his mind*

(286) cf. **Àdrɔ̀ mà tsɔ tùsú ɛ̀mï dri-á rá!** *may God bless you* (lit. *may God spit on your heads*)*!*

VII. The Verb

A. *Root of Verbs, and Prefixes*

646. As a general rule verbs are found in their simple, basic form, i.e. as an open (mono-)syllable, consisting of a consonant and a vowel (C+V), as **ba, bɛ, bi, bo, bu,** which are all real verbs. In addition, there are many others, with the same basic spelling, distinguished by peculiarities of sounds and tones (cf. Vocabulary).

647. There are a few exceptions to this rule: such as (*a*) verbs beginning with, and consisting only of a vowel, as **'a, i, 'i, 'ɔ**; (*b*) verbs with more syllables and with a special tone-pattern ˈ ˈ ˋ, as **ɛ'borǎ** *to besmear*, **ɔkonǎ** *to gather*, **epakǎ** *to cause to come back*, **etsandí** *to vex*.

648. One of the prefixes **a-, e (ɛ)-, o (ɔ)-,** is often added to the simple or root-form verb to modify its meaning (cf. § 346). For instance:

(*a*) Many of the root-form or simple verbs indicate an action or movement away from the speaker.

E.g. **mu** *to go* (away); **dzi** *to take* (to somebody or somewhere)

649. (*b*) The prefix **e-** (or **ɛ-**) when added to these verbs indicates an action or movement in the direction of the speaker.

E.g. **emú** *to come*; **edzí** *to bring* (hither).

N.B. This **e-** (and for that matter **a-** and **o-** as well) will take the same tone as the root verb, while the latter, in such cases, may change from mid to high tone.

650. (*c*) The prefix **o-** (or **ɔ-**) is commonly employed to express plurality in the action (may be a plurality of subjects, objects, acts) or even frequency, intensity, or the like.

E.g. **ɔmú** *a mass came on* (to swarm, crowd); **ɔdzí** *to transport* (by repeated journeys, as of grain)

651. (*d*) For the prefix **a-** no rules can be fixed to regulate its use.

(i) Normally **a-** is used in place of **e-** (with the same function) in some parts of the country (Tɛrɛgo, Omögo, Aringa ...). (ii) Otherwise, single verbs with the prefix **a-** have their original etymologic meaning, always connected with the root-verb. This does not mean that one can use this prefix indiscriminately to form other verbs (consult Vocabulary).

652. Illustrating examples. (*a*) With **a-** :

(287) dzɔ́ asǒ rö rá *the hut has collapsed*

(288) mí a'dú ma àfadzǒ 'bà mǎ drìá ! *pick up my basket and put it on my head !*

(289) tsúpà andï (= api, afu) 'ï rá *the bottle went to pieces (was broken to bits) (smashed)* (whereas **ndï, pi, fu** mean simply *split, crack, slightly break*)

(290) wárágà àsǐ (or ə̀sǐ) 'ï rá *the paper was torn into two (or more) pieces*

cf. wárágà ti sǐ rá *the edge of the paper is* (slightly) *rent*

(*b*) For **e-**, a very simple case, the Vocabulary gives many examples.

653. (*c*) With **o-** (or **ə-**) prefixed verbs offer some variety of meaning: they may express (i) intensity :

(291) ɛ'dɔ́ 'ïmà rúá ə̀nɛ̌-ə̀nɛ̀ *he started contemplating himself all over*

(292) kànì 'bá àzǐ-nï lɛ̀ tî li rá, ɛ̀ri ətî báká sǐ ; ɛ̀i dí 'ǐ álɔ́ rúá, ɛ̀rì dí ŋga sɔ̌ àdzú sǐ *if anyone wants to slaughter a cow, he will thoroughly bind it with ropes, then they fasten it to a peg and then he will spear (stab) it*

(293) əzɔ́ɔ́-nǐ ra má vǒ ràra ; mí əsǒ dzɔ́ drì ɔ́'dǐ ! *rain is pouring (trickles/flows) in to me (in hut); push (all over) grass anew into the roof !*

(294) á lɛ̀ adri 'dálé ká, àfa àzǐ-nï ə̀gà dí ma sǐ *I did want to be there, but something occurred to prevent me*

N.B. Also ə̀gà . . . sǐ *to detest, abhor something*

(295) mï ɛ̀ndzə̀ əlí *you are telling me all lies*

cf. é li ti ɛ̀ndzə̀ *you lied*

(ii) Frequency of actions, repetitive action (often related to intensity) :

(296) 'bá ə̀lǒ ɛ́mvó mà ɛ̀tí ésákǎ-rö (i.e. ɛ̀i ésáko mà ndú ə̀lǒ) *they made holes in the bottom of the pot to make it a distiller* (of lye)

(297) ɛ̀ri ò'bu əndzɛ drùdrù *daily he removes jiggers (from his foot)*

(*d*) Plurality in various senses, as mentioned above :

(298) ə̀lí-nï àfa əya *the wind moves things*

(299) ə̀lí ə̀lù àndrò mə̀ɛ́mbɛ̀ wɔ́rɔ́ vàá *the wind today caused all the mangoes to fall to the ground*

(300) ə̀lí ə̀gǒ (= ə̀bìi) kàká wɔ́rɔ́ vàá *the wind has beaten/laid down all the maize*

(301) dzi édzá ò'bǎ dzɔ́ 'aléa *he brought firewood and put it in the hut*

(302) ɛ̀ri mǎ pá ə̀gbǎ *he keeps on beating my leg* (as if drumming)

(303) ɛ̀tɔ́ə əsǒ otsí 'ï pá trɛ́ *the hare* (running) *pricked his foot with many thorns*

(304) èbìyɔ́ mbàmba–nï ə'bǎ *the spider spins its web*

654. Besides plurality, intensity, and frequency, o- prefixed verbs may express the concept of causality, cf. above, examples 299 ff. For example 299 we may say:

ə̀lí drí sǐ mə̀ɛ́mbè ə̀lù wɔ́rɔ́ vàá *through the power of the wind all the mangoes fell to the ground*

Cf. also **mvi** (= ġə̀ə) *to return, i.e. to go back*

emví (=ɛ̀gə̀ə) *to return, i.e. to come back*

ɔmví (= ɔ̀gə̀ə) *to return, i.e. to give back; to answer; also to return* (of many)

or **fï** *to go in*; **efï** *to come in*; **ɔfï** *to go in* (many), *to cause to go in*; **fɔ̀** *to go out*; **ɛ̀fɔ̀** *to come out*; **ɔ̀fɔ̀** *to go out* (many); *to cause to go out*; but **ɛ̀ì tí ɔfɔ́ n̄drí sǐ** *they exchange a cow for goats.*

B. *The Parts of a Sentence and their Relative Positions*

655. The *subject* of a sentence is, as a rule, placed at the beginning. However, mostly for purposes of emphasis, quite frequently the object is placed before the subject, outside the sentence proper, as it were; then, at some convenient place in the sentence, the reference particle **nï** or **ànï** is inserted to refer back to the object if necessary.

(305) àɲá du (= ŋga)-zà ɛ̀ì dzi lȋlï, i.e. ɛ̀ì dzi àɲâ lï 'bílía 'dɔ̌fárá-rö *they bring* (from excessive rain) *germinating corn and* (well moistened) *cover it in a hole* (or *pot*) *preparing leaven*

(306) ma átïì-nï tǐpi-rǐ 'bá ɛ̀ì ɔmvɛ á'bí *he who begot my father, they call him/(he) is called grandfather*

656. The case of a *double subject* is interesting: one part with **pi** is placed at the beginning, while the other part with **bɛ** is placed at the end of the sentence (cf. § 443):

(307) ɛ̀tɔ́ə pǐ mu ɔ́ɲa tɛ̌ Émvúléti bɛ *the Hare with Emvuleti* (his wife) *went to tend* (and collect) *termites*

657. As a rule, if a sentence contains more than one type of object, the *indirect* or *dative* object is placed before the *direct* or *accusative* object. A *postpositional* object is placed after other objects or towards the end of the sentence; the same is generally true of other modifications.

658. Examples:

(308) é mu má nï (= drí) mvá 'dàrǐ tsə ! *go and beat that boy for me!*

(309) é nɛ̀ má nï kàbìlə̀ ɛ̀ndì ! *look for a sheep for me also!*

(310) mǐ e'dú má nǐ émvó mà mu ànǐ ǐǐ ɛ̀bɛ̀ (= ɛkɔ) mvu-zà-rö!
pick up the pot for me so that I may go with it to fetch water for drinking!

(311) mǐ ɛ̀bɛ̀ 'ǐ drǐ tárà ɔ̀do pâ ŋgókóa! *pour kerosene on his foot!*

(312) é mu má nǐ àfa a'ǐ àfa drí (= vǒ) 'dà! *go to ask something for me from so-and-so there! (go and ask someone over there something for me)*

(313) àma mǐ ɛmbâ Lógbàrà ti sǐ *we are teaching you* (the) *Logbara* (language)

(314) 'bá ɛ̀l ɛ'bó sǐ ámvú 'ǎ *they till the field with a hoe*

N.B. ɛ'bó sǐ is commonly placed after 'à; it is stressed here.

The position of the *verb* and the *direct object* are determined by the rules of CIA or CCA respectively (see § 333).

C. *Multiplicity of Verbs*

659. It is quite a common feature of Logbara speech to find in one and the same sentence two or more verbs, apparently of equal rank, following each other without any connecting particle.

(1) Usually the sense could be expressed just as clearly by one of the verbs only. This excess of verbs, therefore, appears to be mere pleonasm. On the other hand, the multiplicity of verbs serves as a rhetorical device, giving a more vivid or dramatic picture of the action. The DO is sometimes placed between the verbs. Examples:

(315) é mǔ dzi 'bǎ èvǒ 'dǐ dzóa 'dálé! *take this basket to that hut/room!* (lit. *go take and place this basket . . .!*) mu and 'bà could be dropped)

(316) èi 'dǔ dzi éwá ɔ'bǎ mònà ɛbɛ ɛ̀róa, èi ti-nǐ ɔ'bǎ à'bǒà bbí sǐ *they put a pot of beer in the granary and covered it with banana leaves* (lit. *they lifted, took, and placed . . .*)

(317) mǐ àvù mu ma àfa e'dǔ! *(stoop, go and) take up my thing!* (*pick up . . .*)

(318) á mu àfa 'dǐ trǒ 'ǐ oru 'ǐ yà? *ought I to (go, remove, and) hang up this thing?*

(319) kàni é 'du 'bá àzí 'bɛ vàá, mǐ 'bá mba-zà nǐ: mǐ 'bá ɔkpó ɛbɛ-rǐ'ǐ *if you* (catch and) *throw a man to the ground* (wrestling), (that means) *you are a strong man indeed*

660. (2) In many cases this accumulation of verbs is actually an accumulation of shortened sentences or complementary phrases.

(320) mǐ e'dú ɛ́ɲá edzí 'bâ ɲaa 'ǐ! *take polenta to the people to eat!*

(321) èi 'bǎ lésú kǒkò *they let* (lit. *placed*) *milk* (to) *coagulate*

(322) ma éréká bǐ tri mâ rúá *I* (take and) *rub ochre on my body*

(323) 'du ɛ̀rì 'bɛ vàá àfú-á sǐ *he* (took and) *threw him to the ground in wrestling*

(324) èi 'bá bǐ sɛ Árúwá *they seized and took (dragged) a man to Arua* (prison)

cf. mǐ èbǐ ɛsɛ èri 'dɔ́lɛ́! (catch and) *draw him near* (here)!

(325) ɔbǐ tí drɔ wɔ́rɔ́ *they* (caught and) *drove all the cattle away*

(326) é tǔ mu àŋá 'bǐ'bǐ-rö èndǐ kóyeá! *mount, go, and collect corn in its cobs* (from granary) *with the basket!*

(327) mǐ edzí 'bǎ pǎrí-nǐá! *return it to its place (take and place* ...)!

(328) ɔlǐ-nǐ ŋgà 'du èri ɛré rö vàá pǐǐrǐ *the wind will* (rise and) *carry it* (paper) *all off and disperse it anyhow (blow it all over the place)*

(329) é dzi má nǐ tíbǐ drǐ àtsíá! *take the savoury and put it on the fire for me!*

661. (3) Two verbs of identical meaning are frequently used side by side in the same way, although one of them would be quite sufficient—pure pleonasm.

(330) mǎ drì dza àvǐ (or àvǐ dza) rá *I have forgotten it*

D. *Auxiliary Verbs*

662. (1) We met with auxiliary verbs, such as **mu, emú, 'yɛ, ŋga**, when speaking of the future tense (§ 365).

Verbs treated under 'multiplicity of verbs' may, at least in part, be considered under this heading also.

What are here called *auxiliary verbs* are all verbs which also function as main verbs, semantically and syntactically.

663. (2) Besides the above-mentioned there are a few others which occur with some frequency as auxiliary verbs, as:

fè (or èfè), vt. *to give*; aux. v. *to give leave to* ..., *to cause to* ...

ko (seldom used alone), *to leave, let*; *to give leave to* ...

'bà vt. *to put*; aux. v. *to leave, to place* ... *and allow to develop* ...

ɛ'dɔ́ (rarely used alone), *to begin, start,* ... —*ing*

ɛ'bí (apparently not found alone), *to come from* ...

664. Examples:

(331) é fè mà adri dáanï! *let him be alone!*

(332) mǐ èfè á 'bì éwá 'dǐrï! kà 'bì dǐ rá, èrì dǐ 'yɔ: 'éwá 'dǐ alu-alu' *allow me to taste this beer! after/when he has tasted it, he will say: this beer is fine*

(333) é fè á li mǐ nǐ zá! *let me cut meat for you!*

(334) é ko mà ɔvö (= adri)! ɛ'yɔ́ yɔ! *let it/him be! never mind!*

(335) é 'bà ko 'dé, é mu ndɔ̀! (put and) *leave it there, and go* (then)!

(336) é 'bà ɔ́ŋɔ́fǐ vǐvï (= zɔ̌)! *let the fingernails grow!*

(337) é 'bà té mǎ drì ɛtsí (= ga) sǐ drìɔ? *have you been trying to vex me?*

(338) òmú àzǐ-nï ɛ'bí ɛŋgá Gùlúa ; èri àmvé 'dǐ *a guest has come from Gulu; he is outside here*

(339) ábélésó èri ɛ'bí èfö̀ 'bá 'aléa 'délé *an intestinal worm comes out of a man's bowels*

(340) kànì mï ɛ'bí tí drɔ-rï-á 'dálé, mǐ ŋga emú má vö̌ ! *when you come from driving the cattle out, you will come to me!*

(341) ɛ'bí ndrâ 'ǐ ndzɛ 'dó 'ǐ, asi ɛmví 'dólé kö: i.e. 'ǐ-nï èri drɔ-zö̌ rá rǐ'ǐ *he tried to steal away from here, so that he might come back no more*: (that is why) *he drove him away*

(342) kànì é 'à ámvú rá, ásé 'dàrï ɛ'dô maa pǐ̈rí àlö *when you have tilled the field, the* (collected) *grass* (from it) *starts rotting all together*

665. (3) dri kɔ, drì tsɛ *to set out* (on one's way or journey).

(343) ɛ'dó ŋgà drì kɔ kö = ɛ'dó ŋgà muu kö *he has not yet started on his way* (drì is here an auxiliary noun)

666. (4) The auxiliary verbs 'yɛ *to do*, ɛ'bí (= apa), and sometimes lè *to like, want*, are often employed to express the idea of 'to be about to', 'to be on the point of. ...'

(344) ma ɛsú mvá ɛ'bí drà sǐ *I found a child about to die*

(345) á 'yɛ má tǐ (= sɔ) sǐ rá ; 'yɛ 'ï tǐ sǐ rá *I was on the point of committing suicide; he was about to commit suicide*

(346) á 'yɛ ndrâ wárágà sǐ mǐ vö̌ *I was about to write a letter to you* (á sǐ kö *but I did not write*)

(347) á 'yɛ ndrâ mu èmï véllé 'dálé, má âô dǐ mu kö *I was once about to come to you, but in the end I refrained from going*

(348) lè té 'yɛ emú rá, àzó ɔ̀gà dǐ sǐ *he had* (it) *in mind to come, but illness prevented* (him)

(349) 'yɛ té mu ɔ̀dzǐ rö rá, sáwà li (= ɔkɔ, dɛ rö) rá *he thought about taking/he was about to take a bath but the time had passed*

(350) ágú 'yɛ té mu Árúwá áánï, âô dǐ mú ko yé *a man was apparently about to go to Arua* (a moment ago), *but in the end he remained*

(351) á lè té èmï ɔtré ndondondo kö ! *I should like you not to make such a noise!*

(352) á mu té/ndrâ rɔ̀ (= 'dɔ̀) 'bɔ tê dǐ ma ɔvö àzó⸌rö *I should have gone by now, but I was sick*

E. *Notes on Some Special Tenses and Moods: Té*

667. (1) Té (in Tɛrɛgo, &c. = tá) is a frequently occurring particle or adverb of time indicating the near past (within the day); it is placed *after* the *verb* of the sentence (cf. § 383). Examples:

(353) á mu té 'bɔ *I have already been* (gone) *there*

(354) á mu té ráa 'bə, ma èɡɔ̀ rɔ̀ vɛ́llɛ́, ma ɛsú èri kö: èri-nï
emú-zŏ-rï̀ ɛsú dè á mu 'bə (emú má vɛ́llɛ́) *I went
earlier but came back again, as I did not find him: when he
came along, he found I had gone* (*he arrived in my absence*)

668. (2) Té (tá), placed *before the verb* of the sentence, is often found
in 'hypothetic' sentences, i.e. in sentences expressing an unreal
condition or supposition, as of an act, maybe, planned but never effected
(cf. § 471).

(355) kànì té ma mí'ï̀, ma té mvi àkúa *if I were you, I should have
gone home*
(356) ma té mu sòfòría əlɛ-rḯá 'àá (say Árúwá) *I thought about
going over there* (say, to Arua) *to buy a metal pot*

669. (3) Té in the construction S–té–DO–V–'ï ká! meaning: . . .*wish
. . . had . . .! . . . should have . . .!*
A sentence of this type expresses 'a desire which was entertained but
not satisfied'.

(357) ma té 'dɔ̀ ï̀ mvu 'ï ká! *I should have liked to drink water now!*
(358) mḯ té fɛ̀ má nḯ mï̈ 'ï ká! *I wish you had given me* (some)*!*
(359) ma té tábà sɛ'ï ká; mḯ èfɛ̀ má nḯ bɛ! *I should have liked to
smoke! would* (= bɛ?) *you not give me* (some)? *i.e. won't
you give me something to smoke?*
(360) mḯ té má nḯ fúnò edzí tsḯ ká! àbírḯ-nï̈ mà̀ fù̀-fu *you ought
to have brought me groundnuts! I am hungry*
(361) ma té 'dɔ̀ (= rɔ̀) éwâ mvu 'ï ká, kɔ̀ré-nï̈ fu ma káï̀ *I would
have drunk beer a moment ago, I had a great longing for it/was
very thirsty*

670. (4) Té (tsɛ́, lŏ) in the construction: S–V–tsɛ́–DO–ká àsï̀à
(CCA) meaning: something like *why! how! surely!*
A sentence of this type expresses a rhetorical question and at the same
time a reasoned affirmation about an event of the past which seems to
be in apparent contradiction to a later or present situation or proceeding.
Examples:

(362) é 'yə tsɛ́ ɛ'yó 'dï̀rï̈ mŏkɛ́ ká àsï̀à!? *how!? you have already
said this correctly!*
(363) é mu tsé 'dálé rá ká àsï̀à?! ɛ'yó ŋɡɔ̀ ɔ̀gà mḯ nï̈ drì atri-zŏ
nï̈ yà? ma ɔ̀rà ɛ'yó tḯ mu-zŏ 'dálé *why! you have been
there before! what hinders you from going back* (again)? *I am
musing in vain on the matter of going there*
(364) é ŋɡà tsé ɛ'yó 'dï̀ 'yə rá ká àsï̀a? à'do ɔ̀mbɛ̀ mï̈ ti ɛ'yó 'dï̀
'yə-zŏ nï̈ yà? *why! you've already happened to pronounce
yourself on the matter* (given your opinion)! *what prevents
you* (your tongue) *now from speaking out?*
(365) é ŋɡà té ɔ̀lŏ drìə kö àsï̀a! *why did you not say so before!*

(366) é sǐ lǒ wárágà rá ká àsǐa?! ŋga àvǐ ŋgɔ́ ŋgɔ́-nǐ rö yà?
why! you have written it already! how was it forgotten ?

(367) èmï òvù tsírí à'do sǐ yà?! è nè ma ká àsǐa! *why are you
dumbfounded* (as though surprised)? *you have, to be sure,
seen me before !*

N.B. Tentatively: té, near past (within day), tsé, indefinite past.

F. *Special Verbal Constructions*

671. (1) The verb, as a part of speech, is very simple in Logbara, at
least, as far as conjugation (tenses and moods) goes, but the verb as part
of a sentence, i.e. in its syntactic association with other words, is a different
matter. It is this kind of varied association with other verbs which is also
responsible for a variety of meanings and important idiomatic expressions:
and this in itself presents considerable difficulties. Phrases of this kind
are not easy to analyse or to translate with exactness.

(2) Another important matter is the construction of verbs or sentences
which, in Logbara, is sometimes very different from our own. For instance, we would say 'to sacrifice a sheep to the ancestral spirits', while
the Logbara says 'to sacrifice the spirits with a sheep' (corresponding to
our 'to propitiate the spirits by means of a sacrifice . . .').
It is for the purpose of guidance in this matter that the following verbal
expressions and constructions have been set down. Other similar ones
will be found in the Vocabulary.

672. (3) Aó (or awǐ) . . . ko; or àó (= awǐ) . . . ko yé. Here there are
two verbs of almost identical meaning. Aó or awǐ means, etymologically,
'to continue', 'persist in a state' . . . ko corresponds to 'to let be', 'to leave
alone'. Both verbs can be used singly with their original meaning. The
combination àó . . . ko (yé) means (a) *to stay behind* (somewhere), (b) *to
fail* or *omit to do . . ., to continue leaving . . . a thing* (or *position*) *unchanged.*

673. The two verbs used singly:

(368) awǐ èi véllé àkúalé àzɔ́⸜rö *he stayed behind at home sick*

(369) mvá rï awǐ ŋgòá yà? (rï *to continue*) *where did the child
stay so long?*

(370) éwá-nï àó tálá-nï-á (fïfí-á) kírrikírri (èrï èdú⸜rö) *the beer
(rather thick) clogged* (in) *it* (the tube for drinking beer)
firmly

(371) éwá atsε (= ko rö, li rö) 'dálé tsí *beer was left behind there*
but éwá ko (= li) rö 'dálé kö *beer did not remain back there*

674. Tonic characteristics: àó, when immediately followed by ko,
adds a mid tone to its high tone (thus: àǒ ko . . .). But if ko is placed
farther back in the sentence, and is in its turn preceded by a verb, this
latter has to take a high tone in addition to its lower one (as before the
relative pi).

(372) áó (also a'á) 'áá 'dálɛ́ ko yɛ́ or aô ko 'áá 'dálɛ́ *he stayed behind there*

(373) áó láá rö ko 'áá 'dálɛ́ *he remained there to sleep*

(374) má áó tɛ́ màákò ŋ̣áá ko yɛ́ *I omitted to eat potatoes a moment ago*

(375) awɨ̌ emú sàbítì sɨ̌ ko yɛ́ *he failed to come on Sunday*

(376) é ŋga àzí té-rɨ̀ rá yà? á ŋga ko yɛ́ or má áó ŋgaá ko yɛ́ (àvɨ̌ má nɨ́ rá) *have you done the work referred to? I did not work* or *I omitted to work (I forgot it)*

(377) é lǒ àma ti-á mvá àzí-nï bɛ: mɨ́ 'yɔ kènì: àma ɔ̀lǒ ɛ'yɔ́ 'dɨ̌ pɨ̈rɨ́; - àma áó ɛ'yɔ́ àzí-rɨ̀ lǒ ko yɛ́ *you told me and another boy; you said, we ought to tell everything; viz. but now we omitted to tell some words/thing* . . .

(378) áó ɛza àlö-rɨ̀ ɔ̀lǒ ko yɛ́, má áó nï lǒ ko yɛ́—áó àvɨ̌ mà drì rá *he omitted to confess a sin, I failed to tell—I forgot*

(379) ma awɨ̌ etsá 'dɔəlɛ̀ ko = ma áô ko 'áá 'dáalɛ́ *I missed coming here = I continued to stay over there*

(380) áó 'yɔ̌ ko yɛ́ sc. lǒ 'bá àzí-nï mà ti-á kö/nɔ̀sɨ̌ drì-nï-á àvɨ̌ rá *he omitted to tell/he told nobody/he probably forgot*

675. (4) drì (èdrì) . . . nɨ́ (e)dzi/(ɛ̀)fɛ̀ *to send, transmit.* In the above, as in this case, we have another instance of 'multiplicity of verbs'.

(381) má ándrɨ́í èdrì má nɨ́ àŋ̣áfőrá, ɛ̀fɛ̌ 'bá àzí drí rá *my mother sent me flour, delivering it to* (by means of) *somebody* or *my mother sent me flour via somebody else*

(382) é drì mà mvɨ́í nɨ́ àfà dzi 'dálɛ́! *send something to* (take to) *my son there!*

676. (5) àfa sɨ̌ ndɛ 'bá sɨ́ or ndɛ 'bá àfa sɨ̌ sɨ́ *something is denied to* . . . (Ac. kɛŋ). This verb is generally rendered by an impersonal construction. What is denied is expressed with the postposition **sɨ̌**, and the DO expresses the person to whom it is denied.

(383) ŋ̣áaká 'dɨ̌ sɨ̌ ndɛ àma sɨ́ *food is being denied to us*

(384) ndɛ mvá 'dɨ̀rɨ̈ ŋ̣áaká sɨ̌ sɨ́ *the child was denied food*

(385) ɛ́ŋ̣á mɨ̌ nɨ́ kö yà?—ndɛ má ŋ̣áaká sɨ̌ sɨ́ (əmvɛ ma kö, ŋ̣aa a'dúlɛ) *is there no polenta for you?—he* (or *it was) denied to me food* (he did not call me, he ate alone)

(386) ɛ̀rì mu mà ndɛ ŋ̣áaká sɨ̌ sɨ́ *he will refuse me food* (contrary to the laws of hospitality)

677. (6) The verb 'to be full' (and kindred terms) is given in what we might call an upset order, thus: the Logbara turns 'a vessel is full of water' into 'water is full in the vessel'.

(387) ɨ̌ ga ɛmvó-á (or ɛmvó sɨ̌) tré or ɛmvó-á ɨ̌ ga tré or ɛmvó ɨ̌ bɛ tré lit. *water is filling up in the pot* or Engl. *the pot is full of water*

(388) tí lítsɔ́-á (= lítsɔ́ sɪ̀) tré = tí ga lítsɔ́-á (= lítsɔ́ sɪ̀) tré
or lítɔ́á tí tré = lítsɔ́ tí bɛ tré lit. *cattle are filling in the byre;* Engl. *the byre is full of cattle*

(389) ìi ɛ̀ri tsúpà mà 'aléa ágâ dù-á *water in the bottle is half-full*
cf. é 'bà ɛ́ɳá ágâ dù-á ! *put the polenta in the middle* (of people)!

(390) ìi ɛ̀ri tsúpà mà 'aléa ágá vǒ sɪ̀, atsɛ wɛrɛ ɛ̀ri-nǐ ga-zɔ́ *the bottle is almost full of water, there remains little that it be full (to fill)*

(391) ìi ɛ̀ri tsúpà mà ɛ̀tí-á ɛ̀lɛ̀ *there is only a little water in the bottle*

(392) ìi ndɔ̂ mà 'aléa ágá-á *the pail is half-full of water* (lit. *water is half-full in the pail*)

678. (7) gà . . . -kɔ́ sɪ̀ *to refuse to.* . . . 'To refuse' is gà . . . sɪ̀; if it refers to an action, i.e. a verb, kɔ́ has to be added immediately after the verb; kɔ́ has no meaning of its own; it is a purely constructional particle.

(393) gà má nǐ ɛ́ɳá fɛ̀ kɔ́ sɪ̀ *she/he refused to give me polenta*
cf. ń'n̩ gà mǐ nǐ . . . fɛ̀ kɔ́ kö *no, he did not refuse to give you*

(394) gà mu kɔ́ sɪ̀: gǎ (= gàkǐ) emú kɔ́ sɪ̀ *he refused to go: they refused to come*

(395) gǎ ɛ̀ì ko rö kɔ́ sɪ̀ *they refused to separate (leave each other)*

(396) cf. èmï àgátà gà 'dínï à'do sɪ̀ yà? *why do you dispute/quarrel in this way?*

(397) cf. gà má nǐ ɛ́ɳá sɪ̀ *he refused me polenta*

679. (8) Miscellaneous peculiar verbal constructions:

(a) é tö (= sɔ̀) pá 'dǐá! *stand* (lit. *fix leg*) *there!*
á lɛ̀ pâ tö (i.e. oru-lɛ́ sɪ̀) *I want to stand* (i.e. upright)

(b) é mu o'dû kə àkúa! *go home to sleep!* (cf. o'dúkə̀ *voice*)

(c) t'àǐ kə (= sɪ̀) 'bá tsǐ àfa sɪ̀ *he was surprised (astonished)/he marvelled at something* (lit. *surprise caught a man at*)

(d) li rö kö = atsɛ kö = awǐ kö *nothing remained over*
oyú . . . dri-nǐ li 'ï ɛmvɛ̀rö; (ə-)lii 'ï ko päria-rö (= päri-päri) *a pimple . . . a white spot stands out on his head; to form* (vn. irregularly) *roughly round(-ish) patches* (of grass), *water* (lake), *bare spots*
kànì 'bá 'à àɳá ɛ̀ri ɔli rö ko päripäri *when corn is sown, single empty spots form among the growing corn*
li rö vn. *to form an exception, stand out distinctly, to be conspicuous, striking among* . . . (anything)

680. (e) ɛ̀ri ɔ́rǐ ɔ̀wǐ ǹdrí sɪ̀ lit. *he sacrifices/propitiates the ancestral spirits with a goat* (sheep); Engl. *he sacrifices a goat to.* . . .
ɛ̀ì á'bíi mà ɔ́rǐ ɔ̀wǐ (or ɛdɛ̂) ǹdrí sɪ̀ *they sacrifice (to) the ancestral spirits with a goat*

(f) 'bɛ àríà ɔ́ní sɪ̀ pí *he threw a stone at the birds* (lit. *he threw at the birds with a stone*).
é 'bɛ ɔ̀tsɛ́ ɔ́ní sɪ̀! lit. *throw the dog with* . . . Engl. *throw a stone at the dog!*

(g) 'bà èmvò átápì nï lit. *he has put on mourning for his father*; Engl.
ditto, or *he is in mourning for his father.*

(h) kù drì-nï-á or àfa àzí 'bà tì-nï-á to cover (put something over it).
èì dí kǔ drì-nï-á *then they covered it over*
mí tì-nï-á àfa àzí 'bà! *cover it;* lit. *put something over/on/at its
opening!*

(i) to kindle a fire . . .
èì àtsí 'ì áisέ sì *they make up fire by means of* (a) *grass* (-bundle)
èì àtsí 'bà áisέ sí-á *they set fire to the grass*

Adverbials

681.

ndrâ ètú-rì sì = sàbítì ndrâ 'dà sì i.e. aga vútinìá sàbítì àlö
rá *the other week* or *the other Sunday*, i.e. *a Sunday has passed since*
sàbítì ètúrì sì 'dì sì = sàbítì ádzê-rì sì i.e. aga ŋgà véllé-nìá kö
(the) *last week,* (the) *last Sunday*, i.e. *no Sunday has passed since*
εsú ma dè ŋgà àkúa = εsú ŋgà dè ma àkúa *surprisingly he still
found me at home*
tu (a'á, ε'bí ε'dέ) pätí sía *he climbed* (*lived in, fell from*) *the tree*
èì ηərὲ sö báká sía *they are threading beads on a string*
èmï edzí ǹdrí á'dìá nï ayu-zö báká sía! *bring a goat to free so-and-so
from fetters!*
àfa 'dì mâ nï rô! *this is mine, mind!* (*shut up! do not ask for it*)
'dì əkə té 'yə lè 'bə *this he has already said/stated before*
èì mvá àzíni bε etsá àma-rí/àma-véllé àkúa *he came to my village
with another boy*

682. *Note on verbal tones:* exceptions (ref. §§ 343 (i), 347, 356).

A verb in the infinitive, depending from (a) an imperative, or (b) a
verb in the past tense:

(1) Does not take the additional, otherwise regular, falling (high intermediate) tone after the high tone of the end syllable.

(398) é mu mì àfa εdε (for έdê)! *go to adjust thy things!*

(399) mu 'ímà àfa εdέ (,, ,,) *he went to adjust his things.*

(2) A raising (intermediate) tone is added to a mid-tone of the end
syllable of a verb. Examples:

(400) mu ma pǎrí εdzǎǎ (for εdzaa) *he went to spread my mat.*

(401) mu àtsí əvö (for əvö) ásέ sì *he went to light a fire with grass*

(402) 'bá 'bà ε'dó máǎ (for maa) 'bə *the corpse started to rot.*

C. J. S.

PART II. VOCABULARY

FOR USERS OF THIS VOCABULARY

USERS of this Vocabulary should bear in mind the following:

1. The 'Logbara' of today represent a very varied collection of peoples or, more correctly, of originally distinct divisions of the Ma'di race. Historically there were at least three clearly distinct tribal waves which came into the country independently, from different regions and directions (cf. Introduction).

2. The result is that these three main divisions spoke and still speak Ma'di dialects, but they differ considerably in details, especially in their vocabularies.

3. The present Vocabulary has attempted to collect words of various dialects used at the administrative central area of Arua. As is to be expected under such circumstances, the dialects of Áìvò and Pàdzùlú formed the main and basic source of the Vocabulary.

Hence the fact is that one can very often hear several entirely, or sometimes only slightly, different words for the same object. The Áìvò–Pàdzùlú dialect is, as has been mentioned, mainly represented. Mostly, however, different words, especially of the large and important Terego–Omugo and north section and others (Adömi, Oluko) have become well known and understood and have, therefore, often (though not to any degree of completeness) been recorded.

4. As a consequence one may perhaps find in the Vocabulary (a) a word which the boy or native adviser may not know; this must be expected. It should be remembered, however, that the word in question, nonetheless, came from the tongue of some Logbara; (b) a word may be found written differently in various places because various words are actually in use or because, to some extent, the pronunciation is often not very clear; (c) differences in intonation have similar results.

5. Opinions expressed in examples represent the opinions of the natives, not necessarily those of the author.

6. There is still plenty of scope for further study and analysis of the Logbara—or Ma'di—language beyond the present work.

Morphological notes. (a) A-, e(ɛ)-, o(ə)- are important frequently recurring prefixes in Logbara; it is impractical and impossible to list all the combinations of these. In the different districts, moreover, the same prefix is not always employed with the same criterion. Therefore, when a verb with a given prefix is not found in its alphabetical order, (a) the verb in its root-form or without prefix, or (b) the same verb with another of the above-mentioned prefixes could be consulted.

Their general meaning is as follows: e- (T. = a-), direction of the action towards the speaker; o-, plurality (subject or object), frequency-repetition, intensity of an action; a-, particular meaning but, as a whole, not definable.

Use of Brackets

In many cases their significance is apparent from the context (indicated by '=', 'or').

Within a word a letter or syllable bracketed indicates that such a word may be pronounced either with or without the bracketed elements. Example:

'bǐ(kǝ) *hair*, means that for *hair* 'bǐ or 'bǐkǝ are in use: often in one region one form is used for preference, in another region the other form.

Within a sentence a particle in brackets means that such a particle may be used or not at will (without, generally, adding anything to the meaning).

Abbreviations employed

A.	Arabic (origin)	poss.	possessive
a.	adjective	prd.	predicate(-tive)
Ac.	Acooli	prn.	pronoun (*dem*/onstrative/, *ind*/efinite, *rel*/ative)
Ad.	Adömi		
Al.	Aluur	prs.	personal
av.	adverb	pstp.	postposition (≅ preposition)
BC.	Belgian Congo		
cj.	conjunction	q.v.	*quod vide* = which see
ex. =	e.g., example	S.	Suaheli (origin)
f.	from	sby.	somebody
fig.	figuratively	sg.	singular
lt. lit.	literally	s.-s.	so-and-so
MN.	Ma'di–Ndri	sth.	something
NE	north-eastern part of the country	T., Tom.	Tɛrɛgo (= Tɛrɛgo–Omugo)
n.	noun	V.	Vòra
Ol.	Oluko	vn.	neuter, intransitive verb
o.-s.	one-self	vt./vr.	transitive verb reflexive verb
p.	person		
pl.	plural	≅	approximately equal to
Plu.	Pàdzùlú	Y.	Yɔlɛ

VOCABULARY

N.B. The prefix **a-** (used regularly in Tɛrɛgo–Omugo instead of the **e-** in general use elsewhere) is a frequently recurring verbal formative. Only the more common verbs of this category are listed here: for others the root or stem-word provides sufficient explanation.

á, pl. **à**, prs. pron. I, we.

-á, ubiquitous locative postpositional suffix: in, to, from; **èri dzó-á** he (she, it) is in the hut; **mu àkú-á** he went home; **fï dzó-á** he went into the hut.

'a, more stressed **'alɛ́**, n. inside, interior; belly; **é wɛ dzó 'alɛ́!** sweep the room! **'aléá** (also **'alɛ̆á, 'alɪ́á**), **'alɛ́-nï̈-á** (also **'a-nï̈-á**) in (within, inside...) it; **fï lítsóá** or **fï lítsó 'aléá** he entered the cattle-pen; **èdzé 'dì̈ mà 'alɛ́á à'do yà? àfa 'alɛ́nïá yɔ** what is in this calabash? there is nothing in it (i.e. it is empty); **ɔ̀kó** (or **tí**) **mà 'aléá mvá tsí̈** or **ɔ̀kó 'alɛ́** (or **mvá**) **bɛ** the woman (cow) is pregnant.

'à (= **'yà**), vt. to till; **mú ámvú 'à** they went to cultivate the field.

'a, vt. (1) to bloom; to start forming or putting forth fruit; **'dó̆ 'a àŋgà 'à̈'a**; **èri tsä̈ä-ru** eleusine is just starting to put forth fruit; it is un-developed; **'dì̈ 'dó̆ 'ắpi 'à̈'arì̈'ï** (or, **'bɔrì̈'ï**) this is eleusine beginning to form (formed); **'dó̆ 'a dɛ 'bɔ...** is already formed; (2) to produce abundant fruit; **pätí mà éfí̈ 'à̈ tö̆** the tree is abundantly laden with fruit; (3) **ávâ 'a** (= **'ya**) to breathe.

a'á or **'a'á** (Tom. = **ɔ'á**), vn. to stay, abide, dwell; be found; **ɛ́dró̆nï̈ 'a'á ásɛ́ 'aléá** the mouse lives in the grass.

'ắá, a 'á, av. yonder there, beyond (thus, a valley, valley-like depression, river); **èri 'ắá** he is there beyond; **á mu tɛ́ sòfàría ɔlɛ 'ắá Árúwá** I went a moment ago yonder to Arua to buy a cooking pot; **zɔ a 'álɛ́** (**'ắálɛ́**) **'dà** he crossed over there (other side of the river).

á 'a! intj. no! let it be!...

a 'bá, a tree (very hard wood); **èì ɔsì̈ ɛ́dzá-¹rö** they split it for fire-wood.

àbà, or **abá** (= **aza**), vn. to be (behave, act) perplexed, embarrassed, confused, muddle-headed, dumb-founded, aghast, stupefied; (stressing av.: **lìi, bǎälì̈, kì̈rr, lǎäì;**) **àbà ɛ'yó sì̈ àbà-àbà** he speaks confusedly... **mí̈ àbà kö bǎälì̈, é mu àfa 'dì̈ e'dú!** do not behave absurdly, go and take up the thing! **àbà** (= **àdì**) **ìyí sì̈** he ran heedlessly into the river (drowning, avó̆); **àmà dí̈ ắó àbà-àbà** we are staying here like fools; **èmï 'bá àbàzà** (= **azazà**) you are idiots; **ɔ̀kó àbàzà** slovenly woman.

abá = ɡa, vn. to over-flow, -run, inundate, flood; **ìyí abá àkúá** (or **dzóá**) **lìi** the (rain) water is flooding the village (hut) in a thorough muddle; **'bá mà ɔ̀'bí abá** (= **ɡa**) **àndrònï̈ 'dó̆nï̈ yà!** what a crowd is strolling about here today!

a 'ba rö a 'ba-a 'ba, vt./vr. to consist, be formed of distinct layers

N

or strata; à'bŏà păti a'ba rö a'ba-a'ba the banana stem is made up in layers; 'bá a'ba rö a'ba-a'ba people are crowded (closely) together.

àbàbà = èdìà, n. epilepsy.

à'bàkùndàa, n. a kind of pigeon.

àbálá, n. competition; 'bàkǐà—... bɛ they entered into competition with; èi ndzo à— sǐ they competed in running; adri-nï à— sǐ kö there was no competition.

á'bálà(ŋg)á, n. wild vine; á— èri pätǐ rǎpi rǎra-rǐ the á— is climbing trees.

à'batà, n. (wild) duck.

àbé, n. (1) club, cudgel; àbélèkúkú large stick (for various uses); ma 'bá ǵbǎ àbé sǐ I beat sby. with a club; (2) handle; ɛ'bó àbé èrī pätǐ ɛ'bô sö-zŏrǐ a hoe handle is a stick for fixing a hoe; ëlï àbé handle of knife.

à'bé¹ = ǎfú, n. wrestling; andzi 'dàǐ à'béá those children are wrestling.

à'bé², n. kind of small humble-bee; èri fǐ pätǐ mà ògóá it enters (lives) in tree-holes; ósɔ̀-nï tsǐ (ànyú ósɔ̀-lɛ́) it has honey (like bees).

à'bé³, n. a climber; pätǐ rǎpi áǵúi mà rùárǐ which climbs other trees.

a'béfɛ, T. = ólófɛ, n. bridge, or also ladder.

a'bɛlɛ'bua, n. small kind of wild pigeon.

à'bĕlĕká, n. a shrub; èri eŋgǎ ótókó driá; èi sí dzǐ ànǐ it grows on termite hills; they rub (clean) their teeth with it(s sticks).

á'bélémvó = á'bókó, n. cheek.

ábélésó, n. (1) earthworm; á— èri atsǐ ozóó mà 'aléá it moves about in rain; (2) tapeworm.

àbì, n. wall; dzó m. àbì hut wall.

à'bǐ, n. kind of thatching grass; dzô tï-ző.

á'bíi, n. grandfather; ancestor; á'bíi-ərí, n. spirit of ancestor; á'bíi(w)á, n. (sometimes for) ancestral shrine and sacrifice.

a'bï = là'bǐ, n. (1) ritual food (ɛ́ŋá tíbí bɛ) eaten by women and children, 4 or 3 times, after a period of 4 (boy) or 3 (girl) months from delivery; eaten partly in village, partly on riverside; 'bánǐ ŋa ìyí-tìárǐ, èrinï derö-zŏrǐ they eat the remains on the riverside; (2) monthly periods (menstruation) after the first (= alǐ): èri a'bï sù or a'bï bɛ she has menstrual flow.

àbìdzóá (-dzóa), n. small house-mouse; èri ɔ̀ŋǐ'bí -nï ɛza rá it spoils trinkets (and other things).

àbbílli or á'bíi mà à—, n. spirit of ancestor; à— (or á'bíi or ərí) dzó ancestral shrine.

ábío or óbío, n. kind of incense tree.

àbírí, n. hunger; 'bá à— bɛ a hungry p.; à— fu má kái I am very hungry; à— 'dɛ nǐ a famine arose.

à'bö = èndzò, àyá, n. lie; mí à'bö bɛ tǒ you are a great liar; é raa ma à'bö sǐ you deceive me with lies; á lè mǐ à'bö kö; á gà mǐ à'bö mâ bbílía sǐ I hate your lies; I refuse to hear your lies.

à'bó(kó), n. additional payment of bride-wealth záa mà à'bó; 'bá fɛ̀ mǐ zíi mà à'bó rá yà? have they brought the bride-wealth for your daughter?

a'bő (cf. 'bö), vt. to cover, conceal; dzó (or pätǐ) a'bő 'bá àzínǐ tsǐ the hut (tree) hides sby.; erítí a'bő ètú(sǐ) tsǐ clouds overcast

the sun; ɔzɔ́ɔ́ a'bɵ̌ (= asɛ) àŋgɵ̀
tsɪ̌ rain (-water) covers/inundates
the ground; má ɛ̀rɔ́ a'bɵ̌ (or 'bö)
yǎbí sɪ̌ I am covering the granary
with grass.

à'bòà, n. banana; à— ɔ̀tsɛsɪ́ bunch
of bananas.

à'bòá = à'bɵ̀lɔ̌, àlàbà, n. (wild)
pigeon, dove.

à'bɵ̌'bɵ̌, n. simple mixture (not
cooked) of leavened flour with
water; milk or mashed bananas
are often added; à— mvu to
drink the mixture.

ábɔki, n. Nile perch (Lwoo gúùr).

Á'bókɔ́, prop. name of a girl (for
whose mother the full bride-
wealth has not yet been delivered).

àbɔ̀rɔ̀kɔ̀ = bɔ̀rɔ̀kɔ̀ q.v.

á'bu, n. valley; á'bu'alɛ́ = á'bulɛ́
river-bed, channel; valley; á'bu
iyí bɛ the á'bu (-valley) has water;
á'buti side of valley; mountain-
slope, hillside; á'buti ɛ̀lɛ̀rɪ̌ the
lower hillside, á'buti órúrɪ̌ the
higher hillside; má àkú ɛ̀ri
á'butiá gúrú ɛ̀lɛ̀ my home is
down on the lower hillside.

à'bù = ɔsɛ, ŋgozà, a. fat, thick,
stout; pánï ɔsɛ̀rö, ɛ̀ri mà áda
à'bù-à'bù his leg is thick, his
person is stout (opp. ɵ́ízà).

a'bú, vr. to cower (or squat) down
(in corner or the like); to bend
forward (or to the ground); a'bú
(= ako) 'ï pätí rùá he cowered
down behind a tree; bɵ̌rà 'dɪ̌ a'bú
'ï ɛ́drónï a'bú-a'bú: ɛ́drɔ́ bɪ̌zɵ̌
the cat crouches down for a
mouse, to catch it; a'bú 'ï a'bú-
a'bú he cowers down on his face.

à'búkùru, av. on one's face; é la
ɛ̀ri à'— place it on its face! la rö
à'— he lies on his face.

á'bulɛ́, á'buti..., see á'bu.

adá, vn. (of fruit) to stunt, spoil,

fail to develop (from drought...);
adázà = àdáláká, àdárákàla,
dàlàká (⸱rö), a. stunted (withered), undeveloped (pods...); ɔ́sɵ́
àzɪ́ 'dɪ̌ 'a àlârö, àzɪ́ 'dɪ̌ mà
rùáti àdá'rö (ɔdïzà or diri-
kpârö) some of these beans are
well developed, others have shrivelled; bɵ̀rɵ̌sɵ̌ dà(là)ká stunted
pigeon-peas; àfa adápi 'bɔrɪ̌,
'bá èi ɔmvɛ dàlàká (T.) what
failed to develop they call dàlàká.

ádaa, a. (1) real, proper; Lógbàrà
ádaarɪ̌ a real Logbara; (2) true;
ɛ'yɔ́ á— the right, true word,
question; truth; ɛ'yɔ́ 'dɪ̌ áda-
ádarɪ̌'ï this is the real truth/
question; (3) right; drí á— the
right hand.

adá-adá, n. dropsy; 'bá adázà,
rùánï ɛ̀ri adá-adá a dropsical
p.: his body is swollen (unnatur-
ally).

ád(r)ámánáká = T. á'bánáká,
n. night-jar or goatsucker.

àdèti or àdàti, amuti, av.; èmi
emú má vɵ̌ à—! come to me by
turns!

adi¹, vt. (1) to beat, knock (with fist
or the like); (2) to crush, squeeze,
squash, bruise; ɔ̀kó ɛ̀ri zá adi,
ɛ̀rinï ɔwïï (or ɔ̀ndɪ̌ï)-zɵ́ the
woman beats the meat to pull off
pieces from it; èi zá-fàlá adi ɔ́ní
sɪ̌ they crush (flesh-) bones with
a stone.

adi² (=raa), vn. to flow, run (current); ìyínï adi mávélé dzóá
adi-adi (rain-) water runs into
my hut; àrínï adi-adi he is
bleeding; má òmvuléa àrínï
adi-adi (= rara) I am bleeding
from the nose.

ádí¹, n. tradition; ádí mbàzànï
ǹdze rɪ̌'ï tradition which old men
relate; 'bá á'bí mà (ɛ'yɔ́ or) ádí

èdrǐ sby. transmits (hands down) the traditions of the ancestors.

ádí², n. in ádî ndzɛ to remove a spell which has caused illness of a boy . . . by an old man; the mbàazà says 'má 'aléá ɛ'yɔ́ tsí: mâ mǔ ndzɛ mvá 'dà mà drìá (i.e. ádî ndzɛ)' or 'mâ mu ádî ndzɛ mvá 'dà mà àzɔ́ sǐ' 'there is ill-feeling in my heart (which has caused illness), let me go to remove the spell from the sick child'; èri ádî tsə or vǔ éríndíkə sǐ; èri ádî sö dzɔ́tilía he takes éríndíkə leaves, spits on them and brushes the sick person's legs (feet) with them; the ádí-removing leaves are fixed outside the hut above door; only the old man himself can remove them.

à'dï? int. pron. who? à'dï lö mínî nǐ yà? who has told you?

àdì, vn. to have a fit of choking; àdì ìyí sǐ he choked from water (momentarily), to choke, suffocate.

á'dí (= lɔ̀tè), n. parasitical plant; á'dí èri pätí mà rùá the parasite grows on a tree.

àdí T. = áyáká, q.v.

a'dï (or ɛ'dï, ətsi, əmbé), vt. to (tie into a) knot, connect, fasten; kànì bákánǐ tsɛ 'ï rá, èì a'dï a'dï when a rope breaks, they connect it; a'dï báká mà ti tsí he knotted tightly the ends of the rope; a'dï mâ drí báká sǐ he tied my hands with a rope.

à'dí, n. war; àŋgǒ ándrâ drìərì à'dírö in the past there were wars; à'dî 'di-zǒ to avenge; èri à'dî 'di 'bá 'înírì mà ɛ'yɔ́ sǐ he takes revenge for one of his men.

à'dí, n. bell; à'dí 'bá 'ǐ tí (mà) ombéá a bell sby. ties to the neck of a cow.

à'di, in ìyí à'di, n. source, spring,

fountain; ìyí-à'di èì 'yɛ ɛdɛ́ rá they will clean the spring; ìyíà'dinï ra the spring runs.

a'dí, vt. to cook; boil (used generally for preparing sauces); èri ŋgà tíbí (zá, moòndrɔ́kɔ̀lɔ̀ . . .) a'dí a'dǐ (ìyí sǐ) she is still cooking/preparing the sauce (meat . . .) (with water).

á'dǐá, indef. pron. s.s.; a certain person.

àdïïkà, n. grass widow ɔ̀kó à—; èri ɔ̀kó ágúpi gǎpi sǐrǐ'ï she is a woman who refused her man/ divorced; èri vínï fɔ̀ àmvé ùú 'bǎ èndì: vínï ágúpi tɔ̀kɔ́ esúzǒ she goes out again to place/ offer her arm (courting): in order to find a man again.

á'díkɔ́ or á'dyɔ́, n. same as ɔ́'dɔ́kɔ́'dɔ́, q.v.

ádïlï (-bbí), n. a cultivated vegetable (A. molachia) known for the viscous stringy quality of its savoury/tíbí.

ádíó, T. a tree; mbǎmba, ə'bí mbèlè kö is very hard, is not easily bored.

à'do? inter. pron. what? à'do yà? à'do yə what is the matter? nothing happened; à'do sǐ yà? or à'do ɛ'yɔ́ sǐ yà? for what reason? why? à'dò-rö? for what purpose? mí àfa 'dï ɛdɛ́ à'dòrö yà? for what purpose do you do/ adjust this? à'do(ŋg)árè yà? when?

àdə = ɔ̀do, n. oil, fat, grease.

adɔ́, vn. to be soft/overripe (fruit); pàipài adɔ́ mènèmènè, lè mǎma the pawpaw is soft/overripe, is about to rot.

a'dɔ́, vt. to drink the last dregs; má a'dɔ́ dzɔ́lɔ́nï 'dɔ́rɔ́kɔ̀lɔ́, tsa mánǐ kö, I gulped down the last dregs, it was insufficient.

àdòkòdòấ, or mènốmènốấ, n. very small brown termites.

àdətáa (cf. də rö), n. modesty.

àdrà, n. anger; vexation, wrath, spite; ágú 'dà àdràrö (= à—bɛ) that p. is angry; mvá 'dǐ mà à— tӧö this boy is very angry; é 'bà à— 'dǐ-nï à'do sǐ yà? why do you get in such a passion? ... so enraged?

àdrá, n. some disease, as a cancerous sore (caused by a spell against a thief); à— ŋa má òmvu wórɔ́ the à— has eaten away my nose completely; 'bá 'bà à— ògù sǐ, i.e. èrinï àfa ògù sǐ 'bá 'bà à— èrinï sby. puts a spell for theft; because he has stolen, they put a spell on him (and some disease will catch him); à— wàá to remove the à— disease.

àdràdrà(-lúfɛ) = mbèɛlú, n. green grasshopper with long tapering head.

àdrágbùrù, n. caries (believed to be a worm 'èrìàgà' and produced by ekáká sugarcane); à— èrìàgà: èri sí mà ésû ŋa, 'bá tùsúnï ànï rằra the à— is a worm, it eats/destroys the nerve of teeth and causes abundant saliva to run.

àdrákà = ɛŋatá, ɛŋákeŋá, n. famous Ma'di poison (prepared for secret internal or external dispensation); èi orî li à—-rö/ɛŋatâ-rö 'bá ɛŋa zɔ̌ they cut up snakes for the preparation to administer it to people; ká ànï mǐ ɛnyǎ, mǐ ŋga drà rá if they give it to you, you will die.

àdràkàdrà = ɔ́nɔ́kɔ́nɔ́, n. praying mantis (Mantis religiosa), èri ndzéndzénï (kùlú) it is a variety of locust.

ádrɛ́ (kɔ̀) T. = andra, n. tongue.

ádrìi or ádrípi, n. brother; á—àzí cousin; clan-member; for addressing anybody: friend.

'ädrì, n.? kidney; a piece of meat (of killing) reserved to mbàazà èi ŋa nǐ to elders of the community.

adri = əvö, vn. to be, stay; a—mâ drìlǐá he is in front/ahead of me; adrípi-trátrárɪ̀ that exists, lives continually: eternal; a—àìkɔ̀ bɛ to be happy, glad ...

àdró, àdróã or ìyí àdró = ŋgarikadíyò, n. water-ghost; an imaginary spirit who is believed to dwell in rivers; èri àlíàrö; èri ìyí 'aléá; èri 'bá bǐ àzɔ̂-rö it is short, lives in water, catches people (while bathing) and makes them sick (the ɔ́dzɔ́ finds out and removes it with sacrifice); (the spirit is described as having a large head with long hair; with only one eye, ear, nostril, arm, leg; there are several kinds of them).

Àdrɔ̂, n. God (the Creator), divinity; À— 'bá ò'bǎpirɪ̀, God who created man; èi À— ɛdê (= əwǐ) ǹdrí sǐ they sacrifice a goat to God.

àdrɔ̀, vt. to put one upon another, to pile, heap up; mǎ àdrɔ̀ àfa à—à— I am piling up things; àfa 'dǐ àdrɔ̀zàrö these things are one upon another/piled up.

àdrɔ̀, n. maternal uncle; àdrɔ̀-mvá/àdrɔ̀-andzi sister's children (at feasts/killings one of them has to come to cook the meat); mu 'ǐ àdrɔ̀á (or àdrɔpíá) he went to his maternal uncle's; cf. ádrói.

ádrɔ̀á = ágɔ̀á, tségɔ̀á, ɛ́- or ègɔ̀á, n. adze.

ádródró = dródró, ándróndró, n. leech; èri 'bá àrí ndzùndzu;

tinï ïrrì it sucks one's blood; it
has two mouths (both ends).

ádrói or ádrópi or ádrúi, n.
sister's child; mother's brother/
uncle (on addressing each other!);
mâ ádrói la ! ɛ'yɔ́ ŋgóní yà? my
nephew! what is the matter?/or
what has happened?

àdròòri, n. brown/red ochre; à—
'bání eɡalé 'bíliárì; ɛ̀ri ɳakû-rö
it is clay a p. digs in caves; mvá
'dï tri à— drìá (or rúáa) sì,
tsàandí (or drà) sì the boy has
rubbed brown ochre on his head
(body) from grief (at death).

àdrópá'dírí = pìrìlía, n. whirlwind; ɛ̀rì ŋga pìrìrö; ɛ̀rì ɳakú
(= fúlúlú) ɔmvɔ́ ébíkɔ bɛ oru:
ɛ̀rì dî ŋga èì bɛ lőrrő it rises
straight up; it gathers dust and
leaves in its height: it rises with
them in a whirling column.

ádú, n. a tree; èì émvó avö ádú
bbí sì; émvó-nï mba tö they
stew leaves of this tree in a (new)
pot, to make it more resistant.

a'dú, vt. to take and put on a p.'s
head; mî a'dú máni iyí 'bǎ mâ
drìá! lift/put (me) the water on
my head (women fetching water).

à'dú, n. (1) black glossy ochre
(used for polishing earthenware);
à'dú èì àní émvó mà tî 'i they
polish the rim of pots with it; (2)
gold; gloss; ɔyɔ mà à'dú glossy
buttocks of monkey.

à'dúkù = ɔ̀'dúku (q.v.), n. edible
pulp covering stone of stone
fruits.

á'dúkúlɛ, n.(? = alóma-alóma)?
spleen; ɛ̀ri ɔɡó mà rúa(á) it is on
the liver.

a'dúlɛ, av. (also a'dúkúlɛ sì, cf.
ndrɔ) (1) alone; é mu mî 'í a—!
go alone! (2) distinct, different, by
itself, special.

adza (or ɛdza), vt. to spread out
(as for showing or airing); má
a— bɔ̀ŋgɔ́ ètúá I am spreading
the cloth in the sun; Índì a— àfa
dzɛzàrö the Indian (merchant)
exposes/exhibits things for buying.

àdzamati or àdzɔmati = kɔ̀-
muti (q.v.), n. knee joint.

ádzê, av. yesterday; drà á— he
died yesterday; ádzê-kárì, a. of
yesterday.

àdzɛ̀, n. (1) merchandise, goods for
sale; è dzé à— mŏkɛ́ ɔ̀mbà
kókɔ̀rö! do buy goods in an
orderly way, without quarrelling!
Índì èì à— ozí the Indians sell
goods; ɔ̀kó 'dïrï 'bâ ma àdzɛ̀
dzɛ-ríá this woman pesters one
to buy goods; (2) àfa àdzɛ̀-nï (záà
dzɛ-ző) bride-wealth; ɛ̀ri àfà
dzi àdzɛ̀nï he is taking bride-
goods (to the bride's father).

àdzɛ̀li (or -ɛ̀)kó, n. flute; à— ɔvɔ̌
to blow a flute.

àdzéríkɔ̀lí = àdzíríkɔ̀lí, n. potsherd: fragment or piece of pottery
or bottle; à— ɛ̀ri àfa andíröpi
'bɔ-rì ... sth. that has broken to
pieces.

àdzì (= drìléba), n. favour, for-
tune, good luck; 'bá kà mî lɛ̀lɛ̀,
éfíní mî mà àdzi tö if people
like (or favour) you, that means
you are lucky; má à— su tö I am
very lucky; mî à— (or drìléba)
yɔ (or ... su kö) you are unlucky.

àdzí, n. (1) taste, flavour; tíbí mà
àdzí alu tö the taste of the sauce
is very pleasant; (2) smell, odour;
àdzí-nï ndrì tö its fragrance is
very agreeable; mî àdzí-nï sɛ
ɔ̀mvu sì you (draw the) smell/
scent with the nose; àdzí-rö or
àdzí-àdzí, a. pleasant, agreeable;
(3) good name in: 'bá mà àdzî di

to defame, calumniate, offend;
àdzî-di-tá, n. defamation, calumny, slander.

adzí, vt. to put forth, mention a p.'s name; **mí mâ rú a— à'do sî yà?** why do you take my name in vain? (in my absence; Ac. **kwòtò η̣íη̣).**

àdzì, n. large bird (? eagle); **èrì η̣ga gèrìkò 'bùá 'dà sî** it draws its way (circles) up in the sky.

ádzídzì, n. ? = óyá-lòrókà, or two similar plants; cf. **lòrókà.**

àdzíkò n. (1) (larger) potsherd or, sometimes, expressly made similar earthenware used as frying-pan; diminut. names: **àdzíkõã, àdzí-(rí) kòlí, àdzòkòlí, émvó-àdz—;** (2) knee-pan; **èri kòmutíá** it is on the knee.

àdzíη̣gùrú = odru-ɔgbɛ, n. a large (about 4 ft.) peppermint-like plant; **pánï kòη̣gòlòkòrö** it has a stiff stem; **àdzí-nï ɔvö-zö àrì-kàrì-rö** it is pleasant smelling; the **ɔ̀ɔdzó** (sorcerer) uses its twigs variously in his rites: **èi ànï εη̣atáà tsɔ, nòsì àdrá wà-zö** by sprinkling or brushing the body they treat poisons or spell diseases (magic).

àdzírà, n. fairly thin pulpy sauce of mashed beans with **mɔ̀nd-**leaves and simsim; **èi ósǒ a'dî mɔ̀ndrókòlò sî; èi ósǒ mà 'alé 'bî'bi lópérèá sî; kànì 'bî ìyí sî 'bɔ, èi 'alénị́á áη̣û 'bɛ àdzí-ràrö** they cook beans with (cut up) **mɔ̀nd,** vegetables; then they stir it with the stirring stick; when they have stirred it well, they add sesame to make it **àdzírà.**

àdzórɔ́á = a'yɔ̀ɔró, n. ground squirrel; **èri ɔ'á ótó'bílía** (i.e. **éfúrú'bòá)** it lives in holes of broken-up termite-hills; **rùánï èri**

ndíríá drírì-lɛ́ it is grey (as a dikdik) with white spots.

àdzú, n. spear; **à— òtolò** fishing spike; **à— sí** edge of; **àtsólì mà à—** (Acooli spear) small blade with long neck; **ɔlïrï(ã̄)** a 12–15 cm. spear (blade and neck together); **à— ándríí** 20–25 cm. spear (blade larger).

ádzu, n. poles to support mud wall; **á— èi ànï dzô tsɔ** or **àbì si** they build a hut, hut-wall with it.

Àdzúá, n. name given by a mother who was threatened with a spear by her man.

àfa, n. thing, something; belongings, property; **àfa 'ípì (= 'íí)** owner of things, i.e. rich man; **àfà-àzó** sick painful spot (on body); **àfadrí,** n. s.-s.

àfá = ámvú, q.v.

àfa(d)zó, n. any basket, recipient; dimin. **àfa(d)zóã** small . . . .

afálá, indef. prn. (= á'dị́á), s.-s. (name forgotten, unknown); **a— mí emú 'dɔ̀á, ε'yó tsí,** N.N. come here for a word.

àfî (cf. **fî),** vn. to burst, explode; **a'ú-ġbɛ àfî kpǔ̃úá** (or **rá) àtsị́á** an egg exploded with a bang in the fire.

afî, vn. (1) to be stunted in growth (animal, plant); **'bánï afí-afî, lɛ̀ zò kö** the individual is stunted, he would not grow; (2) to fail to put forth (seed); **'dǒ afî rá** the eleusine did not come up; (3) to vanish, disappear; **afî ndró** (or **'bɔ)** it vanished as if by magic/into thin air.

àfó, n. pride, conceit, haughtiness; **àfó bɛ** or **àfô-rö** proud, vain (glorious); **mí àfó 'dínï à'do sî yà?** why are you so proud/haughty? **èi àfó 'bǎ ε'yó sî, èi èη̣à rö èη̣à** they make show/

boast in talking; M. À'í'bɔ̀á èri àfó'bánï, M. A. is a conceited fop.

àfɔ̀, vn. (1) to moulder, become/be musty rúánï ɔdza-rö ɛmvèrö it becomes whitish; (2) to become pale, fade (of strong colours).

áfóká, av. completely; andzi ɛrɛ́ èi á— àn̯ú sǐ, àn̯ú lè èi ɔzà-ɔzà the children dispersed in all directions from the bees who wanted to sting them.

àfósàrà T. cf. ɔ̀fósàrà.

äfu = ari, vt. to strive, scramble, fight, compete eagerly for ...(acc.); andzi èi fúnò äfu (or rě, arì) the children scramble for groundnuts (thrown to them); äfútáa = aritáa, n. scramble, struggle.

àfúá or àfútáa, n. wrestling.

àfùfù, vn. to ferment, bubble up/ work (in its first stage); ɛwá 'bánǐ zɔlɛ́ ɔ'dírǐ èri àfùfù-nǐ, freshly strained beer starts fermenting (fermenting next day or so: ɔdráko).

áfúrútsìká, n. gadfly (?).

àgà, n. larva.

àgà (kŏmú sǐ), vn. to crawl; òdékòlɛ́ ŋgà àgàzàrö the baby still crawls.

aga, vt./vn. (1) to pass by; ágú àzínï aga 'dɔsǐ, sby. passed here; (2) to pass over (drìlé sǐ); aga iyí drìlé sǐ pá sǐ he passed over the river with a (deliberate) step; (3) to surpass, overcome; aga ma zɔ̀tá (or ɔŋgú) sǐ he exceeded me in growth (swiftness); (4) to pass (time); sáwà or ètú aga rá the (proper) time is passed.

aga rö (= àsì, api, andï rö), vr. to split, crack (av. trà).

ágáa, n. centre, middle; èri iyí 'alɛ́á ágáa he is in the middle of the river; ágáa n̄dúa centre, central point (of space, current,

opinion); dzɔ́ ágáa n̄dúa in the centre of the hut; ágávɔ̌-(sï), av. almost full; of average-convenient size.

ágáa = kpɔ̀yɔ̀, av. half-full; ɔ̀ndó èri èróá á—durrah half fills the granary.

ágá-ágá, av. reciprocally; ɔmvɛkí èi ágá-ágá 'má ádrói' 'má ádrói' they call each other reciprocally 'my ádrói' (which means 'uncle'/mother's brother only/as well as 'nephew' by the same); ɔ'dakí rö ágá-ágá they insulted each other.

àgà, àgà-àgà, àgàrö . . ., a. (1) badly, in a bungling manner, roughly done; 'ǎ ámvú àgàgàrö they have tilled the field badly; ɔkó 'i àn̯á àgà-àgà (= àgà ŋgúrúkàrö), the woman ground the corn coarsely; cf. àn̯áfɔ̌rá àgà the flour is coarse (badly ground); (2) (surface) rough, coarse; bǎò mà dri àgàgàrö the board's surface is rough.

àgaa = àgǎí, àgäpí, n. neighbourhood, surroundings; má à— . . . place near me; èri mï àgǎí-á ɔ̀gɔ̀gɔ̀ he is close beside you; mǐ ɛsɛ́ mï èn̯ï má àgäpíá 'dǐa! draw here near me! dzɔ́ à— the side of a hut; èri 'bá má àkú (mà) àgǎí těpirǐ he is the guard of my home; àgǎí-á see Grammar, § 496.

agǎi-rö (= ɔgbó), vn./vr. to become disconnected, lost with the rest (cf. ɔgbó).

à(ŋ)gàlàká, see gàlàkà.

ágálɛ́ or ágɛ́lɛ́, n. pudenda or private parts.

agalɛ, cf. agɛlɛ.

agaro-vùú, a. collapsed, broken in; ɔ́tɔ́kɔ́ 'dǎ a— (i.e. drà rá, 'dɛ 'bílé 'alɛ̌á), that termite-hill has broken in (is dead/empty of termites).

àgátà, n. public flat denial, argument, protest; **àgátà-rö**, a. stubbornly denying; **à— ga**, vn. to deny, refuse obstinately, protest plainly; **'bá à— gǎpi** one protesting.

ágǎti, n. chest, breast; **ǎ— mà lɔ́kìri** sternum; **órí èì ndzo ǎ— sǐ** snakes run (move) on their breast.

agbá, n. a tree (*Sarcocephalus esculentus*); **éfínïrì ésésénï** its fruits (of tennis-ball size) release/ contain viscose.

àgbà = **andi**, vn./vt. to break (and go to pieces: **määrù**); to crack; **à— dí 'ï määrù** (or **'bə**); **èrì dí éríkɔ̀rö**; **mà 'bɛ̀ dí** (**éríkənï**) **áséá** it (falling to the ground) cracked; it is now split, let it be thrown into the grass; **àgbà ɛ́mvó rá** she broke the pot.

àgbàkà, n. a large basket (**èvǒ** or **àfazó áŋgǔrí**).

ágbárágbù, n. jaw; **á— ándrárì** (= **ákpákù**) lower jaw; **á— órúlérì** upper jaw.

ágbǎrí, av. without reason, for vain pretext; without plan, at convenience; **é tsə èri ǎ—** you have beaten him without reason; **mǐ əmvɛ mvá 'dìrï ǎ— àfa 'dìrïá 'ï yà!** have you called the boy in vain for this thing here? **mâ ŋgà mu 'dálé ǎ— ká, àzí àzínï mâ drìlïá tsï** I shall go there at my convenience, I am engaged now.

ágbàtárá = **gbátá-gbátá**, n. disorderly, confused discussions, when all speak at once **èì ɛ'yɔ́ dríâ ndzɛ éwá drì-á**... on beer-drinking-bouts.

àgbɔ̀, vn. to bark; **ɔ̀tsɔ́nï ɔ̀gbɔ̀** the dog barks.

agbɔ́ = **tra**, vt. to fold; **èì ŋgà bɔ̀ŋgɔ́ agbɔ́-agbɔ́** they are still folding clothes.

àgbûá (Ad. **rùgbɔ̂**), n. great bustard.

ágbúlúká-ìí, n. waterbag of afterbirth; **ìyínïrì èfï vàá** its water sheds on the ground.

ágê, T. **=⁻ádzê**, av. yesterday.

agɛlɛ = **agalɛ**, n. inside of...; as **drí a—** palm of hand; **pá a—** sole of foot; **ti a—** (red) inside of lip.

agó, vt. to bow, bend (a single thing); **mǐ agó pätí mà drì agó-agó!** bend the top of the stick (or wood, tree...)! **agó 'ï**, vr. to bend, warp, twist, turn; **rï agózàrö** he sits cowering.

àgɔ̀, vt. (**= ègɔ̀ vélé, tra**) to bend... inside (more sticks...); **èì àbɔ̀rɔ̀kɔ̀ àgɔ̀** they bend sticks or/and grass (set in circle) inwards to form a roof or shelter (as: **àrïíá tɛ̀-zɔ̀** to scare birds off crops); **àma dzó mà drì àgɔ̀** we are bending poles inwards and tying the frame of the roof.

ágɔ́, n. (1) = **ágúpí** man/vir; (2) = **átá** male; **ǹdrí ágɔ́** he-goat; **tí ágɔ́** = **mǒnío** bull; **a'ú ágɔ́ lɔ̀lɔ̀** cock, &c.; (3) **drí—, pá ágɔ́** thumb of hand, foot.

àgɔ́, n. melon or edible pumpkin(?); **àgɔ́-bbí** leaves of the plant; **àgɔ́—** or **nd(z)ɔ́lɔ́ fɔ̀** its flower (every part serves as a vegetable).

àgɔ́á = **àgɔ́bá, àgɔ́áká, àgúákɔ́** (cf. **àŋàkàŋà**), n. bug; **èri 'bâ ndzǔndzu** it sucks a man's blood.

àgobi, àgobïã, or **àgobi-àgobïã**, n. tiny black birds (feeding on green seeds of small plants).

ágɔ́fɛ, n. shrub with long thin sticks which are used for roofing

granary; èri päti rŏérŏérì èrɔ́
mà tì tsə (or mbɛ) zŏ.

agɔgɔfi = agɔləgɔ = agɔləfi, n.
ìyì a— waves (or whirlpool) of
river, strong current and whirling;
ìyì ágɔ́fɛ also.

ágɔ́gà, n. a kind of sweet potatoes;
á— mà 'alɛ ɛkaˀrö kìlɛ a'ú-gbɛ́
mà 'alɛ́ its inside (pulp) is reddish
yellow like an egg's inside (yolk),
hence: yellow(ish).

agú-zà-rö a. concave, bending
concavely; gbɔ́lɔ́ èri a— the
shingle is concave(ly hewn).

ágú, pl. àgu, n. man/homo
(Mensch); individual; ágú 'dà
that individual.

ágúi, ágíi, n. friend, comrade; mí
èfè mání àfa 'dìrï ágú sì! give
me this out of friendship! àma
mvá 'dà be ágúìrö I and that
boy are friends.

ágúpi, pl. àgùpi, n. man/vir,
husband; àgùpi andzi boys (male
children).

àgúrú or ɔ̀gúrú, (cf. agúzà) n. a
(carved-hewn) wooden plate.

à'í = à'íɳá, à'ítìzà, à'ítìká,
à'ítìpá, n. lye (from ashes ɔ́fɔ́-
tàrö); salt; cf. à'í-sú or zá-sú
broth; à'í-sîrö (= draazàrö)
bitter, unpleasant.

à'ǐ, vt. (1) to believe, agree,
accept; má à'ǐ mí ɛ'yɔ́ kö I do
not believe your words/statement;
mï à'ǐ tɔ̀əkɔ̂rö you believe unreasonably; (2) to answer, react
(to call, question); à'ǐtáa, n.
belief; answer.

a'í, vt. (1) to ask for; to pray sby.;
èi káanï wárágà a'í 'bá àzï drí
(= vɔ̌) they may perhaps ask
paper from sby.; (2) to receive,
accept delivery of; é mu bɔ̀ŋgɔ́
a'ǐ 'bá àzïnï (or mánï)! go to
receive a cloth for sby, (me)! má

a'í ǹdrí má ágúi drí rá I re-
ceived a goat from my friend; (3)
to collect, gather; a'í tí mà lɔ̂dè
ègáä sì, zú 'alɛ́ 'yazɔ̌, lɛ́sú
tɔ̀zö they gather cows' urine in
a calabash, to rinse out the gourd
in which to put milk.

à'íi or à'ípi or à'í-àzí, n. wives of
one man or of brothers call each
other thus: rival (polygamy),
sisters-in-law.

à'íiɔ́ or ɔ̀dzíiɔ́, av. in the later
morning hours; ètú tsa à'íiɔ̀rö
the sun has reached the pleasant
morning stage; yöö à— àmba sì
he is basking in the morning
sun.

à'í-ɔndzɔrɔ́kɔ = ĕkíkía, n. small
black ant; èri 'bá tsî-tsï it bites.

ai, &c., see ayi, &c.

àkà, av. at random, spontaneously,
of one's own initiative; mu 'í drì
sì àkà, ɛ'yɔ̂ zi kɔ́kɔ̀rö he went
at his peril, without asking; àkà sì
deliberately, knowingly.

aká = àmbá, a. big, mature,
grown-up; old; important; mo-
mentous; ɔ̀kɔ́ àká old lady; 'bá
àká ándrâ drìɔ great man of the
past; àɳá àká/àmbá or ándríi
thickly set spike of corn; ma atíi
mà ráɳá àká, èri àfó 'bǎ ànï the
ox of my father is fully grown, he
is proud of it; ɛ'yɔ́ àká important,
serious matter.

aká (1) vt. to dissolve, melt,
liquefy; ma aká ɔ́sɔ̀ 'dìrï àtsí sì
I have liquefied this fat on the
fire; (2) vn. to dissolve, &c.;
sàbunì aká ìyí sì the soap dissolved in water; é 'bà ɔdo ètúa
mà aká-aká! (= é 'bà ɔdo mà
aká ètúa) take the fat into the
sun to melt! (aká = ra here); (3)
vn. to be weak, extenuated, flabby
(though possibly fat); ma aká

əndí sỉ aká-aká I am (old and) weak and (therefore) untidy; mu rùá akáza sỉ kö, mu rùá mbazà (or əkpɔ́) sỉ he did not walk feebly but powerfully; (4) vn. (= mènèmènè) to be soft, lithe, supple, slender; à'bɔ̀à aká-ạká mènèmènè the banana is (over-) soft.

àká-ŋgáláká (cf. àká), a. of an extraordinary size; màākò èri à—; kà əŋgɔ̀rɔ̀kɔ̀ ɔ̀lò 'anï kö, èri àlârö the potato is enormous; if worms have not hollowed it, it will be excellent.

àkànyà, n. donkey.

àkárá, n. a sharp-pointed hard wooden spike; èri kəŋgələkɔ̀rö; èi ànï tí sɔ̀ it is very hard; they may stab a cow with it.

àkáráfí, n. cooked (but dried) food for travelling (cf. Ac. pɛ́kɛ viaticum) consisting of ɔ́sɔ́ pi ɔ̀ndó bɛ pi àṇú bɛ beans, durra, sesame.

àkéké or àtsétsé, n. roar of laughter; à— guzɔ̀: 'bá pírïnï guzɔ́ əkpɔ́ sỉ a peal of laughter, when all laugh noisily.

àkỉ = àkíkỉ or əfífíá, n. small pustules, pimples: àkỉ ɛŋgá mỉ andratiá your face is covered with pimples.

àkíndía, n. a kind of red durra (with close bunch/ear): alu tɔ̌ is very pleasant to eat.

àkỉ-rỉ S. = lɔ̌kìrï, a. clever; cunning . . .

àkɔ̀ or kɔ́kɔ or kɔ́kɔ̀rö, pstp. without, lacking; mỉ bbílé àkɔ̀ tɔ̌ you are extremely deaf (really or figuratively: obstinate).

àkò, vn. to be/become thick or dense; e'dí (or tíbí)nï àkò, or emúzɔ̌ èdûru àtsía gruel becomes thick on the fire.

ákə'dúku, n. a horned caterpillar (brownish).

àkpà, = əmbɛ́, vt. to compress; press different objects together.

àkpἆ (= mvá-àkɔ̀ǎ), n. tweezers; . . . ti-bbí ɔ̀tỉzɔ̌ for pulling out hairs of beard.

ákpäkù, n. lower jaw, part of chin.

àkú, n. home; village; àkúa to, at, from home; àkú'bá countryman; àkúarỉ of home, of the village; 'dỉ 'bá àkúarỉ these are people from home; àkú-drì or rî-drì, n. courtyard (of village).

àkù, vt. (1) to wink, beckon (with hand, tongue, . . .) (cf. èkù); (2) to collect, snatch in too great quantity (in eating, thus prejudicing others); mí àkù 'bánï tíbí kö! do not snatch the savoury away from people! (3) to do the rough part of tilling; èri ŋgá 'alɛ àkǔ ɛ'bó sỉ he digs and breaks up the field with a hoe; əkónï ŋgazɔ̌ emúzɔ̌ tsəzɔ̌ mɔ̌ké bɛnï the woman then beats it nicely (smooth); ma ṇaakú àkǔ 'bílía (cf. kù) I am raking earth into the hole.

akú, vt. (1) drì to cover over, conceal (carefully; cf. òpì cover); mí akú drì-nï tsỉ! conceal it well! (2) ti akú to turn upside down; èri émvó mà ti akǔ (vàá) she puts the pot upside down.

aku, vt. to shut, cover with . . .; aku èrimà ti tsỉ he covers his mouth (with hand).

àkúfí, n. leavened corn, leaven, yeast; èi à —ɛdɛ̌ éwá ərozɔ̌ they prepare leaven for making beer; éwánï 'alɛ ṇa à— sỉ the beer works through leaven; éwánï dra à— sỉ beer becomes sour through leaven.

àkufi-àkufĩå or àkufi-àrĩá n. sparrow; èimà dzɔ́ gónï ór

àzìnï tégòlà tálá its abode is a
hole in a tree, or among tiles.
ákúkù = àkùlúkú = (əlí) òlukúkù, n. sudden short gusty
wind; á— εŋgápi àmbôrö
àŋgö εzápi storm rising powerfully and causing damage; or
érìtí εŋgápi əzʋʋ́ pì ʋ̀lí pie: 'dì
ákúkù-nï clouds with rain and
wind make a storm.
akúma = arambako, n. hard
clear clean place on the side of
village (for spreading corn . . .);
in this place children lure and
collect ákúrúmba termites for
tíbí.
ákúrúmba, n. termites collected
on akúma (q.v.): ʋ́ɳa akúma
drìá.
àlá, a. clear, clean, pure; ecclesiastical: holy; dzʋ́ 'dì mà 'álé
àlárö the inside of this hut is
clean/the hut is clean; 'bá àlárì
saints; àlátátárá or àlátárârö very very clean, brilliant.
ala, vt. (1) to cross; alazà, a.
crosswise, transverse; pätí alazà
cross; gìrì alazà cross-way; é
mu gìrì alazà 'dì sì! take this
side-path! (2) to cross, thwart,
interpose obstacles; əzʋʋ́ ala mà
drìlé tsí; mà mu ŋgʋ̀ sì yà?
rain crossed my way; how should
I go!
alá, vt. to mix/season a savoury
with simsim or the like; èri zá
à'í-sú (or any tíbí) alá áɳú (or
mànìà) sì she seasoned meat broth
with simsim . . . oil; alá tíbí aláalá she seasons the savoury.
ala in ètú ala, av. in the afternoon
(about 12–6 p.m.).
àlàbàdrìʋ́ = làbàdrìʋ́, làbʋ̀drí
T. = ʋ̀ndátá, n. the big redheaded lizard.
àlàká, n. dried gàlàkà-grass (used

as kind of torch); à— èri kàlàbà
'wípi 'bərì, ʋ́ɳa̤ tεzʋ́ it is dried
'kalaba' grass (burning) for collecting termites.
álálàa, n. sparrow-hawk.
álánda, n. cake of termites; ʋ́ɳa
'bání a'dí 'bərì; èri 'baárö; èì
ə'wí-ə'wí ètúa termites after
having been cooked (and in cake
form); they dry them in the sun.
àlàpàlà or àlàpàpà, n. butterfly;
'bá à— esú pätí fʋ̀ mà drìá one
finds butterflies on flowers.
àlátárá or àlátátárá, a. (see àlá)
very clean, pure; ìyí 'dʋ̀ mà
mïlé àlátárá`rö(=ndrì̤ tʋ̀ʋ̤) this
water looks very clean.
'alé (cf. 'a), inside, interior; tsúpà
mà 'alé pírïnï the (inside of)
bottle is empty; 'aléa, 'alïa in;
'alé-nï-á in it; éká 'alé part between two joints of sugar cane or
the like.
'alé? inter. prn. how is it that . . . ?
how could/should . . . ? é 'du té
mâ búkù 'alé? how is it that you
took my book?
álé, n. reflection of self-accusation,
self-reproach; èri 'í álê dε (depressed/low-spirited) he indulges
in brooding self-reproach.
àlè¹ = ʋle, dzε, vt. to buy, marry.
àlè², vn. to pass (sth.) through sby.'s
legs; àlè 'bá mà pálá sì (part of
magic ceremony).
àlí, n. a small part, half; àlö
àlí bε one and a half; àfa dzʋ́lʋ́
kʋ́nï 'bá nï kolé àlíokʋ́-nï the
remains of a thing people have
left over is a (small) part; àlínï ko
tsí half remained over ($\frac{1}{3}$ or $\frac{1}{4}$?).
àlì = lʋ̀ndrè, n. colobus monkey; àlì atsípi pätí sía sì the
colobus which walks on trees.
álìì = ágíi, n. companion, thing
that matches with another; búkù

'dà mà álíinï ŋgòá yà? where is the companion of those books?

álí or ólí, n. *Acacia seyal* or *Holstii*; èri otsí bɛ it is thorny.

alï, = a'dï, vt. to connect, knot; mí alï báká (tï) tsí! connect the rope (end)s! ma ásé alï ṅdrí 'ï-zǒ I knot up grass to fasten goats at.

ali, vt. (1) to divide, cut to pieces and distribute; mâ mu ɛ́ká 'alɛ́ ali andzi nǐ let me give (share) out sugar-cane joints to the children! (2) to cut across, take a side-path; má ali gèrì wɛrɛ 'dò sǐ I am taking this short side-path; gèrì ali²rö-ali (= alazà) side- or cross-way; à'dïpì èì ali (=aga) 'dànǐ yà? who are passing there? mvá àlö ali dzó andratiá sǐ a boy passed in front of the hut.

alí, vn. to attain womanhood (by first occurring menses); záa 'dǐ alí rá; ɛtsó àlèzàrö rá this girl is grown-up; she can marry; èri alí bɛ or alí-alí or mba 'bɔ she is grown-up.

àlí¹, n. act of fornication or adultery; grave legal-social offence of parents; àlí 'bǎ to commit fornication or adultery; 'bà àlí 'bá àzǐ mà záamvá (or òkó) sǐ (= bɛ), he committed fornication (or adultery) with sby.'s daughter (wife); ɛ'bé 'î drìá àlí (záamvá sǐ) he contracted debt for fornication; àlí 'bá adulterer or fornicator; àlí-mvá illegitimate child; mvá 'dǐrï 'bánï ndrâ tilé àlîrö 'dǐǐ a child they begot by fornication/adultery.

àlí², n. trouble, hatred, hostility; àlí ndǎ 'bá vǒ to start/provoke animosity, hatred; á lè àlí kö I do not want trouble, hatred; àlí'bá adversary; é sò pá (= mí ɛ'dá

mí) àlí 'dǐ mà drilía! take yourself the responsibility for this crime!

àlí = káí, n. customary fine for fornication or adultery; èì mónió àlö fě àlîrö: 'bánï àlí 'bàzǒ záamvá bɛ rǐ they pay an ox for fornication, for having had illegitimate intercourse with a girl.

álí, n. a. deep; ìyí 'dǐrï álí (bɛ) (= álîrö) this water is deep; àŋgǒ á— (= gúrû-ru) the place is deep (low-lying).

àlí(ìá), a. short; 'bá àlíìárǐ short person, dwarf; gèrì àlí sǐ by a short way, short expression.

àlí-àtsáai = ɛ́wá ìyí, n. the dregs of edzí, i.e. third beer; èì mvu 'dáanï they drink it anyway (without ceremony or pay).

àlíbɔ = àlíòá, n. partridge.

àlïkàlï, n. frog (with bulging eyes, largely webbed toes and wide jumps).

àlǐkí, n. roll made of sticks (àrífɛ) and fixed on opening of granary; èì èrô tǐ tsɔ à— sǐ; èì à— rùá ndrǎ báká sǐ they make the rim of granaries with it; the roll of sticks itself is wrapped up with rope.

àlǐkó, n. stubble of grass (after cutting kàlàbà) in the veldt —áséa.

àlío, a. poor, needy, indigent, penniless; ágúpí àṇàpá òkô dzɛzǒrǐ kókòrö èri à— (= ódzóló) a man without cattle to marry a woman is indigent; má àlío mvánï I am the child of a wretch.

àlíóá = àlíbɔ, q.v.

àlíría, n. (1) young woman (before having had a child); (2) first child of a woman; mvá 'bánǐ tì kàyórǐ a child born as first.

àlö, num. 1, one; **àlö-àlö** singly, one by one; **àlözőrï** the first.

álɔ́, n. peg (to fasten cows, goats); **mĭ ɛ̀fɛ̀ mánĭ tĭ álɔ́ àlö ɛ̀ri 'ĭ zŏ** give me a peg to fasten the cow to!

àlò (cf. **lò**), vt. **àfa drĭ àlŏ** to reduce, break up lumps of earth; **ɛ̀i ŋaakú** (or **ɔ́tɔ́kɔ́**) **mà drĭ àlŏ** (= **g̊àga**) **ɛ'bó sĭ** they break lumps of earth (termite-hills) to pieces with a hoe.

alɔ́, vn. to be/become slack, loose, shaky, not firm; **alɔ́zà** very shaky.

álófɛ (or **àlófɛ, à'béfɛ, àpífɛ**), n. bridge; ladder; any large strong timber used as support for some over-structure.

àloko, n. (1) particular kind of tattoo (**ɔ̀tsɛ**) of girls; (2) a kind of sweet potatoes.

aloma-aloma, n. (1) a kind of tattoo on breast; (2) **drɛ́ká a—a—** a large kind of mushroom.

alóma-alóma = T. **ɛ́mvɛ̀ àloa**, n. diphtheria; **a—a— 'ĭ 'bá olíkò** diphtheria compressed one's windpipe.

àlɔ́ɔri T. = **drĭ'bá.**

àlotoko or **àlokoto**, n. creeper with bean-like fruits; beans and leaves eaten eagerly; stem used for fibre, or burned to obtain lye/salt; **àlotoko-bbí** or T. **òlògbùá-bbí** leaves-vegetable of former (is planted).

àlotsɔkö = **mólá**, n. a large fat field mouse; **ăg̊átinï ɛmvɛ̀rö, rúánï òkàkòkà** its breast-part is white, its body brownish (eaten by many).

àlú, n. reed-rat (Ac. **anyïïri**).

alú, vt. to curse, execrate, bewitch; **'bá àzĭnï mĭ alúzŏ; ma alú ɛmĭ 'dĭ̀: 'á drà a'dúlɛ kö, è drà má vŏ sĭ ndĭ̀ !'** I curse you

thus: 'I will not die alone, you shall die after me also!' **alútáa**, n. curse; **'bá 'dà drà alútáa sĭ** the man died from a curse.

alu, vn. to be of pleasant taste, palatable, agreeable; also: **àdzínï alu tŏ** very much relished, appetizing.

àlú-g̊bɛ́, n. infertile egg; **a'ú-g̊bɛ́ ɛ̀rinï ɔdzá kö 'dĭ** when eggs do not develop (into chickens).

àlùkàắ, n. plant with (round) tuberous root which continues to multiply; leaves similar to those of an onion; root with pleasant odour.

álúrùá, n. quail.

álúrù-'dŏ or **lúudrì** another **lâŋgò 'dŏ**, n. kinds of eleusine.

àlúrùzú or **àlúùzú** (also **àlîzú**), n. gourd-bottle; **ɛ̀ri kéré: ombɛ-lékɔ̀nï èzĭrö: tinï kùlùru (ŋgö-lŏrö)** it is a gourd: the neck is long and thin, the head is enlarged and round.

àma full size prs. pron. we, us; **àma-drĭ...à(ma)mà,**poss. our(s).

amá = **pɛ̀**, vt. to choose, select; **ɛ̀ri 'ĭ tĭ amắ tĭ àzĭnï mà 'alĭá** he is sorting, picking out his cows among others.

àmá = **ɔ̀ndí**, a. dirty, untidy (used only for **ti** face); **mĭ̂ ti àmá²rö, é mu ɔ̀dzĭ !** your face is dirty, go and wash!

àmakà, a. rotten; **kànï zá mᾰma, ɛ̀i ɔmvɛ zá a—** when flesh is decaying they call it rotten flesh; **mòɛ́mbɛ̀ à—** rotten mango.

àmali, a. calm, gentle, soft, well-behaved; **'ɔ'ápi 'yɛrɛ** that which behaves quietly; **tĭ à—** placid cow; **mvá à—,** i.e. **ɛ̀ri 'ɔ'á ɛ̀ndzìtáa sĭ** obedient boy; he is respectful/well-educated (opp. **àmbò**).

àmaŋgali, a. bad-smelling, stinking; **'dàaká àmaŋgali˄rö (ŋgù-zàrö)** excrements stink.

àmarà or **àmorà** or **èdïïa,** n. epilepsy.

àmbá = mbàazà, 'wàarà, dèzà, n. old, grey person; **èrimà drìá ɔ̀zɔ̀fɔ̀rɔ̀ tsï** he has grey hairs/he is hoary.

amba, n. a very harmful weed; **fönï ɛka fɔ̀rɔ̀** has reddish-yellow flower; **èri ɛbíkɔ** it has large leaves; **èri ɔ̀rï fùfu; ŋaaká pírï èi atrú-atrú: àŋgɔ̀nï ambàrö** it chokes seeds; it stunts corn, because the ground is invaded by **amba.**

àmbé, n. (1) gruel stirred up with milk (large quantity) **'édí 'bánï ɔsalé lésú sïrï;** (2) (= **kàfőa, àmbéré)** remnant of a hoe; (3) (= **àmbérèká)** fried bean broth; **ɔ́ső 'bánï osí rá 'dìi, 'bá èri 'i eníkèni: 'bá èri ɔsa ìyí sï** they fry beans, grind them fine and mix them with water.

ambí, vn. to become/be cool, cold; **ìyí, àŋgɔ̀ ambí-ambí** water, it is cold; **ɔ̀kpɔ́ ambízàrö** left-over food of yesterday is cold; **àŋgɔ̀ ambí ndró** the place is cold—empty (abandoned).

àmbó, n. person of age, position, authority; master, lord; **'bá àmbɔ̀rörï, 'bá ro èri rá** p. of position, they revere him; or **'bá èi òrì-òrì** they fear him (cf. Ac. Làdïït); a. much, large.

àmbò, n./a. obstinacy, intractability; **-rö, -rï** obstinate, unyielding, disobedient; **mvá 'dïrï àmbò bɛ** (or **-rö), eri 'bá áŋgírï 'dìi mà ti ko** this boy is obstinate, he disregards the words of the elder.

ámí, n. a climber; **èri pätí ɛŋgápi**

ìyí-tìá; èrì ra pätí àzïnï mà rùá sï; 'bá ànï èróti sɔ̀ it is a plant growing by the riverside; it creeps/climbs up some tree; it is used for the rim of a granary.

àmía, àmí'bá, n. assistant, associate in fieldwork (invited from the wayside in friendly, joking manner); **mï èri ɔmvɛ'àmía' gìrìkɔ ámvú vélérï sï** you call him **àmía** from the path on the side of the field. If he has accepted, he afterwards becomes 'amia'ba' at a simple meal.

àmïnï = màrarà, n. mirror; **à— èi ànï 'bá lǔ** they look at a p. with it.

amo, n. (1) heap of earth for planting potatoes: **èi mààkò sö amo 'a** (or **drìá); é lì amo mààkò saző** pile up heaps to plant potatoes; (2) heap of weeds of field, burned later **amo ámvu drírï, èi ŋga ɛvɛ-ɛvɛ.**

àmó'dőá, n. a kind of eleusine.

àmorà, same as **àmarà,** q.v.

àmorè, a. not ready-cooked; **ɔro e'dí/a'dï ŋaaká— àmorè-rö** she stirred the gruel/cooked the food—not getting it ready; **éŋá 'dïrï àmorè-rö** this polenta is not ready-cooked; **àfa anípi** (i.e. **àtsíá) körï** anything not fully cooked (i.e. on fire) is **àmorè** (Ac. **numu).**

àmórèká, n. prong-like ornament (of glass, metal...); **èi tsòfàríà mà ɛríkò 'di àmórèká 'rö; èi sǔ tìá: àzïnï bbía, àzïnï ɔmbɛlékɔ̀á** they forge a piece of aluminium-pot into a prong-like cone and fit it in lip, or on ear or neck.

ámukɔ, n. heap of weeding; **ásé ɔ̀kóèi nï tra pärí àlőárï, èinï ŋga emú ɛvé àtsí sïrï** grass which women gather (in field clearing) which then they will burn.

àmurö or **ɔ̀kó àmurö**, n. recently married young woman; **ɔ̀kó èìnï ɔlɛlɛ́ ɔ'dïrï̀**; **á mu mâ àmurö-(g̊)aa** I went to my fiancée (still at her father's).

amuti = **àdàti, yŏkö (sï̀)**, av. by turn; **andzi èì a— ŋġa** (or **'ä̀**) the boys work/till by turn; =**andzi èì ámvú 'ä̀ a—** (or **yŏkö) sï̀**, the boys till the field by turn; **andzi èì tí ɔtsɛ̃̀ yŏkö sï̀** they herd cattle alternately.

àmvà, amvo, ru T. vt. to cover, copulate with.

àmvɛ́, av. outside, away; **fɔ̀ à—** he went out or away; **mvá àmvérï̀** the boy who is outside.

ámvíi or **ámvípi**, n. sister; **ámví àzï̀** half-sister.

amví, vt. to touch, finger, handle; **èri mâ drì a— a—** he handles my head (cf. **ɔló** to lightly touch, graze).

amvi, vt. to repeat (an action), to do over again; **èri 'dɔ̀-fárä̃** (or **àn̠áfɔ̃rá) amvi onï driá** she is grinding over the eleusine (other …) flour again; **èì ámvú amvi ɛ'bó sï̀** they scratch over the field again with a hoe (to cover up seeds); **èríbí a—** to chew the cud, ruminate.

amvo, vt. (1) = **bï̀** to catch, embrace; **ɔ̀kó a— mvá tsï̀** the woman embraced the child; (2) (of male animal) to cover (female), copulate; **ǹdrínï a— a—** the goat (**áġó**) is covering.

ámvú = **ŋġá**, n. field (for cultivations); **èri ámvû ga, á— 'ä̀** he thoroughly digs, tills the field.

amvú (= **andzú**), vn. to dissolve (in water…); **à'ínï amvú ìyí sï̀** salt dissolves in water; cf. **à'í kà**

ɔvö tíbí mà 'a̠léa, 'bá ɔmvɛ aso-aso from salt in savoury they say **asoaso: à'í aso rá yà?** is it pickled with salt?

Ámvúléti, prop. name of Mrs. Hare (of fables).

ánákù̀lé, n. palate.

ándá, av. by chance, accidentally, suddenly; by good luck; unexpectedly; **á mu á— zá driá** on a sudden/by good luck I came upon 'flesh' (i.e. game); **mï̀ etsá á— dzɔ́ mádrírï̀á** you arrived at my hut by chance.

àndɛ̀, (1) vt. to annoy, vex; **mï̀ à— má ɛ'yɔ́ sï̀ 'dínï àsï̀ rɔ̀?** why do you annoy me in this way with talking? (2) vn. to be tired, annoyed; **ma à— kái** (or **rá**) I am very tired.

àndèsé (or **-sá**) = **ɔ̀rɔ̀táa** n. compensation, remuneration (for service done).

andï or **àndï̀ 'ï** = **ɛtsɔ 'ï**, vn. to break, go to pieces; **tsúpà a— 'ï rá** the bottle broke in pieces; cf. **ɛ́mvó mà ti ndï̀ 'ï rá** (a piece from) the rim of the pot broke off.

àndì, vn. to muddle, confuse words or names in speaking (= **abá**); **mï̀ à— (or abá) ɛ'yɔ́ 'dï̀ sï̀ à— à— (abá-abá)** you have got tied up with your words.

àndï̀, n./a. strange (to one's clan or tribal group), foreigner; **'bá à—** a stranger/foreigner (in wide or strict sense); **atsí àŋġò àndínï̀á** he travelled to a foreign country; **mï̀ àndínï̀** = **mï̀ dzúrúnï̀** you are a foreigner!

ándɔ́ or **ɔ̀bìlàkà ándɔ́**, n. hyrax; **èri ɔvö ónî ġóá** it lives in mountain caves.

andra or **andre** (also **ɛ́dre**), n. tongue; **mï̀ esɔ̃́ mï̀ andra!** put out your tongue!

àndrà = **ambé**, vt. to wrap (or tuck) up/round: **èri bàlàŋgíti àndrǎ 'ǐ rúáa tsǐ** he wraps a blanket round his body/himself.

andrá, av. down, below, in the valley; in lower lying country; **dzó èridrí a— 'dà**, his hut is down there; **andrálé**, a. lower; **ti andrá-lé** lower lip (opp. **örúlé**); **sí andrá-lé**, lower tooth/teeth; **'bá andrá-rǐ** or **andrálé'bá** or **andráláa**, n. low-land people (i.e. Tɛrɛgo–Omugo, &c. = T.).

ándrǎ, av. the day before yesterday; formerly; **á— drìə** in the past, long ago; **èri ('bá) ándrǎ-drìə** (= **'bá ɔ̀kpɔ́lɔ̀nï**) he is a very old man.

àndràndràlúfɛ = **mbɛ̀mbɛ̀lúku**, n. large green locust with long tapering head.

andralí or **andrɛlí**, n. dew; **a— 'a ásɛ́ rúáa** dew is on grass.

andrápïrö (cf. **áúpï**), n. aunt (mother's sister).

andrati, n. forehead, face; **andrati-á**, av./pstp. in front, ahead of; **èri ma andratiá** he is in front of me.

andrɛ, see **andra**.

ándríi or **ándrépï**, n. mother; female; **ǹdrí á—** she-goat; **a'ú á—**, **tí á—** hen, cow.

ándríi in **àṇá ándríi**, n. a kind of eleusine.

andrí, vt. to (go to) visit or see; **mu èrimà ándríinï andrî** he/she went to see his/her mother.

andrí, vt. (1) to whirl, sweep away; **ɔ̀líinï àfa andrî** the wind whirls things away; **ɔ̀kó èi àṇá milé (andrí)ndrî** (= **vo**) **kóbì sǐ** women clean corn by causing wind with a **kobi**-fan; (2) to swing, move in a circle (rite).

àndrí (cf. **ndri**), n. oracle, magic power, charm; **àndrí 'bâ ndrizǒ-rǐ** charm to bewitch people; **èri àndríbɛ, èri 'bá ɛnǎ** (= **ndri**) he possesses magic, he bewitches people with it; **àndrí 'bǎ** to consult means of magic (as **è'yá-fǐ**, q.v.).

àndrò, av. today; **mu à—** he went today; **àndrò-rǐ**, a. of today; **ètú àndrò-rǐ mǒkɛ́** today's sun/weather is nice; **'yə tɛ́ ɛ'yó 'dǐrï kilé àndrò-rǐlé** he told the matter as if (it was) of today.

andro, vn. to become or be soft, to crumble easily; **é kà màäkò sö àtsía, èrì dí a— mə̀ənə̀** (or **mɛ̀nɛ̀**) if you put potatoes in the fire, they become soft.

ándró, n. (heap of) ruins; abandoned village site; **á— èri àŋgò dzó ùwù-zǒ rá-rǐ'ï** 'ándró' is a place from which they have moved the huts; **àŋgò fǐ àkú á—: 'bá àkúa yə** the place is an abandoned village: there are no villagers.

àndró[1] = **àndrótáa**, n. address, speech; appeal, instruction, sermon; **àndrô ndzɛ** to address, appeal, have a sermon; **má átíinï mánǐ à— ndzɛ** my father gives me instructions; **ɛmbápinï à— ndze àndrò** the teacher is giving instruction today.

àndró[2], n. in **bǐ 'bá mà à— tsǐ** to be generous with a p.; **bǐ àndrónï tsǐ** he was generous with him (forgiving him or giving him something).

àndró = **drətáa**, see **ndrə**.

àndrù = **àtə̀**, vn. to start rotting, decay slightly; **ónya à—à— (ŋgùŋgù)** termites start rotting (smelling; collected the day before).

àndrúkù or màndrúkù or óndù-rúá, n. pangolin.

andú or àndù, vt. to fool, make fun of; to wrong; àndù ma rá he has fooled (or wronged) me.

àndzà = à'yà, vn., to be jealous; mî milé àndzà mási you are jealous of me.

àndzá, n. penis; à— mà àwáfí gland of penis.

àndzé-àndzé =ɳàɳa = tồtồ = dồdə, n. 'hopeless case', irreclaimable; unmendable; mvá 'dǐ wereáárö à—à— this child is small: an incurable case! é 'bǐ Lógbàrà ti ɛmbá tǐ; mî dí àlö ɳáàɳa! you try in vain to learn Logbara; you are a hopeless case!

andzi, pl. of mvá, n. children.

andzi = aɳi, vt. to crush, squeeze flat; a— ógáálírí drí sǐ he crushed a flea with his fingers; èi öró a—a— (pá sǐ) they crush a snake under foot.

àndzì or à— 'bìrìtì or àndzírítítí, a. thick, strong (as paste-board, timber...); lítsó mà gbólóà—'b— pen shingles are thick and strong (opp. èpéèrö thin—transparent).

àndzí, n. member of a clan or tribal group; Pàdzùlú à— a Padzulu clan-member.

ándzíríkáandzi, = ńdzí, q.v.

andzö, (1) vt. to break down; undo; èri dzó òkurǐ a— rá, èri ə'díni ɛdé 'ǐ he is breaking down the old hut and making a new one; (2) vn. to sever from, break with; òkó a— 'ǐ ágúpi bɛ rá the woman severed herself from her man (cf. əndzö).

ándzörökò, n. trinkets, knick-knacks; finery; èi əmbɛ òpílía, əmbɛlékòá, nòsì páa, nòsì dría they fasten them on waist, neck, legs, hands.

àndzù, vn. to be washed clean, polished; rùáni à—à— he is clean.

àndzù = amvú, vn. to dissolve, liquefy; à'íni andzú (= àndzǔ, amvú) iyí sǐ salt dissolves in water; ósəni à— ètú sǐ fat liquefies in the sun.

andzu, vt. to tie, fasten; èi bòngó a— báa sǐ they tie the cloth with a string (rope); ópílɛmvó èri àni bòngó a— a belt he fastens with the cloth.

ándzú = ambízà, a (1) cool, moist, wet; àngò 'dàri ándzú màákò sazó the place is (suitably) moist for planting potatoes; (2) ásí á— peaceful, meek, calm; 'bá ásí ándzû-rö (= á— bɛ) (= ambízàrö), əmbàni yə a gentle (mild, sweet) person, he does not quarrel.

àndzùkù-ru, n. éɳá à— polenta made from corn not previously roasted éɳá 'báni ànyá əsí körǐ.

àni, rel. av. with it, by that, for that reason, &c.

ani = atsí, vn. to spoil, get spoiled or damaged (of ripe fruit; by unfavourable weather), deteriorate; 'dó, à'bòà, &c., ani-ani eleusine spoiled (in rain and fell to the ground and burst out), bananas got spoiled (after ripening).

aní (cf. ni), vn. to transform, convert (into appetizing food by cooking); éɳá or e'dí aní 'bə the polenta or gruel has curdled; ədza rö kòzàrö; kà aní kö alu kö it becomes (mass of food on cooking) thickened and brownish (colour of finished food); if it does not curdle, it is not palatable.

ááni, bíni ááni or kaáni ááni, av. perhaps, possibly, maybe: fǐ 'aléníá ááni it (he, she) possibly entered (or went into the hut) it.

aní = àsɛ́ = ɔ̀bɛ́lɛ́, n. a black-grey scaleless lungfish (cf. ó'wï).

àní(b)ó, n. (1) = àmía, q.v.; (2) a stranger who arrives later and associates with or assimilates to an original group.

ắníkắní or ɳ̀àrákòá, ɳ̀iɳ̀ìá, òdù-dù mắndắrí, n. a wild plant (with hardened stem) ɛ̀ri ɛŋgá áséa it grows in the bush tsɛ́nɪ̀ (alone); èiɳɔ̀-ɳɔ̀ drí sɪ̀: éfɪ́nï enɪ̀rö kɪ̀lɛ́ mànïàlɛ́: èi ànï tíbɪ̂ ɳaa they break it (ear with seeds) off by hand (on harvesting); the grains are small and black like mania's (slightly larger than poppy's).

ànìkání = ànikáni or (poet.) èbì-yóo (-mbàmba), n. spider.

ániniá or anínía, av./a. staring/glaring fixedly (commonly absent-mindedly); mï á— nɪ̀ 'dínï à'do ɛ'yó sɪ̀ rɔ̀? why are you staring absentmindedly like this? mvá 'dàrï ániniâ-rö that boy is puzzled (in a daze).

ànío, n. a tree (Sapium ellipticum).

ànɔ́ or ámbá, n. a harmful weed; ànɔ́ mávélé ámvúa tsí, àɳ̀ání kaző kö there are 'anɔ'-weeds in my field so that the corn does not grow; àŋgò ànɔ̀rö/ámbârö area infested with 'anɔ'-weeds, hence: barren, deserted ground.

àŋgà (similar 'wï, oŋgú), vn. to dry (hard, stiff; at sun, fire); é fɛ̀ mà à— 'dïá ɔ̀gɔ̀gɔ̀, é dzi pắrí àzïa kö! let it dry here, do not take it elsewhere! ma rúá àŋgắ ètúá I dried my body in the sun; èi zá àŋgắ àtsí drìá they dry meat over the fire.

aŋga (= ɔva, ɛŋgá), vn. to boil, bubble up; to effervesce; ìyí

'bánï bɛ̌ àtsía ɛɳá ìyîrörɪ̀ ɛ̀ri a—a— the water they put on the fire for polenta is boiling.

àŋgà or ŋgà, av. yet, still; à— kö not yet; ɛ̀ri ŋgà 'dïá ɔ̀gɔ̀gɔ̀ he is still here; àŋgà ŋgà kö it is not yet dry.

àŋgálà or àìŋgá or fɛ́fɛ́, n. a. restless, fidgety; unmanageable, bustling; ágú 'dà rïï vàá kö,àŋgálànɪ̀ tɔ̀: ɛ̀ri atsí tɔ̀ that man cannot sit down, he is very restless: or he wanders about the whole time; tí 'dɪ̀ àŋgálà-rö (= mà à— tɔ̀) this cow is unmanageable (always separating from the rest).

àŋgàràbà = ndzèrùndzèrù, n. a savoury of beans (or the like) roasted, squeezed, or ground and cooked in water with the addition of some oil.

àŋgáríɔ̀á, n. small wild pigeon.

àŋgbà-zà = ɔka-zà(q.v.) = ɔmŋgba-ɔmŋgba, a. of greenish-reddish colour.

àŋgbakà = ɔ̀bằu, n. hyena.

àŋgbắlắo, n. ravenous p., glutton; mvá 'dà à— tɔ̀ that boy is a glutton.

àŋgílí(ká), n. a tree (Parinari curatellifolia) with edible fruits.

áŋgɪ̈́rí, a. big, large; of large quantity; 'bá á— very old person (often slightly weak-minded; preferably engaged to sacrifice to the spirits); ɛ́mvó á—á—(=ɔ̀yɔ̀ɔpi-ɔ̀—) very large pot(for beer...).

àŋgò, n. soil, ground; area, place, country; weather: earth, world; àŋgò-milé weather-outlook; à—trà: a'úátá èi tsérè ɔ̀'bɛ̀: ɛka ɳ̀ằarù dawn/daybreak, (when)the cock crows: distant red; à— tàa: à— àtɪ̀ (or ɔ́ú) 'bɔ it is full-clear day; à— kúrù (or pɪ́rɪ̀ mà) drìá all over the world.

aŋgɔ́, vn. to itch; **mâ rúánï a—a—** I feel itchy; **à'íríbɛnï a—'bâ rúáa a—a—** scabies itches on a p.

áŋgulú, T. (more common **óŋgulú**), n. big larva (found in waste-heaps).

àɲà, vn. to turn unfavourable; deteriorate, degenerate, grow worse; **ásínï àɲà mánï 'bɔ** or **àɲà ásí mánï 'bɔ** his feelings have turned against me; **mâ bélɛ́nï àɲà-àɲà** my sore has grown worse.

àɲá, n. cereals, corn/grain; **àɲá-(e)fï** grains of corn; **àɲá-fǒ (-fǒ-)rá** flour; **àɲá-sí ('anï amvízǒ)** (coarse or fine) grain of flour (judging by touch); **àɲá'bí'bí** corn cut and kept (still in its ears); **àɲârö** fertile, producing much corn; **àŋgǒ 'dï àɲârö** this ground is very fertile; **àɲá-kɔ̀rɛ fu ma kál** I have a great longing for cereal-food (after, say, long feeding on potatoes).

àɲà'bá, n. man-eater ('*kulia-bantu*' of public belief).

àɲá'bíɔ, n. mouse of veldt and granary (**ɛ̀rɔ́á**) (eaten).

àɲá-dzó, n. granary (= **ɛ̀rɔ́**); stomach.

áɲáká, n. stiff prickly hairs of some grasses; **á— ɛ́ká (or ɔ̀zó) mà rúáa, ɛ̀ri 'bá ɔ̀sɔ̀-ɔ̀sɔ̀** prickles of maize- (or reed-) stalks, it stings.

áɲáka, n. deposits of beer (in pot); **àfa rḯpï ɛ́wá ɛ̀tïárï ɛ̀i ɔmvɛ áɲáka-nï nɔ̀sì káɲá'dǒ: ɛ̀i dḯ dǎ vàá** what is deposited at bottom of beer, they call **áɲáka/dregs**: they pour it away (on to the ground).

àɲàkàɲà, n. blood-sucking vermin; **à— àfa tḯpï dzóarï** that multiplies in hut (as: **àgɔ́aká** (bug), **ɔ́gálírí** (flea), **ɔ̀'bú** (gadfly larva, jigger)).

àɲá-ndrî, n. kind of eleusine.

àɲá-ŋgárɛ̀ (cf. **ŋgárɛ̀**), n. time of harvesting corn; **à—ŋ— ɛ̀i atsí bàdàrö** at such time people go wandering off (no work and plenty of food).

aɲáó = **ŋgúru**, n. wild beast (large carnivora).

àɲàpá, n. animal; animals for marriage; **à— àkúarï** domestic, **à— áséarï** wild animals (excluding anyáó).

àɲá-ríɔ́ríɔ̀, n. kind of gecko (?).

àɲá-ti-bbí, n. 'beard' of corn (germinating exposed to moisture).

àɲï, cf. **ɛ̀ɲï**.

áɲíi, n. father-in-law.

áɲḯ, n./a. irony, sarcasm; ironic (mostly offensive); **ɛ'yɔ́ áɲïrö** angry—ironical words/speech; **'yɔ mánï áɲḯ** he says the opposite ironically; **áɲḯ ɔmvi (or ɔ̀tḯ)** to give an evasive answer/shuffle a bitter rejoinder; **mḯ mánï áɲî 'yɔ à'do sḯ yà?** why do you speak with irony?

aɲi, vt. to rub between hands (to obtain clean grains); **ɛ̀i 'dǒ (ɔ̀ndó, ɔ́sǒ ɲḯríkïa) aɲi-aɲi** they get eleusine (durra, small beans...) ears clean by rubbing between hands.

Àɲḯipi, n. a tribal group towards Rhino Camp.

Àɲïirá or Ètɔ́ɔ À—, n. name of Mr. Hare (of fable; cf. Mrs. Hare, Amvulɛ́ti).

àɲɔ̀, vt./vn. to break; **pätï àɲɔ̀-àɲɔ̀** the wood/stick broke; **é di ɛ̀ri rúá àɲɔ̀** you have beaten him most thoroughly; **àɲɔ̀(táa) = àndɛ̀táa, ɔ̀rɔ̀táa**, n. weariness, stiffness; 'bá àzínï ŋɔ̀'ï ŋɔ̀ŋɔ̀, sby. is weary, 'broken'.

aŋú, vt. = erí, q.v.

àŋú, n. bee; àŋú ósɔ̀ (or sú or ɛ́ŋá) honey; àŋú òdärї wax; àŋú éfї single bee; àŋú ò'bú bee larvae; àŋú 'bá dŏdŏ bees sting.

áŋú, n. simsim; áŋú ósɔ̀ simsim-oil; áŋú dàaká chaff from sesame cleaning; áŋú zɛ̀ or zɛ̀ká dregs from simsim-oil straining; áŋú ɔ̀dŏ ndzi-zŏ drí sї̀ to squeeze out simsim-oil with hands.

áŋû-ba, n. strainer (of cloth or plaiting screen); á— èi ànï ɛ́wâ zɔ they strain beer with it.

àó¹ (or àwї́), n. kind of creeping reed-grass (containing sugar); èi àó ɛvɛ́ à'î-rö they burn it to obtain lye = àó à'ї̀ zɔ̀ (Shilluk apaajo).

àó² = ɔ́ó or ɔ́ótáa (cf. ɔ́ó), n. crying.

àó³ (or awї́), av. at the last moment, by chance (happening); àó ... kö yé no longer; má àó mu kö yé, má andrîi àó ɛtsá tsî I am no longer going as my mother happened to arrive (cf. next).

àó⁴ (or awї́) ... ko, vn. to persevere in; persist in, to stand out for, to continue being ...; 'bá zɔ̌pi körї àô ko àlïíá one who does not grow, remains short/stunted; 'dï àô dí ko 'dï, asї dí zɔ̌ kö this (individual) remains at a standstill (stunted), he does not grow any more; àó àkúaa he continues staying at home; àô ko 'dálɛ́ he stopped there; wárágà àó iyí driá the paper stopped (floating) on the water; kàmìnï asї 'bá sï̀ kö, èri àô 'bâ ŋaa 'ï a lion does not care for (respect) a man, he persists in eating man.

a'ó, vn. (1) to yawn; mï̀ a'ó-a'ó 'dïnï! you are yawning like that! (2) to stutter; èrì a'ó ɛ'yó sï̀ a'ó a'ó he stutters on speaking.

à'óï-rö or à'wî-rö, vn. (1) to become or be dry; (2) (= èdú, kólóŋá) to be(-come) thick, dense; e'dí 'dï à'oîrö, the gruel is thick.

àóɔkó (more common ɔ́ókó), n. anger; èrì 'yɛ àokó (or àóɔkó) sï̀ (= bɛ) he acts out of spite; à—ŋa èrì rá he lost his temper.

àó = àótà, àwḯtà, n. property left; inheritance; àfa mánï̀ kolɛ̀ mávélɛ́rï̀ èri àónï; mvá mávé-lɛ́rï̀ dí má àô ŋa nï̀ mâ pàría things I leave (dying) after me are the inheritance; my child will eat my inheritance (= inherit) in my place; àfa mà àótà inheritance of things.

apá (cf. pa), vn. (1) to flee, (make one's) escape; é kà mu apá kö, òdrúnï̀ ŋga mï̀ fu rá if you do not make off, the buffalo will kill you; (2) (= pa 'ï) to escape alive, avoid death apá (or ɛ'bḯ) drà sï̀.

ápà, n. elevated flat wooden frame; ápà ɔ̀ndó ɔ̀'bàzŏ for airing durra.

ápàrákà, n. nuisance, prank; crazy trick; silly/mischievous, &c., acts; é 'bà á— àfa 'dï sï̀ kö! do not indulge in silly tricks here! 'á— mà tíbí àgóbbí 'pumpkin leaves are the sauce of mischief' (saying); ètóɔnï̀ ápàrákà-rö the hare (of fable) is cunning.

àpắrìtì = àkúti, n. the side/ flank of cleaned village space/ court; à— pàrí ókòrŏŋyà ddàzŏ it is the place to pour off refuse or sweepings; má mààkò saa àpắrìtì-á 'dïá I am planting potatoes on the waste-heap here.

ápàtá, n. groin/inguinal (region and) gland; **ma á— àzôrö** (= **èkèkèlé**) my inguinal gland is swollen.

apí = **trà**, vn. to be satisfied, satiated, full; **apítá** (= **tràtáa**) **éɳá sì rì** being satiated with polenta.

api, vt. to cut open, slit; **api rö**, vr. to split; **kàlámò api 'ï rá** the pencil split in two.

àpífɛ = **òlófɛ**, n. strong timber for some particular supporting purpose: bridge; ladder; base of cupboard.

apinaka, n. ant-bear; **tinï mbî-lîrö** its mouth is tapering off; **a— èri 'bílé ɔvá àmbôrö** it digs big (obliquely running) galleries; **èri màà'kò, óɳ,â ɳa** it eats (harmfully) potatoes, termites.

ápípïïá, n. tumour, morbid swelling; abscess, tumescence; **ápí-pïïá-nï 'bá èpi nì** a tumour causes swelling; **èri 'bá òpì ɔrɔ-á sì ndîïrí, ndúa sì, lómàá sì, milíá sì ùúgbúlúkù-ètí-á sì** it (may) causes tumours all over on buttocks, hind parts, flank, eyes, armpit; **ápípïïá-nï èpi tsɛnï 'dáanï** a tumour comes without apparent cause.

àpŏrà, àpŏr-à'í, à'í, n. terms for commercial mineral salt; **à'í-ògárí** salt in block.

apfû (-zàrö), a. decaying, rotten, crumbling away; **mba kö** not solid; **óní a—** brittle stone; **àɳá ap(f)ú ètú sì a—a—** (ripe) corn spoils in the sun (falling easily to the ground—on field).

à(p)fúrútò = **érífúrá**, n. dust; **èri ɳga òlí sì** it rises by wind.

ára = **ìyídrìpuuru**, n. water lily; **ára ráápi ìyí drìá** creeps on the water.

àrà, n. python; **àrà zánï tíbîrö** its meat serves as sauce (is eaten by many); **ósònï árò nï** its fat is medicine; **àrà-ábǎ(u)á**, n. a smaller kind of python.

ara, vt. to spread and arrange surface smoothly (and compactly); **mí ara mààkò ar-ara mà ò'bà 'ï wórò!** arrange the potatoes (in pot) so that they may all fit in; **ara…dri** to smooth surface and cover it (with durra, or other leaves); **é kà àɳâ lî 'bílía (éwârö), mï drinï ara tsí** when you press corn into a hole (for beer preparation), you smooth its surface, covering it.

àràkàlé = **àràkèlé** = **àtràkàlé**, n. free space between branches of any kind of ramification (as between fingers, prongs of a fork, on tree); **sí à—** gap of teeth (lost); **pätí à—** bifurcation on tree; wooden fork (for building); **'bá 'dà sò pá pätí àràkàléa** that person stands in the fork of the tree.

àràkílíyò = **àràkílíkɔ** = **àràwïä** = **àyuuri**, n. glossy starling (or blackbird).

arambakɔ = **ákúma**, q.v. n. smooth hard spot over a termite dwelling; **drìnïä adri réè/kpɛ-mŋgbɛlɛ/ndïï(tí)rí/àlá** it (the place) is bare (clear).

äráû, n. red Hussar monkey (Ac. **àyòòm**).

aráúâdrĕká, n. small reddish inedible mushroom; **bbínï èri wɛrɛ ɛkàrö; pánï rŏĕrö ɛmvĕrö** its pileus (cap) is small and reddish; its stalk thin and whitish.

àràwǎɳá, n. briar (its knotted root used for balls **pàɳà**).

àràwïä, cf. **àràkílíyò**.

àrè = **àdì**, vn. to suffocate, choke (with sth. sticking fast in throat);

àrὲ έŋá sǐ he had a choking fit from (eating) polenta; drà àrὲtáa sǐ he died from suffocation (believed quite uncommon).

àrí, n. blood; àrínǐ raa he is bleeding; 'dǐ má àrǐ this is my blood (i.e. child); pätí àrí (= sú) sap of tree; 'bá mà àrí-ti ɔfὲ̌ to (take) revenge for a killed p.; 'bá mà àrí pὲ̌ to celebrate the killing of an enemy.

arí, n. drum; é mu arǐ tsə! go and beat the drum! arínï ɔ́ð (ɔkpɔ́ sǐ) the drum resounds (powerfully).

arí, vt. (1) to contend, strive; andzi èì fúnò arí-arí the children are struggling for groundnuts (thrown to them); á 'bà má àfa 'dǐrï ko arízàrö I have given/left my things to be fought over; (2) (= ɛtɔ́ = pa = e'dú) to rescue, save; arí (= e'dú) mvá rá he saved (as snatching from water) the boy.

arï, vt. to sow; èì áŋú ɔrï arï-arï they are sowing sesame seeds.

ǎrǐ, vt. to prop, support; ǎrǐ té àfa 'dǐrï ká, ŋgà asó rö (= ɛ'dé) ndɔ̀ he had (first) propped up the thing, but still it fell down; ma pätí ǎrǐ dzɔ́ rúá I am propping a pole against the hut (-wall); ǎrǐ rö, to be caught (as falling fruit on tree).

àrï-àrï sǐ = ágá-ágá, av. reciprocally, mutually; àma àma ozí àrï-àrï sǐ we are questioning each other in turn.

àrǐ, a. abundant, copious, plentiful; 'dɔ̌, &c., ὲri àrǐ eleusine is plentiful (on field, in granary . . .).

arí-zàrö, a. hoarse, husky; ɛ'yɔ́ 'yɔlɛ́ tá (kí) rǐ sǐ o'dúkənï ədza rö arízàrö his voice became hoarse, because he had been talking so much.

àrǐïa, n. bird; à— gbɛ, sɔ́bí bird's egg, tail.

àrǐïatsɛtsɛ = àrǐïálɔ̀ɔkɔ́, n., a snake (= ?örí-óhulú).

àrǐbá, n. vein.

àríbío = oriio, n. a tree (with hard and tough wood).

àrí'bɔ́ = arï'ba, n. enemy; à— ὲri 'bá 'bâ'dǐpirǐ an enemy is a man who kills man.

arǐdrὲ̌ká, n. a very small, thin (edible) mushroom.

àrǐfɛ, n. a shrub yielding good twigs/rods for plaiting; ὲri pätínï wɛrɛ-wɛrɛ; èì à— ndrǎ àlǐkǐrö, èì ὲróti mbɛ ànǐ it is a slender stick, they wrap them round into a roll and make the rim of a granary with it.

àrǐka = ásí-àzó, n. dysentery; mï sɔ̌ àrǐ-rö, èì ɔmvɛ à— when you evacuate blood, they call it dysentery.

àríká, n. a grass with strong stem, boys make arrows with; à— ὲri έndὲrὲfínï àrǐïa tsàazɔ̌ the 'arika' is an arrow to shoot birds with.

àrìkǎrì, a. àdzí à— sweet-scented, fragrant, perfumed; ɔdo pi èì mbásàlà bɛ (àdzínï) àrìkǎrì-rö onion fried in oil has a strong smell.

àrílɔ̀kɔ́, n. a warbler, a thrilling songster; kà emú ɔ́ɔ́ mívélé àkútiá, ὲri ò'dù nï if it comes to sing beside your village, it is a bad omen.

àríoti = àróti = màríti or màróti, n. compensation, reparation; revenge; kànǐ 'bá àzínï 'du àfa mídrírǐ rá, ὲri àfa mídrírǐ mà à— ɔfὲ̌ if sby. has taken away your thing, he will compensate you for it; ὲri tábà 'du àfa 'dǐ mà àríotǐ-rö he took a cigarette

in compensation for this; **á gba
(mânǐ) má àríoti I** (for my part)
have struck as revenge; **èri 'ǐ à—
'yɛ (ga, 'bɛ, tsɔ, ə'dǎ . . .)** he does
it (cuts, throws, strikes, insults) in
turn/as revenge; **éŋa ńdrâ ɛ́dró,
ɛ́dró emú 'ímà à—ŋa** you have
once eaten mice, now mice (by
night) come to gnaw at you for
revenge; **àríoti ɔ̀fɛ̌** to compensate.

àrípá, n. spike—spear, or arrow
with slightly indented flanks.

àrɔ̀ or **àarɔ̀,** num. eight, 8.

áaró or **ɛ́ɛró,** n. medicine.

àrɔ̀-àrɔ̀, vn. to spring/put forth
(young shoots); **ásɛ́ (or àŋá) àrɔ̀-
àrɔ̀** grass (after fire) (corn) springs
up; **pätí 'bánǐ drì ga rárǐ, èri
àrɔ̀-àrɔ̀** a tree whose top has been
cut puts forth new shoots.

àró, a. unripe, green; **àŋá . . . ŋgà
àrɔ̂rö** the corn is still green; **èri
ŋgà kǎka** it is still only developing.

áró = áróndzɔ̀lá, ɔ̀ndzɔ́, n. a
wild lily; **èì ɛ'bǐ əva ásɛ́ 'alɛ́a**
they dig it (the root) in the bush;
èì ɔlánǐ sǐ mvá drì ɔ̀dzǐ (or mɔ̀)
they (crush and mix in water and)
wash a newly-born baby's head
with its root.

aró, vt. to take up/lift sth. (heavy)
with laborious care; **èì àfa ndzì-
zàrǐ aró-aró** they lift up a heavy
thing carefully; **mǐ edzí àfa
'dàrǐ, mǐ aróaró!** bring that
thing, but carefully!

àròkpà, vn./a. (1) showing/having
new sprouts; **àŋá (or ɔ̀rǐ wóró)
èri à—** the corn (or any seed) is in
its first sprouting; (2) **mvá à—**
baby after some months (supported it can sit upright) is strong,
fat.

àrənì, n. growing-up young female

(animals); **tí à—** a fairly big
heifer; **ńdrí à—, a'ú à—,** &c.,
young female goat (or lamb),
chicken.

àrɔ̀rɔ̀á, n. a large bird(? black ibis);
rúánǐ ënǐrö, tinǐ èzɔ̂rö-kəŋgələkə it is black with a long coarse
beak; **pánǐ àbatà pá lɛ́** it has
duck-like (web-) feet; **èri fǐ ìyí
ǹdúa è'bí ndǎ** it dives into water
in search of fish.

àrótá = èndzìtá (cf. ro, èndzì),
n. awe, respect, reverence; **ɔ́pí 'dǐ
mà à— èri àmbó: èì ɔ́pí ro tɔ̀**
the respect for the chief is great;
they respect the chief very much.

àrú (cf. ru to arrest), n. prison;
'bá bì (or ru) èri àrûrö sby. has
arrested him (seized for prison);
èì mu èri ɔndzɛ tí sǐ àrúa they
go to liberate him from prison
with a cow.

arú, vt. in **'bá mà drì arû (= ri)**
to domineer, prevail; to be
despotic; punish/impose atonement; **èri èì mà drì arû (or rì)**
he domineers over them.

Àrú, n. a river close to (SW.)
District's h.q. (B.C.); Aru, too.

àrú-àrù = àrútsú = àró (q.v.), a.
soft, tender, green: **mba ŋgà kö,
èri ŋgà àrɔ̂rö** it is not yet strong
(hard), it is green.

Árúwá, n. a small steep hill within
'Arua', WN. District's h.q.

Ásà, n. river rising E. of Arua; **mu
Átsá mà 'alɛ́a; Átsá ra kpɛrɛ
Mǐìrǐ mà 'alɛ́a** it runs into the
Atsa which reaches the Nile.

àsà, vn. (1) to be/look/appear hazy,
misty (lightly) cloudy; vague, indistinct; **àŋgɔ̀ 'dà àsà-àsà
(≅ ɛmvɛ̀rö)** that area looks misty;
àfósàrà sǐ àŋgɔ̀ àsà-àsà it becomes dim from mist; (2) (of
sight/eye) to see vaguely, indis-

tinct; ètúnï 'bà 'bá mà milέ àsà tsí, nè àŋgò wɛrɛ the sun makes one's eyes hazy (dazzles ...) so that one sees little; èri milέ àsà o'dú sǐ tsí his eyes are dim from sleep.

àsá = **àdzí**, n. good name, fame; **àsâ ndzɛ** to slander, calumniate (= **àdzî di**); **ma àsá yɔ** I have no name/reputation, i.e. I am unknown.

asa, vt. to prepare neatly the portion(s) of ɛ́ɳá—with the respective **tíbí**—on tray to present to sby.; **ɔ̀kónï ɛ́ɳá asa kóyi tǐá** (or **'alěa**) **dzi ágúpí drí; èi 'bá ámvú 'ǎpi ɔ̀yá sǐ 'dǐǐ mà ɛ́ɳá asa-asa** they portion polenta (and savoury) for the (few) hired field-workers.

asa, ɔsa (cf. **sa**), vt. to slap, smack a p.'s face, to box a p.'s ear over and over again.

asa, vt. to open (rather widely); **mǐ asa ti tsí = é 'yɔ ɛ'yó tsítsí, mǐ ɔ̀vù tsírí kö!** do open your mouth, do speak, do not keep silent! **èri ti asa o'dú sǐ** he opens his mouth wide in sleep; **àma asa á'dǐání aga** we made place (opening) between us to N.N.

àsákàlέ = **èsékèlέ, àsalá** = **èsɛlέ**, n. (1) line of division/demarcation, limit, boundary; line or space between; **ámvú mà à**—(= **lɔ̀kìri**), boundary line of fields; (2) **é mu bá 'dǎǐ mà àsalá awa, èi ɔ̀mbà 'bǎ** go and separate those people, they are fighting; (3) **é tsɔ àsákàlénï ìrrì, nna!** divide it in two, three (equal) parts; (4) **mâ dzó pätí (mà) àsákàlěa** my hut is in between the trees.

ásákàsà = **talakpà**, a. insipid, flat, tasteless, savourless; **ɛ́ɳá ásákàsà-rö, alu kókɔ̀rö** this polenta is insipid, not agreeable;

à'í tsa 'alénǐá kö there is not enough salt in it.

àsárɔ́, n. a tree (*Acacia sieberiana* or *A. tortilis*); **otsíní èzɔ̌rö** it has long thorns.

àssé, n. a medium-sized fish.

asέ = **atri, ɔga**, vt. (1) to bar, obstruct; **mǐ émvúléti asέ tsí; é dà mǐ mání émvúlétiá rá!** you are blocking the view (say out of window); do get out of my light! **mǐ asέ mání dzótilέ kö, ma ànï (mâ dzóa) àzî ŋga** do not block up the door-opening, I am working by it (-s light); (2) to hide, conceal (physically, organically); **bɔ̀ŋgɔ́ asέ ndô tsí, á nè èri kö** the cloth conceals the pail, I cannot see it; **èri milέ asέ tsí** he obstructs (shields, screens) his eyes; cf. **milénï èri asέ** (= **àsà**) **o'dúzù búkù làzǒ ètúkàárǐ sǐ tsí** his sight is impaired from continued reading in the sun; (3) vn. to be impaired, diminished, spoiled; **olíkɔ̀nï asέ tsí** his voice is impaired/hoarse.

ásέ, aísέ, n. (1) grass; **ásέ èbirǐ** green/tender grass; **ásέ à'wǐrǐ** dry grass; **mǐ edzí mání ásέ ɔmbézàrö** (or **drià**) **àlö!** bring me a bundle of grass! (2) veldt, bush; **mvá àvě áséa dɔriá** the boy went astray in the bush hunting.

àsɛtí, n. constellation girdle of Orion lit. **à sέɛ tí ɔ̀kóa!** let us take cows for the bride/wife!

àsì¹ (cf. **sì**), vt. (1) to knock together; **mǐ àsì àmà drì** you knocked our heads against each other's; (2) to fill in; **àsì dzó drì 'yǎbí sǐ 'bɔ** he has pushed grass into the roof of the hut already.

àsì², vn. (1) to stop short, interrupt (journey, &c.); **má té 'yè mu Árìŋgàá, ma àsì Kóbókɔ̀á** I was to go to Aringa, but I stopped at Kɔbɔkɔ; **mu àsì agaa awí drì atri vélé** he went and stopped half-way and came back; **mï àsì àzí sì à'do sì yà?** why did you stop work? (2) to end, terminate; **ndzìlá mǔpi Kàmbìàfariá mu àsì iyí tìá** the road to Rhino Camp ends at the riverside (Nile); **Ròkɔnï mà àngǒ àsì Àyà sì** Rokɔni's territory terminates at the river Aya (B.C.); **é ndzo àsì ko ŋgɔ́á yà?** how far have you run (lit. you run stopped left off where)? (Ac. **g̈ik**).

àsì, vt. (1) (= **andï**) to tear, rend; **àsì kàràtasì, bɔ̀ŋgɔ́** he tore paper, cloth; (2) to split, cleave, crack; **mï àsì pätí kö!** do not split the wood! **àsì ɛ́dzá 'bɔ** she split the firewood; **èì ǹdrí mà 'alɛ́ àsì** they are ripping open the belly of a goat; **àsì rö**, vr. to split, tear; **bɔ̀ŋgɔ́ àsì rö àsì** the cloth rent.

ásí, n. (1) mind, disposition; way of thinking; feeling, sentiment; opinion, view; conviction; **ɛ'yó mï ásía ŋgǒnï yà?** what is your opinion? **emú ásí sì** he came of his own will/freely; (2) **èri ásí ndrǐndrì** he is glad, pleased, content; **ásíni ɔ̀kpɔ́** (or **mbàmba** or **tɛ̀tɛ**) he is courageous, fearless; **ásíni kɔ tǒ** (= **ɔ̀ɔ́kɔ́ bɛ** or **àdrà bɛ** or **ɔ̀mbàrö**) he is excited, angry; **ásíni ambí 'bɔ** his heart/feeling is cold, i.e. he is dead; or fig. he is resigned, quiet; (3) **ásí-drìlɛ́** pit of stomach, manifestation of life; **èrimà ásídrìlɛ́ ambí** (or **àvɛ̀**) **'bɔ** the pit of his stomach (witness of life) is cold/dead: he breathed his last; **'bà ásí drìnìá** he craves after it.

así, vn. to care, have regard for (**sì**); to be anxious, concerned about (**sì**); to be solicitous for (**sì**); **mï así ma sì kö à'do sì yà?** why do you not care for me/disregard me? **andzi 'dì, èmï así ɔ́pí sì kö yà?** boys, have you no regard for the chief! **así àfa sì** (**kö**) to take (no) care of.

àsí, n. (1) unyieldingness, stubbornness; **mvá 'dì àsîrö** this child is wayward, inflexible; **mï àsí ndɛ̀ àngǒ rá** your stubbornness outdoes everything; (2) constancy, determination, persistence, assiduity; **mï àsí yɔ** you have no perseverance; **èri àsí 'bǎ sùkúrú rùá** he perseveres/is steadfast at school (in spite of difficulties): to insist, stick to, adhere **àsí 'bǎ**.

asi, av. again; else, further, more; **èì dí asi ànï à'dò 'yɛ yà?** what more can they do with it! **asi...kö** no more, no farther, nothing else; **asi lɛ̌ kö** they like it no more; **á 'yɛ asì mu ddíká kö** I may go no more! **má asi 'bá àzǐnï mà àfa ɛdé kö** I shall deal with other people's affairs no more; **asi ɔvá kö** he dug no more.

ásìkû, n. a smaller kind of owl (cf. **ɛ́máa** the bigger one).

àskarì (? = **ɔtsépì**), AS., soldier, guard.

asö, vn. to be tasty, seasoned with salt; to have a good relish; **à'í asö** (= **dra**) **tíbí 'aléa rá**; **èri emú 'bá tiléa ndrìzàrö** salt is seasoned in the savoury; it becomes pleasant in one's mouth; **lésú asö- asö** (= **dradra**), **alu àni tǒ** milk has become sour and thus delicious.

asǒ, vt. to demolish, pull down; to break down; **asǒ dzɔ́ òkurì 'bɔ, èrì ŋgà mu ɔ́dírì si** he has demolished the old hut, he is going to build a new one; aső 'ï, vr. to break down, collapse; dzó drì orurï aső 'ï the ceiling of the room collapsed; dzó, èró, pätí... aső 'ï rá the hut, granary, tree... collapsed, crumbled.

àső, n. denunciation; indictment, case; àső 'bá àzí mà rùá a case against a p.; èì àsô dzi ópí vő 'dálé they took the case to the chief there; èrì àső 'dì mà ɛ'yó ôlô he is discussing the case; èrì àső 'dì mà ɛ'yô lì he decides the question; àső sö, vt. to accuse, denounce, betray; sö mâ rùá àső rá he betrayed/denounced me; sö àső mvá àzïnï mà rúá; èrì àsôrö he denounced another child; he is treacherous (also giving away others' secrets); Yuda èrì àső sö Yesu mà rùá Judas betrayed Jesus; èìmà àső mání tô their charges against me are bitter; àső (= òlòlòá) ndè (àŋgö) rá treachery/denunciation is extremely common.

àsò, vt. (1) to raise, lift sth. with a prop; èrì èró-ti àsô (= zï) (è)ré sï she lifts (i.e. opens) the roof of the granary with the prop; (2) to support, prop up with; èì dzó drì àsò, kà mu ɛ'déző kö sï they support the roof/ceiling of a hut, lest it fall down; (3) drì àsò rö to be or stay in line; èì mu drì àsòrö (= kpïï lố àlö) they march in straight line; èì búkù 'bǎ drì àsòrö they place the books in line (on shelf).

àsòrò, n. a tree with whitish-coloured bark, covered all over with long white thorns.

átá, átápi, átíì, or átípi, n. (1) (átíì) father; ma átíì, my father! ma átíì ma tïpirï my father who

begot me; (2) (átá) male (of animals); a'ú átá (= lôlô) cock; (tí mà) mőnió átá a bull, &c.

àtá, T. (= òbí), n. kind of.

átá-mvá, n. the elder 'brother' among men of seniority (same as átáláə).

átáláə or átálɔ́ or átólɔ́, n. head-man or chief p. of any community; fig. kà adri ədzəlôrö tï, èì əmvɛ àŋgö 'dì mà á— even if he was an (old) bachelor (with his own home and associates) they speak of átáláə; also 'bá àŋapá bɛ èrì átámvá or á— a rich man is an authority; átálɔ́ 'bání èrimà rú èndzìző tőrï (= àkú) dignitary whom people esteem.

átáŋákə, n. large locust (eating of which is reserved for elders) (Ac. òcɛnnɛ).

átáògú, n. uncle (father's side).

àtï, vn. (1) to cease, stop; əzóó àtï rá the rain stopped; (2) (= dza) to recover, heal; rùání àtï mőké or àzóní àtï rá he has recovered (from illness); bélé àtï 'bə the sore is already healed; mvá milé (or rùá) àtï rá the child has recovered; (3) vt. (= awa, cf. tï) to portion out, distribute; àtï éɳá àtï-àtï she portioned out the polenta; (cf. é tï éɳá! take up a bit of polenta!).

àtì, vt. (1) to lean against (rùá); àtì àdzú dzó rùá he leaned the spear against the hut; àtì 'ï àbì rùá he leant against the wall; má àtì rö àtì, á kà mu ɛ'déző kö I leaned against something (rest-ing) lest I should fall; (2) to prop, support (with hand or other); mï àtì tsí, kà muzó gòröző kö hold/support it lest it fall down!

atí or etí (1) vt. to knead (= work); to tread, stamp (with feet); mï atǐ ə̀drí ráká, mǐ ɛdé pàlatà (or é si ɛ́mvó) ndə̀ you first work the clay, then you make tiles (pots); ə̀drí atǐzàrö well-kneaded / treaded clay; (2) to give the finishing stroke; àfa àvò mïnǐ mu atǐ-atǐrǐ'ï a sick (or wounded) animal ... you go and finish it off.

àtí (or àtě), n. (1) (attire, bearing) politeness, propriety; àfa mïnǐ 'yɛ àtǐrö 'dǐ ə̀ndzí your deportment is not pleasing; èri 'ïmà rùá àtí tǐ: èri àtǐrö he dresses his body with care, he is smart; é ŋa ŋaaká àtí sǐ do eat with propriety! (2) diligence, care(fulness), intelligence; 'bá 'dà èri àzî ŋga àtí sǐ that man works with industry; àtí mà adri àzía tsǐ! = mà ŋga àzí àtí sǐ! care should be shown at work! àtî-rö, a. clean, polite; presentable; decently or properly behaved.

atï, vt. to tie, fasten together (bundle); mǐ atï tsǐ, kà mu (zǒ) ayu (or ɛré)-rözǒ kö! tie them together properly, that they may not loosen (and scatter)! èi ɛ́dzá, màåkò-bbí atï they tie to a bundle, firewood, potato-shoots.

ati, vn. to vacillate, move (or rock) to and fro; 'bá 'dàrǐ atii ɛ́wá sǐ (ɛ́wá èri fûfu) that man staggers from beer (is drunk).

àtí'bɔ́, n. client, poor man who attaches himself to a wealthy host, servant, slave; mǐ à— mádrí you are my slave.

àtïlǐkö = àtölǒkö, MN. kǐndə̀ (ŋaaká a'dǐzǒ), n. fireplace (for cooking).

atö[1] (cf. tö), vt. to step, tread (put one's foot), stamp, trample on; èri órí atö he treads on a snake; ma atö 'alénǐá (or drïnǐá) pá sǐ I put my foot in (or on) it.

atö,[2] T. (cf. ətö), vt. to take one by surprise; ma atö èri iyía ə̀dzïröriá (pǐlílǐrö) or: ... ma àfa ò̀gùrïá I surprised him: taking a bath (naked) or: stealing my things.

atǒ, vn. to squat, sit back on heels; ma atǒ-atǒ I am squatting on my heels.

àtə̀ = àndrù, vn. to start rotting.

átɔ́lɔ́ = átátɔ́gɔ́ = átáláo (q.v.), n. person of authority, master of a place.

àtölǒkö, n. (1) kind of small termite-hills; ɛdzíríkɔ́ 'bà dzɔ́ àtölǒkə̀-rö the termites (special kind) make their abodes in form of miniature hills; (2) the former (brought home) or similarly formed blocks of clay used on fire-place (to put pots on); ká à— ò̀tǐ èl ɛ́mvó 'bà drïnǐá ŋaaká a'dǐzǒ having arranged fireside blocks, they put the pot on it for cooking.

àtràkàla, pätí àtràkàla, n. bifurcation, tree's branching-off; branch.

atri[1], vt. to obstruct, prevent, exclude; èmï ɛ́mvéléti a— (=oga) you are obstructing the light-opening (as window, door); mǐ a— mánǐ gèrì you obstruct my way (or outlook).

atri[2] dri (= (è)pà dri), (1) vn. to return; mǐ a— (=è̀gə̀) dri vélé ('də̀á or 'dálé)! come (or go) back! (2) vt. to cause to return, head off, cut off; mǐ a— mánǐ ǹdrí (or tǐ) 'dà (mà) dri vélé! head off the goat (or cow) there for me (Ac. ŋə̀lə̀ wì).

atrú, vn. to be stunted (in growth); to languish (pine or wear) away; pätí 'dǐ zə̀ kö, atrú tsǐ this plant does not grow, it is stunted.

Átsá, n. name of a river.

átsálá(ká), n. a basket; á— ɔ́mbî kɔzɔ́ or á— èì ànï ɔ́mbî kɔ the (large) basket for catching locusts.

àtsàvɔ̀ = àzàvɔ̀ q.v.

atsɛ¹, vn. (1) to remain, be left over; a— àlö one remained; àfa atsɛ́pirï dzɔ́lɔ́(kɔ́)nï what is left of food is a remainder; dzɔ́lɔ́(kɔ́)-nï : ɛ́ŋá dzɔ́lɔ́ a— tsí a remainder of polenta was left over; a— wɛrɛ it will soon...; a— wɛrɛ ɔzɔ́ɔ́nï 'yɛ̀ 'dî'dì (= èsöèsö) it will soon rain; (2) to remain behind; ma ádríì a— (better áó) vélé my brother has remained behind.

atsɛ², vt. to stand around, surround, encircle, encompass; 'bá mà àgáí a— or 'bá àgaa a— to encircle people; atsɛ̃́ òdrú mà àgáí atsí sï̀; èì àgáínï a— kúrù they encircled a buffalo with fire; they surrounded him completely; 'bá a— á'dïá mà ámvú àgaa people have surrounded s.-s.'s field (with their fields or other).

àtsɛrɛ, n. very large sore (possibly with several openings); èrì su tò it is very painful.

àtsétsɛ́ (=àkékɛ́) n. loud͏ laughter (especially of women).

atsí, vn. to walk, march, journey; andzì emú a— arí sï̀ the boys came marching at the beating of a drum; mï atsî drɔ kìlé ɔ̀tsɔ́lɛ́ you are sauntering about like a dog; atsí'bá n. rover, roamer.

atsí (cf. orí), vn. (1) to form a rusty crust on iron; aya atsíatsí ŋaakú sï̀ the iron has got a rusty crust from the earth (it lay in it a long time); (2) (cf. ani) to become worm-eaten, rotten from long lying in granary; àŋá atsí-atsí the corn has spoiled.

àtsí,¹ n. fire; à— ti 'bǎ to light/ kindle a fire; à— eŋû to put out/

extinguish fire; à— bì 'bɔ fire has caught/blazes; àtsî-rö a. (a) warm, hot; (b) ti àtsî-rö talkative, verbose; mvá 'dì ti àtsí bɛ the child talks much; or using bad/offensive language; N.B. àt-síkà, n. smoke; àtsíkà èrì ŋga lɔ̌ɔ̈rɔ̌ (or ndrí-ndrí/dírrrr) smoke rises in puffy (or thin) columns; àtsí-áŋáka = lɔ́kɔ́fɔ̌-rá = élí = érí = fɔ̌rá, n. charred grass; àtsí-fɔ̌rá = ɔ́fótá, n. ashes; à—ɔlɔ̌ŋgö = àtsí-fúlɔ́ = àtsí-ɔlɔ̌ = àtsí-sí, n. glowing charcoal; àtsí-kölɔ̌ = àtsí ɔlɔɔlo = àtsí-pèlèŋgú, n. charred wood-end (àtsínï vɛzɔ̌'bɔrï'ï the fire having finished burning).

àtsí² (cf. tsï⁵), vn. to be fond of prying, inquisitive; to be forward, meddlesome; mï milé à— (= tɔ) ŋgà tò, mï 'dîɔ nè mádrí rá! you are extremely inquisitive ...you will instantly have to deal with me!

átsí, n. (1) small hut in the middle of cattle-pen; á— lítsɔ́arï'ï; 'bá laa rö ànï they sleep (or keep small calves, goats) in it; 'bá átsî si(lítsɔ́a mà) ágáa they erect it in the middle of the pen; (2) ɛ̀rɔ́ or dzɔ́ á— granary's or hut's roof.

àtsífe, n. a magic stick for divination; à— èrì ɔ̀ndó páráká mà drílé the 'atsife' stick is a piece (between two joints) of a durra stalk; àtsífɛ̀ ndri to rub/consult the 'atsife' stick; ɔ̀kó èì à— ndri ètrɔ̀ women also consult the ...; 'bá àtsífɛ̀-ndrípirï the soothsayer by means of ...; èì séntè fɛ̀ àtsífɛ̀-ndrizɔ̌ tsí they pay for consulting. ...

átsíkɔ̀ = átsímvó, n. temple (side of forehead).

àtsɔ́ = àmbέ, NE. = ε'bó, n. hoe.

atsɔ́, vn. to limp; to be crippled, lame; 'bá atsɔ́pi or 'bá atsɔ́zàrö or atsɔ́əpá a lame/limping person.

àtsɔ́fà = mosɔ́á = kasɔ́á, n. excrescence (on elbow, knee ...).

átsúkùrú = àrɔ̀rɔ̀á, q.v.

atu, n. oar (Rigbɔ).

átúfε = əlófε = álófε, q.v.

àù = àɔ̀, àdrɔ́-òrí = kákúlε, n. red soil/ochre; ɲaakú εkarĭ'ï.

àú = àwí, vt. to scorch, singe, burn; èi yékéá àǔ àtsí sǐ they singe (dispersing) the ferocious big black ants with fire; èi àɲú àǔ they singe bees (for honey).

au = awï, vt. to cast the skin; órí au 'dɔ̀ or órí awï ko ŋgɔ̀'bɔ̂ or órínï 'ímà 'bíkə ŋgɔ̀'bòrĭ ko 'dǐá or koko 'dέ or trɔ̀ ko 'dέ the snake has sloughed; órí auzà, rúá auzà parts of rough skin coming off.

a'ú, n. fowl; a'ú-átá cock; a'ú-kàrĭ or a'ú-àrənĭ fem. chicken; a'ú-ándrii(tĭpi'bərĭ)hen (started laying eggs); a'ú-ǵbε egg; a'ú 'bíkə feathers of ... ; a'ú-àɲá = áŋgulú large larvae from waste-heaps; (àpáràtiá or àŋgɔ̀ maazà-rĭá) called fowls' food.

àù, n. lust, lewdness; 'bá àurö or aù be lewd person; ɔ̀kó àuru èri ɔ̀kó atsípi bàdàkàrö or ɔ̀kó láá-rö-pi áɡúpí àzĭnï bε bàdà-kàrö a harlot, a woman roaming or sleeping with men at random; èri àu bε (said of man also) he/she is lustful.

àú-àú or àúkàù, a. (1) báká àú-àú unevenly, coarsely twisted rope; (2) rúá àú-àú to have a rough surface (as: skin from some disease).

àúbbí, n. a kind of vegetable; 'bá dzi à— 'bá ámvú 'äpirĭ drí kö they do not bring 'aubbi' vege-tables to fieldworkers.

a'ûgukù, n. kind of grub (= ɔ́ŋgulú).

àùkàù, a. édzá á— (= nĭïrĭ) light brushwood as firewood.

àú-ŋgúrúkà = àgàrö, àgàgà, a. àɲá-sí àú-ŋgúrúkà coarsely ground corn.

áúpi, n. aunt (father's sister mï átíi mà ámvíi).

áúrε-áúrε (?) = úra-úra, q.v.

àúrúɲà, n. scum or thickened skin formed on (semi-) liquids.

àúsérε, n. spider's web; èbìó èri à— bǐ the spider spins her web.

áutsέ = áupá, áərɔ́pá = áùrù-pá, màlǎo, n. abandoned field; fallow field (temporarily at rest); á— ŋgá 'bánï 'àlé drìərĭ; èri tsúrú'dɔ̀ áutsêrö it is a field formerly tilled, now uncultivated.

àvá = kɔ̀rε, vítsɔ́, èlí, n. desire, longing, yearning after; passion; ma ándríi mà àvá fu ma kái I am extremely homesick for my mother; àfa 'dǐ mà àvá(ɲazàrö) mánï yə I have no desire for this (for eating).

ává, n. (= àvìvì, T.) breath; ávâ 'a to breathe; mvánï ŋgà kírí ávâ 'a, drà ŋgà kö the child is still breathing, it is not yet dead; 'bá édri nï ávâ 'a nǐ a living man breathes; é 'a ává kö! hold your breath! 'a ává díká kö he breathes no more (i.e. he is now dead); ma ávâ vö tɔ̀əkó I am just blowing; èri ávâ se òmvu sǐ he smells with the nose; ávâ ndzε to sigh; ávâ lǐ to (take a) rest; àma ŋgà ávâ lǐ! let us take a rest/breath! é sɔ̀ ɡárì mà ává! pump the cycle!

àváfï, n. fresh new shoots of a

plant; à— ɛ̀ri ɛŋgá ɔ̀rï 'bánĭ
salé ámvúarĭ mà 'aléa shoots
come forth from seeds they
planted on the field.

àvĕ or **àvĭ**, vn. (1) to get/be lost;
to go astray; **ágú 'dà àvĕ áséa**
that man went astray in the bush;
(2) **'bâ drì àvĕ = 'bá tàbì àvĕ**
to forget; **'ĭ tàbì (or drì) àvĕ rá**
also **'ĭ drì dza ànï rá** he has forgotten (about) it; **ɛ'yɔ́ 'dĭ mà àvĕ
mĭnĭ (or mĭ-drì) kö!** do not
forget the matter! **drì-àvĕ** or
drì-àvĕtá, n. forgetfulness; **'yɛ
drì-àvĕ sĭ** he acted out of forgetfulness.

avĭ, vn. to play; **è mú avĭ!** go to
play! **andzi èĭ avĭ** the children are
playing; **bɛ̀ndérɛ̀nï avĭ-avĭ ɔ̀lĭ
sĭ** the flag flies in the breeze; **mï
avĭtá ndè àŋgŏ rá** your playing
surpasses everything.

avĭ, vn. to breathe/rest; **mï àndè
rá mï ŋgà avĭ** you rest from
weariness; **é kà oŋgû ndzo, mĭ
mu avĭ ndɔ̀** after you have run,
you go to rest/breathe again.

àvivì, n. (1) **àtsĭ-à—** radiation or
flow of heat (from near fire); **àtsĭ-
à— sĭ mĭ rùánï drĭdrï; mï
tsúrú'dɔ̀ à— vö 'alénĭá mà ɔ̀ri
benì (ɛŋgá àtsĭ-ándrĭí vŏ)** you
feel hot from radiation of (a
relatively near) fire; you blow now
on it to mitigate it (it comes from
a mighty fire); (2) vapour, evaporation, exhalation (of odours) (**à—
lŏ ɔ̀mvu sĭrĭ**, 'avivi' only for the
nose); **ɔ̀do 'dĭ mà à— ŋgù
ɔ̀ndzí** this oil smells bad; **dzɔ́ 'dĭ
mà à— ŋgù ɔ̀ndzí; èĭ ɔdré sŏ
'anĭá 'áánï** the smell of this hut
is bad, they may have urinated
in it (cf. **àzáŋgà**); (3) T. (= **ává**)
breath; **ɛ̀ri ɔvö à— kɔ́kɔ̀rö** he is
without breath (i.e. he is dead).

àvítsɔ́ or **àvútsɔ́**, n. a dance; **èĭ
à— ɔŋgŏ tö** they are dancing
'avitsɔ'.

avɔ, MN., n. = **a'dá-a'dá**, q.v.

àvŏ, n. (1) dead body, corpse, carcass; **'bá àvŏ, tĭ àvŏ-nĭ** a man's
or cow's carcass; **'dà àvŏnĭ** that is
a corpse/dead p.; **mï ɛ'yɔ̂ ndrâ
'dà mà àvŏ agâ mánĭ (or mâ
drìá) à'do sĭ yà?** why do you
rake up old stories of a dead p.?
(2) **àvŏrö: àfa édri berĭ a'dúle**
said of living things; sick, enfeebled, dangerously ill, hope-
lessly ill; **'bá 'dàrï àvŏrö** that
man is dangerously ill.

àvɔ̀, vn. **àvɔ̀-zà**, a. (1) (living being)
enfeebled, swollen; **'bá àzɔ́ bɛ
rùánï àvɔ̀-àvɔ̀** a sick p. is puffed
out, swollen (out), flabby, lan-
guishing; (2) (plants, &c.) withered, faded, wrinkled, shrivelled
(not rotten); **kànì é sĭ kàká
èbĭrö, é 'bà ɛ̀róa; kànì ɔ'á vŏ
sĭ na, mï emú 'bà ètúa ndɔ̀: ɛ̀ri
adri àvɔ̀zàrö (rùánï tsúrú'dɔ̀
ɳuzàrö, àrĭnï ndzu 'bɔ: rùánï
ɔtra-rö-zàrö)** when you pull off
corn-cobs still green, you put
them in the granary; after three
days you put it in the sun: it is
faded (grains fall off quickly) (it is
now faded; the sap is withered, it
is shrivelled); **àdzínï ɛ'dó rö
ɔdzắ ndó** its taste begins to
change.

avŏ = abó, ɛmvú, vn. to drown;
**iĭ kà tĭ áŋgĭrí, é kà 'dɛ 'anĭắ,
mï avŏ rá** if a river has risen high
and you fall into it, you will
drown.

avö, vt. to stew; **ɛ̀ri mààkò avö
émvóa** she is stewing potatoes in
a pot; **moka ɛ̀ri lɔ̃dè avŏpi 'bɔrĭ
'ĭ** stale cow urine.

àvŏtà, n. presentation of a head of

cattle to a maternal uncle on the occasion of a death; 'bá drăpi 'bə-rĭ ma à— (= à'bókɔ́) fĕ, èrì ɔ́ózɔ̌ (ádróí nï) the offering of a cow for mourning (it is killed at the funeral dance).

àvù, vn. (1) to stoop, bend down; mĭ àvù mu ma àfa e'dŭ! bend down, go and pick up my thing! (2) (= rï) to sit on, to cover eggs, to hatch; a'ú (ándríí) àvù (= rï) ġbé drìá 'bə the hen has sat to hatch.

àwà¹, vr. to quarrel, wrangle, contend, dispute, argue; andzi 'dàĭ èì àwà rö àwà-àwà those boys are quarrelling; èmïnï èmï àwàzɔ̌ 'bá àzĭ bɛ when you are disputing with sby.; ɔ̀kó èì àwǎ ɛ'yɔ̂ 'yə òmbà sĭ the women quarrel speaking angrily.

àwà², vt. to crush, squeeze, grind (beans or the like: dry or moist); èì ɔ́sɔ̌ à'wĭrĭ àwà (óní sĭ) they grind dried beans (on stone: maybe for cleaning them from chaff).

awa¹, vt. (1) to distribute, serve out, portion out; awakĭ 'yé dràá sĭ they distribute arrows at funeral (ceremony); èri éņá awa she serves out polenta; 'bá awa ɛ'bó 'dĭĭ klásì vɔ̌ sĭ klásì vɔ̌ sĭ they distributed these hoes by classes (school children); (2) to divide, separate; 'bá 'dà awa 'bá asákalá aw-awa that man separated them.

awa² rö, vr. to clear up (setting in fair); àŋgɔ̀ lĕpi 'dĭpi ɔzɔ̂rörĭ 'dii kö, èri awa'ï rá it was about to rain, but did not, it cleared up.

àwa-'dínï! O.K., that's right! that's it! it is true! àwa-'dĭnĭà or àwa 'dĭ 'fɔ̂ə! also (especially after meals) àwa'dĭ-fɔ̂ə! àtsĭ drĭ (or vɛ) mï rá! thank you! (lit. you had a beneficial fire-kitchen!); also used for 'all right then; it serves you right!'

áwárápá, n. scorched durra stalks standing on the field after harvesting.

awĭ¹=ɑ́ó, vn. to remain behind; awĭ ko he stopped and remained; awĭ Árúwá 'dálé vɛ́lɛ́ he remained behind at Arua; ètɔ́ə awĭ dri atri vɛ́lɛ́ the hare stopped and turned back (fable).

awĭ² (i.e. 'bílɛ́), n. hunting-pit; ġǎ awĭ òdrú kìdzîá, èì bĭ zɔ̌ they dug a hole on the buffalo track to catch them; àņàpá dría ɛtsɔ̌ 'dezɔ̌ 'alénĭá any animal may fall in.

àwĭ¹, n. gathering of elders in commemoration of death of an age-mate (arranged by the latter's relatives by killing an ox and inviting them); tí 'dà 'bá lĭ àwĭa that cow they kill for the commemoration; mbàazà okonɑ̀rɔ̌ àwĭa, trǎ rö àwî ņaarĭá the elders are invited for the..., they gather for the communal meal; ɛ'yɔ̂ ndzɛzɔ̌ at meal's end speeches are made (about the deceased, &c.; cf. Nuer funeral ceremony). (àwĭ = ádí?)

àwĭ² T. = ádí, n. spell (-disease); àwĭ ndzɛ to remove a spell; 'bá 'wàrà 'dĭĭ tɔ̀ nï nĭ èì àwĭ ndzɛ 'bá àzɔ́'rö mà drìá it is mainly old men, they (who) remove a spell from sick persons.

àwĭ or àwú (alias lòlì), n. reddish-brown clay or ochre; ņaakú ɛkarĭ; èì ànĭ dzɔ́ (or arĭ) rùà tri they daub a hut (or drum) with it; 'bâ tri drà sĭ a person daubs himself for a funeral.

á'wíí, n. sister-in-law.

à'wí, a. (1) dry; ɛ́dzá, ásɛ́ à'wírì dry firewood, grass; (2) (= èdú) thick, dense; ɔ̀drí or ë'dí à'wí (èdú); bè àŋgà ìyí 'aníá wɛrɛ the clay/gruel is (too) thick, they have not yet put enough water in it.

àwí-à'í or àwú-à'í, n. a particular kind of grass used for burning and obtaining salt (lye from its ashes).

Àwíavá, n. early tributary of Enyaó: èrì Ényáó mà é'búsí drìlɛ́.

àwírì (= mílɛ́ tsìzàrö, àùru), a. lewd, lascivious, libidinous, lustful; à— mïnï adrizɔ́ mílɛ́ trìzàrö being lewd; kàrílɛ̀ èì ɛ́zóàndzì ɔ̀bǐ avízɔ́ èì bɛ; ɛ́zɔ́ 'yɔ kènì 'mï àwírìrɔ́' youths catch girls for playing; the girls will say 'you are lewd'; 'bá atsípí 'bá àzí vö sby. going to persons of the other sex; Àùá or Àwíà, proper names of male or female of children of doubtful father (illegitimate).

àwítà = àótà, q.v. ... àfa má átíìnï kolérì (or kó mání 'dǐ) what my father leaves behind (for me); má átíì mà àwí-dzó my father's inherited hut.

àwízyó, n. widow; ɔ̀kó ágúpínï dràzɔ̀ rárì a woman whose man died; in some districts also: widower (commonly ɔ́dzɔ́lɔ́).

àyà, vn. also àyà ŋgɔ́rɔ́ŋgɔ́rɔ́ to bloom, be in flower; àn̪á èrì ŋgà àyàzàrö or fɔ̀rö fóí, 'bà ŋgà éfí kö the corn is still blooming, has not yet started to form grains.

aya, n. (1) iron; aya-zè iron dregs; ɛ'bó 'bánï 'bɛ(= 'di)—lérì mà zè the chips from forging a hoe; ayârö of iron; (2) (= kǎryá) bicycle.

à'yà, n. jealousy; à'yà bɛ or -rö jealous; ɔ̀kó 'bà a'yà à'íì bɛ a woman becomes jealous of her rival (polygamy).

àyá, n. lie; àyá bɛ or àyârö (= ndzɔ̀rö) lying, mendacious, deceitful, untruthful.

áya = áyakáya, n. a kind of reed grass (its stem is sugary) coming up in swampy ground (dɔdɔ): ásɛ́ dǔpi ìyí (dɔdɔ) mà 'aléarì áya or á(yá)ya.

ayá, vn. ayázà = ɔ́ízà a. weak, feeble (f. disease, age); 'bá ayázà or ɔ̀kpɔ̀kɔ́kɔ̀rö, èrì 'ye dɔ̀lɔ̀dɔ̀lɔ̀ —or èrì mu trɔ̀ŋgɔ̀-tr—an enfeebled p. moves unsteadily, shakily.

áyáká, n. (= àdí) special basket for fishing ɛ̀'bí bǐzɔ́.

àyákà = dòtà, ëzíkëzí, tsùrútsùrúa, n. liffa.

àyákáká, av. only (to exclusion); àma sùkúlù andzìrö à—, andzì tɔ̀ɔkɔ́ 'aléníá yɔ we are only schoolboys, no other boys are in; 'dà ɛ́zó andzì à— there are only girls there.

àyàkílíkì(lì) = ɛndìlìkà, n. tassellike skin excrescences under neck of goat (or on ear of some p.) ṅdrí ombɛlékòá.

à'yälu, n. swelling on knee: à— pì ma kö̀mùá; kànì pì dɛ́ 'bɔ èrì ɛ'dô vì 'bǎ when the swelling is complete, it starts forming pus.

áyámvó, n. temple; sa má á— rá he boxed my ears.

à'yaro, n. ground squirrel.

áyáya = kǎdzúa, n. chicken-pox.

ayɛ́ or ayɛ́bbí, n. collective term for 'leaf-cloth' of women; ayɛ́ sǔsù ŋgókóa leaves they don on back-parts (and front); such leaves are in particular: ɛbíkɔ, àgélébí, ètɔ́kɔ́bí, ɔ̀lébí, à'bɔ̀àbí (èì ɔ̀sì ayɛ́bbîrö banana leaf is cut in strips for the purpose).

áyí=máaikə, n. a tree; èl èdö àtsîrö laazö they light fire (with it) for lying down.

áyi, n. rainy season; àŋgö áyìrö it is now the wet season; əzɔ́ɔ́nï 'di áyi sì rain falls during the 'ayi' season (April–November about).

áyï = ɛsélé, n. line; é sa màákò áyï àlö! plant potato-shoots in straight line! màákò mà áyï mu kpii the line of potatoes is straight; èl áyï mà tà mba they keep the line (gymnastics).

ayï¹, vn. to run, pour out, scatter; 'dö-fï ayï àfadzó éríkò mà ètï sì; kànì àfadzó éríkò mà 'a sì, dönï ayï mvárrá vàá (tròtrö) eleusine runs out from a cracked receptacle; if the receptacle is cracked, eleusine will steadily run out; 'dö éfïnï ayï mà rùá ayï-ayï eleusine grains keep shedding on me (on carrying).

ayï², vn. to separate, sunder, divorce; ɔ̀kó ayï rá the woman abandoned her husband = ɔ̀kó ayï rö ágúpí bɛ separated from husband; ágúpí ayï (vt.) 'ïmà ɔ̀kó rá the man divorced his wife; ayïtáa, n. divorce; ɔ̀kó mà a— èrinï ayïzörï'ï woman's divorce by which she abandons her man.

ayï³, vn. to come, shoot, sprout forth (ɛŋgá); to bloom, put on ears (of corn); ɔ̀ndó ayï 'bə the durra has put on ears.

àyï = ndïïrï, av. frankly, openly, publicly, under one's nose/eyes; má ɛmbá 'bá à— I have taught people publicly.

àyïïà, n. mother (intimate term); à— ogú = ándrápìri aunt (mother's side).

ayïïärə = óŋgbírí, n. small ornamental bells (tied on ankles); èl

əŋgô tö a— sì they dance with bells on the ankles.

àyíkàyí, n. down; èri tsï a'ú 'bíkə táláa it is among fowls' feathers.

àyïkï, n. long flowing hair; mvá 'dà mà à— drïá tsï that (white) girl has flowing hair; à— drìbbî ko andzi mà drïá 'dáanï fà-kókɔrörï hair uncared for, uncombed, on a child's head; lɔ̀lɔ̀ mà à— (àyɔ́kï T.) cock's comb.

àyìkò, n. joy, delight, happiness, gladness, content; 'bá adri à— bɛ, ɔ̀mbà kɔ́kɔrö people are happy, without quarrelling.

àyípi, a'wî, n. sisters-in-law call each other so (man's ónyïïzï).

ayípi = ayï = èrífɔ́rá, n. fine dust (carried by wind); àfa ayïzàrï sth. dusty.

àyíríbɛ, also à'íríbɛ, n. itch, scabies; àyíríbɛ-nï fò mà rùá fɔ̀fɔ̀ itch broke out on me; à— ɲa má káyì rá; lɛ̆ vì'ï 'dáanï 'dáanï 'ï ko 'ï kö it irritates me all the time and wants to be scratched continually.

àyìrà = àyìrìgó (cf. ndàátá), n. large red-headed lizard.

ayísɛ = ásé, n. grass ayísêrö grass-covered.

áyiti, n. beginning of fieldwork; á— ŋgárï time/season of beginning of . . . ; á— ŋg— = mbá əzɔ́ɔ́nï ɛtsázörï the month the rain begins; á— o'dú àɲá fàzörï the time to dig in seed corn; èl ɛ'dó ámvú fà á— ŋgárï they start to dig over the field at the beginning of the rainy season.

àyízɛ̀, n. kind of graminia with sharp-edged leaves.

áyo = 'ï, stressing particle.

ayó, vt. to order, charge, send, command; 'bá ayó má ayó-ayó = 'bá pɛ̀ mà tï pɛ̀pɛ̀ I have been sent (lit. they sent me); ayó 'dɪ̀: 'bá tɪ pɛ̀zɔ́rɪ̀ an order, when one sends; ayó or ayótá, n. order, command(ment); ayó fɛ̌ to give an order.

ayô, vt. to make use of; á ŋgà bòŋgó 'dɪ̀ ayô díká kö I won't use this cloth any more! mɪ̂ ŋga màrárà 'dɪ̀ ayô díká yà? will you use these spectacles any more?

áyó = líkíɳ̩á, n. yams.

àyɔ̃́ɔ̃́á = àzí, n. work; é mu à—! go to work; àndròrɪ̀ à— (or àzí) o'dú ssu 'ï today is Thursday (4th day of work); àyɔ̃́ɔ̃́á 'yɛ (or ŋga) or ayô to work.

à'yólò, n. small green parrot (?).

à'yɔ́ró or à'yáró, n. ground squirrel; sóbínï tàyàrö its tail is bushy.

ayu, vt. to untie, unfasten, undo; má bòŋgó-bá ayu I unstitch the cloth; mɪ̌ ayu báká! untie the rope!

ayúkù, n. kind of mane below neck and breast (of some goat . . .); kàbìlò átá mà a— èrì 'yɛ gògògò the mane of the ram is swinging.

áyúrú = rókókòá, ɳarôróa, n. a small carnivore (living in clusters); èri a'ú mbǎ it ambushes fowls; òtsó tsa èrinï òmbà sɪ̌ kö a dog cannot overwhelm them (they attack all together).

àzá¹, T. = àzó, n. sickness.

àzá² = àzámà(nà)ká, màazá, ɳàazá (kà), n. a tree (*Bauhinia thonningii*; Ac. ògáli); bákánï èri ó'bíkə 'aléa its (highly valued) fibre is contained in its bark.

àzà¹, vt. (1) to blind, dazzle; ètúnï 'bâ milé àzà-àzà (dìtáanïrɪ̀) the sun dazzles one's eyes (its shining); (2) to light up, illuminate

(from a distance); àtsínï àŋgò àzà wóró ɛmvɛ̀rö the fire lights up everything to a distance.

àzà² (also ɛ̀zà), n. (1) sympathy, commiseration, compassion, pity; mvá 'dà mà àzà (ɛga) mání tò I feel great pity with that child; or 'bá 'dà mà àzà kə ma tsí, mâ dɪ̂ 'yɛ à'dɔ̀rö (or ŋgónï) yà? I feel pity for that p.; what shall I do? ma àzà kə èri rá; fɛ̀ mání mòɛ̀mbɛ̀ àzà sɪ̌ he has compassion on me; he gave me a mango merely out of pity; (2) to support o-s., care for o-s.; 'bá èl àzî ŋga ɛdrízǒ or àzà kəzǒ (i.e. àbírí sɪ̌) people work to help/support themselves/for their livelihood; mâ mu ma àzà kə! let me go to relieve/open my bowels!

aza, n. weak-mindedness, idiocy, imbecility; 'bá 'dà mà aza òndzí the craziness of that man is very pronounced; mvá 'dàrɪ̀ aza bɛ; èri 'bâ tsə aza sɪ̌ tsɔ̀tsə that child is mad; he strikes one out of imbecility; mɪ̈ aza-aza or mɪ̈ aza bɛ or mɪ̈ azàrö you are crazy.

àzáŋgà, n. exhalation, evaporation; dzó 'dà mà à— ŋgǔ òndzí the air of that hut stinks (= àdzí).

àzá-orí, n. a poisonous snake; òmbànï tö it is ferocious; èri 'bâ ga kál; 'bá drà ànï rá it bites dangerously; one dies from it.

àzàvô (-rö), a. (1) tasteless, unsavoury, insipid, flat; ɛɳá 'dɪ̀ àzàvôrö this polenta is insipid; (2) neglected, careless, untidy (opp. àtɪ̂rö); é kà mɪ̂ rùá àtɪ̂ tɪ̂ kö, àfa mɪ̂ rùá 'dɪ̂ ə'á àzàvôrö (or àtsàvôrö) if your p. is not tidy, things about you are in disorder.

ázávȍȍ, n. slovenliness, sluggish-ness, dullness, sloven; ȍkó ázá-vȍȍrörȉ asȉ ȁfa sȉ kö, ȅri ázávȍȍnï a slovenly woman does not care about things, she is a slut; é kà nȉ ɛ̨â 'ı (or àzî ŋga) sȉ kö, mï ázávȍȍ-nï if you are unable to prepare polenta pro-perly, you are a sloven.

àzí, n. work; àzî ŋga to work; ȅri àzî ŋga ámvúa he works on the field; àzí'bá or ámvú'bá (!), n. a (real) worker; 'dȉ àzí mȉdrí, 'dȉ àzí mádrí kö this is your business, not mine !

àzí(-nï), indef. prn. another, somebody; 'dȉ àzînïrȉ this is somebody else's; é 'bà àzíní díká, 'dȉ tsa kö put in another, this is not sufficient; fȅ 'bá àzï-nï he gave it to another.

azi[1] (cf. zi), vt. to ask a person(-'s consent) about; àdzȅ azi to in-quire about bride-price; andzi mú ézó-andzi azi (ùú 'bȁ) boys go to ask (flirt) girls (for arm-support or other).

azi[2], vt. (1) azi 'bâ tïá to order, command a p.; ópí azi té àmȁtïá kènȉ: àma emú mùsórȍ 'bɛ the chief ordered us to bring the taxes; (2) to instruct, inform, ad-vise; mï ɛ'yó azi àmȁ tïá kènȉ: àma emú drù sȉ kö you in-structed us, not to come tomorrow; ȅri azi mvání mȍkɛ́: 'á kȍ̂ dȉ èmï 'dȉ, mâ dȉ mvȉmvi !' he told (taking leave) them nicely saying: 'I leave you here now and go back !'

azia, num. 6, six; aziazȍrȉ or aziȁrö sixth.

ázíïrrȉ, num. 7, seven; ázíïrrìzȍrȉ or ázíïrrirö seventh.

àzó (= T. àzá), n. disease; pain; àzó bȉ ȅri tsȉ he became sick;

àzȍ̂rö or àzȍ bɛ, a. ill, sick, pain-ful, aching; mâ rúa àzȍ̂rö I am sick; 'bá àzó bɛ a sick p.; àzȍ̂ ta, vn. to sigh, moan (from pain).

àzȍ (-rö), T. = èezȍ̌, a. long, tall; àzȍ kȍndróndró or kàdrùkà-drù, T. = èzȍ̌ ŋą̂á (-rȉ) very long or tall.

àzù = asé, vt. to obstruct, cause trouble, obtrude; àrí àzù (or asé) ma òmvu tsí (nȍsì òdiiká sȉ) blood (bleeding) obstructed my nose (maybe from a chill); èkéllȅ àzù ma ȁgȁti tsí cough (bronchitis) blocked my chest.

B

bbà, n. female breast; (= bbàdzȍ́ or bbàdzórȍ́vȍ) udder; kȍdzȁȁ-nï ŋgà bbà ndrȍndrö the calf is still sucking.

bba-rȉ, a. (1) plain, frank, correct; é lȍ mání ɛ'yó bbarȉ (sȉ)! tell me the plain truth! 'dȉrï bba this is right; (2) industrious, active; orderly, tidy; ȍkó bbarȉ a dili-gent, careful mistress of the house; bba-ndrɛ or ȍkó bban-drȅrörȉ a paragon, strong woman (cf. Prov. 31, 10 sqq.); (3) well-behaved, gentle, obedient; mvá 'dȉrï bba, àgátànï ya this child is well-educated/kind, he would not refuse . . .; ásí-bbarȉ kind, generous, fine, elegant; 'bá ásí-bbarȉ a well-disposed, mannered, well-bred p.; (4) drì-lé-bba, n./a. good luck; fortunate, lucky; blessed.

bá = báká, n. rope, string, thread; ósù bá tendon of bow; tí bá . . . rope to tie a cow (in pen).

'bà, vt. to put, place; 'bà búkù médzà drìá he put the book on the table; é 'bà mvá vàá ! put the baby on the ground! (1) tì 'bǎ to (put the) cover; 'bà émvó tì tsí she covered the pot; é 'bà àfa drì 'bà'bà! cover it! (2) àfa mà tì 'bǎ àtsí sǐ to kindle, set alight sth.; é ɡa tìbìrítì, é 'bà tábà mà tì ànï! strike a match and light the cigarette with it! (3) to form; bɛlɛ 'bà ɛ̀ví 'bə the sore has formed pus; éfí-nï 'bà 'ï rá grains have formed; (4) bbílɛ 'bǎ 'anïá or ásí 'bǎ drìnïá to pay attention; á 'bà mâ bbílɛ̀ kö or á 'bà ásí drìnïá kö I did not pay attention to it; (5) used in numerous verbal compounds as dzì ... 'bà take to ...; 'bǎ tíbí drï 'ï they set the savoury (on hearth) to warm it up; 'bà...ko to leave; 'bà 'ə (= 'yɛ) = ɛ'dó to start.

'bá, pl. 'báɛ̀ì, also 'bǎäpì, n. man, i.e. homo; human, person; indef. pron. somebody; 'bá mà 'bá or 'bâ 'bá man's relation, kinsman; 'bá àzïnï somebody; another one; 'bá àzïnï yə or 'bá àbö yə nobody; ëlïnï 'bâ drî lì a knife cuts a p.'s hand.

bàbàlì, n. nonsense (words, conduct); é ko b— dzà, b— ɔ̀ndzí stop this silly talk, confusion is bad.

bǎbǎlì, n. kind of undergrowth, shrub (its stems, sticks used for hut-building); b— ɛ̀ì ɛ̀rô tsə ànï, ɛ̀ì ŋgà bǐ ɔ̀drí sǐ they wattle a granary with these sticks and daub it with clay.

badaa, a. spacious, roomy; dzó 'dïrï badaǎrörì 'ï this hut is spacious; Eklesya mà 'alɛ́ badaǎ-rö the church is spacious; n. sleeping hut.

bàdà, bàdàkà, a. trashy, trifling, worthless; useless, unavailing; 'dï àfa bàdà-nï this is rubbish;

bàdà-rö, av. at random, without reason, incoherently, crazily; mï atsí bàdà-rö a'ú (or ǹdrí)-lɛ́ you walk/idle about like a fowl (goat; said of females).

badrìdrìôrö = kəŋgəlôrö, mbàmba, a. hard; kànì màákò əzó kö ɛ̀ì əmvɛ b— when a potato is not roasted they call it hard; showy, sustained.

bàaikɔ̀, n. kind of dance; ɛ̀ì b— tö they dance 'baiko'.

báká or bá, n. rope, string, &c.; é 'ï b— tí mà əmbɛ́á! tie a rope round the neck of the cow! 'ï tí b— sǐ they fasten cattle (in pen) by ropes; ma rö ayu báká-sía rá I am freeing myself from fetters (by indemnity).

bàkàsìsì, A., n. present, remuneration; mâ mu èmï tábà awa bàkàsìsì-rö I shall give you cigarettes as a reward.

'bálá'bálá = èpékèpé, a. light.

bálákándí(a), a. tìnï b— it is thin.

bǎälì (cf. àbà), a. perplexed, puzzled; ma àbà dí ko b— I am still bewildered.

bǎlì(bǎlì), av. not quite full; lésú ɡa kéréá b—(b—) milk fills almost the calabash; ɛ́ɳ̀áó ɡa bǎlì the E— river is not quite/is almost full.

bàlì-bàlì, av. restless, fickle, shuffling; ɛ̀ri atsí b—b— he walks shufflingly (turning here and there).

bàalo, n. kind of mid-size bean.

bǎò, n. timber, plank.

'bara, 'barakala, 'rö, a. wide-flat-thin-light; kóyì 'barǎ-rö the winnowing trail-basket is ...; wárágà 'dï 'b— the sheet of paper is. ...

'bàràá = èdrîdríia, n. sparrow-hawk.

Bǎärì, n. the Aluur (i.e. people who came from elsewhere; 'Baar' Ma'di).

bàtànìà, A./S., n. blanket.

bɛ¹, pstp. (together) with; è mǔ àkúa èri bɛ! go home with him!

bɛ², av. gently pressing; please ...; é fè èrinï bɛ! please give to him!

'bé, T. = óní, n. mountain; 'Bé Étì Mt. Ethi (arabized: Gebel Woti).

bè, èbè, vt. (1) to draw; ɔ̀kónï ìï bě érèdzé sì the woman draws water with a calabash; (2) to distribute, portion out to; èri tíbí bě kàbèlé sì she serves up savoury with a ladle; (3) to pour, fill in; mǐ èbè mánï ìï! pour water in here for me! (cf. kə, ɛkó).

'bɛ, vt. (1) to throw away or at; to fling, hurl; é 'bɛ 'dálé! throw it away! é 'bɛ àrïïa óní sì! fling a stone at the birds! (2) àŋgǒ mà tì 'bɛ to hedge, fence in; 'bɛ ámvú 'dà mà ti otsí sì (tsï) he marked the limits of/or hedged in/the field with thorns; èi màákò mà tï 'bɛ ɔzǒ sì they hedged in the potato (-field) with reed-stalks (cf. tsɛ, lï); (3) (= di) to forge; ɛ'bô 'bɛ to forge hoes; (4) è'bî 'bɛ to catch fish (with hook); (5) to pay (imposts, &c.); lwalò, mùsórə, désìmà 'bɛ to pay, deliver road-contribution, taxes, church penny; (6) to overcome one; o'dú 'bɛ má rá (= ma ɔvö o'dû kə) I am overcome with sleep/am sleepy; éwánï mǐ'bè'bɛ ndè dï mï kái the beer (drunkenness) throws you to the ground (for sleeping), your senses are gone; (7) to take before the public authority; èi ɔkô 'bɛ dòánìá rúnï sìzǒ búkùá rï they take the woman before the counsel to take

down (officially for marriage) her name; (8) 'bɛ rö, vr. to throw o-s. into, to rush; à'yóró 'bɛ rö 'bílïaa the ground squirrel flung herself (rushed) into a hole.

bébéré or bérébéré = aza, n. weak-mindedness, craziness; 'bá b— bɛ a crazy, silly person.

bèdɔ̀kɔ̀ = bɔ̀dɔ̀kɔ̀, kpòo, av. dripping, running; 'bɛ mî drì àrï bɛ b— óní sì he hurled a stone at your head causing the blood to run.

bɛkɛ, n. a kind of woodpecker.

bɛlɛ = bilɛ, n. sore; wound; b— milé = ŋabilɛkɔ, scar; b— ŋgù-ŋgù the sore smells bad; 'ï b— dza kö his sore is not healed; mâ b— (milé)nï àzóàzó (or sûsu) my sore is painful; mâ dría b— tsï I have a sore on my hand; mǐ pá bɛlɛ'rö your leg is sore; b— mà àmakà putrescence of a sore.

'bèlè('bèlè), vn. tender, delicate, yielding, pliable; ɔdékóá 'dï mà rùá 'bɛlèrö (= akázà) the baby's body is tender, delicate.

bèndérè, A.S., n. flag.

besèn, Engl., n. basin; b— ìyí bɛ, the basin contains water.

bì = dà, vt. to bow, bend, press down; ɔlíkà bì ásé (or ɔzǒ, pätï) vàá the wind bent down the grass (reed-stalks, tree); tínï áísé ŋaarïá, áísé àzï 'dàï èbi rö vàá while a cow feeds on grass, some bends down (under her); bǐ gǐrì ǎgáti sì (áséa) ɔmbí bǐ (= kə) zǒ (or -rïá) they flattened out a path with their chests (in the grass) while catching locusts.

bì¹, vt. (1) to catch, seize, hold fast; clasp round; kànì é bǐ tí, é kô dǐ èri dzà! if you cannot hold it fast, let it go! ɔbǐ drɔ tí wórɔ they caught and drove off all the cattle; (2) to daub (tying it so), line, coat, plaster; èi dzɔ́ bǐ ə̀drí sǐ they daub a hut('s wall) with clay; bǐ ɛ́mvó mà ti tsí (i.e. èi àdzíkə̀ 'bǎ tinǐá tsí, èi bǐ ə̀drí sǐ) they fastened up the pot's opening (i.e. they put a potsherd on the opening and line it with clay); (3) bǐ sɛ to (catch and) pull, drag, trail; èi 'bá bǐ se Árúwá they are dragging a man to Arua (prison); (4) bǐ (= èkpà) ásí to clasp (with arms) one's lower chest (for cold, pain); fig. to take courage, take heart; to endure, put up with, hold out, persevere; é bǐ(or mí èkpà) mí ásí tsí, é 'bà ɔ̀rì kö! hold out with courage, do not fear! (5) 'bá mà vúti bǐ to follow a p.; è bǐ mâ vúti! follow me! (6) 'bá àndrɔ́ bǐ to be generous with a p./to treat a p. generously; bǐ àndrónï tsí he treated him generously; é bǐ má àndrɔ́ (or ásísílé)(ɛ́ɲ̣á sǐ) tsí be generous with me (with polenta)!

bǐ² or bǐbǐ, vn. (1) to be(-come) dark; àŋgǒ bǐ 'bə it has become dark; àŋgǒ bǐbǐ it is dark; (2) àtsí bǐ rá (or drà, eɲ̣ú rá); mí əvö àtsí èri dì ànï! the fire went out/died away; blow so that the fire may flame/blaze up! (3) to be(-come) dirty; bə̀ŋgɔ́ bǐpi bǐbǐrǐ á lɛ̀ kö I do not like dirty clothes; ìyí mà milɛ́ bǐbǐ the water is turbid, muddy.

bi = ǵbɛ, vt. to shove; ɛ'yɔ̂ bi 'bá àzí mà drì-á (or rúá) to put/lay the blame of sth. upon a p.; kànì 'yə ɛ'yɔ́ ə̀ndzírǐ rá, èrì bi 'bá àzí mà rúá if he has uttered sth. bad, he imputes it to another; bi ɛ'yɔ́ 'dǐ bǐbi he is exculpating himself and imputing others.

bbí, n. (1) ear (outer); bbílɛ́ or bbítálá inner ear; 'bá ɛ'yɔ́ ɛri bbílɛ́ (or bbítálá) sǐ man hears with his ears; bbí ėdö lobe of ear; bbí-drìlɛ́ upper rim of ear; (2) leaf; päti-bbí leaf of tree (or of any plant); (3) drì-bbí head hair.

'bǐ or, more commonly, 'bíkə, n. (1) hair of body (man, animal) 'bǐ 'bá rúá-rǐ; ṅdrí 'bǐ goat hair; kàbìlò 'bǐ wool; (2) a'ú 'bí(kə) feathers of fowls, &c.; (3) ɛ̀'bí 'bǐ scale of fish; (4) päti 'bǐ or ɔ́'bɔ́kə bark of tree; (5) ɔ́sɔ́, fúnò 'bǐ pod of beans, ground-nuts...; (6) àɲ̣á 'bǐ husk, chaff of grain.

'bì, vt. to taste; éɲ̣á mà àdzí 'bǐ or tíbí à'í 'bǐ, nə̀sì tsa rá (nə̀sì) tsa kö to taste the polenta, or the savoury, to see whether it is sufficiently salted, to try, test.

'bì, vt. (1) to bore, drill a hole; Lógbàrà 'bi päti 'yé sǐ the Logbara bored wood with an arrow; ò'bi'bírí ə'bǐ bǎò 'bə the wood-beetle has bored the plank all over; (2) to stir, twirl, revolve rapidly, whirl (between hands: food); èi ɛ̀'dí, lésú 'bi lòpére sǐ they stir gruel, milk with the stirring-stick; èri mààkò 'bi lésú sǐ she mashes potatoes with milk.

'bǐ'bǐ, in àɲ̣á 'bǐ'bǐ, n. ear/spike of corn; (cf. àɲ̣á éfĭfí grains); èi àɲ̣á 'bǐ'bǐ dì óní sǐ they clean (thrash) corn with a stone (small quantity; of a larger quantity tsə kàlì sǐ beat with a stick).

'bǐ'bǐïa, n. bat; 'bǐ'bǐïa-òpì wing of bat; umbrella.

'bǐ'bíə, n. star; 'b— 'bùárǐ stars in the sky; èrinï dìzɔ́ àtsí-lérǐ 'ï which shine like fire.

'bíkə, see 'bǐ.

bilɛ, see bɛlɛ.

bbílɛ́ (cf. bbí), n. inner ear (organ

of hearing); èrimà b— yɔ (= 'bá ɛ'yɔ́ ɛrípi kö-rì) he has no ears, i.e. he does not heed/obey orders.

'bílé, n. (1) hole, pit, cave, cavern; èri 'b— ɔvâ he digs a hole; (2) grave; èi 'bílê ga 'bâ sazŏ they dig a grave to bury a person.

'bílé'bílé, n. kind of tunnel or subway; 'bá gìrì 'alé lŏ man digs a way in it (ground).

'bìlí (or -ɛ́), n. log as chair, native chair; rï 'b— drìá he sits on a chair.

bìlìbìlì, ëni b— (= kúkúrûrö or biritsitsi), a./av. jet-black.

biliṇ̀árö, a. well rounded; mvá 'dì mà 'alé b— this child has a well-rounded belly (satisfied).

'bíɔ, n. very small bit; 'bá èfè mánï zá 'bíɔ they gave me a very small bit of meat (kàdà a large bit).

'bìɔwá, n. small, thin white kind of (underground) yams (cf. líkíṇá large brown kind).

bìirì, av. causing or leaving streak, weal, mark on body; gbà ma b— he has beaten me leaving me covered with weals (or striped).

bïïrï, av. (= ì̀-ìì) delaying too much, overtime, becoming late; má ɔvö 'dɛ́ 'dálé bïïrï yà? have I delayed too much there? bìrï -bìrï, av. steadily, fixedly; nè èri b—b— he kept on looking at him.

'bìríndà (= tálí, S.?), n. marvel, miracle; Yesu Kristu mà b— tŏ, ɔdzá ànï iyí éwârö the miracles of our Lord are many, so he turned water into beer (wine).

bírísì, S.A., n. mat (cf. lɔ̀kɔ́ndrɛ́).

bìiti, n. (1) fleshy growth (in sore); (2) (= zèlé) hind parts; (3) (= fïti ɔ́sɔ̀rörì) T., fat on entrails (animals).

'bítɔ (= kála), n. place on one's side; èri ma bítɔ́á he is beside me.

'bítɔ́ (kì), n. a large tree (Daniellia oliveri); sù 'b— mà bbí she put on 'bitɔ' leaves.

bìzŏöa, n. small square basket with handle (b— pá); èi b— tsà étsétsɛ́rɛ́ sì they make a 'bizooa' with splinters of durra stalks.

'bò, vt. to milk into one's mouth; andzi èi lésú 'bŏ èimà tilëá the children milk milk into their mouths.

'bö, vt. (1) (= mö) to cover over, (en)case; (= zì) to hide; èi èrɔ́ mà rùâ 'bö yǎbbí sì they cover over the granary (body) with 'yabbi' grass; 'bö (= zì) 'ï rá he hid himself; (2) (= ɛtsí) 'bö ma ɛndzɔ̀ sì he deceived me with lies; (3) (= sa) to slap; 'bö èri drí sì he smacked him with his hand.

'bɔ, av. particle of past tense; pointing to achievement of action; dɛ 'bɔ it is now finished; mu 'bɔ he has gone already.

bŏa, av. on one's flank under shoulder; ɔ̀kó bì (or du) mvá bŏa the woman holds/carries the child on her flank; á kpɔ̀ 'ɛ́ bŏa I hold the arrow under my arm; èi sìríbá sù bŏa they carry the amulets under the shoulder.

bóbúa, n. àṇá b— a white kind of eleusine.

bɔ̀dɔ̀ (kɔ̀ = bèdɔ̀kɔ̀), av. dripping with; èrimà drí àṇú sûrö b— his hand is dripping with honey; rùánï ɔvö ìyîrö b— he is dripping with water (coming out of river); ìyí pie b— water is running down.

'bŏdŏrŏ(-rö) = ètsì-ru, a. cloudy; àndrò àŋgŏ 'bŏdŏrŏ-rö, ètú ɛná-zŏ kö-rì the sky is overcast today, when the sun is not visible (ɛríti sì on account of clouds).

bòodrá = əya (ŋga), n. yaws.

'bələ, a. convexedly curved.

bŏlŏkŏ, n. large wild pigeon.

bə̀ŋgɔ́, n. cloth; èi b— sử, or trŏ vàá they put on, or take off a cloth.

bòn̪à = dzìn̪à, av. stiffly erect; sɔ̀ pá bòn̪yà he stands stiffly.

bŏrà, n. cat; for calling: búsù-búsù (S.?).

'bŏrŏ́ = 'bá or ágú, n. man (homo), person, individual; (Lɔgiri: ɔ́ní).

'bŏrŏ́, av. ɛmvɛ 'b— snow-white.

'bŏrŏ́, n. offence, guilt, wrong; èri 'b— à'ĭ 'ĭ rùárĭ sĭ he admits his offence/guilt.

bbŏrŏ̀-bbŏrŏ̀, av. muttering, grumbling; mĭ 'yɛ b—b—(ə̀mbà sĭ = mĭ ənɔ́ ŋgúrúŋgúrú) you are grumbling (anger).

'bə̀rɔ́, n. a large grasshopper.

'bɔ́rɔ̀á, n. a short thin pied poisonous snake.

bə̀rɔ̀á, n. kind of indigenous manioc, wild or cultivated.

bə̀rɔ̀dzɔ́vò = bə̀drɔ̀dzɔ́, n. living hole (underground) of mice.

bə̀rɔ̀kɔ̀, n. miniature grass-hut; èi ànïn̪aaká ámvúarĭ mà àgàĭ tĕ they guard the corn on fields in them.

bbŏrŏ́ndŏ́ = lógárí (q.v.), 'rö, a. isolated, secluded, unsocial; 'bá bbŏrŏ́ndŏ́'rö, 'bá 'a'ápĭ a'dúlɛ-rĭ (kind of) hermit/p. of singular habits/tastes, one who lives alone.

bŏrŏ́sŏ́, n. pigeon pea (Ac. lapɛna).

bòotá (= T. máau, mɛ́ɛo), n. butter; èi lésû tsə (or ɛdɛ̂, a'dĭ) bòotârö they churn milk to butter; èi b— a'dí-a'dí ədzá rö lésú-ədɔ̂rö they then melt the butter to ghee.

'bú, n. hole; ɛ́drɔ́nï 'bílɛ əva 'búa a mouse digs a hole in the depres-sion; 'búa in the hollowed ground; àn̪á 'búa kà dĭ drà 'bə, èi dĭ əmvɛ 'dŏfárá when the corn pressed into a hole (in the ground) is sour, it is called leaven.

'bù, n. the sky, heaven; àrïanĭ ŋga 'bùá sĭ birds fly in the sky.

bbu-, pref. for adverbs of time; bbu-drìə long time ago; mu bbudrìə he went in the past, long ago; in olden times; bbu-ǹdrâ some time (or also days) ago; má ɛtsá bbùǹdrâ I arrived some days ago; bbu-ndɔ̀ in the (far) future; bbu-mvârö at the time of childhood.

búua, n. a dance; èi búuâ tö they are dancing 'buua'.

bùuá, n. a kind of very small bird (finch?).

búbù¹, n. kind of dewlap between hindleg and belly of cow; tí mà b—.

búbù², av. in the very act; á bĭ ògúoo b— I caught the thief in the very act (of stealing); má esú èri b— I found him unexpectedly; á bĭ mĭ b— 'bə I caught you in the very act.

bùbù-ɔ́zɛ́, n. occasional rain out of season; bùbù-nï 'di ə̀kɔ̀fɔ̀ ráká, ïyĭonĭ ŋga emû dĭ ndɔ̀ an occasional rain (also called bùbù-ïyí) comes first, then the rainy season will come regularly.

búudrì, n. arm-joint (at shoulder ɔ̀pì); búdriá or ɔ̀pì-drìá, av. on the shoulder.

búkù, Engl. n. book.

bbúlú(ku), n. (large black) ground hornbill; èri ə̀ndá bɛ it has gills.

'búlúkɔ́, n. name of a large tree (with large black seeds).

'búlúkɔ̂rö (= àrɔ̂rö), a. green, not yet fully ripe; kaa rá mba ŋgà kö it is developed but not yet mature, ripe; bŏrŏsŏ èri 'b— the pigeon peas are not yet ripe.

'buundú, n. red morning sky; 'b— èri emú nǐ (àŋgŏ èri ekǎrö) or 'b— ɛré rö rá the sky reddens, grows lighter (towards dawn).

'búrô, n. a ritual hole (about 1 yd. in diameter and 2—3 in. deep) dug in the ground; pit dug for the chicken oracle; lǐ a'ú 'b— 'a drà àmadrí ndàazŏ, nòsì kànì à lè drǎ rá he killed a fowl in the hole to investigate our death, when we are dying (sick).

bbùrù, n. kind of weaver bird; very small, feeds on seeds.

'bùurú, n. av. home; mu 'b— (= bàrú, T.) or mu àkúa he went home.

bùrù-bùrù, av. with flickering flash; àŋgŏnǐ lǐ b—b— it is lightning in flashes.

bùrudzì (= gok), S. n. bugle, horn; b— vö to blow the bugle.

búutì, Engl. n. canvas slippers/ boots.

D

Dà¹ = táamvŏ, n. pipe; mǐ aɳǐ tábà dà mà 'aléa! crumple/ crush tobacco into the pipe!

dà², vt. to pour out (or into); é dà vàá! pour it away! é dà ìyí 'ïmà rúá! sprinkle him with water! èi à'í dǎ tíbí 'aléa they put salt into the savoury; àma áɳú dǎ òkpórŏa we pour sesame into the bag; dà 'ï vàá, vr. it was spilled.

dà³, vr. (1) to withdraw, retire from…; é dà mï rá! á lè mï nĕ kö be gone! (get thee hence! get out from my sight!) I do not want to see you; dǎ èì rá they have withdrawn; (2) drì (è)dà to return.

dà⁴ (= bì), vt. to bend, bow down; òlǐ dà pätí rá the wind has bent down the tree; rö dà, vr. to bend, incline; to slope, slant; pätí dà 'ï dà the tree is bent; dzó 'dà mà àbì dà 'ï dà the wall of that hut is sloping; é dà mǐ dà! bend down! àŋgŏ Éɳáó mà tìá dà 'ï dà the ground on the side of the Eɳao is sloping.

'dá stressed 'dálé, av. there, yonder; té èri tsǐ 'dá (if not stressed at all 'dà) he was there a minute ago; á mu té 'dálé rá I went there a moment ago.

'dà¹-rǐ, pl. 'dàǐ, demonstr. prn. that/those; av. there; èrì mu 'dà there he goes.

'dà², vt. to avoid (taboo); òkó èì a'ú 'dǎ ǹdrí bɛ women avoid (eating) fowls and sheep.

'dà³, vt. to lick; taste (= 'bǐ); èì à'í or áɳú 'dǎ they lick salt, sesame; òtsénï ìyí 'dǎ-'dà (= mbĕmbe) andra sǐ a dog laps water with its tongue.

'da, vt. (1) rû 'da to (give a) name; à'dǐ 'da mǐ rú 'dǐnǐ yà? who has given you such a name/called you so? (his mother); (2) (often ə'da) to call a person names, insult, revile 'bá àzínǐ 'dazŏ; 'datáa or ə'datáa, n. insult; (3) ŏ'dókó'dô 'da to tell stories, fables.

daaká (= sórŏ, zè), n. waste, refuse, offal, leavings; àɳú d—, wax; à'í d— (ŏfŏtá à'í), dregs of (ash-) salt; àɳá 'bánï ɛdɛ éwârörǐ mà d— flour residue/dregs from beer-making; (polite term for excrement).

dǎälì, a. depressed, hollowed; àŋgŏ d— the lower part of an elevation/hill; depression in the ground; ŋgŏrú-d— upper–lower part.

dàlì-dàlì, a. quivering; ɔ́da(lo)-kɔ́da èrì d—dàlì-rö the after-birth (or also entrails) is a quivering mass.

dáamvó (cf. dà¹) (= pámvó; kɔ̀tsɔ́), n. pipe.

'dáanï, av. without more ado; unceremoniously; of his own free choice; mu 'd—, lὸ ɛ'yɔ́ kö he went at his own discretion without saying a word; Múŋgὸ 'bà èrì 'd—'dà: rúánï rὸêrö 'd— tsɛ́nï God made him so by mere chance/accident: he is thin/slender accidentally; é ko èrì 'd—! leave it alone/to his own discretion.

dàrabà or dèrabà (fr. Engl. driver), n. driver (of motor-cars); mótókà tì dzɪ́pirì who takes along a motor-car.

dàràŋgbà = kpàràkpàrà, -rö, a./av. extending/hanging (over) bulkily, heavily.

dàarì or dàara (MN.), stiff hair of tail of some animals; èwá d— the stiff hair of elephant's tail; ὸdrú d— buffallo's (tail or) mane hair. (cf. kúrúsá).

dè¹, dèrè, cj./intj. of surprise: is it then/after all/really...! mï dèrè àfa 'dɪ 'yɛ! is it you then, after all, who did it! mï dè èndzὸ lï mánï you have lied to my face then! (cf. rúmu).

dè², dèzà, vn./a. old (animal or anything); worn out; 'bá (or ὸkó) dèzàrö old man (woman); also ὸkó òkurï dèdè a very old lady; dzɔ́ dèzà old dilapidated hut; á lè àfa dèzàrö (or dèpi rá 'dï) kö I do not want old worn-out things; èrì 'bá dèzà (rï) he is an old man.

dɛ¹ = alú, vt. to curse, imprecate; invoke evil upon, threaten; 'bá 'dàrï ὸndzí, dɛ ma rá: 'é drà

fɔ̂!' that man is bad, he cursed me, 'may you die!'

dɛ², vt. to complete, finish, terminate; or to be finished; 'bílé dɛ mánï andzi rá/or 'bá ènɪ́kinï the grave has taken away all my children (or everybody); dɛ̆ ámvú rá or 'ǎ ámvú dɛ 'bɔ they finished (tilling) the field; ámvú dɛ rö 'bɔ the field is finished (tilling).

'dɛ¹, vn. to die, perish, succumb; 'bá 'dɛ 'bɔ the person died; gbà 'bá àzɪ́ kàlí sɪ̌, 'dɛ rá he struck him with a stick, he died (from it); èrì ŋgà 'dɛ̆'dɛ he is dying.

'dɛ², vn. (1) to fall (from some height); sɪ̂nɪ̌ 'dɛ it hails; èdiɔnɪ̌ (i.e. pátí éfɪ́nï) 'dɛ fruits from ... fell to the ground; mɪ̂ sɪ̂ 'dɛ 'bɔ your tooth has come out; étí éfɪ̂ 'dɛ vàá tamarind fruits fell down; (2) to break out (disease, &c.); àbírí 'dɛ ándrâ rá a famine broke out in those days; (3) 'bá mà vútiâ 'dɛ to follow a p.; é mu ŋgà drìlé, mâ ŋgà 'dɛ (or mu) mɪ̂ vúti sɪ̌ rá go ahead and I shall follow you.

'dé, av. (1) (= 'dɪ̆á) there (at some mentioned place...); (2) 'dé...'dé partly ... partly; here—there; 'dé gúrú (or dǎälì) 'dé ŋgörö partly hollow, partly rising (uneven ground).

débè, S. = ndɔ̂, n. a jar.

dèdè or èdíï, n. grandmother; mâ d— or mâ dèdèá or mâ èdíï my grandmother! má a'á mâ (è)díï vὅ I have been staying with my grandmother; á mu mâ (è)díï mà dràá! let me go to my grandmother's funeral/tomb.

déènὸ = gbándzá, q.v.

'dɛrɛ'dɛrɛ (cf. sérèsérè), av. level, smooth; mɪ́ ɛdé ŋaakú mà drì 'd—'d— rö! make the surface of the earth smooth (with hands)!

dîi or èdîi, n. grandmother; mvá 'dî mà èdîi this child's grandmother.

di, vt. to beat, knock; (1) (cf. Ac. dìinò) to forge iron ayà di; àdzû di to make a spear; èi ókâ di èi vö àtsî sî they forge at the forge (-bellows) blowing fire; (2) (= òdzì) to wash; èi bòŋgô di they wash a cloth (i.e. beating); (3) to knock, hit; èri mâ milê di he strikes my eye; di mâ sí trú he knocked out my teeth; (4) to thrash; òkónï àŋâ di óní sî the woman threshes the corn (a small quantity at a time) with a stone; èri àŋá 'bíkə berî di óní drìá she threshes corn in its husk on a stone (to clean it); (5) àdzî di to defame, slander; di àmbó mà àdzí rá he slandered the Big Man/authority/headman.

dîi, av. secretly, clandestinely; stealthily, furtively; é zì dîi áséa! hide it by stealth in the grass! mà 'bà dîi 'dálé, mà εená kö! let it be put aside secretly, that it may not be seen!

di, vn. (1) to catch (fire), to blaze up, to break out in flames; àtsínï dî lè (-lè) the fire flares up; édzá èbìrö, àtsí dì ànï kö the wood is green, therefore the fire does not catch; (2) to flicker, flare; (if at a distance = gu); (3) to shine (of bright object); èri dî ndrì-ndrî it shines brightly.

dï, vt. to annoy, vex; ε'yó dï èri rá the matter has made him weary; àŋgô nï mâ dîdï I am tired (or sick) of the place; mî ε'yónï 'ye mâ dï, mïnï 'bâ tsə(lérî) sî I am getting weary of you, if you beat a p.

dî, cj. av. then, afterwards; now; à mû dî! let us go then! è mû dî ìî! goodbye! so go then! tê dî... but now.

'dî, 'dïrï/'dîî, demon. pron. this/these.

'di, vt. (1) to kill; 'di 'î ádrîinï rá he killed his brother; 'bá 'bâ-'dîpirî a murderer; (2) àdzû 'di to throw a spear; 'di àdzú èwá rùá he speared an elephant; (3) əzóónî 'dî'di it is raining; əzóó 'di 'bə it has already rained.

dìidîi, av. swinging, balancing; kìtándà-nî 'dε ma bε d— the bedstead sinks swinging with me (on it).

dîïá, av. carefully, smoothly, wholly; é dzi d— (= 'yékè) mà àgbà rö kö! carry it carefully (say a glass) that it may not break! ko éŋá d—, εló rùánï kö he left the polenta intact, he did not touch (i.e. take from) it.

ddíká, av. (1) again; é 'yə d—! say it again! (2) (local) farther on; é mì àfa 'dî 'dálé('rö) dd—! push this thing farther away!

dìnàdìnà (= akázà), a. av. sticky; elastic.

'díni, av. like this, in this way, thus; 'yə 'd— rá he did say so; 'díni táandí precisely (actually) so; just like this.

'díə, av. instantly (= tsúrú'də).

'dîpi, av. thus, so; mî edzí 'd—! bring me like this (pointing out the quantity desired, the size, with gesticulating hands).

'dîirrrí, av. (= píripírí), whirling; àdrópá'dírí-nî ŋga-zó 'dîirrírî the whirlwind rises (whirlingly).

dïrïkpa'rö (= ədï-ədï = àdáláká = ənìzà = dèzà), a. (1) (man, &c.) old, shrivelled, wrin-

kled; (2) worn, threadbare, shabby
(cloth, &c.).

'də, 'dərï/'dəï̈, demon. pron. this
here (at back); èri 'də he is here
(on the other side); mï̈ emú 'də!
come here (on this other side)!
'dəá, av. here (= 'də); 'dəpi like
this (show with hand); dzɔ́
èmï̈ vélérï̈ ŋgəpi yà? how big is
your hut? èri 'dəpi ('bá èi e'da-
e'da) it is like this (show with
hand).

'dɔ́, 'dɔ́lɛ́, av. here; in/to this place,
this way, hither; ɛ́ri a'á 'dɔ́ he
has been here; mï̈ emú 'dɔ́lɛ́!
come this other way/to this place;
èri 'dɔ́lɛ́ he is on this other side
(not in your direction).

dò, vt. (1) ti dò to kindle, light sth.;
é mu ámukɔ́ ti dǒ! go and set
fire to the heap of grass! é mu
àtsï̈ edǒ émvú ètḯá! go and light
fire under the pot! ásé ti dò to
fire the grass; é dò àtsï̈ ɔ́tàliá
sía! light the small lamp! (2)
(insect) to sting; touch with sth.
sharp or painful; àn̩ú-nï 'bá dǒ
bees sting; (3) (= sö) to dip in;
ma ɛn̩á dǒ (or ˋsö) tíbí 'a(léa)
I am dipping polenta into the sauce.

'dǒ, n. eleusine; ma ándríi mu
'dǒ adza my mother went to
spread eleusine (to sun and air,
for drying).

də, də rö, vr. to keep silent (in
discussion); to be modest or
moderate, reserved; to moderate,
restrain o-s.; kànï zi rö 'dálɛ́,
ɛlɔ́ àfa kö: èri 'ï̈ də 'dú'dú when
he draws aside (silently), without
touching anything: he is bashful/
unassuming, mum; 'bá 'dà èri
'yɛrɛ, o'dú pírí sï̈ èri 'ï̈ dɔ̌-də
that man is very reserved/un-
assuming, he always behaves
humbly; é də mï̈ də! or é də mï̈

tsírḯ (≅ mï̈ òvù tsírḯ!) keep
quiet/restrain yourself! é mu ɔ́pí
vǒ dəzàrö (= àdətá sï̈ or ɛ̀nd-
zìtáa sï̈)! go to the chief respect-
fully/humbly! dətá, àdətáa, n.
bashfulness, modesty, modera-
tion, humility, reserve.

də, cj. if; də mï̈ oŋgú tö, èmï̈ mù
drə rö èri bɛ rá! if you are so
fast, go and race (each other) with
him!

'dò, vn. to rise, repeat with one;
kàni ává mï̈ 'aléa trɛ́, mï̈ tinï̈
'dǒ if gases fill your stomach up,
they rise with you; 'bá àzï̈nï̈ ɛ́wâ
ti 'dǒ beer repeats with him
(aufstoßen).

dò, vn. to get fixed (for use); to
be/get ready/suitable/settled for
...; dzɔ́ 'alɛ́ dò 'bə the interior
of the hut/room is ready-fixed;
gï̈rï̈kə dò 'bə the road is com-
pleted/ready; bəŋgɔ́ 'dï̈ dò 'bə
the cloth is now ready (ironed,
&c.: for use); edǒ gï̈rï̈ mávélé
ámvú 'alɛ́ sï̈ (or mà àgǎi sï̈)
they have made/produced (by
continued walking) a path through
my field (or: on its side).

dòáni, n. (A.S. diwan) assembly of
authorities for public discussions,
council; place of assembly; é tö
èri dòániá! take him before the
assembly (with his case)!

dədə = gǎrípàrí, n. swamp.

dədərə-bá, n. a long rope; d—
ṅdrí 'ï-zɔ̌ èríbía long rope to tie
goats in the grass (for feeding);
èzɔ̌ dəidə extending at great
length (rope).

'dǒfárá, n. leavened dough for
beer-making 'd— ɛ́wâ-rö.

dòkà, or dòkáni, A.S. n. shop.

dəkə-dəkə or dərə-dərə, -rö, a.
weak, lean; rickety; loosely fastened.

dɔ̀ko-nï ≅ kà adri 'dïnï, conj. phrase: it is better; ... had better (with hortative); d— á mu 'dálɛ́ kö I had better not go there; d— mï ɛ̀fɛ̀ mánï àlö! you ought to give me one! drìga'dïï(T.) (= kà adri 'dïnï) à mví àkúa! we had better go home!

'dɔ̀kɔ́rɔ́, T. (= 'dɔ̌fárá = kàràwà), n. flour leavened with ground àkúfï; èì àkúfï àwǎ 'dɔ̌fá-rö they grind 'àkúfï' for leaven.

dólïdólï, av. going to pieces; ɔ̀nyɔ̀ 'ï d— it broke to pieces.

dɔ̀lɔ̀dɔ̀lɔ̀, av. shaky (cf. ayázà).

dólómò, n. a tree on river-sides.

'dóresï, intj. used in phrases as àwà'dï fɔ̀ manï ɛ́wá mà ti 'd—! may the breaking wind (belching) from beer do me good! (cf. 'dò).

'dóresï, indf. pron. the individual of a moment ago; 'd— mu ŋgɔ́lɛ́ yà? where did our companion who was with us just now go?

dɔɔri, n. hunting; à mú dɔɔrïá àṇàpâ gbï! let us go hunting to kill animals!

'dɔ̌rɔ́'dɔ̌rɔ̌ = kátrí, a. even, level, smooth; gǎ dzɔ́ mà ǹdú 'd—'d— they cut the grass-end of hut level—straight; mï e'dölò àŋgɔ̌ 'dï 'd—'d—! do level out the ground here!

dɔ̀rɔ̀dɔ̀rɔ̀, av. loosely; not firm; bákánï 'yɛ d—d— the rope hangs loosely (pending); àŋgönï yǎ d—d— the earth shakes (earthquake).

'dɔ́rɔ́kɔ̀lɔ́, av. to the last bit or drop; a'dɔ́ ɛ́wá dzɔ́lɔ́ 'd— he drained it to the last drop (beer).

drà, vn./n. to die; death; drà sɔ̀ èri kái death struck him mercilessly; 'bá drǎpirï dead person; mu (əŋgɔ̌ tö) 'bá drǎpirï mà dràá he went to (dance at) a dead person's funeral/to visit a grave-side; 'bá sá èri 'bílía 'bɔ they have already buried him.

dra, drǎdra, drazà = òká, vn. to be(come) acid, sour; ɛ́wá dra 'bɔ the beer has (fermented and, as required) become sour; dra mǎ sísɔ̀á it set my teeth (jaws) on edge; dra òkáŋgálí extremely sour, bitter; ásí-nï drǎdra (i.e. òmbàrö) he is quarrelsome, fond of picking quarrels.

drà, n. kind of dance; èì mu drà tö they are going to dance 'dra'.

drǎdràvá, n. lump of clay shaped into miniature hut, into which a trouble (illness)-bringing spirit of a deceased is caused to move by a sacrifice; dzɔ́ 'dï èì bi ɔ̀drí sï made from clay; the spirit yàkáni.

dràŋgà = kɔ̀tsɔ́, n. pipe; 'bá tábà se d— sï they smoke tobacco with a pipe.

drí, pstp. genitive: of; dative: to, for.

drí, n. hand (comprising forearm); drí-lèdzô index or forefinger; drí-áda (tà ṇa-zɔ̌) right hand (for eating); drí-lèdzí (= edzí) (zá bïzɔ̌) left hand (for picking up meat at meal).

drì¹, n. head; drì'bá = kàïɔ̀rì = T. àlɔ́ɔ̀rì, the first-born; dribbí head-hair; cf. Dribbídu famous ancestor of the Terego-Logbara stock (with peculiar hair); drì-ndzá, n. bashfulness, modesty, humility; drì-ndzá kɔ èri tsï he is abashed, ashamed; saying: drì-ndzá nya ɔ̀ndɛ́ bashfulness ate the nerve (i.e. hinders pluck); drì-ndzá yɔ (or kɔ́kɔ̀rö) devoid of all (sense of) shame; shameless, unabashed; impudent, brazen-faced; profligate; **drìlé,** n. top, tip, extremity; **pá-, drí-...(mà) drìlé** tip of toe, finger; av. in front, ahead, before; **é mu èi bɛ drìlé!** go ahead with it, i.e. continue! **drìlé (= dritsépi = ódzíə),** n. messenger; delegate (esp. for marriage arrangement); **'bá mŭpi ópí mà pàrïa ɛ̀ri ópí mà drìlé** a person going in place of a chief is a chief's messenger; **driléa/drìlïa,** pstp. in front of; **ɛ̀ri mâ drìlïa** he is (or stands) before me; **á tsâ mu-zó kö, àzí mâ drìlïa tsí** I cannot go, I am busy (lit. work is before me); **drìlé-bba** or **drìlé mŏké** (lit. the front is pleasant, good) lucky; good luck; **Ò'dírikpò mà drì- lébbanï tsí; Ò'dírikpò** is lucky; **drìlé ɔ̀ndzí,** n. bad luck; un- lucky; **mâ drìlé ɔ̀ndzí, ma esú ɛ̀ri (drìlé ɔ̀ndzí sì) kö** I am un- lucky, I did not find him (through ill-luck); **drì'bâ-ti = yïla,** n. descendant, offspring; **'bá dribbï kókɔ̀rö** or **'bá drì ŋgbə** bald- headed person.

drï², cf. **èdrì,** vt. to transmit.

drï, vn. (va.), (1) to warm up, to be warm; **é mu ìyî drï** or **é 'bà ìyî drï** or **é 'bà ìyí àtsïa** go and warm the water! or put water on fire! **àŋgò drï dzóa drï** it is warm in the hut; **ètú drï̂-drï** the sun is hot; **mâ rúá drï̂drï** I feel hot; **á lè ìyí drïzàrörï kö** I do not want warm water; **á lè ìyí drïpi drï̂drï-rï'ï** I like warm water; **'bà ìyí àtsí drïá drïzàrö** she put water on the fire to warm it; (2) (= **vɛ**) to burn; **àtsínï drï 'bâ rúá** the sun burns one; **ètú sílénï mâ drï̂drï (= vɛ̂ve)** the sun's rays burn me; (3) to blind, dazzle; **ètúnï 'bâ milê drï̂drï**

the sun blinds one's eyes; **drïtá,** n. warmth, heat.

drïia, indf. prn. all.

drïadría = ɔndzayìa, T. = **kà- màlárà,** A., n. red Cayenne pepper/paprika.

drìga'dí, T. = **dòkoni,** q.v.

drïká = èdríká, T., n. mush- room; **d— ɛ̀ri ŋga ótókó drìá** a mushroom grows on ant-hills.

drílékó = óꞯúrúbí, óyúrúbí, 'bíkə, n. chaff; **àꞯá d—** chaff of corn.

drìlé-ti, n. = **drì-'bâ-ti,** cf. **drì.**

drìiə, drìə-drìə, av. before; early; in the past; **ò'bíti d—d—** early in the morning; **mí èfò drù ò'bíti (sì) d—d—!** come early in the morning! **ǹdrá-drìə** long ago, in the (distant) past; **'bá ándrâ drìə 'dï̂ mà ɔ̀rï kírí ŋgà tsí** the true descendants (seed) of the people of the past are still extant; **drìòwú sì** long long ago.

drísísí, n. pilfering, thieving; **mí d—bɛ,** or **mí drísísí'rö (= ògù- ru)** you are going pilfering/ stealing.

drɔ̀, vt. to heap (or pile) up; (1) to put one upon another; **èi bɔ̀ŋgó drɔ̀** they are piling up cloths; **èi édzá drɔ̀** they heap up wood; (2) vn. to be covered with rash, weals, streaks; **ɔndrokɔndro kà mí dò, mî rúánï drɔ̀drɔ̀ (or drɔ̀- bììrì)** or **drɔ̀zàrö** if the 'ɔndro- kɔndro' ants bite you, your body will come out in a rash.

drə, (1) vn. to wander, roam, rove; **mvá 'dï̂ drə tò, lè àzî ŋga kö** this child is always tramping about; he does not like to work; **mí átíinï̂ drə kìlé ɔ̀tsó-lé, ɛ́wá ndä̂** thy father roves about freely like a dog in search of beer; (2) vt. to drive away/off, to put to flight;

é drə èì àmvé ! drive them away !
ədró (for plurality); àŋúnï ma
ədró ədró bees are chasing me;
(3) to drive to, take to; drə tí
ökó-á he drove cattle to bride's
parents (for marriage);(4) 'bá mà
ètï drə to pursue sby., &c. ;(5) vn.
to haste, hurry to do; èrì drə
éŋâ ŋa he hurries or goes rashly
to eat polenta (not even washing
before).

dródró (commonly ádródró), n.
leech; kànì bɛlɛ mî pá tsï, èì
dródró 'bǎ àrïnï ndzu when
you have a sore leg, they put on a
leech to suck the blood.

drözí, av. the day after tomorrow;
d— àzï 'dà sǐ after three days.

drù, drùsǐ, av. tomorrow; mà mu
àkúa drù ! he ought to go home
tomorrow !

dù = tə, drï, vn. to be (-come)
slightly or lukewarm; ìì dừdù ètú
sǐ the water is slightly warm from
the sun.

du, vn. to sprout; to come(or shoot,
spring) up; ərïnï dừdu the seeds
shoot up (where they fell); àŋá
du ámvúa fórí (= fədî) 'bə the
corn has come up in bright tender
sprouts on the field; 'dö, əndó,
päti du mökế eleusine, durra,
tree grew well; dừdu, duzàrö
overgrown, covered with tall
grass; sprouted; àŋgö (or áisé)
duzàrö = àŋgö du tö the place
is overgrown with grass; ásé du
ámvúa grass grew on the field.

'du, vt. to take up, lift; to take
away, remove; carry off; əlí 'du
nǐ the wind has carried it off; 'du
'bǎ to take and put elsewhere;
ma kálâ 'du 'bǎ àmvé əzóó íyí
a'í-zö ànï I place the tesht outside to collect rain water with it;
e'dú (T. a'dú) to take up, lift; to

put on one's head; zá àdzínï
e'dú ru ndrrí a pleasant odour of
meat is wafted about; e'dú 'ímà
édzá she took up the wood (on
her head).

dúdù, S. (= ò'bu), n. chigoe or
sand flea; d— fï 'bâ pá the
chigoe burrows into one's foot;
ká èri ɛndzɛ 'bə èì əmvɛ ò'bu
when removed (alone) they call it
'ò'bu' (cf. ógálírí).

'dú'dú, av. very quiet (as a mouse),
mum; də rö 'd— he kept still.

'dúkù, n. hiccup; 'dúkù-nï ma
sìsì hiccup knocks me/it gives me
hiccups.

dúllú(ä) = àlí(ä), n. a stump of
anything; drí d— stump of arm
or hand (maimed); əfô ŋa èrì drí
dúllú ('rö) leprosy has eaten
away his hand to a stump; päti
dúlûrö a piece of wood : a cudgel.

dúlú-dúlú = dólídólí = kótsí-
kótsí, av. into small pieces.

dùmù, a. close, heavy, sultry
(weather); àŋgö dí əvö d—; ètú
yə, əlí yə the weather is sultry,
without sun or wind.

dúrù = èrítì, av. much delaying,
loitering on the way; mu dúrù
he went away and stayed out (too)
much (opp. tsàkà, púru, kàlà-
wù).

dúutì, n. a kind of edible mushroom (large).

dzà, av. with ko: to leave alone;
é ko oŋgú dzà (= rá) leave off
from hurry !

dza, vt./n. to turn; (1) to turn or
twist round; mvánï a'ú mà
əmbɛ dza (drí sǐ) the boy has
wrung the fowl's neck (with his
hand); cf. əŋga, or dza 'ímà milé
mökế he turned/turned his eyes
correctly; (2) vn. to heal; mâ drí
ndrâ pïpirǐ dza rá my hand

which was swollen before has healed; **mâ bɛlɛ lɛ̀ dza (rö) kö** my sore refuses to heal; **dáwà ndrâ mïnï 'bằ rï̀ sï̀ dza ànï rá, de 'ï 'bɔ** because of the medicine which you applied it has healed, it is finished; **mâ rûâ dza (= àtï) rá** I have recovered; (3) vn. **drì dza** or **àvě**; **'ï̀ drì(tà) dzá (or àvě or àvě̀ dza) rá** he has forgotten it.

dzárà (= **dzɛ̀ké**), n. game of hazard (largely indulged in by Logbara); (**ódrúsï** cowry shell, serves as dice); to play at dice: **d— 'bɛ** (= **gbï̌, g̣bà**) or **ódrúsï 'bɛ sente sï̀** (for money); **mí emú à mú d— g̣bï̌!** come let us go and play at dice! **kànì 'bá àzínï mà bɔ̀ŋgó tsí, ɛ̀ri trö fɛ̌ g̣bà rá dzárà sï̀** if a p. has on a cloth (or animals, even wife) he will take it off and put it in for the game.

dzɛ = **ɔlɛ**, vt. to buy; **ǹdrî dzɛ** to buy a goat; to marry; **lɛ̀ ɔ̀kô dzɛ** or **ɔlɛ** he wants to marry a woman.

dzɛ̀ké = **dzárà**, q.v.

dzɛ̀rɛ̀(kò), n. thicket (of trees, reed-stalks, &c.); **d— pätï trǎrö- pï pằrï àlǒárï̌** trees gathered in one place; **ɔ̀zô dùdu àmbôrö 'bá ɔmvɛ d—** reed-stalks grown in quantity are called thicket.

dzi, vt. (cf. **edzí, ɔdzí**) to take, bring to . . . ; **á dzi 'bà èirï̌** I took it to their home.

dzí (dzí óɳa, dzí ɛdzíríkó), n. one kind of termites.

dzï = **ɔ̀mɔ̀kó**, n. enmity, hatred; **dzï àmanï̌ 'bá 'dï̌ bɛ tsï̀** there is enmity between me and this man.

dzí, T. = **wóró**, av. all.

dzï̌[1], vt. to sharpen; **ma elï sí dzï̌** I am sharpening the knife; **ɛ̀ri sí dzï̌** he rubs (cleans) his teeth (with a special piece of wood).

dzï̌[2] = **ndzɔ**, vt. to express; **ɔkónï**

ósǒ dzï̌ the woman expresses the pulp of beans (mash).

dzíibú, n. the network of corridors in termite-hills or elsewhere where snakes and mice live; **d— ɛ̀ri pằrí óríni ɔvözörï̌ (órï 'bílé)** it is the place (hole) in which snakes live.

dzìɳà = **bòɳà**, av./a. stiff—erect **ɳáɳákò'bï̌ ɛ̀ri bbíkó bɛ d—** the **ɳ—** caterpillar has stiff (bristly) hair.

dzíríbbi (= **g̣íríbbi, T.**), n. plant used as vegetable.

dzìrìlí, T.? = **ndrùndrùá,** n. (?) zibet cat.

dzírílí, n. shout of joy (**àìkò**); **èi d—** (= **lúlú**)**'g̣a àɳàpá bï̌ rï̀ mà àìkò sï̀** they shout the 'dzírílí' for joy of having laid hands on a game animal.

dzìrö, a., twilight; **àŋgò̀ d—** (= **òníkòni**) . . . **'bánï fözǒ o'búti sï̀ rï̌** when people go out in the morning.

dzò (= **'yò**), n. snake poison.

dzó, n. hut, house; **dzó'alé** interior of hut; **dzó-drì** roof of hut; **dzó'bólókò-ètï̌** = **dzó'bílé (kò)- ètï̌** (or **-ǹdú**) veranda; **dzó- ètálá** draining channel for rain- water on side of hut; **dzó-pálá** or **dzó-ètílé** the ground from the hut towards the water place; **dzó-'íi**, n. owner of hut, head of family; **dzó** hut, family (-group); **dzó-tálá** or **dzó-milé** window; **dzó-ti-lé** door (-opening).

dzó-bi commonly **dzáróvò**.

dzòdzòkì, n. phantom, spectre, ghostly appearance; **Aluru èi ɔfǒ rö dzòdzòkì-rö nï̌** it is the Aluur (and some other people are believed to have this capacity) who can transform themselves into phantoms (i.e. by night).

dzɔ́fɛ, n. 'yɛ́ d— shaft of arrow.

dzɔ̀fó, T. = òn̠ìfé, òn̠ìàfa, n. trinkets, knick-knacks.

dzɔ́ló(kɔ́), n. remains (of food &c.); mvá ko én̠á mà d— tsǐ the child left some polenta over; áisɛ́ (ɛ́dzá) d— atsɛ tsǐ grass (firewood) remained (over).

dzɔ́lókɔ̀-ètǐ or **dzɔ́bɛ́lékɔ̀ ǹdú**, n. space round hut under roof; veranda.

dzörǒ, n. hand-bag, basket.

dzɔ́róvǒ, n. nest (of bird); hole (of rat, snake); àrǐan̠ǐ rǐ dzɔ́róvǒ-á birds sit in nest.

dzùlú'ru (1) (= ɔ̀lìru), av. on one's back; ágú 'dà laa 'ǐ d— that man lies on his back; ɛ'dɛ d— he fell on his back; (2) (= gɔ̀lǐ'ru) crookedly, incorrectly; èri ɛ'yɔ̂ ndzɛ d— he speaks incorrectly.

dzùlú(ku)'ru, a. relatively (rather) too long; a'ú ti d— the fowl's beak is long; ɛ́mvó ti d— the pot has a long neck; mǐ drì d— your head is (backward) protracted (insult).

dzúrú, n. distinct clan or tribal group, foreigner; é mvi èmïrǐ, mǐ dzúrúnï (or àndǐnǐ) go back to your country, you are a stranger.

dzuru, a. (1) (= áŋgǐrǐ, tsóla) abundant, plantiful; 'bá 'ǐ àndrɔ̀ én̠á d— they have prepared plenty of polenta today; (2) (= ndɛ́nǐ) bigger, taller; L ... èri mánǐ d— (= zɔ mánǐ ndɛ́nǐ), L ... is taller than I.

E

N.B. The prefix e- (ɛ-) may be added to almost every verb beginning with a consonant. Meaning: (as a rule) an action, &c., proceeding in the direction of the speaker, as mu to go; emú to come. If, therefore, a verb is not found under e-, look for the root-verb.

é, prs. pron. short form; thou; é fǐ! go in!

è, prs. pron. short form; you (pl.); è fǒ! go out!

èɛ (= ɔ̀ə; angrily m̃m̀), intj. yes.

έ'ὲ (= á'à, m̃'m̀), intj. no.

ɛ'ɛ̀! (= wûwú!), intj. alas! what a pity; (expression of pain, sorrow, disappointment); ɛ'ɛ̀! mâ bɔ̀ŋgɔ́ àsǐ rö 'bɔ! alas! my cloth is already torn!

ébbá = èbàrǐɔ, n. bushbuck (Ac. rǒdà); ándrǐinǐ ɔ'yónǐ yɔ the female has no horns; ébbá'rö, a. dapple, piebald; white- and brown-spotted; 'dé ɛka 'dé ɛmvɛ (ɛ́— mà ùwúrá) here brown, here white (bushbuck-colour).

ɛbbá-àrǐa, n. hoopoe.

ebbabǎ = ɔlɛ, ɔdzá, etsǐ, vt. to deceive, cheat; èri 'bá e— èndzɔ̀ sǐ he deceives one with lies; mǐ ma e— tɔ̀kɔ́ you are just flattering me; ɔ́dzɔ̀ɔ-nǐ 'bá e— the diviner practises deception upon people.

ebabà (= ebetà) rö, vr. (1) to differ from ...; àma ti àlörǐ e— Térégò bɛ 'ǐ we differ from Tɛrɛgo in language; (2) embarrassed, puzzled, confused; e— rö 'ǐ drìá rá he is confused in his head.

èbè = ɛkɔ, vt. to draw (water); ìyí èbèzǒ òkèlé sǐ with a calabash.

ɛ'bɛ́, vt. to miscarry, or be miscarried; tǐ ɛ'bɛ́ ádzɛ̂ the cow miscarried yesterday; ɔ̀kɔ́ 'dà mà mvá ɛ'bɛ́-ɛ'bɛ́ (= fɔ̀ rá), mbánǐ tsa ŋgà kö the child of that woman was miscarried, the months were not sufficient; 'í lĕ tí (mvá) ɛ'bé-zàrörì ŋa kö he dislikes (he says) eating from miscarried calf; ɛ'bé-zà, a. flabby (of such flesh).

èbì, (1) vt. to join, attach, fasten (with glue), to glue on; má kàrtási èbì ésésé sì I am joining papers with glue; émvó kà andi rö rá, èì ɔ̀bì ésésé sì if a pot has cracked, they join it with glue; (2) (= 'dɛ), vn. to die.

èbi, a. (1) green, unripe; = 'wípì körì; ǹdrí lĕ ásé èbi (-rì) the goats like green grass; (2) raw, uncooked; àfa a'dípi-kö-rì; á lĕ zá èbi (-rì) kö I dislike uncooked meat; (3) wet, soft; àŋgò èbìrö ìyí sì the ground is wet/soft from water; bàŋgó ɛ̀rì èbìrö ɔzɔ́ɔ sì the cloth is wet from rain.

èbì(yá) [= o'díia], chisel; èbì kìtɔ̀pɔ́lɔ́ (or ŋàŋgàlà) ɛdé-zǒ a chisel to carve a stool (from one block).

èbì (= èbìyɔ́), n. (in fables) (1) spider (= ànìkání); èbì ɛ̀rì báká sĕ-ɛs the spider spins threads; èbì mà báká cobweb; Èbìyóombámbá proper name of spider of fables; (2) cannibal.

è'bí, n. fish; è'bí mà éwí (sóbí) fish's fin/tail.

ɛ'bí, vn. to start; to come from; ɛ'bí ɛŋgá = ɛ'bí emú to come from; ɛ'bí ɛŋgá àzía, ɔŋgɔ́á (or ɔŋgɔ́-ŋgɔrìá) he comes from work, dancing.

ɛ'bi or ɔ'bi = osí, ɔyo, vt. to roast, grill; àŋá èbi èì ɔ'bi àtsí sì (òtakà mà 'aléa) éŋâ rö fresh/tender corn is roasted on fire (in potsherd) for polenta; kànì 'wì (orò-orò), èì mũ 'i ɛ̀rà drìá when it (the fresh corn) is hardened, they go to grind it on a stone.

èbìia, ɛ́sɛ̀ è—, n. a green locust (eaten).

èbíkèbí, a. of nice, smooth, healthy surface (ndĕrĕ̀-zà-rö).

ɛbbíkɔ, n. detached leaves of plants (bbí when on plant); paper.

èbìŋáa, n. commonly tǐndírì glow-worm.

è'bìŋa(w)a = ɔ̀'dìá, n. ibis.

èbìòá = óbáŋguru, n. kind of planted tuber similar to common potato (taste more like manioc).

ébbíró or ébbíríwá, more commonly óbbíró, n. rhinoceros.

ébbíro, n. a tree.

è'bò, vn. to ferment, rise, work; to effervesce, bubble up (= ɛgbé); to boil over.

ɛ'bó, n. hoe; ɛ'bó àbe handle of hoe; ɛ'bó sɔ́ tail of hoe (used also as chisel); èì sö àbe sía they fix it on to the handle; ɛ'bó ámvú 'à-zǒrì 'ï hoe for tilling the field.

è'bó, n. woody creeper; atsí vàá sì it creeps on the ground.

ɛbölǒ, vt. to frighten (as child); threaten; ɛbölǒ ɛ̀rì tsɔzǒ, kà èfǒ kö he threatened to beat him, unless he confessed.

ɛ'borà̀, ⇌ tri vt. to smear, smooth; èì dzɔ́ mà 'alé ɛ'— ŋaku (or wórɔ́tɔ̀) sì they smear the floor of a hut with clay (cowdung); ɛ'borà̀ eví sì to whitewash with chalk; èì ŋáadrì mà drì ɛ'—ɛ'— they smooth the surface of the barrow (tomb).

ɛbɔtuatua, n. hoopoe (?).

è'bù or ɔ̀'bù, vt. to plan, have in mind (some design); àma è'bù ŋga àzí ɛ̀rɔ̂ tsɔzǒ, nɔ̀sì dzɔ̂ sizǒ we are planning to construct a granary, or to build a hut.

ɛ́'bu commonly á'bu, n. valley; ɛ́'bu 'aléa within the valley.

έ'búsí, n. beginning (upper end) of valley or river; Éη̨áó mà έ'— the source of the Enyao river; ìyí έ'— drìlέ the start/source of river.

έ'dà, n. spleen.

ε'da, vt. to show; to point at; to manifest; mǐ ε'da máni έ'dá! show me the picture! ε'dá, vn. to appear; 'bá drì ε'dá áséa 'dálέ a man's head shows/is visible there; àtsǐ ε'dá ndrǐ a fire shows flickeringly there; έ'dá, n. picture, photo; mǐ edzí έ'dá ε'dâ mâ tíá mǒkέ it is nice, that you have brought a picture to show me; mǐ ε'dá máni έ'dá! show me the picture!

εdε, vt. to disregard, disdain, despise; undervalue; make fun of...; εdε ε'yó mâ tíá-rǐ εdε-εdε he scorns words from me; èri ma εdε-εdε he makes fun of me.

εdέ, vt. (1) to make (ready), produce; ma εdέ bɔ̀ŋgó 'bə I have now made the cloth; èró εdέ to make a granary; lɔ̀kìri εdέ to devise an expedient/shift; (2) to adjust, arrange; εdέ (rö) ɔ̀η̨ì bε he arranged it (himself) elegantly, he made it pretty; mǐ εdέ ε'yó èlmà vúti sǐ (kìlέ èi εdέ lέ 'dà lέ) do (or speak) as they have done; (3) to repair, put in good order.

ε'dέ, vn. to fall (to the ground nearby); pätí (or mvá) ε'dέ vàá a tree (boy) fell down; ε'bí ε'dέ pätí sía he fell from the tree.

e'dí¹, vt. to raise, erect; èl dzó pätí e'dǐ they erect poles for a hut (by driving/ramming them into the ground); èl èró e'dí àη̨â nǐ they erect a granary for corn (by driving poles, &c., into the ground and fixing the body of the granary upon it); èl kaali e'dǐ a fence.

e'dí², n. gruel; e'díərö-ərö or əsa-əsa or tε (T.), to stir, prepare gruel.

edí, vt. (1) to poke (in a spear-like fashion) sth. against; mǐ edí ma kàlí sǐ kö! do not poke a stick at me! (2) T. (=Plu. elí) to tickle; mǐ edí ma kö! do not tickle me!

edǐá = pàrífεsí, n. stand in hut on which to store fuel:... édzâ drəzǒ.

edǐá, n. (1) main pillar (in centre) to support roof of hut; (2) T. = gbèléfε stick, cane; é—(= àbééá) ɔ̀kó àmbóni atsí-zǒrǐ 'ï a cane with which old women walk about; é— drìni lǐ-rözàrö (òlíŋgóló'rö) cane whose head is shaped like a ball (knob).

èdǐä, èdǐdǐa, n. epilepsy; èri 'bá ə'bε vàá it throws a man to the ground (into fire, &c.).

é'dìò, T. = tsúrú'dǒ, av. soon, quickly, immediately; mâ mu é— I will go at once.

èdío = èdíəkó, èdíkó, n. a tree (Vitex cuneata) with black cherry-like fruits; 'èdío-fε' ('εdio' tree) name of place of C.M. Aruwa.

èdírílí, n. hornet (wasp); rùáni ëni̇rö, n̈dúni εka the chest-part is black, the back part reddish; èri 'bá ədò-ədò (zàzà) it stings; è— mà hɔ̀rɔ̀ŋgótɔ̀ hornet's nest (with eggs and larvae).

èdo, n. (1) bbí èdo lobe of ear; (2) pá èdo heel; drí èdo wrist.

èdò (cf. dò), vt. to light a fire àtsǐ èdǒ.

ε'dó, vt./n. to begin, start; ε'dó εmbátáa 'bə he began teaching already; à'dí ε'dó rá war broke out; ε'dó εŋgá to come from...; ε'dó ámvú 'ä 'bə they started already tilling the field.

e'dölð, vt. to level (rough ground); ndzìlá (or 'bílέ) e— to fill up/in a road (a hole) levelling (≅ ɛrɔkà, vt. to smooth).

ɛdɔlɔ or ɔdɔlɔ or ɔdilɔ, n. sausage tree (*Kigelia Aetiopica*).

èɛdrá or èɛdríi, n. mother-in-law.

èdrákùlé, n. black-head (bird); è— èl ɔndzayià ŋaa èndì it eats (fruits) even red pepper.

èdrání(g)ɔ́ or ɔ̀kɔ́ àká (= àmbɔ́), n. aged woman; è— 'dà etsá 'dà the old woman arrived there.

èdrè, vt. to set upright, in correct position; mí è— àfa 'dì mŏké! put this thing here in order! mí è— ɔdrá öru! put the bamboo upright! mí è— mï pii! raise yourself up/stand upright! èdrè-zàrö, a. in right/straight position, upright, erect.

èdréká commonly dréká, n. mushroom.

èɛdrí or ŋáŋá, n. water scorpion (*Nepa cinerea*)?

èɛdrí, n. razor; è— drìbbí fàa-zɔ́ for cutting hair; è— tsï rá the razor is sharp.

èdrì, vt. (1) to send, transmit; è— mání wárágà bɔ̀ŋɔ́ èfè-zɔ́ he sent me a letter that he would give me a cloth; ádí èdrì-zɔ́ to transmit traditions; (2) to translate; èri Lógbàrà ti èdrì he translates in Logbara; èri mâ ti èdrì ɔ́pí drí he exposes my case before/to the chief; 'bá ti èdrìpirì translator, interpreter; (3) to connect, join ends; to increase; èri báká èdrì àŋàpá 'bɛ-zɔ́ he joins ropes to lay out for game.

èdrí; milɛ́ è— (or ǹdú) a look askance/aslant, sidelong glance; mï ma lù milɛ́ (ǹdú) è— sï you look askance at me.

édri, n. life; rùánï ŋgà ɛ́—/rùánï ɛ́— ŋgà tsï he is still alive; édri`

rö alive; mï ŋgà 'bá ɛ́—, é dè ŋgà kö you are still nimble/full of life, you are not yet old.

ɛdrí 'ï, vr. to escape with one's life (cf. epá, ɛtɔ́); ɛdrí , vn. to live.

ɛdrí, vn. to be(come) warm, hot; ètú ɛ'dɔ́ (=tsa) ɛdrí 'bɔ the sun has become (pleasantly) warm (ab. 8 a.m.); ɛ́ŋá ïi ɛ— 'bɔ the water for polenta (stirring) is now hot.

ɛdrîdría, n. sparrow-hawk.

ɛdrɔ́, n. mouse, rat; ɛ́— ásía = àŋábía; ɛ́— dzóa = àbìdzóa veldt, domestic mouse.

ɛdú = à'wï, a. dense, thick (of fluids); tíbí or e'dí èdú`rö the savoury, gruel is thick; mà bè 'alénïá ïi ddíká! put in more water! (cf. only ɛ́ŋá à'wï!); ásí èdú`rö courageous, fearless.

e'dú (cf. 'du), vt. (1) to provide oneself with, to take for o-s.; mí e'dú ŋaká mïní mï drì-sì-rì kö yà? have you not provided food for yourself on your own account? (2) to invent, assert light-heartedly; mï ɛ'yɔ́ e'dú mï ásí sì mï ásí sì/or mï ɛ'yɔ́ e'dú mï drì sì you simply invent things (light-heartedly)!

édzá, n. firewood, fuel; ɛ́— òù (= òwï) to collect wood; é sö ɛ́— émvó ǹdúa! push wood under the pot!

edzá (cf. adzá), vt. to spread out, lay before; mí e— mání mï ŋgókó, á lè nè turn/show your back to me, I want to see it!

èdzè, èdzèkò, èdzèlé, lómà, kálá, n. side, flank; ɔvö má èdzèléa he is on my side; èdzè-fà (là), n. rib; èdzèdriá, av. on one's flank; laa rö èdzèdrìà to lie on one's flank; dzɔ́ èri pätí èdzèkòá the hut is beside the tree.

èdzé (= ètsé), n. fairly large calabash; è— ɛ́wâ nɪ́ gourd-bowl for beer; èdzɪ̃́iá, n. a smaller bowl.

èdzèlékò, n. kind of ...; division, part, side of ...

èdzèlèkó (alias: àdzìlikó, T.; èdzàlàkó), n. kind of flute, small horn whistle, hollow-hand flute; èi èdzèlèkó'rö ɛbarïò mà ə'yó (ədjófɛ) ɛdɛ̂ 'ï (= g̀òkɛ́) they make a whistle from a bushbuck's horn.

èdzi, ɛ́wá èdzi, n. light-second beer (Ac. tiŋ); èi è— sɛ fïfï sï they draw/drink 'edzi'-beer with grass-tubes (straws).

edzi rö, vr. to resemble; e— èi e—e— (= òsï-rö-òsì) they resemble one another.

èdzí = lèdzí, a. drï è— left hand; é 'du búkù drï è— sï èndì! pick up a book with your left hand also!

èdzìdzi ('rö), n. framework (of building, basket, &c.); dzó (mà) è— framework of a hut (without any finishing touches, roof, &c.); àfadzó è— a basket-frame; ... 'bâ ŋga ŋg̀à àzí rúánɪ̃́arï dɛ kö they have not yet finished work on it.

édzío, n. a kind of white durra; ɛ́— èi 'ï ɛ́wá˄rö, nòsì ɛ́ɲá'rö they grind it for beer, for polenta.

ɛɛdzíríkó, n. white ants, termites; èri dzô mbɛ̀mbɛ they eat huts, &c.

èdzò, vt. to stretch; èi bá(ká) è— èzó'rö they stretch out a rope; mï è— rö è—; ɛ́ kə ádzɛ́ o'dú kö yà? you are stretching yourself; did you not sleep yesterday?

ɛ̀ɛdzo, n. twins; andzi osɪ́pi òkó mà 'a ìrrì èi əmvɛ ɛ̀ɛdzó two babies born to a woman at the same time are called twins; òkó osi ɛ̀ɛdzó'rö the woman has borne twins (apparently with no special ceremonies).

édzó or édzófɛ, n. kind of thin reed-grass with very strong stalks; ɛ́— 'yɛ̂ sö-zŏ, 'ɛdzo' stalks for fixing on an arrow-blade; èi 'yɛ̂ sö ɛ́— sía tsï; èi àɲ̀àpâ g̀bï ànï they fix an arrow-blade on and (go to) shoot game with it; 'yɛ́ ɛ́— ndɛrï òkpó'rö kəŋgəló'rö; ndɛ̀ òzŏ òkpó sï rá this arrowshaft is strong and hard, surpassing ordinary reed-stalks; àdzú ɛ́— (or pätɪ́) shaft of a spear.

éfɪ́, n. (1) fruit (of any plant); grains; pätí mà éfɪ́ fruits of a tree; 'dŏ mà 'aléa éfɪ́'rö = éfɪ́ tsï the eleusine has developed fruit/grains (satisfactorily); (2) meaning of words ɛ'yó mà éfɪ́; é ndzɛ ɛ'yó 'dï mà éfɪ́ kɪ́lɪ́lɪ́! give the exact meaning of this word!

ɛfï¹ = etsï, vt. to lay (or put) by; to make up a sum (by laying aside small amounts at a time); ma sìlíŋgì ɛfï bòŋg̀ô dzɛ-zŏ I lay by money in order to buy a cloth; sìlíŋgì ɛfï 'ï tsa kàlï nna the shillings have accumulated/ gathered to the sum of 30s.

ɛfï² = tri ≅ ndzò, vt. to (be) smear, grease, daub over (with oil or anything); èi a'dú ɛfï émvó rúá they daub over a pot with 'a'du' (mica); èri sàbúnï ɛfï páa (or driá) he smears soap on his legs (head).

efɪ́¹, vt. to terminate or finish the last remnant of ...; efɪ́ ámvú mà ti he finished (the end of) the field; efɪ́ dzó drì dɛ rá he gave the finishing touch to the hutroof.

efí², vn. to come in (cf. fí); mí efí dzóa ! come in (the hut, room)!

έεfì, n. innumerability, countless number; ɔ́ŋa (or àŋú...) 'dì mà έ- étö̀ the termites (bees) are innumerable; mòɛ̀mbɛ̀ 'dì έɛfìrö̀ (έɛfì nì tö̀) the mangoes are countless.

èfö̀ (cf. fö̀), vn. (1) to come out; mí èfö̀ (dzɔ́ mà 'aléa sì) àmvé! come out (from the hut)! ètú èfö̀ 'bə the sun has risen; (2) to start, depart; á kà èfö̀ ètúnï èfö̀rìá, ma ɛtsɔ́ Mísà ɛri-zö̀ mö́ké (or... ma etsá sùkúlùá mö́ké) if I start at sunrise I can well hear Mass (... I arrive at school in time).

éfórá, n. kind of very small termites (swarm about 8 p.m.).

efötirì or efökörì (commonly àyíríbɛ), n. itch disease; e— ŋaa ma scabies has affected me.

èfú, n. large kind of termites; èfúnï ɛŋgá èfúrúgbòá àŋgö̀ sàrà sì the 'ɛfu' swarm from 'efurugboa' (holes) early in the morning.

èfûfúã, n. very small white termites; èì èfö̀ ɔ̀ndré sì they swarm in the evening; (chickens and birds are fond of them).

èfúrúgbɔ̀, n. holes (labyrinth) of an abandoned (and partly crumbled) termite-hill ɔ́tɔ́kɔ́ drăpirárì mà p̆àrí (hidden recess for mice, snakes, ground squirrels, or the like); èfúrú(g)bòá, av. in, from holes in abandoned termite-hill.

Ɛga, n. name of a river, tributary to the Enyao; Ɛga fï Ɛ́ŋàó mà 'aléa the Ega flows (enters) into the Enyao.

ègá, n. mid-size calabash bowl; ègá ɛríkɔ̀ the bowl is cracked;

mí edzí máni ɛ̀gáã éwá ɛ̀bɛ̀zö̀ bring me a bowl to draw beer!

ɛgá¹, vn. to be angry with, scold; mí ɛgá (or awä̆) mâ drìá 'dínï à'do sì yà? why did you scold me like this? mï ɔ̀ndzí, ma ɛgá mï drìá àni I have scolded you, because you behaved badly.

ɛgá², vn. to be stingy, shabby; 'bá 'dìrï ɛgá 'ïmà éŋá sì this man is stingy with his polenta (he eats it alone without inviting . . .).

ɛgá³, vt. (1) vn. to rise; recover senses, regain consciousness; 'bá àvö̀rörì ɛgá nì the (apparently) dead person recovered/got up; (2) to spring, gush up; ìyí à'dinï ɛgá nì,/ìyíní ɛgá ìyí-à'di-á springwater gushes up/the water comes from the source; (3) vn./vt. to remember, recollect, recall; ɛgá ɛ'yɔ́ 'bə the matter (word) recurred to him; ma ɛgâ dï 'bə I now remember; it just came to my mind; ɛ'yɔ́ ndrá àvĕpi ɛrinírì ɛgá 'bə the word/matter he had forgotten returned to his mind; mu á'dïáni ɛ'yɔ́ ɛgâ he went to remind somebody of a thing (to call/bring to a person's mind).

ègà = etsï, ɔsé, vt. (1) to sew, repair; èri 'dà 'ï èvó (or àfadzó) (ɛríkɔ̀) ègä̂ he is there repairing, mending, joining his cracked pot; (2) restore, cure.

ègárákɔ̀, ègaràka, ègórókɔ̀, ègárásɔ̀, ègárísɔ̀, n. crab; èri ìyí mà 'aléa she lives in water (or holes burrowed under water).

ègbè, n. cold; è— èri 'bâ fùfu cold 'kills'/afflicts a man.

ègbɛ = ándzú, ambïzàrö̀, a. cold, damp; not bitter; ǹdzú è— the melon is tasty; ŋaaká è— (àtsí kɔ́kɔ̀rö̀) the food is cold; è— n.

tà è— cold food left behind from the day before.

ɛ̀gbɛ́, n. peace; ásí è— peace of heart, peacefulness, happiness; àŋgǒ è— (= à'dí kɔ́kɔ̀rö) there is peace (in the country) (Ac. kwèe).

ɛgbɛ́, vn. (1) (= àgbɔ̀) to bark; ɔ̀tsɛ́nï ɛ— nì a dog barks; (2) to ferment, rise, work; to effervesce, bubble up; ɛ́wánï ɛgbɛ̂ the beer works.

ɛ̀gbɛ̀kɛ̀gbɛ̀ (-rö), a. bad-smelling, stinking; àfa 'dà mà àdzí ɔdzá 'ï è— that thing has become bad-smelling.

ɛ̀gbɛ́rɛ́(kɛ), n. kind of termites (swarm at daybreak).

ɛgbï =ɛŋgá, vn. to come up, shoot, spring forth (any plant); pätí ɛ— 'bɔ the tree has come up.

ɛgbölɔ̀ = ɔtrɛ́ zɔ̌, more commonly ɛbölɔ̀ (q.v.), vt. to scold, chide a p. ('bá driá); ɛ̀ri ɛbölɔ̀ 'dínï à'dï mà driá yà? against whom is he (esp. drunken persons) inveighing thus?

ɛ̀gìrò-rö, a. dark (in the evening); àŋgǒ è— it is dark.

ɛ̀gɔ̀ = ɛ̀dà (cf. gɔ̀, dà), vn. to come back; mï̃ ɛ̀gɔ̀ (drì) vɛ́lɛ́! come back!

ɛ̀gɔ̌ = gɔ̌, ɔ̀gɔ̌, n. specially thick/ heavy sloping board with holes through central ridge; ɛ̀ɛgɔ̌ tí mà tílɛ̀ ɔ̀pìzɔ̌ the plank with which to close the cattle pen.

ɛ̀gɔ̀à = ádrɔ̀á, kɔ̀yía, n. adze; ɛ̀l ɛ̀gɔ̌ pa è— sì they rough-hew a pen-door plank with an adze.

ɛ̀gɔ́lï (-rì), a. crooked, bent, mis-shapen (hand, leg . . .).

ɛ́gúgú, n. a child born after several who have died; proper name may be Dràzù; fem. Àvŏró.

ɛ̀l, pers. pron. they; them; ɛ̀i-drí (or -vɛ́lɛ́ or -nï), to, for them; ɛ̀idrí-rì theirs; ɛ̀imà ándrïí their mother (or ándrïí ɛ̀idrírì).

ɛ'ïl, ɛ'ípi, n. owner, proprietor; ɛ̀ri tí 'dà mà ɛ'ïl he is the owner of that cow.

e'ï̃ rö gà = ɛŋà rö, vr. to boast, brag of sth. (àfa sì); mï̃ e'ï̃ mï̃ búkù sì gà you prided yourself on the book; mï̃ mï̃ e'ï̃ rö tɔ̀ you give yourself great airs; e'ïïá or e'ïtá, n. pride, vain glory; vanity.

ɛ̀ikï or ekï, pers. prn. = ɛ̀l q.v.

ɛ̀(y)íkì = ɔ̀rà, vn. to reflect, to think; to muse (on), ponder (over), revolve in one's mind; to mourn (for); to grieve (fret) over/about; ɛ̀ri ɔ́ó ándrïí sì, ɛ̀ri ɛ'yɔ́nï ɛ́íkì-ɛ́íkì he cries for his mother, he is grieving about it.

ɛ́íkïï, n. large reddish ant (feeding much on sugar).

ɛka¹, a. red; brown; ɛka ndri-ndri, ɛka ndíli-ndíli, ɛka wïrï red as blood, crimson; ɛka wàrà-wàrà dark red (brown); tí ɛkàrö the cow is brown/fallow.

ɛka² rö, vn. to adhere, stick to (-á); e'dí kànì eka rö 'bá driá kö, dè (-rè) ŋgà ɛri àmorèrö if gruel does not stick to one's finger, it means it is not yet ready (= ɛtɛ́ ŋgà kö).

ɛká, vt. to help, assist; ɛká ma rá he assisted me; mï̃ ɛká 'bá kö you do not render aid to a person; ɛkátá, n. use, value, utility; búkù' dìmà ɛkátá yɔ this book is of no use.

ɛ́ká, ɛ́káká, n. sugar cane; ma ɛ́kâ ndzu I am (chewing and) sucking sugar-cane.

ɛká-fɔ̂rá = ɛká-sɔrɔ, n. waste, refuse (of chewed sugar-cane).

ɛ̀káráká, n. a kind of undergrowth yielding strong and hard poles/

posts; èì ànï lítsô 'bε they make cattle pens with it.

ékέ! intj. exclamation of surprise/ disbelief.

èkèkèlέ, n. swollen gland; è— 'bá pí-pi-rì εkεkεlε causes swelling.

èkélè, n. cough; è— ɡa to cough; ɡa ádzέ è— tǒ he coughed badly yesterday.

èki, T. (=èì), prs. prn. they, them.

ékïkíá = àyí ɔndzɔrɔkɔ, n. small black common ants.

èkïlà, vt. to wrap round; to twist, lay across; mï è— àfa 'dïrï è— è— (báká sì)! wrap up this thing with string! mï è— pá è— you are putting one leg upon the other; mï è— báká mà adri ɔkpɔrö! twist a rope with another so that it may be strong! órí è— mâ pá a snake has coiled round my leg; è— rö: pätí rö èkïlă-rö-pi 'ï álíi mà rùárì a tree which climbs up another (companion) tree, twisting round it.

ékílíŋgbì = éŋgbílía, n. kind of slide-bolt or -stop or spring (for releasing a mechanism, a trap); mï εkpí (= εló) ék— nï! do release the (slide-) stop! piece of light wood fixed to fishing-lines to observe movement of catching fish, or the like.

εkó (cf. kɔ), vt. (1) = èbè, to draw water, &c. (from river, pot . . .); mà si iyí èbè iyía I go to the river to fetch/draw water; (2) to sweep; mï εkó dzó 'alé! sweep the room!

èkpà¹, vt. (1) to press together; to compress; mï è— tsí! press them together! è— rö, vr. to crowd (or join) together; to press (or squeeze) close together; àfa 'dì è— rö kírikíri these things

stick tightly together; kànì sínï è— rö tálánï yɔ; sí àrĕkàlénï yɔ when the teeth are close together (in the ordinary way) there is no space between; there is no teeth-gap; tí zá mà ósò è— (or eka) 'ï émvóa tsí fat of beef sticks to the pot fast; mvá è— rö 'ï ándríi mà rùá the baby clings (nestles, snuggles up) to his mother; (2) (= εló) to touch (press) lightly (to call attention); è— ma (drí sì) he touched me (with his hand); (3) to summon up (all) one's strength; mï è— (= εmbá, εté) ásí tsí! pluck up your courage!

èkpa², n. è— ti bbî ndzε-zŏrì 'pincers' to remove hair of beard.

èkpéré = èndrà, ègatá, n. stinginess, niggardliness; mï è— tötö thy niggardliness is very great; 'bá èkpéré'rö a stingy person; è— pi èndrà bε wóɔró àlö, 'εkpεrε' and 'εndra' mean all the same; è—: ŋaaká mïnî ŋaalé a'dúle, mïnî 'bá àzínî ndε-zŏ sì stinginess, when you eat food alone refusing it to another.

èkpétékè (-lékè), av. innumerable, countless; έsísí ezŏ (= 'a) è— (= έεfì nï tǒ) the mulberry tree produces countless fruits.

èkpì, vt. to press down; mï è— tí drì tsí, èrì mù ŋga apá kö! press down the head of the cow (to be butchered) that it may not get up and run off; mï è— ássí tsí! be courageous!

εkpí = εló, vt. to set free, release, let off (say gun) (cf. **ékílíŋgbì**).

èk'pî = èk'pê, n. concavity formed by knee pressed back (of some p. at fully stretched leg); 'bá èk'pî bεrì a p. with such a peculiarity.

èkpò¹ (also **èkpà**), vt. to touch lightly (to attract attention); to beckon, wink, and the like; **è— ma rá** he has touched/beckoned me.

èkpò², vt. to take (bring, carry, convey, deliver, transmit) sth. to a p.; **mï è— té ɛ'yó 'dï edzí 'alé yà?** how (? why) have you conveyed the news?

èkù, vt. (1) to scrape (rake, scramble) together; **èi fúnò èkǔ** they scrape ground-nuts (dried in the sun) together on the ground (with hands); (2) (= **èkpò** or **òkpò**), to wink, beckon, attract attention in some way.

ekú, vt. (1) to mention one's name; **èri mâ rú ekǔ** he is calling my name; (2) to stun, stupefy; **èi 'bâ bbilé ekú-ekú èinï òtré sï** they stun people with crying/heated discussions.

èlá(kí), n. shrub/tree (*Zizyphus mauritania*) (Ac. làŋo).

èlè, av. (opp. **'bùá**) below, at the lower end, bottom; down-hill, &c.; **mvá mu tí bɛ èlè 'dálé** the boy went with/took the cattle down there (towards valley); **médzà ètía èlè** down underneath the table.

ɛlɛ¹ = **òfö, òdza**, vt. (1) to replace A by B; **mï ɛlɛ 'bá 'dï ɛlɛ-ɛlɛ!** replace these people with others! **é mu mvá tí òtsépi 'dà ɛlɛ!** go and relieve that herdsman/cowboy! (2) to exchange; **àma àfa ɛlɛ-ɛlɛ 'bá 'dà bɛ** we are exchanging with that man; **àma ɛlɛ ndrí kàbìlò sï** we exchange a goat with a sheep.

ɛlɛ², vt. to deceive, cheat; **ɛlɛ ma ásí** he cheated me.

èlé = **àtsíkoló**, n. charcoal; **èi ànï ɛ'bô di** they forge hoes with it.

èlɛkɛndré or **éndrékɛndré, n.** chameleon.

elegí = **eledzí, odzí, n.** gallbladder; bile; **èribìrö** it is green.

(é)lélé, n. = **kàtá**, q.v.

èlèlèwírè or **lɛlɛwírè, n.** vagabond, vagrant.

élélu = **èrìagà, n.** a large caterpillar with thorn-like hair; **èri dzuru; èri 'bá vù 'ïmà otsí sï** it is large; it scratched one with its thorns/hairs.

ɛlɛlú, n. a woody creeper with valuable fibre; **(báká) èri pätí răpi (găpi) vàálé sï** a plant that creeps on the ground; **èi ànï èró tï sɛ** with its fibre they tie/make the rim of a granary.

éléséré(á) = **ésérévá, n.** kind of mouse living in trees **a'á pätí sía/goléa.**

éléú, n. = **élïò**, q.v.

ëlï, n. knife; **ëlï pílí(àbɛ kókòrö)** short knife without handle; **ëlï òkpólò** worn-out (or stump of a) knife; **ëlï pätí sí pɛèzò** a knife to point the end of a piece of wood.

élí, n. (1) dry season; **élí ètúnï kazörï** when the sun shines (without break); **àŋgò àmvé 'dïrï élínï** the weather outside (in general) is of the dry season; **élí ètú drï tò** in the dry season the sun is very hot; (2) (= **wàŋgì, wàdrì**) year.

èlí = **ò'dú, n.** thigh; lap.

eli = **ɛlɛ, òdza**, vt. to change; **'bá eli pàrínï** a p. changes his (hut's) place.

ɛlí¹, vt. (1) to break and scrape together, pick up; **èi édzá ɛlí ogara sï** they break/chop wood with the axe; (2) to frown at a p.; **èri milé ɛlí (≅ etö) 'bá drìá** he frowns at a p.

ɛlí², vn. to blow; **òlínï ɛlí-ɛlí** the

wind is blowing; òlǐ εlǐ dzóa dàrísà sǐ the wind blows into the room from the window.

εlǐ³, vt. to tickle; á lè mà εlǐ ma kö ! I do not want to be tickled.

elï = εdró, vt. to deny, refuse; to overlook (in distributing); ma ándríi elï ma έɳá sǐ my mother has excluded me from polenta.

eli, vt. to trip a p. up (by putting out a leg or the like); eli ma eli oɳgú sǐ (i.e. pá sǐ), ma ε'dέ ànï he tripped me up when I was running (with his leg), and so I fell.

εlí, vt. to take by surprise; ma ándríi εlí ma rû my mother has taken me quite by surprise; òmú emú ma εlí àkúa a guest arrived unexpectedly at my home; òmú εlí (= ato) èri tsǐ a guest came surprising him.

èlǐfírí or èlǐ commonly lǐ, n. gluttony, greed; lǐ fu mǐ kái: mïnï mu 'bá àzǐ mà àfà ɳaazǒ èelǐ sǐ, mïnï 'bá àzǐnï ndε-zǒ sǐ, èkpéré sǐ you are extremely greedy: when you are going to sby. to eat out of greediness, while you refuse another (food) out of stinginess.

élíka(v)a, n. any kind of corn/grain (of a poor quality) which ripens during the dry season 'dǒ, &c. kǎpi élǐ sǐ; éfǐnï wóró ɳírǐá'rö all the grains are very small.

ëlǐkëlǐ, av. to within a small margin (of finishing); ga päti ël— (atsê dǐ wεrε èrinï ε'dézǒ vàá) he cut the tree until there was very little left (to cause it to fall); εlǐ àbε ë— he trimmed the handle leaving it very thin.

èlǐkïlí = òndzókònzdó, ndzò-làndzòlà, a. smooth, polished, glazed.

élǐ-mà-ìyí, av. dry-season water; ozóó έ— occasional/irregular rain of the dry season; cfr. ozóó áǐ-mà-ìyí the proper rain (of rainy season).

εlímákərə, εlíókərə, εlímákua, n. swallow; ε— àkírǐ (= lókìri)-nï tò, èi εré rö àɳgò drìá pǐrï; èi etsá élǐ sǐ the swallow is very clever; they migrate all over the world; they arrive here during the dry season.

élímandrendre or élíndende = lígalíga, n. dragonfly.

élǐə (= óló, T.), n. a fig tree (Ficus gnaphalocarpa); élǐə-ozína, n. sycamore fruit; (it has large leaves; when growing it is often entangled with the Ficus natalensis (laro) tree; èri sú bε it yields a sticky juice); èi εdé kpàkpà (kàrà-mándà) rö they make shoe-soles with it.

εlípá, n. a shrub (Annona chryso-philla); large leaves; edible fruits.

èlìpìtrì, n. barn-owl (?).

εlírígà, n. the millipede.

èlo, n. tuft of feathers on head of some birds; a similar dancing ornament; yú(kú'dù) 'dù mà èlo the feather-tuft of a 'yuku'du' bird; èi yúkú'dù mà 'bíkə òsǐ èlòrö, èi ànï oɳgó tö they arrange 'yuku'du' feathers in tufts and dance with them.

èlò, vt. to direct, lead (singing, dancing...); oɳgó (or ezítá) èlò to lead dancing (praying).

εló, vt./vn. (1) to turn, hang downwards or obliquely; èri drí (or drì) εló vàá he lets his hand (head) hang down; mǐ εló tinï vàálé ! turn its (of a pot) opening downwards/turn upside down; (2) to go downwards; 'bá εló (or emú) -pi ìyí drìərǐ'ï a man who in the

past went down/over to Bunioro-
Buganda; èrì mu ɛlórö-zà-rö
he goes down the slope; (3) to
put on a slope, obliquely; mǐ ɛló
bǎò put the plank at a slope! ɛló
rö ɛló = ɛlózàrö or ɛló 'ï
laazàrö to be steep (slightly) inclined; àŋgò ɛló-rö-pi kú-
kúlú'ru a steeply inclined ground.
ɛló¹ = èkpò, vt. to touch lightly.
èló², n. scrotum; èló éfí testicle;
mónió (or ǹdrí) átá kàni èri
èló ɛbɛ (i.e. 'bá o'du kö), èri tí
(or ǹdrí) agə when an ox (or goat)
has its natural scrotum (testicles
not having been removed) it is a
bull (buck); èi èló o'du èi tínǐ ko
raˌ̣àrö they remove the scrotum (testicle) and leave it as an ox;
èi ko tí agə'rö they leave it a
full male.
èlòə, n. óna̦ èlòə young whitish
termites (before swarming).
éló = élía, q.v. 'bá óŋgólónǐ n̦aa
'ï, èi éfíni wǐ people eat the pulp
and spit the grains out.
ɛmáa, n. owl (great-horned?); èri
fərətəa'rö it is greyish.
ɛmbá¹, n. fishing or hunting net;
ɛ— èi àni àn̦àpâ (or ɛ'bî) 'bɛ; èi
ɛ— 'bɛ àn̦àpá ní (nòsì ɛ'bí ní)
they lay/throw the net for game
animals (or fishes).
ɛmbá², vt. (1) to teach, educate;
ɛ— ma rá, or ɛ— mání ɛ'yó he
taught me (in sth.); ɛ— 'ï mvá he
taught (exhorted, punished) his
child; ɛmbápi teacher; èmbátáa, n. teaching, instruction; mu
èmbátáa he went to the lesson;
(2) (= ətó) to pull o-s. together,
to tighten, to gather one's strength;
mǐ ɛ— ásí tsǐ (i.e. mǐ ásíni
mbazó kəŋgələkə òri kókòrö)
pluck up your courage! (that your
heart be strong/fearless); mǐ ɛ—

mǐ kúrèkúrè ká, é ndzo ndò!
tighten (brace) your muscles, then
run!
èmbétékérè = èmbétété'rö =
ɛtémbéré, q.v.
èmbílí(a), n. narrow watercourse
(into which several small ones
collect) leading to a fishing-
basket-trap called 'embili' hence
ǹdúnǐ èmbílí(a)'àrö its lower
part is narrowing/tapering.
émbílía, n. small piece of wood
attached to fishing-rod (for ob-
servation of movement? = ká-
fórá).
ɛmbǐlǐká, n. Chalcides seps (Ci-
cigna): lizard with two pairs of
very small legs (at distance) (cf.
mbèlèndzùkù = òsùmìnìkà);
or T., term for lizard.
émbílíkó, T. = dzólókó, n. rest,
remnant.
embó, vn. (1) to jump; e— pätí
mà sía (or driá) he jumped from
the tree (high up, or from a
branch); (2) to spring, stand out,
surpass.
éméɛko = mǎikə, n. a large tree
(Combretum binderanum) (áyí
similar).
èmǐ, prs. pron. you; èmǐ-drí,
èmǐ-vélé, èmǐ-mà, èmǐ-ní (-rǐ)
your, yours; èmǐ-rí at your home
(village).
èmì (cf. mì), vt. to push up
(hither); oyú-nǐ n̦aakú èmì the
mole pushes up earth (on bur-
rowing əvá).
ɛmi¹ = drǐ, tə, dù, vt./vn. to
warm up (slightly/lukewarm); iyí
ɛmi yùu the water is lukewarm;
ma mâ rùá ɛmi (= àŋgǎ) àtsí
sǐ I warm myself at the fire; mǐ
ɛmi iyí mà drǐ àtsí-àtsí! warm
the water so that it may be hot!
bòŋgónǐ dí ɛmi (ètúa) 'dà the

cloth there (in the sun) is warm; ìyí mà ɛmi yùu! have the water warmed (slightly)!
ɛmi² = 'wï, àŋgà, oŋgú, vn. to dry; bòŋgó ɛmi 'bə the cloth is dry; mà rúá iï-rö, ɛmi ŋgà kö my body is wet (from rain), it has not yet dried.
ɛmó = tra, əko (cf. mo), vt. to put together, gather, assemble; mix; mí ɛmó ȅi pí àlö! put them all together! ɛmó rö tú àlö they all assembled in one place; ìyí 'dàï ɛmó rö tú àlö those rivers (water courses) all join together.
ȅmò, vt. to sip (as liquid food . . .); ma e'dí (or tsái) ȅm̀ I am sipping gruel (tea; possibly just a draught).
emú (cf. mu), vn. to come; mí emú 'dòá! come hither!
ɛmvɛ, a. white; 'bá ɛmverï the white man; 'ï sí ɛmvɛ'rö his teeth are white; ɛmvé, vt. to make white; mï mà rúá ɛmvé ȅfótá sï you are making me white with ashes; mí ɛmvé ma kö! do not make me white! ȅri bòŋgó ɛmvé sàbúnï sï he makes his cloth white (washing, ȅdzï) with soap.
ɛmvɛléti = ɛmvɛ mà gïrï, n. outlook, prospect, vista, access or admittance (of light, air); asé (= atri, a'bó) ɛ— tsï he has obstructed the light; é ko (or dà) mï ɛmvɛléti-á rá! withdraw from the light-way! é ko mání ɛ— (= ɛmvɛ mà gïrï)! let light come in!
ȅmvè, n. large ring (for arm, leg, &c., mostly for women); sù ȅ— pá she put a ring on her ankle/ leg; ȅ— òkó mà pá-rï'ï a ring on the woman's leg; ȅ— ȅi dïdi ȅri ayá'rö they forge it; it is iron.

ȅmvéréfí = ȅtsòròfí, n. a small fish (of common rivers).
ɛmví¹ (cf. mvi), vn. to come back; ȅi mu àkú andrî, ȅi ɛ— drùsï they went to visit home, they will come back tomorrow.
ɛmví², vt. to build, form little by little (of termites); ȅdzíríkó àto-lóko-nï ɛmvî nï termites build their hills (by degrees).
ȅmví¹ or évï, n. chalk; ȅ— ȅi dzó (mà rúá) ɛ'börȁ ànï they white-wash a hut with it.
ȅmví², n. clay containing alkaline; ȅ— ɳaakú tínï tsï ìyíárï, 'ɛmvi' is a clay cattle go to lick at the water-side.
ȅmvìá, n. (= mólá) wrist-ring; ȅ— dría arm-ring (= ándzö-rökö).
ȅmvìa = ȅmvéréfí, q.v.
ɛmvó¹ = ɛmbó, vn. mí ɛmvó vàá! jump down!
ɛmvó², vn. to swell; drínï àzó'rö, ɛ— 'dïpi his hand is painful, it is swollen like this.
ȅmvó, n. pot (general term); ìyílé ȅ— or mö'dà water-pot.
ȅmvò, n. sorrow, grief; mourning; əvö ȅ— bɛ to mourn, sorrow, grieve; ma ásínï əvö ȅ— bɛ I am feeling grief; ma əvö ȅ— sï tö I am very much grieved, sorry; ȅ— 'bȁ to start/put on mourning; kànï 'bá àzínï drà rá, nòsï mï átápi drà rá, mï ȅmvònï 'bȁ if somebody has died, may be your father, you start mourning; ȅ— əkə rá mourning is over; 'bá trá-rö ȅ— sï or 'bá mú ȅmvòá (or drȁá) people assembled/ went to funeral rite (after three days for male, four for female).
ȅmvõã, n. orphan; 'bá átá drȁpi rá, àyïànï vínï dràzö rá-rï, mvánï 'dï ȅi əmvɛ ȅ— a child

whose father and mother have died is called an orphan; **kànì mvá àzínï ɛmvõã⊥rö, ɛ̀i ɛ̀ri ətsɛ̂** if a child has become an orphan, they take care of him.

ɛɛná = **ɛnɛ́, ɛ'dá, ɛndrɛ́,** vn. to be visible; to show or reveal o-s.; **ɛɛná wɛrɛá** it/he is slightly visible; **àfa ɛɛná kö, àŋgö̀ bìbì** things cannot be seen, it is dark; **ɛ— kìlɛ́ drìnï àvè̀ rá lɛ́** he looks as if he had forgotten it/he gives the impression of having forgotten it; **ɛ— mání rá** it is visible to me/I can see it.

énátá, n. a bundle of magic medicines (put on top of a bamboo on a path; against offenders).

ɛ̀ndɛ̌lɛ̌kà, n. (1) excrescence on ear-lobe (**bbí è̀dóá**) or elsewhere; **è̀— bbía, ɛ̀i mólá sǔ bbía** an excrescence on the ear, because they applied a brass ring to the ear; (2) (= **àyàkílíkìlì**) tassels of skin and hair on neck of a goat.

ɛ̀ndɛ́rɛ́, n. quiver; **è̀— 'yɛ̂ tə-zö̌; əŋgɔ́ tözö̌** quiver to put arrows in; for dancing; **è̀— ɛ̀i tsï tí enïrïkə sì** a quiver which they make from cow hide.

éndèrèfí, n. (**andzìnï**) piece of grass stalk used as arrow (by children); **ɛ́— àríá tsà** (= **gbï**) **zö̌** to shoot birds.

ɛ̀ndì¹, cj. also; **mí emú mávö̌ sì è̀—!** come to me also! **mâ mu vínï è̀—** I shall also go.

ɛ̀ndì² (cf. **ndì**), vt. to collect, gather (with both hands); **é tu ɛ̀rɔ́ mà 'aléà mu àŋá ɛ̀ndì kö yà?** did you not go into the granary to collect grains?

ɛ̀ndí, a. deserted; desert; **'bá kà adrì 'a-nï-á yə, ɛ̀ri àŋgö̀ ɛ̀ndí`rö** where nobody lives is a desert; **'dà àŋgö̀ ɛ̀ndírì** that is a desert.

ɛndí, n. a tree with edible fruit.

ɛ̀ndìkìndì = **mbèlè,** av. quickly, immediately; **etsá è̀—** he came quickly.

ɛ̀ndìlìkà, see **ɛ̀ndɛ̌lɛ̌kà.**

ɛ̀ndrà = **ɛ̀kpɛ́rɛ́,** n. stinginess, meanness, avarice; **'bá è̀— bɛ, -rö** a niggardly p.; **'bá è̀— kɔ́kɔ̀rö** a generous p.

ɛndrɛ́, T. = **nè̀,** vt. to see.

ɛndrí, n. spirit, mind (≅ **ásí**); **ma endrí** (or **ásí kɔ̀rɛ**) **ɔ̀tì rá** I am uneasy in my mind, dismayed/I feel terrified.

ɛ́ɛndrì, n. shade (away from sun's rays); **éndrì-léndrì,** n. shadow (dark figure projected by body against light rays); **pätí mà ɛ́ɛndrì** shade of a tree; **ɛ́— àŋgö̀ ɛtúnï əvözö̌ 'anïá yə-rì** a place where there is no sunshine; **á mu tê rï éndrìá** I went to sit in the shade.

ɛndú, vt. to wrong, injure, damage (a p.'s right), take advantage of (overreach) a p.; **'du áŋgírí fɛ̀ mání gaã: ɛndú ma ɛ—ɛ—** he took much and gave me little: he wronged me.

ɛ̀ndzà, n. laziness; **è̀— bɛ** or **-rö** lazy; **ɛ̀ndzà-rö, lè̀ àzî ŋga kö** he is lazy, he does not like to work; **àzí sì à 'bà è̀— kö** we were not lazy at work.

ɛndza¹ (= **etsandì**), vt. to vex, annoy; worry, harass, molest; **ɛmï ɛndzá ma kö, è dǎ ɛmï rá!** do not vex me, get away! **mï 'bá ɛ— tö̀** you are a bore/tormentor; cf. **mí ɛ— ma kö!** do not trouble me!

ɛndza², (1) **'bâ drì ɛ—,** vt. to (put to) shame; to confound, confuse; **mï mâ drì ɛ—ɛ—** you confound me; **mí ɛ— mâ drì kö!** do not put me to shame! (2) **dri-ndzá,**

n. shame, bashfulness; **drì-ndzá kɔ** (or **bì**) **èri tsí** he feels ashamed; **èri 'yɛ drì-ndzá sì** he acts out of shame/confusion; **ma drì-ndzá tò** I feel ashamed/abashed; **èri drì-ndzá kókɔ̀-rö** he is devoid of all (sense of) shame; **dri-ndzá sì òkùkù drà ra** the tortoise died from bashfulness (excess).

èndzì = **òrì** vt. to revere, venerate; to respect, esteem, honour; **mvá 'dà è— 'ï átíïnï tsí** that child reveres his father; **èndzì-zà-rö** or **è— bɛ**, a. respectful, reverential, submissive; **èndzì(t)áa** or **àrotá** respect, regard; esteem, deference, honour; authority, prestige.

èndzɔ̀, n. lie; **mí è— bɛ** or **è— -rö** or **è— 'bá** you are a liar; **ɛ'yɔ́ è— rö** a lie; **é li** (= **lò**) **mání è— kö!** do not tell me lies! **è— mà pá àlí** lies have short wings/legs; or **è— sì Ò'díri mà pá àlí** O-'s legs are short for lies.

èndzɔ̀ròfí, see **émvéréfí**.

èndzǔ, n. a shrub (*Grewia mollis*) with long thin twigs yielding good fibre; **èì èndzǔ'ga báká'rö èrô sɛzɔ́** they cut 'endzu' for fibre to make granaries.

ɛndzú, vt. **'bá mà rú** or **'bá mà ɛ'yɔ́ ɛ—** to praise, glorify, extoll one's name/utter words of high praise/blessing; **mï 'bá àzí mà rú ɛndzú 'díní 'alɛ́ yà?** how do you praise somebody in this way?

ëni, -rì, a. (1) black, dark (object); **ǹdrí ënirì** black goat; **'bá ënirì** black people; (2) (= **bìbì**) dark; **àŋgò ëni'rö, èri nìni** (**bìbì**) it has become dark (night).

ëní, vt. (1) (= **fu**) to rub, efface, obliterate; **mí à'do ëní yà?** what are you erasing? **mí ëní** (or **é fu**) **rá!** rub it out! (2) (= **ɔwɛ́**) to wipe off; **mí ëní mî rùá!** wipe yourself clean! (3) vr. to brush, graze against; **ɛmvó ɔ̀ndì ëní rö mâ rùá** the soot on the pot has brushed against (soiled) me.

ɛni = **ɛnilà** = **ekilà** = **oni rö**, vr. to get entangled, wrapped up.

ëní or **íní**, n. night, darkness; **àŋgò ëní'rö** (= **íní bɛ**) it has become night; **mâ ŋga ɛŋgá atsí ëní sì** I shall start travelling by night; **ëníia** (**aɠa**) at midnight; **ëníia 'bá dríia o'dúa** by (mid-)night everybody is asleep.

enï better **enïrïkɔ**, q.v.

ëníkění = **onókòno**, av. a. (1) fine (of powder...); **èri àɲáfôrâ 'ï** (or **amvi**) **ë—** she has ground (over again) the flour finely; (2) soft, smooth; **àŋgò ë—**, **èri tsíɲá bɛ** the ground is soft because it is strewn with sand; **bɔ̀ŋgó ëníkění'rö** the cloth is soft.

eníkení, av. (cf. **dɛ**) completely, perfectly; **nì ɛ'yɔ́ e—** he knows the matter perfectly well (cf. preceeding).

enïrïkɔ = **enï**, n. skin; leather/ boot; **'bá e—** man's skin.

ɛŋga, vt. (1) to awake, rouse; **mí ɛ— mvá o'dúa 'dàrï, mà emú ɲaakâ ɲaa!** rouse that boy from sleep, that he may come to eat! (2) to lift, raise; **èri drí ɛ— ööru** he raises his hands.

ɛŋgá, vn. (1) (often **ɛ'bí ɛ—**) to come, originate from; **ɛ'bí ɛ— èirí** he comes from their village; (2) to start, rise; **ɔ̀línï ɛ— nì** the wind is rising; **ɔzɔ́ɔ ɛ— 'bɔ** the rain has started; **e'dí ìyíní ɛ—ɛ—** the water for gruel is rising/ boiling; (3) to germ(inate), sprout forth, spring up; **'dǒ** (or **pätí**) **ɛ—**

'bə the eleusine (tree) has germinated; (4) to fly hither.

èŋgbèlèkè or èŋgbéléké, n. chimpanzee; sɪ̀ rö 'bá ádalɛ́ it is like a man.

éŋgbiléŋgbì, see mbìlembì/ -ŋgbì.

éɳá, əɳókə polenta; éɳá əva to stir/prepare polenta; éɳá (è)sá polenta without tíbí (sauce: poorest meal); á ɳa éɳá dzóló I have eaten (in the morning) the remains of (yesterday's) polenta (fairly common).

èɳà rö àfa sɪ̀, vr. to boast, brag, vaunt (o-s.) with . . .; mɪ́ mɪ́ èɳà rö mɪ̃ mvá sɪ̀ you are boasting with (= proud of) your child; 'bá èɳăröpì tö one who boasts much, big braggart; èɳàá, èɳàtá, n. boasting, pride.

ɛɳaɳ̆á = ɛɳakeɳa, ɛɳatá, (= àdrakà, T.), n. poison mixtures/preparations (much in use among Logbara/Ma'dì); ɛɳa, vt. to poison; ɛɳa má ɛɳaɳ̆á sɪ̀ she poisoned me (with a poison).

éɳàki = hərəŋgótə, n. grass (stem) used for divining: èì àtsɪ́fɛ̀ ndri ànɪ̈.

èɳ̈ì, èɳïia'rö, a., av. pstp. near; mvá 'dà èri èɳïä 'dà that boy is near there; ma àkú èri èɳïìrö vàá 'dɪ̀ my village is down here, near; àma Dàwúdì bɛ èɳï-èɳï (əgə̀-əgə̀) I live near Dawudi.

Ɛɳàó = Ónàó, Ánàó, n. river starting at Vöra (near Aruwa).

ɛɳú, vt. (1) to extinguish, put out (fire); é mu àtsɪ́ ɛɳú! go and put out the fire! (2) to cool down; ɛɳú ìyí àtsɪ́rɪ̀ ìyí ándzú sɪ̀ rá she cooled the hot water with cold.

ɛpa, ɛpakà = èdà, ègò, atri; dri ɛpa, vn. to come back.

èpé(kèpé)rɪ̀ = làùlàùrɪ̈, a. light, thin, threadbare, shiny, shabby; transparent.

èpì = èkpà, vt. to pinch, bruise, squeeze, crush, press against (sɪ̀); mɪ̈ mâ drí èpì pätí sɪ̀ you pinch my hand with the wood; mɪ́ èkpà (èpì, tö) mâ pá kö! do not crush my foot! mɪ̈ ma èpì (èkpà) 'dɪ̀! you are treading on me!

ɛpí rö, vn. to be proud, to boast, swagger; mɪ́ ɛpí mɪ̈ gà (= kö); mɪ́ 'dɛ́ 'bá ádarɪ̀ yà! do not be conceited; you are just an ordinary man! mɪ̈ ətsóə tòəkó; mɪ́ ɛ'íi (= ɛpí) mɪ̈ wɛrɛ! you are a mere dog; do not be so proud! ɛpíɪ́á, n. pride, haughtiness.

èrá, T. = èró, q.v.

èrà, = óní, n. stone, rock; mountain; éràfɪ́ gravel; èrà mvá a greater stone; é mu mánɪ́ èràmvá e'dú 'dà! go and pick up that stone for me!

éráká, n. red ochre (ìyía in rivers); èì é— əsa ədo sɪ̀ they mix up red ochre with oil; əkó èì éráká tri rùáa ɛkàrö women smear themselves red with red ochre.

érákákàlíó, n. a red weaver bird.

érálɛ́, T. = sí è—or sí àràkàlé, n. natural small gaps between teeth.

èré, n. (1) shrub yielding good sticks for bows; èré èì edɛ̃ ósù-rö they make bows from 'ɛrɛ' sticks; (2) (= ré) pole (with forked end) for opening/lifting the granary roof; èré èróti zìzŏrɪ̀'ï pole with which to open the granary.

ɛré, vt. to disperse, scatter; ɛré ma àfa wórə́ bàdàkàrö he scattered all my things at random; ǹdrí ɛré rö áséa the goats dispersed in the grass; andzi èì ɛré-zà-rö the boys have dispersed.

ɛrɛ́á = ərɛ́á, n. ankle.

érèdzé, dim. érèdzíĩã, n. a smaller calabash (cf. ètsé).

ɛrékɛrɛ = trãtrã, av. shattering in innumerable fragments (to break).

érénika, éróniká, òníniá, n. special stone (quartz); ɛ̃— èi ànï ɛ́mvó rûâ tri they rub the body of a pot (rim) with it.

èri, prs. prn. he, she, it; him, her; èri-drí, -vélé, &c., his, her, its; èridrírì his, hers; èrirí at his home.

ɛri¹, vt. to hear; 'bá àzí mà ti ɛrizǒ to hear/obey a person; ɛri ɛ'yɔ́ átíi mà tiá rá he obeys his father; ɛriá, ɛritá, n. hearing, obedience.

ɛri² = osi rö, vr./n. to bow down, stoop; mǐ ɛri mǐ èlè! stoop down!

ɛrí¹, vt. to keep back, detain, delay; mǐ ɛrí ma mívélé dzöa you delayed me in your room (by talking, &c.); ɛrí rö, vn./r. to remain behind, delay; ɛrí 'ǐ àkúa 'dã (èrinï awǐ-zǒ) he remained behind at home.

ɛrì² (cf. irí), vn. to repent (of sǐ); ma ɛrí ɛza, manì ɛdélérì sǐ 'bə I repent of the wrong I have done; mǐ ɛrî dǐ 'bə? do you repent? ɛritá, n. repentance.

ɛrí rö (cf. rǐ to sit), vn. to move in, to settle, hover (birds); àrǐïa ɛrí 'ǐ 'bùá 'dálé; èi ɛrí èi èlè: tökí ŋgà pá ŋaakú drìa kö: atsákí ŋgà bɛ (= kpɛrɛ) ŋaakú drìá kö birds are hovering in the sky about to settle; they are not yet (standing) on the ground.

eri = aŋú, vt. to tighten; èri wààta¹rö, èri 'bâ sí erí-erí it is sour, it sets one's teeth on edge.

èerí, n. uncultivated ground; àŋgò 'bánï 'à-lé·körǐ soil people have not cultivated.

èrî¹, n. clear/clean space on the side of a village (for dancing, &c.); àŋgò 'bánï əŋgô tö-zőrǐ, èi əmvɛ èrî a place for people to dance is called 'ɛrî'; 'bá àŋ̣á ɛdza èrîâ (or èrîdrìá) they spread corn on the 'ɛri' (for drying); èrîdrì, n. compound of/in village; àŋgò àlá àkú 'aléa 'dǐ èri èrîdrì the open/clear place within a village is an 'ɛridri'.

èrî² sǐ = əkpɔ́ sǐ, av. strongly, vigorously, energetically, with force; é 'yə ɛ'yɔ́ èrî sǐ (= èrî-mà-kə sǐ)! speak aloud! é ndzo èrî sǐ! run fast! èri àzí ŋga èrî sǐ he works energetically.

èrìagà, n. caterpillar; èri àzâ-bbî ŋa it eats leaves of àzáká shrub.

èríbí, n. freshly growing grass (say after first rains); dzi ǹdrí 'ǐ èríbía, ǹdrí mà ŋaa è— bɛnǐ he took the goats and tied them in the grass, that they might eat from the fresh grass; è¹rö a. green.

èríbínì, n. a green non-poisonous snake.

érífiá = órifía (or úã), n. small kind of wasp (painful stinging).

érífőrá, élífőrá, áí(p)ì, n. dust (as raised by wind); é— ɔ̀líni 'du ŋaakú 'aléa-rǐ; 'dɛ 'bâ miléa dust the wind raises from the ground; it falls into one's eyes.

éríkə̀, n. crevice, cleft, fissure; ma ɛ́mvó èri é— bɛ my pot is cleft, split; bə̀ŋgɔ́ éríkə̀rö the cloth is torn.

èrikiki-, èrikəkə¹rö, av. of a pungent bad smell; àdzíni èri-kikǐ-rö it smells bad.

erindi = ərindi, n. spirit; Àdrô èri ɛ— nǐ God is a spirit; 'bá mà ɛ— human soul.

éríndi(kə), n. a common creeping grass (Eragrostis milbraedi, and

Cynodon transvaalensis) ásέ răpí vàá sǐ used in ritual ceremonies; vǒvö é— sǐ to spit on 'erindi' leaves and pass them gently over one's body (kind of blessing).

érindrɛ, ǒrindrɛ, n. perspiration.

ériti or eríti, n. cloud; é— atri ètú milé tsí clouds have covered the sun.

èriti = dúrù, av. being long in coming; mu è—; ga emví kɔ mbèlè sǐ he went and was long in coming back; he would not come back quickly.

έɛró, óɔró, áaró, n. medicine (native and other).

èró, n. granary; èró 'bánï àn̠á 'bà-zǒ-rǐ'ï granary in which people put their corn.

ɛrɔkà = e'dolò, vt. to level out rough ground.

èró-líri, n. special granary (with supports of 1·5 m.) for reserve provisions (for time of need; of husband).

érónikấ, see érénikấ; óní èlíki-líri a polished stone.

ɛrú = bǐ, vt. to catch; mâ mu àrǐïá ɛrú I am going to catch birds.

èrù or èndrì (T.), ɔndrì, ɔrú, n. a large vulture (feeding on pigeons, lambs, snakes, small game, &c.).

éru! intj. surprise (disagreeable); calling attention; éru! éru é bǐ! halloo! catch it!

ɛrúgbɔzǒ = áfúzǒ, av. with great eagerness; àfà n̠azà ɛ—.

Èruwấ, prop. name of a river.

èsá, n. polenta eaten without savoury (wretched meal); έn̠á èsá dry polenta; έn̠á èsá ('rö) ko (= li) ï tsí tíbínï yɔ dry polenta, without savoury, was left over (say, in the evening for next day's breakfast; commonly έn̠âsá).

ésáko, n. pot with perforated bottom; é— à'í tǐ-zǒ-rǐ'ï with which to lixiviate lye (alkalized water).

ésὲ, n. various kinds of larger locusts; ésὲ alu tǒ locusts are very tasty.

ésέ(sέ), n. viscous juice, glue; ésέ ὲri pätí (i.e. ágbá, ɔ'bɔ́ló, láaró) súnï; 'bá àrǐïã ɔ'bà ésέ sǐ glue is the sap of (certain) trees; they catch birds with it; àrǐïã mu ón̠à n̠a, 'dɛ ànï tsí birds go to eat termites, and fall upon it (becoming caught).

ɛsέ[1] rö (cf. sɛ), vr. to draw near; mí ɛsέ mí ɔgɔgɔ má vǒ come nearer to me!

ɛsέ[2], vt. to bewitch (cf. lὲɛké).

èsélé, èsékèlé, n. space; distance between; boundary; 'bá sö pätí èsékèléa they plant trees on the boundary (space between); ɛ'yó 'dǐ 'ɔvö' pi 'adri' bɛ mà è— n̠gónï yà? what is the difference between (the words) 'ɔvö' and 'adri'?

èserí, n. small brown bird with red legs and long tail.

ésésévấ, éléséréa, n. kind of squirrel (living in trees); edzí èl ɔláa bɛ it resembles an 'ɔlaa' (a similar animal?).

èsì, vt. to transplant; ma mòèmbὲ èsì I am transplanting mangoes.

esi (cf. sì), vn. (1) to descend from; mí esí vàá! come down; ma ɛ'bí esí pätí sía I descended from the tree; (2) also esí, vn. to be delivered; mvá esí (commonly osi or tǐ) 'bɔ a child was born; (3) esí rö (more common ɛsέ rö) to draw near.

esí rö, vn. to be(-come) entangled (on growing, &c.) in grass (or bush), to be interlaced; părí 'dà

ásé ɛsí rö ɛsí the place is all entangled with grass, bush ... ; ɛsí-
ríkìsìrì rö av. entangled, interlaced, inextricably confused.

ésísí, n. mulberry shrub/tree; ɛ̀rì
gbï ɔ́tɔ́kɔ́ drìá it grows (for preference) on termite hills.

èsɔ̀ (cf. sɔ̀) (1) vt. to pour; mɨ́ èsɔ̀
(= èbɛ̀, èdà) ìyí mâ drìá! pour
water on my hands! (2) vn. to
pour down; ɔzɔ́ɔ́ èsɔ̀ 'bɔ it has
started raining; (3) to hang down
heavily; ǹdrí èsɔ̀ tré 'bɔ, ɛ̀rì 'yɛ̀
tì tsúrú'dɔ̀ rá the goat is heavy
with young, she will very soon
bear young; ǹdrí mà bbà èsɔ̀
dàràŋgbà the udder of the goat
is drooping heavily.

esɔ̀ (cf. sö), vt. to put (or push) out;
to reach out; mɨ́ esɔ̀ mɨ̀ andra
àmvé! put out your tongue!

èsɔ̀, vt. to balance on one's head;
ɔ̀kó èsɔ̀ ìyí émvó sɨ̀ drìá, ŋga
(nɨ̈) ɛ'dé kö; bɨ̀ drí sɨ̀ kö a woman
balances a water pot on her head,
so that it will not fall, though she
does not hold it with her hand.

esú¹, vt. (1) to find; esú silíŋgì:
drìlénï bba he found a shilling,
he is lucky; (2) esú rö or esú ti
'bá bɛ to meet a p.; àma esú ti
(or rö) mɨ̈ bɛ I have met you/we
have met; esú ma dè ŋgà àkúa
he found me (by chance) still at
home.

esú², n. nerve (cf. àríbá vein).

ésúlékɔ̀, n. the concave back of
knee-joint.

esúti (cf. esú¹, vt.) juncture; (1)
ìyí e— or ìyí ɛtsí-ti confluence,
junction of rivers; (2) joint (of
limbs ...) (3) e— ágíi bɛ meeting
with a friend.

ètà = ɛwí, vt. to tempt; try to
induce; ɛ̀rì 'bá ètà ɛ'yɔ́ ɔ̀ndzírì
sɨ̀ he tempts one with bad things;

A... ètà ma ɔ̀gù sɨ̀ A ,... tempted
me to steal.

ètálá, n. dzɔ́ è— the slightly
sloping ground at the side of a hut.

ètátá, n. rain-torrent; ɔzɔ́ɔ́ è— nɨ̈
ra gɛ̀rì (or àkúa) sɨ̀ a rain
torrent runs on the way (in the
village = ètátánɨ̈ ra ètálá sɨ̀).

ètátâdrɛ́ (ká), n. a mushroom (not
edible).

ɛté (cf. tɛ) (1) vn. to be ready
cooked (e'dí); e'dínï ɛté ŋgà kö,
mà 'bà àtsɨ́a ddíká! the gruel
is not yet ready, have it put on the
fire again! (2) vt. to steady; mɨ́
ɛté (= ɛmbá) ásí tsɨ́! pluck up
your courage!

ètɛkpɛrɛrɨ̀, a hobbling, limping
'bá è—.

ɛtɛmbɛrɛ, ɛ̀mbɛtɛkɛrɛ̀, otukudu,
a. shallow; ìyí mà ǎlí ɛ̀rì ɛ—,
= ìyí mà 'alɛ́ ɛ— the water is
shallow.

ététéŋgùlé, n. tadpoles.

ětɨ́ or ítɨ́, n. tamarind tree (Tama-
rindus indica); ětɨ́ e'dí mbɛzɔ̌
tamarind fruit to eat with/in gruel.

Étì, Bɛ́ Étì (sometimes Óti), n. a
high peak at Tɛrɛgo ('Jebel
Woti').

ètɨ́¹, n. (1) (= éfɨ́) meaning; mɨ̈ ètɔ̀
(é ndzɛ) ɛ'yɔ́ 'dɨ̀ mà ètɨ́ kílílí you
have explained the meaning of the
word correctly; (2) reason for;
é ndzɛ mánɨ̈ ètɨ́nɨ̈ rá! tell me
the reason for it! (3) (= ǹdú)
origin, descent, extraction, an-
cestry; àma (mà) ètɨ́ (èì bɛ) pɨ́rɨ̈
àlö we are all of the same descent
(clan).

ètɨ́² = ǹdú n. (1) space under ...;
pätí ètɨ́ space under a tree; ètɨ́a,
pstp. under; é rɨ̈ pätí ètɨ́a! sit
under the tree! (2) back/hind
part of ....

eti = tö, to knead; èì ɔ̀drí eti

pá (or **drí**) **sï** they are kneading clay with feet (hand).

ètì = **emó**, vt. to put together, pile up something in a disorderly way; **èri búkù ètï** (= **emó**) **pïrï àlö bàdàkà** he throws all the books on a heap.

ètï[1], vt. to pick, pluck, collect (fruits); **èri pätí éfï ètï** he is plucking fruits (from a tree); **mï ètï mání mòèmbè nna 'dï** you have plucked these three mangoes for me.

ètï[2], vt. to portion out; **é fï éɳá ètï 'bá 'dï ̈ nï!** go out and share out polenta to the people!

ètï[3], vn. (1) (= **ε'dé**) to fall by drops or the like; **sïnï ètï mï drïá** it hails on your head; **əzɔ́ɔ́nï ε'bï ètï** (= **ε'dé**) **'bùá 'délé** it starts raining up there; (2) **ètï g̀èrìá** to drop in (or reach, by chance) on a way/path.

étírïkɔ́, **átírïkɔ́**, T., n. (1) snail; **é— ándrïí** female snail; **é— dzó** snail-shell; **é— èi ànï àdzíkɔ́ 'alé əfá** with a snail-shell they level the inside of pots (on making new ones); (2) oyster (cf. **kàbèlé**).

étírïlï, n. cricket; **é— 'bílé** hole of a cricket.

ètisí (**kə**), n. pad (of grass or cloth) on head; **ìyí 'bà zɔ̈ drìá** to put water (pot) on it (for carrying), or other (Ac. *otac*).

ètɔ́ə, n. the ordinary small hare; a larger one (hare or rabbit) is called **è— òdúlùkú**; Mr. Hare's (of fables) proper name is **è— àɳìirá**; Mrs. Hare is **Ámvïléti**; **èri əndzó ə̀tsɔ́-lé** it runs like a dog.

etɔ̈ = **εsé**, vt. to pluck, tear off (fruits); **mâ mu à'bòà etɔ̈** (= **εsé**) I am going to break off bananas (bunch).

etó, vt. to fix on; **ma mílé etɔ̈ Zak.**

mà drìá I fixed my eyes upon (= frowned at) Zak.

ètɔ̀, vt. to set right, adjust; (1) to repair; **mï ètɔ̀ èrɔ́ átsí 'dï ɔ́'dí** (**átsífε sï**) repair the granary with 'atsi' sticks again; (2) to fix, fasten (on **sía**); **ma ε'bɔ́ ètɔ̀** (= **sö**) **àbé sía** I am fixing the hoe on the handle (cf. **édzó**); (3) to explain, elucidate, define (cf. **ètï**[1] (1)); (4) vr. **ètɔ̀** (or **ε'da**) **rö** to make o-s. answerable/responsible for; **mï ètɔ̀ mï àlï mïnï 'dï mà drìlía!** also **é sɔ̀ pá àlï mïnï . . .** make yourself responsible for (take upon yourself) this fight of yours! (5) to aim at, go/keep straight to a line/direction; **mà ètɔ̀ pätï 'dàrï kílílí!** keep straight on in the direction of that tree! **εtə** (!) **dzó 'dà mà ti kpìi** he moved straight on to the door of that hut.

εtó = **arí**, vt. to assist (in danger), to save; **èmï εtó ma** (= **è pá ma**), **kàmìnï mà ɳa**, or **ŋgúrúnï ǹdrî 'du 'dɔ̀!** help me! a lion is about to eat me, or: a wild beast is carrying off a goat here; **εtó ma drìə rá** he once saved me; **'bá 'dà emú à'dï nï εtó yà?** whom is that man coming to save? (his presence is annoying); **εtópï** saviour.

ètɔ̀ə-ónï, n. asbestos (amiantus); **è— pə̀röpə̀rö-rö** the asbestos is breakable/decaying.

ètrè, T. = **èvï**, q.v. gadfly.

étri, **étrïá**, n. kingfisher; **é— mà ti èzïí eka pie**; **rùánï lóbékè: ëni sï εmvε sï** the kingfisher has a long, thin red beak; its body is chequered black and white; **òpï drïlénï sùràsùrà** the front part of the wings is blue.

etrï 'ï etrï, vr. to purpose, determine, protest (to omit doing, &c.; cf. **'yə̀ sɔ̀**).

ètrɔ̀ = èndǐ, av. also; ma emú tɛ́ ètrɔ̀ I have also come.

ètrúndzílïrö, av. on the brink, verge, edge of . . . , on the point of falling off sth. 'bà 'ï è— he stood/ sat on the edge of sth. (in a perilous position); 'bá rǐpï pǎrí ɔ̀ndzía-rǐ/kànì pǎrí (àŋgɔ̌) tsa èrinǐ kö, èrì rï̈ è— one sitting in a bad (dangerous) place is on the point of falling.

etsá, vn. (1) to arrive, reach (hither); to satisfy; mǐ átíi e— ádzɛ́ rá yà? did your father arrive yesterday? (2) to arrive at some point; e— à'yiiɔ sǐ it is some time after 8 o'clock.

ètsákì, T., av. in countless pieces.

ɛtsaandǐ, pl. ɛtsáandì, vt. to vex, annoy, trouble; mï̈ ma ɛ— tö you are annoying me greatly; èmï̈ ɛtsáandì ma kö! do not vex me! ètsáandí, n. grief, affliction, trouble; mǐ ɔvö è— sǐ à'do sǐ yà? why are you grieved? è— bɛ grieved.

ɛtsara (= azi), vt. to send word, inform; ma ɛ— ndrâ mï̈ mï̈ ándríi mà tiá rá I informed you some time ago through your mother; ɔ́pí ɛ— ma nǐ, á mu 'í vö drùsǐ the chief sent me word to go to him tomorrow.

ètsɛ́, n. calabash bowl; dim, ètsɛ́ã; è— èri ágávɔ̌ sǐ the bowl is half-full; 'ɛtsɛa' is for drinking beer è— éwâ mvu-zɔ̌rǐ.

ètsɛ, vr./vt. (1) to be absent at, fail to attend; to omit, miss; ma è— o'dú ïrrì I was absent (at work . . .) two days; mï̈ è— ɛmbátáã (sǐ) rá/or ɛmbátáã è— (= aga) mï̈ mà drìlɛ́ sǐ you did not assist at instruction/ . . . escaped thee; (2) to forget; ɛ'yɔ́ manï̈ tɛ́ (ko) ètsɛ̌ rǐ, ma egá (= ɔ̀rà, esú) tsúrú'dɔ̀

the word I had omitted/forgotten, I remembered it now; (3) = atsɛ to remain back, be left over.

ɛtsɛ = ɛ'da, vt. (1) to show, indicate; mï̈ ɛ— mánǐ gïrǐ mǔpi Màràtsàá-rǐ! show me the way to Maratsa! (2) to explain, reveal; mï̈ ɛ— ɛ'yɔ́ 'dǐ mà ɛ́fí pùù rá! do explain to me the meaning of this word clearly! ma ɛ— mǐnǐ ǹdúnï̈ Lógbàrà ti sǐ I have explained its meaning in Logbara to you; ɛtsɛtá = ɛ'datá example, illustration; ɛ— sǐ e.g.

ɛtsɛ́ (cf. tsɛ), vt. to break (or snap) off; ɛ— báká rá he pulled off the string; to tear (or pull) out/up; mǐ ɛ— ásɛ́! pull up the grass!

ɛtsɛ́kɛ́lɛ́ndrè, n. = ɛ́tsïtsí, ɛ́tsï̈kïtsí, q.v.

ɛ́tsɛ́kïtsí, n. large black ants; ɛ́— èi 'bá dǒdò ɛtí sǐ they sting a p. with their back-part.

ɛ́tsɛ́tsɛ́ré, n. splinters (of rind of durra stalk or the like); ɛ́— èi ɔ̀ndó páti wuu (ɛ̆lï sǐ): èi dǐ fa, èi dǐ tsà ndɔ̀ they 'skin' durra stalks (with knife): they rub it: then they plait them; ɛ́tsɛ́tsɛ́ré-fɔ̌rá waste chips from 'ɛtsɛtsɛre' cleaning.

ètsɛ́-ïrǐkɔ̀, n. piece of calabash; è— bánï̈ ɛdɛ́ ɛ́ŋá ɔfá ànï̈ they make it to scratch polenta (from pot) with.

ètsì-ru, a. cloudy, dark, gloomy, depressing; àŋgɔ̌ è— it is cloudy; àŋgɔ̌ èfɔ̌ tɛ́ ɔ̀'bíti sǐ è— it was cloudy at daybreak.

ɛtsí = ɔlɛ́, ɔdzá, vt. (1) to deceive, cheat, mislead; mï̈ ɛ— ma tɔ̀ɔkɔ́, mï̈ ɔ́pí mvá kö you are simply deceiving me, you are not a chief's son; (2) to delay, detain, put off; 'bâ drì ɛtsí-zɔ̌ (Ac. galo); mǐ ɛ— mâ drì kö, á lɛ̀ mu àkúa!

do not detain me, I want to go home!

εtsi, vt. (1) (= òpì) to close; to lock, shut firmly; mí ε— dzótilé (or sàndúkù ti, kɔ́pɔ̀lɔ̀, ëlï mà sí) tsí! shut . . . the door (lid of trunk, padlock, knife)! (2) ε— rö to meet with (bε); àma ε— àma mï ádríi bε gïïrìá I met your brother on the way; (3) to join (as ends of string); èi ǹdrí báká (-ti) ε— (= a'dï), they join the (torn) ropes of the goat; èi ə'bɔkɔ́ ε— they fasten the string net for baby-carrying; (4) (= əsa) to join up things; to throw together, mix up; èi ε— dría àlö they join or mix them all up; (5) ε— 'ï wεrε it is almost closed (slight opening remains), the ends almost meet; (6) to encircle, enclose, form a circle . . . ; andzi èi päti (or dzɔ́) àgàï ε— the children form a circle round a tree (hut) (joining their hands: playing); (7) ε— rö ε— to feel giddy: mâ milénï ε— rö ε— I am feeling dizzy (eyes clouded).

εtsí(kí)tsí, εtsékítsí, εtsíkilí, n. large black warrior ant (biting and stinging?); εtsïtsí-nï 'bá zǎ the 'εtsitsi' stings/burns one; (Ac. məərə) έ— èi mu ɔ́dzíríkɔ́ ndǎ ɔ́tɔ́lɔ́kɔ́a they go to catch termites in their hills; έ— àlío a similar large bad-smelling ant (moving singly, the former in endless processions).

εtsíkirí, εtsímákɔərɔ̀, píripíría, n. 'whirling round oneself' (playing child); giddiness, dizziness; mvá 'dïrï e— 'bi the boy turns in a whirl; e— rï mâ ǹdrí ə'bέ (or εtsí) nï giddiness continues to throw my goat to the ground.

εtsɔ́¹, vt. (1) to reach sth.; mâ drí ε— rá my hand reaches it/there; mï ma ndrǎndrà (milé èdrí sì), mï ε— bbílé má vɔ̃ kö you look askance at me, you do not turn your ears towards me (i.e. do not pay attention); (2) ε— . . . zɔ̃ to suffice for, be able to; ma ε— kúrsi 'dì εdézɔ̃ kö I can/could not make this chair.

εtsɔ́² (cf. tsə), vt. to shut up; mí ε— εróti! shut up the lid of the granary! dìrísà ε— rö tsí the window shut (by itself or wind).

étsofí, étsukí, T., n. oil-yielding kernel/fruit of 'mala' tree.

étsərɔ̀fí, n. a small fish of country rivers; è'bí mà è— ŋgókónï ŋgɔ̀'bɔ̀-ŋgɔ̀'bɜ̀rö the 'εtsərɔfi' fish has an uneven back.

etsú = ekú, to abbreviate sby.'s name to a short pet name; èi 'bá mà rú e— ásí ndrìzà sì they adapt/abbreviate one's name out of intimacy; e.g. Gabrieli becomes Gábì etsútáa sì by abbreviation; rú etsúzà abbreviated/ pet name (familiar name).

étù = ɔ́kɔ́rɔ̀ŋgə, n. borassus palm.

ètú, n. the sun; (= o'dú) day; ètúnï èfö-èfö the sun rises; ètúnï 'dὲ 'dε the sun sets; ètúnï èförìá at sunrise; 'bù-ǹdú (sì at) dawn, daybreak; the early twilight; ma èfö té àŋgɔ̀-trà sì or éní sì or a'úátánï tsεrε 'bεzɔ̃ 'dì I started in the early morning, or: at cock's crow; mï etsá ètú ŋgɔ̀pi yà? at what o'clock did you arrive? ètúkà, n. sunshine (ètúnï kazɔ̃ when the sun shines); ètúfε, n. excessively long period of sunshine; ètúfεnï kàka, əzɔ̀ɔ́nï 'di körï sì the .un shines excessively, while the rain does not fall; ɔ́lέεɔ́nï ètúfε sɔ̀ nï the sorcerer causes the drought (opposite of rainmaker); **ètúsílé,** n. the bright pleasant sunshine (after about 8 a.m.); **ètúnï 'bàzǒ 'bâ vɛzǒrï, mǐ dí ètúsíle̊ yöö** when the sun has begun to warm you, you go to bask in the sunshine; **ètú 'dɛrïá (? = ètú-párá** or **-ana)** the sun about to set; **ètú sǐ** in the daytime; **ètú-zùu** av. all day (long).

etú¹-etú = tùtu, pǐpì, vn. to swell; **ásínï etú-etú** his belly is swollen, raised (cf. next **etú).**

etú² (cf. **tu),** vn. to come up, mount; **mǐ etú mávǒ 'bùá 'dǒ!** come up to me! (say, on a tree); **ɛ̀'bínï etú Ényáóá** fish swim up the Enyao river.

ɛ́ú = ɛ́wía, ɔ́lóa, gɔ̀lí, n. fishing hook.

ɛvé (cf. **vɛ),** vt. to burn up; **èi ɔkörǒnyà ɛvɛ̂** they burn the sweepings (rubbish).

évérékɔ́, n. space where grass has been burned; **èri àɳgǒ àtsínï vɛlé 'bɔrǐ'ï/ásé vépi ɔ́'dí'rö** a place the fire has burned down/ the grass burned recently.

èvǐ, = vǐ, ɔ̀vǐ, n. cattle (gad)-fly i.e. **èdrú òɳú** buffalo fly; **èvínï 'bâ tsǐtsï** the gad-fly bites man.

èvì or **vì,** n. purulent matter, pus; **èvì ɓï ndrrì** pus bursts forth.

éví, n. kind of white clay, chalk.

eví, vn. to fall obliquely, slantingly; **ɔzɔ́ɔ́ eví ɔ̀lí bɛ** the rain came slantingly down with the wind.

èvísakö, n. furrow on back (along spine) of man.

èvǒ, n. fairly large (square) basket; demin. **èvǒã** a small 'evo'; **ɛ́mvó èvǒ mà 'aléa** a pot in a basket; **èvǒ àɳá lɔ̀ɔzǒ** basket for harvesting corn.

evǒ (cf. **vö),** vt. to (expel by) smoke (out); **èi édrɔ́ evǒ àɳádrilékɔ́ sǐ**

they smoke out mice from hole (burning chaff near hole and fanning the smoke into it).

ɛ́wá, n. beer; **ɛ́wâ zɔzǒ** to strain beer; **(ɛ́wá mà) èdzí** second beer.

ɛ̀wá, n. elephant; **ɛ̀wá drí** proboscis of elephant; **ɛ̀wá²rö = ɔkpɔ́'rö,** a. difficult (in general); **(èi nï mbèlè kö).**

Ɛ́wǎdrì, prop. n. district east of Aruwa.

èwǎdrì (ɛlǐ), n. (beginning of) dry season: when the winds are strong: **kànì ɔlínï lǐ tǒ** (about November).

èwáfà, n. (1) shrike; (2) name of a district (Maratsa); **È— tsû** market of 'Ewafa'.

èwasìdù, n. a large tree (with thorns on stem).

Ɛ́wávíɔ́, name of a small river, tributary of Ɔsǒ.

èwélè-, èwéréwélè-, èmbétété 'rö, a. almost completely flat; **ǎlí kókɔrǒ** without cavity or depth.

ɛ́wí(a)¹, n. fishing-hook; **ɛ́wí ɛ̀'bí pɛ̀zǒrǐ** hook for fishing; **èi kǒlú** (or **ɔdɔ̀) sö ɛ́wí sía, èi ànï ɛ̀'bí 'bɛ** they fix grasshoppers on the hook and angle for fish with it; **ɛ́wíã** small hook.

ɛ́wí², n. (1) edge, corner; **dzɔ́ (mà) ɛ́wí** corners or angles of a hut; **ɔsǐ pätí ɛ́wínï ɔsǐ-ɔsǐ** he shaped the wood (furniture) with edges; (2) long tattoo marks (on face . . .).

ɛwí, vt. to set (or to show a p. by) a (good or bad) example; to enlighten, teach, give a lead (good or bad); **'bá mà bbílé ɛwí** (or **ɔsɔ̀)** to whisper into one's ears, to insinuate, induce, seduce; **ɛwí 'bá,** or **ɛwí 'bánï ɛ'yɔ́** to insinuate . . . ; **ɛwí dí mánï 'bɔ̌; ɳga ká: àma nɛ̌ ɛri bɛ rá!** he has shown me now; wait a bit, he will have to do with me! **ɛwízǒ òbí**

ə̀ndzí sǐ to scandalize with bad example; mɪ́ ɛwɪ̆ ma ɛ̀'yɔ́ ə̀ndzírǐ sǐ kö! do not seduce me with bad talk!

ɛ'wɪ̆¹ = ɛrí, vt. to keep back, detain, withhold a p. with talk or ... delay; ɛ'wɪ̆ ma ámvúa ètú-zù he kept me on the field the whole day; mɪ̈ ɛ'wɪ̆ ma 'dɪ́nɪ̈ à'do sǐ yà? why do you delay/compel me thus?

ɛ'wɪ̆² (commonly 'wɪ̈), to dry, parch; 'bâ zá ɛ'wɪ̆ àtsɪ́ sǐ they dry flesh on fire; enɪ̈rɪ̈kə ɛ'wɪ̆-zŏ ètúa to parch a skin in the sun.

ɛwitsà = əfo, vt. to exchange; to change; mɪ́ ɛ— mání silíɳgì 'dɪ̀rɪ̈! do exchange this shilling for me! èì tí ɛ— ǹdrí sǐ they exchange a cow against goats.

ɛ'yá, n. a tree (its seeds are put in fire or in potsherd on fire and consulted; àndrí ə'bé-zŏ observing their behaviour; if they explode an avenging excursion or enterprise will succeed; the other way, if...) ɛ'yáéfɪ̆, the seeds for oracle.

ɛyá, n. a woody creeper (with thorns) (yielding fine sewing fibre); ɛyánɪ̆ ra màákò bbí lɛ́; èì ànɪ̈ èɡáã or ètsé ... tsi (or ... àfadzó tɪ̆ mbɛ) it creeps like potato leaves; they sew (cracked) calabashes with it (or fix the rim of receptacles).

ɛ́yǎ = àyɪ̆̀a, n. mother (familiar); ɛ́yǎ mâyê! mâ ándrɪ̆́ mâ yê! my mother! my mother!

eyakiyà (= more commonly əyakɪ̆yà?), n. earthquake; ɛ̀ri àɳgò əy-əya it shakes the earth.

ɛ'yɔ́, n. word; speech; reason, opinion; à'do ɛ'yɔ́ sǐ? why? for what reason? ɛ'yə̂ sö to report (or retell) gossip, slander, tell-tale; á nì mɪ̈ ɛ'yɔ́ rá! I know your thought/intention/opinion; ɛ'yə̂ 'yə (or ndzɛ, ə̀lò) to speak, discuss; ɛ'yɔ́ ètɪ̆ lɪ̈ to judge, decide (a question); ɛ'yɔ́ ɡbɛ 'bâ drɪá to impute a th. to a p.; ɛ'yɔ́ ètɪ̆ ndzɛ (or 'du, òtɪ̀) to discuss a case; ɛ'yɔ́ èti ko-zŏ dzà to drop a case; ɛ'yɔ́ àvɪ̆ (= dza) 'bə the word/matter was forgotten.

ɛ'yɔ́-éfɪ̆, n. report, detailed account, minutes; ma ɛ'— áda 'dɪ̀rɪ̆ ndzɛ 'ɪ̈ I am giving here the true account.

éyío or éɪ̆yó, n. crocodile.

ézá = ɔ́lá, ètɪ̆, ǹdú, yɛ̈ɛ̈lá, n. root, origin, descent, extraction, birth; àma ɛ́zá (or á'bɪ́) Dribbídu our origin (ancestor) is 'Dribidu'.

ɛza, vt. to spoil, upset, ruin ..., Eccl. to sin; ɛ'bɔ́ ɛza rö rá the hoe is ruined (worn); ə̀lɪ́ ɛ̀ri wárágà ɛza-ɛza (or ɛrɛ-ɛrɛ) the wind has blown the papers into disorder; ɛza 'ɪ̈ rá he became spoiled (moral).

èzakìzà (rö) (similar tsandɪ̆-rö), n./a. compassion, commiseration, pity, sympathy; to have compassion for; to take pity on; compassionate, charitable to; 'bá 'dà a'á mání èzakìzà-rö = ɛ̀ri mání ètsándí bɛ I have compassion on that man; also 'bá 'dà mà ɛ̀— mání tŏ.

èzɛ́ (1) èzɛ́²rö, av. 'for all that, on mature consideration'; ásɪ̂ mu Árúalɛ́ rá; éfɪ̈nɪ̈ mu èzɛ̀rö; ɡà tɛ̆ mu-kɔ́ sǐ, mǔ dɪ́ 'dáanɪ̈ he went to Arua of his own free will; that is he went on mature consideration; earlier he refused to go, then he went all the same; (2) èzɛ́-nɪ̈ tŏ = èzɛ̀rö, a. tough, tenacious; émvó àfanɪ̈ a'dɪ̆zŏ 'alénɪ̆́a mbɛ̀lɛ̀ körɪ̆̀'ɪ̈, ɛ̀ri èzɛ́ a thing that does not cook quickly in a pot is tough.

èzèkèzè = **tsùrútsùrúa, tságòa,** n. luffa.

ezí, vt. to pray; **'bá Àdrɔ̃ ezí (téo sì)** one prays to God (with a gourd-rattle); **ma 'a èzíá** I was at prayers.

eezí! intj. it is true; certainly (expression used by eyewitness).

èzíï (-rì) = **róέ,** dimin. **èzíïã,** a. long (and thin, slender, delicate at the same time) (cf. **èzɵ̈ö**).

ézío, n. lover (boy or girl, when engaged, call each other and are called so by others); **mã̀ mu é— andrí** I go to visit my betrothed.

èzɵ̈ö (-rì), a. long (and relatively thick); **ndàndã̀ mà tinï zɵ̀ èzɵ̈örö** the snout of a shrewmouse grows long and (relatively) thick; **èzɵ̃ p̆ětsɵ̀p̆ětsɵ̀** long and unsteady (moving).

eezó (cf. zɵ̀), vn. to increase, produce, propagate (of any 'living' being); **'bá e— àŋgɵ̀ drìá kákàɵ̀rö** people have greatly increased in the area; **ɵ̀tsέ e— andzi bɛ kárákàràrö** a dog produces many puppies.

èzɵ̀ɵ́, n. hog; **è— sì (rö) ɵ̀pégɵ̀ lέ** a hog is similar to a pig; **è— ɵ́kúrúsá** bristles of a hog; **è—mà sì èzɵ̃rö** the hog has long teeth.

èzɵ̀ (cf. zɵ̀), vt. (1) to bring (or train) up; rear, raise; **ándrïi drà rá, ɵ̀kó àzínï èzɵ̀ mvánï** the mother died and another woman brought up the child; (2) to educate; **mvá 'dìrï ásí ɵ̀ndzîrö, tsa zɵ̀-zɵ̃ 'bá tɵ̀ɵkó drí kö** this child has a bad character, he could not possibly grow up with ordinary people (i.e. only with his mother); **ágú 'dì fè sì ándrïi tsa èri èzɵ̀-zɵ̃ kö 'dínï à'do sì yà?** why has this

p. written that his mother had been unable to educate him?

ézó-andzi, also **ɵ̀kó-andzi** (pl. of **záa-mvá),** n. girls.

èzɵ̀sí, n. glandular swelling of groin or armpit; **èzɵ̀sí pì ma nì** my inguinal gland is swollen.

F

fà, vt. (1) to cut (hair); **fà mâ dribbí rá** he has cut my hair; to shave; (2) to grub (up), scrape, rake; **èi áŋ̩ú fã̀** they are scratching a sesame field (to cover seeds in it); **èi 'dɵ̃ fí rì 'alénìá; kà dí rì 'bɵ, èi fã̀fà** they sow eleusine seeds in it (field); after they have sown it, they scratch it over; **ámvú fà-zɵ̃** to scrape/rake a field.

fa, vt. to clean; to cut, trim, dress surface of sth. (from any roughness or unevenness); **èri màákò rúâ fa** (= **kpɵ̃, rɵ̆, ɵli**) she peels, cleans potatoes (before or after cooking); **èi ósu** (or **ɵ́ŋ̩ófí, mbégò bá) ɵfã̀** they trim/dress an arrowshaft (fingernails, a sisal rope (just finished)); **fa gaa, ko àzínï tsí** she cleaned a few, leaving the other part.

fàlá(-kɵ́) sometimes **fà** only, n. (1) bone; **f— 'dì mà 'áá ɵ̀do yɵ** there is no marrow in this bone; **lɵ́mà fà** or **lɵ́mà mà f—,** n. rib; **f— mâ lɵ́màá** my rib; **ópílé f— coccyx (cf. ò'dúti);** (2) **pätí fɛ** (or **f—)** stem of tree (bark removed).

fàrásì, A.S. horse; **àkàŋ̩à sɵ́bí tàyàrì'ï** donkey with bushy tail.

fè, vt. (1) (cf. **èfè)** to give; **é fè té kö à-sì yà?** why did you not give it before? (2) **fè...'bá dría** to consign (in a p.'s hand); **fè tí èrimà dría** he consigned a cow to him; (3) **fè+hortat.** to allow, permit, let;

to cause; **é fɛ̀ á mvi àkúa!** or **é fɛ̀ mánî rúkúsà á mu àkúa!** allow me to go home! (4) **drì fɛ̀zö** to pay attention; **á fɛ̀ drì ɛ'yó mvá 'dìnï 'yɔ rì ɛrí!** I paid attention to hear what this boy said; (5) **tógbɔ̀-rö fɛ̀** to lend (against pawn); **èri g̀à àfa fɛ̀kó 'bánî sì** he refuses to give sth. to a man.

fɛ, T. = pätí, n. tree (in general).

fë, vn. (1) to wear out; **ɛ'bó** (or **élísí, ɔ̀gara…) fëë rá** the hoe (edge of knife, axe) is worn out; (2) to become deserted, abandoned; **àŋgö̀ fë ndrrró** (= **ìyíi**) (i.e. **'bá 'alénîá yɔ**) the place (country) has become completely deserted (nobody lives in it).

fí¹ (= commonly **éfí**, q.v.), n. especially in combinations as **drìbbí-fí** a single unit (as a single hair).

fí², n. intestine, bowels; **tí fí** a cow's bowels; **fí bùlúdzɔ̀** (= **olíma**) the colon.

fì (= **hwɛ̀ɛ, T.**), vn. to burst; explode, blast; **à'dì 'yɛ 'dìnï nì yà?** **fìfì** who has done that? it burst; **ɛ'yá éfí ɔ̀fì** the 'eya' grain exploded (on fire); **ɔ̀vínï fìfì** it thunders (lit. the lightning explodes); **fì trà** it flew open.

fï¹, vn. **fìfì = ambí-ambí,** vn. to be cool, fresh; cold; **ìyí** (or **lésú**) **fìfï** the water (milk) is cold; **àŋgö̀ fïzàrö** it is cold.

fï², vn. (1) to go in, enter; (cf. **efí** to come in); **é fï dzóalɛ́!** go into the hut (room)! (2) to penetrate (body, mind, &c.); (3) **'bá mà pàría fï zö** to succeed a p.; **fï átíí mà pàría** he succeeded his father.

fï³, vn. to form, develop (under ground; of tubers, ground-nuts…) **màákò** (**gbándà, söŋgó**) **fï 'bɔ**

the potatoes (maniok, groundnuts) have already developed (i.e. well-formed).

fífí (= **hwìá**), n. kind of reed-grass with empty (tube) stalks (Ac. **òbòot**); **'bá káanï f— sì ìyî sɛ** a p. may drink (draw/suck) water with a 'fifi' tube; **èi fífíá tsà töö̀rö** they plait 'fifia' stalks into hives; **f— èri ìyî gbóa** it is found along rivers.

fíàfíà (**-rö**) = **alu,** a. (of taste) pleasing, agreeable; **à'í 'dɔ̀ mà sí fíàfíàrö, alu tíbí bɛ tö** the taste of this salt is agreeable, it is delicious in savour.

fö̀, vn. (1) to go out (cf. **efö̀** to come out); **è fö̀ àmvé!** go (ye) away/ out! (2) to go away; cease, disappear; **ìí 'dì mà àtsí fö̀ rá** or **ìí 'dì mà àtsínï ambí rá** the heat of this water is gone/it has cooled down; (3) to come out or appear (in some peculiar aspect): as, to bloom, show up with (buds) flowers; **àŋá èri ŋgà kírí fö̀-rö** ('dáanï) the corn is still fully blooming; (4) similarly: to grow (turn, become) grey, white; **'bá àmbó fö̀ mbàzàrö** (**èri ɔdzá ɛmvɛ̀rö**) the old man has grown grey (he turned white); **'bá àmbérï mà drìá fö̀ö** (= **ɔzɔ̀fɔ̀rɔ̀**) **tsí** (= **èri fö̀ bɛ**; only **àŋá èri fö̀ rö!**); **fö̀,** n. flower; **èi yabí fö̀ ndzɛ tɔ̀ bɔ̀ŋgó 'aléa laa-zö** they pick the (cotton-like) flowers of yabi grass and pack it into a bag (as pillow) for lying down; **ɔ́ónï ɛrï fö̀ ku… ku 'ku' 'ku'** we hear sounding (knocking).

fö̀ = ŋ̣ï, vt. to rub; **fö̀ ɔ́fótá 'ìmà rùá** (= **ŋ̣ï 'ìmà rùá ɔ́fótá sì**) he rubbed himself with ashes; **mï dzó 'alɛ̂ fö̀ö** you are rubbing/ scrubbing the floor (to dust).

fɔ̂! intj. please! **mǐ ɛ̀fɛ̀ mánǐ, fɔ̂**!
give me, please! **'dǐ té ɛ'yɔ́
ádanï** (or **tsɛ́ áda) fɔ̂**! that was
the truth, I am pleased!

fɔ̀ =**aŋgə-aŋgə**, vn. to come out
in a rash and cause itching; **mâ
drínï fɔ̂fɔ̀, ma vǐvì** my hand
itches, I am scratching.

fɔ̀ə(r), av. brightly shining; sparkling, gleaming; **àfa ɛná ko fɔ̀ə**
sth. is seen hazy–bright; **àfa
ɛnápi ɛmvɛ fɔ̀əə** sth. looking
whitish/hazy; **àŋgɔ̌ ɛ'dá Árúwá
fɔ̀əə** (distant) Aruwa looks hazy/
misty.

fɔ̂dǐ and **fɔ́rí**, av. (related to **fɔ̀ə**),
in bright, white shoots; **àɳá 'du
f— 'bə** the corn (put aside for
germinating leaven) has germinated in bright white shoots; **ɛrítí
ɛ'dâ ko 'bùá fɔ́rí** the (light) clouds
appear up there bright/hazy.

fɔ́lɔ́fɔ́lɔ̌, av. all to pieces; **óní ɔ̀fǐ
f—** (= **fɔ́rɔ̀fɔ́rɔ̌**) the stone broke/
crumbled to pieces.

fɔ̀ŋgóà, kǐfúŋgà, A.S., key.

fɔ̀ɳìfɔ̀ɳì, fɔ̀ɳìfɔ̀ɳì, fùɳìfùɳì, also
T. **fɔ̀(nì)fɔ̀nì**, a. **àŋgɔ̌ 'dɔ̀rï
fɔ̀ɳìfɔ̀ɳì-rö** the ground is pale/
grey (from pulverized stones, and
easy for digging).

fɔ́ɳɔ́kɔ̌ (or -**kɔ̌**), n. crumbs, fragment, bit, odd bits; **ɛ́ɳá f—** scraps
of polenta.

fɔ́rá, n. powder (of any kind);
àɳá-fɔ́rá corn powder, i.e. flour;
ɳakú (or **ɛ́rí**)-**fɔ́rá** ground dust;
pätǐ f— sawdust; also **fɔ́ra** rubbish, waste, refuse; **fɔ́rá'rö** in
powder form; **árɔ́ fɔ́rárö** medicine in powder.

förö-zà, vn./a. worn by rubbing;
defaced; ground down; baldheaded; **ágú 'dà mà drì förö-
zà-rö** that man's head is bald.

fərə, fərətə(tɔ̌)rö, a. **ɛmvɛ f—**

dirty white, (ash-) grey; yellowish
grey.

fɔ́rɔ̀fɔ́rɔ̌, same as **fɔ́lɔ́fɔ́lɔ̌**, q.v.

fu¹, vt. to kill (properly and figuratively; **'di** to kill with arms, only);
to try hard, to press hard; **àbírí**
(or **ìyí-kɔ̀rɛ, əzɔ́ɔ́** ...) **fu ma kái**
hunger (thirst, rain) press me
hard, I am very hungry (thirsty,
caught in rain); **əzɔ́ɔ́nï ǹdrí fu
'dà, mà mu ètrɔ̌** the rain strikes
the goat (tied there in the grass),
go and set it free (to take shelter).

fu² **ru** (= **rö**), vr. to wrestle,
struggle with; **è mû fu ru**! go
and wrestle! **kànì à fu àma mvá
gaa 'dǐ bɛ, tsa mánǐ (àfúa sǐ) kö**
if I wrestle with this small boy,
he will be no match for me;
àfúã-àfútá, n. wrestling; **ndè èrì
àfúã sǐ** he defeated him in wrestling; **à fu té àma á'dǐánï bɛ rá,
à ko àma rá** I have fought with
NN., we have now separated;
a'ú gbɛ fu ru rá the egg broke.

fu³, drì fu, vn. (1) to meet with a p.
(**'bá bɛ**); **à fu drì 'bá àzínï bɛ
gìrǐà** I met a person on the way;
(2) (= **tsa**) to suffice, be sufficient;
ɛ́ɳá 'dǐ fu drì 'bá möödrí sǐ rá
this polenta is sufficient for ten
people; (3) to be up to standard,
perfect; **fu drì tsǐ: àfa áŋgǐrí
tsápi mǐnǐ rá** it is amply sufficient: such a quantity will suffice
for you; **mvá 'dà mà ɔkpɔ́ fu
drì tsǐ** the strength of that boy is
well up to standard; **nì àzí báònï
fu drì** he knows the work of
carpentry fully.

fúlúdúdú, av. **àlí f—** short and
thick, plump, buxom.

fúlúlú, n. fine dust (carried about
by wind).

fúnɔ̀, n. ground-nuts; **ma fúnɔ̀
əpǐ** I am shelling ground-nuts.

fùṇìfùṇì = föṇìföṇì (q.v.), a.
grey, dust-, dirty-grey; əyəə mà
'bíkə fùṇìfùṇì-rö the grivet
monkey is grey.
fùrùfùrù, a. soft (to touch).
fúrúfùrù, n. lungs.
fútúfútú'ru, a. foamy; ɛ́wá mà
óbúrúsòṇì ɛŋgá f— the froth
rises foamy from the (working)
beer.

G

gà, vn. to crawl, walk on hands and
feet; èrì gǎ-gà vàálé sǐ he (baby)
is crawling on the ground.
gà... sǐ, vn. to refuse; ò kó gà ǹdrî
zá sǐ (èndzìtá sǐ) the woman
refuses goat-meat (as also sheep,
fowl)(taboo, with awe); gà +verb
+kə sǐ to refuse to ... ; gǎ emú
kə sǐ they refused to come.
ga¹, vn. to be full; (note peculiar
construction: i.e. things are full in
-á or sǐ): bòŋgô ga sàndúkù-á
tré, mǐ əmǐ vàálé! the trunk is
full of cloths (in Logbara only:
cloths are in a completely filling
quantity in the trunk), press them
down! é bè ìyí ɛ́mvóa, ìyí mà ga
ɛ́mvóa tré! fill the pot with
water! (Logbara lit. pour water in
the pot, that water may be in a
filling-up quantity in the pot!) ìyî
ga ɛ́mvóa tré; èrì ga trée kpɛrɛ
ɛ́mvó mà ti vǒ sǐ our: the pot is
brim-full (Logbara lit. the water
is full in the pot; it is filling up
fully up to the brim); tî ga lítsóa
(or lítsó sǐ) tré, also; tí lítsóa tré
cattle are in a filling-up capacity
in the pen (our: the pen is full of
cattle).
ga², vt. (1) to cut, hew; ga pätí
ògara sǐ he cut a tree with an
axe; (2) to dig (cf. 'bílé); mà ga
óṇa mà 'bílé mǒkɛ́! one may

dig a nice hole for (collecting) termites! (3) to bite (of snake); líṇï
mâ ga ɛ́nï sǐ the 'li' (snake) bit me
by night; (4) to ache; mâ drìnï̀
gàga my head aches (I have a
headache); (5) ga rö to split,
crack; burst; zúkùlû ga rö rá
the gourd has split; (6) to strike/
scratch; é ga tìbìrítì! light (lit.
strike/scratch) a match!
ga³, vn. (startle, alarm)(1) èkélè ga
to cough; (2) to cry/shout (as for
notifying death); èì lúlû ga 'bánï
drà sǐ they shout death-notice;
(3) ga tsï to give a sudden start,
to 'stop breathing' at (Ac. ŋaàŋ);
á ga tsï èrinï ma ɛlí-rï̀ sǐ I gave
a start when he took me by surprise; ɛrindi-nï̀ ga tsï kìlé gbï̀
èrì gbï̀ lé he got out of breath as
if he had been shot at; 'bá
òndzírï̀ kànì nĕ kàlï̀ èrì ga tsï
if a bad man sees a stick, he gets
alarmed.
gaa⁴, dim., gãã, a. small, little;
few; gaa kaṇà-rö (T. gaa (ká)
ndíârö) very small ...; á lè mvâ
gãârï̀ mà emú má vǒ I want a
small boy to come to me.
gǎgǎ = kórékɛ or kórókɛ, n.
crow, raven; èrì ënïrö, ómbé-
lékòṇï ɛmvèrö it is black with
white neck (breast).
galáá, T. = óní, n. snake (general
term).
gala'bá, n. the grey-brown spitting snake (cobra?); èrì 'bá tsï
ŋgbí, 'yoonï tòò it bites a p.
painfully, it is very poisonous.
gàlàkà or ògàlàká = kàlàbà, n.
one kind of tall graminia (cf.
àlàká).
gàṇà = gàgáṇà, a. restless, capri-
cious, thoughtless, wanton; vague;
mï̀ mà g— tö you are utterly
thoughtless (in moving and touch-

ing everything); **ɛ̀ri atsí tɔ̀** he rambles/loafs about lightheartedly.

gaṇagaṇa'rö, a. shaky, tottering, unsteady; **mvá 'dɪ̌ atsí gaṇagaṇa'rö** the baby walks shakily.

gàràlà-rɪ̀, gàɪ̀gáɪ̀-rö, a. having abnormal sideways extensions or accessories (as a cross, aeroplane . . .) in relationto its other dimensions.

gáráma = àtràkàlɛ́, n. branch; **pätí g—** branch of a tree.

gáͬrì, n. bicycle.

gáͬrí, n. rainbow; **g— nɪ̈ ɔzɔ́ɔ́ 'alɛ́ àsɪ̈** the rainbow stops the rain; **ɛ̀ri ɔzɔ́ɔ́ milɛ́ ɛrɛ rá, ɔzɔ́ɔ́ 'di ànɪ̈ kö** it disperses the rain which therefore does not fall.

gbà = tsə, vt. to beat, strike; **é gbà édrɔ́ kàlí sɪ̈!** strike the mouse with the stick! **ɛ́'dá gbǎ** to make a photo (picture); **ɔ̀gbà,** vt. to ward off; **ɛ̀ri 'yɛ́ ɔ̀gbǎ kàlí sɪ̈** he parried the arrow with a stick.

gbagbà, gbagbǎ = kùànà, n. (1) trap (of any size); (2) gallows (of the Government).

gbálá = gbárálá, T., n. arm ring (of ivory or iron).

gbandà, n. cassava or manioc root; **èì g— sa 'bílɪ̈a, ṇàṇa** they dig/plant cassava in (the earth) (a tuber), for eating.

gbándzá (= déènò), A.S. n. loan, debt; **á lɛ̀ mɪ́ ɛ̀fɛ̀ mánɪ́ sìlíŋgì àlö gbándzârö (or déènòrö)** I wish you to lend me 1s.; **fɛ̀ gb'- rö** to lend, loan; **('du) gbándzâ ṇa** to borrow sth. of; **mvá 'dɪ̌ 'du mâ déènò sìlíŋgì àlö** this boy borrowed 1s. off me; **ɛ̀fɛ̀ (or edzí, əmvi, ɔ̀gɔ̀) ŋgà mâ àfa kö** he has not yet returned my property (paid his debt); **'du mâ bɔ̀ŋgɔ́ gbándzâ²rö; ɛ̀rì 'yɛ əmvi .'íì**

vɔ̌ he borrowed my cloth; he will return it to its owner.

gbàŋgìlò, n. gad-fly; **g— nɪ̈ gbé sɔ̌ tí mà ŋgókóa; tínɪ̈ ɔ́ǎ ndzo oŋgú drìá** the 'gbaŋygilo' lays her eggs on the back of cattle; cows start running.

gbàrà = tsootí, av. instantly, at once; **mu rá etsá g—** he went and returned immediately.

gbàràkà, n. the floor of a granary **(ɛ̀rɔ́ g—** the whole supported by four legs); **g— ɛ̀ri ɛrɔ́ ɛtɪ̈; èì g— tsǎ ɛlɛlú sɪ̌ g —** is the bottom of the granary; they plait it with 'ɛlɛlu' sticks.

gbàrànàarö, a. fully rounded off; **mvá 'dàrɪ̈ 'alɛ́ bɛ g—** that child has a full-rounded belly.

gbǎärù, av. with noise; **ɛ'dɛ́ rá ṇɔ̀ 'ɪ̈ g—** it fell and broke noisily.

gbé, n. egg; **a'ú gbé** fowl's egg; **a'ú gbé mà ɔ́bɔ́rɔ́kə (= ɔ́'bɔ́kə, hɔ̀rɔ̀ŋgɔ́tɔ̀)** the shell of a fowl's egg; **gbé sɔ̌** to lay eggs (cf. **rɪ̈, əga).**

gbɛ, vt. to vomit; **ɛ̀ri lésû gbɛ** he vomits milk; **ɔ̀tsé ɔgbé àfa ɛrinɪ̈ ṇa 'dɪ̌ì vàá** the dog has vomited what it has eaten.

gbè, vn. to draw or pucker up one's mouth for weeping; **é gbè té à'do sɪ̈ yà?** why were you about to weep a moment ago?

gbɛ, vt. **ɛ'yɔ̂ gbɛ** to impute, attribute fault . . . to; **é gbɛ ɛ'yó mâ drìá** you have put the blame for the matter on me.

gbèɛ́ = ɔ̀bálákɔ́, n. the jackal; **ɛ̀ri oŋgû ndzo tɔ̀** it runs very fast.

gbèléfɛ, n. name of a cane growing on riversides and used as walking-stick especially by old persons; **ɔ̀kó àmbó èì atsí g— sɪ̈** old women walk with a cane.

ġbéré, n. a fairly large calabash; ġ— èri èġá àmbónï; èri pï kérềrö 'gbɛrɛ' is a large calabash; it grows like a pumpkin; ġ— lésú or ɛ́wá ɔsó (= dà) ző for pouring/ portioning out milk, beer.

ġbï¹, vt. to shoot (arrow, gun); àmà mu àṇ̀apâ ġbï ásɛa 'dálé zârö, ṇaazàrö we are going to shoot game on the veldt for meat, to eat.

ġbï², vt. to produce honey; àṇ̀ú ġbï sú bɛ törő mà 'aléa bees produce honey in the hive.

ġbï³, vt. to plait; èi bírísì ġbï they plait mats (for lying on).

ġbï⁴, vn. to grow, develop; päti mà mvá èri ġbï-ġbï päti mà rùa a small plant (parasite) comes forth/grows on the body of a tree.

ġbítíġbítï = tókítóki, a. even, regular, smooth; dzó mà drì rùáni èri ġ— the (grass) roof of the hut is even (not in steps).

ġbó¹, n. side, flank (below armpit); á kpɔ̀ búkù ġbóa I held the book under my shoulder/arm.

ġbó² = á'bulé, n. valley, depression along watercourses; iyí ġbótiá on the side of rivers; iyí ġbóa = iyí-tiá on the bank/side of a river; èri iyí ġbó 'à kákâ-rö he cultivates the side of the river for maize.

ġbö, vt. (1) (= ali) to divide; ġbő dzó 'alé irrì they divided the interior of the hut into two; dzó mà 'alé ali ru irrì the hut is divided into two; (2) to push/ shove aside, to elbow (one's way through . . ., or) aside; é ġbö andzi 'dï amvélé! push/elbow the children away!/outside.

ġbəkə, n. well-beaten track, way, road (= ndsìlá); ġ— èri ġèrìkɔ̀ 'bá ádarï pinï tí bɛ atsí-ző àni

tȍrȉ a way which man and cattle alike walk on.

ġbólé, n. corner; angle; dzó (mà) ġ— corner (or angle) of hut/room.

ġbɔ́ló, n. roughly hewn plank to lie on: bedstead; ġ— 'báni laa-ző-rï plank for man to lie on; èri bằo Lógbàrà-nï ɛdé-rï a board the Logbara make.

ġbólókɔ̀-ètí = ġbílítɔ̀-'bí, T. ɔ̀wílé(kɔ̀)-ètí, n. armpit.

ġbȍṇà, a. long and flowing; ndrí 'dà mà 'bíkə ġ—(ġ—)rö the goat has long flowing hair.

ġbóroa, n. dark-grey very poisonous snake; ɔ̀mbàni tȍ, èri 'bâ tsïtsï it is very fierce, it bites man.

ġbərətə, n. old, decrepit, infirm; tí ġ— old bony cow.

ġbúlúku, n. (large black) ground hornbill.

ġɛlɛkűã, n. ball-gourd calabash (with small opening on top); ġ— tí (mà) lésû zə-ző ball-calabash for milking cows.

ġềrì, ġìrì, ġềrìkɔ̀, n. (1) path, way, road; ġ— ŋ̀gɔ̀ sȉ yà? by which way? ġ— mu-ző Árúwá-lé-rï ŋ̀gɔ̀? which is the way to Arua? (2) fig. direction; way, manner; place; ġ— wɛrɛ sȉ by a short way, in short.

ġì = dzì, T. Y. . . . same as 'i (q.v.), vt. to hang up . . .

ġi = dzì, T. Y. . . . same as 'i (q.v.), vn. to take refuge behind; . . . àma ɛġí bàrádzàá 'dólé ɔzóó sȉ we took refuge from rain under this veranda; dzì pa rö 'bá àzï vő he fled to sby.

ġi, Y. = drí hand.

ġìlìġìlì (= dzìrö), a. at twilight, in the dusk; àŋ̀gȍ èri ġ—, lè bȉ ɛnȉrö it is dusk/dawning (the day is breaking) . . . the night is setting in.

ginəkɔ or ginəkɔ́á²rö, a. meagre, lean, emaciated; mvá 'dï̀ ginəkɔ̂ rö (òízà-rö, əsɛ kö) the child is lean (not fat).

gìɲí, n. particular dance; g̈— tö to dance 'giɲi'.

gírígírí, ꞌrö, a. of a lumpy, knotted, gnarled, knobby surface; ə'bɛ́ or ə̀'bà 'ï̀ g̈— it looks lumpy.

gìrìlíti = gìrìlɔ́, n. attack of indigestion; ɛ̀ri g̈— 'dɔ̂ he is suffering from (an attack of) indigestion.

gɔ̌¹ rö, vn. to fall down (losing balance); ɛ̀ì pätí gâga; pätíníꞌ gɔ̌ rö (= ɛ'dɛ́) ànïꞌ they cut a tree and the tree then falls down; mvá wɛrɛ́á 'dï̀ gɔ̈rö nïꞌ the small child falls to the ground; é kà éwâ mvu tɔ̌, mïꞌ ɔ̀gɔ̌ rö ɔ̀gɔ̌ if you drink much beer, you fall down; ɛ̀ri 'ïꞌ gɔ̌ 'dálɛ́ it is sloping/falling thither.

gɔ̌², vt. to shovel; ɛ̀ri (tí mà) wɔ́rɔ́tɔ̀ gɔ̌ he is shovelling up/out (on his knees, with both hands) cow dung.

gö = atíꞌ, vt. to give the last stroke/push/finishing stroke towards defeat or death; é gɔ̂ díꞌ ɛ̀ri göɲökö! give him the finishing (death) stroke (or decisive stroke to defeat)!

gɔ̌ = a'bïꞌ, n. the rest from a'bïꞌ; ɛ̀ì a'bïꞌ ꞌa gɔ̌ ꞌrö they eat the rest of an 'a'bi' meal.

gó = gólɛ́, n. a hole in a wall, tree, or anything; àríꞌïá nïꞌ ti goá birds nest in tree-holes; (gólɛ́ the inside excavation/space; gó the opening appearing outside).

go, ègo, n. heavy, rough-hewn board with an elevated crest in the middle; through this elevation three holes are made for poles; this piece of hurdle serves to shut up the opening of a cattle pen ɛ̀ì tálánï̀ lɔ̌ nna; ɛ̀ì ànïꞌ lítsɔ́ tilɛ́ 'bǎ, òpì-òpì; go lítsɔ́ tilɛ́ 'bà-zɔ̌rï̀.

gɔ̀, ègɔ̀, vn. to return; ɛ̀ì díꞌ gɔ̀ (= atri) drì vélɛ́ they go back now.

gə̀'bɛ, dim. gə̀'biǎ, n. a basket.

gɔ̀'dɔ̀, n. kind of durra; ə̀ndó gɔ̀'dɔ̀-rö ɛ̀ri ɛkȁrö the 'gɔ'dɔ' durra is red.

gə'dɔ, gɔkə'dɔ, a. bent, curved; pätí 'dï̀ gə'dɔ-gə'dɔ²rö this tree is crooked.

gógóá, n. a kind of midge.

gökɛ, n. (1) (= túlúlúa) large (cow...) horn used for blowing 'bá vȍvö; (2) (= tsɔ́lɔ́kpɔ́) small horn (sometimes the hoof of a cow tí-pá) used for keeping oil, glue; g̈— ə'yó 'bá ànïꞌ ésɛ́sɛ́ sɔ̌ a horn they pour in glue.

gɔ̀ókɔ̀, n. [kitchen; or] quite rudimentary temporary shelter, or hut-frame with grass spread on it as roof (without walls); ɛ̀ri dzɔ̂ laa zɔ̌rïꞌ'ï̀ or, according to others, also tà a'díꞌ-zɔ̌rïꞌ'ï̀ a 'hut' to lie in; . . . to cook in.

gólɛ́ (cf. gó), n. hole (space inside; maybe under water); ɛ̀'bínïꞌ fïꞌ zɔ̌ used as refuge by fishes (among river grass) or other animals.

góolíꞌ, n. a well-pointed stick or pole to make holes; g̈— 'bílɛ́ ɛga zɔ̌ to 'cut' holes.

gɔ̀lí-gɔ̀líꞌ, gɔ́níꞌ-gɔ́níꞌ, gɔ̀nɔ̀-gɔ̀nɔ̀, a. bent, crooked, tortuous, twisted (of wood/tree, stick, rope, way, talk . . .).

gɔ̀lìꞌ, n. fishing-hook; g̈— ɛ̀'bíꞌ 'ï̀ zɔ̌ hook for fishing.

gɔ̀lɔ̀kɔ̀, a. very high; ásɛ́ g̈— very tall grass.

gǝmbɛrɛ = ɛnï (rikǝ), n. hide, skin, coat (prepared); g̈— laa-zǒ to lie on.

gǝndɛ̀, n. arrow with barbs; 'yɛ́ 'dï gǝndɛ̀-rö, ɛ̀ri sô bɛ this arrow is a 'gǝndɛ', it has barbs.

g̈ǝní-g̈ǝní = g̈ǝlíg̈ǝlí, q.v. a. ǝná (or ǝmí) 'ï g̈—g̈—rö it (road, river, tree) moves/goes along winding/meandering in zigzags; ɛ'yǝ́ g̈—g̈— obscure, confused, evasive, words/talk.

gǝnǝ̀-gǝnǝ̀ = g̈ǝlí-g̈—, q.v. ɛ̀zǒ g̈—g̈— long-curved, twisted.

gǝnǝ-gǝnǝ, gǝnǝkǝ, g̈ǝlǝkǝ = ɒ̀ízà, a. lean-sick, thin, decrepit, infirm; ǹdrí g̈—g̈— a meagre goat (about to die).

gönörö, g̈önökörö, 'rö, a. contracted, cowered/squatted down; tra 'ï g̈öŋ̈ökö he cowered down.

g̈örà, a. long, shaggy, waving, floating; ɛ̀ri drìbbí bɛ g̈— she (a white girl) has long waving hair; ǹdrí-ǒ'bí ǝŋgǒ tö-zǒrǐ ɛ̀ri g̈— g̈— rö the dancing quiver-stick is long and shaggy.

g̈örɛ̀, g̈ùrɛ́, n. small receptacle (of bark stripped off a tree, or the like) used for churning milk ɛ̀ì lésú sǒ ànï; ɛ̀ì ɛ́sɛ́ sǒ ànï àrǐïá ǝ'bà-zǒ they pour glue in it to use it for catching birds.

g̈ǝrí-g̈ǝrí = kǝ̀rí-kǝ̀rí, tsìŋ̈í-tsìŋ̈í, a. variegated, streaky, striped; ǝ'dó lɛ́ as a leopard.

g̈örilo, ɒ̀ì-g̈—, a. lean, thin, meagre/ill; 'bá ɒ̀ìpì ɒ̀ì-ɒ̀í-rǐ an emaciated, ill-conditioned person; ǝ'dó ɒ̀ì-g̈— the leopard had become lean.

g̈ǝr'ǝbílǝ̀ kàníkàní, n. whidah-finch, -bird; sǒbínï ɛ̀zǒ it has a long tail.

g̈öróŋ̈a (a distant variety of yams? this produces the tuber in the ground, while . . .), n. a climbing plant producing tubers on the plant with likewise tuberous roots (both eaten); g̈— ɛ̀ri ka pätí sía (on the tree); ǒlánï fï 'búa its tuberous root develops in the soil.

g̈u¹ (= dì), vn. (1) to (give) light, to shine (forth); àtsǐ gu (or dì) lɛ̀ɛ-lɛ̀ɛ the fire beams, radiates brightly; (2) to glitter, gleam, sparkle; búkù 'dǐ mà ti gu ndrǐndrǐ (= 'yɛ ndrǐndrǐ) the (gilded) edge of this book gleams; tìndiirì ɛ̀ri gu ŋ̈á-ŋ̈á-ŋ̈á the glow-worm gleams (at times).

g̈u², ǝ̀gu, T.Y., n. lower part of spine, lumbar region.

g̈u³, vn. to laugh; é gu 'bá àzínï (mà drìá) kö! do not laugh at (deride, make fun of) other people! á gu tɒ̀ǝkó I laughed for no special reason; ɛ̀ri gu mání tsìŋ̈àa he smiles at me (all over his face).

g̈ùu, g̈ùumù, or g̈ìimà, av. shaded; àŋgǒ ɛ'dé (pätí-bbì sǐ, erítí sǐ) g̈ùu it has become shaded (through tree foliage, clouds).

g̈ùbɛ̀rɛ̀ = 'bbàràá, n. sparrow-hawk.

gufà, ɒ̀gufà, n. backbone or spine.

g̈ûg̈űűá, n. midges; ɛ̀ri a'á ìyí mà drià 'bùá, ɛ̀ri 'bá tsǐtsǐ they stay above the water, they bite.

g̈úrú, a. depressed, concave; àŋgǒ g̈— low-lying ground, depression, deepening (as of lakes); 'bílé 'alé g̈— the hole/cave is deep; àŋgǒ g̈—g̈— ɛ̀ri 'bílêrö a depression is as if excavated; ɛdzɛ̀nï g̈— its side is hollowed, cut out, concave; àŋgǒ g̈— ǝmbɛ̀-nïrǐ the hollow between clavicles (on neck).

guti, ŋ̈gúrùkúti, n. same as gufà.

H

hái! intj. surprise 'is that so! very well, then!' ɛ'yó à'ĭ-zŏ expression of approval.

hàohào, hàhào-rö, a. coarse, rough; hard-stiff; bǎŏ èri h—, èri 'bá òsì-òsì the plank is rough, it scratches; bòŋgónï àŋgà-zŏ h— 'dĭ (ètúa) when a cloth dries stiffly (in the sun).

háŏhàŏ, a. light, of small weight; bòŋgó h— rö the cloth is light.

hɔɔ = huu, hwáhwa, hwéhwɛ, a. (1) hollow, empty inside; (2) not tightly or closely set, loosely (with gaps) set; dzó drì hòòrö (hùùru) ɔzòónï tĭ ànï (or tĭtĭ) the hut-roof is not compact enough, rain trickles in; ɔzòó tĭpi dzó-drì huurĭ sĭ rain trickling from loosely set roof; àfa 'dĭ tálá lŏ rö 'bɔ, ɛná hùùru this thing is pierced (by insects . . .), one sees through; a stone worn out by grinding so as to be partly transparent, is hɔŏ- or huù-rö (or hórɔ-hórɔ, q.v.).

hòrò-hòrò- = hàohào-rö, a. hoarse, rough, husky; mĭ olíkò h—h—rö your voice is hoarse.

hórɔ-hórɔ, hɔrɔkɔtɔ, ˟rö, a. light, thin, loose, threadbare transparent (from poor make or structure); atsɛ́ hórɔhórɔ (pérɛ-pérɛ), èrì 'yɛ dĕdè it became/ remained quite thin (some article, or stone), it will soon be consumed/ finished.

hórɔ(ǎ)kókŏ-rö = mù, a. noise-lessly, unnoticed, unobserved, stealthily; é 'du hórɔ-kórŏrö à'do sĭ yà? why did you take it without the least noise?

hòròŋgótò, hòròŋgótò, òhórókótɔ, sórókɔ, i.e. = atsɛ́pirĭ, n. the

remains (after the contents are removed; hence) hornet's nest; àɳ̊ú h— honeycomb; kànì ndzu àɳ̊ú mà ósò rá, atsɛ́pi 'dĭ èì ɔmvɛ àɳ̊ú-h— after having removed the honey, the comb remains; a'ú-gbé h— eggshell.

hùù-ru see hɔɔ.

hwàai ká! T. = ŋgà ká! háai! mǎtĭ! be calm! leave off, please! let it be! sorry, sorry! excuse me!

hwèɛ, T. = fĭ, vn. to burst, explode.

hwéhwɛ̀rö, see hɔɔ.

h(w)éré = wórɔ́, av. all.

hwérɛ, av. quickly, instantly; é ŋga ɛ'yó sĭ h— (= mbèlè) ká! start immediately with the question!

hwèrè, av. rustling (on stroking, sweeping . . .); àŋgŏ wɛɛ lé (or zŏ) yófé sĭ, èrì 'yɛ h—(h—) on sweeping with a broom, it rustles.

hwĭ́, av. of a sudden, abruptly, with a jerk; vŏ hwĭ́ he blew it off abruptly; 'du àfa 'dĭ hwĭ́ all of a sudden he snapped it; ŋga hwĭ́ 'bɔ he departed all of a sudden.

hwĭ́á = fĭfĭ́(á), n. kind of reed grass/stalks (hollow); a hive prepared with such stalks but not yet occupied by bees.

hwĭ́lĭ́lĭ́'rö, a. ɛmvɛ h— snow-white, brightly-white; m̀bá èr ɛmvɛ h— the moon is/shines bright(ly).

hwĭlĭ́, a. half-, in part cleaned, shaven; mvá 'dĭ mà drì h— the child is half-shaven.

I

ĭ¹ (= gĭ, T.), vt. to light, kindle fire; é 'ĭ àtsí lèɛ, 'bá nĕ àŋgŏ ànï! light a blazing fire, that one may see by it! 'ĭ àtsí àtölŏkŏá she kindled fire in the hearth;

əvï (or àtsí) 'ï àŋgŏ the lightning (the fire) has lit up the place.

'ï² (T.Y. = gì, dzì), vt. (1) to fasten, tie to (-á) with rope; é 'ï tí ə'yóá (or əmbèlɛkòá)! tie the cow by its horns (or neck)! mĭ ə̀ 'ï tíĭ lítsóa (álɔ́ mà sía)! fasten the cattle in the pen (to their pegs)! é 'ï ǹdrí 'dìrï 'dé (= 'dĭá)! fasten the goat there! (2) to hang up; á 'ï kĭfóŋgà 'bùá 'bə I have hung up the key; 'ï bòŋgɔ́ oru they hung up the cloths; 'ï rö to hang o-s.; 'ï 'ï bá sĭ he hanged himself with a rope; (3) è'bĭ 'ï-zŏ to fish/angle.

'ï and e'ï (T.Y. = gï agï, dzï adzí) (≃ apa), vn. to escape (danger), to take refuge (or shelter) with a p. (or under one's roof); mĭ e'í rá you escaped safely (hither); 'bá àzínï 'ï (= ɛdrí) dzɔ́ 'aléa ndrí a man succeeded in taking refuge in the interior of the hut.

'i, vt. (1) properly: to grind (corn...); then: to grind and cook; to prepare (food) àɳá, ɛ́ɳá, ɳaaká ³'ï zɔ̌; ɛ̀ri ŋgà àɳâ 'ï'i; dɛ ŋgà kö she is only just grinding the corn (food), it is not yet ready; ɔ̀kó 'i ɛ́ɳâ zá sĭ the woman prepared polenta with meat; é 'i àɳá mbèlɛmbèlè, 'bâ ɳa ɛ́ɳá ànï! grind the corn quickly, so that people may have their polenta! (2) to polish (by rubbing, grinding surface); ɛ̀i émvó tĭ 'i à'dú sĭ they polish the brim of the pot with black ochre.

'ï, prs. pron. he, she; him-, herself (when it refers to the speaker or the person introduced; with reflexive verbs 'ï = rö; tsə 'ï (= rö) rá he struck himself; 'ïmà, 'ï-drí, &c., his, her . . . .

ïï, ïï-ïï (= bïrï-bïrï), av. steadily, attentively, eagerly; tínï ìyî mvu ïï-ïï, ìyí kɔ̀rɛ fu té ɛ̀ri kái the cow drinks water steadily (protractedly), because she was very thirsty; é sɔ̀ pá ïï, á lɛ̀ mĭ ti ɛrí! keep on standing, because I want to hear you.

ii a lightly stressing particle after imperative; è mû dí ii! so you go then! kèni, á mu ii! they say, I may go!

ïï (1) vt. to let drop on/in, place; pour; é ïï àfadzóa! pour it into the vessel! ma bùrŏsŏ əmvŏ ïï àfadzóa I am collecting (with both hands forming cup) pigeon peas and pouring them into a vessel; ɛ̀i àkúfï ïï éwá 'aléa, éwá mà dra ànï; (2) vn. to drop, fall lightly; əzɔ́ɔ́ ïï ddíká it drizzles again; əzɔ́ɔ́nï ïï-ïï it is drizzling; əzɔ́ɔ́nï ɔ̀ïï-ɔ̀ïï it drizzles (more) heavily.

'ï rö, vr. (more commonly e'ï rö, q.v.) to boast, brag, vaunt (of sĭ); ɛ̀ri rö 'ï'ï he is boasting; 'ï rö (= 'ï) 'ïmà mvá sĭ she bragged of her child; 'ï or 'ïtá, n. boastfulness, vainglory, pride; ɛ̀ri 'ï (or àfó) bɛ he is boastful, proud, talking big.

'íi or 'ípi, n. owner, proprietor; dzɔ́ 'dĭ mà 'íi-nï à'dï 'ï yà? who is the owner of this hut? àfa 'dĭ mà 'ípi (or 'bá) ɛ̀ri ŋgɔ́ yà? where is the owner of this thing?

ïi (= ? ìyí), n. water; ïi mvu-zàrö water for drinking; ïi bòŋgɔ́ ɔ̀dzì zɔ̌ water for washing cloths; riverbed: ïi gɛ̀rì, ïi lɔ̀ré, ïi ɔ́rĭlɛ́, ïi kiritâ, ïi kùlé; water-fall: ïi kùrù; wave (whirlpool): ïi éfï or ïi ágɔ́gɔ́fï; ìyí kɔ̀rɛ fu ɛ̀ri kái he/she is very thirsty; ïi àraa running water; ïi àlĭó-rĭ, ïi tsi-päri̇̀, ìí líröpìrì, ìí bằlì stagnant water, lake (= ? ìí líröpärï).

ìí-drì-puuru, plu. n. lotus flower; èrì ə'ằ ìí pá sŏpì tsírì mà 'aléa it is standing upright in the water (roots in the ground below).

ídzío, see édzío.

ìíka, n./a. early beans, &c., planted on waterside ósŏ ìíka 'bánï 'ằ/fằ ámvú ìí-g̣bóá m̀bá nna sìrì'ï, èì əmvɛ ìíka grown on waterside, sown in March.

ì(y)íkì = ərà, see éíkì, vt./vn. to think, ponder; èrì àfa àzínïìíkì or èrì ìíkì àfa àzínï mà drìá he is reflecting/meditating...on sth.; ìíkî = əràtáa, n. thought, reflexion, meditation, rumination (probably the form éíkì is more commonly used).

ílégí, ílézí, see elegí.

ìílìmà or ì(l)ímàì̇̀(?), a. əzɔ́ɔ́ ì— drizzling rain; əzɔ́ɔ́ ìílìmà-nï ɔ̀ï̇̀ it is drizzling.

ìí-əŋgəŋg̣ɔ̂ã, n. bird; Hydrometra paladum (?).

ìí-púrũɑ̃́, n. bird/snipe, woodcock (?).

ìrrì, num. 2, two; ìrrì-zŏrì second.

ïrí (more usual ɛrí), vt. (1) to repent (of sì̇̀); èrì ïrí ògù sì̇̀ rá he repents of stealing; mï̇̀ ïrí 'bə yà? do you repent? ïrí atsítáa Átsì-drìá bɛ-rì sì̇̀ rá he regrets having walked with 'Atsidria'; èrì ŋga ïrí drì-ndzá sì̇̀ rá he will repent out of shame; (2) to delay; to cause a p. to delay (in any way); mï̇̀ ïrí ma kírikíri 'dínï à'do ɛ'yó sì̇̀ yà? why do you keep me back (say working on field, almost) forcibly? (see ɛrí).

ítí̇̀, see étí̇̀, n. tamarind.

ítri, see étri, n. kingfisher.

ìí-tsakȫa or ìítsa-rùánìá-kö, n.

a mud- (mole-) cricket (with a waterproof 'cloth-covering'); èrì əvö ɔ̀rɛtékɔ̀ 'aléa it lives in mud (water not reaching its body, says the name).

ítsɔ́, T., elsewhere lítsɔ́, n. cattle pen.

ítù also ótù commonly étù, n. borassus palm.

íví, éví, ímví, ɲáɲá, n. alkaline soil; n̄drí èrì íví tsï̇̀ goats lick alk. ground.

ìyá-bǎ-yə, ìyá-yə, bǎ-yə! kind of intj. 'nothing happened'! 'there is nothing to be found!' ìyá(bǎ) àfa 'dá yə! 'there is nothing' (answer to some curious inquiry). N.B. For other possible ì- words see under y-.

K

kà¹, pl. ká (= kànì with distinct construction), cj. if; when, whenever; andzi ká àzî̇̀ ŋga kö, esú àfa kö if the boys do not (unless the boys) work, they will not find anything; n̄drí kà èríbî ɲa 'bə, mï̇̀ ètrɔ̀ èrì àkúa when the goat has eaten grass, you unfasten it to go home.

kà²/kâ mu...zŏ kö, cj. in order that...not; lest...; dzí 'bá 'dìï̇̀ hóspítáliá, kâ mu drằ (zŏ) kö they took the p. to the hospital, so that they might not die (cf. Grammar).

kà³(-nì) trə...tě,...(trŏ), cj. even if; although (cf. Grammar).

kà⁴, vt. (= tsà) to intertwine, -lace, plait; èrì ásé kằ (= tsằ) èró-drì 'bö-zŏ he interlaces grass to cover the roof of the granary.

kà⁵ (cf. rì̇̀), vt. to use sparingly, economize (for lack) (said of savoury at meal); èrì tíbí kằ he takes very little savoury (with polenta).

ka¹, vn. to shine; **ètú ka àndrò rá** (**əzɔ́ónï adri-zɵ́ yə-rǐ sǐ**) we have sunshine today (i.e. no rain); **ètúkà kǎka, əzɔ́ónï àlö-nï yə; ŋaaká nï ɔ̀drà pǐrǐ rá** the sunshine goes on without any rain, so that the corn dies completely.

ka², vn. to become hot; **àyà àtsía 'délérǐ èrì ka ɛkǎrö** the iron in the fire there is becoming red-hot.

ka³, vn. (1) to start forming, developing (of fruit); **àŋaánï ŋgà kǎka; àŋá ka ŋgà kö** the corn is still only forming, it is not yet developed; (2) to produce in (great) quantity; **pätí 'dǐ mà éfǐ ka** (= **'a, eezó**) **wǐïrǐ** the tree is full of fruits.

ka⁴, vt. to bewitch; **ərí ka** (= **fè àzó**) **'ïnǐ nǐ; 'ï kà tǐ li rá, 'ïmà àzɔ́nǐ ŋga əkə** (= **àtǐ**) **rá** a spirit (of a dead p.) has bewitched him (made sick); when he has killed an ox, his illness will cease! **'ǐ ŋgà pa rö rá** he will escape (death).

ká, particle of colloquial/polite question; **mǐ ti edzǎ 'dólé ká yà!** will you, kindly, turn this way!

kàabèlá, kèbèlé, n. oyster (-shell, used as spoon?), or similarly spoon-shaped piece of calabash; **èi ètsé ɛdě kàabèlârö 'ï, èi ànï éŋá əva** they prepare a piece of calabash as a spoon and stir polenta with it.

kàabìlə̀, n. sheep.

kàdà, a. flabby, drooping (of a soft solid mass); **elí mádrí zá k—** (= **akázàrö**) they cut me a nice piece of pendent flesh; **áŋú 'bánï sǐ érà driárǐ sǐ, èri k—** sesame which they grind on a stone, it

moves (as a solid mass) up and down (**k—**).

kàdrì-kàdrì, a. supple, long and flexible (up and down).

kàdrù-kàdrù = **kɔ̀ndrɔ́ndrɔ́, T.** (Plu.: **èzɵ́ pĕtsɔ̀pĕtsɔ̀**), **èzɵ́ k—-k—**, av. very long, tall.

kàdrúɔ̀, n. an adolescent youth; a girl calls 'her boy' **mâ k—**; he calls her **mâ àmúrúo**.

kǎdúa = **ókpɔ́á**, n. paunch or stomach (of ruminants); **tí mà k—** a cow's stomach.

kǎdu-kǎdu = **kǎmu-kǎmu**, av. (of eyes) opening wide and closing (nervously); **mǐ milénǐ 'yɛ k—-k—** your eyes blink nervously.

kàdzàránì, A. n. Indian cane.

kǎdzúa = **áyáya**, n. chicken-pox (?); **èri 'bâ ŋa** it 'eats' man.

(é)káfórá, n. piece of light wood attached to fishing-rod.

káftèn, n. from Engl., captain; **k— 'bá drì tsépirǐ: pìríndì lípirǐ** captain who leads, who blows the whistle.

kàfűűá, n. stump of a hoe; **èri ɛ'bó atsépirǐ'ï** it is the remains of a (worn-out) hoe.

kàfútò, n. foam, froth; **èi 'bá tǐ-tǐ ká, kàfútò-nï èfɵ̌ ndɔ̀** when they throttle a p., foam comes forth (from his mouth); **kàfútò-nï ɔ̀mì rö 'bâ tiá** froth forms on one's mouth.

kágbùlu (= **èríbbí**), n. fresh new grass (**àrɔ̌rö** not yet grown up) (as after a grass burning).

káagɔ̀rɔ̀, n. a shrub (sticks much used for roof frame); **k— èi ànï kǎría ɛmbě** they tie up the wooden frame of a roof with it.

kái, av. very much, extremely (connected with certain verbs for causing pain/suffering); **éŋá mà kɔ̀rɛ fu ma kái** longing (hunger)

for polenta torments/presses me
very hard.

kái = **àlí**, n. illegal sexual intercourse, adultery (Ac. luk); **àlí 'bǎ**
(to commit fornication or adultery); **èì tí fě àlö àlî rö** (= **káî
rö**) they give/pay a cow for a
transgression with the other sex.

kâií, n. stupid fellow; **mïnï kâiî
fô!** you are a stupid fellow all
right.

kàikə, n. a larger kind (common)
of beans (Ac. **mùràŋà**).

kàíərï, n. first-born (man, animal).

kááka! = **ùú-lulu!** intj. exclamation of surprise.

kaaká, kaakâ-ŋa (= T. **lèsèrí,
mòndóàŋa, mŋgbáyïá**), n. maize.

káákà = more common **ləka**, av.
in **lì ləka** to speak roughly,
rudely; **é lì mánï k—** (**ləka**)
'dïnï à'do sï yà? why do you
answer me so rudely?

kákàó ('rö) = **kárákàràrö**, q.v.

kàkú, T. (= Plu. **kàú**), n. kitchen
(or additional hut of compound);
k— dzó éŋâ 'i-zőrï hut in which
to prepare polenta/food.

kálá, n. (1) side (of room...); **é laa
mï káláá!** lie down on the side
(not in the middle of the room
ágáá or **ágá (ǹ)dúa**)! (2) **sí k—**
molar tooth; (3) **dzó mà kǎléa**
(or **ôókòá**) at the side of the room.

kàlá, kàlâ, or **kàlê,** n. pen-fence
of thorns; (1) **èì k—** (= **bàrànà
V.**) **'bɛ otsí sï, èì tí əfï 'anïá
əzóó sï** they make a pen with
thorns to drive in cattle at time of
rain (near **lítsó** proper; for cleanliness' sake); (2) sometimes a
division in **lítsó**; (3) S. (= **kalaya**)
kind of iron plate for earth work.

kálà, n. Engl. collar; neck-piece of
shirt, &c.

kàlàbà = **ɛ́ndèrèfí, gáláká,** n.

a kind of tall grass (still **èbìrö**
green).

kàlàfɛ, n. number, sum-total **ʒ
k—!** read the number!

kàlákàlá = **ərɛ́, 'rö,** a. watery.

kàlámò, S.A., n. pencil; **k— sí**
pen-nib.

káláņá, n. muscle; meat without
bones (for kitchen).

kǎlǎtì = **èdzèlékò** = **á'bulé,** n.
riverside; **ìí mà k—** area close
to riverside, shore.

kàlàtúsì, n. eucalyptus tree; **k—
rȍè, kà adri èzȏrö, èri aká-aká**
the eucalyptus tree is thin, when
it becomes long, it is pliant (it
bends easily).

kálé(-ěa), n. side (cf. **kálá**).

kaali, n. enclosure, courtyard (of
hut or village); **k— dzó àgáí tò-
zȏ rï'ï** a fence planted round a
hut; **k— tìlé** fence entrance;
sometimes hedge for fields.

kàlí, n. thin stick, cane; **àdzú mà
k—** shaft of a spear; the 'tens':
k— îrrï 20; **k— nna** 30; **k— ssu**
40; **k— tääú** 50; **k— ázía** 60;
k— ázîîrrï 70; **k— àrò** 80; **k—
óròmì** 90; **k— nna drìnï ssu**
35; **kàlíïa** small stick.

kàlíïa, n. ritual miniature hut (foot
or less diam.) fixed on top of a
stick and placed in the courtyard
on occasion of a sacrifice (sheep,
fowl) for a sick child or woman;
dzóadzóa the same, fixed in the
roof inside a hut.

kàlí-kàlí, a. sweet (sugar, honey...).

kàmɛ́ɛ̌ or **kèmɛ́ɛ̌** (S. **kìdzókò**), n.
spoon; **k— éŋâ ŋaa-zőrï'ï** spoon
to eat polenta.

kǎmì, n. lion; **k— óŋófí** lion's
claw; **k— 'bâ ŋa** eats man.

kàmurè, n. a kind of white durra.

kàndalà, E.S.A., n. candle; **é 'bà
k— mà tì tsí!** light the candle!

kàandí 262 kátárá

kàandí, Baŋgala = mùpirà, n.
rubber ball, football; èri òlóŋgó̆-
lô̆-rö it is round.
kàandú or kàandí, n. name of a
tattoo design on face.
káanï, av. while … the better;
rather better; the best … ; 'dìrï
ə̀ndzí, káanï 'də̀'ï that is bad
but this is good; k— 'dì ndrìnì,
'dà ndrì kö; mí èfè k— mânï
'dìrï'ï! while this is suitable that
one is not; you had better give me
this one! bə̀ŋgô̆ bá 'dà sì k— ma
ópílé nï this cloth-belt fits my
waist best.
kàni, cj. when, if; k— vínï 'dínï
mâ ko dzà! if things are like
that, let me leave it! k— tró, cj.
even if (cf. Grammar).
káŋgá, n. èri kére èzô̆-rörì,
Lògò èi ànï əŋgô̆ tö it is a long
gourd prepared as a wind instrument used by the Ləgə at dances.
kàŋgárà, n. sweet beer from ə̀ndó
(or 'dô̆) pi sùkári ŋgúrù bε
(sùkári mà zô̆ŋgó̆rö́kò) durra
(or eleusine) and deposit of sugar.
kàɲàa-rö, av. (after a few adj.)
very; ə̀ndzí k— very bad; ugly.
káɲáà-rö, av. in gáá k— (= but
wεεréâ-rö) very small, few.
kàɲíkàɲíïã, n. widow-bird.
káɲíra, n. tail-hair of elephant.
kaao, n. a very large reddish locust.
kàokào, n. tall graminia grass with
sharp hair (otsî rö); 'bíkónï 'bá
ə̀sò-ə̀sò its hairs prickle.
kápà (S. mùsípì), n. girdle, belt;
k— èi sù ópílía they put round
the waist.
kápìa, n. Abdim's stork (Spheno-
rynchus abdimii); black and white
wings.
kàrátà, A.S., n. playing cards.
káarákàarà-rö = káakàaó('rö),

a. many; àfa k— ε'dé vàá a number of things fell to the ground.
káráká'bô̆, n. wooden sandals;
k— atsí-zô̆ páa-rì'ï sandals to
walk with on foot.
kàràŋgá, n. (1) a kind of locust;
(2) (= ŋgàaràká, lùlù, T.) beer
in a stage of preparation.
kàráŋgà, kàláŋgà, n. a kind of
large ground-nut.
káráwa = dô̆fárá, q.v.
kărí or kărî (= àrənì), n. young
female animal; tí k—, a'ú k—
young cow (heifer), hen; kărî-
á(nï), n. still younger fem. animal.
kăría, n. (1) dzó k— frame of a
hut (or roof); èi k— əmbê̆ báká
sì they make/fasten up the frame
with ropes; (2) circle; a. round;
(3) bicycle.
kăárí'bá, éfí'bá, n. k— èri àŋgò̆
'ípi the owner/occupier of a
place, area.
kărilè, n. a youth, young man.
kàrìdzó, n. = kìrìdzó, q.v.
kăáru, av. noisily; á tsï màákò
wátârö k— I ate raw potatoes k—.
kăárù, a. hard, raw; not ready
cooked; ósô̆ 'də̀rï k—k— rö,
a'dî ŋgà dε kö these beans are
raw/hard, they are not ready
cooked; 'dò éwáti k—, vn. he
belched from beer.
kărúkărú, n. cartilage.
kasóá, see àtsófà.
kàtá, (é)lélé, n. flat rocky space
(where women gather to grind
their corn) (Ac. lèlà, Al. cánà).
kàtákàtá (= mbìrì-mbìrì), av.
confusedly, pell-mell, higgledy-
piggledy; 'bánî ndzo-zô̆ mb-
mb— əsa-rö-əsa k—k— people
run higgledy-piggledy mixing up
confusedly.
kátárá, n. leather boot or shoe;
k— dε 'bə the boots are worn out.

kàtî, n. opening of lítsó(tilé): tí kàtîı or lítsó kàtîı opening of cow-pen.

kǎáti = dzó-ti-lé, n. opening of hut; mí òpì kǎáti-lé tsí (tìkò sì)! shut up the hut-opening (with the door)!

kátrǎ = hwére, av. instantly, quickly, without delay, immediately; é gò drì k—! go back immediately!

kátrɛ, n. metal (copper, brass ...) wedge- or nail-shaped ornament fixed in upper (rarely lower) lip; sǔ tìárì which they put into the lip.

káatrí(ĭ), a. (1) short, dwarfish; (2) level, smooth; li pätí káatrí he cut the wood level/smoothly; li drìbbí k— he cut the hair leaving a crown of hair.

kátrìa = àmórèká, q.v.

káatsì! ≅ ʼy(ékè) intj. (ironic) all right! k— àmà mu nè mï bɛ rá! all right, we shall see each other (meet, some day)! (threat).

kàú = gòókò, n. kitchen kàú dzó éɲâ ʼi-zó ʻkauʼ is a hut for cooking.

kawà, A.S.? n. coffee.

kɛ, T. (= tsɛ), vt. to tear, break; ndrí kɛ báká rá the goat has broken the rope.

kěákěá, n. kind of inedible mushroom; é kà ɲa rá, mï ɔgbɛ-ɔgbɛ, or mï ogu ànï kǐá-kǐá; maybe mï ànï drà ɛsú if you eat it, you will vomit, or you will start (idly) laughing; you may die.

kêkê or kêkéI or kàìkáì or kěyè-kéyé, n. sieve; k— àɲâ ya-zó a sieve to winnow (or fan) corn; èì àɲâ ya k— sì, èì sìní ya they winnow corn (the coarse part) with a sieve.

kèkélè[1], n. very large kind of basket.

kèkélè[2], a. hanging down loosely;

bòŋgó ʼdì mà ti k— the end (fringes) of the cloth (curtain) is hanging loosely (cf. kèlékélè).

kɛlɛdzuko, n. = óyá, q.v.

kèlékélè, kèlérékélè, a. hanging down, being suspended from; bòŋgó èri kèlékélè-rö (èri è'ìzà) the curtain is drooping/is suspended; n. see-saw; à mú (àma) kèkélè ya! let us go and swing (ourselves) on the hanging rope.

kɛmèkɛmè = akázàrö, a. lithe, pliant, supple, easily bent.

kěnà-kěnà, indf. prn. all (= ná wóró...).

kènì, pl. kénì conjunctional phrase ... say(s) that; andzi kénì: à mví àkúa! the boys say: let us go home! (report).

kèŋgerè = áiâro, n. bell; a bicycle-bell says (fantasy): ayanï endzó ʼdì; é ko gěrì rá! a bicycle is coming; clear (leave) the way!

kèŋgèrè = kètrèkètrè, av. slidingly; mvá ʼdì èri gǎ (or àgǎ) k— the baby crawls (sliding on the ground).

kérɛ = zú, n. gourd-bottle; èì lésú tò kéréá (or àlúrùzúa) they pour milk into the gourd-bottle; kérǐá a small one.

kérè = tsérè, n. the shrill shout (in falsetto voice) characteristic of far-off communication; k— ʼbɛ to utter the shout.

kérɛkérɛ, av. (to break) to splinters, small pieces; òvï òsì pátí k— the lightning has torn the tree to splinters.

kɛtɛkɛtɛ, n. = tsíkíndà, q.v.

kèyèkéyè, n. same as kêkê q.v.

kï = tï, T., vt. to swallow; kï éɲá ʼwïrí he swallowed the polenta in gulps.

ki (MN.) = **fu, 'di,** vt. to kill; **ma
mî kìi** I will kill you.

kìdrìkìdrì, av. swinging up and
down; **gắrì əya rö mî bɛ k—**
the bicycle moves slightly up and
down under you(r weight).

kìdzî, n. (1) spacious port or landing place; **k— wàalàrö** the port
is spacious; **k— 'bánï ali-zŏ ìí
'dà mà drìlé sì** a port where
people pass over the river; (2)
(rare) (= **gbəkə**) **òdrú mà k—**
the path used by buffaloes (especially to go to the riverside).

kìdzí(k)ɔ́, n. a particular dance;
à tŏ k— 'ï (= Ad. **áyo**)! let us
dance 'kidzikɔ'.

kílàkílà, n. vegetable and a slimy,
stringy sauce from such a plant
(? molachia); **k— èrì ndzɔ̀zà-rö**
the 'kilakila' sauce is slimy/runny.

kìlé, cj. like, as if; **èrì k— 'ï átíl-lé**
he is like his father.

kìlibá same as **kílyò,** q.v.

kílíkìlì, n. **àyà k—** tassel tuft;
ǹdrí mà àyà k— goat's tassellike excrescence on neck; **drí
(àyà) k—** a sixth finger on hand
(like tassel).

kíllílí, av. straight, upright, level-
straight; just, correct; **sò pá k—**
he stands upright; **é lò mání
k—!** speak to me frankly, correctly!

kilikpa, a. see **kpakadìlì.**

kílyò = **kilìbá,** n. (1) string of
'metal' beads for waist; **èì k—
sù ópíléa-rì'ï** they put a 'kilyo'
round their waist; (2) (= **àdrɔ̀bá**)
thin neck-ring.

kìrr, av. cf. **abá.**

kíirí = **èrìitì, pí,** av. for good,
definitely; **mvi 'ïmà àkúa k—**
he went home for good; **ópí fè
mání ǹdrí k—** the chief definitely gave me a sheep; (2) **k—**

(placed before the verb), still; **mî
ŋga k— a'á 'dálé yà?** will you
still/definitely (?) stay there? **èrì
ŋgà kírí tsí yà?** is he still alive?

kìrìdzô, n. a woman lately con-
fined/in childbed; **əkó mvá
osípi ó'dírì, èrì ŋgà kìrìdzó˙rö,
rï ádúbí drìá** a woman lately con-
fined is still in childbed (state),
she sits in the 'adubi'; **èrì éņâņa
kàmèɛ sì** she will eat her polenta
with a spoon (oyster-shell).

kírikíri = **kídikídi, òzí,** n. a
humble bee; **èrì ŋga ótókó
óņanì ŋgazŏrì mà əmbɛtiá** it
comes out on the side of termite
hills; **èì èrì alá áņú sì bè'dò-
bè'dò, èrì dí ega ədô-rö** they
(roast and) mix it with simsim, it
becomes fatty.

kírri-kírri = **títi, trítrí,** av.
firmly, tightly; **é bì ágú 'dà
k—k—!** hold that man firmly!
**mí əmbɛ k—k—, kà mu ayu-
ru-zŏ kö!** tie it tightly, lest it
loosen!

kíríkìrì = **mà tŏŏ,** av. urgently,
importunately, persistently; **á 'bà
ópí drí k— tĕ** I made urgent
representations to the chief but
in vain; **k— á'dïá èfè mání
kàlámò** when asked persistently
he gave me a pencil.

kìrìkɔ́ = **tïrïkɔ́, - sì,** av. firmly
(adhere); **áņú sìzàrì (awí ogá
rö) kìrìkɔ́ sì, èrì awí ánákùléa
(èrì 'bá tì-tì)** ground simsim (on
eating) jammed firmly, it remained
in the throat (it chokes one almost); **áņú éfí ga rö kìrìkɔ́ sì,
èrì awí sí àrìkàléa** simsim
(grains) stuck fast, remaining
among the teeth.

kìrìmà, n. = **rìetsà kìrìmà a'ú
átá mà páá** spur on cock's leg.

kìrìtsà = **pìrìtsà,** n. spur or spur-like (bony) excrescence of leg of fowl, goats, &c.; ankle (of man).

kìtándà, A.S., n. bedstead.

kìtìpálá or **kìtɔ̀pɔ́lɔ́**, n. native plaited stool (made from **óvu**, kind of ambatch, for frame and **rǎpú**, splits from a palm-tree stem or bamboo).

kìtɔ̂ = tzòê, tölò, n. àdzú mà k— spike.

kö, adv. not; no.

ko, vt. to leave (off), stop, cease; to abandon, let be (alone) **ko . . . dzà**; **é ko dzà!** stop! leave it alone! **ko mvá kö** she (mother...) did not abandon the child; **kó èri a'dúlɛ** they left him alone; **é ko gìrì** (= é sɛ mï rá)! withdraw from the way! **ko rö**, vr./vn. to remain over (aside); **ko rö kö** there did not remain over; **è kó èmï rá!** draw aside!

kò, vn. to curdle, clot, coagulate; **lésú kò rá** the milk coagulated; **á lɛ̀ lɛ́ (-sú) kòzàrï mbɛ 'ï** I want to eat curdled (thick) milk.

kə¹, vt. (1) to sweep; **é kə dzɔ́ 'alɛ́ yɔ́fɛ́ sǐ!** sweep the room with a broom! (2) to draw water; **ǐ kəzɔ̌** (= bɛ̌); (3) to sleep **o'dû kəzɔ̌**; **é kə (o'dú) dzɔ́a 'dé!** sleep there in the room! **o'dú 'bɛ èri rá** or **kə ('bɛ) o'dú rá** he fell asleep; (4) (= bǐ) to catch; **mú ɔ́mbî kə** they went to catch locusts; **àzɔ́ kə èri rá** sickness caught him/he became sick; (5) **tǐ kə (àtsǐ sǐ)** to catch fire, blaze; **dzɔ́ kə ti** (i.e. **àtsǐ sǐ) vɛ̀vɛ** the hut caught fire and burned down; (6) to seize, catch/take hold of (esp. fig. of passions); **ɔ̀mbà kə èri tsǐ** anger caught him/i.e. he became angry; **'bá mà àzà kə** to take pity on sby. (cf. **àzà**, n.); **àmbó mà tǐ kə** (or **bǐ**) to catch up with/con-

sent/obey authority's words or orders, &c.

kə² **drì** = ɛ'dɔ́, vn. to start (make) for; **ágú 'dà kə drì mvi ndɔ̀** (= **ágú 'dà ɛ'dɔ̂ dǐ mvi**) that man went and turned home.

kɔ́ɔ̀á or **kɔ̀kôá**, n. egret.

kóbi = **kóyi**, n. kind of winnowing tray; **ɔ̀kóï èi ànï àɲá o'bǐ** women winnow corn with it.

kóbǐá, **kóyǐá**, n. very small tray for portioning out polenta; **k— ɛɲá ɔva-zɔ̌rǐ** trays to distribute polenta.

kɔ̀bɔ̀lə = **kɔ̀bɔ̀lɔ́kɔ̀**, **kɔ̀bənɔ̀**, **kɔ̀bɔ̀nɔkɔ̀**, **kɔ̀mɔ́nɔ́kɔ̀**, **kàmànà**, n. dewlap.

kòdíà, n. a cow which has calved quite recently.

kódìà! or **hódì!** S., intj. hullo! (to call attention); answer **kàríbù!** come in!

kódi-kódi, av. only; **á lɛ̀ 'bá àlö k—k—** I want only one p.

kòdì-kòdì, a. dense, thick (opp. ɔ̀ré); **e'dí kòdì-kòdì-rö** the gruel is thick.

kódɔ́ = **mòkàrà**, n. three (or more) days old (i.e. already too sour) beer; **ɛ́wá k—** = **ɛ́wá ɔ̀drá** = **ɛ́wá mòkàrà** old sour (bad) beer; (opp. **ɛ́wá àfùfù** the new fresh beer) (ready for consumption).

kɔ̀ɔ́'də = **kɔ̀ŋgɔ́rə**, q.v.

kódra = **pàrí**, M.N. **kələ**, n. papyrus plant; mat from papyrus.

kɔ̀dzáã, pl. **kɔ̀-andzi**, n. calf (**tǐ mvá**); **k— àrɔɔnì** fem. calf; **k— ágó** male calf.

kó(y)ǐá, cf. **kóbi**, **kóïǐá ɛɲá drì** (or tǐ) **sö-zɔ̌** to cover polenta.

kɔ́kɔ́, **a'ú k—** or, better; **a'ú mɔ̀lɔ̌**, q.v.

kɔ́kə, -rǐ, ²rö, a. being without; **ɛ̀lï sí-kɔ́kərǐ** blunt (without

edge) knife; **mvá milέ-mba
kókɔrɪ̀** (or **-rö**) boy without intelligence, not clever.
kɔkɔ́á, n. bogey, bugbear; **k—
έri andzi wɛrɛ mà drì etsí-zɔ̌**
bogey for frightening/fooling small
children; **k— 'dɪ̀: èri mɪ̌ ŋaa
tsúrú'dɔ̀**! the bogey-man is
here, he will eat you up immediately! (to silence crying children).
kɔkɔ́á, n. woodpecker; **k— èri
pátí mà tálá lɔ̀ ɛndì** it makes
holes in trees.
kɔkɔlɔ̀-rö, av. by force, forcedly;
'du mɪ̈ k—? did he take you by
force?
kókɔ́rɔ́, n. front part of lower leg;
pá k— tibia.
kɔkɔsì, S. (**kikwasi**) safety pin; **k—
otsɪ̂ ndze-zɔ̌** . . . to remove thorns.
kɔkɔtɛ = **kɔŋgɔ̀lɔ̀**, a. rigid, stiff;
mba k— he is (dead and) rigid.
kɔlíkɔlí, n. pied wagtail; **k— ɔ́ó
kènì: 'sí ɔ̀ŋ̩ì yɔ, sí ɔ̀ŋ̩ì yɔ'** the
wagtail (singing like a canary)
sings: 'the teeth are not nice'
(ɔ̀dàtáa insult).
kólóa, T. = **égɔ̌á**, a. adze.
kɔlɔa = **kɔlɔŋga**, **ɔ̀kɔlóa**, n. bird
of about pigeon-size, body green-
ish, wings red; **k— mà ɔpìnɪ̈**
(**sí drilέ**) **ɛka-ɛka** (a bee-eater?).
kɔlɔ̀bá = **kɔlìbá**, **ogali**, n. skin-
cloth of woman mourning death
of a grown-up son **èi k— sǔ
ɛmvɔ̀ sɪ̌-'ɪ́mà mvá àkárɔ̀ mà
drà sɪ̌**.
kɔ́lɔ̌'bɔ̌, n. a popular vegetable
(*Hibiscus sabderiffa*); **k— ɛŋgá
a'dúlɛ, àmbónɪ̈ èi rɪ̌rɪ̀** it comes
up alone, mostly it is sown; **k—
drầdra** the 'kölö'bö' is acid (Ac.
mmàlà-kwáaŋ); cf. **láakà**.
kɔ́lɔ̌kɔ́lɔ̌ = **kɔ̌mùkɔ́mù**, av.
going to pieces; **ŋ̩ɔ 'ɪ̈ k—** it went
to pieces.

kɔlɔ̀-kɔlɔ̀ = **ɔ̀lɔ̀kɔlɔ̀**, av. loosely,
slackly, not tightly; **é sɔ̀ k—**! fix
it loosely! **ɔmbέ k—** (**rö**) he tied
it loosely.
kɔ́lɔ́lɔ́[1], a. restless, without self
control; **ásɪ́ kɔ́lɔ́lɔ́-rɪ̀** (also **kɔlɔ́-
kɔlɔ́** or **kɔkɔlɔ̀** or **rùtsùrùtsù**)
he is excited, restless, fussy/puts
hands on everything.
kɔ́lɔ́lɔ́[2], n. a savoury of beans
cooked and seasoned with salt and
fried onion.
koloŋa = **kiliŋa**, a. dense, thick
(of liquids); **e'dí** (**edú**) **k—** the
gruel is thick.
kɔ̌lɔ̌táa = **kɔ́lìtέ**, n. newly (up to
about a month) born calf; **tí tɪ̌pi
àndrɔ̀ 'dɔ́nɪ̈ èi ɔmvɛ k—** what
a cow brought forth today is
called 'kölötáa' (also T. **kɔ̀dzá
ɔdrɔ̀kɔ̀**).
kɔlú better **kùlú**, q.v.
komará, n. shea tree (*Butyro-
spermum parkii*); **k— nɪ̈ akɔ̌ ɔdɔ̌-
rö** the shea-butter fruit dissolves
(on cooking) to oil.
kɔɔmɛ = **'bɪ̀lɪ̀**, **ɔgɔ̌ɔ̃**, n. chair,
stool.
kɔ̀mɔ̀nɔkɔ̀, **tí mà k—**, n. dewlap
of cow (see **kɔ̀bɔ̀lɔkɔ̀**).
kɔ̌mú, **kɔ̀múti**, n. knee; **k— mà
àdzìkɔlí** knee-cap; **k— sì-zɔ̌
vàá** to kneel down; **é sì k— vàá**!
kneel down!
kɔ̌mùkɔ́mù, **kɔ́lɔ̌kɔ́lɔ̌**, av. breaking all over (in many parts); **'bá
àzìnɪ̈ ɛ'dέ pátí sía k—** a man
fell from a tree breaking his
bones.
kómvó, **ɔ́kómvó**, n. reversed clay
cup-like trap to lure termites
from their holes; **'bá k— si
ɔ́ŋ̩a-nɪ̈ ɛ'dέ-zɔ̌** they build
'komvo' traps for termites to fall
into.
kónakóna = **tέkὲtέkὲ**, av. cleanly

(white); ɛmvɛ kóɳàkóɳà snow-white.

kónákóná, n. a miniature calabash bowl (ètsíä); 'bá k— sĭ ɛ́wá 'bĭ one tastes beer with a 'konakona'.

kòndróndró = kàdrùkàdrù, av. àzə k— (T.) = (Plu.) èzó pĕtsə̀pĕtsə̀ very long.

kə̀ə́nə̀, n. see kə̀ŋgə́rə.

kóŋgóa = kólóo, Tom. n. adze (= ádrə̀á).

kəŋgələ(kə) (1) 'rö coarse, stiff; bə̀ŋgó k—, èri 'bá òsiòsi the cloth is coarse, it scratches one; bə̀ŋgó mà ti mba kəŋgələ̀ rö the edge of the cloth (as collar) is hard and stiff; (2) av. tightly, firmly; solidly; mĭ óɳa əmbĕ ebbíkə sĭ k— (= kirikiri) wrap the (collected) termites tightly in leaves! (3) stubbornly (dispute sth.).

kə̀ŋgórə = kə̀ə́'də, kə̀ə́nə̀, n. primitive wooden mallet/rake for farm work; rake; èi ámvû tsə k— sĭ they beat the field even with a rake.

kóɳà, n. corner; angle; edge; (of hut, room, case . . . .).

kə̀ɳíkə̀ɳí, a. of different colours; variegated, piebald, motley (of colour or drawing/design).

kŏɳikŏɳi = kŏɳukŏɳù,líɳà, T., n. constellation of Pleiades.

kŏɳókò = fŏɳókò, n. very small quantity of; éɳá k—, e'dí k— a small quantity/a bit of polenta or gruel.

kópə̀, A.S., n. metal cup, bowl (= kikopo).

kópə̀lə̀, S., n. padlock; tä̌árí mà k— padlock of a trunk.

kə̀rɛ, n. (natural) craving, longing; fondness; ĭi k— thirst; éɳá k— hunger for polenta; ɛ́wá k— fondness of beer, &c.; fu ma kái

or ndɛ̀ ma rá overwhelms/tortures me/I am very thirsty, &c.; 'bá 'dà emú tábà k— sĭ this man came along because of eagerness for a cigarette; ándrĭi mà k— fu èri kái; apá ànï àkúa he was homesick for his mother, so he escaped home.

kórékɛ, n. raven, crow; k— k—! é ɳa fúnò kö! crow, crow! do not pick ground-nuts (on the field)!

kərí, n. serval cat; k— mà rúánï sì ə̀'dó lɛ́ the serval cat's body (colouring) resembles the leopard's.

kə̀ərí-kə̀ərí = kə̀ɳí-kə̀ɳí, a. variegated, striped, &c.; á lɛ̀ bə̀ŋgó k—k— 'dàrï'ï I want that cloth there with stripes (? from kərí).

kə̀rə̀ a kind of dance; á mu kə̀rə̀á! let me go to the 'kɔrɔ' dance!

kərə = rŏɛ́, a. (said of man) slender, slim, thin; 'bá k— a slender p.

kòròbá, A. = ròbí enïrïkə hippo whip.

kərəgbələ = gbərətə, a. lean, meagre—sick; tí k— or tí òízà old sick lean cow.

kótà, n. a three-cornered wedge stopper or plug; k— ĭi tĭ sö-zó to stop a water receptacle (bottle, &c.); k— éɳá drì sö-zó to cover polenta.

kətɛ̀, n. the bony part of the tail; tí k—; kətɛ̀rö = mba tò very strong, of pith and marrow, compactly vigorous.

kòtó = áɳûba, n. beer-strainer.

kótsí-kótsí or kə̀tsí-kə̀tsí, av. mbèlè k— very quickly; èri nĭ mbèlè k— he knows it quickly, or fluently.

kótsí-kótsí = kítsíkítsí, av. (1)

to the last remnant; (2) (= dólí-dólí) all to pieces.

kɔ̀ɔtsó, n. water-pipe; k— tábà sɛ-zőrï̈ pipe with which to smoke tobacco; k— mà ɛ́mvőårö ɔdrî si'ï̈ the cup of the water-pipe is made of clay.

kó(y)ì and kóyïá, see kóbi; kó(y)ì àŋá o'bï̈-ző basket-tray for winnowing corn.

kɔ̀yɔ̀-kɔ̀yɔ̀ = yɔ̀kɔ̀-yɔ̀kɔ̀, av. loosely, not closely fitting; mï̈ ɔmbé k—! tie it slack!

kɔ̀yɔ̀(á), wékḛá, tɛ́ó, n. gourd-rattle for shaking at magic rituals; ɔ́ɔdzɔ́ɔ-nï̈ k— ya nï̈ it is the diviner who shakes the rattle.

kóyɔ́a, n. a kind of red durra (of the tsàràkàlà species).

kpakadili = tilikpa, kilikpa (i.e. sḛzàrö), a. adhesive, sticky, glutinous, viscous; gbándà ɛ́ŋá ɛ̀ri k— polenta from maniok is sticky.

kpákòá, n. tweezers.

kpåkpå = kàràmándà, n. wooden sandals.

kpålúfá, T. = pá mà fàlá, n. lower part of leg, below ankle (? of cow); 'bá mà k— (?) man's tibia.

kpàrà, kpàrà-kpàrà = dàràŋgbà, av. (to hang) heavily, low-massed.

kpɛmŋgbɛlɛ, av. (1) with noise (when sth. falls àfa-nï̈ ɛ'dɛ́-ző-nï̈-rï̈); (2) = ṅdïrí, hard and blank, clean (cf. ákúma); ... drïnï̈ a tsḛ̀ dí k—his head has remained/become bald.

kpɛmŋgbɛrɛ²rö, a. very hard (say ground for digging); àfa mbåpi mbåmbarï̈ sth. very hard.

kpɛrɛ, pstp. as far as, until, reaching; mu k— Árúwá he went as

far as Aruwa; é ga ɔ́drɔ 'dï̈rï̈ k—vàá! dig up these weeds to the very roots.

kpɛ̀rɛ̀ = ŋgɔ̀lí, n. kind of sickle/knife (paŋga); k— ɛ̀l ànï̈ ásɛ́ vɔ̀ they mow/cut away grass with it.

kpɛrɛ-kpɛrɛ = pérɛpérɛ, av. (1) without delay, immediately; é mu ɔ́pí vɔ̀ k—k— go to the chief without delaying on the way! é ŋga k—k—! rise/start immediately! (2) (= tsɛ́) perfectly well; ma ɛri k—k— I have heard (or understood) it perfectly well.

kpɛ̀tɛ̀ɛ¹ = kpùtsù, av. drenched, soaked; atri dri bɔ̀ŋgɔ́ bɛ k— he came back with a drenched (from rain) cloth; ɔzɔ́ɔ́ fu ma bɔ̀ŋgɔ́ bɛ k— the rain wetted me and my cloth through/or drenched me to the skin.

kpɛ̀tɛ̀ɛ̀,² n. the proper Logbara native ɛ́wá beer ɛ́wá kpɛ̀tɛ̀ɛ̀.

kpɛtɛ, av. empty(-handed), for nothing, for love; mà dí 'dɔ̀ drí sì k— here I am with empty hands (say after working 'iia' in Buganda).

kpii, kpi-kpi = pii or pipi, av. straight ahead, in a straight line; level.

kpɔ̀, also pɔ̀ = zì, vt. to hide away, conceal; 'bá àzínï̈ àfa ògŭpirï̈ kpɔ̀ ko 'dá, emú pírínï̈ one who has stolen sth. hides (and leaves) it away there, and comes along empty-handed; é kpɔ̀ (or 'bà) ko àfa 'dï̈ mï̈ vɔ̀ 'dɛ́! hide this at your place! kpɔ̀ rö, vr./vn. kpɔ̀ rö ɔ̀ri sì ɛ́drɔ́ 'bílía he concealed himself, out of fear, in a rat's hole (fable); kpɔ̀ (= zì) 'ï̈ pätí rùá he hid behind a tree.

kpɔ̀kpɔ̀ = kpɔ̀lɔ́-kpɔ̀lɔ́, av. n. excitedly, flurriedly, nervously; 'yɛ k— (ásí fùfù or tsùrùtsùrù) he acted in a nervous hurry; mïnï ya-zɔ̌ ɔ̀rì (or àzí) sì when you hurry out of fear (or work); ɛ̀ri 'bá kpɔ̀lɔ́-kpɔ̀lɔ́ bɛrì he is an excited/hysterical person.

kpɔ̌lɔ̌ = tsǎkù, q.v. ɔ̀dó àndzù k— the oil was absorbed leaving a spot.

kpərɔ́ = kpərɔ́kɔ̀, n. a rushlike plant with triangular stem and bushy head; drìnï tàyàrö əmi lɛ́ similar to papyrus (but much shorter); ɔ̀kó ɛ̀ì tsɛ zǎ (or ɛvɛ) à'î-rö women pull it out, burn it to obtain salt (by distilling its ashes).

kpɔ́ərɔ́ = wɔ́ərɔ́, a. all, the whole quantity; ma əmvó k— I gathered up (in cupped hands) the whole.

kpɔ̀yɔ̀ = aɡaa, av. half-full (or less); ìí ndɔ̂ 'a k— the pail is partly full of water; dzɔ́lɔ́kɔ̀nï ko 'ï k— a (small) amount (covering the bottom) remained over.

kpǔũã, av. cracking, with a stunning noise; ɡbà drìnï kàlí sì k— he gave him a numbing blow on his head with a stick.

kpúmɡbúlú (vàá), av. flowing/ bubbling over; ɛɡbé k— vàá it (beer) overflowed; à'día 'bâ mu kpúmɡbúlú people went to war in mass (all).

kpumɡburu, av. with a dull noise; ɛ̀bìónï 'yɛ arí bɛ k— the spider fell in the drum with a dull noise.

kù¹, vt. to fill in, cover up; 'bá dràzà ɛ̀ì 'bǎ 'bílé 'aléa, ɛ̀ì ŋaákú kǔ drìnïá tsí they put a dead man in the grave (hole) and fill it up with earth; mï ŋaákú kǔ àfa ɔ̀ndzírì mà drìá you throw earth over (cover) an ugly object;

kù², vt. to remove, take away; mï emú wɔ́rɔ́tɔ̀ kǔ! come and remove the dung! ándríi-nï 'yə: 'mï edzí ɛbbíkə bbí, á kù mvá zɛ̀ ànï!' the mother says: bring me leaves that I may remove the filth of the baby! é kù ìí kùlɛ́, ìí mà raa ànï! clean the bed that the river/ water may run off!

ku¹, vn. to be, become deep; ŋaákúnï drə 'ï ɔ̀ndì sì, 'bú-nï (or 'bílɛ...) ànï kǔku the earth crumbles away and the hole deepens in this way; ìí mà 'alɛ́ kǔku (álîrö) the water is deep; àŋɡɔ̌ (or 'bílɛ́) kǔku (or álîrö), the place is steep (the hole is deep) (vertically); kuzàrö or ku vàálɛ́ ndrii (or ɡúrú) to be steep/deep.

ku², vn. to move or stand aside; ɡɛ̀rì lúrúārì sì é ku ɡɛ̀rì ɡárì-nï rɛ̀ áiséa! as the path is narrow clear the way for the cycle! àɡátà 'dì mà kǔ dí mî-nï! the discussion (the right in it) may stand for you (you are right)!

ku³, vn. to be, become dark; àŋɡɔ̌-nï ku (= bǐ) ndɛɛ rá (i.e. ákúkúù tsí a storm is on), it has (is) become (-ing) darker.

ku⁴, vn. (1) to resound, ring, echo; à'dí àmadrí 'dì ku ndɛ̀ rá our bell (of school) has rung properly already; (2) rú ku to be renowned, famous; rúnï ku tɔ̀ his name is much talked of; ávítá sì Nyàpɛɛa mà rû ku tɔ̀ for games 'Nyapɛɛa' (secondary school) is renowned; rû kuzà famous, renowned; 'bá rû kuzà a famous man; Àdrɔ̌ mà kutáa the glory of God.

kùànà = ɡbaɡbà, ɔ̀ŋɡà, n. trap of mice (and other) much in use for ritual purposes; ɛ̀ì ànï édrɔ́ 'bǎ ɛ'yɔ́ ɛ̀tï ndà-zɔ̌ they place it for mice, in order to divine secret causes of a disease or other matters (by observing the movements of the animals).

kùbú = kàbóti, S. n. a heavy rain coat; laa 'ïmà k— sï he lay down with (or on) his 'kubu'.

kùdìà, n. a cow which has calved recently tí tïpi ó'dírï èi ɔmvε k—; lésúnï ŋgà εkârö (= otsïfï) its milk is still reddish.

kúkù, T. = kàú, q.v.

kúkúlû-ru, a. steep, precipitous; Étì k—, Mt. Eti is steep; tutáa (= tuzà) nï ɔ̀kpɔ̀rö its ascent is difficult.

kúkúrú- = kúkùrùlúkù, kúrùlúkù (-rö), av./a. àŋgò bï k— it is pitch-dark.

kúkúté = kúŋgúté, a. thick (and strong; of cardboard, timber . . .); èegó 'dï k— this timber is thick.

kúkúti, n. the raised ground near a river; k— èri ŋgörö-rö the river bank is elevated; ìi (mà) kúkúti-á close to the bank.

kúlà, n. a field site prepared in advance (to be cultivated when the rains set in); 'bá tsúrú'dɔ̀ k— mà 'alέ ǵbǎ (or àkǔ or 'bε) now (beginning of March) people prepare a 'kula'/field (later ámvú 'ǎ).

kùulú = ndzεε, ndzεnzdε, n. grass-hopper, small locusts (gener. term).

kùlù-ru, a. thick/strong (of long, round object); pätí k—, báká k— the tree, rope is thick (opp. rŏέ).

kuludúdu, av. forming into a kind of ball, coil, lump; 'bá tra báká k— they wind a rope into a ball (or coil, roll); àɲ̂û lï rö k— bees (after swarming) mass together into a ball/lump (on a tree).

kùlúkùlú = tsùlútsùlú, n. turkey.

kùlùŋgbù or kuluŋgbu, n. a clog or short heavy piece of wood (to imprison, or hamper one's movement); k— èì 'ï tí gàɲ̀àrörï mà ɔmbεléa they tie a clog to the neck of a straying cow.

kùlùŋgbú, n. k— èri ɔmbí g̱bé bε-rï the 'female locust' full of eggs.

kúlúɲ̂á²rö, a. thick, knobbly (roundish); 'úà'úà mà drì k— the hornbill has a round head.

kúmù, kúmùá, n. snag (jagged projecting stump or point on the ground); k— sì mâ pá drìlé a snag has stubbed my (big) toe.

kurè-kurè, av. to fulness, completeness; only in: mvá mba k—k— ɔkó mà 'a 'bə the baby has fully developed in the woman's womb (near delivery).

kúrè-kúrè, av. collecting one's energies; εmbá (or ɔtó) 'ï k—k—; εmbá 'ïmà rùá kɔŋgɔlə ká, èri ndzo ndɔ̀ he contracted his muscles (in preparation for some exertion); he first braced himself, then he started running/racing.

kúrù, av. all over the world (an area, country); àŋgò drìá k— all over the world; 'ïmà rú ku órɔ̀ drìá k— his name is renowned all over the world.

kúrúkúrú, av. ëni k— quite, black dark; àŋgò bï ëni k— it is pitch-dark.

kúrùkúrù, av. completely, perfectly; ma akú mǎ milé k— I covered my eyes completely; é wεε àkúdrì k—, àzï-nï εnápi nï yə sweep the courtyard neatly, that nothing (improper) may be seen in it!

kúrúsέ, kúrúsǒ, n. thick hair, bristle; k— èzó mà 'bíkə 'kuruse' is called hog's hair; èwá mà 'bíkə

sóbía èì ɔmvɛ k— an elephant's
(thick, stiff) tail bristle is called
'kurusɛ'.
kútû-ru, a. short stunted (often
crippled); águ 'dà mà ùú k—
(= ɔtra-zà-rö) the arm of that p.
is stunted/maimed/contracted.
kúuti = kúkúti (≃ á'butì), n.
ìí mà k— elevated bank of river
or water's edge.
kùyà = dằärù (-rö), a. to be
lying scattered on the ground;
pätí bbí k— ɲaákúa the leaves
of the tree are lying about on the
ground.

L

là¹, vt. (1) to cut into small pieces;
'bá zá là ɲïrïɲïrï a man minced
up the meat; (2) to make incisions
(as tattoo); ɔtsɛ 'bání là an-
dratiárï tattoo marks a man cuts
on his face (&c.).
là², vt. to count, read; á nì làtáa
(or làzɔ́) kö I cannot read/count.
là³, vt. to shout one's clan call; 'bá
àzïnï súrú 'ï-vélé-rï là a man
shouts his own clan's call (at
dancing, hunting).
laa¹, vn. to lie down; mvá laa rö
lằàlaa the baby is lying down;
mï adza pằrí laazɔ̌ vàá! spread
the papyrus mat on the ground for
lying down! vt. to lay down flat;
é laa mvá vàá à'búkùrú! lay
the child down on its face!
laa², vt. to fling, hurl; ὲri pätï laa
'dálɛ́ he hurls the stick away.
lá or èlá, n. tall shrub with edible
berries (Ziziphus mauritania).
lằ¹ or lâ¹ = pằrí, kɔ́dra, n. papyrus or mat made from papyrus.
lằ² = lâ² = làŋgá n. place of assembly for men of the village; pằrí a'á-
zɔ̌ tɔ̀rï 'ï place where people sit

about; around the fire for basking
(in bad weather) pằrí àtsî yoo-
zɔ́rïá; as láà lítsó-ti-á assem-
bling place at the entrance of the
cattle-pen. During the hot season
the 'la' sitting place is under a
large tree.
làbàdrìɔ́ = làbɔdrí, àlàbàdrìɔ́,
q.v.
lá'dámù = lálámù, é'dà, or álό-
malóma, n. spleen; l— tí mà
'alɛa, àmbó èì ɲa nἲ the spleen
of a cow, old people eat it.
lằäì = bằäìì, lἲï, kìrr, av. (cf.
lἲï) bewildered, perplexed.
láká'bù = àrú, n. prison (from
English 'lock-up'); ὲri láká'bù-á,
'bâ tsï mààkò wátâ-rö 'dáanï
ɔzɔ́ kɔ́kɔ̌-rö he is in prison where
people eat raw potatoes—without
roasting.
láakà = káalà, T., n. 'sabdavilla'
vegetable; pods and seeds of
kɔ̌lɔ̌'bɔ̌ a decoction of which is
used as seasoning of 'ɔso' beans.
làlà, av. quickly; mï ayu báká
làlà! untie quickly the rope! é
mu làlà! go quickly!
lálámò = é'dà, T., cf. lá'dámù.
láŋgó 'dɔ̌, n. a kind of white
eleusine.
làaó, n. dressed skin; cloth.
làpὲ = lὲpὲ, ɔ̀lὲpà, ɛlɛpὲ, n. a
shrub (Stereospermum kunthianum)
yielding good sticks for work.
láaró, n. the cloth—Ficus (natalensis or/and F. thonningii) tree
(Ac. kitoba).
láasì, S., thin light kind of cloth—
ĕníkĕnîrö bright and soft.
làùlàù-rö, a. light (weight).
lὲ¹, vt. to like, love; ɔkó 'dï lὲ 'ïmà
mvá tɔ̌ the woman loves her
child very much; mï atíì lὲ mïnï
atsí-zɔ̌ kö; mï adri àŋgɔ̌ 'dïá
'dɛ́! your father does not like you

to wander about; do remain in this place!

lè², def. v. (with hortat.), it is convenient, necessary ... that; **lè mïnï atsí kö, mï àzô-rö** you ought not to walk (travel) about, because you are sick; **lè 'bá pírí mà ɛrí àmbó (mà) ti!** everybody has to obey the (words, orders ... of the) elders! **lè káanï é** ... you had better ... you ought rather ... it is preferable that you ....

lèdèrè, n. = lodari, q.v.

ledi, n. (1) ambatch-wood; (2) oar; (3) a stirring stick; **1— tíbí 'alé ɘsa zǒ** a stick to stir the savoury (in cooking).

lèɛdzô, n. forefinger or index; **à'do ɛdé (or 'yɛ) mî 1— nï yà?** what is the matter with (disease) your forefinger?

lèdzóɘá, n. a magic poison (ɛɳa-ɛɳa) of the ɘdzó kind.

lèɛké, n. avengeful spirit of a deceased (Ac. cen); **1— ka èri nï nï or 1— nï èri ɛsé nï** a deceased spirit has bewitched him; **èri 'bá ɘdzǎ** he upsets one.

lêkèmbé, n. small musical instrument played by hand.

lèlê, lèlèá, n. tooth-brush or -stick (from a special shrub); **1— sí dzï (or ɘfá)-zö** a stick to clean (rub) the teeth.

lélé = néné, réré, av. with impressive effect; **ɘvínï ġà 1—** it lightens (powerfully); **àtsïkà-nï ɳïɳï 1—** smoke rises thickly.

lêlé, T. = tsèrè, rè, av. distant, far-off.

lèɛlèɛ, av. brightly, dazzlingly; **ġu (or dì) 1— (ɛmvɛ tǒ)** it shines brightly.

léléa = óní àtsí, n. spark.

lèlékè (alias ólèlê, ólè), n. path (of mice in the grass); **ġïrïkò édró-**

nï mu-zǒrï'ï, 'bá ɘmvɛ 1— the path mice walk in is called 'lɛlɛkɛ'

lèlèó or lèlèġó, n. planet Venus (especially as morning star; as evening star it is sometimes called **áġɘlïröá); 1— èri èfǒ ètú-ếní drí möödrí** it rises at 4 a.m.

léléti = ếlíléti, T. = tïkótïkó, òtùnï, n. slow/blind worm; **èri mu drílé tsí ... vélé tsí** it moves (equally) foreward or backward.

lémékó = lámbérékó or lém-(b)érékó ... n. black area where grass has been burned.

lééɛnì, E. = áï, Lgb. n. compound (with many lines of huts).

lèɛpè, n. cfr. làapè.

lèrè-lèrè-rö, a. shiny, glossy.

léesú or léɛ, n. milk; **èl 1— zɘ (T. za)/or èl tï zɘ léɛsú'rö/èġaa (or èkéɛá, ètsía) sï** they milk a cow into a gourd; **èl 1— tsɘ kérɛ sï ɘdǒ (or bòotâ) rö** they churn milk in a calabash to get butter; **1— 'dï kòópi 'bɘ rï** this is co-agulated milk.

léɛti, T. MN. = tálá, n.? hole, path.

li¹ vt. **tí (or zá) li** to butcher, cut up a cow (or meat); **àbírínï ma ásí li 'dóní nï yà!** how hunger does hurt me!

li² = 'bè vt. to define, fix boundary, delimit; **é li àŋgǒ (or ámvú) mï vélérï!** define the boundary of your ground (field) clearly!

li³ rö, vn. to remain over/cut off; **ɛɳá mà èsá li (= ko) 'ï rá** a bit of polenta was left over; **li-rö-pi or atsé-pi-rï**, n. the rest, remaining part; **àŋá li 'ï ko párîâ-rö** corn (on field) failed to come up in some places (sporadically); **ï li-rö párîâ-rö or ï lípirï or ï li 'ï párí** water that remained back in spots, i.e. lakes.

lĭ⁴, ɛ'yɔ̂ lĭ to cut question, judge; àmbónï ɛ'yɔ̂ lĭ the authority judges; ɛ̀ndzɔ̀ lĭ to lie, to tell lies; é lĭ mání ɛ̀ndzɔ̀ kö! do not tell me lies! = é lĭ mâ tĭá ɛ̀ndzɔ̀ kö! 'bâ drìa (or rùá) ɛ̀ndzɔ̀ lĭ to slander, calumniate.

lĭ⁵, vt. to barter, to trade; ɛ̀i àน̦â lĭ ɛ́wá (or n̍drí) sĭ they barter corn for beer (a goat) (= ɔmvó).

lĭ = ɛ̀lĭ, n. very poisonous glossy black water snake; ɛ̀ri a'á ɔzŏá, nɔ̀sì áyáá it lives among reed-grass (when disturbed it rises and swells its head); lĭnï 'bâ ga ndzàlĭ, 'bá 'dɛ ànï rá it bites very badly, one dies from it (in a few minutes); lĭnï ágû drɔ tsĭ the 'li' pursues the male.

lĭi, av. (1) immovable, spell-bound; àbà (or sɔ̀ pá) lĭi he remained perplexed (upright); 'bɛ o'dú lĭi he fell fast asleep; àน̦gŏ-nï a'á lĭi it has become calm (without wind); (2) (= dĭi) completely; drì-nï àvĕ lĭi he has completely forgotten (about it).

lĭ (1) vt. to roll (along sth.); é lĭ pätí (or pípà, gắrì) 'dálé! roll this wood (pipe, cycle) there; (2) vn. in ɔzɔ̀ó-nï (or àน̦gŏ-nï) lĭ it thunders/the thunder roars; àน̦gŏ lĭpirĭ, n. the thunder.

lĭ¹, vt. to wipe (clean, dust) off; lĭ ĭi 'ïmà rùárĭ bɔ̀น̦gó sĭ he wiped the water off his body with a cloth (towel); ɛ̀i ɔ́kòrön̦à lĭ-lĭ they dust; é lĭ médzà mà drì rá! wipe the table!

lĭ², vt. to pack, gather up, to grasp (seize) with hands and take... ɛ̀i àน̦â lĭ 'bĭlĭa, ɛ́wâ-rö they gather corn into a hole, on behalf of beer (preparation); bɔ̀น̦gɔ̂ lĭ-zŏ to pack clothes (for moving); é lĭ àfa 'dĭĭ wɔ́rɔ́ àmvé! pick up these things and take them out-side! ma emú ma àfà lĭ àkúálé rá I shall pack up my things and take them home; mĭ elĭ (= ɛ̀tì) น̦gŏlŏ mĭ vŏ sĭ! gather up a good part for yourself! é lĭ (= mĭ adza or ɔ̀tì) àน̦á (àmvé) ètúa! take the corn into the sun (out-side)! ɛ̀i ɔdrî lĭ ɛ́mvô si-zŏ they take up clay (and roll it) for pot making.

lĭ³, vt. to prepare heaps (singly or in rows) for planting potatoes; ma màákò lĭ̈lĭ; ma àน̦gŏ lĭ (or tra), ma màákò 'bbí sö drinĭä I prepare heaps (of earth) for potatoes and I will put in potato leaves; the same màákò amŏ lĭ.

lĭ⁴, vt. lĭ 'bá ɔ̀yɔ̀ sĭ to cause a p.'s solemn promise (ɔ̀yɔ̀) to be broken (bringing punishment up-on him); á sɔ̀ ɔ̀yɔ̀ tsĭ, ágú 'dà lĭ mání I solemnly promised, that man caused me to break my word.

lĭí¹ (or ɛ̀lĭí, ɛ̀lĭífĭrĭ́), n. fondness, eagerness for sth. ɛ́wâ lĭí fu ma kái a great longing for beer con-sumes me.

lĭí², av. by drops; ĭi 'dɛ lĭí the water fell by drops.

lĭí³, av. in sö lĭí to surpass, excel...; 'bá sö lĭí 'bá 'dàĭ-nĭ́ a man has outwitted those people (say kàrátà sĭ in playing cards); 'bá sö mùpírà lĭ-rö they played the football match victoriously.

lĭà-lĭà = tsŏkŏtsŏkŏ, av. brim-full; ĭi ga trɛ́ lĭà-lĭà the water is up to the brim of the vessel (i.e. the vessel is brim-full of water).

lĭálĭá, av. shining/reflecting; mà-rárà mà 'alé-nĭ́ 'yɛ 1—1— the mirror reflects light.

-lĭa or, better, -lĕa, from suffix

-lɛ́+á in; oɳúkuɳú fɨ̌ 'ïmà
əmvu-lɨ́a a fly went into his nose.
líbìrà or sìndánì, A.S., n. needle;
l— bə̀ŋgɔ́ sə̀-zɔ̌ needle to sew
cloth.
liidà = lúutè, q.v.
lɨ́dɨ́rɨ̌ = pá-ədzú, n. calf of leg;
gbà èri lɨ́dɨ́rɨ́-á he struck him
on his calf.
lígalíga = àɳá-rɨ́ərɨ́ə, élíndèndè
or élímándrèndrè, n. gecko;
l— lè tòtònɨ̈ ə'á èróa the gecko
prefers to stay in the granary;
(probably by confusion) sometimes, dragonfly.
líkíŋá, n. yam.
líkɨ́tɨ́ = èdrándrèkóa, n. small
pocket (of trousers), bag.
lɨ̌lɨ̌; sí l— or ə̀tsɔ́-sí, n. canine
tooth.
líndalínda = òlúkútúrù, n. ant-
lion; òlúkútúrù èri 'bílé əva
a'á-zɔ̌ 'ɨ̈ the ant-lion makes a
hole (in the sand) to stay in (and
catch food) (alias dragonfly?).
liŋgə(-rəkə), n./a. upper-most
part/top of an elevation or hill; sə̀
pá àŋgò l— 'dɨ̌á he stands on
top of the hill.
liŋgə̀(-rö) = túrù(? = T.lò'dó),
a. àŋgò l— (or ŋgörò)-rö raised
place in hut to lie on; i.e. 'bá
ɳaákú əmvɔ̌ pàrí àlɔ́á dzó
'aléa laa-zɔ̌ they pour earth (and
trample it) in the back-part of a
hut to lie on.
líɳà = kòɳikŏɳi (q.v.) a. glossy.
lɨ́rɨ̌, a. very long (exceeding normal); pätí zɔ̌pi èzórɨ̌ èri l— a
tree that grew very tall is 'liri';
mvá lɨ́rɨ́rɨ̌ (opp. dúlúrɨ̌) a very
tall (short) boy.
Lɨ̌irú, n. a mountain between
Ofóddè and Àrìŋgà: ə̀fóddè pi
mà àsálá Àrìŋgà bɛ-rɨ̌-á.
lɨ̌itrɨ̀, in ètû l— = ètú trá (or

zù), av. the whole day long; àma
ə'á dzóa ètû l— we stayed the
whole day in the hut/room.
lɨ̌itsɔ́ (also lɨ́i), n. cattle-pen; l—
tínɨ̈ kə-zɔ̌rɨ̌ pen for cattle to
sleep in.
lɔ̌, av. only (placed before the word
of reference); 'yə lɔ̌ ɛ'yɔ́ àlö he
said only one word; lɔ̌ mvá àlö
only one child; 'bá lɔ̌ mòrókölɔ̌
ɳaa 'ɨ̈ they eat only m— (q.v.);
ólù ədo lɔ̌ trizàrö castor oil
is only for rubbing o-s.
lɔ̌[1], vt. to tell, narrate, explain; inform; é lɔ̌ mánɨ́ àfa mïnɨ̈ nɛ̌
kɛ̌nàkɛ̌nà! tell me about everything you have seen! lɔ̌ mánɨ́
ɛ'yɔ́ rá he has communicated the
matter to me; lɔ̌ 'bá mà tiá rá
they informed him, announced
it to him; ə̀lɔ̌, vt. to narrate in
detail, discuss, talk over.
lɔ̌[2] = 'bi, vt. to bore a hole, pierce;
édrónɨ̈ ólè lɔ̌ sí sɨ̌ the mouse
cuts holes (path through grass)
with its teeth; èi bbí mà tálá lɔ̌
(= sə̌) 'yɛ́-sí sɨ̌, èi ndzía sə̀ ànɨ̈
they pierce the ear with the point
of an arrow and fix in a ring; èi
'bílé ə̀lɔ̌ fúnò sa-zɔ̌ they make
holes (in the ground) to plant
ground-nuts.
lə̌ = là, T., vt. (1) (zá, tɨ́) to cut
up into small pieces, mince (zá
meat); to butcher, dismember;
'bá pɨ́rɨ́ èi tɨ́ lə̌ the people are
dismembering an ox; (2) to incise;
ə̀tsɛ lə̌ (or ə̀sɨ̌) to tattoo; èi mvá
'dà mà andrati lə̌ or èi ə̀tsɛ lə̌
mvá 'dà mà andrati-á they
tattoo the front of that boy; (3) to
harvest; èi àɳá lə̌ they are cutting/
harvesting corn.
lŏö, av. in cloud-form; kànì é
mvu tábà, é vö (= wi) àtsíkà ti
sɨ̌, èri ŋga lŏö when you smoke

and blow out the smoke it rises like a cloud.

lóá = **lómɔ́ɔ́**, T., n. hartebeest

lòbá (MN. **liku**, Ac. **òtɛ̂ŋ**), n. a tree (with fatty fruits; *Lophira alata*).

lóbéké = **kərikəri**, **ndzindzi**, **ə'bézàrì**, a. variegated, checked, spotted, of various colours; **bɔ̀ŋgó 'dà ɛ̀ri lóbéké'rö** that cloth is checked.

ló'béréko=**ló'biriko**, n **dzó̩ l**— or **dzó̩ ó̩'bírə** (= **lémérékó**) a small stick fixed on top of a hut.

lóɔ̀dè̩, lìɔ̀dè̩, n. stale urine of animal (**tí ə̀dré**); **l**— **mökaa** (**avŏpi 'bə rì'ï**) **drâdra òkáŋgáli** stale urine is extremely bitter/ sour.

lódári = **ò̩kà**, **ádúrúbá**, **lè̩dè̩rè̩**, n. a woody creeper (with strong tuber), yielding good fibre (of a bitter taste, not eaten by ants) (Ac. **ànónó**); **lódári-bá sì̩ ɛ̀i áɳ̊û tï** (**pätí rúá**) with 'lodari' fibre they fasten sesame (to drying frame).

lódíyo = **gbɛ̀ɛ́** (q.v.), n. kind of jackal.

lɔ́də = **mùkà**, **bélé lóŋgó̩də**, n. large obstinate sore (on leg).

lɔ̀ə̀dri = **lòodí**, n. dor (-beetle); **ɛ̀ri tí zɛ̀ ò̩lì̩ pá sì̩** it rolls cow dung along with its legs.

lò̩fŏ̩ = **lò̩kìri**, n. subterfuge, excuse, pretext; deception, imposition; **mï̩ mâ l**— **ò̩fŏ̩ 'dí̩nï à'do sì̩ yà?** why do you disclose my subterfuge like this? **á lɛ̀ mì̩ lò̩fŏ̩ kö** I do not like your deceptions; **sŏ̩ l**— **kéni àzó̩ rö** they made the excuse (pretext) that they were sick.

lógári = **bbŏ̩rŏ̩ndŏ̩**, a. solitary, lonesome; isolated, unsociable, secluded; **mï̩ ə'á lógári'rö, mï̩**

ɳaakâ ɳaa lógári'rö you are unsociable, you take your food alone; **'bá lógári'rö** a solitary, recluse, hermit.

lɔ̀gbó̩, n. heglig tree and fruit (*Balanites aegyptiaca*).

Lóoi, n. prop. name for **Lówi**, nicknamed **Kákóa**.

lə̩ka = **káàkà**, av. roughly, rudely.

lò̩kíà = **tsóà**, n. a weaver bird.

ló̩kírà = **mŋgbilímŋgbì: ùú l**—, n. elbow.

lò̩kìri, n. deception, outlet, expedient, cunning, trick; **mvá 'dì̩ mà l**— **tŏ̩** this boy is very cunning; **ɛ̀ri l**— **ɛdɛ̂** he is playing a trick = **ɛ̀ri̩ 'ye l**— **sì̩**.

lò̩kìrï = **àsákàlá**, n. boundary, limit; **ámvú (mà) l**— boundary/ line of demarcation of field; **é sö pätí lò̩kìrï-nïá!** plant sticks as demarcation.

ló̩kó̩fŏ̩rá, n. see **àtsí**.

lò̩kónd(r)è̩ (cf. **ndéndé**), n. a tree/ palm; mat made from its leaves.

lò̩lì = **ɳáŋgbì̩rì**, i.e. **ɳaakú ɛkarì** n. red soil; **ɛ̀i 'bâ sa 'anì̩á** they bury a man in it.

lɔ̃lɔ̃ = **lò̩gó̩lò̩gó̩**, **a'ú átá**, n. cock; **l**— **tsa ɛtú 'ídrí̩rì̩ là̩ 'bə tsérɛ̀ sì̩** the cock can indicate daybreak with its crow.

lólòá = **ó̩lè̩**, n. **ɛ́dró̩ l**— hidden path of mice in the grass.

ló̩əma, n. side, flank; **ɛ̀ri mâ lóɔ̀máá** he is on my side; **l**— **sí**, n. rib.

lò̩mbŏ̩, n. (1) = **líkíɳá**, yam; (2) a bird.

ló̩mérɛ, n. special man's field (beside his wife's) for special occurrences.

lóɔ̀nd(r)è̩, n. colobus monkey; **ɛ̀ri ɛ̀ni sì̩ ɛmvɛ sì̩** it is black and white; **'bíkónï ɛ̀ri ɛ̀zŏ̩ gò̩rà** its hair is long and flowing; **ɛ̀ri a'á**

ɔ̀tséá, ɛ̀rí atsí pätí sía sǐ it lives
in the forest, goes in trees.
lòongà, T., = ɔ̀ngà, gbagbà, n.
a trap.
lóngbóró, n. tree with large edible
fruits; éfínï 'bá ɛdɛ́ kétɛkɛtɛ̀ rö
from the fruits one gets a kind of
castanets.
lɔ̀ngbɔ̀tɔ̀ more commonly mɔ̀-
ngɔ̀tɔ̀, n. affected cervical muscle.
lɔngɔ̀lɔngɔ̀ = ólɔ̀lɔ̀, n. lapwing,
plover; àíkí (= ɔ̀lǒ) bɛ driá
göràgörà it has a flowing tuft on
its head.
lòpérɛ = lòpérɛ́á, n. a stick with
cross-like prongs at the end, used
for stirring/drilling savoury (cooking); èl ósǒ mà 'alê 'bi l— sǐ
àdzízàrö they stir beans to a
mash with a l—.
lɔ̀rê, n. swampy waterbed at spring
of river; íí mà à'dí mà l—; mà
íí lɔ̀rê sǐ línï ra-zǒ the bed of the
water of the source; one may
drain a bed that the water may
run off.
lɔ̀rókà or lɔ̀rékǎ, n. a large plant
with lancet-shaped leaves (*Amo-
mum korarima Dan.*); èrì ka
ǹdúníá èlè it produces its (triple
capsule) fruits on the ground
(from the roots); óyó l— a smaller
kind in watery ground (bundle of
tiny fruits under water); óyó l—
èl àní órí ɔ̀wǐ the 'ɔyɔ loraka'
they sacrifice to the spirits.
lǒörr-ǒ, av. in a puffy column
(smoke) (cf. àtsíkà).
lɔ̀tèɛ ≈ á'dí, n. (?) walking-stick
(of old men); l— kàlí mbàzànï
atsí-zórì'ï a stick with which old
people walk.
lù¹ (1) vt. to look, glance at; guard,
look upon, after; é lù mání ǹdrí
'dìí èndì! look after these goats
for me too! (2) vn. to detach and

fall; mòémbènï lǔ trù ɔ̀lí sǐ
many mangoes fell to the ground
in the wind.
lù², av. unobserved; á 'bɛ lù I
dropped it unobserved (stealthily).
lúbú, n. gourd-ball receptacle; l—
ɔ̀do tɔ̀ɔ-zǒ . . . to fill in oil.
lúudrì, n. kind of eleusine.
lúfɛ, n. ordinary stick to stir
polenta l— éɲá ɔvazǒ; èl 'anǐ sɛ
l— sǐ they stir it with a 'lufe'
lukú = òlúkú, n. l— mvá drì
sö-zórì small special basket to
put on baby's head (when carried
on mother's back).
Lúukù, n. a mountain ('bé) on the
Àdzíia–Mà'dí-Ndrí boundary;
Ólúkɔ̀ people.
lúkúkuà = àdrópá'dírí, mágárágá, pírípíría, n. whirlwind.
lúkútúrù = púrúa, n. ant-lion;
èri a'á tsíɲá mà 'aléa lives in
sand.
lúlú, n. alarm; lúlù ga to give the
alarm.
lǔlù, vn. (1) to pulsate, throb; àfa
àzó mà l— èri sǔsu the throb-
bing of a painful swelling; (2) ? to
cause to emerge, to push up (beneath).
lúuná, n. a fish-like water snake
(? eel); èri rò la è'bí driá it lies
on fishes (!?).
lùurú, àɲá l—, n. not yet well-
formed eleusine.
luurú, n. fog; l— engápi àtsíkà
lé 'dì ò'búti sǐ fog that rises in the
morning like smoke.
lúrú(ǎ), a. narrow; émvó mà ti
lúrú ǎ the opening of the pot is
narrow; gìrì ásé 'aléa lúurúárì
sǐ the path through the grass
being narrow.
lúurúm(b)é = mìindzí-mbé, bà-
dì-b—, ɔ'bé rözàrö, ɔ'bé rö l—,
gɔrígɔrí, q.v.

lúutɛ̌ = líidà, T., n. rough grass circle (nest for fowls); 'bá aísɛ̂ tra kárîârö; a'únï gbɛ́ sɔ̌ 'alénɨ́á they gather grass into a circle; fowls lay eggs in it.

lúutsé, n. part between two joints (body, bamboo, &c.); ɔ̀drá mà 1— ɔ̀ŋgbùlûmbù mà 'aléa a bamboo's joints; lúutsé-nï zɔ̀ dzì'ï ko the 'luutsɛ' grew short.

M

ma, prs. prn. I; me; má-drí or má-nḯ to me; má-drí or mânḯ my; má-rḯ or má-vélɛ́ or má-vɔ̌ at my home, of my home's; mádrí-rỉ, mânḯ-rỉ, mávélɛ́-rỉ mine; mâ-nḯ on my part; á lɛ̀ mâ-nḯ kö I for my part do not like/want it.

mà¹, pstp. genitive, 's, of; ágú 'dà mà mvá (or dzɔ́, &c.) that man's child (or hut); it is often dropped as, ágú 'dà mvá (or dzɔ́).

mà², part. of hortative, 'may..., ought...'; mà mú rá! let them go!

màa³, vt. to hope, expect, look for, be confident; rely on, confide in; to trust; constructions: (1) àfa màa zɔ̌ 'bá drí (or 'bá vɔ̌) to hope/expect/await sth. from; ma àfa màá mḯ vɔ̌ 'dínï à'do sỉ yà? é ga àma nḯ àfa fɛ̀kɔ sỉ how is it that I rely upon you for sth., and you refuse to give it to us?! é màa mádrí rá ádàarö, má emú fɛ̌ rá! do depend upon me absolutely, I will give it to you! (2) 'bá màa zɔ̌ (àfa sỉ) to confide in a p. (for sth.); á màa mḯ tɛ̌ I relied upon you in vain; èri átá màá sìlíŋgì sỉ he looks to his father for money (shillings); (3) á màa mḯ vɔ̌ màákò tɛ̌ I expected potatoes from you in vain; èri

'ï ándríi-nḯ màá ɛɲ̣á sỉ he is reckoning upon his mother for polenta; á kà Múŋgù màá rá or á kà ma màá Àdrɔ̌ drí rá, Àdrɔ̌nï ma ɛkâ rá if I put my trust in God, God will help me; àma pírí rö màá Àdrɔ̌ sỉ (or vɔ̌, drí, nḯ), ètsáandí (= màtó) sỉ we all rely on God in our troubles; màatáa, n. hope, confidence.

maa¹ = ɛdɛ, vt. to disregard, despise, to disdain, undervalue, neglect; èri mà̀ màma = èri ma ɛdɛ-ɛdɛ he despises me (as inferior); maa ma fú = ɛdɛ ma he disregarded me.

maa²...fú (Ac. rɛ̀ɛm), vn. to be wanting, deficient in; to be in want of; dzó ma ɔ̀zɔ̌ (or ásɛ́) fú the hut (builders) is in want of (more) reed-stalks (grass); ágú 'dà mâmaa tí ɔ̀kɔ̌ dzɛ-zɔ́rỉ sỉ fú (i.e. tí tsa kö) that man is in need of (more) cows for marrying.

maa³ = sï, vt. to pester (with bothersome or endless begging, soliciting, &c.); ágú 'dỉ 'bâ maa tɔ̌ (àfa a'ízà sỉ) this man pesters one (with begging).

maa⁴, vn. to go, or be spoiled; à'bóà maa 'bɔ the banana is already rotten; máápi mamarỉ or maazà, a. rotten, spoiled; á lɛ̀ à'bóà máápi mamarỉ kö I do not like rotten bananas; mà maa rá it may moulder (or fall to dust)! (imprecation).

màbísò or màbúsò, A.S., n. (Lgb. àrú)prison; bỉ 'bá màbísò-rö (or àrúùrö) he arrested a man.

màdàmàdà = mɔ̀dɔ̀mɔ̀dɔ̀ = dì-mòdìmò, a. swampy; ɔ̀rété rö ɔ̀săpi iï bɛ 'dỉ èrì dỉ 'ye àŋgɔ̀ màdàmàdà-rỉ mud mixed with water (it) becomes swampy.

Mà'dí, n. oldest and largest tribe of the Upper Nile, of which the Logbara are a division.

mà'dikà'dí, n. a large ficus tree (*Dracena steudneri*); èri kìlé láaró lɛ́ it is similar to *Ficus natalensis*; súnïrï̀ ɛsɛsɛ̂-rö its sap is sticky, viscid; elastic (mùpírà lɛ́ like rubber).

maafí = màràfí, ə̀mə̀rə̀fí, n. particular grass with fine stalks (for broom).

màgắlì (or -là), S., n. cart.

mágárágá, n. (1) name of a spirit; èri Àdrónï he is a spirit; èri ŋga 'bùá sï̀ àtsï̂ bɛ he descends from the height in fire; èri 'bá ə̀sə̂ ə̀yə̀ sï̀; èri 'bá sə̂ lómáá he affects (magic) a p. by a spell; causes pain in flank; (2) (= àdrópá'díri) whirlwind; èri afí pätí ètíá, i.e. pätí èrinï a'á-zö̆-rï̀ mà ètíá it comes to rest under a tree, i.e. under a tree where it lives; (3) ? (= mágáráká) pneumonia (?).

màgbə̀rə̀ = gbəgbə, a. incurable, malignant, virulent; kà dza kö if it does not heal.

mä̆äikə = ɛmɛ́ɛko, n. *Combretum binderanum*, a large tree with broad leaves bbínï päku or 'barà-rö.

mákátà, A.S., n. court; m— mà 'aléá mï pá sə̂ 'bá àmbórï̀ mà miléa at a court you stand before the authorities.

mààkò, n. potato; á mu m— sa I went to plant potatoes; èri m— bbî tsɛ he breaks off potato tops (for vegetable); m— 'bĭkə potato skin; mí əpí m— mà rúá rá! peel the potato(es)!

màlááa, n. *Pseudocedrela kotschyi* a tree whose fruit (étsofí) contains an oily kernel; èì étsofí mà rúá mbɛ; 'ï éfínï òò ('wḯ) vàá they eat the fruit, its kernel dries

on the ground; but èì éfínï sï̀ e'dí əro with the (squeezed) kernel (added) they prepare gruel.

máládzá = mà'yàlà, yòmà, dzï̆, n. hatred, enmity; malevolence; èì m— 'bǎ 'bá àzï̆ bɛ they have fallen out with each other, they are bitterly opposed to each other.

mälå̆u or málɔ́ə, T., n. a tree; mbazà kə́ŋgə́lə̀rö is very hard; ə̀kó mvá ɛbɛrï̆ ɛtsə́-nḯ ɛɳâ 'i-zö̆ édzánï sï̀ kö a woman with child must not cook her polenta with this fuel.

mälå̆u, n. the empty field after harvesting; ə̀ndó páráká pámvó 'bá əmvɛ m— the stubble-field of durra is called 'malau'.

màlì, a. kind, gentle; mï ássí mà ndrï̀ m— you are gentle/kind; 'bá màlìrï̀ (= àmali) a gentle person.

màalö̆rə̀ = màaríllɛ̀, n. a large tree; èì ɛdê ɛ́sê-rö they use it (its sap sú) as glue.

má(n)dzáka, n. Guinea worm; m— fípi 'bâ pá-rï̀: èrinï fə̂ mâ pá fə̂fə̀ the worm that penetrates one's leg; it makes my leg itch.

Màndzéndzɛ́, n. Maŋgbetu (distinguished by the Logbara for the elongated backs of their heads).

màni-màni = ə̀nìkə̀nì, a. av. indistinct, vague (visible); àŋgə̀ m—m—, ètú 'dɛ̂ dḯ 'bə it is dark, the sun has set (ə̀mú-nè-rö-tê).

màniá (Ac. làmolà), n. kind of grain planted for its oil yielding seeds (like simsim); m— ëni black kind; its white counterpart yɛrɛo.

máaɳá, n. monitor lizard or Nile Varane; m— wa (= mbo) ïí 'aléa a monitor jumped in(to) the river.

Mányáwá, n. a river; M— 'dε Sèwá mà 'aléa the 'Manyawa' falls into the Sewa.

määo, av. high (of heap...?); 'bá drɔ̀ àfa 'dà m— they piled things there high up.

marára, A.S., n. glass; mirror; m— ma nè-zɔ̃́ mirror to look at myself.

màarí, n. a small round gourd (used as blowing instrument); èri pɨ̀ àpǎrìtɨ́á it grows (swells on) on one's farm ground; èi m— vö ɔ́ŋgɔ̂ tö-zɔ̃́ they blow the 'maari' (sometimes made of wood) for dancing.

mǎärí, n. loan, things lent; m— 'íi creditor; mɨ́ èfè mánɨ́ ṅdrí mǎärî rö! give me a goat on hire, i.e. hire me a goat! mâ m— mɨ́ vɔ̃́ tsɨ́; mɨ́ ɔ̀gɔ̀ mâ ŋgá (or àfa) 'í! you have borrowed things from me; give me my things (property) back! mà mu mâ m— a'ɨ́ let me go and ask for my things which have been lent; é 'du (àfa 'dɨ̀rɨ̈) mǎärî-rö! take it (this thing) on loan! mǎärí-tɨ̀ (or àrío-ti) fɛ̌ to pay for thing lent/borrowed, to repay/refund a loan...; mɨ́ èfè mâ mǎärí-tɨá repay my loan! mvu ɛ́wá mǎärî-rö he drank beer on loan; èri sénti fɛ̌ mǎärí-tɨ̀-rö he paid money for the loan/thing lent; èri mǎärí-tɨnɨ̈ (= àrío-tɨnɨ̈) ɔ̀fɛ̌ rá he has repaid the loan, or for things lent.

marɨ́ɔ, n. mahogany tree (Khaya grandifoliola); èri ɨ̀f-tɨ́á it grows on the riverside; kànì èri wɛrɛ, èi ɨ̀ɛrɔ́ e'dí-zɔ̃́ when it is still small, they cut it for fixing up a granary.

mǎäró, n. large and tall white mushroom; èdrɨ̈ká 'bánɨ̈ dzɨ̈ 'dà à'do (è)drɨ̈ká nɨ̈ yà? èri m—

nɨ̈ what kind of mushroom is it they are bringing there? it is a 'maaro'.

márú = márúkɔ́, n. in ámvú m— old field (which has been some years under cultivation); kànɨ̀ é 'à òkûru if you till an old field.

määrù, av. 'that it broke'; di 'ɨ̈ ádrɨ́i mà drì m— he struck his brother's head so that it broke.

másá, n. a tree.

mátákà (? or mákátá) S. = késì, E., n. question, case (before tribunal); èi m— ndzε they bring in a case (or accusation); m— li to decide a question.

màatô = tsàandí, n. trouble, grief, affliction; mishap; ma m— 'bǎ I am in distress, grieved; á zi mɨ́ m— sɨ̌ I ask you out of distress; á mà àfa 'dɨ̈ mɨ́ vɔ̃́ m— sɨ̌ I hope for this thing from you in my trouble; èrì dɨ́ m— mǎ 'bá 'dà vɔ̃́: lè 'ɨ̈ mà fɔ̀ rá: 'ɨ̈ mà: ɔvo tsàandí 'dà mà 'aléa kö he relies on that man in his trouble: that he may be relieved.

màvùlù, S., n. large box or trunk; màvùlùru-rɨ̀'ɨ̈, a. voluminous.

mà'yàlà (= à'yà), n. jealousy; rivalry; jealous feeling; èri m— 'bǎ ma bɛ he is (or has become) jealous of me.

màazá = àzámàká, àzámànàká, ŋàsákà, n. a tree (Bauhinia thonningii).

mba¹/mbá, n. moon; month; mba èri 'bùá; èrì mvɛ ɛ́nɨ́-nɨ̈ the moon is in the sky, it lightens/ whitens by night; mba egá 'bɔ the moon has reappeared; mba-sɨ́ the newly appearing moon; mba-sɨ́ɔvo ègélò 1st quarter; mba aɡa ṅdúa 2nd quarter (half-moon); mba tsa àmbó 'bɔ or mba etsɨ́ ŋgúrúa 'bə full moon/3rd quarter; mba əndrí 'bə: èrì èzíǎǎrö; èrì dí èfǒ àŋgǒ trà sì the moon is in its 4th quarter: it is long and thin: it rises now in the early morning; mba dɛ 'bə the moon is finished, i.e. new moon; ədzá 'ï ayíalê-rö it has turned to the west; mba si ǹdúa 'bə (or ǹdúalê-rö) the moon has turned to the east (3rd phase); mba èri ŋgà mba-sí ('rö) or aga-ǹdúa it is the 1st, 2nd phase; mba o'dú the month's (last) day, i.e. paying day.

mba², vn. to develop; grow bigger and stronger (according to nature); à'dï mba 'bə nǐ yà? tí mvá mba nǐ what has grown bigger? the (cow) calf has developed well; àkónï mbâmba, èri ŋgà mu osí-osí the woman has become big (with child), she will (ere long) give birth.

mba³, vn. to be strong, firm, steadfast, energetic, active, forceful; to be hard (of ripe fruit...); mí ásí mà mbâmba! = mí ɛmbá ásí tsí! pluck up your courage! strong, tough (say of paper, timber ...); milê-mba, n. intelligence, sagacity; cleverness, shrewdness; mvá 'dï mà milê-mba tsí this boy is clever; ɛdé milê-mba sì he has done it with cleverness.

mba⁴; ...mà tà mba, vt. to protect; keep; preserve; é mba mvá 'dï mà tà tsí (or mǒkɛ́)! guard this child well! 'ï átíi-nï èri tànï mba rá his father protects him; é mba ma tà! assist me! àfa tà mba-zǒ to keep, lay up, preserve; ma àfa fè mínï, tà(-nï) mba zǒ I give you a thing for safekeeping; mï èfè mï àfa 'dïrï, á mba tànï tsí you gave me this

thing of yours and I have taken care of it.

mbà, vt. to lie in ambush for; 'bórà-nï ɛdró mbǎ the cat is lying in wait for a mouse; 'bá lɛ̌pi 'bâ 'dípi-rǐ èri mu 'bá mbâmbà one who wants to kill a p. waylays him.

mbà'bú, n. guinea-pig.

mbàa-rö = bàa-rö, av. at random, heedlessly, without aim; èri atsí m— (= bàdàkà-rö) he saunters heedlessly; mï òlò ɛ'yónï m— you talk nonsense.

mbàa-zà, n. an old man; kànì 'bá dèdè èì əmvɛ m— when a man is (very) old, they call him 'mbaa-za' (= 'bá dɛ̌pi 'bə-rǐ'ï); mbàazà 'wàarà elders, principals (of a village), very old men; m— órǐ àwǐpi-rǐ'ï old man (often even weak-minded) who offers sacrifices to the ancestral spirits.

mbɛ¹, vt. to eat, nibble, gnaw at (used for eating fruits or things not cooked); to lap (almost liquid food); èì e'dî mbɛ lésú (or sùkarì) sì they eat/lap up gruel with milk; 'bá ětí, mòèmbè... mbɛ̂mbɛ they enjoy eating tamarinds, mangoes, &c. (sweetmeats).

mbɛ², vt. to tie, fasten; bandage; ma mâ drì àzȇrörǐ (ə)mbɛ I am swathing (wrapping round) my sick arm.

mbɛ³ 'ï, vr./auxil. to start, set about doing; àrà mbɛ 'ï mvì ndȏ the python set out to return in the end (fable).

mbégò, S. = ədzó or tȍrȍbáŋgì, n. sisal (fibre); é mu m— bâ fa! go and unravel the sisal fibre!

mbèlè (-mbèlè), av. soon, quickly; é ndzo m—! run quickly! mà mu àkúa 'dálé rá, mà emví m—! let him go home but come back quickly! mí emú m—m—! do come quickly!

mbɛlɛndzi, mbɛlɛdzodzo, mbè-lɛ̀dzòkò, àmbìlìká, sùmìnìkà, (ɔ́lɔ́tɔ́kɔ́, q.v.) = mbèlɛ̀(n)dzù-kù; n. kinds of lizards; m—rùánï ɔ̀ndzɔ́kɔ̀ndzɔ̀-rö, vínï lɛ̀rɛ̀lɛ̀rɛ̀-rö its body is slippery and also shiny.

mbèlú=mbèmbèlúko, àdràdrà-lúfɛ, n. a smaller green locust with prolonged conical head-piece.

mbèerrí, av. sickly, infirmly, in-dolently; atsí m—; ɛ̀rimà rùánï akázɔ̌ aká-aká-rï̀'ï he walks shakily; he is ailing.

mbètè̀, n. finger-ring.

mbï = tsùlá, n. island; patch of grass with clean surroundings; kànì ásɛ̂ tra 'ï ŋɔ́lɔ̂rö èì ɔmvɛ mbï when grass is growing to-gether (in an isolated place) they call it an island; mbïèrì àŋɔ̀ lí-rö-pi ïì mà àsalá-rï̀'ï an island is a piece of land cut off in the middle of water.

mbi rö, vr. to copulate, have sexual intercourse (of man only); 'bá èì mbi rö men copulate; mbí rö 'bə they had coitus.

mbïlɛ́mbì (pointed), n. in ùú m—elbow; ti m— chin.

mbïlí, n. = sɔ̀rɔ̀, q.v.

mbïlï-rö, mbïlímbïlï-rö, a. taper-ing, diminishing in thickness to-wards one end; kàlámò mà sí m— the point of a pencil is taper-ing; ɛ́drɔ̀ mà ti m— the snout of a mouse is tapering.

mbïrï = mbïrí = ɛ̀kpétɛ́kɛ̀, av. numberless; manifold; otsí mà súrúti m— there are many kinds of thorns; Lógbàrà mà súrúti m— there are many different clan (or tribal) groups among the Log-bara; ɔ́mbí etsá m— locusts

arrived in great numbers; ïì ndɔ̂á m— dɛ ŋgà 'ï kö there is much water in the pail, it is not yet finished.

mbïrïti = òŋgúrùkú, n. the coc-cyx.

mbírò, n. oil-palm (Elaeis).

mbo (= mvo, waa), vn. (1) to bound, bounce; jump (over); kǎmì mbo ɔ̀kó mà drìlé sï̀ the lion jumped over the woman; é mbo ïì mà 'a (= 'alɛ́a) 'dálɛ́! jump into that water! é mbo pätí mà drìà (= drìlɛ́) sï̀ ándzí-ríkáándzï (mà ɛlɔ̌ mï pá mà rùá kö)! jump cleanly over the tree-trunk (that it may not touch your foot)! tí mbo rá the cows jumped over the enclosure/pen and were off; (2) to resist, rebel against (sï̀); mbó ɔ́pí sï̀ they rebelled against the chief/ruler.

mbóróá, a. too short (remainder of sth. naturally longer).

mbúrúmbúrú, a. (1) (= ŋgúrú-ŋgúrú) growling, grumbling, muttering; ɛ́ri ə'yó m— he is mumbling to himself; (2) fag-end, residue; á li kàlámò mádrírï̀ m— I have cut my pencil to a mere stump.

mɛ̌ɛ̌'dïá or mɔ̌ö'dɔ̌á, n. a kind of eleusine.

médzà, A.S., n. table.

mɛ̀nè (-mɛ̀nè), a. soft, fluffy; supple, pliant; gently/lightly (cooked); avɔ̌-pi m—m— lightly stewed.

meenóa = ɔ̀dòkòdɔ̌á, n. very small whitish (very destructive) ant/termite; m— mbɛ bǎò dɛ 'bə the 'meenoa' termites have eaten the timber; m— ɛ̀ri ɔ́dzú-rúkɔ́ nï the 'meenoa' are termites.

mɛ̀ò, n. string-net-bag (to hold in calabash, pot, &c.); èì kɛ́rɛ̌â sö mɛ̀ò mà 'alɛ́a, èi dí 'ì päti rùá 'bùá they put a small calabash into the string-net-bag and hang it up to a wooden peg.

mépò, E., n. map; m— ɛ'dá àŋgò driri̇̀ a map is a picture of the earth.

mëëri, n. the Nile (river); lake.

mï, prs. prn. thou; thee; mí-dri, -vélé, -nï, to thee, thy (cf. Grammar); mî-nï for thee; as regards thee; (cf. poss. prn.).

mì, vt. to push away; (cf. èmì hither); é mì mvá vélé! push the child back! mí èmì 'dólé! push it this way! má tî sɛ, é mì (=drə) tí mà vúti máni (or...máni tí mà ǹdú)! I lead the cow, you push (or drive) it from behind (for me)!

mï = pï, vt. to twist, wring, turn (forcibly); èri mvá mà bbî mï he twists the boy's ears; èri a'ú mà òmbèlɛ́kò mï he wrings the fowl's neck (killing); èi bákâ mï they twist ropes.

mi = milé, q.v. mâ mi my eye.

mí'bíndzɛ́á = mílɛ́ndzèko, q.v.

milé = mi, T., n. eye; look, aspect, appearance; m— fí eyeball; m— ëni the pupil of eye; m— 'bí eyelashes; m— óŋgóró'bí (or 'bə) eyebrow; m— ógú eyelid; m— èdri corner of eye; (1) aspect, appearance; ii mà m— bìbì (or bì ëni tsitsi or ëni rö), əsá 'alɛ́ni dri sì the appearance of the water is/it looks/dirty; they stirred it with the hand; àŋgò-milé the atmospheric outlook; àŋgò-m— (èri) əzòòrö it looks like rain; (2) living aspect; èri milé bɛ i.e. milɛ́ni ndzɛ rö kö (or dɛ/ambì/drà ŋgà kö) he has still his living eye, i.e. is still alive (he is not yet dead); (3) surface,

touch milɛ́fí; bòŋgó 'dì mà milɛ́fí aká-aká (=mènèmènè) the surface of this cloth is soft; (4) milɛ́ sight; ònderɛ̀ ŋa mâ milɛ́ rá small-pox has blinded me; 'bá milɛ́ àtsï berï person with shifty roving eyes/fickle, restless person (especially girls); (5) milɛ́ti bony projection round eye; face, front; ònderɛkó ŋa mvá 'dì mà milɛ́ti nì small-pox has disfigured this boy's face; (6) mark (of disease), sore; mâ pá milɛ́ àzóri'ï the painful sore on my leg; (7) variation: 'bá milɛ́ drǎpirï a blind person; àŋgò milɛ̀-rö pírïnï, 'di kö the sky is gloomy/ overcast, it does not rain.

mílɛ́ndzèko (or -a) = mí'bíndzɛ́á, ŋ̀àŋa, n. water-mite.

mindre, n. tears; èi òó m— sì they cry with tears; m— òó-zò- ri'ï tears from weeping.

míŋ̣ímíŋ̣í (ᵃ rö), a. minutely, finely (spread, made...); (as an area covered all over with various small things/leaves...).

mìindzí-mìindzí = kòríkòrí, q.v.

mìríndà = òndòa, n. cleverness, ability; clever trick, mystification; èri m— edzí 'bá ebbabà- zò he makes a show of cleverness to cheat people.

mïiró, n. cream; lésú m— kòpi drinïá rì cream of milk which collects on it.

mŋgbàa (-rì) (= kílílí, ádadà), a. true, real; á 'yə (ɛ'yó) m— I told the truth; 'dì ɛ'yó m— this is the truth; àtsï m— real (not painted) fire.

mŋgbí, av. completely, decisively; fatally; mvu ɛ́wá m— (atsɛ́pi- nï yə) he drank the beer altogether (without leaving any over).

m̀ŋgbí, av. ? totally; mvá 'dàrï vélé m— that boy is the very last.

mŋgbírí-mŋgbírí = kótsíkótsí, av. to the last bit; èrì ɳa ètóənï m—m— he ate up the hare to the last bit (fable).

mŋgbə, a. prd. (1) open; mí əpì kǎtílé kö, é ko m—! do not shut the door, leave it open! n. m— drìá open spaces (right and left) on front (without hair); (2) hollow (empty within); 'aléní èrì m— its inside is hollow; àfa 'dǐ mà àràkàlé m— the interstices of this thing (fork) are open; (3) free; mǐ drílé m— (mí àzí kókŏ̀rö) you (-r forehead) are free (without work).

m̀ŋgbú, av. all, totally; m̀— 'díní exactly so; 'bá wóró èikí əmvɛ m̀— 'díní (i.e. líkíɳá) everybody calls it exactly so (l—).

mò (or mò̀), vt. to compress, press together; mò tì tsí he compressed his mouth (lips); èrì 'ǐ drí mǒ (better ətǒ, əmǒ) ma sì-zǒ he compressed his hand (to fist) to strike me; mò rö, vr. to cower, squat down (in a corner); má má mǒ ásɛ ètǐa I am cowering down under the grass.

mö, vt. (1) (= 'bö) to coat, dress over; èi èrǒ mö ásɛ sǐ they cover the granary with grass; (2) to make up in packages; 'bá ésɛ̀ mö ásɛ sǐ they pack up locusts in grass; (3) to cover over; àfa àzǐ mà drì mö to cover sth. over; (4) (= ə̀mì) to treat (a sick, tired p.) with (hot) water, wash; èrì 'ïmà mvá mà rùâ mö, àzə̀-rö she treats her child with water as he is sick.

mə̀, vt. to pour into one's mouth; èi éwá (or ə̀ndó) mə̀ tìléa (ɳaa-zǒ) they pour (with cupped hand)

beer (durra grains) into the mouth (to eat).

mò'dà = mùnà, mònà, ïïlɛ́mvó, tídzó, n. waterpot; èi dǐ ànï ïi bè they draw water with it.

mə̀də̀-mə̀də̀ = dìmì-dìmì, mà-dà-màdà, q.v.

mŏ̈ödrí, num. 10, ten; m— drìnï àlö 11, eleven; m— zǒrǐ tenth.

mò̀ɛ́mbè̀, S ?, n. mango (tree and fruit).

mŏká = wànŏká, T., n. stale cow urine; tí mà lŏ̀dè̀ ádzêrǐ m— cow urine from yesterday; (calabashes are washed out with this the first time).

mò̀kàrà, n. (1) (≐ máládzá, mà'yàlà = dzì) ill-will, spite, malevolence; enmity; mí ma m— lï à'do sǐ yà? why are you spiteful to me? mïnï yòmá 'bà-zǒ 'bá àzí mà rùá, èì əmvɛ m— if you begin to hate sby. they call it 'mokara' (enmity); (2) sometimes (= ə̀drá(kóá), kódó) two (or more) days old beer (bad).

mŏké (mŏ̈öké), a. (= 'yɛ́ɛkè), av. good; nice; well, all right.

mŏkóá, n. a very much appreciated savoury (tíbí); e.g. èì ósǒ a'dǐ mŏkóá'rö they cook/prepare beans with oil; or kàìkə avözà èi əmvɛ m— stewed beans they call 'mokoa'; èì a'dǐ àpórà'í sǐ 'dáanï they may prepare it with lye-salt.

mola, n. (1) yellow metal, brass ring, &c.; molǎrö brassy, yellow; (2) (in some parts) a kind of rat.

mə̀lô = kókó, n. a'ú m— miniature hut for fowls; a'únǐ laa-zǒ tì-zǒ 'anǐá in which fowls nest and lay (eggs).

mŏ̈öndŏ̈, n. white foreigner (apparently kinder term for ò̀gá-rà'bá).

mòndrà=mòndàrì, T. (=omú), n. fully developed pupa just before the imago or fully grown insect issues (of bee, &c.).

mòndrókòlò, n. a vegetable plant (*Hibiscus sativus*; A. bamia; Ac. òtígû); it is prepared with simsim, kàikǝ-beans and lye-salt(à'ítìká).

mòndzókǝ̀, n. àagó m— the soft pulp of a melon or pumpkin (with seeds).

mǒnìǒ-drěká = mòrǒ-drěká, n. a small, white, edible mushroom.

mǒnìó also múnìo, mǎnìó, mǒnìgǒ, n. ox; m— átá bull.

mǝ̀nǝ̀ = mènè, q.v.

mǒönǒ, n. a skin disease, rash; èrì 'bâ mbɛ rùá it affects (rough, red or grey-whitish spots) one's body (skin).

mǝ̀ŋgǝ̀tǝ̀ or lǝ̀ŋgbǝ̀tǝ̀, n. sleeping-sickness disease (with enlarged neck muscle).

mòpírà, S., n. football, and any rubber ball or article; èì m— tsǝ àbálá sǐ they have a football match.

mòrá = obí, n. large pot for beer preparation émvó éwá ǝrǝzǒ-rǐ.

mòrè = àmórèká, n. (lower) ear-jewels; àfa 'bánǐ sǔ bbía-rǐ a thing they put on their ear-lobes (cf. ndzǐǐa).

mǝ̀rǒ, n. old place of lítsó, marked by heaps of cowdung (wǒrótǝ̀) and, occasionally, mushrooms growing well on it, the mòrǒ-drěká.

mǝ̀rǝ̀dúfò, S., n. commercial term for a strong cloth (bǝ̀ŋgó ǝkpórǐ).

mǒrókòlǒ, n. a liquid savoury concoction of water, simsim and ash-lye; 'àŋgǒ dùrù' if beans are added (squeezed).

mǒrǒlǒ, n. (1) pulp; àfa (as è'bǐ) a'dípì tékètékè 'dǐ gbï rö mǒrǒlǒ'rö a thing (fish) they overcook turns into pulp; (2) lésú mǒrǒlǒ (drǎpì kö-rǐ not sour) èrì tsúrú'dǝ̀ kéré mà 'alěa kòzà-rö: alu tǒ sweet milk now in a bowl to coagulate: very nice.

mǒrǒtö, n. dry cow droppings mixed up with earth wǒrótǝ̀ tǐnǐ zɛ ǒ'dírǐ (fresh cow dung) etsí-rö-pì (= ǝsáröpì) ɳáakú berǐ, 'dǐ m—; àagó nǐ pì ànǐ mǒké melons swell well on it (manure).

mosóá, n. = àtsófà, q.v.

mòtéré, n. slices (of manioc, potato); ǝlá mà m— 'bá 'bà 'wï ètúa slices of manioc people put to dry in the sun.

mòtsé = ɳàadzò, n. oribi gazelle.

mòtsélé, S., n. rice.

mù, av. invisibly, undetectably; ma àfa 'dǐ àvǐ mù, á ndà èrì tǐ my thing was lost completely, I searched in vain for it.

mu, vn. to go (away; cf. emú to come); aux. vb. of future; ǝzóónǐ mù 'dì rá it will rain.

mùlùrù (T. = mùrùlù), a. fresh; lésú m— (=wa) fresh milk (not sour or coagulated).

múnékè (= T. óda), n. afterbirth (of animal).

mùsóǝrǝ̀, S., n. taxes; m— 'bɛ to pay taxes; ópí-nǐ m— a'ǐ/= tra the chief collects taxes.

mút(r)è, n. a particular dance; mà m— tö ! let them dance 'mute'

mùtùkárì, E.S., n. motor-car.

mvá, pl. andzì, n. (1) child; ágúpì mvá boy, son; zǎä mvá girl, daughter; offspring; the form mvíì, much in use, for mvá (for intimacy); (2) young of any animal (or plant); tǐ mvá calf;

kàbìlɔ̀ mvá lamb; a'ú mvá chicken, &c.; (3) small piece of...; ɛ́rà (or óní) mvá small stone; (4) drí mvá, pá mvá finger, toe.

mvà, vt. to clear of grass (ground, with hoe...); mu àŋgɔ̀ mvà (= mvɔ̀, vɔ̀) he went to clear the ground of grass.

mvakomvakoa = àkpââ, n. tweezers.

mvàrrà, (1) av. in steady flow; mànìà mà éfì ɔfì m— 'simsim' grains (put on fire) exploded in continuous succession; (2) n. A.I.M.'s H.Q. (Arua).

mvɛ, vn. (1) to be white, clear, bright; lésú mvɛ tɔ̀ milk is very white; (2) to shine; àŋgɔ̀ mvɛ mba sǐ ɛmvɛ there is clear moonshine; mbanǐ mvɛ ɛ́ní sǐ the moon shines by night; (3) vt. to make white (rare).

mvíí, intim. form of mvá; mâ mvíí 'ï my son; Rɔ̀kɔnï mvíí'ï Rɔ̀kɔnï's son; emú 'dǐá ko mvíí-nǐ 'dɛ́ she came here and left her child there.

mvi, vn. to return, i.e. go back (cf. emví to come back); əmví to give back; əmví 'bá mà ti to answer a p.

mvɔ̀, vt. to gorge o-s., eat one's fill (of solid food only); mvá 'dà ɛri ŋaaká mvɔ̀ tɔ̀ that boy eats his fill; ǹdrí-nǐ àŋáfɔ́rá mvɔ̀ the goat gorges itself with flour.

mvo, T. = mbo, q.v.

mvu, vt. to drink; è mú àmbó mà ɛ́wâ mvu! go to drink beer at the elder's.

N

N.B. Here are listed only words pronounced generally with initial n, while under ŋ will be found words which are pronounced with n in some dialects (Tɛrɛgo) as ɛ́ŋâ ŋa or ɛ́nâ na.

ǹñ = ɛ̃̌ɛ̃, intj. yes.

ná or nná, indf. pr. all.

nna, num. 3, three; nna-zɔ̌-rǐ the third.

na, (1) vn. to avoid, shun; ɛ̀ri adzú/'yɛ́ na he avoids a spear (by skilfully manœuvring his body); (2) (= ko, dà, sɛ, si rö); vr. to step aside, make way for; é na rö rá, ma mâ àfà ɓbï 'dɛ́lɛ́ 'dì move aside that I may throw my th. over there; ɔdrú-nǐ endzó 'dà, é na mǐ rá ɛ̀ri ɛ́dǐɔ mǐ fûfu a buffalo is coming there; get out of the way, it will kill you!

nàáfé, T. = ŋɔ̀fé, n. axe....

nàgá or nàá, T. = ŋ̀àá, n. beast of prey; é nɛ̀ nàá endzó 'dìɔ! look out! a wild beast is coming running towards us!

ndà, vt. to seek, search; 'bá mu pätí ndàrǐá 'bɔ sby. has already gone out in search of wood.

ndakà, n. kind of red durra ɔ̀ndó ɛkarǐ.

ǹdálǎ (? = ǐi-drì-puuru), n. a plant growing in/on water (?lotus) ɛ̀ri ŋga ǐi mà 'a; 'bá ɛ̀ri mbɛ̀mbɛ they eat it (? its root); n— ɛbíkɔ ɛŋgápi ǐi drìá 'bùá-rǐ its leaves spread up upon the water.

ndàlàkà, n. a bird of the milvius kind (?) ɛ̀ri yúkú mà ɛ̀dzɛ̀lɛ́kɔ̀.

ndala(-wa) more commonly walanda, a. flat broad (wide); àfa ndala'rö ɛ̀i ɛmvɛ àdzíikɔ́ (ɛ́ŋá əva-zɔ̌) a flat thing is called a potsherd (to distribute polenta); àŋgɔ̀ n— (or walanda) a plain (area).

ndàndằ = dzɔ̌dzɔ̌, n. shrewmouse; n— mà ti zɔ̀ ɛzɔ̀rö the shrew-mouse's snout is long;

àdzí-nï èri èríkɔ́kɔ̀rö (= ŋgù-zàrö) it has a bad smell; kànì mu gèrìkɔ̀ alɪ̈́, èrì mù 'dɛ gèrìkòá if it goes across a path, it will die on the way.

ndătá = ndɔ̌tɔ́, à(yì)ràtà, àyìràgɔ́, á'yotá, n. the same as (or young ones of?) ɔ́lɔ́tɔ́kɔ́ or álátá large red-headed lizard.

ndè, vt. (1) to outrun, outmatch, surpass; mvá 'dà ndè ádzê ma oŋgú sɪ̈́ rá that boy outran me yesterday; (2) to defeat, overcome, subdue; àzɔ́ ndè èri rá disease has overwhelmed him/he is very sick; (3) to be beyond a p.'s ability; ɛ'yɔ́ 'dɪ̈́ mu mɪ̈́ ndě rá this question (matter...) will be too much for you; to be unable, incapable, unequal, inadequate for; av. surpassing all; o'dúkonɪ̈́ ku ndè rá its sound surpassed everything.

ndɛ, vt. to refuse, deny a p. a thing; mvá 'dɪ̈́ ndɛ ádzê ma ɛ́n̥á sɪ̈́: n̥a a'dúlɛ, əmvɛ ma kö this boy denied me polenta yesterday: he ate alone without calling me; é ndɛ ma (éwá sɪ̈́) sɪ́ you refused it (beer) to me.

ndɛ́ = ádanï, av. properly, exactly speaking; really, actually.

ndɛ-rɪ̈́, pl. ndɛ-èi or ndɛ'dɪ̈̀ (= té-rɪ̈́/té'dɪ̈̀), dem. prn. the afore-mentioned, -seen, -discussed...; mvá ndɛrɪ̈́ ŋga etsá à'do-ŋgárɛ yà? when will the child we were talking about arrive here? mvá ndɛrɪ̈́ (= mvá-nïrɪ̈́) etsǎ 'dɔ̀ that boy is arriving here; é tsə andzi ndɛ'dɪ̈̀ à'do sɪ̈́ yà? why did you beat the boys who were here before?

ndɛ́ndɛ́, n. palm growing in swamps (Phoenix reclinata; Ac. òtëët).

ndɪ̈̀, vt. (1) to pinch, tweak a p.; ndɪ̈̀ ma ɔ́n̥ɔ́fɪ̈́ sɪ̈́ he pinched me with the fingernails; (2) to pull/break off (small parts); é ndɪ̈̀ zá fɛ̌ mvá 'dà mà dría! pull off some meat and put it in that boy's hand! mɪ̈́ èndɪ̈̀ èri nɪ̈́ ddɪ́ká! break off some more for him! ndɪ̈̀ rö, vr. to break away, off; é bɪ̈̀ émvó baba, tinɪ̈̀ kà-zɔ̌ mu-zɔ̌ ndɪ̈̀-rö-zɔ̌ kö! catch the pot carefully, so that its rim may not break off! émvó mà ti ndɪ̈̀ 'ɪ̈̀ rá a part of the pot's rim broke away.

ndî see èndî, av. truely, really; ndɪ́?! really?!

ndɪ́, a. drî ndɪ́ (= áda) right hand; drî ndɪ́ àmanï ɛ́n̥á ètɪ̈̀-zɔ̌-rɪ̈̀ right hand with which to break off polenta; wòɔ́kɔ̀ drî ndɪ́á on the right-hand side.

ndii, ndiiɪ́, av. ndi, ndindi-rɪ̈̀, a. silent, quiet, reticent, taciturn, reserved; mvá ndi (-ndi) rɪ̈̀; èri gǎ ɛ'yɔ́ kɔ́kɔ̀rö àkà a taciturn boy, he refuses wantonly without saying a word; èri n̥ɪ̈̀ ndindɪ̈̀rö he smiles quietly; ɔlɔ̌ ɛ'yɔ́ 'dɪ̈̀ 'ɪ́mà véléa ndii they talked over the matter secretly in his absence; ágú 'dɪ̈̀ emú má vɔ̌ ndiiɪ́ 'dɪ́nï; lè mâ 'dɪ̈̀ 'di yà? this man came so cautiously/stealthily to me; does he want to kill me? mɪ́ adri (or òvù) ndii! keep silent, cautious! 'bâ dɪ́ a'á ndii the people kept quiet/peaceful then; əvo-zɔ̌ ndii, i.e. ə'yətá kɔ́kɔ̀rö to be quiet, peacefully, i.e. without much talking (= tsɪ̈́ɪ̈rɪ́, iyàa).

ndindía, n. plague; pestilence; àzɔ́ 'bánï ədrà-zɔ̌ ndindirɪ̈̀ a disease of which people die without people knowing it.

ṅdɪ́ɪ̈rɪ́, ndɪ́tɪ̈́rɪ́-rɪ̈̀, a. (1) clean, neat, proper, tidy (= àlá); àŋgɔ̌ ndírí=ɔ́kɔ̀rɔ́ŋ̣à kɔ́kɔ̀rö the ground is clean—without dirt; (2) clear; àŋgɔ̀ milɛ́ n—, i.e. ɛ́rítí milɛ́nı̣́á yɔ the weather is clear, bright, i.e. no clouds in sight; (3) clear and distinct, intelligible, plain, lucid; é 'yɔ ɛ'yɔ́ n—! i.e. é 'yɔ ɛ'yɔ́ ɔ̀yɔ̀kɔ̀ló sı̌ kö speak clearly and distinctly, do not whisper!

ǹdíríá = ɔ́vá, n. dikdik gazelle (Ac. amuur); a. dark-grey (as the 'ndiria').

ndítí (̊= àlí, kútú), a. short, a small part only visible; mà sɔ màákɔ̀ bbí vàá (bbínı̈) mà adri ndítíâ-rö (= àlíârö)! plant the potato shoots in the ground, so that only a small part remains visible!

ndítítírı̣́á (cf. ndítí) (also tùkùtúkú), n. short man, dwarf, pigmy; 'bá zɔ̆pí àlíarı̌ people grown short; facetiously called ·'é nɛ̀ ma wé ŋgɔ́ yà?' lit. from how far did you see me? (if told that he was observed at a good distance, he is pleased, otherwise he· takes offence); n— rö, a. dwarfish.

ndɔ̀, av. afterwards, ultimately, subsequently, in the end; má emú 'dòá ndɔ̀ I shall come here in the end; ndɔ̀rı̌, a. later, of the future; 'dı̌ àzí àmanı̈ mu lɛ́ ŋga lɛ́ ndɔ̀rı̌'ı̈ this is the work we shall go to do afterwards/later.

ndɔ́ɔ́, n. pail (debe).

ndó, ndóndó, a. different, distinct; ɛ'yɔ́ 'dı̌ı̈ ndóndó these words are different (in meaning).

ndólí-ndólí, a. long-stretched; àfanı̈ rö èdzò-zɔ̆ èzɔ̆ n—n— sth. reaching a good (relative) length; ɔ̀tɔ̀nɔ̀kɔ̀ èdrè 'ı̈ ɔmbɛlɛ́ n—n— (= ndɔ́tɔ́nɔ́) the snake

stretches out its neck very long; mı̌ olí àfa 'dı̌ n—n— (= ndɔ́tɔ́nɔ́) à'do sı̌ yà? why do you cut the things so long?

ndòlò = ɔmá, n. female genitals, vulva.

ndɔ́tɔ́'dɔ́, n. swelling, protuberance; 'bâ ɡba drinı̈ n— a man struck his head causing a swelling.

ndɔ́tɔ́nɔ́, a. = ndólí, q.v.

ndɔ́tɔ́rɔ̀ = ɛ'ba-àrı̣́a, n. hoopoe.

ndɔ́tɔ́rɔ̀(à)-rö = ɔtúkú'dú, èkpétérè, ɔ'dɔ́tɔ́rɔ̀, a. of little depth, not deep; álínı̈ n— = álínı̈ yɔ there is no depth; ɡa 'bílé n— he dug a flat/not deep hole.

ǹdɔ́tɔ́tɔ́, av. in heaps, clusters, piles; 'bă àfa n— they put things in a heap/piled. things up.

ndrâ, av. time ago, in the past (very elastic term); n— (òku) drìɔ̀ long ago, in the distant past; n— ɔ̀kɔ̀rı̌ sı̌ in the past—in the beginning; n— ètú dɛ vútinı̣́á kárákàràrö 'bɔ many days have since passed; mu n— dɛ̀rɛ̀ drìɔ̀wú sı̌ = n— drìɔ mu dɛ̀rɛ̀ drìɔwúsı̌ he went thus long long ago; ndrâkárı̌, a. of old, of the past; 'bá ǹdrâkárı̌ the ancestors.

ndrà¹, vt. to cast (furtive) ·glances askance; èri mvá àzínı̈ mà búkù ndrǎ he is casting a sidelong glance at another boy's book (cribbing from); to leer at sby. (out of the corner of the eye), to look askance at; 'bá 'dà n— ma milɛ́ èdrí (or ǹdú) sı̌ that man looked (contemptuously) at me out of the corner of his eye; mı̌ má n— 'dínı̈ à'do sı̌ yà? why do you look thus askance at me?

ndrà² = dà, vt. to pour (out); mà ndrǎ ɔ́sɔ̆ mà ı̌ vàá, mà ŋa ádarı̌ áyò (= 'ı̈)! mà ndrǎ vàá àkú má 'alɛ̆a 'dɛ́! strain off the water from the beans and eat them! let it be poured out in the yard there! èì ə̀do ndrᵃ̀ émvóã mà 'aléa they strain oil into a small pot.

ndrà³, vt. to wrap round; èì ə̀mbé ndrᵃ̀ they tie round a circle of sticks (with rope) (to fix it on top of hut).

ndrákúndrákú, a. thievish; mᶤ̀ drí ndrákúndrákú῾rö your hand is larcenous.

ndrᵃ̀lì, av. indistinct, confusedly; ma ɛri n— I did not hear it clearly.

ndràndràlúfɛ, = àdràdràlúfɛ, mbèmbèlíku, n. a large locust with long-pointed head.

ɳ̀drí, n. goat; n— ágó, -átá he-goat; n— kᵃ̀ri, -ándríi she-goat.

Ñdrí'bá, n. name of a tribal group of Áìvò; it is a segment of the original large Ma'di division called Mà'dí-Ñdrí or Goat-Ma'di.

ndri, vt. to winnow, fan (by wind); èì àɳ̯â ndrí-n— èrî driá (ə̀línï ókŏ̀rŏɳ̯à 'du rá) they fan corn in the stamped ground (the wind carries off the chaff).

ndrᶤ̀¹, vn. pleasant, agreeable, giving pleasure; (1) (sight) nice; mï andrati n— kö, mïnï osilérᶤ̀ sᶤ̀ (or ə̀ndí bɛ) your face is not nice because of your tattooing (being dirty); gu n—n— it shines brightly; ètú egbí (or èfŏ) n—n— the sun rose brilliantly; (2) (smell) èri ɳgǔ mání ndrᶤ̀zàrö it smells nice to me; àdzínï èri e'dû rö (ə̀lí bɛ) mání (or ma ò̀mvuá) ndrrᶤ̀; nə̀sì èì zá a'dᶤ̀ aánï its fragrance comes to me (in my nose) agreeably; perhaps they are cooking meat; (3) (weather) àɳgò̀ ndrᶤ̀ dzóa ndrᶤ̀ = dzó 'alé ndrᶤ̀ndrᶤ̀ it is comfortable in the

room (nicely cool); (4) (condition) satisfactory, adequate; má ëlï 'dᶤ̀ n— tŏ my knife ('s edge) is good, satisfactory; kànì é rᶤ̀ (ə̀rï) 'bə, èri ɛɳgá n— tŏ once you have sown it, it will turn out well; (5) (moral) calm, gentle; èmï ásí mà ə̀vö ndrᶤ̀zàrö (i.e. é 'bà ə̀mbà 'bá àzᶤ̀ bɛ kö)! be quiet/gentle (i.e. do not start to quarrel with others)! ásí ndrᶤ̀zà, n. loving kindness, mercy.

ndrᶤ̀²-àfa, ə̀ɳ̯ᶤ̀-àfa, àfó-àfa, n. trinkets, knick-knacks.

ndrri, av. very deep; 'bú ku (≡ fï) vàálé n— the hole is deep and steep.

ndrí, cf. ɳgà (ndrí ká).

ndrí¹, ndrí-ndrí, av./a. (1) (of distant flickering fire) shining through, at intervals; àtsï ɛ'dá n—n— fire shows there flickering; (2) mílé n—n— restless, never resting, unquiet, uneasy, continually moving; mᶤ̀ mílé n—n (or àtsï) tŏ your eyes are roving around restlessly; é ko mílé n—n— (or àtsï) dzà! mílé n—n— èri ə̀ndzí don't be so inquisitive; restlessness is bad; be quiet! mᶤ̀ adri ɛ'yéré! mᶤ̀ ndrí-ndrí-â-rö, i.e. mᶤ̀ àfa òbᶤ̀ tŏ you never rest, you handle everything; (3) sharp(-pointed); sìndánì sí n—n— the needle's point is fine; ëlï ə̀kó drírᶤ̀ mà sí n—n— the edge of the woman's knife is sharp; (4) causing sharp, spasmodic pains; èrᶤ̀ 'yɛ n—n— lómáá it causes sharp pains in the flank.

ndrí², av. with sudden stealthy movement; bŏ̀rà 'ï (= dzi, T.) n— the cat escaped/ran to safe refuge all of a sudden.

ndrí-ósə̀-rö, a. faint, languid; n—

ósð de rö 'bâ dría kö, èri ŋgǔ
dánï dánï the smell of goat fat
takes a long time to disappear from
one's hand, hence ɔzɔ́ɔ́ 'dï àtï
'dɔ́ kö, èri ndrí-ɔ́sɔ̀rö this rain
does not stop, it goes on drizzling.
ndri, in àtsïfè n— to consult the
magic rubbing stick; if the rubbing 'ring' [of grass] sticks im-
movably (sɔ̀) on a subject, it
indicates guilt/doom; má 'yɛ drǎ
'dɛ́ kö, àtsïfɛ ka mánï bba I
shall not die of it, the magic stick
was favourable to me; vt. (= enǎ)
to bewitch; èri 'bâ n— àndrí sï
he bewitches people with charms;
'bá àtsïfè ndrípirï the rubbing-
stick diviner.
ndrî or ndríɔ̀ or ɛ́'dïɔ̀, av. afterwards, later on (during the same
day); (kind of formative particle
of near future).
ndríndrí, av. ɛmvɛ n— (our) it is
snow-white.
ndrìkíndrikí, av. unsteady, shaky
(of walk, pace); èrì 'yɛ n— he
walks unsteadily; said of áfa lɛ̌pi
drǎpi dràdràrï if almost about
to die.
ndrìmà-ndrìmà, a. (1) dark,
gloomy; àŋgɔ̀ n—n—rö it is
sunless (cool), gloomy; erítinï
ètú mà milé asɛ́-zö tsï (light)
clouds cover the sun; (2) dark
(after sunset); àŋgɔ̀ n—n—:
'òmú-nè-rö-tě sï' it is dark; 'a
guest can no longer be recognized'.
ndrí-ɔ̀drà, n. a very small mouse
(of fields); èri ti pätí sía (or
ò'díti 'alɛ́a) she brings forth
her young on a tree (or under a
mound of earth).
(è)ndríio = ndrí-ɔ́'bí, ndrí-
pɔ̀dɔ̀, ndrío-tibbí, n. quiver
resembling bundle of sticks (or

grass stalks; or maybe real quiver-
èndɛ́rɛ́-filled with grass) covered
with a long-haired and -tailed
skin of colobus; n̄— ɔŋgɔ̀ tö-zö
for dancing entertainment only.
ndrí-vu-ņ̣írí, ndrívuyɔ́rɔ́, n.
very small (black with whitish
breast) bird (finch).
ndrö[1], vt. to suck; mvá (or kɔ̀dzǎ)
nï 'ï ándrïi mà bbà n— the baby
(or calf) sucks its mother's breast
(udder); èri tàmtámù n— (or
mbɛ) he sucks sweets; endro, vt.
to suckle; ɔ̀kó 'dïrï mvá e—
bbà sï the woman suckles her
baby at her breast.
ndrö[2], vn. to smoulder; àtsï n—
ɛka or àtsï tsï ņ̣àai, i.e. èri àtsï-
fúlɔ̀rö the fire is smouldering, i.e.
burns slowly and without a flame
(as under ashes), is incandescent.
ndro, vt. to enlarge (from inside);
èì 'bílé (i.e. mà 'alé) ndrɔ̀ndro
ɔ̀drɔ̀dzɔ́ sï they enlarge the interior of a grave for the dead's
'chamber'.
ńdró, av. àŋgɔ̀ n— desolated,
wretched, afflicted, disorganized
place; mï átíl ko àŋgɔ̀ n— your
father (dying or departing) has left
the place a prey to wretchedness/
desolation; 'bá ɔ'yɔ́ 'alɛ́nïá òku
drìɔrï lɛ́ kö; 'bá ɔvö ànï
ètsáandí sï nobody's directing
voice, as of old, is heard in it;
people are disconsolate/comfort-
less; àŋgɔ̀ fï ndró the place (or
country) has become desolated.
ndrɔ, vt. to slander, backbite;
'bání 'bá àzï n— zö vélɛa (i.e.
èrinï ɔvö-zö yɔ-rï sï) when one
slanders another behind his back
(i.e. he being absent); èmï 'bâ
n— kïlé ɔkólé you are back-
biting/defaming people like women; mï bbílɛ 'bâ ndrɔzà sï

yɔ 'dĭ̀! mĭ̀ mù n— àmvé 'dálé
à'dúkúlé sĭ̀! are you impervious
to (advice against) slandering
people? go away and slander for
yourself! èi ɛ'yɔ̂ n— 'bâ rúá
they are slandering (against) people; ndrɔtáā, n. backbiting,
slander.

ndrɔ¹, vt. to remove, take away
cautiously/stealthily; ma ëlĭ̈ n—
sö dzɔrôá I abstract the knife
and put it in my pocket; n— té
mvá 'dĭ̀ mu èi bɛ 'dálé he took
the boy away unnoticed and went
there with him.

ndrɔ² (= tú àlö), av. all together;
etsá n— they arrived together;
ndrɔ-ndrɔ, av. side by side; éi
atsí n—n— they walk side by
side.

ndrɔ̀kɔ̀('dɔ̀)rö ≙ ndrɔ̀kɔ̀sɔ̀-rö, a.
of considerable length (of its
kind); màákò mà amo n— rö
the damlike strip of potatoes
(field) stretches a long way (maybe
the whole length of a field); said
of long shed, &c.

ndrɔkí-ndrókí, a. in zigzags; gĭ̀rĭ̀
mu n— (= gòlígòlí) the road
goes in zigzags.

ndrɔlè, a. oblong (as a cucumber).

ndrɔ̌ndrɔ̌lɔ̌, av. cold; àŋgɔ̀ ambĭ̀
n— it is very cold.

ndrɔsɔndrɔsɔ, a. stretching, extending in slimy/clammy/stringy
threads; or particularly long; as
a donkey's head (ndrúkù, mbɛ̀sɔ̀-
mbɛ̀sɔ̀-rö).

ndrù, T. vt. = ndà to seek.

ndrúkù-ndrúkù, ndrúkùsù-ru,
a. extending downwards; gà zɔ̌
èlè sĭ̀ n—n— to drag/creep
lengthily on the ground; dzɔ́ mà
áisé ndrúkùsùru the roof grass
reaches deeply down (towards
ground).

ndrûndrúa = dzĭ̀rĭ̀lĭ́, rörɔ̌a, n.
zibet cat.

ǹdú = ètĭ́, ɔ́lá, n. (1) lower part
of; posterior; pätí ǹdú the lower
part of a tree; or place/ground
under a tree; (2) track, trace;
káayò (?) ŋgaa 'dálé, ndúnĭ̈
àvĕ̀ rá the stork flew away there
and its trace was lost; ǹdú-á =
ètĭ́a, pstp. under, beneath; mvá
laa rö ko pätíǹdúa 'dà the child
lay (and remained) under that tree.

ndzá, drì ndzá, see ɛndza² (3).

ndzàai, S., n. bhang, hemp; ágú
'dà sɛ n—; èri tsúrú'dɔ̀ aza àni
that man smokes bhang; he is now
stupefied from it.

ndzáiyá, more commonly ɔ́ndz-
záiyá, n. Cayenne pepper; èi n—
'i à'í bɛ tú àlö they grind red
pepper together with salt.

ndzǎlí, ndzǎlía, av. (1) (= kái)
very badly; tsɔ èri n— he beat
him very badly; (2) wholly, the
whole; ndĭ̀ àfa 'dĭ̀ n— they tore
off the whole.

ndzǎrùndzǎrù, ndzàindzàai, n.
a particular savoury; èi ɔ́sɔ́ osi-
osi àtsí drìá, èi dĭ̀ ɔ́sónĭ̈ àw-
àwà oní drìá they roast beans
(in a pot) on fire and then pound
them on a stone; (to which they
add water).

ndzɛ, vt. (1) to take, bring out from
(inside..., beneath...); é n—
mání àfa sàndúku mà 'a 'dĭ̀!
take out sth. for me from the case!
mĭ̀ ɛndzé ndrâ ma iía drìɔ rá
you pulled (saved) me once from
the river; n— pätí àfa 'dà mà
ètĭ̀arĭ̀ rá they removed a piece
of wood from beneath that thing;
(2) ɛ'yɔ̂ n— to speak; é n— ɛ'yɔ̂
mĭ̀ ásía 'dĭ̀! give your opinion
(thoughts in your heart)! (3) to
remove (generally); é n— (also

zì) lítsɔ́ tilé rá! remove the door
of the cattle enclosure! èi ádî n—
drìnɨ̌lá, ɛ̀rinɨ̌ ŋga (or àtì, atsí) zɔ̌,
they remove a spell from him that
he may rise (heal, walk) again!
(àzɔ́ sɨ̌); (4) castrate (= o'du);
ɛ̀ri ǹdrî(tí...)ndzɛ̀ndzɛ(=o'du-
o'du) ráaò rö they castrate a goat
(bull) male; (5) ndzɛ rö, vr. to
come off, sever, separate, detach;
n— rö andzi mà ɛ̀sɛ́kɛ̀léa (or
'aléa) rá he separated from the
boys; elɨ̈ mà àbé n— rö 'bə the
knife's handle came off.

ndzɛndzɛ, n. the common smaller
grass-hopper; n— ɛ̀ri sǎsà
(= ngǎŋga or mbɔ̀-mbo) the
grass-hopper flies (or jumps).

ńdzɨ́, ńdzɨ́-ndzɨ́, ńdzɨ́kərə, av.
over sth. away (without touching);
ǹdrí mbo àfa àzɨ́nɨ̈ drì sɨ̌ ń—
the goat jumped cleanly over the
thing away.

ndzì, T. = zì; dzɔ́tilé ndzɨ̌ to
open a door.

ndzì, vt. (1) to compress, express,
squeeze; ɛ̀ri bɔ̀ŋgɔ́ (mà) lɨ̂ n—
he squeezes water from the cloth
(wrings cloth); ɛ̀ri apípiá mà èvì
ɛndzɨ̂ he squeezes pus from a
sore; (2) to choke, throttle, suffocate; ɔ̀kó n— mvá zö-rɨ̌á (esú
mvá osi àvɔ̌-rö) the woman
suffocated the baby in labour (the
baby was still-born); (= tɨ̌tɨ̌,
dzɨ̌dzi).

ndzɨ̌ = ndzo, vt., ndzɨ́rɨ̌ ndzɨ̌ or
ndzɔ́rò ndzo, T., to hiss (dis-
approvingly); é n— ma ndzɨ́rɨ̌
sɨ̌ à sɨ̌ yà? why do you hiss me? =
mɨ́ mánɨ̈ ndzɨ́rɨ̌ ndzɨ̈yà?

ndzi-ndzì, ndzɨ̌zà, vn. to be
(-come) heavy; àfa 'ɨ̈ ə'bépi n—
n— sth. overwhelmingly heavy.

ndzɨ́ndzɨ́ = kɔ̀ríkɔ̀rì, a. variegated (of colour, design, &c.).

ndzɨ̈ɨa, n. small earrings; n— 'bá
sù bbía (numerous close fitting)
rings they put in the (upper) ear.

ndzìlá, n. (larger) road; à mú n—
sɨ̌! let us go by the (public) road!
n— ŋaakú əmvó-zɔ̌ kàlâ sɨ̌rɨ̌
road made by pouring earth with
iron plates.

ndzɨ́ndra (or -dre), n. a kind of
termites (swarming about 7–8
p.m.).

ǹdzɔ́ = ɔ́rɛ̀ɔ́, n. aloe (?) plant; (or
= ədzɔ́?) (or nopal?).

ndzɔ̀ = e'börà, vt. to daub,
plaster; èi dzɔ́ 'alé n— tí wɔ́rɔ́tɔ̀
sɨ̌ they daub the interior of a hut
with cow-dung.

ndzo (1) vn. to run (away); orí tsɨ́,
é n— rá! there is a snake, run!
mà n— oŋgú sɨ̌! run fast! (2)
(= ndzɛ, ga), vt. to get hold of
by suddenly snatching from a
mass with one's five fingers as
ɛ́ŋá esá, àŋú n— to snatch from
polenta, honey (unpolitely); n—
drìnɨ̈ ŋaàò to snatch uncouthly
from it.

ndzə 'ɨ̈, vn. to break open; mâ pá
àzɔ́rɨ̌ mà milê n— 'ɨ̈ n— my
sore leg has broken open.

ndzɔ̀(-ndzɔ̀), vn. to be slippery,
slip off; búkù ndzɔ̀'dɨ̌à! look out!
the book is slipping off! ɛ̀'bí mà
rùá n—n— a fish is slippery;
rùánɨ̈ n— ɛ̀'bí mà rùá lé it is
slippery like a fish.

ndzɔ̀zà, ndzɔ̀ndzɔ̀là, ńdzɔ̀là-
ndzɔ̀là, -rö, a. smooth, polished,
sleek; slippery; slimy, ropy, muci-
laginous; àŋgɔ̀ ndzɔ̀zàrö the
ground is slippery.

ndzɔ́andzɔ́a, a. sour-bitter; n—
drǎdra, ɛ̀ri mɨ̂ tɨ́ ŋǎŋa it is
bitter eating/biting one's mouth;
n—n— kɔ̌lɔ̌bɔ̌ vélérɨ̌ alu tò;
ɛ́ká drìlé alu kö the sour taste of

Hibiscus is pleasant; of the top of sugar-cane it is not.

ndzɔ̀kà-ndzɔ̀kà ≈ **mɛ̀nɛ̀-mɛ̀nɛ̀ -rö, a.** flabby, flacid; flexible, supple; **tí mvá ɛ'bézàrï̀ mà zá n—** (**mba kö**) the flesh of a miscarried calf is flabby/without consistency (**tɔ̌ɳ̱àtɔ̌ɳ̱àrö**).

ndzórò, ndzo = **ndzï, ndzírï̀,** q.v.

ndzu (1) vt. to suck; **ò'dó** (or **ò'bú**) **nï 'bá àrï̀ n—** the leopard (larva of gad-fly) sucks one's blood; **èì ɔ̀ndó párâ** (or **éká**) **n—** they suck durra-stalks (sugarcane); (2) vn. to leak, ooze out, trickle away; **ìí n— bɔ̀ŋgɔ́ mà rúá** water is sucked up by cloth; **ɔzɔ́ɔ́ ìí tï̀pì àŋgɔ̀-gúrú 'dï̀ mà 'aléarï̀ n— rá** the rain-water that collected in the hollow has dried/oozed away; **ìí n— ètú sï̀ rá, àŋgɔ̀ ɛ̀rì à'wï̀rö** the water has oozed away in the sun, the ground is parched (= **àŋgɔ̀ ndzuzà** parched ground).

ndzú, n. small kind of melon (eaten when green); **'bá ɛ̀rì sâsa ámvútiá/àzïnï̀ àpǎrìtiá** they plant it on the side of fields/or village.

nɛ̀ = **ndrɛ̀, ndrà, nì,** vt. to see; **á pè tɛ́ mánï̀ tinï̀ Árúwá ɛ'bó nɛ̌** I sent him for me to Arua to look for hoes.

nï, particle (cf. Grammar, §§ 556 sqq.) (1) characterizes subject in CIA; (2) suffix: its, his, hers; (3) (**nï**) pstp. of dative: to; (4) pstp. **'-nï** for, as for... part; (5) for stressing any part of speech.

nï̀, def. v. for stressing: 'it is...';... **nï̀ yà?** interr. 'is it...?' **à'dï-nï ma ɛdɛ nï̀ yà?** who is it who fooled me?

nì = **nɛ̀, lù,** vt. to know; to fix, look fixedly at...; recognize; **ɔ̀kó nì 'ïmà mvá rá** a woman knows/

recognizes her child; **ɛ̀rì 'bá nï̌** (= **nɛ̌, lù̀**) he looks at/contemplates a person.

ni¹, vt. to carry on back (**ŋgókóa**); **ɔ̀kó-nï mvâ ni ɔ'bɔkó sï̀ ŋgókóa** the woman carries a child on her back by means of straps; **é ni à'bòà mà páti mï̌ ŋgókóa!** carry the banana plant on your back!

ni² = **bï̀,** vn. to be (-come) dark; **àŋgɔ̀ ni 'bɔ** it is now dark; to be dirty, stained; **bɔ̀ŋgɔ́ ni 'bɔ** the cloth is dirty.

nii³, vn. (1) (= **kaa ɛka**) to become/be ripe; **à'bòà nii dí 'bɔ** the banana is now ripe; (2) (= **ɔfö, a'dï̌**) to be ready-cooked; **éɳá, e'dí, &c. ni 'bɔ** polenta, gruel &c. is ready (opp. **wátáa, èbì**).

nni, ìnni, n. a snake.

nìimà (**-nìimà**), av. wearily; laboriously; **gárì tö-zɔ̌ n—n—** to drive/push a cycle (say, uphill) wearily.

nɔ, vn. to thunder; **ɔzɔ́ɔ́-nï̌ nɔ** (= **lì**) **nï̌** it (the rain) thunders.

nɔ̀, nò, vn. to mutter, grumble; **rùmúníô** (= **ò'dí**) **ɛ̀rì nɔ̀ dzó 'aléa rrrú 'dï̌** the harmonium rumbles (sounds) in the room; **'bá 'dà ɛ̀rì dí nɔ̀nɔ̀** that man grumbles; **bɔ̌rà-nï nɔ̀nɔ̀** the cat is purring.

nɔ́fí = **ɛ̀ndrà,** n. stinginess (with food); **n— bɛ** or **nɔ́fí'rö** niggardly.

nɔ́nɔ́kɔ̀ = **kɔbɔ̀lɔ,** q.v.

ŋ

ŋgà (seldom **àŋgà**) = **drì, T.,** av. still; yet; **ŋgà ká** (T. = **drì ká** or **drì sɔ́**)! not yet, not so far as that! **ŋgà ká, é tɛ̀ wɛrɛ!** not yet, wait a moment! emú ŋgà (T. amú drì) kö he has not yet come.

ŋga¹ = 'yɛ, mu, aux. v. of future tense; mâ ŋga emú rá I shall come.

ŋga², vn. (1) to rise; é ŋga pâ tö oru sǐ! or é ŋga orulé sǐ! stand up! è ŋgâ mu 'dálé! stand up and go there! (2) (= sǎ, ɔsǎ, ɔŋgǎ) to fly; àrǐïa nǐ ŋga ópípí sǐ birds fly with their wings; to swarm (termites); ɔ̃ɳa nǐ ŋga ɛ́nì sǐ (some) termites swarm by night; (3) àzî ŋga to work; ma àzî ŋgâ̂ŋga I am working; é ŋga à'do àzí yà? what were you working at?

ŋgá, n. (1) (= àfá, ámvú), n. field; é mu ŋgá 'ǎ! go and till the field! má àzí ŋgá drî ŋga I am working at cultivating the field; (2) (= àfa) thing; mǐ e'dú mání ŋgá 'dǐ! take up this thing for me! ndrɔ́ èìmà ŋgá nǐ ndii, má ɛri kö they have arranged their business (chitchat, rubbish) secretly, I did not hear it; mǐ ŋgá mà a'á! keep your rubbish to yourself! ɔ'bɛ́ ŋgání rö = 'bá ɛ'yɔ́ sɔ̌pirǐ a chatterbox.

ŋgà or ŋgà ndrí...ká (= ɔká; T. drì ká), vn. to threaten, intimidate; ŋgà ndrí (= ndrîɔ) èrinǐ ká he threatened him; ŋgà èrinǐ ká (or ndrîɔ): èrì mu nɛ̌ rá he intimidated him: he would see! ŋgà mínǐ ká: àma emú nɛ̌ mï bɛ rá... we will see each other! the same: ŋgàkâ lï to intimidate, threaten; á lï èrimà ŋgàká (= ɔmɔkɔ́) I threatened him.

ŋgàbàŋgàbà, av. moving up and down; 'yɛ ŋ—ŋ— it moves up and down (at dancing; flying; branches moved by wind).

ŋgàká = ɔmɔkɔ́, n. threat; ŋ— lǐ to threaten; èri Simoni mà ŋgàkâ lï èrì tsɔ (or 'di) zɔ̌ he threatened to beat (kill) Simoni.

ŋgálá = kɔlɔi, tsùlùtsùlù, a. impatient, excited; 'ïmà ásí ŋ— tɔ̌ he is very excited, cannot control himself (and wait a moment).

ŋgálákí = ŋgáláfí, T. = nyɔ̀rɛ̀, n. beads; necklace of; waistband of beads.

ŋgáŋgá = kirikiri, trítrí, av. firmly, tightly, strongly; é bǐ ŋ—ŋ—! hold him fast! mǐ ɔmbɛ èri bá sǐ ŋ—ŋ—! tie it tightly with rope! mvá 'dǐ ɳa 'ï ɛ́ɳá sǐ ŋ—ŋ— (= gbarakaɳa; 'alɛ́nǐ dǐ àtrákà) this boy ate polenta until he had a well-rounded belly.

ŋgarakadíɔ, n. shooting star; èrì Àdrɔ́ nǐ it is a spirit (in their opinion); ŋgärikädíyò èrì ŋga àtsǐ bɛ (spirit living in rivers) it comes as fire.

ŋgárákádzǎ or ɔ̀ŋgáráká (-dzà), n. striped mouse; ŋgókó-nǐ kɔ̀ríkɔ̀rî-rö its back is striped.

ŋgárè̀, av. at the time of...; à'do-ŋgárè̀? at what time, when? àɳú ŋ—, ɔndó ŋ— at the time of simsim or durra harvesting; ámvú 'à ŋ—, ɔ̃ɳa (ŋga) ŋ— at the time of field tilling, of swarming of termites.

ŋgbéŋgbɛ́ = kírikíri, av. definitely, energetically, decisively; ɔmbɛ́ èri ŋ— they tied him (or it) properly; lɔ̌ ɛ'yɔ́ ŋ— (ɔkpɔ́ sǐ) he spoke firmly.

ŋgbɔ́lɔ́, dzɔ́ ŋ—, n. a quite empty, unfurnished hut/room.

ŋgbɔ́lɔ́kɔ́, drì ŋ— (heads) skull.

ŋgèyèŋgéyè, n. small, broad-bodied fish.

ŋgìlíŋgília, also tùkùtúkúa or 'é-nè-té-ma-wɛɛ-ŋgɔ́yà?', n.

pigmy, dwarf; 'bá àlía 'dìì (short men).

ŋgɔ, inter. pr. (1) ŋgɔ́? ŋgɔ̀á? where? whence? whereto? mvá èri ŋgɔ́ yà? where is the child (boy, girl)? mǐ mu ŋgɔ́ (á) yà? á mu tέ 'dέ kö; ma tέ driə lö̌ 'də where are you going? I did not go anywhere; I have been here the whole time; (2) ŋgɔ̀'ï? which? 'bá ŋgɔ̀ èi kaká ɔpí nǐ yà? which (of the children, persons) will husk the maize? (3) ŋgɔ́-nǐ? ŋgɔ̀ŋgɔ́-nǐ yà? how? in what way/manner? ɛ'yɔ́ mǐ-vɔ̌ 'dέlέ ŋgɔ́nǐ yà? 'dǐ ŋgɔ́nǐ yà? what is the matter with you (at home)? what is this? ɛ'yɔ́ 'dέ yə nothing happened; (4) ŋgɔ̀ sǐ (= drí)? of, in, by which...? èmǐ ɛ'yɔ̂ ndzɛ ti ŋgɔ̀ sǐ yà? in which language do you speak? (5) ŋgɔ̀pí? how much? 'bá əva έŋá ŋgɔ̀pí yà? how much polenta did she make?

ŋgö = əsɛ, à'bù (opp. óí), vn. to be(-come) fat, stout, well-fed, corpulent, plump; 'bá 'dǐ ngɔ̂ŋgö this man is stout; voluminous.

ŋgɔ̂'bɔ̀, n. the slough; orí ắû ko ŋ— the snake has shed/cast its skin (cf. óhɔ́rókɔ́tə).

ŋgɔ̀'bɔ̀, ŋgɔ̀'bɔ́-ŋgɔ́'bɔ̀, -rö, or 'bɔ̀-ŋgɔ̀ = əga-zɔ̌, a. of uneven, rough surface; έyío mà rùá (i.e. ŋgókó) ŋgɔ̀'bɔ̀-rö the crocodile's back is uneven; 'bá (or ɛ̀'bí) mà rùá-nǐ əga-rö ŋgɔ̀'bɔ̂ŋgɔ́'bɔ̀-rö a (sick) man's (fish's) body is rough/scabby (scaly).

ŋgɔ́əí = ŋgörö, q.v.

ŋ̀gókó, n. back (of anything); nii àfa ŋ̀gókó-á she carries a thing (baby...) on her back; atsí ŋ̀—ŋ̀— sǐ he walks backwards; ŋ̀gókó-á, pstp. behind; after—in one's absence; é mu dzɔ̂ ŋ̀gókó-

á! go behind the hut! mâ ŋ̀gókó-á behind me, or in my absence (after I had left); etsá ópí mà ŋ̀gókó-á (= vútɪá) he arrived here after the chief (or in his absence); (Ad. gɔ́lɔ́-á; Mitsu. gɛrïa); ŋ̀gókó'dò-rö humped, hunchbacked; drî ŋ̀—, pâ ŋ̀— back of hand, foot.

ŋgòlέ (or -lí) = pɛ̀rɛ̀, n. large knife with long handle, kind of sickle; ŋ— àŋgö və-zɔ́rï to clear ground (of long grass).

ŋgòlè-ŋgòlè, av. (ɛŋgá, əva, aŋga ŋ—ŋ—) bubbling over (in boiling pot...).

ŋgɔ̌lɔ́¹, -ắ, a. tiny; smaller, less developed individual of...; 'dǐ ŋ— rǐ'ï, this is a small one; börà àkárǐ ndè ɔbálákɔ́ ŋgɔ̌lɔ́ắrǐ rá a fully grown cat is bigger than a young wild carnivore.

ŋgɔ̌lɔ́², ŋgɔ̌lɔ́-ŋgɔ̌lɔ́, -rǐ (cf. ólɔ̌ŋgɔ́-ólɔ̌ŋgɔ́), a. round.

ŋgɔ̌lɔ́³-rö, av. together; andzi mà ɲaà ɲaaká pírí ŋ— (wɔ́rɔ́ tú àlö)! the children may all eat together!

ŋgɔ̀lɔ̀-ŋgɔ̀lɔ̀-rö, av. restlessly moving, tramping or roving about; tí èri ŋ—ŋ— the cow roves about (separating from the rest).

ŋgörö = ŋgörökö'dö, ŋgörölö, ŋgɔ́əí, ⸱rö, a. raised, elevated, hilly; àŋgö ŋgörö-rǐ hilly ground without rocks (έrà kókɔ̀rö); uneven, rugged, coarse; óní ŋgörölɔ̌rö, 'bá etú drinǐá ɔkpɔ̀ sǐ the mountain is rugged, it is climbed with difficulty; also ŋgörökö'dò-rö humped, &c., piled up.

ŋgù¹, vn./vt. (1) àdzí-nǐ ŋgù to smell/it smells; èri adzínï ŋgù (= sɛ) òmvu sǐ he smells it with his nose; àdzínï ŋgù ndrrrǐ it smells pleasant; (2) ŋgǔ-ŋgù, vn.

to smell badly, stink; **à'bǒà maazà** èri ŋ—ŋ— a rotten banana smells bad; **dzǒ 'dì mà 'alé** ŋ—ŋ— it smells bad in this hut; **ŋgù-zà,** a. bad-smelling, stinking.

ŋgù², vt. **ŋgù 'bá, ŋgù 'bá àdzí, ŋgù 'bá (àdzí) ɔ̀ndzí** to hate a person (no present tense!); **mvá 'dà ŋgù ma tǒ** that child dislikes me very much; **é ŋgù ma 'dínï à'do sǐ yà?** why do you dislike/ hate me thus?

ŋgúù¹, ŋgúi, n. ant-lion.

ŋgúù², ŋgúi, ŋguyù, ŋgùvì, n. small black kind of termite (**óɳa**).

ŋgulù = ɔ̀mbùrùkù, ɔ̀mbǒrǒkǒ, T., n. foot-and-mouth disease (cattle, goats...); **èri tí** (or **ǹdrí**) **mà tǐ ɳâɳa, nɔ̀sì èri ǹdrî pâ ɳa** it affects the mouth of cows, or the legs of goats, &c.

ŋgúlùá, n. small-pox; **èri ŋ— bɛ** he has small-pox.

ŋgúlúŋgúlú, n. tree of the gawawa variety.

ŋgúru, n. beast of prey; **ŋ— tsï 'bá rá** a ferocious animal has mauled someone.

ŋgùrúbě, n. (wild) pig.

ŋgúrúkà, nv. **àgà ŋ—** rough, coarsely (ground); **àɳá 'dì èri àgà ŋ—** this corn is coarsely ground.

ŋgúrùkúti = guuti (also **ɔ̀ŋgú-rúkúti, ɔ̀ŋgúrùŋgú**), n. small of the back.

ŋgùrùmà, n. stale collected termites; **àndròrǐá 'bá èri 'bǎ éfǐfî-rö, èrì dǐ àndrù-àndrù; 'bá mu èri sǐ ɳaa drùsǐ** they lay (the collected termites) aside for the day (**ŋgùrùmà**), they start smelling; they make them into pulp and eat it the next day.

ɳ

N.B. A large part of Logbara country uses **n** instead of **ɳ** (Tɛrɛgo).

ɳa or **ɳaa,** vt. (1) to eat; **mu éɳâ ɳa** he went to eat polenta; **tí ɳa ásɛ́ rá** cattle ate grass; (2) to affect; cause pain; gnaw, consume, undermine (a p.'s health); **bélénï mâ pâ ɳa nǐ** a sore makes my leg painful; **ótsátsá—, ɔɔyá èri 'bâ ɳâɳa** yaws—eat away a p.'s body.

ɳàï-ɳàï, a. rough (from sand or the like); **á rï àŋgǒ ɳ—ɳ— rǐ mà drìá** I sat on a rough place (sandy . . .).

ɳàá = ɳàga, àɳaàó (same as **ŋgúru**), n. wild/ferocious beast; **ɳàǎ ɳa mâ ǹdrí éní sǐ** a wild animal has eaten my goat by night.

ɳá'bílékó, n. scar, cicatrice; **bélé ɳ—** scar of a sore/wound; **ɳ— ǹdrá mádrírǐ èri èndǐ** an old scar of mine is still here.

ɳǎdrì = ówï, T., n. tumulus on grave; **'bâ sa 'bílíárǐ mà ɳ—** grave-mound of a man they have buried in a grave.

ɳa-dzó = 'alé, n. belly/stomach.

ɳàadzò, ɳàadzòǎ, mòotsè, n. oribi gazelle; **ɳ— mà rúánï èri ɛkǎrö, ɔmbɛ-nï lírí; èri rǒé** the oribi is brown; it has a long and slender neck.

ɳafe, n. axe.

ɳafé, n. walking-stick.

ɳaaká = tà, n. food (of man); **àfa 'bánǐ ɳa ti 'aléarǐ èi dría ɔmve ɳaaká** what man eats in his mouth (cooked!) they call it all food.

ɳaakú, n. earth, soil, clay; **èi ɳ— sǐ dzɔ̂ bǐ** they daub huts with clay.

ŋ̀àlíà, ŋ̀àlíkà, ŋ̀àlíàká, n. remnant, small quantity remaining over of any food; ɔ́sɔ́ —, àŋ̩á ... mà ŋ̩— left over beans, corn... ; mà a'dí ɔ́ŋ̩a mà ŋ̀àlíkàá 'dìàrì̀! let these left over termites be cooked!

ŋ̀àambí, n. dancing entertainment (ávítáa), (for women only): ŋ̀àambî tö; èì ògúrú sì ŋ̩àambíá they (kneeling) rub wooden slabs; or standing: èì kòyò ya; kòyò kà ɘvö èridrí yɘ èri drî sa áyò they shake the gourd-rattle (kòyò kéré); if they have no rattle they clap their hands.

ŋ̩ámŋgbí = kǐríkǐrí, av. firmly, strongly.

ŋ̩ámŋgbìrì̀ = lòlì, n. red soil (mostly with gravel); é kà ŋ̩aakú 'bùá ënirì̀ 'dìrì̀ ɘvá rá, mǐ dí mu ŋ̩— esú̩ when you have dug and removed the black upper soil, you will find the red ŋ̩—; ɔ́ní 'bánï ɘvá dzi 'dà ndzìláãrì̀, èri ŋ̩— (= ŋ̩aakú ɛkarì̀) bɛ the stones (i.e. gravel) they dig and bring to the road are found mixed with 'nyamŋgbiri'.

ŋ̩ámúkɔ́, n. open grassland for pasture; pàrí pätí kókɔ̀rö tínǐ ŋ̩aa-zɔ́ rì̀ place without trees for cattle to graze.

ŋ̩àŋgàlà, n. native (carved or) plaited stool.

ŋ̩aŋgiŋ̩aŋgi, n. small (ornamental) chain put on neck èì ŋ̩— sǔ ɘmbéá.

ŋ̩àŋ̩á = àndzé-àndzé, n./a. a desperate/hopeless case; incorrigible, past mending; mǐ àlö ŋ̩—! you are a hopeless fellow.

ŋ̩áŋ̩àkò'bí, n. black caterpillar; ŋ̩— èri ënìrö bbíkɔ́ bɛ dzìŋ̩à the 'nyanyako'bi' is black with long erect (stiff) hair; èri 'bá áú-áú 'ǐ bbíkɔ́ sì̀ it stings one with its hair; èri atsí vàá sì̀ it moves on the ground.

ŋ̩ào-ŋ̩ào-rö, a. loose, slack; not compact or cohesive; easily detachable or crumbling (opp. tìlikpa or sɛzà).

ŋ̩árékǐ = èmà, n. target (?); àfa ġbǐ-zà sì̀: èri mà ŋ̩áríkǐ tò at shooting: he is of extraordinary ability, luck.

ŋ̩àzákà = àzámàká, n. q.v.

ŋị̀[1]—rö-ŋị̀, vn. (1) to be restless, fidgety; Ò̩kpɘyɘnǐ ŋ̩— O. is fidgety; (2) to move restlessly; mvá 'dǐ èri 'ǐ ŋ̩ǐ̩ŋ̩ǐ̩ ètí sì̀ the baby crawls/moves on his posterior (unable to stand: tsa pá sò zɔ́ kö); ŋị̀-kìrìkìrì rö, a.

ŋị̀[2], vt. (1) to rub; èì ŋị̀ à'ídènì sì̀ they rub (him) with iodine; (2) to rub/squeeze; èri mvá mà òmvû̩ ŋ̩ǐ̩, kà mu ɘwí-zɔ́ kö or òdìká sì̀ she rubs/squeezes the baby's nose so that it may not cry, or on account of its cold; (3) to crush, crumple; èì enïrïkɘ̀ ŋ̩ǐ̩ŋ̩ǐ̩ ɘ'bɔ́kɔ̀-rö mvâ ni-zɔ́ they crumple (tan) a dry skin for leather-straps to carry a baby (on back); ŋị̀ rö ŋ̩ǐ̩ŋ̩ǐ̩, vn. to break up/be broken up, reduced to pieces or powder; tábà 'bánǐ mvurì̀ ŋị̀ rö ŋị̀-ŋị̀ or tábà ŋị̀ 'ǐ wɔ́rɔ́ tobacco which people smoke is reduced to small pieces (powder, in pocket): it is pulverized.

ŋị̀, vn. (1) to burn low; àtsí mà ádarì̀ dì nï kö, èri dí ŋị̀ àtsí-kàrö 'dúù a proper fire does not burn/blaze, it smoulders with much smoke (cloud-like); (2) ɘvǐnï ŋ̩ǐ̩ŋ̩ǐ̩/ŋị̀ lélé it lightens; (3) to smile (in subdued manner, with closed lips ndindìrö); èri ŋị̀ mánǐ ŋ̩ǐ̩ŋ̩ǐ̩ he smiles at me.

ŋíŋgírikí, a. small, minute but numerous (as seeds of tobacco, pawpaw).

ŋïïəá = ŋïïrï, n. thread-like intestinal worms; èri ŋíïríâ-rö sì rö kìlé wízì-lé; ɛmvɛ̀rö: èri 'bá 'aléa it is tiny and small (about 1 cm.) thread-like; it is white: is found in human beings.

ŋírí, ŋíríá, n./a. very small, little; little things; àfa 'dïrï ŋ—ŋ—mbïrï (= èkpétékè = ètsákí) these are innumerable minute things; ŋírïnï té è kó 'dïï (i.e. màákò mà ŋ— èì ko garíá 'dálé), èrì dí oŋú (= ədɔ́ èì ədɔ̌) ètúkà sì these small things (waste potatoes) you left back (on the field on digging), have now hardened—dried in the sun; cf. 'bí'bíə 'bùá'dïï ŋírïŋírí èkpétékèlékè the stars up there are tiny and numberless.

ŋíïrì, n. panpolin (?).

ŋíríkyà, ɔ́sɔ̌ ŋ— = ɔ́sɔ̌ tsïkïrí, n. a small kind of beans.

ŋɔ̀, vt. to break; á mu áséa édzá ɔ̀ŋɔ̌ àtsî-rö I went into the veldt/bush to break/make/collect wood for fire (firewood); ŋɔ̌ gèrì áséa əmbí bï-zɔ̌ they broke/trampled a path through the grass on catching locusts; ŋɔ̀ 'ï ŋɔ̀ŋɔ̀ to break or be broken; to be tired.

ŋafɛ, ŋafé, see ŋafɛ . . .

ŋəndɔ̀, T. (? S.) = 'aya-dzɔ́-drì-pa-zɔ̌ or aya-'bìlé-ɛpá-zɔ̌', n. hammer; ŋ— èri aya mùsù-marì ddì-zɔ̌ a hammer is an iron implement for driving in nails.

ŋərè = ŋgálíkí, T., n. beads; string of beads (for neck, waist); záá 'dï əsé ŋ— nï the girl has threaded beads to string; èì ŋ— sǔ əmbɛ-á they put the string of beads round the neck.

ŋu, oŋú, vt. to wither—shrink, hardening and discolouring, to dry and fade; pàìpáí bbí 'dï ŋûŋu the leaves of the pawpaw have faded and withered and changed colour.

O

N.B. The prefix o (ə) is commonly attached to verbs, when a plurality of persons or things (be it as subject or object) or a mass is expressed; it often expresses also intensity, frequency, repetition of an action. Verbs with the prefix o- are here given on account of their frequency or particular importance or meaning. O- may, however, be added to every verb.

ɔ̀ɔ̀ or ɔ̌ɔ̌, intj. (à'ïtáa assent) yes.

'ə, T., elsewhere 'yɛ, vt. to do . . . ; èrì mu à'dò 'ə yà? what will he do?

ɔ́á, T., alias ɛ'dɔ́, q.v. (cf. gbàŋgìlò).

ə'á or 'ə'á (more commonly a'á), vn. to stay; mostly: to have been staying, be found; mï 'ə'á bəŋgɔ́ ədzï ìíá 'dálé you have been washing the cloth at the river; ésè-nï ə'á ɔ̀ndó bbí tálá the 'ɛsɛ' locust stays among durra leaves; kàni àzí yə, mï 'ə'á 'ə'á when there is no work, you simply remain idle.

òàŋgì or wàŋgì, T. = élí, n. dry season, year; é ŋàà dí ò— rá you are still eating by this year (i.e. still alive!).

ɔ́bá or ɔ́báŋgòlo, T. (= ɔ́ndú), n. knotty excrescence, knot, lump; ɔ́bá èrì àfa pïpì 'bâ rúá, fípi ddíká kö a lump that rises on one's body and does not go down.

ə'bà (cf. 'bà; pl.), vt. (1) to set, put

aside; **mí ȯ'bà èi dzóa !** put the things aside in the room/hut! (2) to place, put (in position); **èi ɛ́wá if ȯ'bǎ àtsí drìá ȯtákà sǐ** they place water for beer on fire in a pot; **àrïǐä-nï dzɔ́rɔ́vȍ ȯ'bǎ pätí sí-á** birds build their nests on trees; (3) to create; **Àdrɔ̃ ȯ'bà àŋgȍ nǐ** it is God who has created the earth; (4) **àtsí ti ȯ'bǎ** to set on fire, ignite (an area); **àmà mu áséa àtsí ti ȯ'bǎ !** let us go to the grass to set it on fire ! (5) . . . **milɛ́ ȯ'bǎ** to overlay, cover; **ȯzɔ̃ɔ́ ȯ'bà milɛ́, èrì 'yɛ̃ 'dǐ'dì áánï** rain (-y weather) has covered the sky (face), it may possibly rain; **ȯ'bà milɛ́ tȯȯkɔ́** it is covered to no purpose (no rain); (6) to lime, set up snare (lime-twig, -rod); **ɛ́sɛ́ àrïǐä ȯ'bà zȍ** glue to snare birds; **mú àrïǐä ȯ'bà ɛ́sɛ́ sǐ** they went to entrap birds with lime.

ȯbá, ȯbáIákɔ́, ȯbɛ́Iɛ́kɔ́, ȯbɔ́Iȯkɔ́, n. the smaller carnivora (Ac. **ȯgwàaŋ**); **ȯbá mà ȯlɛ̀ èri ásé dùzàrǐ mà 'aléa** paths of carnivora are (hidden) among thick tall grass.

óbáIàú, n. a shrub (Ac. **ȯbvùul**)? or tree, *Mitragina stipulosa* or *M. macrophilla*; its large fruits eaten by birds.

ó'bárádzí (or -ɛ́), **ó'bɔ́rɔ́dzó, ɛ́'bárádzɛ,** n. ? kind of antelope.

ȯbǎù, T. = **ȯbù,** n. hyena.

ȯbɛ́, vt. to tempt; wheedle, talk over, persuade; entice, induce (Ac. **bìtȯ**); **èri ma àfa ȯbɛ́** he is wheedling things out of me; **èi 'bá àzínï ȯbɛ̃ dzi kòlíàbàtò drí ŋaa-zà-rö** they entice a man to bring him to the cannibal to be eaten; **é mu mvá ȯbɛ̃ à'bȍa sǐ, kà mu ȯ́-zȍ kö (sǐ)** try to persuade the child with a banana not

to cry; **ȯbɛ́ ma sɛ́ntɛ̀ kɛ̀nì: 'í ànï mání a'ú fɛ̃** he gives me temptingly a few cents, saying that in this way he is giving me a fowl.

ȯ'bɛ́ (cf. **'bɛ**), vt. (1) to remove, throw away (waste, &c.); **èi ŋaakú ȯ'bɛ̃** they remove earth (surplus); (2) to overwhelm, throw to the ground (say on wrestling); **èi ȯ'bɛ́ rö ȯmbà (avítáa) sǐ** they wrestle fighting (or game); (3) to mix together; **èi ȯlá ȯ'bɛ̃ mùgátirö** they mix together manioc (and other) to kind of bread; cf. **èri báká ȯ'bɛ́** (= **pǐ**) he twists/ twines a rope; (4) **ȯ'bɛ́** (= **ȯsa**) **rö** to alternate, vary (say various colours); **tí ȯ'bɛ́ rö èi ńdrí bɛ èríbí ŋaa-rïä** cows and goats are intermingled on the pasture; **rùá- nï ȯ'bɛ́ rö ȯ'bɛ́** it is of various colours; (5) T. (= **si**) to build.

ȯbɛ́Iɛ̀, n. a fairly large fish (of inland waters).

ȯbɛIɛ = **mbɛ̀Iɛ̀,** av. quickly, immediately; **èmï ȯmvɛ èrí sǐ mà emú ȯ—!** call loudly that they may come at once!

ȯ'bɛ̀Iɛ̀ = **àbɛ́, àbɛ́Iɛ̀kó,** T., **kàIí,** n. thick stick, cudgel.

ó'bɛ́Iɛ́kȯ = **ó'bɔ́Iɔ́kȯ,** n. cheek.

ȯbɛ́rédzɛ́, n. see **ó'bárádzí.**

ȯbɛ́tɛ̀rɛ̀ (= T. **ȯbɛ́Iɛa**), n. a kind of smaller parrot (?); **ȯ— èri ɔ́ŋà ŋa** it eats termites (&c.); **èri àrïǐä pírí mà owǐ** (= **àȯ**) **ȯ'bǐ wɔ́rɔ́** it imitates the voice of every bird.

óbí (= T. **mȯrá**), n. very large pot for preparing beer **óbí ɛ́wá ȯrȯzȍrǐ.**

o'bí, vt. to winnow corn with basket **èi àŋá o'bí kói sǐ.**

ȯbí, n. (1) kind, sort, colour; **bȯŋgó 'dǐ mà ȯbí ɛmvɛ̀-rö** the colour of this cloth is white; (2) nature, character; **mvá 'dà mà ə̀bí mők̆é, ɛ̀ri ɛ̀ndzɛ̀táa bɛ** that child has a good character, it is respectful.

ə'bí, n. mass, multitude, great number; **ə'bí emú àndrò 'dòá** a mass (of people) came here to-day; **ə'bî-rö**, a. many, numerous; **ə'bí-á**, av. publicly, before the people; **'bá tsə ɛ̀ri ə'bía** they have beaten him publicly.

ə'bì (cf. **'bì**), vt. to try, tempt, (put to the) test; (1) to examine; **àma ŋgà ɛ̀ri ə'bì àndró sɛ̀** we are examining him in preaching; (2) to try, endeavour, make an effort; **ɛ̀ri àfa ə'bì kɛ̈ 'aléalé tɛ̈** he tries in vain to swallow it down; (3) to tempt (try to) entice, lead a p. into temptation **'bá àzɛ́nɛ̈ ə'bì ɛ'yɔ́ ɔ̀ndzí sɛ̀** or **'bá àzɛ̈ mà bbɛ́lé ə'bì** (= **ə̀'bù**); (4) to measure, try on; weigh; **ɛ̀ri bə̀ŋgɔ́ ə'bì** he tries on a cloth; **ɛ̀mɛ̈ ɛ̀fɛ̀ mánɛ̈ ɛ́wá á 'bì!** give me beer to taste it! **ɛ̀ì sùkárɛ̀ ə'bì paúndɛ́ sɛ̀** they weigh sugar by pounds; (5) to imitate, copy; (cf. example of **ɔ̀bétɛ̀rɛ̀**).

ə̀bì (cf. **bì**), vt. (1) to press together, compress; **mɛ̈ ə̀bì milé!** shut your eyes! (but: **é bì ti!** shut your mouth!); **ə̀bì ɛ̀ì (mà) drí tsɛ̀** they (two) took each other by the hand; (2) to glue, paste ... together; **ə̀bì wárágà ésé sɛ̀** he joined together papers with paste; **ɛ̀ì àṇú mà ɔ̀därɛ̀ sɛ̀ émvó (mà) ɛ́ríkə̀ ə̀bì** they glue/join a cracked pot (or pot-splits) with bees-wax; (3) (= **eġa**) to recollect, come into one's mind; **(ə̀)bì dì ɛ'yɔ́nɛ̈ 'ɛ̈ driá 'bə** (= **eġa dì rá**) he remembered it (a word); **ma ə̀bì** (= **á bì**) **mà̆ driá pæ̈rínɛ̈ 'bə** its place came into my mind (I re-

membered the place); (4) **ə̀bì ɔ́rɛ́-tɛ̈á** to offer at a shrine; **'bá kà ɔ́rɛ́ éṇá 'ɛ̈ 'bə, ɛ̀ì dɛ̈ mu ə̀bì ɔ́rɛ́-tɛ̈-á** after they have prepared the polenta for the spirits, they go and lay/offer it (in small quantities) before the shrine.

obí (= **ədza**) **rö**, vr./n. to turn (o-s.); **mɛ̈ obí mɛ̈ vélé!** turn your back (hither)! **ɛ̀ri 'ɛ̈ obí 'dɛ̈** he turns hither; N.B. **àma obí àma ɛ̀ri bɛ obí-obí** (i.e. **ɛ̀inɛ̈ atsí-rɛ̆á ɛ̀ì ndàrɛ̆á**) they missed each other (on the way; i.e. when walking in search of one another—in opposite directions); **ásí obí-ző̆**, vt. to change one's mind; **'bá àzɛ́nɛ̈ obí ásínɛ̈ tsɛ̀** somebody made him change his mind.

o'bí (cf. **'bì**), vt. to bore, drill (into wood...); **o'bí-o'bí** or **o'-bízà**, a. worm-eaten, disintegrating (wood ...).

o'bí-rö'bí = **ə̀'bí'bírí** (also **o'bí-bǎo-'bə**), n. wood-beetle; **o—nɛ̈ pätí mà 'aléa o'bí** the wood-beetle works its way into the wood.

ò̀bìkò̀bì, a. (dirty) grey-black.

əbiə = **abiə**, n. incense tree, and resin **pätí mà sú** (*Canarium schweinfurthi*).

óbíró = **óbírwá, ábío**, n. rhino-ceros.

ò'bíti = **ò'búti-rì**, a. of the morning; **ò'— sì**, av. in the morning; **ɛ̀tú-nɛ̈ ŋga ɛ̀fò̆-rɛ̈-á ò'búti 'dɛ̈** the sun rises in the morning.

ɔ́'bó, n. big wild pigeon; (**ɛ̀ri etsá élí sɛ̀** comes in the dry season (?).

ə'bo, n. time of swarming of termites **óṇa ɔ́'bo; ɛ̀tú óṇa-nɛ̈ ŋga-zőrɛ̀; əzɔ́ɔ́ 'dɛ̈ ə'bɔ̆-rö** this rain causes termites to swarm.

ə'bóɛ̈ = **ɛ'bó**, n. hoe.

ɔ́'bɔ́ = **ò̀gúrú**, n. boat, canoe; **ɔ́'bɔ́ atsí-ző̆ ɛ̈ 'aléa-sɛ̈-rɛ̈'ɛ̈** boat with which to travel on water; **atu kàlí ó'bɔ́ pɛ̃-zǒrì'ï** oar is a stick with which to push a boat.

ó'bókɔ̀, see **ə'bələ**.

ó'bókɔ, n. (1) (= **əgǒrǒ'bàlá**) bark of tree, &c.; (2) **orí mà ó'**— sloughed skin of a snake; **ɛ̀'bí mà ó'**— fish-scale (i.e. what envelops) cf. **ə'bɔ́rókə**.

əbɔ̀kɔ̀, n. kind of large-size beans; beans and leaves very much appreciated.

ə'bəkɔ́ = **ó'bùká, ó'baká**, n. leather (or other) strap-apparatus for carrying baby on back **mvǎ ni-zǒrì**.

ó'bókɔ́á = **ólúdzóvá**, n. a small pear-shaped cucumber; **'bá ɛ̀rì sa ámvúa; ɛ́fĩnï ndròlɛ̀-rö** it is grown in fields; its seeds are flat-oblong (*Cucumis prophetarum*).

əbɔ́kɔ́bɔ́, Mtsa = **ésísí**, q.v. plant with edible black berries (mulberry shrub or tree?).

əbələ or **əbɔ́lɔ̀kɔ́**, n. = **əbá**, q.v.

ə'bələ = **ə'bələmvo, ó'bɔ́lɔ́kɔ̀, á'bókɔ̀, á'bélɛ́mvó**, n. cheek.

ə'bəló = **ə'bóá**, n. a big tree; **èi ə'bóá mà sû ga ésésê-rö'ï àríïã ə'bà-zǒ** they cut the 'ɔ'boa' tree for its viscose sap for catching birds; **súnï ɛ̀rì ésénï** its juice is viscous.

ə'bɔ́rɔ́dzɔ́ (= **dzí**) = **ɛ́'bárádzɛ, ó'bárádzé**, q.v.

ə'bɔ́rókə = **ə'bɔ́, ó'bókə, óbɔ́r-ókə, ə'bɔ́rókɔ́tə**, n. (1) bark (of tree); (2) rind, husk (of grass, &c.); **əndó ə'**—, **yabí ə'**— rind of durra...stalk; (3) shell (of egg, &c.); **òkùkù mà ó'**— the tortoise's shell.

ò'bu, n. larva; **ò'bu ɛ̀rì ti ǹdrí mà driá** a larva develops in a sheep's head; **ɛ̀rì 'bâ lɔ́mâ ndzǔndzu** it (gad-fly) sucks one's flank (at night); **a'ú ɛ̀rì ò'bù ŋaa** fowls eat larvae; jigger; insect.

ə'bù, vt. to (try to) seduce, pervert; **mǐ ə'bù mâ zíi (nï) rá!** you have seduced my daughter!; **mǐ ə'bù ɛ̀rì kö, é ko mà a'á 'dɛ́!** do not seduce him (her), let him alone!

ò'búti, see **ò'bíti**.

o'bú rö, vr. to bend, lie on one's face; **ɛ̀rì 'yɛ** (= **o'bú**) **'ï o'bú rö o'bú ò'búkùru** = **ɛ̀rì laa rö ò'búkùru** he lies on his face; **mǐ o'bú mǐ!** bow down! **ò'búkùru** = **à'búkùru**, av. on one's face.

òbù-òbù (cf. **òbù** or **òbǎu** hyena) = **òbìkòbì, ònìkònì, òtrìkòtrì, -rö**, a. dappled, piebald, variegated; **tí mãnǐ òbù-òbù emú 'dɔ́ bɛ̀a?** does my dappled cow come here? **tí mà rùá sì rö òbù drírì lɛ́** the cow's body (colour) resembles that of a hyena.

o'búrú, av. later, some day, in the end; **mǐ ŋga emú má vélé dzó nɛ̌ o'**— **rá** you will come to see my hut some day.

ó'búrúsɔ̀, n. foam, froth; **ó'**— **etúpi** (= **ɛŋgápi**) **éwá mà driá** foam that forms on beer; **èi lésû zə ó'**— **bɛ** they milk, making froth.

ó'búrùtú, ó'bútùru, ó'búlùtu, à'búlùtu, á'bélɛ̀'búa, ('Loi-ti') lɛ̀'bíàdáààdáa, n. names for a kind of caucal bird; **bbíkɔ̀-nï sì rö yúdù drírì lɛ́** its plumage resembles that of the caucal.

òbù-'úǎ'úǎ, n. the wild dog of the bush.

ə'da (cf. **'da**), vt. to indulge in bad language against, insult; **mvá 'dà mà ə'datáa əndzí; ɛ̀rìnï mǐ ə'da-zǒ ti əndzírì sǐ** that boy's way of talking is shocking: he insults one/you with bad language.

óda, ódakóda, ódalokóda, mudɛkɛ, munɛkɛ, n. afterbirth; tí
mà ódanï ŋgà esî dàlìdàlìrö
mvá mà véléa a cow's afterbirth
hangs wobbling after the calf.

òdärì, n. wax; àŋú mà ò— beeswax; anurúá mà ò— ground
bees-wax.

ðdɛ, n. rain-worm; ðdɛ èì ànï
è'bî 'bɛ ɛwí sï they angle with
rain-worm on hook.

ə'dɛ (cf. 'dɛ), vn. to fall (of many
small...); əzóó-nï ə'dɛ-ə'dɛ
heavy raindrops are falling.

òdé, a. young (still small; said of
anything); mvá 'dà èri òdêrö
(akázàrö) that boy is young/
delicate; 'bá òdérï young/weak
person.

òdééá, n. a kind of bird of passage;
èri emú ɛ́lí sï it comes in winter/
dry season.

òdékðá (cf. òdé), òdékðlíá, òdékùlé, n. quite young baby; òdé
osi àŋgà ó'dîrö; èri ŋgà akázà
(or ɛkâ) rö a baby born only recently; it is still weak/red; mvá
òdékölíà-rö, ŋgà ó'dîrö newly
born baby.

odi, vt. to beat with fist; ðkó èì
odi rö odi-odi women (on fighting) belabour each other with
fists.

òdì, n. (strong, thin) top shoot;
ðndó mà drìlé ayï-zórï durra
tops expanding, its tiny stem is
called òdì (cf. òsárá); childrens'
arrows.

ò'dí, n. musical instrument (with
metal tongues on wooden case,
&c.); èì ò'dí tsə they are playing
the...

ó'dí, a. new; àfa ó'dírï a new thing.

o'dí = òdídi, n. inflammation of
ear-drum (which becomes white);
èri adri vìrö: èri erá vìrö it

forms (white) pus; a pus-like
matter runs out.

ədi, vn. to be(-come) wrinkled,
shrivelled; 'bá dɛ̌pi 'bərï mà
andratinï ədi-ədi the face of an
old man is wrinkled; ósö ədizàrï
shrivelled beans.

ə'dí, in ə'dî ŋaa or ə'dí ətó, vt.
to intrigue, scheme, plot against;
mï èri mà ə'dî (or ɛ'yô) ŋaa (or
ətó) èri 'di-zó... you are plotting
against him to kill him (thrash,
rob); 'bá mà ə'dî ŋa = ti (or
ɛ'yó) ətó 'bâ rúá; past t. ətó
ɛ'yó 'bâ rúá they plotted/schemed
against sby.

ə'dìá, ə'dìá-ə'dìá, n. umber bird
(*Scopus umbretta*); ə'— èri ópí
àrïïá vélé àmbórï; kà lè tïti
àrïïá èì èri vélé dzô si nï; emú
ɛ́lí sï the umber bird is a great
chief among the birds; when it
wants to hatch, (all) the birds will
build its nest; it arrives in winter.

ó'díiá = ɛ́'bósó, n. a chisel; èì
pätí tálá lö̌ ó'— sï they cut holes
in wood (or iron) with a chisel.

ə'di'dð = tsúrú'dð, av. just now;
àma ṅdú mï bɛ ə'— = àma
ṅdrí tsə rö mï bɛ tsúrú'dð you
will have to deal with me instantly
(challenge).

òdiiká, n. a cold, chill, catarrh
(òmvusí in the nose); ò— di
(= bï) èri rá she suffers from a
chill; èri ò— tsə he is sneezing;
mïnï tsə 'dï ò— nï yà? is it a
cold that makes you sneeze?

ó'dípí, n. a group of relations,
kindred (clan sub-group); àma
mï bɛ ó'dípía (= ó'dípî-rö, ó—
nï) you are of my kindred group
mï mâ ó'dípí-dípí; àmà mu
àma ó'dípíá we are going to our
(tribal) brothers.

òdirì = òdärì, n. wax; àŋú-nï

ò— sǐ dzótilé 'í-drírǐ asɛ̌; èi
'bílɛ́tilɛ́ 'dǐ ə̀bǐ pírí ò— sǐ tsí;
èi dí ko wɛɛreá bees cover the
entry of their hole with wax; they
leave over very little (hole); èi ò—
sǐ ò'dí ə̀bǐ people adjust 'o'di'
(-instruments) with wax.

ə̀díríkpà = àdárákpàlá = ədizà
-rö, a. wrinkled; 'bá/ə̀kó àmbó
'dà mà rùá ə̀díríkpà-rö/ədiədi
that old person/woman is very
wrinkled.

ò'díti = ò'dítiko, ò'dúti, ògaako,
n. clod, lump (of earth); ámvú
ò— a roughly dug field (preparation).

ò'díti-àríǐã, n. a bird (bee-eater?)
nesting under a lump (of anything); èri ò'díti 'álɛ́ àkǔ or
èri ti ò'dítiá it scratches open
a clod of earth or the like (under
a stone), it hatches in clods of
earth.

ə̀do, n. grease, oil (of any kind); tí
ə̀do = bòotá butter; ár̩ú ə̀dó
simsim; àr̩ú ə̀do (= ósə̀), honey;
kə̀máará ə̀do shea-butter; ólù
ə̀do ricinus (castor) oil; mbírà
ə̀do palm oil; màlâ (or ótsufí)
ə̀do heglig oil.

ódə́ə, n. a strong high climber; èrì
ra pätí ágíi mà rùá it creeps up
a fellow tree; monkeys like its
fruits very much əyə lè mbɛ tǒ;
'bá àn̩í tikə̀ tsə they plait doors
with it; súnǐ èri ésêrö its juice
is viscous. (*Vitex cuneata*, ? also
V. madiensis, cf. èdío, Ac. òy-
wɛ̈ɛlô.)

ə̀do rare for èdo; pá èdo, n. heel.

ədó rö ədó (cf. də), vn. (1) to move,
behave softly, noiselessly; bǒrà
nǐ 'i ədó mu-zǒ édrɔ bǐ-zǒ a cat
moves quietly when catching
mice; (2) = on̩ú to wither, become soft and dry (of surface;

losing the harsh freshness—and
becoming better for food); mààkò
ədó èi ədó/ = on̩ú-on̩ú = dǐdí,
i.e. rùá-nï dï-zà-rö the potato
has withered.

ə̀dó (T., ə̀dóə), n. leopard; èri
n̩drî tsï it 'bites' goats &c.; ə̀dó
mbérémbéré, n. cheetah; èri 'bá
ásí ələ it frightens a man (by
mewing and spitting, but runs
off); èri n̩drí mvâ n̩aa it eats
kids.

ə̀'dò¹, n. a kind of dance; mà tö
ə̀'dò áyo! let them dance 'ɔ'do'!

ə̀'dò², n. (1) T. (= án̩ǐ) lò mání
ə̀'dò he gave me an evasive, un-
suitable reply; (2) system, style;
custom (!? = Ac. òŋɔɔn); 'bá
òkurǐ mà ə̀'dò ndó the ways/
customs of the ancestors were
different; sǐ dzó 'dǐ ə̀'dò (=àtá,
òbǐ) ndó sǐ they built this hut in
a different style.

ó'dóá or 'dǒ'dóá, n. the young
unfledged migratory locust; ó'—
èi mbȯmbo the 'ɔ'doa' are only
hopping (not flying); à mú ó'—
kə átsálá sǐ! let us go and catch
young locusts with the basket!
(sometimes called ədə̀kədə̀).

ó'dókó (-'dó) = ó'dǒkó, á'díkó,
á'díə, n. story, fable, legend; 'ètó
mà rú sǐ' about the hare; 'bá
ó'— 'da they tell stories.

ódə́ló, ədəlǒó, n. sausage tree
(*Kigelia aetiopica*).

ə̀'dótórò, a. not deep; ií mà álí
ə̀— (= èn̩ï) the water is shallow.

ódrá, n. bamboo (*Oxitenantera
abyssinica*); ó— 'dǐ mânírǐ'ï
this bamboo is mine.

òdrá, n. food left behind from day
before (generally); ér̩á ò—, e'dí
ò— remains of polenta, gruel; 'bâ
n̩aa àfa ò— ádzɛ̂ 'bǎ ràa (or
'dà) 'ï people eat remains laid

aside during the night (as breakfast); έwá ò—.

ɔdradraa, n. a large tree with small edible fruits.

ɔdrákòdrà-rö, a. sour, bitter.

ɔ́drá'dǒ, n. a kind of eleusine (with wide spikes).

ɔdré, n. urine; tí sɔ̌ ə— rá the cow shed water; ɔdré-dzɔ́adzɔ́a bladder.

ɔ̀drǐ, n. clay, loam; ɔ̀— tö pá sǐ to stamp clay with feet; ɔ̀— ɛ̀ri iía/'bîlέ mà 'a clay (for pots) is found in water/in holes; é mu ɔ̀— tǐ, mà emû si έmvô-rö! go and collect clay that they may make pots with it! ɔ̀drî si-zɔ̌ to work/form clay into pots, &c.

ɔ̀drí, ɔ̀dría, T., n. a kind of black heron (along swamps, at dry season).

ɔdrǐ-ɔdrí, vn./a. not well stewed; mààkò ə— halfcooked potatoes.

òdrǐ, T. = ɛ̀drǐ, vt. to increase; fíisí 'bá mà òdrǐ ddíká! the fees have to be increased again!

ɔ́ɔdrɔ, ɔdrɔmɔnɔkɔ, n. kind of stubborn weed; ɔ́— ámvúa 'dòá ɔ̀ndzí; ámvú 'dà ndrǐ 'dɔ́ kö the weeds in this field are ugly; the field is in bad condition.

ɔ̀drɔ (cf. drɔ̀), vt. (1) to heap upon other; èì àfa ɔdrɔ̀ ágúí mà drìá, ágúí mà drìá they heap things upon each other; mǐ ɔ̀— àfa mvá 'dǐ mà drìá 'dǐnǐ kö! do not pile up so much on the boy's head! 'bǎ ɔ̀drɔ-zàrö they put them on a heap; (2) ɛ'yó ɔ̀drɔ (=tra) 'bâ drìá to calumniate, slander a p.; (3) to prepare in great quantity; ɔ̀kó 'dà ɔ̀drɔ ko έŋá àfadzóa tré that woman heaped up polenta in a receptacle.

ɔdrɔ́ (cf. drɔ), vt. (1) to drive away; mǐ ə— ma kö! do not

drive me away! (2) to beat up/about; à mu ádzɛ̂ àŋàpá ə— we went yesterday to beat up game; ɔ̀tsénǐ àrîïä ɔdrɔ̀ the dog drives off birds.

ɔ̀dróa, pl. ɔ̀dróa-andzi, n. girl.

ɔ̀drɔ̀dzɔ́, n. (1) common dormitory for youths and, separately, girls; andzi ɔ̀drɔ̀ rö 'anïá children crowd, huddle together in it; èì laa rö ɔ̀drɔ̀dzóa they lie/sleep in the common dormitory (in centre villages only); (2) birds' nests (birds are said to lie in collective nests (?)); àrîïá èì laa rö ɔ̀drɔ̀dzóa birds sleep in common nests; (3) well/closely adapted chamber for corpse in grave (either in the side or at bottom; to be walled off before covering in grave); eɡa 'bîlé ɔ̀— sǐ, mà sa ɛ̀ri ɔ̀— sǐ he dug a grave with chamber, to bury him in it.

òdrú, n. buffalo; edzí ò— mà ə'yó ɡɔ̀kɛ̂ rö he brought a buffalo horn for the purpose of a blowing horn.

ɔ́drúɡbé = ɔ́ríríabbí, q.v. ótúrbé peppermint plant (Cymbopogon apronardus).

odrúkodrú, n. toad; o— ɛ̀ri ɔwáɔwá (= ɔmbo-ɔmbo = ɔ̀tǐ-ɔ̀tǐ) ǐ tíá the toad/(frog) jumps at the water-side.

òdrùŋa, n. brass wrist-ring.

odrúsí = ódrùsí, odrísí, n. cowry-shell; mǐ ɛ̀fɛ̀ mání o— mà mu ànǐ dzɛ̀kɛ̂ 'bɛ! give me cowry-shells so that I may play at hazard! èì o— 'bǎ ŋɔrɛ̀ rúá ɛ̀rinǐ ndrǐ-zɔ́ they put cowry-shells on their bead-string to look nice.

ò'dù, -ru, a. ominous, portentous; being an omen of evil; kànì mǐ esú ɡala'bá mǐ esú ò'dùru if

you meet with a 'gala'ba' snake,
it is meeting with a bad omen.

o'dú¹, n. day; **o'dú-zù**/= o—
drí́a, o— tää ... everyday; always; continuously.

o'dú², n. sleep; o— kə (or 'bɛ), to
(fall a-)sleep; o— kə ma tsí́ I am
sleepy; 'yə ɛ'yó o'dú milɛ́ sɨ̀ he
talked in his sleep; ɛ́ɳá o'dû
kəzŏrɨ̀: 'bánɨ̂ fï-zŏ o'dû kəzŏ
dzóa-rɨ̀'ï evening meal, when
people are to enter the hut to
sleep; ma o'dû kə I am sleepy.

ò'dú, n. thigh; ò'dú fà (-la), thigh
bone; ò'dú-fà-sí (≙ ò'dú-ti or
ópíléti) head of femur; 'é li mɨ̂
ò'dúfàsí gàràlàrɨ̀ï vàá' = mɨ̂
ò'dúfèsí gàɨgàɨ̂-rö your thigh
(or lumbar) region is unbecoming-
ly large (ə'datáa insult).

o'du, vt. to castrate; ɛ̀ri ǹdrí or tí
o'du he castrates a he-goat, a bull.

oddú, (1) vn. to be (-come) soaked,
drenched; wet through; mâ
bə̀ɳgɔ́ o— ɨ̀ sɨ̀ my cloth is wet
from water; àɳgɔ̀ o—o— the
ground is soaked; ɔ́sŏ o— 'bə the
beans are now soaked/soft; (2) vt.
to wet, sprinkle; mɨ́ o— mɨ̂ rùá
'dínï à'do sɨ̀ yà; ɨ̀ dɛ'ï rá yà?
why do you only just sprinkle
yourself; is the water finished (to
wash properly)?

òdú, n. credit, loan; mɨ́ ɛ́fɛ̀ mánɨ̂
séntɛ̀ òdûrö! give me money on
loan! lend me! é 'à mánɨ̂ ámvú
òdûrö (= òdú nï), mâ ɳga emú
màríti (= àríóti) nï ə̀fɛ̀ ndə̀!
till the field for me on loan, I will
then compensate you! (cf. gbándzá).

òdùdù = òdùkòdù, n. moth, &c.,
larvae (eating paper, cloth, &c.).

ódúbí= òtubí, n. a narrow 'chamber' (generally under the ɛ̀rólírí)
fenced in with sticks, palings, or

the like, in which a woman with
a new-born baby stays during the
day—for washing, &c. (? better
ádúbí).

o'dúkə̀ = o'díkə̀, n. voice; sound;
mɨ̈ o— àmbó or àká your voice
is big, i.e. low; o— ɳírí́a or
wɛrɛ́á small or high voice.

ó'dúkó, n. news, tidings; mɨ̈ ɛri
ɛ'yó 'dà mà ó— rá yà? or mɨ̈
ɛri ó—'dà rá yà? have you heard
that news/rumour? 'bá àmbó mà
drà mà ó— (or ɛ'yó) etsá má
vŏ nɨ̀ the news of the big man's
death has reached me.

o'dúko'dú, n. (generally smaller)
caterpillars; ɛri ɔ́sŏ bbí mbɛ
pírɨ́ it eats up the (tender) leaves
of beans.

ə'dúkù (more common apparently
à'dúkù), n. pulp of fruits; komará, ɛdíəkɔ́ à'dúkù the edible
pulp covering the stone of shea-
butter fruit and others.

òdúrú-rɨ̀, a. deaf; mvá 'dɨ̀
òdúrú˞rö, ɛri ɛ'yó kö this child
is deaf, it does not hear speaking;
mɨ̂ bbílɛ́ òdúrú˞rö you(-r ears)
are deaf!

o'dúti, see ò'díti.

ɔdzá (cf. dza), vt. (1) to turn sth.;
mɨ́ ɔdzá mɨ̈! turn round! mɨ́ ə—
= ɛló) tinï vàálɛ́! turn it upside
down! á lɛ̀ sàà 'dà ə— (= əpi)
'dílɛ́ I want to adjust that watch
according to this one; (2) ti ə—
to interpret; Lógbàrà ti ə— zŏ
to translate Logbara; (3) to exchange, interchange (for places);
mɨ́ ə—'bá 'dɨ̀ ə—! do exchange
these people (or: send others in
their places)! (4) (= əlɛ́, ɛtsí) to
cheat, make fun of; mɨ̈ ma ɔdzǎ
(= ebabǎ, ɛtsí) you are making
fun of me! (5) to develop; a'ú gbɛ́
ɛ̀rinï ə— kö 'dɨ̀ (i.e. àlú gbɛ́)

when an egg does not develop (blind egg); ə—ə— rö, vn./r. (1) to turn round; (2) to exchange places; (3) to pass each other by without meeting (walking on the same path in opposite directions); (4) to recover; rùá-nï ə— rö mö̆kɛ(=àtï̀'bə)he recovered well.

ə̀dzì, vt. (1) to wash; mu bə̀ŋgó ə̀dzì he went to wash the cloth; é mu mï̀ rùá ə̀dzì! go to wash yourself/to have a bath (= mï̀ ə̀dzì rö)! (2) to soak, wet; əzóó ə— èri rá the rain has soaked him.

ə̀dzi (cf. dzi), vt. (1) to transport a quantity of ... (by repeated journeys); (2) ə— mádrí tsï̆—gà à'ï̀ kə sï̀ òvú àkà sï̀ he keeps silent on purpose—he would not answer.

odzí, odzíka, n. bile; gall-bladder; o— èri əgó mà rùá the 'odzi' is on the liver; or o— èri tí ('bá) mà ásíá is in the pit-region of a cow (man);ᶦ... o— dra òká the bile is bitter; àmbó èì mvu 'bâ rə-zö̆ big men drink it for the purpose of bewitching sby.

ə̀dzí (= àrï̈, àrïbà, T. dzíbò), n. (1) great anomalies of surface, of line (say boundary), curves, &c.; (2) cavity, cave, hole, burrow, den = óní tálá, óní mà gólɛ́; ə— èri ótókó mà 'aléa a hole in the inside of termite-hill; ə— ŋgúru-nï 'a'á-zö̆rï̀ den in which a wild beast lives; (3) indentation, incision, cut, notch (in anything); (4) crooking, bend, turn; corner (= kóŋà); bǎò mà ə— edge on timber or furniture; ámvú mà ə— mu tö̆ the border of the field is sinuous/very irregular; ïí-nï raa ə— sï̀ the river runs/flows in windings/turns.

ə̀dzìàtá, ə̀dzìmàtá, n. baboon

(Ac. biim); ə— èri óní ùù ágátìá 'bá ə'bɛ́ (= tsà)-zö̆ the baboon gathers stones keeping them on his breast to throw at people (said to be very daring).

ódzíə, n. (1) intermediary, go-between for marriage arrangements; ó— nï tï drə ə̀kó-á the match-maker drives the bride-wealth cattle; (2) in general: messenger (of any kind); apostle.

ə̀dzíó =à'yïə, av. in the late morning about 8/9–11 a.m.; ètú ə̀dzíə̂-rö or etsá ə— sï̀ it is the pleasant morning sun.

ə̀dzə̀, n. divination craft; ódzóə èri àzí ə— drírï̀ ŋga the diviner does the work of divination; ódzóə èri 'bá drăpi 'bə 'dï̀ï mà ò'dúkə̀ zi the magician asks/consults the voice of deceased; sö mâ drí ə̀dzə̀á he has put my hand (has introduced me) into the craft of magic.

ódzóə¹, n. magician; medicine-man; ó— àtsífɛ-ǹdrípi the rubbing-stick diviner; ó— nï 'bá ɛdɛ̆ mìríndà (= tálï̀) sï̀ the medicine-man treats people in a mysterious way/marvellously.

ódzóə², n. midwife; ó— èri ə̀kó bï̀ mvâ zö-rḯá the midwife helps a woman at child-birth; ə̀kó emúpi ə̀kó àzíní bï̀-rḯá mvâ ti-rḯá-rï̀'ï, èri ódzóə nï a woman who comes to help another woman at delivery is a midwife.

ə̀dzó = T. tö̀rə̀(or ótö̆rə̆)-báŋgì, n. name of various plants with onion-like bulb-root or similar, with long and broad pulpy leaves (some lily-like); kind of sisal-like leaves are used for ropes; ə— èri mbásálà-lɛ́ it is onion-like; 'bá bbíní atsɛ̂: mvuzàrö nòsì ŋgù-zàrö òmvùá: èri áró they tear off the leaves (and crush them), then boil and express them) in water) for drinking or for smelling because they are a medicine; **'bá lɔ̌ sú-nïrï̌ mvu 'ï** only its (expressed in water) juice is drunk; **'bá atsɛ́pi wɛrɛ drăpi dràrï̌, ɛ̀ri egǎ ə̀— sï̌ rá** one near to dying is revived through this medicine. Its varieties are as follows:

ə̀dzɔ́-ə̀dzɔ́ɔ̃́á, n. (1) leaves obtained from various 'ɔdzə' plants; (2) mysterious/magic charm (in form of fruits or crushed leaves) thrown at a person and causing magic disease or initiation to sorcery itself; **ə̀—ə̀— 'bá ùú əmbɛ́pirï̌** the 'ɔdzə' affects one's arm (especially); **ɛ̀i ə̀— 'du ï̌ àtsï̌ sï̌** they treat it with warm water; in other cases this 'ɔdzə' effects **ɔ́dzɔ́ə ádaarï̌** i.e. initiates a p. into sorcery/makes him a sorcerer.

ɔ́dzɔ́lɔ́, n. (1) poor, needy, destitute in the sense that he lacks cows, &c., for marrying; **'bá ɔ́dzɔ́lɔ́'rö ə̀kó kɔ́kə̀rö** a poor man has no wife; hence (2) bachelor; widower; **ágúpi ə̀kónï̈ dràzɔ́rárï̌** a man whose wife died.

odzú, n. in **pá (mà) odzú** calf of leg.

odzúrúkɔ́ more commonly **ɛdzíríkɔ́,** n. termite; **ɛ̀ri ɔ́tɔ́kɔ́ ɛmví nï̌** it forms/constructs (by slow patient work) earth-hills.

ə̀fà, vt. to scrape, rasp; scratch and clean away (**ɛ'bɔ̌ sï̌** with a hoe); **'bá mu ɔ́ŋa ə̀fǎ** they go to clean round a termite-hill and dig a hole to collect swarming termites in; **mu dzɔ́ pə̀rí ə̀fǎ** he went to clean the place for a hut.

ə̀fá, vt. to clean off (all surface

unevenness of sth.) (**ëlï̈ sï̌** with a knife); **ɛ̀i ə̀tsɛsïïá ə̀fǎ ósùùrö** they trim the 'ɔtsɛsiia' stick into a bow; **ma mâ ɔ́ŋɔ́fï̌ ə̀fǎ ëlï̈ sï̌** I trim my finger-nails with a knife.

ə̀fè (cf. **fè**), vt. to give to many or in quantity; **màríti ə̀fè̃** to indemnify, compensate; **ɛzá-ti ə̀fè̃ ɛzitáa sï̌** to make reparation, atone with prayer for one's sins.

ə̀fï̌ (cf. **fï̌**), vt. (1) to crack, split; **é dzï kaká ə̀fï̌ àtsïa!** take the maize to the fire for roasting (crackling)! (2) to stretch, smack; **ma mâ drí ə̀fï̌** I am cracking my fingers; (3) cf. to flit, leap over (to); **àtsï̌ kà fï̌ (= tï̌) mï̌ rùá rá, é wɛɛ rá!** if a fire-spark flies on to you, brush it off!

ə̀fï̈ (cf. **fï̈**), vt. to cause to enter, to drive into; **àŋgö̀ kà bï̌ rá, mï̌ tí ə̀fï̈ lítsóa** when it becomes dark, you drive cattle into the pen.

ə̀fï̌, vn. to penetrate, permeate, pervade; **drà-nï̈ ə̀fï̌ 'bá rùá rïarïa, dɛ 'ï kö** a disease is permeating a p.'s body chronically, it does not cease.

ə̀fïfïá = àkï̌, q.v.

ə̀fɔ̌, n. leprosy; **ə̀fɔ̌-'bá** or **'bá ə̀fɔ̌ bɛ,** n. a leper; **ə̀fɔ̌'bâ ŋáápirï̌** leprosy which consumes a man; **ə̀fɔ̌ ɔlï̌ mâ drí rá** leprosy has maimed my hands (cf. **kùlúvá**).

ə̀fɔ̀ (cf. **fɔ̀**), vt. (1) to drive out (herd); **kànï̌ ɔzɔ́ɔ̀ àtï̌ rá, ɛ̀i dï̌ tí ə̀fɔ̀ àmvé, mà mu ɛ̀ríbïŋa** when it has stopped raining, they drive out the cattle, that they may go to eat green grass; (2) to bring out, disclose, reveal; **lɔ̌fɔ̀ ə̀fɔ̀-zɔ̌ (= ɛ̀ndzɔ̀ ndzɛ) 'bá àzï̌ mà ti-árï̌ ə̀lɔ̀-zɔ̌ 'bá àzï̌-ti-á** to disclose a deception: to expose to sby. a p.'s lie he told another; **ɛ̀i**

ɛ̀ndzɔ̀ ágú 'dà-nï ndzɛ-rï̀ ɔ̀lɔ̌
they reveal the lie which that man
told.

ɔfö = ɔdzá rö, vn. to be (-come)
transformed, converted into sth.,
or to change into something; ɔfö
rö ŋgúrû̱-rö he was transformed
into a wild beast; ágú 'dà ɔfö 'ï
dzɔ̀dzɔ̀kï̀-rö that man became a
phantom, spectre.

ɔfő¹, vt. to break up (soil) and clean
from grass (ɛ'bő sï̀); ɛ̀ri pätí
n̄dú ɔfő (i.e. ɛ̀l ásê 'yà 'bɛ àmvɛ́)
ɛ̀l dï emú ŋ̱aakû̱ ga (kàkâṉa
n̄dúnïá) he has (lightly) loosened
and cleaned the ground (shaking
the grass and throwing it away),
then they came to dig the ground
(under the maize).

ɔfő² = ɔ̀trɔ̌, vt. to exchange animal
for animal (sï̀); ɔfő n̄drí-átá
n̄drí-ándrii sï̀; 'bâ ŋga n̄drí 'dà
lì rá he exchanged a he-goat for
a she-goat and then killed the
former (the she-goat is returned
to its former owner after she has
borne two kids, which are retained
in place of that he-goat); mï̀ ɔfő
mání sèntè sìlíŋgì sï̀! do exchange cents with me for a shilling!

ɔ́fő, n. funeral ceremony; ɔ́fő tö
to dance at a funeral ceremony;
mu ɔ́főã or mu ɔ́fő tö or mu
ɔ́fő-tö-rïá or mu dràá he went
to the mourning/funeral ceremony
(with dancing, distribution of
arrows to relations and, under
good conditions, of meat to elders).

ɔ́fő-à'ï, n. lye (obtained from ashes
(ɛ̀ri ɔ́fótâ-rö) of burned cow-
dung).

ɔ̀fődzɔ́ = ɔ̀fɛ́ndzɛ́ = gala'bá, n.
big venomous, spitting snake;
greyish-yellow (?); ɛ̀ri 'bá vő-vö
ává sï̀ it blows/spits at a p. (attacking); ɛ̀ri a'á àŋgö óni-rö bɛ

it lives in stony (hilly) ground;
thick; about 4 ft.

ɔ̀fɔ̀kɔ̀fɔ̀, a. restless, turbulent,
fidgety (opp. ɛ'yɛ́rɛ́ calm).

ɔ̀főkőfő, -rö, a. indistinct, vague
(of smell); àdzí-nï ŋgù̱ ɔ̀főkőfő-
rö its smell is indefinable.

ɔ̀fóndzɛ́, n. large tree (Mytragina
stipulosa); ɛ̀l pa arï̂-rö they make
drums from it.

ɔ̀fósàrà (also àfósàrà) = lùurú,
n. fog, mist; vapour; ɔ̀— asɛ́
àŋgö tsḯ the fog obstructs the outlook; ɔ̀— vàá ɛ̀ri lùlù, = ɛ̀ri esí
gògògò) the mist drizzles finely.

ɔ̀fótá = ɔ̀fórá (cf. àtsí-fórá), n.
ashes; ɛ̀tú ɔ̀fótá drí Ash-Wednes-
day.

ɔ̀fúdrì = ɔ̀mvú, n. secret additional exit (in emergency) of mice
(besides the ordinary ɛ́drɔ́ mà
'bílɛ́).

ɔga¹(cf. ga), vt. to pick, break open;
a'ú-nï ɔga ɛmbá-sí sï̀; ɛ̀ri ɛ'dɔ̌
andzi ɔndzɛ-ző, ɛ̀rinï̈ mba
(= zɔ̀) ző the hen breaks open the
eggs at new moon, to let out the
chickens and to rear them.

ɔga² (cf. gà), vt. to refuse; prevent,
obstruct; ɔga mání ɛ́ṉá (ṉaa) sï̀
he refuses me polenta.

ɔ́ga (T., ɔgá), n. tick; ɔ́ga tí
(or ɔ̀tsɛ́) vélɛ́rï̀'ï tick of cattle
(dogs).

ɔ̀gaako = ɔ̀díti, n. a clod, lump
of earth; ɔ̀— ɛ̀l àni tí 'bɛ ɛ̀rinï̈
muző they pelt a cow with it to
make it go on; ɛ̀l víni àrï̀á ɔ'bɛ̌
àni they fling it at birds (to drive
them off).

ɔ̀gàlì = ɔ̀gèlɛ̀, n. a piece of cloth
(worn in front and behind by old
women, especially for mourning);
ɛ̀l ɔ̀— sù̱ báká a'dï-a'dïrï̀ sï̀;
ɛ̀l dï sù̱ ɔ́pílïa they put it on with
a string round the waist.

ɔ́gálĭrĭ(ắ), n. flea; ɔ́— tu mĭ bɔ̀ŋgɔ́á a flea walks up your cloth; ɔ́gálĭrĭ-nĭ ɔdza rö ɔ̀'bûru a flea turns into a jigger (!?).

ògárá, n. axe; èl pätĭ ga (= lĭ) ò— sĭ they cut wood with an axe.

ògárá'bá (= àŋgárá'bá), n. the white man.

ɔgbé, vt. to vomit; èri ɛ́ɳá ɔgbɛ̂ he vomits the polenta.

ɔgbó, vt. to isolate; mĭ ɔ— 'bá ɔ̀fɔ́ bɛ ndó! do isolate the leper! tĭ àlö èri 'ĭ ɔ— tĭ àzĭ 'dĭ mà 'aléá ndó one cow separates from the others; èri tĭ gàɳɳ̀á-rö=tĭ ɔgàĭbɔ tĭ mà 'aléa it is an unruly cow, a cow of singular habits among the rest.

ɔgó, n. liver; ɔgó mà 'aléa ɔdzĭ (= ɔledzi) tsĭ the bile is in the liver.

ɔgo, n. a shrub; ɔ'bɛ́ (= ɔ̀'bà) 'ĭ gĭrĭgĭrĭ-rö its large fruits have a knotty surface.

ògó (cf. gó), n. (1) kind of plank (hewn); (2) hole in the ground for hiding/keeping money ògó àŋgò 'bánĭ silĭŋgĭ dàa-zŏ́.

ògɔ̀ = ɔmvi, vt./vn. (1) to return, give back sth.; mĭ ògɔ̀ ma àfa vélɛ́! give me back my property! (2) to answer (to -tiá); ògɔ̀ ɔ́pĭ mà tĭá he answered the chief; á kà ɛ'yɔ́ ògɔ̀ ɔ́pĭ mà tĭá, mà 'yɛ drĭ-ndza sĭ when I reply to the chief, it ought to be with bashfulness.

ògö (cf. gö), vt. to overturn, overthrow; ɔ̀lĭ ògö àndrò kaaká wɔ́rɔ́ vàá the wind has blown down all the maize today.

ɔ́gɔ̀á = ɛ́gɔ̀á, n., q.v.

ògɔ̆́ɔ̆́á, n. wooden (carved or assembled) native chair.

ògɔ̀gɔ̀, av. (1) near; mĭ emú ɔ̀—! come near! (2) holding on, all along; ɔ'á ma àgǎĭ-á ɔ̀— he is all the time on my side; èri ŋgà àzĭ ŋga ɔ̀— he keeps on working; èri ŋgà Árúwá ɔ̀— he is still continually at Arua.

ɔ̀gɔ́gɔ̀lĭ⸜rö (= gĭrĭ gɔ̀lĭgɔ̀lĭ), a. crooked.

Ógɔkɔ̀, n. people and area of Rhino Camp with Áávò (= Áóvò), &c.

ògɔ́lɛ́, n. channel or the like; èl ĭ ògɔ́lɛ̂ ga ɛ'bó sĭ they dig a water channel with a hoe.

ɔ̀gɔ́lɔ̀á = ɔ̀gɔ̆́rɔ̆́'bàlá, n. dried and separated bark of fallen tree, &c.

ɔ̀gɔ́lóko, n. large reddish or black ant (feeding much on fruit, sugar).

ɔ̀gɔ́lɔ́gbɔ = léŋgbɔ, T., n. libation-stone of cattle-pen; ɔ̀— èri ónĭ lĭtsó-ti-á the 'ɔgɔlɔgbɔ' is a stone at the entrance of every litsɔ; ɔ̀— mà tálá húù-rö the 'ɔgɔlɔgbɔ' has a large hole in it; lésú ... 'bá kà àŋgà dắ ónĭ ndɛ mà drĭá kö, andzi mbɛ́ kö milk (of cow after calving)... if they have not yet shed (some of it) on the stone, children cannot drink of it.

ógú in milɛ́-ógú, n. eyelid.

ògú = gu, n. back lumbar region; ma ògú àzɔ́⸜rö my back aches; ma ògú nĭ ɔrɔrɔ̀ my back is stiff.

ògù¹, n. neighbourhood, the (level) ground nearby; ndɔ̂ èri dzɔ́ ògù 'dà mà 'aléa the pail is in the room (or hut) nearby there; ògù vàá 'dĭ this same locality; ògù kúkúlù⸜rö (= élórózàrö) the sloping side of this site; àŋgò té ògùrĭ élórózàrö the site was sloping ground.

ògù², a./av., aside, apart; mĭnĭ tĭ tsɔ-zŏ́ ògù when you turn round/about; 'bánĭ laa-zŏ́-rĭ èri 'ĭ tĭ tsɔ ògù one who is lying down turns over; é tsə mï ti ògù! turn round!

ògù³, vt. to thieve, steal; ògù or ògùtáa, n. stealing; theft; ògù-zà, -rö, a. thievish; stealthily, secretly; ògúuó, n. thief; mï 'bá ògùru = 'bá àfa ògŭpirï, mï ògúuó thou art a thief; ògù rö ògù ndïïá he made off secretly; ɛ'yɔ́ ògùzà secret arrangements (often: backbiting).

ogú (cf. gu), vn. to laugh; mvá 'dàrï ogú that boy is laughing; ogúŭá = ogútáa, n. laughing; laughter; kànì é gŭgu, 'dï ogŭáá when you laugh, that is laughter.

ógúrï suffix in átá-ó— = átá mà ádrípi father's brother; ma ándríi-ó— = ma átïïmà ádrípi mà ɔ̀kó (?) my father's brother's wife.

Ogugu or Òvú, n. proper name of a child (m. or f.) born after others who died.

ògúrú, n. kind of wooden plate; ò— ɛn̥á əva-zɔ́ wooden plate for portioning out polenta (cf. n̥àambí).

ogúrú-k-òguru, a. roughly uneven; àŋgò o— 'dé ŋgörö 'dé 'dǎäli broken rugged ground, rising and falling.

ɔ́hɔ́rɔ́kɔ́tə = hɔ̀rɔ̀ŋgɔ́tɔ̀, n. shell...; órí ɔ́— slough of snake; àn̥ú ɔ́— honeycomb; a'ú gbé mà ɔ́— shell of egg.

ohulú, n. órí o— a snake; rùánï òbìkòbì ëni sï ɛmvɛ sï it is variegated black (? dark) and white.

ò(h)wéɛló, n. crested crane (its flesh believed to be poisonous); ò— mà òtsùtsùlú the crested crane's peculiar hair-tuft or crown.

ɔ̀ï (cf. ïï), in əzɔ́ɔ́-nï ɔ̀ï-ɔ̀ï drrrr(ï) it keeps on drizzling steadily.

ói, vt. to wipe off with the side of the hand; ɛ̀ri ɛmvó 'alɛ́ óï (drï sï), əmbɛzàrö he wipes out the pot (with hand) for licking; mï óï àfa 'dï vàá! wipe this off on to the ground! ɛ̀ri tïbí óï òtɛkŭá she portions out sauce in small pots.

óï or wï, əndrí, əndzú, vn. to be (-come) lean, thin, emaciated, worn, scraggy; ɛ̀ri óï kái he is extremely thin/ill-conditioned; 'bá óïzàrï a thin, lean person.

ɔ̀'ï (T., ɔ̀dzï) (cf. 'ï), vt. (1) to tie to sth.; ma n̄drí ɔ̀'ï áséa (átsía) álɔ́-ti-á I am tying goats (and sheep) in the grass (hut) to pegs; (2) to hang up; bɔ̀ŋgɔ́ ɔ̀'ï-zɔ́ to hang up clothes; (3) to kindle, set on fire; ɔ̀'ï àtsï n̥án̥a, ɔ́n̥a tèrïá they kindled fires everywhere, for collecting termites.

ɔ̀'ï'ïǎ = òtsákàí, n̄dríàtibi, T., àdìzúrùábi, n. an obstinate weed (especially on abandoned fields; its seeds stick to one's clothes).

oinaa, n. a relatively small beetle with long feelers; é kà ɛ̀rimà rùá əlɔ̌, ɛ̀rì də rö tsï; ə'ya rö kö; sì rö dɛ 'bə lɛ́, dɛ 'ï yə if you touch it, it keeps still; it does not move, feigning death, but it is not dead; ə'yó-nï zɔ̀zɔ̀ its 'horns' are long.

ɔ̀'ïŋgírïkï, a. hard-rinded; hardened; gbándà 'dï à'bù kö, ɛ̀ri ɔ̀'ïŋgírïkï-rö (rùá tinï ə'ïŋgírïkï = kɔ̀ŋgɔ̀lɔ̀kɔ̀rö) this manioc is not thick (well-developed or pulpy); it has a hard rind (almost turned to wood); its suckers are very thin; the body (of the manioc root) is hard and tough.

ɔka, vn. (1) brownish yellow; àgóbbí əkazà pumpkin leaves

are yellowish brown; èrì ɔka éráká-ti sì it is brown—like red ochre; (2) (= örí-örí, àŋgbà-ŋgbà) to be (lightly) rusty; örí, àŋgbà-zà and, especially, at-síatsí imply a detaching rusty crust (of iron); (3) reddish (of clouds); èrítinï ɔka-ɔka the clouds (morning or evening) are red.

ɔ̀kà, n. a climber (yielding good fibre); èrì ra pätí drì sì it creeps up trees; ɔ̀kà 'dì mà áɲáká kà ayï 'bá rùá, èrì 'bá ɔsɔ̀-ɔsɔ̀ (ɲ̀ àɲa) when its powder falls on sby. it causes itching.

ɔ̀ká = drȁdra, a. (1) sour; bitter (Logbara does not apparently distinguish); ɔ̀ká-ŋgálí(ká)-rö bitter; dra ɔ̀ká it has become over-sour/bitter; lésú ɔ̀ká the milk is sour; ɔ̀ká-nï̀ = ɔ̀kà-nï̀ wɛrɛ it is slightly sour; ɛ́wá dra ɔ̀ká-ŋgálíká the beer has become sour/bitter; (2) fig. ill-natured ásí ɔ̀ká̌ = ásí drazà; mï̀ ásí dra/ɔ̀ká mání à'dï ɛ'yó sì yà? through whose influence have you become so ill-disposed towards me?

ɔ́ká, n. the smith's bellows; ɔ́ká-l-émvó aya di-zŏrì bellows' pot for forging iron; sí ɛ́mvó ɔ̀drí sì; èì tinï ɔmbɛ́ ǹdrí enïrïkɔ́ sì; èì kàlî sö aga drìà; èì dí sɔ̀ kàlí sì, èì àtsí vö ànï̀:ɔ̀ndóánï̀ ànï̀ ɛ́mvɛ̀ di they make the (particular) pot with clay; on the opening they tie a (piece of) goat-skin; they fix a stick on its centre, and they work the stick up and down and blow on fire with it: the artisan (smith) forges rings (&c.) in this way; ɔ́ká'bá the smith; ɔ́ká àzí the smith's work; ɛ'bó, ɔ̀gaara, &c. di zŏ to forge hoes, axes, &c.

ɔ̀kélè more common ɛ̀kélè, n. cough; a malignant form (? consumption) of it kíɔ̀kíɔ̀.

ɔ̀kɛlé, ɔ̀kɛlékɔ̀á, ɛ̀tsía, ɛ̀gá, n. small calabash (for drinking): íì mvu zö ɔ̀kɛlía small and decorated; èì rùá-nï̀ lɔ̌lɔ̀ (T., lɑ̌là) àtsí sì nɔsì 'yé sì they incise its body with fire (red-hot iron) or an arrow.

okí, T. = otsí (1) n. thorn; (2) vt. to conceal.

ɔ̀kî, n. wife of...; má ɔ̀kî! my wife; Dàwúdì ɔ̀kî the wife of Dàwúdì.

ɔ̀kó, pl. ɔ̀kóèì, n. woman; wife; ɔ̀kó àmbó (= àká, dèzà) great/ old woman; ɔ̀kópì is sometimes found in place of the former.

ɔko, ɔkonǎ, vt. (1) to gather, sweep together; assemble, collect (scattered things in one place); èì ɛ́dzá or àtsíförá ɔko yófé sì; èì dí emú àtsí dǎ drìnǎ́, èrì dí tsï ɲàai they gather fuel (twigs) or ashes with a broom; then they set fire to it, and it flares up; ɔ̀kónï̀ áisɛ́ ámvú-á-rï̀ ɔkonǎ the woman gathers the grass/ weeds in the field; ɔko tí pírí ɛdrɔ tí àzínï̀ mà 'aléa he gathered all the cows and drove them among the others; (2) ɔko 'ï, vr./vn. to gather; ɔko 'ï tú àlö they all assembled together; ɔzɔ́ ïí ɔko'ï àŋgɔ̌ á'bǔ-ru (= àŋgɔ̌ guru) mà 'aléa rainwater collected in a depression; ɔkotáa assembly; (3) to govern, rule, keep together; ɔ́pí èri 'bá èìdrírï̀ ɔkonǎ pírí àlö the chief rules/keeps his people together.

ɔkɔ́, vn. to end, be finished; ɛ'yó ɔkɔ́ 'bɔ the matter (discussion, speech...) is finished; si dzɔ́ ɔkɔ́ (= dɛ) rá he built a hut, it is

finished = he finished (building)
the hut; àzí əkɔ́ 'bə work is
finished.

əkɔ̀, əkàô, -rì̀, a./av. first; mvá
'dì̀ etsá əkɔ̀ this child arrived
first; ǹdrí drăpì əkɔ̀rì̀ águ 'dà
mà ǹdrí the first goat to die was
that man's.

əɔ́kɔ́, n. annoyance, vexation;
anger, wrath; spite; ə̀— nï̀ èrì
ŋa kái he is very angry; ə̀— ŋaa
àma 'alɛ́ rá = ə̀— kə àma tsí
we were displeased/crossed; we
grew angry/lost our temper; əkó
kànì ə̀— ásínì̀álɛ́ tsí, èrì 'ï tì̀tì̀
when a woman is very upset/
grieved, she will hang herself;
mï̀nï̀ ə̀— 'bà-zồ 'bá àzínï̀
bɛ/=mï̀ ə̀— bɛ, mï̀ ɛdé ə̀— sì̀
when you are angry with sby., you
act out of spite; əkó àzínï̀ mà
mvá kà drà rá, èrì ə̀— 'bằ
águpí-nï̀: águpí fɛ̀ 'ïmà mvánï̀
drằ nì̀ if some woman's child dies,
she will become angry with her
husband, because the man caused
her child to die.

əɔ́kɔ̀, see wɔ́kɔ̀, n. side.

ɔ́kómvó = kómvó, q.v.

əkɔ̀ndɔ̀, n. ostrich; ə̀— 'bíkə
ostrich feathers.

ókóro = T., àgbàlàá, (?) n. oyster.

əkoro, n. massed ball made of
anything; àŋú əkoro a ball or
mass of bee-hive contents.

Ɔ̀kồrồlồ, n. proper name, tributary of Éwávío; Ò̀— 'de Éwávíò
(Mvàrà mà ètì̀lɛ́a) mà 'aléa
the Ɔk— flows into the E—
(below Mvara).

ɔ́kồrồŋà, n. sweepings, weedings,
rubbish; èrì ɔ́— əkonă kə̀ŋgɔ́rə
sì̀ she gathers up the weeds with
a rake.

əkpɔ̀ = mba, n. strength; power;
efficiency/efficacy; kằmì mà ə̀—

tồ = kằmì mà ə̀— tsí the lion
is very strong; əkpɔ̀ bɛ = (!)
əkpɔ̀-rö = èwâ-rö, a. (1) difficult (to accomplish); àzí 'dì̀
əkpɔ̀rö this work/task is difficult;
sɛ́ntɛ̀ mà əkpɔ̀ ndàzà-rö tồ it
is very hard to find money; (2)
strong, tough; báká 'dì̀ əkpɔ̀-rö
(= ə̀— bɛ or mà ə̀— tồ) this
string/rope is very strong; əkpɔ́
sì̀ forcedly.

əkpɔ́ = èg̀bɛ́, n. rest, remains;
éŋá, e'dí . . . əkpɔ́, n. remains of
polenta, gruel (which is eaten
next day); mí edzí éŋá-əkpɔ́
mâ ŋaa ! bring me the remains
of polenta (from yesterday) that
I may eat ('breakfast' they say).

ókpɔ́á = kằdúa, n. paunch or
rumen of ruminants.

ókpɔ́dzɔ́, n. (1) womb; ɔ́— èrì
pàrí mvánï̀ əvö-zɔ̀ ándríi mà
'aléa womb is the place where
the baby is inside the mother;
(2) 'throne'-chamber of termite
queen; ɔ́ŋa mà ándríi-nï̀ fï̀-zɔ̀
'alénì̀árì̀ for a termite 'mother'
to enter/live in.

əkpɔ́lɔ̀(kə), a. old and worn (of
anything); èrì sáwà ə̀— nï̀ it is
a very old watch; 'bá ə̀—.

əkpɔ̀lɔ̀-k-əkpɔ́lɔ̀-rö, av. yielding
only to insistence, importunity;
fɛ̀ mánï̀ ə̀— he gave it to me after
much insisting.

əkpɔ́rɔ́, n. (1) skin-sack; əkpɔ́rɔ̀rö
èi ǹdrí enï̀rïko ǹdzə 'ï for a
skin-sack they pull off a goat's
skin (without cutting it); é dzi
mánï̀ zá 'dì̀rï 'bà əkpɔ́rɔ́a !
bring me this meat and put it in
the bag (for travelling)! (2) shell;
òkùkù òkpɔ́rɔ́ tortoise-shell; 'bá
ɛdɛ̂ ò'dî-rö tsɔ̀tsə they make
'harps' with it (shell of tortoise)
to play.

əkpórókpòrò or àlà kpórókpòrò, n. (insignificant looking) female of ólótókó (large red-headed lizard); kókó or òndàátá ò— male of it.

əkpòrəvò, n. woman big with child òkó mvá bɛ 'aléá-rì.

òku, a. old; of the past; av. before, formerly; é ŋa òku è'bí kö yà? did you not eat fish before! Éŋáó 'bá èi òkù fï ànï wɛrɛ; àndrò tì àmbô-rö, sö (= a'bó) ódrá drì tsí the Éŋáó river did not go deep before; today it has risen high, it covers the bamboo bridge; fúnò òku-rì 'wï 'bə, dä stóòá 'bú 'aléa 'bə the old ground-nuts are dry. they have already poured them into the store; tsɛ 'ï òku (or kó) drìə in the far past, since olden times.

okú¹, vt. to weed; mu 'dó okú he went to weed the eleusine; èri ásɛ ámvú-á-rì okú he is pulling up/ clearing the weeds in the field.

okú², n. shield (generally unknown to Logbara); okú èzô-rö tìkò-rö; èi tsàtsà a shield is oblong and of wickerwork; they plait it.

okú³, sometimes used for akú, q.v.

òkùkù, n. (1) black tortoise of riverside; (2) èkáráká ò— smaller brown/yellow land-tortoise.

ólá, n. (1) root (of tree or any plant); pätí ólá tree root; óədrò ólá; (2) (= yëla, ərí, molá...) descendant, offspring, progeny; èrimà ńdú ɛŋgá-zó-rì ólá what descends from him—descendant.

òláà or òláà dìrì, n. manioc plant and root.

əláa = élésɛ́réá, édró lólòá, n. kind of common squirrel (white and black); living on trees.

ólá, vn. to be playful, joking, not treating a matter seriously; fidgety; 'bánï əlá-zó trìtrìtrì when a man plays/moves restlessly to and fro; èmï əlá (= avï) kö! don't be a nuisance/keep to the point!

əla = ə'ya, vt. to rinse/wash out; èi ɛmvó mà 'alé əla iï sì she cleanses the pot by rinsing it with water.

əla-zà = ala-zà, a. lying crosswise.

əláká, n. (1) poles/sticks for the flat bottom of a granary; (2) pole for lifting/opening roof/door of granary ə— èróti zì-zó-rì (= èrópätí).

òlaŋgi = à'dï, n. bell.

əlé, n. kind of wild banana (Musa ensete); òlé ɛŋgá iïa tsénï; àmvérï 'bá sàsa the wild banana grows on riversides; outside (the waterside) it is planted (leaves used as 'cloth' by women).

əlè, n. magic power, witchcraft; əlè'bá = óléɛo, i.e. 'bá 'bâ rópirì sorcerer, magician, i.e. one bewitching man; one who hems and spits in the beer to bewitch you əsólò wï ɛ́wá 'aléa mïnï əlè rə-zó; əlè rə, = rə to bewitch; əlè tsə to remove a spell; ágú té əlè rópi 'dà èrì dí mu əlè tsə (= əlè lï) the p. (generally old man) who has laid a spell will (have to) come to remove it.

əlé = ədzá, ɛtsí, vt. to mislead, trick, cheat; mï əlé ma kö! do not cheat me!

əlɛ = dzɛ, vt. (1) to buy; à'dï əlɛ mààkò 'dìrï nï yà? who has bought these potatoes? (2) əlɛ àfa mà ti-á or əlɛ àríotinï rö he compensated or indemnified for sth.; (3) to marry a woman with bride-wealth òkó əlɛ or dzɛ.

ólè, lólòá, ólòlê, n. neatly kept passages of mice (ɛ́drɔ́ ólè) or bigger rodents or carnivora; ólè ásɛ́ 'aléarì or ásɛ́ ṅdúa among/ under the grass; sometimes children make similar secret paths in high grass to hide or escape beating.

ɔlɛdzí = ɔdzí, n. bile.

ólésɛ́réa, n. kind of common squirrel living on trees (cf. ɔláa).

ɔ̀lï = ɔdzí, vt. to transfer from one place to another by repeated journeys; mu yäbí ɔ̀lï he went to transport thatching grass (cut before).

ɔ̀lï = ɔ̀lïkà, ɔ̀lïríkà, n. wind, air; ɔ̀lï-nï päti ɔya the wind moves the trees; ɔ̀lïnï ma emvu-emvu the wind blows dust, &c., on me.

ɔlï, n. a whistle; ɔlï lï or vö to blow a whistle, to whistle.

ólï = álï, n. a shrub or high slender tree, with tiny leaves and thorns (*Solanum incanum*.)

olï (cf. lï), vt. to cut up, dress; ma ɔ́ɳɔ́fï olï ɛ̈lï sï I am cutting my fingernails with a knife; to cut up into many (small) pieces; ɛ̀rï ɛ'yɔ́ olï-olï = ɛ̈rï ɛ'yɔ́ olï ɛ̀ndzɔ̀rö he talks differently everywhere (lying).

ɔ̀lïïá = ɔ̀lï-ándzírí, ɔ̀lï-áŋgá, n. (1) shrub with yellow, inedible berries; (2) cervical gland or muscle (Ac. òcɔ̀ɔk).

ɔ̀lïdiá, n. excrescence on hand, eye, &c., wart.

Ɔlïka, n. tributary of Ega river.

olïkɔ = olúkɔ, n. (1) windpipe, trachea; (2) o— ŋgɔŋgɔ Adam's apple.

ɔlïkó, n. kind of caterpillar.

ɔ̀lilïkɔ = ɔ̀lirïkɔ, ɔ̀lïrïkà, àkúkù, n. strong wind, whirlwind; ɔ̀—

ɛ̀ri ɔ̀lï (ɛ)lïpï ɔkpó sï is a wind which blows with vehemence.

òlïŋgóló = lïrözà, ᒾrö (cf. ɔló-ŋgóló), a. round, ball-like.

ɔ̀lïïrï, ɔ̀lïïría, àdzú ɔ̀—, n. spear with short blade and long neck.

òlïrú = dzúlû-ru, av.(1) wrongly, distorted; ɛ̀ri ɛ'yɔ̂ ndzɛ ò— he speaks badly; (2) on one's back; 'bá àzïnï laa rö ò— sby. lies on his back.

ólisi S.?, a. bɔ̀ŋgó ó— light 'amerikani' cloth.

ɔ̀lǒ, vt. (1) to report to a p. about; to tell, relate, retail; confess; (2) ɔŋgɔ ɔ̀lǒ to lead in song (prayer); 'bá àlönï ɔ̀lǒ nï, 'bá pïrï̂ ɛ̀i ɔŋgɔ/or a'ï̈ (a'ï̈ 'bâ tiá), a p. leads in song, all then follow (or agree to his voice...); ɔ̀lòlòá, n. informing, tale-bearing; denouncement; treachery; mï ɔ̀lòlòá tǒ you are a wretched traitor, informer.

ɔ̀lǒ, vt. to make holes; ɛ̀mï ɔ̀lò (= ɔga) 'bïlɛ́ fúnò sa-zǒ! make holes in the ground to plant ground-nuts!

ɔló = ɛló, amví, vt. to touch (over and over again); mï ɔló ma kö! do not touch me!

ɔlǒ, ɛlǒ, vt. milɛ (or ti, drì) ɔlǒ to bend (oneself/e.g. one's eyes, mouth, head) down, stoop; ma milɛ ɔlǒ àŋgǒ nɛ̀-zǒ vàá I bend down to see/search the ground; mï ɛlǒ milɛ vàá ká, é nè ndɔ̀ you bend down (say over book because of poor sight) first, then you see; mï ɔlǒ (tinï) vàá, iȉ 'álénïárï mà raa bɛɛnï (= ànï) you tilt it (say basin) that the water in it may run out; ɔlǒ-zà, a. inclined, sloping, oblique.

ɔlóɔ = ɛlyó, n. sycamore tree (*Ficus gnaphalocarpa*).

ólóa = ɓú, n. fishing-hook.

óəlò'bí, n. depression in front of head; tuft of hair (of man) or feathers (on head) of birds.

əló'bò, n. fresh sprouting (of any plant); ásέ-, kaká-, kàíkó əló'bò fresh/new sprouting grass, maize, beans.

ólófε, n. orig. one-tree-bridge; ladder; èri àfa 'bánï ə'bε ií drìá atsí-zŏ it is a thing they place/ throw over a river to walk on.

əlòkòlò = kòlòkòlò, av. loosely, not very firm or solid; mí a'dï ə—, má emú ayu beenì tie it loosely, I shall untie it afterwards; é sò ə—! fix it lightly! əmbε kòlòkòlò he tied loosely.

əlòlòá, n. see under əlŏ.

ólóòlóò, əlóŋgəlóŋgə, n. lapwing, plover, peewit; èri drì-bbí bε he has a tuft of feathers on the head; ó—! 'bá or Bàrìá dzó ŋgòá yà? peewit! where is the hut of man, of the Aluur? (people ask jokingly, and the bird turns its tuft-feathers in the direction asked for).

əlóŋgbóró, n. a tree (*Strichnos innocua*) producing a ball-like fruit (hard shell, pulp dries and is extracted); ə— mà éfí 'bá əmvε tsíkíndà, ézó-andzi èi aví ànï its fruit-shells are called 'tsikinda' (kind of castanets); girls play with them (two joined with a string).

əlòŋgbórókpò, n. cranium; fà-lákó ómìnï əvö-zŏ 'alénïá-rï the bony covering of the brain; ó— ólò'bí pìε àlö the cranium (inside) and the depression on the head are one (place).

əlŏŋgö, n. (1) àtsí ə— glowing fire; (2) (ósŏ) ə— kind of beans.

əlóŋgò-rö, əlóŋgò-lóŋgò-rö, a. lumpy; whole, undivided; èi ósó a'dï ə— they cook beans whole;

'bánï awá kö-rï 'dï of things one does not usually divide or break.

òlóŋgŏlóŋgŏã`rö, a. round(ish); àfa párí-rï èri ò— something circular is round.

əlŏrókŏ = əbáláko, q.v. əlŏ-rókŏ-nï a'ú bï....

ólótòkó = ólókòtó, n. lizard (generic term).

əlù (cf. lù), vt. to cause to detach and fall down, to shake off; əlí əlù àndrò mòεmbè wóró vàá the wind has shaken off all the mangoes today.

olú, n. big basket with narrow opening tinï èri lúrû-rö: əmbî kə-zö for catching locusts.

ólù, n. castor-oil plant (*Ricinus communis*); 'bá ólù mà éfí a'dï ədò rö ('bá ŋaa ànï tíbí kö) people boil its grains for oil (they do not eat it as sauce); 'bá ànï a'íríbè tri they rub/cure itch with it; ólù 'bí èi ànï àŋâ lï with ricinus leaves they cover grain (for fermenting).

olúkò see olíkò, n. voice.

òlúkútúrù, n. ant-lion.

òlúuó, n. tree with large red flowers (*Erytrina abyssinica*, odiŋ, Ac.); òkpò nï ga-rï-á yə, èri vínï a'bï mbèlè it is not hard for working/cutting; it is also quickly bored.

òlúrù = káŋgá, n. big cow-horn tí ə'yó àmbórï, or also a long calabash 'horn'; 'anïrï ŋgbə (in-side emptied: used for blowing at dances).

òlúrúa, n. a sore toe; ò— odi rö nï the sore toe knocked against sth.

olúti = lúuó, n. a fish with a small round mouth.

əmá = mbíríkò, n. vulva.

əmbà, n. quarrel, dispute, con-

flict; ə— bε or ə—rö quarrelsome,
angry; hot-tempered, irascible;
ə̀mbá̌ 'bà to (start) quarrel, lose
temper; **èri 'bá ə̀mbà-ə̀mbăpirï**
or **ə̀— kə èri tsí** he is a squabbler,
quarrelsome fellow; brawler; **èri
ə̀— sö àma ásíá** he has annoyed
us/has upset our temper.
ómbà = **ò mbáïá, ò mbáïwá,** n.
hamster (of bush); **èì ə'á ó̀tó̀kó̀
é̀ríkò̀á** they live in crevices/holes
of termite-hills.
ə̀mbákà = **àndèmá, àndèsómá,
ə̀rò̀má, ə̀rò̀drí,** n. gift, present;
award (for a service); payment; **fè
mání ə̀— àzí sǐ** he gave me an
award/paid me for a service/work.
ò mbaŋgölö̌ = **álánda,** n. a
(dense, solid) lump of pounded
termites, cooked thus; **'bá ó̀ɳa
sìsì; 'bá kà sì 'bə, èì dǐ ə'bé-
ə'bé('barà̀rö...); èì dǐ 'bǎ a'dǐ-
a'dǐ àtsí-á** they pound termites;
then they make it into flat (or
other) cakes and put it on fire for
cooking; **ó̀ɳa ə̀mbázà-rǐ** or
ə̀mbápi-ə̀mbá-rǐ hard cake.
ə̀mbε (cf. **mbε**), vt. to eat up
(much); to scrape off with bent
finger, or ... ; **èri émvó 'alέa-rǐ
ə̀—** she is scraping off (the gruel
in) the pot; **ə̀— 'alénï tékètékè
'bə** he has already wiped off
cleanly the inside.
ə̀mbέ, vt. (1) to bind, string,
fasten together; **mǐ ə̀— pätí
rúá!** tie up the (split) wood!
έdzá (or **dzó̀ drì) ə̀— zó̀** to tie
together fuel (roof frame); **àfà
dzìlérǐ èì ə̀mbé-ə̀mbé** things to
be taken along are fastened; (2)
to force one (morally) to give in;
to defeat (in dispute, 'case'); **mǐ
ə̀— àma (= é ndè àma) 'bə** you
defeated us; (3) **ti-nǐ ə̀mbέ rö
ə̀mbέ** his tongue/speech is con-

fused/stuttering (unable to pronounce properly).
ə̀mbè-zà-rö, a./av. (1) stuttering
(ly), broken; **mǐ ε'yô 'yə ə̀—** you
speak badly/with difficulty; (2)
invalid; **'bá àvò̀-rǐ vàálé sǐ
atsípi kö-rǐ èri 'bá ə̀mbèzàrǐ**
a sick man on the ground who
cannot walk is an invalid.
ə̀mbε, ə̀mbεlé, ə̀mbεlékò̀, n.
neck and fig.; **drí-ə̀—** wrist (lit.
neck of hand); **ə̀mbε-kúkú** nape;
ə̀mbεti, n. (1) (lower neck with)
shoulder; **dzi pätí ə̀mbε-ti-á** he
carried the wood on his shoulders;
(2) lower end of slope or hill; **óní
mà ə̀mbεti èri dà̌älì/èlè; èri
ásê-rö** the neck of the mountain
(hill) is low down; it is covered
with grass; **ó̀tó̀ mà ə̀mbεti-á** at
the foot of a termite-hill.
ə̀mbé, n. sticks tied to a circle and
put on top of a hut: **ə̀— ndrǎ.**
ə̀mbésù, av. wetted, drenched
through; **kànì é 'dε ïa bò̀ŋgó́ be,
mǐ èfö̀ ə̀—** when you have fallen
into a river with cloth on, you
come out wet through; **ə̀sǒ ma
ïí sǐ ə̀—** he sprinkled water on me,
wetting me through.
ə̀mbí, n. migratory locust; **ə̀— èri
'dô ɳa** the locusts eat up eleusine
(and other); **ə̀— gbé-bε-rǐ** locusts
with eggs in; **'ə̀mbí-zə-kö'** (lit.
the locusts cannot fly across it;
universal name for:) Lake Albert.
ə̀mbílí, n. **ə̀— (=àsǒ) 'bǎ** to betray; **Yuda 'bà ə̀— Yesu mà
rúá** Judas has betrayed Jesus.
ə̀mbíríkə̀mbi = **èì mbi rö mbì-
mbi,** vr. they had sexual intercourse; coitus..
ò mbörò̀ drέká, n. an inedible
kind of red mushroom.
ə̀mŋgbù, n. joint; **éká mà**

əmŋgbù (= lúmŋgbù) the knot-joints of maize (&c.) stalks.
òmŋgbùrùkù = òmvòròkò, òŋ-gòròkù, n. an insect boring pota-toes, &c.
əmèlè = əmìnàkà, ònìakà, n. entwining a competitor's legs with one's own to overthrow him; èri ə— sö águi mà páa he entwines his friend's leg (play or fight).
əmì, vt. (1) to compress; kànì ga tré, mï əmì-əmì when it (say basket) is over-full, you press it down; əmì èi tré tsúkùtsúkù they pressed/squeezed (vr.) closely together (leaving no room for more); (2) (= vù) to massage, knead, rub (body, &c.); ma əmì mvá mà pá I massaged the leg of the child; (3) to calm, appease; soothe, soften; èri 'bá mà ásí əmì he is pacifying a person.
əmì, n. brain; əmì əvòpi dri-á-rì the brain which is in the head.
əmí, n. Cyperus papyrus; papyrus ropes (much in use); əmí dzó dri əmbé (= tïï)-zò papyrus ropes for tying up the frame of a roof.
Òmí, n. apparently the name of some(where?) distant tribe in Belgian Congo; Òmí-ŋgúrú some fabulous people in B.C. whose members can change into wild beasts and as such eat man (cf. Alur Ɖùbàar?).
òmí-àrïïa, n. weaver bird (?).
əmɔkó = əmùkó, mòkàrà, n. ill will, resentment; hatred; 'bá mà ə— 'bà (= tö, lï) ásí-á to bear/have a spite/grudge against a p.; lï ma ə— ásíá he holds a grudge against me in his heart; èri ma əmɔkɔ tö/lï (mâ tà lï) ásía he is spiteful against me; àma ə— mï bɛ tsí you bear a grudge against me.

ómónókɔ = kɔbɔlɔ, q.v.
əmərɔfí = əmàéfí, n. kind of gramminia with strong stems (used for brooms).
òmú, n. guest, visitor; òmú, 'bá etsápi ɔ'dïïrï a visitor, a man who arrived recently; mï ŋga èri dzï ko gïrï-á you will accom-pany/see him on to the way; 'òmú-nè-rö-tï', av. late evening twilight (lit. a visitor cannot be recognized); kànì 'dà à'dï 'ï yà áánï?! who can that indistinctly visible visitor be?
omú = mòndrà, q.v.
òmù-ŋa, vn. to take part at a wedding banquet (as guest); èri əmvɛ 'bá òmùŋa-zò 'í vò he invited sby. to a wedding banquet; àma emú mï òmû-rö òmù-ŋa we came as your wedding-guests (to the banquet); ŋaaká èri-nï 'i 'dàrï òmùŋa-zò that meal she is preparing is for wedding-guests.
òmútrútrúâ-rö, òtrúkù-rö, a. crippled, truncated, mutilated (as by leper) ɔfó ŋaa mï drí (or pá) nï òmútrútrúâ-rö.
əmvà (cf. mvà), vt. to clean (ground by scraping off its unfit surface); mï ámvú əmvà 'bùá sï you clear the field superficially (not moving the soil).
əmvɛ, vt. (1) to call; é mu andzi əmvɛ! go and call the children! (2) to pronounce; mï ə— èri 'yékè you pronounced it pro-perly.
əmvè-zà, əmvè-əmvè (cf. əm-bèzà-rö), vn. invalid(-ed); 'bá àzó-nï bï drìə 'ə'ápi gèrï vàá sï one who has been sick for a time and remains on the ground (cannot rise).
ɔmvi¹ = əgó, vt. (1) to return, give

back (to); mǎ mu àfa 'dàrï ə—
rá I shall return that thing; ɔ̀kó
kà ayï (= andzo'ï) rá, èi tí ə—
rá if a woman divorces, they
return the cattle; (2) ɛ'yɔ́ ə—, or
à'ïtáa ə— to answer, reply; mǐ
ə— mánǐ à'ïtánǐ kö à'do sǐ yà?
why do you not answer my
question? èri 'bá àzǐ mà ɛ'yɔ́ ə—
he answers sby.'s question; (3) to
re-swallow the chewed cud; tǐ èri
èríbí ə— the cow swallows the
ruminated grass.

ɔmvi², vt. to inherit a relative's
wife; èri 'ï ádríi mà ɔ̀kó ə— he
inherits his (dead) brother's wife;
ɔ̀kó ɔmvizàrǐ an inherited wife.

ɔmvi³ = ɔ̀ndrè, ɔri, vt./vn. (1) to
calm down, appease, mitigate; é
mu águ 'dà mà ásí ɔmvǐ! go
and calm that p.! ásí-nǐ ə— 'bə
he is now quiet; lè ɛ'yɔ̂ 'yə ma
bɛ ɔ̀kpɔ́ sǐ; 'ǐ tinǐ ŋga ə— rá he
wanted to speak very strongly to
me; he will calm down; (2) to
soothe, neutralize (say poison
ɔ̀yɔ̀), mitigate; kànì órí ga mǐ nǐ,
'bá ŋga árɔ́ edzǐ 'bǎ milé-nǐá
èri-nǐ ə— zɔ̃ when a snake has
bitten you, they bring a medicine
to apply and neutralize it; (3) to
restrain oneself; ə— 'ïmà ásí
mɔ̃kɛ́ he restrained himself properly; nì 'ïmà ásí ə— kö he has
no command/control over himself, or he is without self-control.

ɔ̀mvó more commonly ɛ̀mvóa,
q.v., n. orphan.

ɔmvó¹ = ɔmbó = ɛmvó, vn. to
jump.

ɔmvó², vt. to collect, gather with
both hands (forming cup) or with
a basket; èi áɳú ɔmvɔ̌ drí (or
èvɔ̌) sǐ they gather up simsim
(from the ground after drying)
with hands (basket); mǐ ə— ɔ́ɳa

dría, mà ko rö kö! collect all the
termites, that none remains back!

ɔmvó³, vt. èdzɔ̀-rö ə— to bear
twins; ɳdrí ə— èdzɔ̀-rö the goat
bore twin kids.

ɔmvó⁴, vt. to barter, exchange (exclusively animal against animal or
corn; cf. ɔfö, ɔ̀trɔ̀); mǐ emú àɳá
ə— mádrí ɳdrí sǐ (mí èfè mání
àɳá, ma mǐ nǐ ɳdrí fɛ̌)! do exchange corn to me for a goat!

ɔ̀mvɔ̀rɔ̀kɔ̀, n. insect infesting
potatoes; èi ɔ̀— rɛ̀ɛ́ màákɔ̀ rùá
rá ká, 'bâ su ndɔ̀ they first
scrape the rot off the potatoes
then wash them.

ɔ̀mvu, n. the nose; ɔ̀— (mà) tílɛ́,
n. nostrils; ɔ̀mvu-sí nasal mucus;
ɔ̀— tsə to sneeze; àrǐ àzù (or
asɛ́) ma ɔ̀— tsǐ I am bleeding
from the nose; é sǐ ɔ̀mvu-sí(vàá,
ɛbíkə sǐ)! blow the nose (to the
ground or with leaves)!

ɔ̀mvú = ɔ̀fúdrì, q.v.

ɔná, vt. to shun, avoid; ɔ́ná (or
ɔná), n. shunning, avoiding,
warding off (missiles); èri ɔ́ná bɛ
or ɔ́nâ na tö he is very able in
avoiding (blow, spear, arrow...);

ɔná'bá, n. hermit, person with
solitary habits 'bá 'bá ɔnápi-rǐ,
èri 'bá ɔná-ɔná: lè 'ə̂'á a'dúlɛ
he escapes people and wants to
be alone.

ɔ̀nákɔ̀ná, kɔ́nakɔ́na, tékètékè,
av. cleanly (with nothing left over);
ma ɔmbɛ ètsǐa 'alɛ́ ɔ̀— I licked
the inside of the calabash bowl
cleanly.

ɔ̀ndá (or -ɛ́, -ɔ́), n. a'ú ɔ̀— cock's
comb or wattle; a'ú átá èri ɔ̀—
bɛ.

ɔ̀ndǎtá, n. the common big red-
headed lizard.

ɔ̀ndɛ, n. nerve; 'drì-ndzá ɳaa
ɔ̀ndɛ' (saying) 'bashfulness eats

one's nerve (? strength, energy for self-defence)'.

ɔndé, vt. to slit open and spread; **èi è'bí** (or **a'ú**) **'alέ ɔnd̂** (= **àsî**) **èri-nî 'wï-ző** they slit and spread a fish (fowl) for drying (**àlârö** well).

ɔndɛrɛ, ǹdɛrɛ̀, n. giraffe.

ɔndɛrɛkɔ́, n. small-pox.

ɔndí, ɔndíríkɔ̀, n. dirt, filth (of any kind); **ɔ̀— fu èri rá** or **ɔ̀— bî** (or **ɛŋgá**) **èrimà rúá tɔ̀** he is very dirty; **ɔ̀— bɛ/nï, ɔndî-rö,** a. dirty; **bɔ̀ŋgɔ́ mídrí ɔndî-rö** your cloth is dirty; **bbílé-ɔndí** ear-wax; **ɛ́mvó-ɔ̀—** soot or pot-black (cf. **ëni**).

ɔndì, vt. to pinch, nip off; **èri ɛ́ŋá** (or **ɛbíkɔ**) **ɔndî** he pinches off small portions of polenta (leaves/ paper); challenge among unequal youths; 'ma mî ti ɔndî tsú-rú'dɔ̀!' or 'àma àmà ti ɔndî mï bɛ rá!' I'll soon have a lip-pinching with you! (kind of fight among Logbara).

ɔndó, n. durra; **ɔndó-páráká** stem/stalk of durra.

ɔndɔ, n. barrenness, sterility; (for either sex); **ɔndɔ̀-rö,** a. barren, sterile; **'bá (tí, a'ú,** &c.) **ɔndɔ** or **ɔndɔ̀rö** barren/impotent human, cow ...; i.e. **típi kö-rî** that which does not reproduce/bear.

ɔndɔ́, better **ándɔ́,** q.v.

ɔndóɔ́, ɔndóá (also **'bá ɔ̀—**), n. blacksmith; **'bá ayà** or **àdzû dípirî èri ɔ́—** one forging iron or spears is a blacksmith; **ɔndóoá ɔka-drí àdzû dípirî 'dî/**or **pàrí 'bánï ayà di rö rî** the forge (smithy or blacksmith's shop) where they make spears/work iron; craftsman.

ɔndòa = **àkírì(-rî, -rö),** a. clever; **ɔ̀— bɛ** = **milέ mbàrö, 'bá àkírì**

bɛrî an able, clever fellow; **mvá 'dî kilásía ɔndòarö** this boy is clever at school; **ɔndòá** (= **ɔndòà**) = **lɔ̀kìrì,** n. artfulness; slyness, deception; mystification.

ɔndɔ̀kɔ́ndɔ̀ = **ɛ́ndɔ̀kíndɔ̀, àm-bɛ́rɛká,** n. a savoury (from fried and ground beans).

ɔndó-párákáa = **bbúrù,** n. a kind of hedge-sparrow (**àkúfì-àrîïa lɛ́** like).

ɔndoróá, n. hedgehog; **rúánï wɔ́rɔ́ otsî-rö** it is covered with 'thorns'.

ɔndràkɔ̀ndrà = **òkàlàkòkàlà,** a. variegated.

ɔndré, n. evening; **ɔ̀— sî** towards/ in the evening; **ɔndré-rî** = **ɔ̀— bɛ,** a. of the evening; **ètú ɔndré-rî** the evening sun; **ma emú ádzê ɔ̀— sî** I came yesterday evening.

ɔ́ndrí (= **óí, ádá)-zà,** vn./a. to be (-come) lean, emaciated, thin.

ɔndrî, vt. (1) to (rub with) oil (pain), mitigate, soften; **á dzi mà drí ɔndrî ɔdo sî** I took my hand to oil it; (2) **'bá mà ásí** or **ti ɔ̀—** to calm, quiet; to comfort; **ɛ'yɔ́ èri-nï ɔ̀lòlérî ɔ̀— má ásí rá** his words (he said) have consoled/ comforted me.

ɔndrɔ̀, vt. to adjust, arrange; **ma ɔ̀— dríbbí tsànóa sî, èri-nï ndrî-ző** I dressed my hair with a comb, that it may look nice.

ɔndrɔkɔ́ sɔ̀ or **sɛ,** vn. to snore; **má ɔ̀— sɔ̀ o'dúa** I am snoring in my sleep.

ɔndròkòndrò, -rö, a. of not un-pleasant taste (not sour or bitter), fairly good.

ɔndrokɔndro, n. small black ants; **èri 'bá zàzà** (= **dɔ̌dò**) it stings one; (similar but smaller **ɛ́rîkîa** or **à'yí-ɔndzɔrɔkɔ**).

əndŭ or əndú more commonly andú, vt. to wrong a p., say, on distributing things; to disregard, make fun of.

óndú = óbá, q.v. n. knotty excrescence (on head/face, &c.).

óndzáííá = ríaría, dríadría, oŋgúaaró, kámálárà, n. red or Cayenne pepper; dra tö is very sharp (? sour).

əndzèló, n. a tree.

əndzí, a. bad (in any sense); ə— kàɲàarö very badly); əndzìvŏ, q.v.

ondzí, vn. to go/get dry; tí or lέsú o— 'bə the cow or milk went dry.

óndzí¹, vn. to be glad, pleased; to be delighted, overjoyed; óndzí-zŏ 'bá azíni bε = àikò zö/= 'bà zŏ 'bá azíni bε to rejoice with another/or others; àrí'bó-ni óndzí àma drà sĭ an enemy rejoices at our death.

óndzí², n. a snake.

əndzìvŏ (cf. ədzí), n. malice, mischievousness, wickedness, spitefulness; 'bá èi mu àtsía ə— sitáni drí sĭ people go to hell through the spite of the devil; əndzìvŏ-rö, a. evil, wicked, malicious; ugly, unsightly, deformed.

əndzö, vt. to carry, remove (with care); mĭ ə— gbándà àmvé, 'wï-zŏ! take the manioc outside to dry.

əndzə = èndzə, vt. to entangle, confuse by lying (cf. èndzə); ə— ε'yó drí (= ε'yə ndzε èndzərö) to confuse a matter ('case') with lies.

əndzó = andzá, T., vt. to press out; mash;...màakò ká avö 'bə, èi ə—ə— after potatoes have been stewed they mash them; èi έɲá-

èsá əndzə lέsú sĭ they mash polenta (failing savoury) with milk; ə— rö, vn. to well or spring forth (under some pressure); to come forth.

əndzó = εndzó, n. big shrub; or also tree.

óndzó, n. dirtying (?! oneself); 'dε ó— bε, drà-ni èri ndĕ rá-rĭ sĭ one being overcome by sickness (loses control of himself) soils (dirties, begrimes) himself.

əndzə, vt. to offend, affront; to hurt, injure; to despise (= εdε); óyéni é 'di ndrâ ma ádríi ni, mï ma (ási) ə— 'dĭ you have killed my brother (unprovoked), you have thus gravely injured me; mvá 'dĭ εri átíi mà ti kö, èri àni átíi-ni ə—ə— (εdε) this boy has not obeyed his father, he therefore offends his father.

əndzófà = əverεkó, n. crust (in pot); èri έɲá (mà) ə— əfà kàbèlé sĭ she scratches the crust of polenta (in pot) off with an oyster-shell.

əndzókəndzó-rö = èníkini, a. smooth, polished, glazed, glossy.

əndzŏrŏgbέ, n. a tree (similar to əndzó); bows, shafts, handles (ósù-, àdzú 'yófέ-rö, àbέ) are made from its shoots or branches.

əndzərəkə, (1) av. (= tré, kákàrö) many; àfa 'bá ε'dá gbàzŏrĭ èi ə— things with which they make fotoes are numerous; (2) a. filthy, dirty, disorderly, untidy; έɲá əndzərəkə-rö, ndrĕ kö polenta is untidily served; àfa ndrĭpi mĭ milía kö rĭ sth. not pleasing to one's eyes; 'i έɲá əndzərəkə-rö she prepared polenta disgustingly.

əndzŭ, n. èndzŭ, q.v.

òndzù, zèlé (finer ndú, ètï̈), n. arse, anus, posterior.

ondzú, vt. to waste, emaciate, exhaust; àzó ə— èri 'bə, rúánï̈ tsúrú'də óízàrö a disease has wasted him, his body is now lean; mvá 'də ə— 'bə this child has lost flesh; əndzúzà = óizà, a. lean, worn-out (cf. ndzu).

òndzùó, n. tree (with very hard wood; not eaten by termites) (*Bridelia sclereneuroides*).

óní = érà, n. stone; rock; mountain—hill; óníï̈, n. gravel; 'ónínï̈' àn̦ú sì-zö-rï̈ hand-stone for grinding simsim; óní-ándríi grind-stone (for grinding); é 'bɛ ə̀tsé óní sì! throw a stone at the dog!

əní = ɛní, ɛnïlȁ, ekilȁ, vt. to entangle; n̄drí ɛnï̈ rö báká sì the goat got entangled in the rope; ənï̈ rö to be twisted; yiéré 'dï̈ mà ə'yó ənï̈ 'ï̈ the horns of the water-buck are twisted; ásɛ́ ənï̈-ənï̈ to knot up grass (-tops).

ə̀nì (cf. nì), vt. to learn, acquire, master (an art, &c.); to endeavour/strive to acquire or practise; ma ġárì ə̀nìə̀nì I am endeavouring to use a bicycle; èri ògárábá ti ə̀nì he is striving to learn the language of the foreigners; mvá èri atsítâ̈ ə̀nì the baby is trying to walk.

ə̀ní = mə̀ní, n. (1) the developing blooming stock of durra (ə̀ndó) (eaten as delicacy); ə̀ndó-nï̈ fö ə̀nì-rö: ə̀ndó-nï̈ 'ï̈ ədzá nì; èi èrì n̦ȁn̦a the durra develops its blooming stock: the durra changes; they eat it; (2) (= àyàkï̈lï̈kï̈lï̈) skin-tassels below neck of goats; èri n̄drí mà əmbɛlékóá.

ònì(k)ònì, a. dirty-grey, dark; àn̦gö̀ ònì(k)ònì-rö it is pretty

dark (morning or evening): it is dawning, dusky; or night sets (= is closing) in.

əni-zà = dïrïkpàa, q.v.

ə̀nə̀ (?), n. kind of tiger finch.

ənó, vn. to murmur, grumble; èri ənȯ à'do sì yà? what is he grumbling for? à'do-nï̈ ənȯ nì? bȯrà-nï̈ ənȯ nì what purrs? the cat purrs.

ȯnȯkȯnȯ = àdràkàdrà, n. praying mantis (*Mantis religiosa*).

onȯkònò = aká-aká, mènè-mènè, a. soft, mellow; supple, pliant; bə̀n̦gȯ mà milɛ́ï̈ o— the cloth's surface is soft (fluffy).

ə̀n̦gà = kùanà, n. the trap-oracle, kind of (ritual) trap; ə̀— ə̀pé ə̀'bà-zö̀ àlíbə bɛ trap to catch guinea-fowls and partridges.

ən̦ga (cf. n̦ga), vn. ə— àn̦gö̀ dza to fly turning in circles; àrï̈á èri ə— àn̦gö̀ dza órú 'dálé the bird hovers round up there (in the sky).

ə̀n̦gá(ráká) = T. n̦gárákádzóá, n. a striped mouse; a. striped, variegated.

ȯn̦gálù-ru = òlȯn̦gȯlȯ, n̦gán̦gá-lù, a. whole, entire, undivided, in one piece (or the like); pálpál 'dï̈rï̈ èri ȯ—, i.e. 'bá àsï̈ n̦gà 'anï̈ kö this pawpaw is whole, they have not yet divided it.

ə̀n̦gbȯ or n̈gbȯ, n. the (mostly bare) two sides of upper front of man.

ə̀n̦gbə̀ = àn̦gbà, əka, vn. also ə̀n̦gbə̀kə̀n̦gbə̀ = T. ə̀n̦gbàkə̀-n̦gbà to be yellowish brown; pátí 'dà mà bbí ə̀—ə̀— the leaves of that shrub are yellowish brown.

ò̀n̦gbù, a. to (tie a) knot; alï̈ áisé ȯn̦gbùrö n̄drí 'ï̈-zö̀ he tied the grass into a knot to fasten goats to it.

ə̀n̦gbùlûmbù, n. knot/joint of

reed-stalks, &c., ə̀zɵ̆ —, ə̀drá
mà ə̀— a knot in reed-stalk, in
bamboo.

ɔŋgɔ́, vn. to sing; n. song; èì
ə—ə— they are singing; àfa
ɔŋgɔ́-ɔŋgɔ́pì-rì̀ a thing for singing (as harmonium, gramo-
phone …); ə— 'dà su tɵ̀ that song
(maybe dance) is very pleasant;
ɔŋgɔ̀ tɵ̆ to dance; tɵ̆ ə— ádzê
they danced yesterday; mu ɔŋgɔ̀-
tör̀á he went to a dance.

óŋgóló or ɵ̆ŋgɵ̆lɵ̆, ŋgɵ̆lɵ̆ or
ŋgɵ̆lɵ̆-ŋgɵ̆lɵ̀, óŋgólómɵ̀, -rì̀,
-rö, a. being an entire, unbroken
mass, a roundish lump or clod, all
together or united; ɵ́sɵ̆ mà ó—
èì gbï lòpérɛ̀ sɪ̀ they stir the
bean-mass (in a pot) with a
stirring-stick; mòémbɛ̀ 'dà èì
óŋgólómörö (i.e. pɜ̀rí àlɵ̆á) the
mangoes there are all together (on
a heap); (cf. óŋgálùru).

ə̀ŋgórɔ́, n. a Nile fish.

óŋgórɔ́-bbí, n. eyebrow.

ə̀ŋgɔ̀rɔ̀kɔ̀ = ə̀mŋgbùrùkù, n. insect boring into and eating
potatoes; ə̀— fï mààkò 'aléa;
ɛ̀ri mààkò mà 'a ə̀lò wórɔ́ it
enters potatoes and bores them
through and through.

ɔŋgú[1]= 'wï, vn. to dry; bə̀ŋgó —,
àŋgɵ̀ o— 'bə the cloth, the ground
is dry; mvá ɔŋgú 'bə/ = mvá
milé tɪ̀ 'bə the (newly born) babe
has become strong.

ɔŋgú[2], n. haste, speed; o— sɪ̀
hastily, in a hurry, quickly; 'dɵ̀
(= kànì) mï o— tɵ̆, à ndzó ŋgà
mï bɛ! if you are swift, let us
have a run! mbɛ 'ï o— drìá he
took to flight/to his heels.

ɔŋgúarɔ́, a. sharp, hot (cf. ɵ́nd-
zálïa pepper).

ɔŋgúlírí, n. a harmless mid-size
snake; ɛ̀ri ə̀dzá rö(! ?) ə̀fódzə̀rö

it turns (in time) into an 'ɔfodzɔ'
(it is believed).

óŋgulú = áŋgulú, n. a large larva
(found in waste heaps) a'ú àn̯á
food for fowls.

ò̀ŋgúlùá = ə̀ndɛrɛkɔ́, n. small-
pox.

ò̀ŋgúrukútì, see ŋgúrukútì, n.
lower part of back.

ɵ́n̯a, n. the flying/swarming termite; ɵ́n̯a ándríi termite queen;
ɵ́n̯a-zòŋgórókò passage—labyrinth of termite-hill (cf. ɵ́kpɔ́dzɔ́);
ɔn̯a tɵ̀ (= 'dɵ̀) to fill mouth with
'ɔn̯a' (they form an important part
of native diet).

ə̀n̯ɛrɛ (= ɵ́n̯í-àzɪ́), n. brother's
wife; husband's brother.

ə̀n̯ì = ndrì̀táã, n. (1) kindness,
goodness, excellency; generosity;
'bá fï 'bùá Àdró mà ə̀n̯ì sɪ̀ man
goes to heaven through God's
generosity/kindness; (2) beauty;
handsome features, good looks
ə̀n̯ì'bí; ə̀n̯ì'bí nï ndrì̀ tɵ̀ his/her
beauty is very striking; bélé ɛza
ma ə̀n̯ì'bí a sore has spoiled my
features; ə̀n̯ì-àfa, n. trinkets,
knick-knacks; finery, jewels; ə̀n̯ì-
nï, -rö, be (= ndrì̀zà), a. kind,
good, generous; beautiful, handsome; well-set, in order, clean;
èì àfa ɛdɛ́ ə̀n̯ì be they prepare/
adjust things neatly.

ɵ́n̯ía, pl. ə̀n̯ì, n. (male) lover, sweet-
heart; ágú emúpì ézóa-rì̀, 'bá
ɔmvɛ ɵ́n̯ía a man visiting a girl
is called (her) lover; záa 'dà mà
ɔ— 'dì this is the lover of that
girl; (cf. ézɔ́: kàrílɛ̀ 'dì mà ɛzɔ́
'dì this is the lover (beloved) of
this youth).

ɵ́n̯í-àzɪ́ = ə̀n̯ɛrɛ, n. sister-in-law,
brother-in-law.

ə̀n̯ɔ̀, vt. to carry exceeding large
portions to the mouth (contrary to

good behaviour); èrì έɲá ɔ̀ɲɔ̀,
i.e. èrì έɲá tĭ àmbó, èrì dŏ
tíbí-á, èrì kï 'wĕĕrí i.e. he takes
up a big piece of polenta, dips it in
savoury, and swallows it gulpingly.

óɲófí fingernail; claw; ma óɲófí
li I am cutting my finger-nails;
óɲófí-sá zì rö hangnail (?).

ɔɲókɔ = ɲaaká, n. food.

óɲŏkŏɲŏ or έɲŏkŏɲŏ, n. a very
quickly growing field weed.

ɔ̀ɲɔ̀kɔ̀ɲɔ̀ more common àɲàkàɲà,
q.v.

óɲú, n. a mythical magic condition
(belief) which affects half the
Logbara tribe: the Lógbàrà
(with), the Mà'dí (without it) 'bá
óɲú bɛ-rĭ èì ɔmvɛ Lógbàrà,
'bá óɲú kókɔ 'dĭĭ èì ɔmvɛ
Mà'dí people with this 'oɲu' are
called Logbara, people without
the 'oɲu' are called Mà'di(Tɛrɛgo).

oɲú[1], n. (1) (cf. the preceeding) kind
of eruption on body; èrì 'bá drì
ɔ̀lɔ̌ it comes out as pimples on
head; (2) abbr. for oɲú-k-oɲú
fly; àma oɲúkoɲú rú etsû we
shorten the name 'oɲukoɲu' to
oɲú.

oɲú[2] (-oɲú) = aka-aka, vn. to
wither, fade, droop; 'dŏ mà bbí
oɲú, ɔzɔ́ɔ́ àkɔ̀ sĭ the leaves of
eleusine are drooping, lacking
rain; màákò té gắ 'bɔ-rĭ'ï, èrì
dĭ oɲú-oɲú: rùánï èrì mu
oɲú-zà-rö, èrì dĭ adri alu-zà-
rö the (sweet) potatoes dug before, are now limp/flaccid and are
very pleasant.

oɲúkoɲú, n. common fly; o—
gbàŋgìlò large green bottle-fly.

óɲúrúbí = óyúrúbí = àɲá-drí-
lékó, n. chaff.

ɔ́ɔ́ from ɔwĭ (1) vn. to cry (weep or
utter—of any animal—natural

voice); cry aloud (with noise); to
sing (of birds); tsɔ èrì tsɔ́tsɔ,
èrì ɔ́ɔ́ ànï he was beaten therefore
he cries; mĭ ɔ́ɔ́ kö! do not
weep!/or do not make a noise!
tí ɔwĭ 'dέlέ the cow lows there;
kɔ̀líkɔ̀lí ɔ́ɔ́ 'dà the wagtail sings
there (like a canary!); (2) vt. to
lament, deplore, to weep (the loss
of . . .); ɔ́ɔ́ 'ĭ díí (= dèdè) she
weeps over her grandmother (who
died).

oɔ̀dɔ-oɔ̀dɔ (cf. wɔ̀dɔ-wɔ̀dɔ =
tsà), av. a. to be watery, stale, insipid, unsavoury; 'bá ɔro té e'dí
mŏké, èrì tsúrú'dɔ̀ oɔ̀dɔ-
oɔ̀dɔ or tsắtsằ (ɔdzá ĭĭ rö)
they prepared the gruel properly
a moment ago, it is now insipid
(it has become watery).

ɔ̀'ólògó = lôgɔ, T. = 'úà'úà, q.v.

ɔpá = ɔpákó, n. a rounded piece
of quartz or rock-flint; ɔ̀pá óní
pa-zŏ, kànì óní tsï kö a rock-
flint for knocking the (grinding-)
stone, when it is not sharp.

ɔpa (cf. pa), vt. (1) to cut away,
carve; 'bánï kìtìpólò ɔpa-rĭ-lé
as when they cut/make a chair;
(2) to talk a thing over and over ad
nauseam; èrì ɛ'yó ɔpa (= ɔ'dú)
'bá mà tlá tɔ̀ he retails a matter
to people indefinitely; chatter and
meddle; èrì ma ɛ'yó ɔpa he is
restating my case.

ɔparafí = ɔ̀pɔrɔfí, óníf́í, n. gravel.

ópásí, n. strongly defined back of
head/occiput; mï ɔ́— mbílĭ-rö
('bá 'dazŏ)! the back part of your
head is tapering (insult; Ndzéndzé
drírĭ of the Maŋgbetu).

ɔpé, n. guinea-fowl; ɔ̀pé mà drì
tòa (= sïzà)-rö the guinea-fowl's
head is bald.

ɔ̀péré̀(w)á = lòpére, n. (1) stirring-
stick (of kitchen); lésú kozàrï mà

'alɛ̂ 'bi-zǒ (stick) to whip co-agulated milk; (2) (bird) swift.

əpè, vt./vn. (1) to pick out, remove; ma ò'bu əpɛ̀ I am picking out a jigger; (2) to surpass; mvá 'dàrï oŋgú (or əŋgɔ́) əpè 'dïnï (aga 'bá àzïnï dría rá)! how that boy excels (surpassing all the others) in speed (singing)!

òpì¹, n. a tree.

òpì² (-drì) = búdrì, n. shoulder; yúkú òpì (shoulder =) wing of kite.

òpì³, vt. (1) to shut; mḯ òpì dzótilɛ́ (or dìrísà) tsɪ́! shut the door (window)! (2) ti òpì to cover; (= opí), mḯ òpì (= okú) tinï (or tsúpà mà ti) tsɪ́! cover it (cork the bottle)! ɛ́mvó mà ti oru; mḯ ti-nɪ̌á àfa àzɪ́ 'bà! the opening of a pot is upwards; cover it (lit. put sth. on its open-ing)! àfa-ti-opí-zǒ or 'bǎ-zǒ, n. cover (lit. sth. to cover); dri-nï òpì-zǒ to cover it over; (3) mḯ òpì (= okú) ɛ́mvó ti vàá! turn the pot upside down (overturn, in-vert, topsy-turvy)!

opi, vt. to cut up, dismember; ɛ̀ri tí mà ùú opi he cuts off the cow's foreleg; ɛ̀i tí opi-opi, ɛ̀i awa 'bá pɪ́rɪ́-nɪ́ (!) they dismember a cow and distribute to everybody.

əpí, vt. (1) to shell, husk; mḯ əpí fúnò! do husk the ground-nuts! ɛ̀ri 'bíkə-nï 'du rá, ɛ̀ri ɛ́fɪ́-nï ko 'ï he removes the husk and leaves the grains alone; (2) to wind up, set right a watch sáà əpí-zǒ.

ópí, n. head-chief, king; ópí mvá a king's child, prince.

òpìlɛ́'bí, n. wing (of a bird); àfa àrɪ̌áǎ-nɪ́ ŋga-zǒ-rɪ̀ a thing by which birds fly.

ópílɛ́ = ópíléti, n. waist, hip region; bòŋgɔ́ 'dà sì káanï mà ópílɛ́-nï that cloth may (possibly) fit my waist; ɛ̀rɔ́ mà ópíléti the lower part of a granary (bulging lightly in circle); dzɔ́ mà ó— earth-filling round the outside of a hut at the bottom; ópílɛ́-mvǒ, n. belt, girdle, waist-belt (enïrïkə-nï leathern); ɛ̀i báká pïï rá, ɛ̀i ŋga kílyò sö rùá-nï, ɛ̀i ànï ɛbíkə sǔ they twist a string, put in metal beads and (if women) put on leaves by it.

òpìrìkà = òpìrìfà, àtsɔ́fà, mò-sòá, n. stiff excrescence on elbow, knee, head, &c.

òpìrìkàlɛ́ = àràkàlɛ́ (q.v.), n. bi-furcation; branch; pätí mà ò— fork, bifurcation on a tree; ò— ɛ̀ri awa rö òndzòròkò branches divide many times.

əpírïkəpírí, av. reluctantly, with resistance; 'bá mvá 'dàrï esɛ̂ sùkúlùá ə— a man drags that boy to school reluctantly.

ərà, vn. to think, reflect (upon drì, rùá); òkó òrà 'ɪ̌ mvá (mà) drià the woman thinks of her child; 'bá pɪ́rɪ̂ ŋga òrà̌ ɛ̀ri sɪ̌ or rùá-nɪ́-á everybody thinks of him/her; òràtáǎ, n. thought; thinking.

óra, n. (1) water lily; (2) = óní, T., stone, rock.

òrá, T., n. granary.

Òráa, proper name of a hill.

Óra, proper name, river running through Oköörö and Ma'di-Ndri country.

ərɛ́¹, a. thin, fluid; (1) fresh (natur-ally thin); lésú wa òrɛ̂-rö the milk is fresh and liquid; (2) thin— watery (i.e. mba kö, akázà be-low its natural consistency), in-sipid, flat; e'dí (ɛ́ɲá, àdzírà) ɛ̀ri òrɛ̂-rö (sɛ wɛrɛwɛrɛ) the gruel (polenta, mashed beans) is in-sipid (of loose cohesion); òrɛ́-nï wɛrɛ i.e. èrì ndɛ́ (= áda-nï) èdû-rö (= tɔ̀tɔ̀ nï) slightly thin, properly (as a whole) it is dense.

òrɛ́², n. a tree; èì ɛdɛ́ ósûrö they make bows from it.

 òrɛ̀(1) vn. (= tì) to swell (of water), rise; ìí òrɛ̀- òrɛ̀ (= tìtì) the water is rising; (2) vt. to grate, scratch off; òrɛ̀ 'ïmà drí ɛ̈lï sì he scratched his hand with a knife.

ɔrɛ́á = ɛrɛ́á, n. (1) ankle; (2) name of a tribal group.

òrɛkɛ́, av. alertly, carefully (guarding); èrì àgáí-nï tɛ̌ òrɛkɛ́ he alertly/livelily watches it (continuously walking around it).

òrɛ́kòrɛ́ (cf. òrɛ́) = ɛ̈líkìlì, a. smooth, polished (water, &c., not running smoothly over it, but in separate drops).

órɛ́mo, n. large tree with long thorns.

órɛ́ɔ́, T. = òdzɔ́, n. kind of aloe (or sisal) plant (leaves with thorny rim).

ɔrɛrɛ̄a (= àdzíŋgùrú), n. the common small peppermint plant; èì ànï àdrá wǎ they remove blotches with it (magically caused and removed).

òrɛt(r)ɛ́ = òrɛ̀tɛ́kò, n. mud, swamp; èì mu òdɛ̀ ndzɛ ìí mà òrɛtrɛ́a they go to take rain worms out of the mud.

òrɛ́tɛ́tɛ́ = òrɛ́trɛ́trɛ́, n. *Hila arborea*, green (or other colour) frogs (living on trees or plants, some of them very small and graceful).

òrì, n. fear; vt. to fear; ma órí òrì I fear snakes; òrì bɛ = òrì-rö, a. timid, apprehensive; faint-hearted; nervous; òríó'bá, n. a coward.

òrí, n. louse; òrí èrì bòŋgó 'aléa tsí a louse is found in cloths.

ori = órí, n. snake; orí tsí, é ndzo rá! there is a snake, run off! orí-nï atsí ágáti sì, the snake 'moves' on its breast; orí kà 'bá ga 'bə, èrimà mílé-nï asé tsí after a snake has bitten a person, its sight remains clouded (as dumb); orí-mà-enïrïkə cast/skin of serpent; orí-óhulú, n. the short, thick sand viper; fable: if cut to pieces, head with slight neck-piece, in water, it will transform to àrïïátsɛtsɛ (= àrïïá-lòɔkɔ́): orí àmbó-àmbó 'dïï mà drì èrì ɔdzá rö àrïïatsɛtsɛ.

ərí= òvù, adrizɔ̌ tsú, vt. to calm down; appease; mitigate (pain); vn. to settle down, subside; mâ pá ərí 'bə my leg ('s pain) abated.

orí¹, vt. to impudently, brazenfacedly take away or occupy sby.'s property; seize, confiscate; ògárábá orí àma ámvú rá the white man has seized our fields (e.g. for aerodrome); ma orí àfa 'dì orí-orí I have appropriated this thing (for myself).

orí² (-zà), vn./a. to be (-come) rusty, rusty-brown; rùánï orí-orí it is rust-coloured (say, a thing burned); é 'bà ndrâ sìn-dánì 'dòì orí-zɔ̌ 'dónï à'dóá yà? where have you put this needle to become rusty like this?

òrï, n. seed; àɲá òrï seeds of corn; èìósɔ̌ òrï rï ámvú-á they are sowing (seeds of) beans in the field; òrï-èvɔ̌ small basket for seeds.

órí, n. ancestral spirit; ghost; má átíi mà órí ka ma nï nï the spirit of my father has bewitched me; órí-dzɔ́ or órí-àbbíllì-dzɔ́ shrine (grass, mud, stone-'hut') of ancestral spirit/ghost; ma á'bíi mà órí or àbbíllì ghost of my ancestor; èri órí àbbílli li he sacrifices (cuts animal) to the ancestor(s); èri má átíi mà órí ɛdɛ̃ (or əwǐ) má-ní a'ú or ṅdrí sǐ he sacrifices to my father's ghost a fowl or goat for me; 'bá si órí-dzó 'dàrï èrimà ɛ'yó sǐ they erected that shrine at his word; órí-ti, n. (1) mouth/word of the ghost; mbàzà órí əwí(=ɛdé)-pirǐ, èri ɛ'yó ndzɛ órí-ti-á the old man who offers to the spirits, he reports/interprets the ghost's wishes/answers; (2) in front of the shrine; ma ɛɳá əwǐ (or əbǐ) órí-ti-á I offer polenta (&c.) before the shrine; órí'ípi (man in charge of the spirits) èri órí-dzó mà tà mbápirǐ the spirits' priest is the guardian of the shrine.

ɔrí = yëla, ólá, n. offspring, descendant of (cf. yëla).

òríà = ərííó, n. a tree (*Terminalia velutina*, or *T. dawei*, *T. spekei*).

ɔrí'bá, n. member of a clan-descent group; ə— èmǐ-ní à'dokə nǐ yà?—Áivò. Áivò à'dokə nǐ yà?—Àrivò; of which tribal group are you?—of Aivo. Of which Aivo clan?—of the Arivo clan; ə— dzɛ èi tsénï-tsénǐ kö clan members do not intermarry.

órígəgə = ərigəgóá ≈ aɳárí-əríó, n. gecko; lè a'á àɳá 'aléa tǒ it likes very much to stay in the (granary) corn.

óríndí = éríndí, n. human soul.

óríndrɛ = éríndrɛ, òndí, n. perspiration.

ɔro = tɛ, T., vt. to prepare, get ready (food . . .); èi e'dí, éwá . . . ɔro they are preparing gruel, beer.

órò, n. world, universe; órò driá (-kúurù) or órò ùúdri kúurù, av. all over the world.

ərǒ, n. hump; móní-átá mà ərǒ

a bull's hump; ərǒ'bá or 'bá ərǒ bɛ or óɳgóróa'bá hunchbacked man (often projecting on back and breast); cf. mǐ əró-ɳgoroko'do⸴rö you are humpbacked!

órò, n. buttocks, back part (cf. ètí, ṅdú lower part of anything).

órə, n. condensed fluid on/in eyes; èri 'ǐ li 'bá milía it gathers in one's eyes.

ərə, vn. to get stiff, to ache from weariness; ma ərə 'bə I feel painfully weary; ərətáa = àɳə-táa, n. (local) weariness (from prolonged staying in one position); stiffness; feeling of being thoroughly done up.

ərəbbí, n. dream; ə— əbǐ ma éní sǐ dream caught me/I dreamt by night.

ərədrí = əyá, n. payment, compensation, reward for an action; interest, profit; kàni 'bá pɛ mǐ ti mu-zǒ afa àzí-nï e'dú-zǒ, kàni mǐ edzí rá, èri ɳgaa mǐní ə— fɛ̃ if a p. sends you to fetch a thing, when you bring it, she will give you a reward; profit (from reselling things).

órófǐ = rókódzí, n. kidney.

órókófà = kókóró(fà), n. part of (man's) leg below knee.

óərəmì, number nine, 9; óərəmì-zǒrǐ 9th.

ərətókə = əretékə, q.v.

ööru, av. above, aloft, on high; é tu ö—! go up/mount! é ɳga ö—! stand up! mǐ ɛɳgá dri ö—! raise your head/look upwards! öörulé sǐ upwards, aloft; àrǐá èi əɳga öru (lé) sǐ birds fly/move aloft; èmǐ etú má vǒ 'bù-á (or ö— 'dòá)! climb up to me! é tu 'bɛ́ driá ööru! do ascend the mountain!

örú, av. higher situated (topo-
graphy); dzó ɛmbápi vélérì
andrá, klási èri örú the houses
of the teachers are lower-lying,
the school is higher up (on slope);
mí ɛ'bí ɛŋgá örú yà? are you
coming from up country? 'bá
örúrì = örú-lé'bá, örúlá highland (towards watershed) people.

oru-oru, kátrà, av. quickly, without delay; mí emú oru-oru!
come at once!

Òrùgbò, n. name of a Padzulu clan
group.

órúkə, n. shrub (yielding very useful fibre for beer-strainer èi ó—
ɛdɛ́ áŋú-bàrö).

órúkórú-èdríká, ólúkólú, T., n.
a kind of mushroom.

òrúa, n. small yellow insect feeding
on ground-nut leaves èri fúnò
'bíkɔ̀ ŋa.

əsa = alá, emó, vt. (1) to stir up/
round (cooking); tíbí əsa to stir,
prepare savoury; èri zá 'alé əsa
lúfé sì she stirs the meat (in pot)
with a stirring-stick; (2) to mix
together (different things); èi 'dɔ̌
pi əsa (= emɔ̌) áŋú bɛ tú àlö
they put together eleusine and
sesame; 'bá əsa ɛ'bó 'dìì pírí
àlö they have put all the (different)
hoes together; kàbìlò 'dì əsa
(= ə'bé)'ì ɛmvɛ bɛ ëni bɛ ɛka
bɛ (or lúurú mbêrö) the sheep's
colour is a mixture of white,
black, and red.

əsá-(zà-) rö, vn./vr. to alternate
with; to take place (as: come)
alternately; andzi ŋírí mà əsá
rö 'bá 'wàrà bɛ = mà əsá èi
əsá andzi ŋírí 'bá 'wàrà bɛ!
let children take their places
alternately with men; kàbìlò 'dì
əsá èi əsá-əsá these sheep
alternate (with goats).

əsákɔ̀sà-rö, a. insipid, flat; as
when without salt à'í kókɔ̀rö.

òsárá = mbɔ̀rà, n. a shrub; èi
ò— ɛdɛ̀ àrífɛ̀-rö a'ú 'bíkə sì they
make with it (play-) arrows with
chicken's feather barb (for direction).

əsɛ[1] = ŋgö, vn. to be(-come) fat,
stout; é ŋa zá mí əsɛ ànï! eat
meat so that you become fat
(stout) with it!

əsɛ[2], vt. to support, guide on moving; èi mvá əsɛ they help a baby
along; èri 'bá milé kókərì əsɛ
kàlí sì he guides (pulls along) a
blind man with a stick.

əsɛ[3], vt. zá əsɛ to cut (lengthwise)
lumps of flesh and spread it; 'bá
zá əsɛ or 'bá zá 'alé api they
cut and spread meat/slit.

əsé, vt. to thread; ma əsé ŋərè
(báká sì) I threaded beads (in
string); mí əsé tí mà ti tsí, kà
mu-zɔ̌ fɔ̀-zɔ̌ kö! fasten the door
of the cattle-pen well, lest the
cattle come out; èi arí əsɛ̂ to draw
tight the drum (strings or ropes).

òsì, vt. (1) (= àsì, òndì) to tear; to
break in (to) splinters; òlínï
wárágá òsì the wind is tearing
the paper; òví òsì pátí ɛrékɛrɛ
the lightning has split/reduced
the tree to shattered splinters;
mà bɔ̀ŋgɔ́ òsì rö òsì my cloth is
torn; (2) to cause ridges/weals on
body; é kà laa rö pàrí mà
ŋgókó drìá, èri mï òsì-òsì if
you lie on bumpy ground, it will
raise weals on you (i.e. èri mï
rúá èpì-èpì it causes swelling on
your body); (3) to draw out,
straighten; ma áyï òsì I am drawing lines; òsì drì'bbí he combed
(his) hair.

òsì, vt. to knock; èri 'bá òsì drí
sì he is knocking a man with his

hand/fist; **èrì pätí ètí òsì** he is ramming (battering) down the earth under the pole (to fix it).

osi (cf. **tì**), vt. to bear a child; and to be born (said of woman only); **ɔ̀kó osi èdzó**/or **andzi èdzòrö** the woman has given birth to twins; **ma ágúì osi má àgåí sì** my friend was born in my presence (i.e. I was already born); **àma osi ma águì bɛ ètú àlö** I and my friend were born the same day; **ɔ̀kó osi (mvá) 'bɔ** the woman was delivered of a child.

osí, vt. to roast, fry; **èrì óŋa** (or **áŋú**) **osí àtsí driá** she roasts termites (sesame) (in pot) on fire; **ma àŋá osí àtsía (ìí kɔ́kɔ̀-rö)** I am roasting corn on fire (without water); **èrì zá osí émvó 'aléa ɔ̀do sì** she is frying meat with oil in a pot.

ɔ̀sí, n. a kind of passiflora tree (growing wild); **'bâ pa màarì̂-rö** they beat it to form a blowing instrument (its stem; much like a pawpaw).

òsì-rö òsì = edzí èì edzí, vr. to resemble; to be like, equal; **mvá 'dì òsì rö mvá 'dà bɛ òsì** this child resembles (collective form) that child; **èì pírí òsì rö òsì** they are all alike, or are equal.

ɔsí-k-ɔ̀sïrï = ɔ̀sïrí-k-ɔ̀sïrï, ɛsírí-k-ɛsïrï ('rö), a. thick, dense, compact; thickly interwoven, inextricable; **ásɛ́ ɔ—, 'bá fï tálánï sì kö** the grass is impenetrable, one cannot walk in between; **pàrí 'dà ásɛ́ ɛsí rö ɛsí** (cf. **ɛsí**).

osí-k-òsì-rö = òsúkòsù-rö, vn./ a. quiet, sedate; inactive, nerveless, weak; **'bá osí-k-òsì-rì̂** a man who does not quarrel, is friendly, acts sedately; does not play; is averse to any excitement, activity, vigour: indolent; **èrì lö rì̂-rï** he only sits.

Ósö̌, n. name of a tributary of **Átsá** river; rises immediately east of Arua.

ɔ̀sɔ̀, vt. (1) to pierce, prick, sting all over; **ɔ̀sɔ̀ èrì ëlï (sìndánì) sì** he pierced him/it all over with a knife (needle); (2) fig. to prickle one's ears, try to induce, impress, seduce, coax, talk over **'bá bïlé ɔ̀sɔ̀ ɛ'yó sì; mí ɔ̀sɔ̀ mâ bïlé kö!** do not try to impress me! **mí ɔ̀sɔ̀ mâ bïlé ɛ'yó 'dì mà 'aléa kö!** do not try to coax me into this matter! **èrì ɛ'yó ɔ̀sɔ̀ mâ bílía** he whispers into my ear (trying to induce me).

ɔsö̌, vt. (1) to urge, press, try to induce; **mí ɔsö̌ ma ɛ'yó 'dì mà 'aléa kö!** do not coax me into this matter! **mí ɔsö̌ ma ògúá kö; mí òku mí ògúó-nï, á lɛ̀ kö!** do not induce me to steal; you are a thief of long standing, I do not want it! (2) to lead astray; **'bâ milé ɔsö̌** i.e. **fɛ̀ 'bá drì tsà nì** to lead (purposely, by talking over) astray; misguide, -lead, -direct; **ètɔ́ɔ ɔsö̌ ɔ̀'dó mà milé nì** the hare misled the leopard (fable).

ósö̌, n. bean(s); various kinds of them; **à'í (sóró) dàka, àtsolimatarì̂, àndíŋakó, mòsòpía, fúnò, sòŋgo** (american pignuts), **lɔ̀kɔ̀dí, ŋ̈ïríkìa** (its leaves **ósö̌bí**), **bòrósó** (Ac. lapɛna), **kàíkɔ; àlótókó** (similar to soya beans); a larger kind is **ɔ̀'bɔ̀kɔ̀; ósö̌'bíkɔ** pods.

óssɔ̀, n. (flesh-) fat, grease; **zá ɔ́—, tí óssɔ̀** fat of flesh, of cow; **óssɔ̀ (-å̂) -rö**, a. fat; **àŋú èrì óssɔ̀-rö** honey is fatty.

əsö (cf. sö), vt. to pour (quantity);
mĭ əsö iĭ bésèn mà 'aléa! pour
water into the basin!

ɔ́sɔ́àkɔ̀rɛ = rótsókò, ɔ́sɔ́àkàɛ́,
tsɔ̀ndzɔ̀, n. kingfisher (and
varieties of it); èi è'bĭ ŋa they eat
fish.

ɔ́sɔ́fí = ɔ́sɔ́mbĭlĭ, sɔ̆ŋgɔ̆lɔ̆, n.
projection in middle of upper-lip.

ə̀sɔ́lə̀, n. an individual who hems/
clears his throat and spits with
much noise (by which means he
bewitches, the Logbara believe).

ɔ̆su, n. bow; ɔ̆su àrĭ̆a tsà-zɔ̆ bow
to shoot birds; ɔ̆su-bá bow-string.

òsù¹ (cf. sù), vt. to put on; èi ɛ́mvè
(or 'bíkɔ) òsù̆ èimà páa they put
rings on their legs (or, women,
leaves).

òsù², vn. to marvel, wonder; to be
astonished, surprised, amazed at;
ma òsù ɛ'yɔ́ mĭdrí sĭ̆ tò I am
astonished at your words; èri òsù̆
ɛ'dá 'dà drí (= sĭ̆) rá (ndrĭ̆-
táa-nĭ̆ rö-rĭ̆ sĭ̆) he marvels at
that picture; ma òsù oŋgú mĭnĭ
ndzo-rĭ̆ sĭ̆ òsù-òsù I am surprised at your speed; ma òsù
màrárà 'dà drí rá I marvel at
that mirror; òsùtáa, n. wonder,
surprise, admiration.

ɔ́súbí(à)mólà, ? n. gymnastics.

òsúkòsù̂-rö, a. (1) = òsíkòsĭ̂-rö,
q.v. mĭ əvö ò— (= mĭ 'a'á
ɛ'yɛ́rɛ 'dĭnĭ) à'do ɛ'yɔ́ sĭ̆ yà?
why are you so quiet, listless?
(2) of food; good, tasty.

òsùmìnikà, n. = mbèlèndzùkɔ̀,
q.v.

ə̀tǎ = azi, vt. to ask for girl's consent mĭnĭ ézɔ́-andzi azi (= ə̀tà)
-zɔ̆; ma èrimà ti ə̀tǎ—èri dzɛ-
zɔ̆ I ask for her consent—to
marry her.

òtákà, n. a small pot; ò— èri 'ĭ-nĭ
ɛ́ŋá əva-zɔ̆ the 'otaka' is properly

for stirring/making polenta; ordinary cooking-pot.

òtäkú'alĭ̆a, òtɛkú, òtɛkú̆a (cf.
òtákà), n. a very small cooking-
pot; ò— èri àfa tíbí a'dĭ-zɔ̆-
rĭ̆'ĭ it is a thing for preparing
savoury; or: tíbí əzɔ̆-zɔ̆ for
pouring/ladling sauce; òtɛkú̆a
tíbí bè-zö kind of bowl for
ladling sauce; èi ɔ́ŋa ɛ́fĭfĭ dǎ
èbĭ-rö 'alénĭ̆a, èri dĭ ŋgù̆
máŋgáŋgálí they pour raw/
fresh termites in it (savoury) and
it smells 'maŋgaŋgali'.

ɔ́tàlĭ̆a, n. small tin kerosene lamp.

ə̀tèkɔ̀té, T. (= ódrúkúdrú), n.
tadpoles (frog).

òtì, vt. (1) to set right, in order; to
adjust, arrange; mĭ òtì yǎbí ti
(or ɛ́dzá ti) mɔ̆ké! put the grass
(or fuel) bundles in order! (2) to
put in line; ma òtì búkù 'dà
òtì-òtì I put the books in order
(say on a shelf); àgu nna 'dà òtì
èi òtì-òtì (èdzèá sĭ̆) those three
individuals went in line (i.e. side
by side; cf. sɔ̆ drì sɔ̀ they follow
one another); dzó 'dàĭ òtì rö òtì
those huts stand in line.

òtĭ¹ (cf. tĭ̆; idea of: drop, dot,
point), vt. (1) to pick, pluck,
gather (fruits); èi mɔ̀émbè (or
fúnò) òtĭ-òtĭ they are picking/
gathering mangoes (ground-nuts);
(2) to set out, spread by bits/
pinches; èi dɔ̆fɔ̆rà òtĭ ɛ́rà drĭ̆a
they set out (by pinches) leaven
(still pulpy) on stone-slabs (for
drying; cf. ɛdzá).

òtĭ² = əmbó, (1) vt. to spurt,
splash; iĭ (or əzɔ́ɔ́) òtĭ mà rǔa
òtĭ water (rain) spurted on me;
əzɔ́ɔ́ òtĭ-òtĭ (or ə̀ĭ-ə̀ĭ) it drizzles
(rather heavily); (2) vn. to hop,
jump, frisk (about); lɔ̀ndrè-nĭ
ə̀tĭ päti sía sĭ̆ the colobus frisks

about on trees; (3) to start (or jump) up; **'bá mà ásí òtǐ òrì sǐ òtǐ** a man started up with fright; **òtǐ ǝvǐ sǐ òtǐòtǐ** he was startled by a clap of thunder; to be upset, startled, puzzled, in doubt; (4) to jump from one to another; **èri ǝmbǒ** (= **òtǐ**) **ɛ'yó bɛ ǝmbó** he (speaking) jumps from one topic to another.

òtǐ³, vt. (1) (= **ǝmbó**) to revive, (re)invigorate; **ma mvá 'dǐ mà ává òtǐ** I am reviving the pulse/ respiration of the child; **mvá 'dǐ mà ávánǐ òtǐ-òtǐ/ ... mà ásínǐ ǝmbó-ǝmbó** the child recovers himself, or gets new strength; (2) **ɛ'yó** (or **áɲǐ**) **òtǐ/ǝmvi ɔ́kó sǐ** to reply angrily or vehemently; **kànì mǐ èrì zǐ tǒ, èri mǐnǐ áɲǐ** (or **ɛ'yó**) **òtǐ** if you ask him too much, he gives an angry answer.

ǝtǐ = **ǝmbé, andzu, vt.** to fasten, tie together; **ǝtǐ sàndúkù báká sǐ** he tied up the luggage case with rope; **ǝtǐ búkù nna tró** he tied three books together; **kànì 'bá lè tǐ lí, èi ǝtǐ báká sǐ** when they want to butcher a cow, they tie it up with rope; **ǝtǐ kǝŋgǝlǝ/kírikíri** he tied it fast, tightly.

òtǐí, n. brother-in-law; **èri a'ǎ òtǐí-rǐ** he is staying with his brother-in-law.

ǝtǐatɔ̀ = **ǝtétɔ̀, ǝtǝnǝkǝ, q.v.**

ǝtǒ, vt. to set right/straight; put in order, arrange, &c. (1) to mend, repair, restore; **àma ǝtó ndrâ àfa 'dǐ o'dú nna sǐ rá** we corrected/fixed this thing before, on Wednesday; (2) to order, settle; **ma ǝtó àfa dríiá 'bǝ** I have regulated/arranged everything already; (3) to pack up; to roll or tie into a bundle; **èri bɔ̀ŋgó ǝtó**

sö-zǒ dzɔ̌rǒ 'aléa he is folding up his clothes to put them in a bag (i.e. he is packing up); (4) **ǝtó 'ï** to make ready, prepare; **ma ma ǝtǒ mu-zǒ atsíá** I am preparing for a journey; (5) to set in order, in line; **ɛmbápi èi andzi ǝtǒ drì àsɔ̀-rö** the teachers are ranging the children in line (one behind the other); (6) = **otú, ɛtú, ɛlǐ** to frown, look angry at; **èri milé ǝtǒ 'bá mà drìá** he frowns at a person; (7) to plot, conspire against **ti ǝtǒ 'bâ rúá** or **'bá mà ɛ'yó ǝtǒ; èi ti** (or **ɛ'yó**) **ǝtǒ Ðdírǐ mà rúá** or **èi Ðdírǐ ɛ'yó ǝtǒ** (e.g. **èrì tsǝ-zǒ**) they are plotting against Odiri (as, to beat him); **èi àmbó ɛ'yó ǝtǒ, èinǐ èrï drǝ** (= **ndzɛ**) **-zǒ** they are plotting against the chief, to drive him away (depose him); (8) to deliberate, discuss, consider **ɛ'yó àfanǐ-rǐ ǝtǒ; kaunsil èi ɛ'yó ɲaakú-nǐ-rǐ ǝtǒ ... fíisí 'bá mà òdrì díká** (or **'bá mà 'bà drìnǐá díká**) the council deliberates about questions concerning the country; perhaps about fees/ taxes to be increased.

ǝto, vt. to tread under foot, trample down; **èrì àɲá fǎ ámvú-á-rì ǝto-ǝto** he is trampling down the corn they have dug in in the field.

ǝtó, n. (1) navel; **èrì ǝtó bɛ àmbórǐ** he has a strongly protruding navel (umbilical hernia, called **ǝtó-dzó**); (2) penis; **mónió mà ǝtó** a bull's penis.

òtöbí, n. afterbirth (of woman only); **ò— kà esǐ kö, 'bá drà rá** if the afterbirth is not delivered, a p. dies; **'bá àzǐ 'dǐ 'bá ɛɲa ò— sǐ** some people 'poison' a p. by means of such afterbirth (cf. **ɔ́da**).

ə̀tə́əbí = ə̀tókə́bí, n. a creeper with leaves used as food; ɛ'bíkə ɛ̀rì ràra its leaves creep around.

ə̀tó (-kó) 'dóá¹rö, a. of small (-er than ordinary) size, undersized, stunted; crippled, maimed; ótókó 'dǐ ə̀tó¹rö this termite hill is undersized; ágú ə̀tókó'dóárǐ an ill-developed p.; 'bá pánï nǐ 'ï 'bà-zǒ kílílí kö 'dǐ, 'bá əmvɛ ə̀tó'dóá; ɛ̀rì atsí tòkòtókó if a p. does not set down (on walking) his feet properly, they call him stunted; he walks shakily/limping; also a pigmy is ə̀tó'dóá.

ótókó, n. termite-hill; ó— ón̩a-nï ə'á (or ŋga) -zǒ-rǐ termite-hill which termites live in (or swarm off); ɛ̀rì ón̩a mà ə̀drǐ lǐ, ákúrúmbâ si-zǒ she rolls clay from a termite-hill to make an 'ákúrúmba' (termite) trap.

ə̀tə̀kə̀tə̀-rö, a. (1) (cf. təzà, dùzà) lukewarm; ìí dùdù ètú sǐ, ɛ̀rì ə̀tə̀kə̀tə̀-rö the water is warmed up by the sun, it is lukewarm; (2) = àtə̀zà, ŋgùzà bad smelling; tíbí ə̀— (=ŋgùzà) the (old) savoury smells bad.

ə̀tolò; àdzú à— the spike (-spear).

ə̀tólə̀kpó, n. fresh shoots of potatoes (escaped collecting on field).

ótǒnǒkǒ, ətonaká, átón̩óvá, n. scorpion (reported from the Sudan only); kànì zà mǐ ètú 'dǐnï, drùsǐ ɛ̀rì 'ï dɛ ètú 'dǐnï if it stings you at this time (of day), it (-s pain) will end tomorrow at this (same) time (? = ótódín̩á).

ətənəkə, n. grey heron (Ardea cinerea); ɛ̀rì édró pi n̩a ólótókó bɛ, ódrúkúdrú bɛ, órí bɛ it eats mice, lizards, frogs, snakes (? serpentarius).

ə̀tón̩ò = ón̩a-ndríi, n. decaying, stale termites; ón̩a èbi 'bánï 'bâ émvóa ɛ̀rì màma, ɛ̀rì dǐ ə̀— uncooked (collected) termites they put in a pot where they start rotting; they are called ə̀tón̩ò.

ətra (1), vt. to roll (or coil) up; èl báká ə̀— they coil up a rope; órí ə̀— 'ï pätí sía a snake coils up on a tree; (2) vn. to be(-come) contracted, crippled; 'bá ətrazà 'bá rápi gĕrì vàá sǐ a crippled p. is a p. who drags himself along on the ground.

ə̀trakə̀trà-rö or ótrákə̀tra = ìtríkìtri, a. tasteless, insipid, spoiled.

ətré, vt. to speak with very loud voice, shout, speak with excitement; or protractedly; èmǐ ətré trátrá 'dǐnï à'do sǐ yà? why do you shout constantly like this? é trɛ ə̀kpó sǐ ma ɛri bɛnǐ! speak aloud, that I may hear!

ətro, vt. to put together; bə̀ŋgó ə̀— to collect the cloths.

ətró, vt. to push up or back; bə̀ŋgó ətró-zǒ to roll up one's sleeves.

ə̀tró (sí) ə̀tró, n. gums (of teeth).

otrúkə, T. = èdzí, q.v. n. light beer; èl o— pi əsa éwá èdúrǐ bɛ they mix light with (proper) thick beer.

ótrúkú (-ǎ) = ə̀trúlú, dúlú, ¹rö (i.e. àlǐa), a. (1) undersized, stunted; 'bá ò— (= àtrúzà) an undeveloped p., as also a pigmy; (2) crippled, maimed (of limbs); 'bá 'dǐ mà pá òtrúkú¹rö this man's leg/or foot is crippled; èdrĕká òtrúkú-rǐ zì ŋgà 'ïmà bbí kö a shut-up mushroom, its cap (pileus) is not yet opened/expanded (it is folded on the stem).

òtrúkúyia, n. black-cap bird (Sylvia atricapilla).

ə̀tsà = ètsà, vt. to complicate,

entangle (by speaking now so
then otherwise); mí ε'yə́ ə̀tsǎ
'díní à-sǐ yà? why do you confuse matters thus?

ə̀tsákáí = ə̀dzìdzìá, T., n. a kind
of weed whose sharp-pointed
black seeds stick onto one's
clothes on passing ə̀— nǐ bə̀ŋgə́
ə̀sə̀-ə̀sə̀.

òtsàkòtsà = òtsòkòtsò, -rö, a.
tasty, savoury; àfa ndrǐpi tə̀-rǐ
something very pleasant.

ə̀tsáə̀tsá, n. a savoury; èi ə́sə̌
a'wǐ a'dǐ; èi áɲú sǐ 'dǐpi (tré)
they cook dried beans; then they
grind a good quantity of sesame.

ə́tsátsá = ə̀yáa, n. yaws/from-
bosia; èri 'bá ɲàɲa it corrodes
a p.

ə̀tsε, n. (1) wood/forest; (2) tattoo
(of forehead); ə̀tsɛ̀ lǐ (or lǎ, lə̌) to
tattoo (by dots).

ə̀tsέ, ɔ̀tsə́ə, n. dog; ə̀— àɲàpá
ədrə́pirǐ a hunting dog.

ətsέ, vt. to guard; mvá mu tí
ə̀tsériálέ 'bə the boy went off to
guard the cattle.

ə̀tsε, vt. to tear asunder, undo
forcibly; èri bə̀ŋgə́ bá ə̀— he
tears up the seam of the cloth.

ə̀tsέ'à'día = ə̀réa, n. ankle.

òtsεsí, n. a natural division of
bunch of bananas à'bóà mà
òtsεsí.

òtsεsíìá, n. a shrub (yielding good
sticks); èi ò— əfǎ ə́sù-rö they
scrape/rub off an 'otsεsiia' stick
for a bow-stick.

otsí, n. thorn; sting; prick; élélù
(mà) otsí ə̀ndzə̀rə̀kə̀ the 'élélù'
caterpillar has many prickles.

ə̀tsí[1], vt. to conceal, keep secret,
hide away (matters); èri máni
ε'yə́ ə̀tsǐ he conceals the matter
from me.

ə̀tsí[2], vt. to take hold of a p.;

èndzà-nï èri ə̀tsǐ ámvú-ti-á
ə̀tsí-ə̀tsí: á 'à ámvú tə̀ö, ma
àndὲ 'bə laziness comes over him
on the side of the field (and he
says): I tilled much, I am now
tired (and stops); àzí-nï 'bá ə̀tsí
èndzàrö work makes/finds a man
lazy.

òtsíànduru = ə̀tsə́óndu, òkí-
àndə̀, n. formication; ò— bǐ mâ
pá tsǐ formication has stung my
leg.

otsífí, T. = otsíkí, n. reddish
milk (after recent calving) of cow;
'bá o— ə̀sə̌ kàátiá they pour it
(some) out at the cattle-pen's
door. (Cf. ə̀gə́lə́gbə).

ə̀tsò = ètsò, vn. to puff, swell up/
out; séntὲ má ètïa ètsə̌ 'coppers'
bulge in my back (-pocket).

Ɔ̀tsóodrì, n. district/tribal group
(17 miles east of Aruwa).

ótsóká = tsòké, T., = ə́ɲə́fí, n.
finger-nail; claw.

Ɔ̀tsə́kə̀, n. tribal group (8 miles
south of Aruwa).

ə̀tsə́kə̀á = émviá, n. bracelet.

Ɔ̀tsə̀kə̀rö, n. female proper name
(expressing time of trouble; male
Tsàadìá).

ə̀tsə̀kòtsə̀kə̀ = tsàandítsàandí,
-rö, a. depressed, dejected; cast
down.

ə̀tsə́lə́ = mə̀lə, n. in a'ú ə̀—, n.
special small hut for fowls; dzə́
a'ú nǐ laa-zórǐ (miniature) hut
for fowls to roost in.

ə̀tsòmòtsómò = ə̀tsòmòtsórò,
-rö, a. one upon the other; mǐ
sí ə̀— (= àdrə̀zà) -rö your teeth
are grown together (one upon or
behind the other).

ə̀tsórə́ = ə̀tsə̀lə́, lə́ə̀tsə, n. édró
ə̀— rat (string-) snare; báká 'bá
nï εdὲ édró bǐ-zórǐ string-work
arranged for trapping mice.

otsu, vt. to shake, jog; èi ɔ́sɔ̃ otsu
(= ədza) ɛ́mvó mà 'aléa they
shake the beans in the pot (over
fire, that the ones on top may also
be cooked).
ótsufí, étsofí, n. fruit of 'mala'
tree.
ótsúkùru, n. anhinga bird; èri
a'á áyá mà 'aléa (mïïrìá) or
kpɔ́rɔ́ táláa it lives among the
long grass of the river (Nile) side;
pá-nï èzɔ̃²rö ɛka; ti-nï ɛmvɛ²
rö, rùá-nï ëni²rö it has long red
legs, white beak, black body.
òtsùtsùrú, n. tuft of hair (on
head); comb-crest of fowl; saying:
'a'ú edzí àyïïá mà òtsùlùrú' the
fowl takes the crest of its mother,
cf. our 'like father, like son'.
òtú(pi) = òtíí, n. brother-in-law.
òtù = òndù, lï = pa, tra, ənï-
ənï ndrí 'ï-zɔ̃ to gather and knot
grass-tops to fasten goats (/sheep)
at èi ásê lï ndrí 'ï-zɔ̃ òtùru.
ótúkúdú = étémbɛ́rɛ̃, q.v. ²rö,
a. shallow; ìi mà 'aléa ótúkúdú²
rö the water is shallow.
òtúlúkùtùlú²rö = tùlútúlù-rö,
a. àŋgɔ̀ ò— hilly country; àŋgɔ̀
gúrú— dǎäli, gúrú— dǎäli
the ground goes . . . up—down,
up—down .´. . .
òtùnì (á) = órí tikɔ́tikɔ́, òtùnì
tikɔ́tikɔ́, əléti-əléti, n. blind-
worm (Anguis gracilis); rùá-nï
ënï-rö, èrì gu ndrïndrï it is
black, glossy; drì-nï 'bá nì nï
kö one cannot distinguish its head
(walks forwards or backwards
equally well, people say).
òù or òwù, vt. to gather, collect;
ɛ́dzá, ɔ́kɔ̀rɔ́ŋ̣à òù to collect firewood, waste/sweepings.
óú (-òú), vt. to give a feeble light,
to diffuse dim (faint, uncertain)
rays of light; àŋgɔ̀-nï àŋgà

óúòú it is growing dusk (the day
breaks, it dawns); àŋgɔ̀ óû dí 'bə
it is already dawning; ò'bíti sï èri
ŋgà 'ye óúòú èri gìlìgìlì
(= ònìònì, bìrìbìrì) in the morning (when) it is growing dusk, at
twilight/the day breaks.
ɔ́ú, vt to peel, shell, husk; èri ɔ́sɔ̃
(ə)'bíkə (or ə'bɔ́kə) ɔ́û she is
husking (peeling, skinning) beans;
èri gbándà 'bíkə ɔ́û she is
skinning the manioc root; to peel
off bark (cf əpí (or sï) fúnò she
picked out ground-nuts).
ò'úá = ò'úó, n. a tree.
óuátá = éuátá, n. a tree.
ò'ú-àdrí, n. a kind of agaric
(fungus); èri ɛŋgá pätí (or ɛ̀kpá-
tilɛ̃) maazà mà rùáa it grows on
decaying wood.
ɔ́vá = ndïrïá, n. dikdik gazelle;
ɔ́váɔ́vá²rö, a. sì 'ï ɔ́vá enïrïkə
lɛ̃ grey, as a dikdik.
ɔva, vt. to stir, prepare; ɔ̀kɔ́-nï
ɛŋ̣á ɔva: àzï-nï àgùpi drí,
àzïnï ɔ̀kóèi nï the woman prepares polenta, one for men, one
(distinct cooking!) for females;
ɔva ɛŋ̣á 'dï àmorèrö, ìi-nï aŋga
ŋgà kö she made the polenta
(leaving it) unfinished, the water
is not yet well absorbed.
ɔvá, vt. to dig, excavate; ɔvá 'bílɛ̃
rá he dug a hole; to dig up/out;
mààkò (or gbándà) ɔvǎ to dig
out potatoes (manioc roots); èmï
ɔvá ɔ́drò mà ɔ́lá wɔ́ərɔ́! to dig
out all the roots of the 'ɔdro' weed!
ɔ́vɛ́rɛ́kɔ́ or évɛ́rɛ́kɔ́, ásɛ̃ ɔ́—, n.
place in bush with recently
burned grass; áisɛ̃ vɛ̌pi àtsï sï
rá èri ɔ́— the place whose grass
burned down.
ɔ̀vɛrɛkɔ́ = ɔndzɔ́fà, n. crust (of
bread); of polenta in pot ɛŋ̣á mà
ɔ̀—.

òvĭ (cf. vĭ), vt. to scratch; òvĭ ὲrimà rúá òmbà sĭ (óῃófĭ sĭ) he scratches him fighting (with his fingernails); òvĭ έzó-andzi lúlú bε: ὲri òfŏ rö ŋgúrù-rö he scratches the girls who cry out in alarm: he turned into a wild beast.

òvĭ, n. pus; ápĭpĭá 'bà òvĭ 'bə the tumour has formed pus.

əví, vn. to push up earth ('búa from the ground/hole); átĭrĭlĭ (or óῃa) əví 'búa: ὲri 'bú mà ti òpì ῃaakú sĭ tsĭ the cricket (the termites after swarming) pushes up earth from its hole: in this way it shuts the opening of its hole with earth.

òvĭ, n. the lightning; òvï-nĭ ga it lightens; òvï-nï hwὲὲ (=àfĭ, àsĭ, lĭ) it thunders; òvï-nï 'bá sŏ (= tsə) the lightning strikes a man; òvĭ àsĭ pätĭ the lightning has struck/split a tree.

òvĭ = òbĭ, n. character, manners of; 'dĭ òvĭ (= òbĭ) mĭnĭ drĭə-rĭ this is your usual character; mĭ òbĭ òku 'dĭnĭ your character has always been like this.

əvö¹ = a'á, adri, vn. to be; to stay; àma əvö/a'á à'bŏà mbε we are eating bananas; mĭ əvö tòəkó, mĭ òvŏrö you stay idle, you are lazy.

əvö², vt. àtsĭ əvö to blow up fire; mu àtsĭ əvŏ ásé sĭ he went to blow up fire with grass.

òvŏ, n. a large basket; òkó tsátsà 'dĭ women make them.

òvŏ¹, n. laziness, idleness; 'bá òvŏrö-rĭ mà ῃa έῃá kö! a lazy man ought not to eat polenta!

òvŏ² = əndzε, vt. to distribute, dole out (food); 'bá sàánĭ 'aléa έῃá òvŏ (= əndzε) they dole out polenta on to plates.

óvu, n. kind of ambatch— light wood (used for very light furniture); óvu bbínï 'bàaràrö it has large broad leaves; óvu sĭ èi kĭtìpóló εdέ with 'ovu' they make stools; ὲri laolao⁺rö it is light (cf. mïrïá 'dĭ le'di on the Nile is the proper ambatch).

òvù, vn. to keep silent; mĭ (pl. èmï) òvù (or adrï) tsĭrĭ! keep silent! 'bá òvù mvá 'dà mà drà sĭ people keep silent on account of that child's death.

ovú (≅ əzó), vt. to roast; ὲri mààkò (a'ú gbέ, óῃa...) ovû àtsĭ-fúlúa he roasts potatoes (eggs, termites...) in the red heat (lŏ: zá əzŏ only: to roast (fry) meat).

ówá (in Àdzíia) rare for common éwá, n. beer.

əwá = əmbó, vn. to jump, leap; əwá-əwá = əlá-əlá, əndzó-əndzó, vn./a. to be restless, excited, troubled, disquieted; turbulent; tí 'dĭrï əwá-əwá, lè mà zə 'ïmà lésú kö this cow is restless, she does not like to be milked; nèsì aza fĭ rùá-nï áánĭ, ὲri ànï əwá-əwá perhaps he has become mentally deranged and is turbulent because of it.

òwàandrò-wàandrò, a. (yellow-) brownish.

əwásɛdù (i.e. èwâ tsε tí), n. a shrub (lit. the elephant cannot pull it out).

ówέrε, n. rod-broom.

ó'wĭ = ó'ï, n. large kind of (?) lung-fish; ó'bókə-nï ŋgò'bó-ŋgò'bó⁺ rö (or tsímvá-tsímvá) it is scaly (whitish-brown); ə'á òrété-kòá it lives also in (dried) mud (cf. aní another kind).

əwĭ, vt. to sacrifice; ὲri órí əwĭ 'bá áda sĭ he sacrifices a real man to the ancestors (lit. sacrificed the ancestors with a man); **èi ɛ́ɳá tǐ rá, éi ə̀'bǎ óní 'dà mà drǐá: èi ə́rǐ** (or **á'bí**) -**nï ə̀wǐ** (= **òbǐ**) they pinch off (a little bit of) polenta and put it on the (appropriate) stones of the ancestor spirits: they sacrifice to the ancestors' spirits.

owí = **óú**, vn. (1) to dawn; **àŋgò̆nï owí-owí** it dawns/grows dusk (see **óú**); (2) to take beans from pod; **èi bə̆ró̆ssó̆ owí** they clean adze from pod.

ə̀wí = **ə́ó, ȧá**, vn. to utter natural voice, cry (animal, man); **andzi ə̀wí 'dà** children cry there; **àríiá-nï ə̀wí 'dà** birds cry (or: sing) there; **ə̀wí**, n. voice, crying; sound; **ärí 'dǐ mà ə̀wí akú** (= **ku**) **ndè̆ rá** the sound of the drum was clearly (to be) heard.

ò̀wǐ, vt. **tùsú ò̀wǐ** to spit; **èri tùsú ò̀wǐ dzó 'aléa** he spits in the hut/room (bad manners).

ò̀wì = **ò̀wù, ò̀ù**, vt. to gather, collect; **èi mu édzá** (or **óní**) **ò̀ù** they go to collect firewood (stones); **mí ò̀wù 'ǐ-nï édzá edzí ɛ̀ndì!** collect and bring him also firewood/fuel!

ə̀wílékŏ-ètí more commonly **wílékŏ ètí**, n. armpit.

ò̀wúu = **ò̀wúo**, n. a large tree (*Ficus ingens* or *F. congensis*).

ó̆yá = **kɛlɛdzuko**, n. the *Euphorbia media* tree; **ó̆yá mà àrí** (or **sú**) **tò̆, drȧdra; bbí-nï yə́** it has much juice, it is bitter (can blind one); it has no leaves.

ə̀ya = **bò̀odrá, ə̀ya-bò̀odrá**, n. yaws or fromboesia; **'bá ə̀ya bɛ** one with . . . ; **ə̀ya-ə̀rò̆kò̆kò̆** remains of yaws (on any part of body: palm of hand, foot, armpit); **ə̀ya-ə̀— mï èdzò ànï wǐ kpii kö** on account of yaws-remains

you cannot stretch your arm (straight).

ə̀yá = **ə̀rə̀drí**, n. retribution, compensation (both for good or bad deeds); **ə̀yá: mïnï 'bá ə̀mvɛ-zó̆ ámvú-á ámvú 'à-zó̆ ə̀yá sǐ** when you call a p. to your field to till the field for a reward (good meal, &c.); **èri ɛ́ɳâ 'i ə̀yátáà-rö** she prepares food for the hired field workers.

ə̀ya, vt. to move, stir, shake; **mǐ mézà ə̀ya à'do sǐ yà?** why do you move the table? **ə̀vǐ ə̀ya 'bá rá, ɡa ànï tsǐ** the lightning upset him, he got out of breath.

ə̀'yá, vt. to shake, jog; **èri èzú** (or **kɛ́rɛ́; ɛ́mvó mà**) **'alɛ́ ə̀'yǎ** she shakes (on rinsing with water) the (inside of the) calabash (pot).

ə̀yakiya = **ə̀yakuya**, n. earthquake; **ə̀— àŋgò̆ ə̀yǎpirǐ** earthquake which jogs the earth.

ó̆yɛ́, also **ó̆yɛ́lá, ó̆yɛ́-nï**, av. wantonly, one-sidedly, unrequitedly, unreciprocally; **á tsə mǐ ó̆yɛ́** I have beaten you without (your) requital; **é pa ó̆yɛ́lá mâ ǹdrí ádzê; 'dǐ ò̀gùtáa pǎría** you have taken away my goat yesterday wantonly; this is in place of the theft.

oyi, see **oi**.

ò̀yíkŏyî-rö, a. ticklish; **èrimà pá ò̀— he feels a tickling in his foot.

ə̀'yó = **ə̀dzɛ́kɛ́**, T., n. horn; **tí ə̀'yó** cow's horn.

ə̀yó, n. a tree.

ə̀yo, vt. to roast slightly; **èi màȧkŏ ə̀yo àtsílɛ́-tiá** they roast lightly potatoes at the side of fire.

ə̀yə̀, n. a plain engagement, pledge, protestation, determination (on one's own account, as e.g. 'nobody shall ever enter my hut!' to make such a resolution **ə̀yə̀ sə̆**; if any outsider acts contrary to such a pledge ɔ̀yɔ̀-lï, punishment for broken pledge falls on the engager ɔ̀yɔ̀ nï su/or ka rá, the engagement caught/took effect; he may die from it 'bá 'dà drà ɔ̀yɔ̀ sï; mï ɔ̀yɔ̀ sɔ̀ tɔ̀əkɔ́, mïnï 'yɛ-zɔ̌ dràzɔ̌ 'alɛ́ yà? you make vainly the decision; do you contemplate dying in the matter? lï ɛ̀rì lïlï; sɔ̀ ɔ̀yɔ̀, drà ànï one contravened him; as he made the determination, he died from it (cf. etrï'ï etrï).

óyɔ́ɔ, n. the grivet monkey; ɔ́—rúá-nï ɔ̀bìkɔ̀bì (= fɔ̀fɔ̀ŋi̩, fɔrɔ̀rö) the grivet is grey; ɛ̀rì ásé-á, ɛ̀rì mu kakâ ŋaa it lives in the bush, it goes (into the fields) to (steal and) eat maize, &c. (Ac. ɔ̀ŋɛ̀ɛrà).

ɔ̀yɔ̀kɔ̀lɔ́(lɛ́) sï, av. whispering; ɛ̀ì ɛ'yɔ̀ 'yɔ ɔ̀— sï they speak in whispers.

ɔ̀yɔ̀əpi, ɔ̀—ɔ̀— = áŋgɛ́rí, a. large (of quantity).

oyú, n. mole; oyú ɛ̀ri a'ɑ́ ŋaakú mà 'aléa; ɛ̀ri ŋaakú ɔvɑ́, ɛ̀ri ŋaakú àmï 'bùálɛ́ (àmvɛ́) the mole lives in the ground; it excavates the earth and pushes it out of the hole; oyú rúá-nï fɔrɔ̀rö; ti-nï àlïïrö; sɔ́bí-nï yɔ it is grey; has a long snout, no tail.

ɔzá¹ = ɔtré, vn. to speak aloud, strongly; to make noise.

ɔzá², T. = ɔzó, ɔ̀'bï, vt. to roast (lɔ̌ àtsïa only in fire), as màːkɔ̀ or gbándà ɔzá to roast potatoes, manioc root.

ɔzɛ¹, Lɔgiri = ɔzɔ̀ɔ́, n. rain.

ɔzɛ² = ɔ̀gò, vt. to push (away) or knock down (vàá); to overthrow, overturn; upset; ɔzɛ ma àfa wɔ́rɔ vàá mɑ̀ dzɔ́a he has overturned everything in my room.

òzí = kírikíri, n. a kind of

humble-bee; ɛ̀ri ɛ̀fö ótɔ́kɔ́ ɔ̀mbɛ-ti-á; ɛ̀tï-nï ɔsɛ̀-rö it lives and comes out from the side of termite-hills; its back part is large.

ɔzì (cf. zì), vt. to hide; ɛ́sɛ̀ kànì rï 'bɔ, ɛ̀ri ɔzì rö ɔ̀ndó-bbï táláa when the grasshopper settles, it hides away among durra leaves.

ozí, vt. to sell; à mú·mɑ̀ tí ozí! let us go and sell my cow!

ɔzìɔ̀zì = sìsìrì, ɔ̀mbùrùkù, T., ŋgulù, n. cattle, &c., disease. ? foot-and-mouth disease of cattle, sheep.

ɔzɔ̌, n. reed stalk; ɔ̀zɔ̌ ïá-rï stalks from the water-side; ɔ̀zɔ̌ dzó ɔmbé (or ɔtḯ) zɔ́rḯ stalks for the framework of a hut; 'bá ɛtsḯ dzó mà àgɑ́ï ɔ̀zɔ̌ sï people have fenced in the hut with reed stalks.

ɔzó, vt. to roast, broil; ɛ̀ì màːkɔ̀, zá ɔzɔ̀ àtsïá they roast potatoes, meat in the fire; á 'bà zá ɔzó-ɔzó àtsí mà 'aléa I have put meat in the fire for roasting.

ɔzɔ̀ɔ́, n. hog; ɔ̀zɔ̀ɔ́ ósɔ̀(-â) rö the hog is fat.

ɔzɔ̀ɔ́, n. rain; ɔ— ïï-ïï nï ïï (ǹdrí ósɔ̀rö = ɔzɔ̀ɔ́-nï 'di ǹdrí ósɔ̀rö) it is drizzling; ɔ— nï 'dï'di it rains; ɔ— nï lïlï it thunders; ɔ— nï efïefï raining approaches (light drops); 'bá ɔ— àsɔ̌pi rain-maker.

ɔzɔ̀fɔ̀rɔ̀ = fö, n. hoariness; mbàzà mà drìá (or drìbbí) ɔ̀— tsḯ the old man is grey (Ac. loaar).

ɔzórófï, n. name of a shrub.

òzúfï, n. a tree with edible fruits (cherrylike; *Vitex madiensis*).

özuku, n. porcupine; ö— mɑ̀ rúá otsí (or 'yɛ́) bɛ the porcupine has quills; ö— ɛ̀ri 'bá tsà 'yɛ́ sï the porcupine shoots at people with quills (arrow); ö— otsí (or 'yɛ́) quill of porcupine; ɛ̀ri gbándà (or màákò) ŋa tŏ it likes to eat manioc (or potatoes).

òzúmŋgbúrúkú = òzùmbúrú-kú, òvúŋgúrúkú, n. several kinds of humble-like wood-boring bees; èri pätí lŏ it bores wood; ? also a kind of hornet.

P

pà¹ = sì, ġa, vt. to knock; á pà dzótilé pàpà I was knocking at the door.

pà² (= dà, ġò, atri) drì, vn. to turn, i.e. go back (vélé); é pà drì mu àkúa! go back home! cf. èpà, èdà, ègò drì (vélé), vn. to return, i.e. come back; and: to cause to come back/to drive back; mí èpà...ǹdrí drì vélé! check/stop the goats and drive them back here!

pa¹, vt. to snatch (or wrest) sth. from; to obtain possession of sth. by intrigue or force; é pa mǎ bòŋgó kòkòlò-rö kö! do not take away my cloth by force! ma ma àfa epa-epa I am taking my own thing.

pa² rö, vn. to flee, escape from; pa rö 'bò or pa 'ïmà drí 'bò he made off (from one's clutching hand); pa 'ï drà-sía rá or pa 'ï drà mà 'aléa rá he escaped death (Ac. obvòt); pa 'ï ándríí mà rúá/or ándríí vŏ he took refuge with his mother (catching hold of her)/or to his mother; 'bá tsa rö pa-zŏ átá mà rúá (átá vŏ) kö yà? can/ought not a man possibly (to) take refuge/shelter with his father?!

pa³ = ɛtó, vt. to support, back, defend; pa ma nǐ he assisted me.

pa⁴, vt. to adjust for some purpose; (1) to beat/knock off, remove by

blows; érà paa àŋâ 'i-zŏ to dress a stone for the purpose of grinding; (2) pätî paa to smooth, dress (by cutting), plane wood.

pa⁵, vt. to fix, fasten (nail or the like); èri álô pa tí 'ï-zŏ he drives in a peg to fasten cows to; èri pätí mà sí pě, èri enïrïkə epa ànï ŋaakúa (vàá) he points sticks in order to fix the hide on to the ground with them; èri mùsù-márí pa pätírùáa he is thrusting nails into the wood; é pa pätí 'dǐ lùsùmárì sǐ! fix these wood pieces with nails!

pá leg; foot; pá èdo heel; pá odzú or lǐdǐrǐ calf of leg; see pá-mvó.

pǎ̈ï, pǎ̈o, n. ebony (Alur pooi); mba ndɛ rá is extremely hard; rùá-nï ënï²rö, ó'bíkə-nï ɛmve² rö it is black, its bark white.

pálá¹, n. a cultivated plant.(of the bamia kind)(2 m. high); 'bá bbí-nï, fò-nï ŋǎŋa they eat its leaves, flowers (as vegetables, cooked); pálá báká its fibre much appreci-ated; p— áŋáká it has prickling hairs.

pálá², n. bifurcation of legs; space between legs/thighs; mvá 'dǐ èri mâ páláá the baby is/sits be-tween my legs; àrǐíâ ŋga mâ p— sǐ a bird flew away from between my legs.

pàlà = kátrà, oru-oru, av. im-mediately, without delay; mí ɛ'bé mí p—; mïnï drì àdà-zŏ! be quick, that you may (soon) be back!

páláắ¹ = ǹdúa, n. the foot, base of...; 'bé p— of a mountain; Árúwá p— at the base of tiny Aruwa (from which the place has been named) hill.

páláắ² = pásáká or pákásá, i.e. àtíbó, n. workman at a p.'s dependence—slave; ópí mà p—, i.e. 'bá ópí mà dríá-rǐ workmen/ slaves in the hand of a chief.

pálé = pá'alé, vǒ or vǒ sǐ, milékɔ́, pá-milékɔ́, n. time; pálé sí yà? how many times! á dzi p— àlö I brought it once.

pá-mvó, n. (1) trace, trail; footprint, -mark; (2) = ŋábílékɔ́ scar, impression (left by wound, &c.); bélé pằrí or bélé pámvó; ndrá drìə-rǐ mà p—, áda-nï dza rö 'bə an old mark after the sore was healed; (3) rest, remnant; mààkò p— potatoes left behind (at digging); mààkò p— 'bá-nï ŋaa-zǒ 'bə-rǐ mà vútiá-rǐ, èi fǒ ətɔ́ləkpɔ́⌐rö potatoes left behind (in field) after people have eaten (the main crop), they put forth new shoots (called ətɔ́ləkpɔ́); small remnants of anything left behind; mï mǎ ámvú pámvó ri you have snatched away the last remnant of my field (i.e. the whole); (4) pámvó sǐ pstp. after; əzɔ́ɔ́ 'di ráká, á ŋgà fǒ àmvélé ndɔ̀, əzɔ́ɔ́ pámvó sǐ/or əzɔ́ɔ́ mà vúti-á after it has rained I shall go out: after the rain; (5) pámvó (= pằrí) àlö sǐ in one place.

páaníkì = láà, làŋgá, n. place of gathering, of staying of people at hot hours (during dry season); àŋgǒ-nï drǐ tǒ sǐ (when it is very hot).

p'áŋgá = drì-rima, ɔ̀yá, n. punishment; é kà ɛ'yɔ́ ɛza àŋgǒ dríá, mǐ ŋgà mu p'— ɛsú Àdrɔ̀ vǒ if you sin on earth, you will find punishment with God.

pàŋà (similar dúmíí, àràwàŋá), n. a kind of briar; from its knotted root (ɔ́lá) they make balls for children to play with; dúmíí 'bá

ɛdɛ̌ pàŋàrö from 'dumii' they make such balls (called also p—); andzi èi p— tsə kàlí sǐ boys play/knock the ball with sticks (golf?).

päo-päo (â) ⌐rö = pɛupɛu, lǎù-lǎù, -rö, a. light; ndzi kɔ́kɔ̌-rö weightless.

pàrà-pàrà, av. shaky, tottering; èri atsí p—p— ɛ́wá sǐ he walks along tottering from beer; á pa ma p—p— I disentangled myself (from sby.'s grip) almost falling to the ground in so doing.

páráká, n. stalk; ɔndó p— durra stalk; èi ànï èvó tsàá they make (intertwine) baskets with them.

paratsa⌐rö, a. only (?) in; ò'dú p— the thigh/hip is flattened (why?).

pằrí¹ = pằrítà, n. place (for anything); dzɔ́ p— place of a hut (cf. dzɔ́ ándró abandoned place of a hut); dzí dzɔ́ p— àzǐ-nï-á they transferred the hut elsewhere.

pằrí² = ɔmí, kɔ́lɔ́, n. papyrus; papyrus mat/sleeping place, bed; mǎ p— laa-zǒ-rǐ my sleeping mat; é dzi pằrí ɛdzà (or 'bɛ)! take the mat and spread it!

päri, päripäri or para, parapara ⌐rö, also päri-à-rö (of small things), a. round, encircled; médzà pärirǐ (òdzí kɔ́kɔ̌-rö) a round table (without angles); áyáká mà ti päri-rö the opening of a basket is round; iǐ lǐ 'ǐ pằrìrö water (of a lake) is secluded all around; roundish.

pằría, pằrípằrî-rö, a. showing spots here and there; sporadically; kànǐ 'bá 'à àŋá, èri ɔlí rö ko pằrípằríârö: èri ka 'álénǐá sǐ àlö-àlö when a man plants corn, this comes up leaving bare patches here and there: it grow sporadically in single places.

pàrífɛsí, n. kind of large shelf for keeping firewood ɛ́dzá 'bà-zɔ̆.

pásì, ? S., n. box- or pressing-iron.

pätí, n. tree; shrub or any woody plant; p— bbí, p— 'bíkɔ leaf, bark of tree; p— mà áda a tree proper; (any) piece of wood.

pätí, n. stem, trunk (of any plant); pätí (or kaká ...) mà pätí trunk of a tree, stem of maize; ɔ̀ndó p— stump of durra stalks (left in field).

pàtsàpàtsà, a. splashing at random; mvá wɛrɛ̆á-rì 'ì ɔ̀dzì ìí sì p— the small child washes himself merely splashing (not in a proper way).

pè¹, vt. (1) to send, order (as to work); ɔ́pí pè 'bá àzí-á the chief sent/ordered people to work; 'bá ǧǎ sì they refused; (2) 'bá mà ti pè̆ to send a p. with a message; á pè mvá 'dì mà ti àmbó vɔ̆ Árúwá I sent the boy to the elder at Arua (with a message).

pè², vt. to bring forward; (1) to angle; mǎ mu è'bí pè̆ (or 'bɛ) ɛ́wì̆ sì I am going to fish with a hook; (2) to get out (from beneath, &c.); kànì ɛ́drɔ́ drà ǧèrì̆á (nɔ̀ sàndúkù ètí̆a), é pè áséa kàlí sì if a mouse dies in a path (or under a trunk), you remove it (cautiously) with a stick away into the grass; lóà èri mì̆ fí ɛ̀pè àmvé the hartebeest (if attacking) pulls out your intestines (with its horns); (3 to choose, select; èri 'ìmà ǹdrí ɔ̀pè̆ he selects, picks out his goats (among others); (4) to extract; èrì mu emǔ mǎ sí pè̆ he will come to extract my tooth; (5) 'bá mà àrí̆ pè̆ to manifest one's joy at having killed a man.

pè³, vt. to (cut to a) point; èri pätí mà sí pè̆ ëlì̆ sì he points the sticks with a knife.

pè⁴, vt. to surpass; é pè ma zɔ̀táã (or drì) sì̆ you surpassed me in growth (by a head).

pè⁵ rö, vr. (1) to withdraw (or retire) from . . ., to remain aside (or back); 'bá àlö mà pè (= wï̆, ko, ku, li, sì̆, trɔ̀) rö 'dɛ́ kö! let nobody withdraw/stay behind at it! è'bí pè 'ì̆ rá the fish got away; (2) to escape notice, from one's memory; éfí̆-nï̆ àzí̆ àlörì̆ pè rö rá (= àvì̆ mǎ drì-á rá) a further meaning slipped from my mind (I forgot it); ɔ̀trò mǎ ǹdrí wɔ́rɔ́, pè rö lɔ̆ àlö he moved away all my goats except one (lit. one only escaped).

pè⁶, vt. to row, paddle; èi ɔ́'bɔ́ pè̆ ledi sì̆ they paddle the canoe with oars.

pë̆, vt. to twist, twine; èi bákâ pë̆ ëlí̆ drìá ɛ́mbá² rö they twist cords/strings on (their) thigh for nets; mí̆ mǎ drì pë̆ à'do ɛ'yɔ́ sì̆? why are you twisting my hand? èri bɔ̀ŋgɔ́ mà ì̆ pë̆ (= ndzï̆) he wrings the water from the cloth.

pë̆/pí̆ = tú (cf. pírí), av. all; pé̆ (or tú) àlö all together; à mú mì̆ bɛ pí̆ (= pírí̆) àlö! let us (two) go together! èmï̆ ɔ'á pé̆ àlö! remain all together! é fè mání̆ wárágà pí̆, é sì̆ àzí̆nï̆ kö! give the whole paper, do not tear off anything!

pépé(á) = pékèpékè, pèpétí, n. ásí p— cavity of breast (below sternum); pépé-sí-fà (-lákó), n. breastbone or sternum.

pèlèlè, av. through from side to side; àdzú ǧa p— the spear pierced (him) through; sɔ̀ tí p— he stabbed/pierced the cow through.

pèlèŋgú, n. àtsí̆ p— charred bit of wood (after fire).

pèrè = ŋgòlé, q.v.

péré-péré, a. thin, fine (paper, triple wood or the like).

pɛrɛpɛrɛ, av. to any place (whatsoever), at random; ɔ̀li 'du wáráɡà p— the wind took the paper in all directions; é mu ɛ̀ri bɛ p—, é 'bà ɛ̀ri 'dǐá kö! go with it wherever you like, only do not put it here! á lɛ̀ mvá pɛrɛpɛrɛ-rǐ I want any boy immediately.

pí! (1) av./intj. hitting, thump, bang; á 'bɛ àrǐá óní sǐ pí! apá rá I threw a stone at the bird bang (hitting), but it ran off; ɛ̀bǐ 'du ɛ̀ri pí áɡátǐá the spider seized him with sudden grip by his waist; ɛ̀i drǎ pí 'yé bɛ (rùáa) dáanï (ndzɛ rö kö) they died hit by arrows on the place (did not remove the arrows); (2)=**pírí** all.

pì[1], vn. to swell; mǎ pá pǐpì my foot is swollen.

pì[2], vt. to make up to size (as expected), to complete; mï ɔ̀fɛ̀ áɡú 'dà mà sìlíŋgì dɛ rá, éfǐnï é pì mǎrí mà ti 'bɔ you have given back the shillings to that man, i.e. you have completed (by small instalments) the restitution.

-pi (= ɛ̀i), added to a noun, means 'N. N. and companions'; ɛ̀tɔ́ɔ-pi mu ɛ̀wá bɛ the hare with his companions went with the elephant (fable).

ᷢpi . . . rǐ formative of subject relative pronoun; who, which (cf. Grammar, § 257).

pi . . . bɛ or **pie**, cj. and; ɔ̀kó pi mǔ záa-mvá bɛ ɛ́dzá ɔko-rǐá the woman and a girl (or her daughter) went to gather firewood; Ɔ̀dǐrǐ pi etsá Mǐrǐá bɛ àma-rí àkúa O— and M— arrived at our village; àmà mu ɛ̀ri pie àkúa I went home with him (lit. we and he . . .).

-pí, indf. prn. suffix; for size, volume, quantity; . . . atsɛ ŋgɔ̀-pí? how much remained back? ɛ̀ri ŋgà-pí (i.e. áŋgírí), ɔkɔ ŋgà kö there is still a good quantity (indicated by hand), it is not yet finished; mǎ ǹdrí ráɳá 'dǐ-pí my he-goat is of this size (shown); mï ɛsú 'bá àzǐ 'dálɛ́ mǐ-pí you have found/met there a p. of your size or quality.

pii, pipi (mostly only **kpii**), av. straight; é sɔ̀ pá (k)pii! stand upright! ɡ̀ɛrǐ pipi-rǐ ɛ̀ri 'dǐ'ï the straight way is this one here.

pílíᷢrö, a. without handle i.e. àbbɛ́-nï yɔ; ɛ̌lï pílí, ɛ'bɔ́ pílí knife, hoe without handle; ma etó ɛ̀ri dzó-á pílílíᷢrö I have removed it at home to make it without handle; also pílílíᷢrö naked; ma atö ɛ̀ri dzóa pílílǐrö, dri-ndzá dɛ/fu ma kái I surprised him naked in the hut, I felt utterly confused.

pírí, pírípírí, indf. prn. all, everybody.

piriᷢrö, av./a. straight (vertically); é ɡa 'bílɛ́ p—! dig a hole straight down; ma ɛ̀drɛ̀ kàlí p— I set the stick/pole upright.

pìrilǐá, àdrópá'dírí, n. whirlwind, tornado.

pìríndì, S. (= dzɛ̀lɛ̀kó, àdzɛ̀lɛ̀kɔ́), n. whistle; p— lǐ (= vo) to blow the whistle.

pírí-nï = ŋ̀gbɔ, a. empty; 'álɛ́-nǐ-á p— (or 'álɛ́ tɔ̀ɔkɔ́) it is empty; ɛmví ǐi-á dri bɛ pírínï he returned from beyond the lake empty-handed.

pírípíría, n. (1) (= lúkúkùa) whirlwind; (2) giddiness; p— rǐ (= a'á) mvá bɛ nǐ (= dri-nï lǐlǐ) the child turned giddy.

pɔ̀ = kpɔ̀, vt. to peel; ɛ̀ri màákò
(or gbándà) kpɔ̀ (= óú̃, rɛ) she
is peeling potatoes (manioc roots).
pɔ̀dɔ̀, n. long, flowing hair; ǹdrí
mà 'bíkɔ̀ ràápi àmbó'rö èi
əmvɛ p— the long flowing hair of a
goat is called 'pədə'; 'bá pɔ̀dɔ̀ long
flowing hair of, say, a (white) girl.
pɔ̀rɔ̀rɔ̀á, S.?, n. aluminium articles (of ornament).
prìtsɔ̀ = p(ì)ritsà, kìrìtsà, rìɛ̀-
tsà, kìrìmà, lɔ̀lɔ̀ rɛ̀gɛ̀, n. spur
(of fowl).
pùù, av. really, truly; ma aga
pùù mí vǒ 'dì sì I really passed
you by here.
puu, vn. to arch the back; bɔ̌rà-nǐ
puu (= pìi) ɔ̀tsɔ́ sì a cat arches its
back on seeing a dog.
p'ùuà, n. a rifle, gun.
púrúa = lúkútúrù, n. lion-ant.
pùrùɔ́, n. kind of grasshopper
(kùlú).

R

rà = rrà, av. the whole night
through; àzɔ́ bǐ ɛ̀ri ɛ́ní sì, ta rrà
(i.e. etsá kpɛ́rɛ́ ò'bíti sì) he was
ill at night, and sighed the whole
night (up to this morning); ɛ̀ri
àzɔ̀ ta rrà he sighed, sick, the
whole night.
ra¹, vn. (1) to flow, run; ɛ̀tátá-nǐ
raa vàá sì the rain torrent runs
over the ground; zá mà ɔ́sɔ̀, kànì
'bá 'bà àtsí driá, ɛ̀ri ràra fat,
if put on fire, flows like oil (ɔ̀do
rö); (2) to creep, climb (of plants);
ɛ́ríndí (kə) ɛ̀ri ásɛ́, ɛ̀ri ràra,
'erindi' is a grass, it creeps (on the
ground); ɔ̀kà(-báká)-nǐ raa
pätí mà rùá the 'əka' creeper
climbs up trees.
raa² = ɛtsí, vt. to deceive; mǐ
emú mà raǎ à'bɔ́ sì you have
come to cheat me with lies.

ra³, ará, vt. to cover, spread over;
á ra ásɛ́ dzɔ́ mà drì-á I have
spread grass on the hut; é mu
drì-nǐ ará ásɛ́ sì! go and cover
it with grass! 'bá dɔ̌fárá mà drì
raa ɔ̀ndó (or à'bɔ̀à) -bbí sì they
cover the leaven with durra (or
banana) leaves.
rääku, n. a kind of papyrus-
bamboo: not-round, very frail
long sticks.
rǎpú, n. splits from *Phœnix
reclinata* or bamboo stem; kìtì-
pɔ́lɔ́ ɛdɛ́ zɔ̌ this (and the former) used for making very light
stools.
ráɲá = ráaó, n. any castrated
animal; tí r—, ǹdrí r— 'bání
ɛ̀lɔ́-nǐ ndzɛ-zɔ̌-rì castrated ox,
he-goat, whose testicles have been
removed; tí ágú-nǐ o'dú-o'du
rì ox whom man has castrated;
'bá ráó-rö eunuch.
ràorào-rö, a. thin, slight (of cloth,
paper); bɔ̀ŋgɔ́ ràorào-rì mbǎpi
kö-rì light cloth without resistance.
ràrào = éwí, ɔ́ó, lɔ́rí, n. ɛ̀'bí mà
r— fin of fish.
rǎù or rǎù ásí drì diaphragm.
rɛ̀¹, vt. (1) to peel, skin; ɛ̀i màákò
rɛ̌ they peel potatoes; dàktárì-nǐ
bélé rɛ̌ màkásì sì the doctor
exposes a sore with pincers; (2) to
rake, snatch up; andzi ɛ̀i àfa
mádrí rɛ̀rɛ̀ (= ari) àyǐi the
children go off with my things
openly.
rɛ̀², rɛ̀rɛ̀, tsɛ̀rɛ̀, äli, T., av. far,
distant; mukí rɛ̀rɛ̀/äli they went
(very) far; ɛ̀i si rɛ̀rɛ̀ they move/
build apart, separate; á nɛ̀ ɛ̀ri
rɛ̀rɛ̀rö I saw him at a distance.
rɛ, ɛrɛ́, q.v., vt. to disperse.
rɛ́ɛ̀, av. bare, barren, bleak; àŋgɔ̀
rɛ́ɛ̀ ásɛ́ kɔ́kɔ̀-rö a bleak spot (of

soil) without grass; ákúma mà drì èrì réè the top of an 'akuma' is bare.

réŋgè, răŋgè, S., see wúrá colour.

rèɛó = séì, élì, n. knife.

rèrè'úà, n. wild dog.

rì = vì, ndì, kà, vt. (1) to pinch off (a small bit); é rì (= kà) tíbí rìrì! pinch off small bits of savoury (at meals)! é rì zá kö, é ndì áŋgírí! do not spare meat, pinch off larger pieces/portions! (2) to economize with . . . èrì séntè rìrì/or séntè mà tà mbàmba he is sparing, economizing money/guarding it.

rrrì, av. giddily; mà drì-nì lì rrrì (or lìlì) my brain reels/head swims.

rï1, vt. to sow; má átìì èrì 'dô (or àɲû) rï ámvúa my father is sowing eleusine (simsim) in the field; èri òrì rï he sows seeds.

rï2, vn. (1) (also ɛrï) to sit; perch; àrïïá rï pätì sìa birds perch on trees; òrï vàá they sat down; a'ú rï ɓé drìá the hen sits on/hatches eggs; ɛ'yó rï drì-nì rá (i.e. ɛ'yó ndè èrì 'bə) the case 'sits' on him (he lost it); (2) to continue to . . .; èrì dì rï ɛ'yó 'dà òrà he continues to think/muse about the matter; rì dì mu ámvúá o'dú táa he continues to go into the field every day.

ri, vt. (1) 'bá drì ri to punish, correct a p.; èrì mvá 'ì-drí-rì mà drì ri he is punishing his own child; àzí 'bâ drì ri-zô-rì penalty work; dri-ri-ma = drì-ri-táa (= p'áŋgá, òyá), n. punishment, correction, fine, penalty (compensation, return, equivalent); (2) ri = òrí to appropriate (by insolence and/or force); èrì mà búkù ri (= pa)

he is snatching away my book (without much ado).

rî, rîdrì, àkú-drì instead of more common èrî, q.v., n. courtyard.

rïïá, n. spurting of spittle; èrì rïïâ ɓï he sprinkles spittle (on spitting).

ríaría1 = óndzáíïá, q.v., n. red pepper, paprika.

ríaría2, av. chronically (cf. əfí).

ríaría, n. disease affecting bones; èrì su 'bá àfàláa 'dálé it affects one's bones; èrì 'bâ pá lì emú èrì dí ɛ'dô su ndò it attacks (first) one's legs (and other parts) which then begin to be painful.

rí'bí = mbítrí, n. blood-sucking horn; èì ànì àrî ndzu they suck blood with it.

rìètsà = òrègè, cf. prìtsò, n. spur of fowl, &c.

rímàkò sì = òkpó sì, èrî sì, av. firmly, tightly.

ríŋgbílí, av. exactly, accurately, indelibly; ma sáwà mà éfí nì r— I understand the meaning/purpose of a watch exactly.

ríŋgbili*rö, av. immovable, fixed on the spot; pätí 'dǎ r—, andzi bï ɛsɛ tí the (big) trunk is immovable, the boys try in vain to drag it.

rìŋgbìli-rìŋgbìli, av. improperly, ineffectually (handling instruments); èrì ŋgâ ga r—r— he (say a dreamer) works the field ineffectually (as he would hold the hoe, maybe, edge turned upwards).

ríŋgə-ríŋgə, av. rolled up, cowering; laa rö r— he lies curled up; tra rö r— òmbà sì he cowers on the ground in his (impotent) anger.

ríɔríɔ, àɲá ríɔríɔ, n. gecko; rùànì yéŋgérékè-rö its body is coarse.

rĩrí, av. thoroughly (by twining a thing around repeatedly with rope ...); inextricably; (= kĩrikĩrí) firmly; mĩ dĩ tĩ èkïlà báká sĩ r—! tie the ox (encircling) with rope thoroughly!

rïíti = kĩrí, tĩlí, trĩtrí, durù, av. definitively, for good; é mu a'á r— 'dálé à'dò 'ye yà? for what purpose have you gone there to stay?

rò, vn. (1) = ŋga to sprout, come forth, grow; èríbé 'dĩ rörò the new grass is coming forth (tender àró˚rö);(2) to be fat, stout (baby); òdékòlïã èri rörò the baby is well-rounded; mvá rǒpi ròrò a well-fed baby.

ro, vt. to respect, treat with consideration ...; ro 'ïmà átĩí, or ópí he respects his father, chief; rotáa, n. respect; authority, majesty.

rə, vt. to bewitch; òlè'bá (i.e. ágú òlè berĩ) èri 'bâ ròrə a sorcerer bewitches man; mbàzà rə èri òlè sĩ the old man bewitched him with magic; èrïmà rúá-nĩ àzó ànĩ àzó-àzó whence he became sick; rə mánĩ tĩ nĩ he bewitched a cow of mine.

rò¹, vt. (1) to court; mu záa-mvá mà ùú rò (or 'bǎ) he went to lie on the arm (as a kind of pillow) of a girl; ùú rò/ or 'bǎ to place arm (a girl's). (2) záa rò-zö or azi-zö to ask a girl's consent (to marriage).

rò², av. or intj. actually, as a matter of fact; mvá rò tá ə'á 'dó; mu ndró ŋgò sĩ áánĩ, 'bá áó èri nè kö the boy was actually here just now; where can he have gone unnoticed, that he is seen no more.

rò³, av. kirr (onomat.); vù bòŋgó drísà 'a rĩ rò he draws the window-curtains back kirrr.

rò! interj., angry exclamation, confirmation of a determination! 'so it has to be!'; àfa 'dĩrï mânĩ rò!(òókó sĩ angrily) this thing remains mine (i.e. I'll not part from it)!

ròà, av. amiss, in vain; gbï ròà, gbï pĩ kö he shot amiss, not hitting.

ròbí, n. hippopotamus; èri mëërïá it is in the Nile.

ròdókò, n. a tree.

rədzí, n. a weed (resembling eleusine; it is believed the latter turns into the former); òsì rö 'dó be òsì-òsì it resembles eleusine.

ròé˚rö, a. long and thin.

rágbó˚rö, a. fat.

ròrgbô, n. stinginess, meanness; èrïmà r— tòö he is very stingy (= èri èkpéré be); èri àfà ŋaa r— sĩ he eats his things meanly (alone).

ròòké, ròòkó, n. a vulture; èrì zâ ŋa; ti-nĩ tsï èdrí lé it feeds on flesh; its beak cuts like a razor.

rökö-rökö or rókò-rókò = rùkù-rùkù, aká, a. soft, tender, mellow; ósǒ bbï kà mbàmba, é 'bà a'dĩ àtsĩa, eri a'dĩ r—r— when bean-leaves are hard, you put them on the fire for cooking and they become tender.

ròlè-ròlè = ndzòlà-ndzòlà, a. slippery (polished); òdrí r—r— (-rö) clay is slippery.

ròléè (?), n. a'ú 'bíkə òlómò (or òlö'bò) or a'ú mà r— down of fowls.

ròŋà-ròŋà = mènè-mènè, a. soft, mellow; màákò avo r—r— potatoes are stewed soft.

rörö, n. long tapering fishing basket; r— è'bí-nĩ fĩ-zö basket for fish to enter (and be caught; other baskets: èmbítïá, bbĩlĩ very big); **èri əzó nï** it is made of (split) reed stalks.

rótsókò = ètsikítsi, n. bird— snipe; **èrì tsa mba nna sï** it arrives in March.

ròwíá ̱rö, =röé ̱rö, a. long and thin.

rú, n. name; **mï rú à'dï 'ï yà?** what is your name? **mã rú Tsíká** my name is 'Tsika'.

ru¹, vt. (1) (= **bï, kə**) to seize, catch, arrest; **àskárì ru 'bá títí** the police caught him firmly; (2) (= **bï, əmbé**), vn. to clot, congeal, coagulate; **ədo ru 'ï tsí** the (melted-down) fat congealed, became thick; **ègbè oru ma tsí** cold 'congeals' (makes me stiff).

ru², vt. to pair, copulate; **móníó ru** (= **àmvà**) **tí kàrïï (-rï) 'bə** the bull had already covered the heifer.

rû = ndró(á), av. unexpectedly, suddenly; unnoticed; **etsá rû** he arrived unexpectedly.

rù = rǎu, av. lapping, sipping; **ma e'dï mvu rù** I take/drink the gruel in sips.

rùá, occasionally **rùbá**, n. body (of anything); **mâ rùá àzó bɛ** I am ill; **rùá(a) (-nï)** pstp. on (it . . .).

rùarùa, a. watery, thin-liquid; **e'dí r—** the gruel is too thin.

ruùá, av. sinking in (as in mud); **á sò pá 'bílía r—** I put a foot on a hole, sinking in.

rùgbə̂ = àgbûá-rìgbə̂, òŋgb(ó)á, n. great bustard (?); **drì-nï tólókpá ̱rö** its head is bare; **èri kùlû ŋa** it eats grasshoppers, insects.

rùkùrùkù-rö, a. (1) soft, yielding; **ámvú akázà-rï èri r—, 'bá tsɛ rö 'anïá tsɛ** a soft (freshly worked) field is yielding, one breaks in; (2) av. rattling; **'bá àzó ̱rö èri**

'yɛ r—, atsɛ wɛrɛ èri-nï 'dɛ-zó a sick p. has the rattling in his throat, when he is about to die.

rúkùsà, S.A., permit; Lgb. **ɛ'yó a'ï** to ask permit.

rúmu = rú-òmú, n. namesake; **mã rúmu: dèrè èmï rú sì rö èri bɛ sìsì** my namesake: it happens that your names are the same (as his).

rutsurutsu, rustu, ̱rö, a. tender, soft, unsteady; **ásí-nï rutsu-rï** he is light, frivolous, wanton, inconsiderate, impatient.

S

sa¹, vt. (1) to dig in (fruit kernels of any kind); **màákò, gbándà, fúnò, ékáká, óső, mòèmbè . . . sa** to plant potato (twigs), manioc (plant pieces), ground-nut, maize, beans, mango . . . ; (2) to bury; **èì 'bá sa 'bílía** they bury a man in a hole/grave.

sa², vt. to smack, slap a p.'s face (with flat of hand)/to box a p.'s ears; **sa ma áyámvó drí sï** lit. he smacked my temple with his hand; **sa mvá 'dǎrï kái rá** he slapped that boy's face hard.

sà¹, vt. (1) to plead/speak for, to side with, back up; **èri ma sà ópí drìléa** he spoke for me before the chief; **mu ópí-nï sǎ ma sï** he pleaded with the chief for me; (2) to assist, advise; **à'dï-nï mu àma sà ɛ'yó əndzí-rïá nï yà? àma atápi-nï yə-á-rï** who will assist us in trouble, as our father is no more; **'bá ma sǎpi yə** I have no support/advocate.

sà², vn./vt. (1) = **wè** to swim; **èri ìï sà (wè)** he swims; **mï laa rö ìï drìá** you lie on the water; (2) to fly; **àrïïá-nï sǎsà** or **ŋgàŋga** the

bird is flying; **ndégè-nï ɛ̀sǎ**
(= **ɛŋgǎ**) **'dà** an aeroplane is
flying in there; (3) to drive off
birds; **mvá 'dàrï àrïîá sǎ**
(= **drə**)**àŋá 'aléa** that boy drives
off the birds from the corn; (4)
vn. **ásí sà 'ï** to be satisfied,
satiated; **ɛ̀rimà ásí sà 'ï 'bə** he
is now satisfied (from eating).
sàá = **sàá²rö, sàká²rö, sàm-
bàlà-rö, wèwè-rö,** av. aimlessly,
at random; **ɛ̀ri atsí sàá²rö**
(= **bàdàrö**), **ɛtsá nï èivélé kö**
he walked aimlessly, he did not
reach home; **é 'yə mání ɛ'yó
sàá²rö** you talked confusedly to
me; **mï àfà 'yɛ sàârö** you do
things at random.
sándǎ, S., n. bag (with draw-
strings); **dǎ àŋá s— 'aléa** they
pour corn into the bag.
sànóà, S., n. comb; **s— drì-bbí
'alé əndzɛ** (= **ɛŋgá**) **-ző** comb to
straighten hair.
sàrà, av. in **àŋgὸ s—** it begins
dawning; **óú ŋgà kö** the day has
not yet broken; **a'ú-átá-nï tsérè
ə'bɛ̌ àŋgὸ s— sǐ** the cock crows
at the beginning of dawn.
sàràsàrà, av. not full; **àfa gǎpi
kö-rǐ 'bá əmvɛ s—** they say that
a thing that does not fill is **s—**; **ǐ
ga tsúpà 'aléa s—** the bottle is
not full of water.
sátï, S., n. shirt.
sɛ, ɛsέ, vt. to pull, drag, draw; (1)
to pull . . .; **é sɛ àfa 'dǐ 'dálέ!** pull
this thing there! **se A'íiá mà bbí**
he pulled A'iia's ear; **é sɛ ma
'dálέ à'do sǐ yà?** why do you
drag me there? (2) **sɛ** (= **sǐ**) **rö,**
vr. to withdraw, retire; **é sɛ mï
'dálέ!** withdraw there! **Ɔkpὸyə
ɛsέ rö 'bə** Ok— has drawn closer;
(3) **ɛrɔ̀ sɛ** (or **tsə**) to prepare and
make a granary; **èi ɛrɔ̀ sɛ pätí,**

báká sǐ they make a granary with
sticks, rope; (4) **arî sɛ** to tune a
drum by pulling its strings; **é sɛ
arí rímàkὸ sǐ** pull the drum
tightly! (5) to inhale; **ávâ sɛ** to
draw a deep breath; **àdzí-nǐ sɛ**
(or **ŋgù**) to take a deep breath (to
smell); **ɛ̀ri tábà sɛ** he smokes
tobacco; (6) **e'dî sɛ** or **mvu** to
sip (drink) gruel; (7) to stir; **ɛ̀ri
ɛ́ŋá 'alê sɛ** (**əsέ**) **lúfέ sǐ** she is
stirring polenta with a stirring-
stick; (8) **sɛ 'ï,** vr. to drag o-s.
along, to move/proceed with
difficulty; **drà, έwá ndè ɛ̀ri rá,
sɛ rö àkúalέ sɛ̀sɛ** overcome by
illness, drunkenness, he reached
home with difficulty.
sɛ-zà = **sɛ̌sɛ, sɛkɛdɛlɛ, sɛ̀kέ-
sέkɛ,** (vn.) a. (1) tough, hard (to
masticate); **zá a'dǐ mőkέ kö, mǐ
tsï tǐ: zá sɛ̀sɛ** the meat is not
well cooked, you cannot bite it,
the meat is tough; (2) tough,
tenacious; **báká sɛ̌sɛ, mu ə'bǐ
atsé tǐ** the rope is strong, one
tries to tear it in vain; (3) viscous,
sticky; **ésέsέ ɛ̀ri ɛsέ** (= **tilikpa**)
²rö the glue is viscous, elastic;
(4) spun out, drawling; slow—
clear; **é 'yə ɛ'yó mbɛ̀lɛ̀mbɛ̀lɛ̀ kö,
mǐ ɛ'yó sɛ̌sɛ!** do not speak so
quickly, speak slowly!
sɛ̀ɛ, sɛ̀ɛ-zà, sɛ̌pi sɛ̀sɛ̀-rǐ (vn.) a.
plain, level; **ndzilá ɛ̀ri sɛ̀ɛrö**
the road is plain; **à lè àŋgὸ
sɛ̀ɛrǐ, mùpírà tsə-ző** we want/
need a level ground to play football.
sέi-sèi, rèeó, n. a dagger-like
knife, dagger.
sɛ̀ndɛ̀, av. sprawling; **rǐ vàá s—,
èdzù pá kpïï** he sits sprawling on
the ground, the legs stretched out;
ɔ̀kpɔ̀rɔ̀vὸ rǐ s— nǐ a woman big
with child sits on the ground with
outstretched legs.

sèērí = kaali, n. fence; èì s— tsə dzɔ́ (or, sometimes, ámvú) (mà) àgàí-á they make a fence round a hut (with small yard) (or field).

sèrìbì = àúsέrὲ, n. cobweb (various kinds); ànìkánì ὲrì s— ɛdɛ́ the spider makes cobwebs.

sέrɛ (-sέrɛ) = 'dέrɛ'dέrɛ, av. level; lining up straight èì rö òtì trɔ́trɔ̀; ìí ga á'búá s— the water (of swollen river) fills the valley to the level of the banks; Ɛɳáó tì/ga sέrὲ (= tré), the Enyao river is full to the level of the shore.

sέsέlɛ́ = ǹdzíiá, n. an ear ornament.

sí, n. point; (1) tooth; mâ sí my tooth; tí sí a cow's teeth; sí-lɛ́ gap in teeth (missing); 'bá sílɛ́ bɛ gap-toothed p.; sî-zá (or ɔ̀ttrɔ̆), gums; sí-sɔ̀ = ágbárágbù, n. angle/joint of jaw; sí-drìlɛ́ edge of teeth; (2) edge; àdzú-sí edge of spear; ëlï ὲrì sí bɛ the knife has a sharp edge; sí-kɔ́kə̀ᵃrö blunt-edged; (3) point (of instrument, &c.); kàlámù sí pen-nib; point of pencil; (4) elevated part; pätí sí up on a tree; àrïïá rï pätí síá the bird perches in the tree; cf. pätí drìà on a piece of wood; (5) the grain (of flour); 'i àɳá mà sí èníkὲnì/ = 'i àɳá tékὲtékὲ she ground the corn fine; (6) flavour ... à'í mà sí drầdra (= ɔ̀ká) the salt tastes sharp/ bitter.

sí, n. hail (-stone); ssí-nï 'dɛ it hails; ssí-nï kàïkɔ̀ tsə hail strikes the beans (damaging).

sì¹, pstp. with, from; out of, on account of, &c.; ëlï sì with a knife.

sì², vt. to scratch; (1) to scratch, mark out; ὲrì mu dzɔ́ ǹdú sì he goes to sketch the plan of a hut (on the ground); to outline; (2) to draw, delineate; to write wárágà sì; (3) to scrape, rub; é sì tìbìrítì! strike, light the match! àfa zïa-nï sì ma bììrì (= drɔ̀zàrö) sth. has produced streaks on my arm.

sì³, vt. to tear; (1) to tear (up); rend (asunder), split; to wear out; é sì mâ bɔ̀ŋgɔ́ 'alé yà? why have you torn my cloth? bɔ̀ŋgɔ́ sì rö trầa the cloth rent with noise; (2) to pull (or tear, wrench) off; mà mu kàká sì ámvúá edzí àkúa I am going to pull off corn-cobs and take (them) home; èì pätí òpìrìkàlá sì they tear twigs off a tree; èì báká sì, ə'bé-zà-rö ǹdrí bâ-rö they wrench off fibre, to twist for ropes for goats; (3) to cut up (in slices); èì mààkò (or gbándà) sì mòtéréᵃrö they cut up potatoes (manioc roots) into slices (for drying and keeping).

sì⁴ (= awí) rö ko to (separate from companions and) lag behind; sì ko 'ï/= awî ko tsúùá 'àlé he remained behind in the market.

sì¹, vn. to fit; (1) to be fit(-ted, adapted, suitable) for; bɔ̀ŋgɔ́ 'dï sì ma rá this cloth fits me well; mbégò sì rö bɔ̀ŋgɔ̂ bá-lɛ́ kö sisal is not suitable for a garment belt; àzí ɳaaká a'dï-zɔ̀rï sì ɔ̀kɔ́ï rá the work of cooking is becoming to women; (2) to meet, suit a p.'s wishes; to be to a p.'s taste, agree with ...; mòémbὲ sì ma tɔ̀: mòémbὲ kɔ̀ré fu ma tɔ̀ a mango is very much to my taste: I am very fond of mangoes; àŋgɔ̀ Árúwá 'dɔ̀ sì ma 'bə I have become accustomed to the country of Arua; àzí sì àndrò-nï má kö I do not feel like work today; (3) sì rö sìsì to resemble, be equal, identical; òlɛ́ sì rö à'bòà bɛ sìsì Musa-Ensete resembles a banana (plant); èri tibbí kókɔ́ᵃrö sì mídrí-rì lɛ́ he is beardless like yourself.

sì², vt. to knock; (1) to knock, rap, tap (as with front of fist); sì ma drí sì they punched me with the hand (fist); sì 'ïmà kòmu pätí rùá tù he banged (with) his knee against a wooden prop; é sì kòmu vàá! bend your knee!/or kneel down! (2) to batter, ram down the ground; èri pätí ètí sì pätí sì èri-nï pá sɔ̀-zɔ̌ mɔ̌ké benì he is ramming the pole in the ground with a cudgel, that it may stand properly upright; (3) to crush, grind, smash (up); èri áɳú (also óɳa) sì érà drìá she grinds/crushes simsim (termites) on a stone; (4) drì sì (= ègɔ̀, atri, epakǎ), vt. to turn, drive back; to refrain, keep back from . . . ; é mu ǹdrí drì sì! go and turn back the goat(s)! é sì èimà drì mu-zɔ̌ 'dálɛ́ (or Árúwá)-rì-á tsí! keep them from going there (to Arua)! é sì mî drì tsí! control your feelings!/keep your temper! (5) 'dúkù-nï ma sì I have the hiccoughs.

sï = ndzɛ, ɛdé, vt. to clean, remove; é sì mï òmvu sí! clean your nose! èri òmvu sî sï àmvé he cleans his nose outside; drì-nï sï-zà-rö he is bald-headed; ɔ̀pé mà drì sï 'ï tsé nì the guineafowl's head is bare by nature.

sì¹, vt. (1) to build; èi dzɔ̂ si they are building a hut; èi óɳà si ɔ̀drí sì, èri-nï ɛ'dé-zɔ̌, ɛndzó-zɔ̌ they make a clay-trap for termites, that they may fall in, for collecting them; (2) to make (pottery); èi

émvó/tídzɔ̂ si ɔ̀drí sì, èi ŋga ɛvé (or ɔvé) àtsí sì they make pots with clay and burn them with fire.

si², vn. (1) to go downwards, descend (as, from mountain, tree); si 'bílé 'aléa vàá 'dálé he descended far down into the pit; tí èi si ìî mvu ìí-á cattle go down to the river to drink; si ìî edzí ìí-á she went down to the river to fetch water; é si vàá! go down! mï esí vàá! come down! (2) to recede; Ɛɳáó si (or ra) 'bɔ the Ɛnyao river has already receded; (3) rarely si = sɛ or dà, vn. to withdraw, pass by.

sí yà? how many? ǹdrí sí yà? how many goats? ètú (sáwà) tsa sí yà? what is the time?/lit. how much has the sun reached? sí-sí yà? how much each? èmï awa mòèmbè sísí yà? how many mangoes have you distributed to each p.?

sidráà, S. = gbɔlɔ, n. bedstead; s— 'bá tï ɔ̀zɔ̌ (or ɔ́drá, édzófɛ) sì, báaká sì they make it by fastening with string reed stalks (bamboo, &c.).

sílé¹, n. ? top; ètú sílé bright sunshine, sunbeams; ètú s— drï 'dïnï! how the sun burns! sí lɛ́, cf. sí.

sílé²: ásí sílé, n. mind; concept, idea, thought; ádzɛ̂ ma ɔ̀rà ásísílé 'examination' mà drìá yesterday I thought about the examination.

sìndání, S., n. needle; ma bákâ sö s— mà tálá I am threading a needle.

sí-nï-á up on it; tu sí-nï-á he mounted it (tree).

síósíó, n. grey-brown locust with long tapering head.

sírĭbá, n. (1) amulet, a charm against disease; èì s— sǔ gbɔlɔ ètĭa dáwàrö they put the charm under the bed as a medicine; (2) poison bag of snake orí mà sírĭbá.

sírĭlĭ = sĭsírĭlĭ, av. extremely; àŋgǒ ambí àndrò sírĭlĭ-rö it is extremely cold today.

sírĭlĭá = sírĭá⌐rö, a./av. very narrow (of opening); ɛná sírĭlĭâ-rö it is visible through a narrow opening/a fissure.

sĭrĭkali⌐rö = badrikiɔ⌐rö, a. upright, healthy and strong, robust, energetic; èrì mu rǔá s— he walks along upright and robust.

sísí, n. kind of mania; it is used, apparently, only in the following two instances: (1) drí sísí kleptomania (lit. mania of hands); mĭ drí sísí (-àfa ògù-zǒ-rĭ) your hand is 'mad' (in stealing/laying hands on everything you see); (2) àṇà sísí mania of copying others' actions; 'dĭ ma mà àṇà sísí tǒ; mĭ milɛ àtsí tǒ; mĭ ŋga ɛ'yɔ́ ɛsú rá this p. has a mania for copying me; you are extremely forward; you will get into trouble.

sǒ = dà, vt. (1) to pour; é sǒ (= tɔ) ĭí tsúpà 'aléa! pour (fill) water into the bottle! èì ésé sǒ p'úá(ká) 'aléa they pour glue into a 'p'ua' hollow stem (for keeping); (2) to cover, coat, overlay; èì pätí sǒ ésé⌐rö they coat a branch with glue; (3) to pass urine; mu ɔdrɛ sǒ or (more refined) àmà ŋgà mu ĭí dǎ went to . . ., or we are going to make water; (4) (ɔsǒ) to pour, throw over; èrì ĭí ɔsǒ pätí drĭá he is watering the plants; sǒ ĭí 'ĭ drĭá he poured water over his head; or: èrì mvá ɔsǒ ĭí sĭ she is pouring water over the child;

èri lésú sö/or zɔ̆ gùrɛ/gélékóa sĭ she pours milk (into something) by means of a (kind of) funnel.

sö, vt. (1) to put/push in; ma drî sö ɔkpɔ́rɔa I put the hand into my pocket; sö mĭ drì ĭĭá he pushed your head into/under water; é sö mà̤ kaká àtsĭa, mà ɔzɔ́ anï! push my maize-cob into the fire for roasting! (2) to fill up, stuff; sǒ ásé dzɔ́ mà drì-á they filled in grass into the roof; (3) àfa mà tĭ sö to stop, plug up; to cork (bung) up; é sö (or 'bà) ti-nï tsĭ! cork it up! èì màakò mà tĭ sö émvó sĭ they cover the potatoes (on fire) with a pot; mĭ èfè àfa tsúpà tĭ sö-zǒ! give me sth. to stop up the bottle; èì ĭí tĭ sö kótà sĭ they stop the water-pot with a 'kɔta'-plug; (4) to poke/ stir a fire; to kindle/light; é sö àtsí rrĭ, mà dì anï ɔkpɔ́ sĭ! poke the fire that it may blaze up well! é sö mà̤ tábà féfò 'aléa! fill up my pipe with tobacco! (5) to dive; sö 'ĭ ĭí ṅdú-á (è'bí-lɛ́) he dived (lit. pushed himself) under water (like a fish); (6) drì sö (= ɛló) to bend (one's head), bow down (vàá); kàni mĭ ɛló (= sö) andrati vàá, èì 'yɔ kèni: sö milɛ vàá when you incline your head, they say, he cast down his eyes; èrì 'ĭ drì sö vàá he inclines/bows his head; (7) to slander, calumniate, defame; to denounce a p. to . . . = 'bá sö 'bá àzĭ mà ti-á; é sö mvá 'dĭrï ɛmbápi mà tiá à'do sĭa? why did you denounce/or slander this boy to the teacher? é dzi mà̤ sö (= tɔɔ) ṇ̩ampára mà ti-á tsĭ you have defamed me before the headman; (8) àsǒ (or ɛ'yɔ) sö 'bá mà rǔá ('bá àzĭ vǒ) to denounce, accuse; to sue, bring (or enter) an action against; sö àsɔ̌ mã rùá rá or sö mã rùá àsɔ̌ ópí vɔ̌ rá he brought an action against me before the chief; à'dï-nï té àsɔ̌ sö 'dínï nï yà? who has ever disclosed matters like this?! á sö ma tsɛ́-nï áda indeed, I betrayed myself (imprudently); (9) ɔ̀mbà sö to incite, egg on; to stir up strife between...; ɛ̀rì ɔ̀mbà sö èìmà ásía ... èìnï rɔ̂ tsɜ-zɔ̌ he is stirring them up to fight among themselves; á sö ɔ̀mbà mvá 'dǐ mà 'bílía ... 'bá àzî tsɜ-zɔ̌ I insinuated/whispered bad things into the boy's ears, that he may beat sby.

sɔ̀ (ɔ̀sɔ̀), vt. (1) to prick, sting; líbìrà sɔ̀ ma nǐ a needle has pricked me; ɔ̀sɔ̀ ɛ̀rì 'yɛ́ sǐ he pricked him repeatedly with an arrow; (2) to stitch, sew; ma bɔ̀ŋgó sɔ̀ sindánì sǐ I am sewing a cloth with the machine; (3) to strike (lightning); ɔ̀vï sɔ̀ tí rá the lightning struck a cow; (4) to overtake, surprise a p. (death ...); drà sɔ̀ ɛ̀rì káyì death took him unawares; (5) to stand, make halt; é sɔ̀ pá kpii! stand upright! é sɔ̀ pá ɛ'yó 'dǐ mà drì(lí)á mí 'ï! do yourself answer/account in this matter!, i.e. responsibility rests with you; (6) ti sɔ̀ to put forth roots ...; àn̩á-nǐ ti sɔ̀ the corn puts forth its first roots ...; 'dɔ̌ sɔ̀ ti ɛ̀rì-nï èfɔ̌-zɔ̌ ànï eleusine seeds have germinated, when it is about to come forth (to surface); (7) drì sɔ̀ to put or fall into line (i.e. one after another!); àma-nï mu-rǐá drì àsɔ̀-rö when we are walking in single file; yúkú ɛ̀sɔ̀ drì (n̩d)rwǐ̈ the goshawks come along in a line;

sɔ̌ drì sɔ̀ they fell into a single file; (8) ɔ̀yɔ̀ sɔ̀ (= etrí 'ï) to pin down an arrangement (arbitrarily; cf. ɔ̀yɔ̀), to put in force a protestation, a solemnly (or simply) or energetically declared determination (without any appeal to spirits, &c.; but automatically the realm of magic takes hold of it, after a few days; ɔ̀yɔ̀ su/ka rá and punishes the protestor, if the arrangement is, in any way or by anybody—bona fide or otherwise, frustrated); é sɔ̀ té ɔ̀yɔ̀ rá 'bɜ; ... mã ŋgà mu àfa 'dà 'du; ... ɛ̀rì ŋga drǎ rá; nɔ̀ ɔ̀vï-nï ɛ̀rì sɔ̀ ànï; nɔ̀ órí-nï ɛ̀rì tsï nǐ ... thou hast set up an arrangement (say, that a certain thing shall not be taken away); now I (or anybody) may take that thing away; (as a result) he (the protestor) may die; or the lightning may strike him; or a snake may bite him; (9) ɛ'yó sɔ̀ 'alé to set or find hindrance, impediment, obstacle; ɛ̀rì ɛ'yó 'alé sɔ̀ he raises difficulties; ɛ'yó (ɔ̀ndzí) sɔ̀ 'a-nï-á tsí áánï, á nì kö there may be obstacles in the way, I do not know; Ɔndzɔmáá sɔ̀ 'alé-nï tsí áánï, á nì kö O— has possibly raised difficulties (to it), I do not know.

sɜ = tra, vt. (1) to collect (contributions); n̩àmpárà ɛ̀rì àn̩áfɔ̌râ sɜ kàíkɜ bɛ ópí drí (or dzɔ́agó drí) the headman collects flour and beans for the chief (subchief); andzi séntì sɔ́pi Ėklésyà-árǐ boys who collect cents in the church; (2) to contribute; yúkú sɜɜkí 'bíkɜ ètɔ́ɜ nï àlö-àlö the goshawks each contributed a feather for the hare (fable).

só = otsí, n. barb; gɔ̀ndɛ̀ ɛ̀rì só bɛ the 'gɔndɛ' arrow has barbs.

sòátà, S., n. flannel.

sóbí = sófé, sábí, sáfí, n. tail (of birds, animals . . .).

sòééri = ǹdíkǎ, n. a grasshopper.

sòfòríà, S., n. (imported) metal cooking pot.

sókà, S., n. sheet; piece of 'amerikani' cloth.

sókólèkɛ = pádzàmà, S.?, n. undergarment, underwear; èi-nï àkpà-zó ìrrìrì sì when they put one over another.

sóksì, Engl. n. socks.

sóŋgóló = ósómbílí, n. small projection in centre of upper lip.

sòrò = mŋgbílí, n. African game of draughts; s— ŋaa to play at draughts.

sóró = zɛkí, daaká, n. dregs, refuse; àŋú s— refuse from honey, i.e. wax; èdzí s— = èdzí zɛkí, éwá s— = éwá ìí mà zè dregs of beer (from straining).

sòróni, S., n. excrement, dung (= zè).

sòròwàlì = páli, S.?, n. trousers —shorts.

ssu or su, ŋumber 4, four.

sú, n. sap; juice; (1) gravy, broth (zá) à'í sú; (2) pätí sú sap (tree); (3) àŋú sú (= ósò, òdo) honey; (4) pus; sú (= (è)vì) bélé mà 'aléa tsí the sore has pus; bélé sú; (5) extract of . . . .

sù, vt. to put on, dress; èri bòŋgó sù he is dressing; mvá 'dà sù mèndalì that child put on a medal; òkó èi ayébbì sù women don leaves; záa-mvá 'dà sù émvè 'ïmà pá that girl put rings on her legs.

su¹, vt. (1) to wash (collectedly); èi líkíŋá (or màákò . . .) su ìí sì they wash yams (potatoes) (all together) in water; (2) = dzì to express (pulp); kàíkò (mà 'bíkó) su to express the pulp of (cooked) beans from covering.

su² = bì, kə, vn. (1) to catch, take effect (charm); òyò-nï su/ka rá the pledge has 'caught' (cf. sò, 8); (2) to prosper, be favourable; àdzì su kö luck was not with me; èrimà àdzì su tsí he is lucky; ma àdzè su tóö my (sale-) business prospers much.

su³, vn. to cause pain, ache; àdrákà-nï su 'bá mà àsí-á 'poison' aches within one's breast; àzô su mâ rùá I am sick; pá-nï sùsu his leg pains.

sùïsùí = sùúsùú, n. very small grey bird, seed-eating (in undergrowth).

sùŋgúrù, n. a mid-size beetle; èri ə'á áìsè mà sía is found on grass.

sùrà-sùrà better ëni s—s—, a. blue.

surú, n. a kind of (slippery) underwater weed (on stones or free in stagnant water) (? Conferva bombycina) ìí-á óní mà rùá, nósì ìí ráápi kö-rì mà 'aléa or ìí kálá ti-á on the side of water; kànì əzôô 'di àmbóⁱrö, ìí kà tìtì, ìí ŋgà ra surú bɛ rá when it has rained heavily and the river rises, the water flows off with the weeds. Hence: surúⁱrö = surúkà-rö, èríbíⁱrö, a. green; ìí mà milé s— the water looks green (from the aforesaid water-weeds).

súrú, n. used for clan, tribal group, kingship group; s— èmïdrí à'do-kò-nï yà? s— àma-drí Pàdzùlú? to which tribe do you belong? I am of Padzulu.

T

tà¹ = ŋaaká, n. food; tà ŋaa-zà food to eat; á lè tà ŋaa I want to eat; ŋaa tà 'bə he has eaten; lï mà tà dε rá he has finished my food.

tà², n. the formal auxiliary noun of some expressions; (1) **'bá mà tà mba** to protect, guard, defend a p.; **é mba mvá mà tà mŏkɛ́!** look after the child well! **Àdrɔ́ ɛ'yɔ́ mà tà mba-zŏ** to observe, execute the word/command- (ment)s of God; (2) to keep, save, preserve, lay up, put by; **ɛ̀ri àŋá (ɔ́sŏ) (mà) tà mba ɛ̀rɔ́-á** he keeps food (beans) in the granary; (3) to threaten, menace a p.; **'bá mà tà** (better **ə̀mə̀kɔ́**) **lï** (= **tï**) (cf. **ə̀mə̀kɔ́**); (4) **g̈bà ma tà** he has struck me, &c.

tàa³, av. brightly; **àŋg̈ò èfŏ tàa** (= **ńdrrá**) there is a bright light.

tá, T. alias **té**, av. (only within the day!) before, a moment ago, just now (past); **atsá tá mávŏ rá** he came to me just now; **tá**, a. **tá-/ té-rï̀** = **táká-rï̀** the aforeseen or spoken-of; **ág̈ú térï̀** the aforesaid man; **wárág̈à tá(ká)rï̀** the afore- mentioned piece of paper.

ta, vn. (1) **àzɔ̂ ta** to groan, sigh; **ɛ̀ri ŋg̈à kírí àzɔ́-nï̀ tàta** he con- tinues to bemoan his sickness; (2) **àfa mà àvâ ta** (**ásí sï̀**) to have a (great) desire, longing, wish for...; to long for; to hanker, crave after (for); **ɛ̀ri ǹdrí** (or **éŋá**) **'dï̀ mà àvâ ta** (**ásí àlö sï̀**/or **'bà ásí drì- nï̀-á**) he longs for this sheep (polenta) (with his whole heart); **é ta 'bá àzí mà àfa (mà) àvá kö!** do not hanker after another's goods!

táa = **tátá, trátrá, zù** (= **pḯrí** all), av. always; **o'dú táa** every day, daily; **ɛ̀ri mu 'dálé o'dú trátrá** he goes there every day.

tábà, A.S., n. tobacco; cigarettes...

lè t—sɛ (= **mvu**) he wants to smoke.

t'ắí, tàí, n. astonishment, amaze- ment; **tàí kə** (= **sï**) **'bá tsí** (= **'bá òsù**) to be astonished, surprised, marvel (at **sï̀**); **tàí kə ma àmbó mà ɛ'yɔ́ sï̀ tsí** I am astonished at the words/speech of the elder; **tàí mà sì** (= **kə**) **mï má sï̀ kö!/ ɛ'yɔ́ nĕ rï̀ sï̀** do not marvel at me!/at what they have seen; **ɛ̀ri àfa ɛdɛ̆ tàí⸜rö** (= **òsùzàrö**) he does amazing, wonderful things.

tákí = **trátrá**, av. continuously, constantly, incessantly, endlessly; **ɛ̀ri ɛ'yɔ́ 'yə t—, olíkə̀-nï̀ arí-arí** he speaks continuously, he is hoarse.

takpala = **talakpa** (q.v.).

tálá, tálé, n. (1) **bɔ̀ŋg̈ɔ́ t—** the transparency (through fine holes) of a cloth; **àfa mà t— 'dï̀** the fine openings of a texture...; **drì-bbí t—** the pores whence the hair comes forth; (2) the (enclosed, shut in) inside, interior of...; space inside...; folds; **bbí tálá** among the leaves of...; **àfa 'dï̀ mà t— hə** (or **mŋg̈bə**) (**mí etsi tsí!**) this thing is open, or hollow, empty... (shut it!); **tálá-nï̀-rï̀ mŋg̈bə** it is hollow inside; (3) hole; **lŏ t— nï̈ rá** he bored a hole in it.

talakpa, tàlàtàlà, takpala, ⸜rö, ada-zà-rö, a. insipid, flat, stale; tasteless (**àdzí-nï̀ alu kö**); **éká 'dï̀ mà sú talakpà̀-rö/à'í⸜rö, alu kö** this (sugar-)cane's juice is tasteless/bitter, not pleasant.

tálí = **'bìrï̆ndà**, n. marvel, miracle, supernatural sight; **ɛ'da 'ï tálí sï̀** she appeared in a marvellous/ supernatural way; **'bá drăpirï̀ rá, ɛ'dắpi ndɔ̀rï̀, àma əmvɛ 'ɛ'da rö àma-nï̀ tálí sï̀'** one who has died and then appears again, we say 'he appeared to us by miracle'.

tàalotàalo, av. scattered here and there; ɔzɔ́ɔ́ ɛ'dɛ́ àŋgà t— the rain fell only in scattered (big) drops; ɛrɛ́ 'ï t— it scattered all about.

táamvó = dràŋgà, n. pipe (for smoking); ɛ̀ri t— sɨ̀ tábà sɛ he smokes tobacco with a pipe.

tándí ≙ áda-rö, tsɛ́, av. truly, really; certainly, surely, undoubtedly; ɛ̀ri t— tsɨ́ = ɛ̀ri tsɛ́ tsɨ́ he certainly is present/or alive; ɛ̀ri t— (= tsɛ́) yɔ, fɔ̂! he is not present, to be sure, please!

tárà, S., n. lamp; mɨ́ àtsɨ́ 'dö tárà-ti-á! light the lamp!

tǎärí, n. any larger trunk, case; 'mɨ́ emú t— mânɨ́ 'dɨ̀ dzí 'dálɛ́!' ɔ́pɨ 'yɔ nɨ̌, mu-zö́ atsiá 'come and take this my luggage there!' says the chief, about to make a journey.

tátá = táa, q.v.

taáú, taawí, number 5, five; àfa 'dɨ̌ mà òpìrìkàlɛ́ t— this thing has five prongs; mɨ́ awa t—t—! divide it by five/giving each five.

tàvì, n.? forgetfulness, weak(ness of) memory; used with àvɨ̀; mà t— àvɛ̌ rá I have forgotten it (= tàvì-nï àvɛ̌ mánɨ́ rá); ɛ'yɔ́ tàvì àvɛ̌ mánɨ́ rá I have forgotten the word; á ŋaa zá o'dú taáú sɨ̀ tàvì (= drì-àvɨ̀) sɨ̀ I have eaten meat on Friday out of forgetfulness.

tàyà, -rö (1) a. with end spreading and forming a tuft; ɔlá mà sɔ́bɨ́ ɛ̀ri tàyà-rö (= gɔ̀ràgɔ̀rà-rö) the 'ɔla'-mouse's tail has a tuft; (2) tàyà, av. scattering (on the ground); à'í ɛ'dɛ́ t— i.e. ɛrɛ́ 'ï ndó-ndó the salt fell to the ground scattering about.

té = tá, T., av. a (little) while ago, a moment ago, just now; àvɛ̌ té mà drìá rá I had quite forgotten about it; é kènì té ma adri kàáti-á 'dɛ́ tsɨ́ you said a moment ago that I may stay there at the door; á nì té àfa 'dɨ̀rï rá I knew this before; té òku, té drìɔ, té 'dà, té 'dálɛ́ formerly, before, previously, already; long ago; at that time, even then; té- or téká-rɨ̀ of before, of that time . . . ; mɨ́ edzí á lù dɨ́ ɛ'dá tákárɨ̀ kö yà? do you not bring me the picture (photo) of that day to look at?

tê dɨ́, av. but, however.

tɛ̀¹, vt. (1) = ɔro to prepare (food); ɛ̀ri e'dɨ́(or ɛ́wá) tɛ she is preparing gruel (beer); (2) zɛ̀ tɛ to fart; mvá tɛ zɛ̀ the child farted.

tɛ̀¹, vn. tɛ̂tɛ, tɛ́pi, tɛ-zà, a. thick; stout, fat; búkù 'dà mà ti tɛ tö̀ (the side of) this book is thick; mvá 'dɨ̀rï tɛ (= ɔsɛ, ŋgö, ǎ'bu) -zà rö the baby is stout/fat; ɔ̀tsɛ tɛ-zàrö, i.e. ɔ̀tsɛ mà pätí-nï du tré, 'bá nɛ̀ ànï àŋgö̀ mɔ́kɛ́ kö the forest is 'dense', i.e. it is full of trees, one cannot see well in it, therefore.

tɛ̀¹, vt. (1) to wait for a p. 'bá àzí tɛ̌; é tɛ ma 'dòà! wait for me here! (2) to go to meet; 'bá drì tɛ̌; é mu mɨ́ átíi mà-drì tɛ̌! go to meet your father! (3) ɔ́ŋa tɛ̌ to tend and collect termites (when they swarm); (4) to (be on the) watch, to attend, to (keep) watch over, to keep one's eye upon, to guard àfa mà àgä(-í) tɛ̌; ɛ̀ri kaaká mà àgǎí tɛ̌ ɔ̀dzìatá sɨ̀ he guards the maize against baboons; ma ŋgà àfa àgaa tɛ̌ I am keeping an eye upon sth.

tɛ̀² = awɨ́, vn. to omit doing . . . ; á tɛ̀ (= ma awɨ́) ɔ̀góoá e'dú ko yé I neglected bringing the chair; á tè edzí ko yé (mà drì àvǐ ànï rá) I did not bring it (because I forgot about it).

tékè-tékè = **ëníkǐnì**, a. (1) fine, minutely; é 'i àn̠á, té mǐnï 'i (-lé) àgà-àgà 'dǐ, 'díká; é ŋga amví t—t—/or é ŋga/'yɛ amví ndɔ̀! grind the corn, you ground coarsely before again; grind it over finely! 'i àn̠á t—t—, àn̠á 'bíkɔ-nï ɘvö a'dúlɛ sǐ she ground the corn finely, so that the chaff was left behind; (2) brightly clean; mǐ ɘdzì bɔ̀ŋgɔ́ t—t—, mà adri ɛmvɛ ndríndrí! wash the cloth cleanly, that it may be dazzlingly white!

téo = **kɔ̀yɔ̀á, wékɛ́á,** n. gourd-rattle of sorcerers.

térrɛ́ = **térétɛ́rɛ́,** av. sluggishly, indolently, inertly, slow-moving; mǐ atsí t—t— 'dǐnï—àzî ŋga kɔ́kɔ-̩rö—à'dò 'yɛ yà? why are you sauntering about—without doing work—like this?

tèrèbúsì = **tàràbúsì,** A.S., n. the tarbush.

tǐ, av. in vain, without avail; á ndà sǐ tǐ, ma ɛsú kö I looked in vain for hailstones, I did not find any.

tǐ¹, = **ndzi,** vt. to strangle, choke; èri ma tǐtǐ báká sǐ he is about to strangle me with a rope; á 'bǐ màákò kǐ tǐ, èri ma tǐtǐ I tried in vain to swallow the potato, it is choking me; tǐ 'ǐ tǐ báká sǐ he hanged himself with a rope.

tǐ² = **osi,** vt. to bear, bring forth (of woman); to be born; ɔkó 'dǐ tǐ 'bɔ the woman was delivered/gave birth; cf. mvá tǐ 'bɔ a child was born (N.B. that woman is still labouring/in travail ɔkó 'dà èri ŋgà kírí tǐtì); ɔkó èri drùsǐ mu tǐ (= osi) mvá rá the woman

will be delivered of a child to-morrow.

tǐ,³ vt. to pick, pluck, gather; **mvá tǐ mùtsùŋgúà ndii** a child plucked a mandarin fruit secretly; èri én̠á tǐ sö mvá 'dǐ mà ti-léa she pulls off (small bits) polenta and puts it in the baby's mouth; ma ɔ́ga ètǐ tǐ rúá I am picking off ticks from a cow; ɘdrí tǐ to dig/break off (from pit...) clay (cf. atǐ); mǐ àfa tǐ 'bá rúá kö! do not be stingy (small bits) with people!

tǐ⁴, vn. to (make) progress, advance; àzí mǐnǐ ŋga 'dǐ tǐ kö or ŋgá tǐ kö the work you are doing here does not progress; the field does not advance; mvá millé tǐ (= oŋgú) 'bɔ the (recently born) baby has grown strong (cf. mvá rúá àtǐ 'bɔ the child has recovered).

tǐ⁵, vn. to drip, trickle, drops are falling; ɔzɔ́ɔ ǐ-nï ètǐ mà drìá rain-drops fall on my head; ɔzɔ́ɔ tǐ dzó-á rain trickles through my hut (-roof); é 'bà émvó ɔzɔ́ɔ ǐ-nï tǐ-zɔ̌ put a pot for rainwater to drop into.

tǐ⁶ = **ɘmvó,** vn. to jump, leap over; èì ɘtǐ-ɘtǐ (= ɘmbó) ɘŋgɔ̀ tö-rǐ-á they jump at the dance; ɘ'dó tǐ áséa èri-nï ma nè-lérǐ sǐ the leopard jumped into the grass when it saw me; àtsǐ-nï ɘtǐ (= ɘfǐ) 'bá rúá (or dzó drì-á) fire (-sparks) leap over on a person (on a hut).

tǐ⁷, vn. to start with fright; to suffer a shock; ɛndrí(or ásí)-nï tǐ rá, ga ànï tsǐ he started with fright and held his breath; ásí-nï tǐ rá, ádríi-nï dràá-rǐ sǐ he was depressed (dejected, low-spirited) at the death of his brother; tǐ ásí to lay/take to heart, to be dejected; 'dǐ ɛ'yɔ́ tɔ̀ɔkɔ́-nï, é tǐ ànï ásí kö (= é tǐ mï ásí kö)! it is idle talk, do not give way/ grieve! é tǐ ásí kö, mï adri tsírí! do not be/look downcast, be of good cheer!

tï¹ = ɛmbɛ́, vt. to tie (on), fasten, to make by tying (with rope); èi dzɔ́ (or èrɔ́) ˄tï ɔ̀zɔ̌ sǐ they tie reed-stalks on to the hut (or granary); èi dzɔ́ drì tï ásɛ́ sǐ they roof a hut with grass (cf. ɔtï).

tï², T. = kǐ, vt. to swallow.

tí, n. cow, ox; head of cattle; tí ándrí cow; tí mvá calf; tí agɔ bull-calf; tí karî heifer; tí ɔ̀do = bòotá butter.

tï¹, n. (1) mouth; beak, &c.; é zi tílé! open the mouth! é bǐ(= mò, ɔ̀pì, ako) ti tsí! shut the door! ti-bbí beard; moustache; (2) language; Lógbàrà ti the Lógbàrà language; ti andrá-lé-rǐ lower lip; lowlanders' language (Tɛrɛgo-Omugo...); 'yɔ ti èi-drírǐ sǐ he speaks in his home language; (3) ti = ti-lɛ́ opening (of anything); entrance; émvó ti opening of pot; täärí ti-lɛ́ the opening of a trunk; dzɔ́-ti-lɛ́ door (i.e. opening) of hut (cf. tǐïkò door for closing); (4) word, command of; mvá èri átíi mà ti kɔ (= ɛri, tà mba) a child hears/obeys his father's command...; (5) category, class; ámvú ti or dzɔ́ ti mǐdrí sǐ yà? èi nna how many categories of fields or huts do you have?— three (i.e. three wives' particular fields and huts); klási ti ǐrrǐ there are (in Arua) two categories of classes (i.e. Logbara and Aluur primary schools); (6) auxiliary or formal object of several verbs, as mu àsɔ̌ sö ɔ́pí mà ti-á he went

to accuse him to the chief; zi 'bâ ti-á he asked a p.; pè mvá mà ti àmbó vɔ̌ he sent a boy to the elder; é dò amo (or ásɛ́) ti! light the heap of weeds (the grass)...! (7)-ti-á postpositional expression; by the side of...; ma ɛsú ɔ́vá ámvú tiá I found a gazelle at the side of the field; ií tiá by the riverside.

ti², vt. to bear, bring forth young (animals); tí tì 'bɔ or tí ti mvá 'bɔ the cow has calved; a'ú ti (or sɔ̌) ǵbé ra the hen has laid an egg; N.B. Of woman ti expresses productivity (cf. tǐ²); ɔ̀kó 'dà àsì mvá sǐ (or àsì mvâ ti sǐ) 'bɔ that woman has stopped bearing; asi mvâ ti ddíká kö:(ti tsúrú'dɔ̀ kö:) èri ɔ̀kó àká she will beget no more: because she is an old woman.

tì¹, vt. (1) to put in line (side by side); èi ŋgà màákò tǐ dzɛ-zà-rö they are arranging potatoes (in little heaps) side by side for buying; andzi tì rö (láinì-á) rá the children have fallen into line; 'bá tì rö kɔ̀rɔ̀á tǐtì people form into lines at 'kɔrɔa' dance; é tì ŋgörö-däälì ŋgörö-däälì! put alternately longer and smaller ones! (2) to set one's hand/signature to a paper; é tì mǐ drí! do (under-) sign! èri 'ïmà drí tì wárágà 'aléa he signs the paper/letter; also lit. èri 'ïmà drí tì mvá 'dà mà drì-á she puts her hand(s) upon the head of that child.

tì², vn. to rise (of water); ií-nï tǐtì the river is rising; Ɛɲàó tì tré ɔzɔ́ɔ sǐ the Ɛnyao river has risen to its banks because of rain; ií tì 'bɔ the water has risen/fills it (a receptacle).

tí-àrǐïa, n. the black savannah

bird; èì emú éli̱ sì they come during the dry season.

tibbí, tibí-tibí, T., n. beard; èi̱má tibítibí edṹ mbèlèrö their beards grow long quickly.

tíbí, n. savoury (in many compositions; essential part of meal).

tibìrítì, A.S., n. match; é ga (= sì) t—, é 'bà tábà mà ti̱ ànï! strike the match and light my tobacco (: pipe, cigarette . . .) with it!

tìdà-tìdà, tìkà-tìkà, a. sticky, gummy; ésé 'bá ànï àrï̱a ò'bà èri̱ t—t— the glue/lime they lay out for birds is sticky.

tídrò, n. a tree.

tídzó = i̱ílémvó, n. pot (for fetching water).

tí-èvï̈ = tî-wí, áfúrútsìká, n. gadfly; èri̱ tí etsi it stings cattle.

ti̱kò, n. almost flat woven basket; (1) a net- or mat-work as domestic utensil; t— 'bá tsə àri̱fɛ sì, àn̠á tà mba-zŏ (dzóa) they make it with 'arifɛ' sticks, for keeping corn (in hut); t— 'bá ànï màákò ədzí flat basket people transport potatoes in; t— 'bá 'bá àzôrö 'bà dri̱-nï-á dzi-zŏ dàktárì-á, nòsi̱ árò-á a wicker-work stretcher to carry sick men to hospital or for medicine; (2) flat hurdle- or piece of wattle-work used as door; é tsə máni̱ tï̱kò kătilï̱a, 'bá kătilé òpì ànï make a wattle-door for me for a door-opening, that one may shut the opening!

ti̱kótïkó = əlétiəléti̱, n. black snake about a foot long (said to suck one's blood); ma ɛsú t— è'dù sì: kànì mï̈ ɛsú èri̱ gi̱ri̱-á, 'bá àzí̱ èmï-vélé-nï drà rá I have found a 'tikotiko', a bad omen: if you meet one on the way, sby. of your people will die.

ti̱kòmbá (?), n. shield.

tilikpa, a. toughly coherent, tenacious, glutinous, sticky; òdrí émvô si-zŏrï̱èri̱ ëni̱'rö, tilikpa' rö (= sɛzàrö) clay for making pots is black and tough/sticky.

tílírï̱á = tírílï̱á, T., gòká, n. long-horn blowing instrument.

ti-mŋgbìlímŋgbì = ákpáku, sísófà, n. chin (lower jaw, projection).

tìndiiri̱ = èbin̠aa, n. glow-worm; èri̱ atsí énï̱-nï it moves about by night.

típílákö, n. a kind of termites.

ti̱iri̱(lì), av. all on fire/ablaze; 'bá dŏ àngŏ ti̱iri̱ (i.e. àtsí àmbó sì) sby. set/light the place all over on fire.

tò(ö), also ŋgà tò, av. very much, utterly; töö-nï, av. chiefly, particularly, especially; e.g. (a) tònï évérékó-nï əvö éli̱ sì 'burnt places' are found chiefly during the dry season; (b) búkù 'dì áŋgi̱rí tònï 'dì-nï nì̠ (= ndè 'dì-nï ͏nì̠) this book is very thick compared with this other; (c) é fè tònï mvá 'dà nï you have given the main part to that boy; (d) tònï (= áda-nï) á lè drùsi̱ emú skúlù-á kö above all/in short: I do not want to come to school tomorrow.

tö, vt. to tread; (1) to press down by treading; to stamp down; to tread, step, stamp on or under feet; á tö édró drà rá I trampled on a mouse, it died; ma òdrí tö pá sì I am treading the clay with feet; tö galaá pá sì; (2) to suppress . . .; á tö (= àzù) 'bi̱lé ti tsí I stamped down the opening of a hole; ? = tö ɛ'yó 'dì mà ti tsí, löö kö he suppressed/concealed the matter, he did not reveal it; i.e. 'bá àzí̱nï 'yə ɛ'yó ma àgàía,

á tö (= òvù) drì-nï tsí sby.
spoke in my presence (of important matter), I kept it close; (3)
to kick; àkàɳà tö (= yï) 'bá pá
sï a donkey kicked a man with
its leg; tö ma pá sï he kicked me
with his foot; andzi 'dàï mòpírà
tö those boys kick/play football;
(4) special; tö pá to stand (upright); to stop; tö pá 'áá ïï tiá
he is standing yonder on the riverside; pätí tö pá the tree stands
upright; ɔŋgɔ̃ tö (lit. to step a
song =) to dance.

tɔ̀, vt. to put into...;(1) to fill, pour
into; é tɔ̀ lésú kéréá (= ɔ̀zúa)/
tsúpàá! é tɔ̀ 'alénïá! fill the
bowl/bottle with milk! pour it
in! yékéá tɔ̀ rö bɔ̀ŋgɔ́ tálãa the
large brown ants have crawled
over the cloth; (2) to mark, plot
out; é tɔ̀ tí mà àgãí kàlê
(= kaali) sï! stake out the (rain-
season) pen for the cattle! é tɔ̀
kaali pätí ɔ́'dí sï làalà! thrust
new sticks into the fence quickly!
èï lítsɔ́ tɔ̃ (= e'dí) tí-nï laa-zɔ́
they make a pen for cattle to lie
in;(3) to lodge a complaint against;
tɔ̀ ma ɔ́pí vɔ̃ (or mákátàá) ǹdrí
mà ɛ'yɔ́ sï he brought in an action
against me before the chief (the
office) for a goat; á mu èri tɔ̃ ɔ́pí
vɔ̃ I went to sue him to the chief;
edzí ɛ'yɔ́-nï tɔ̃ (= ɔ̀lɔ̃) mâ tiá
he reported the matter (as a theft)
to me.

tɔ, vn. to be(-come) lukewarm; é
'bà ïï tɔ àtsí drìá! put the water
on the fire to warm up! ïï drípi yùu
'dï (= drípi wererï) 'bá ɔmvɛ
tɔ̃tɔ water slightly warmed they
call lukewarm; é mu ïï 'bã àtsía
mà tɔ werɛ! go and place the
water on the fire that it may warm
up! ïï tɔzà/tɔ̃tɔ 'bá ànï rùá

ɔ̀dzï they wash themselves with
lukewarm water.

tòa = ɔlɛ, a. bald (-headed),
shaven; bàbá mà drì tòa the
grandfather's head is bald; mï
drì èri tòa (rö) your head is bald;
àŋgɔ̀ tòa a barren/grassless
place/area.

tɔ́gbɔ̀, n. a delivery of guarantee,
security; pawn; mï èfè mání
silíŋgì taáú t— (rö)! give me
5s. as guarantee (of your words)!

tɔkítɔkí[1] = kɔkɔ́á, n. woodpecker;
èri atsí pätí rùá atsí-atsí he
walks up the trunk of a tree.

tɔkítɔkí[2] = tɔŋgítɔŋgí, mŋgbé-
mŋgbé, kíkí, kɔŋgɔlɔkɔ, ŋgáŋgá, av. hard and smooth (surface
of sth.); tightly, strongly joined;
mï ɔtí (= ɔmbé) t—! tie it
tightly! dzɔ́ mà drì èri t— the
hut roof (grass) is compact and
smooth.

tɔ̀ɔkɔ́, av. to no purpose, at random; idly; ma ɔ'á t— I am staying idly; á fè kö t— I did not give
it for any special reason (Ac.
nɔ̀ɔnɔ).

tòkòtókó = ɔ̀'yo-kódjo — ɔ̀'yo-
kódjo, av. limping; otsí kà pá
ágálé-nï ɔsɔ̃ nï, 'bá atsí t— if
a thorn has penetrated one's foot,
one limps.

tɔ́lɔ̀, n. àdzú (mà) t— a (spear-)
spike; èïnï àŋgɔ̀ (or è'bí) sɔ̃ they
fix it in the ground (or stab fishes)
with it.

tólókpá = kpémŋgbélé, sïzà, a.
bare, denuded; hairless; bàbá
mà drì-bbi tólókpâ-rö the
grandfather/old man is bald
(-headed); ɔpé mà drì tólókpâ-
rö the guinea-fowl's head is bare;
èwá mà rùá t— the elephant is
hairless.

tɔlɔkpɔ = tàlàkpà, óïzà, a. lean,

thin, emaciated; 'bâ rúá tələkpə-
rö a man is lean (sick, hungry).

tɔŋgítɔŋgí = tәkítәkí, q.v. tight,
rigid; aká nï kö not soft.

tŏn̨à-tŏn̨à = munamuna, T., a.
without consistency; detaching
easily, crumbling.

tɔ́rà = ɔ̀dzɔ́, n. indigenous kind
of fibrous plant (sisal variety).

tŏörŏ́, number 100, hundred; t—
nna 300.

tŏörŏ́, n. bee-hive; t— èi tsǎ fífí
(á) sǐ báká sǐ they make a hive
with 'fifi' sticks and ropes.

tŏrŏbáŋgì, T. = mbɛ́gɔ̀, S.
(akin to ɔ̀dzɔ́), n. sisal; t— bá
sisal fibre, rope.

tŏrŏlŏ, a. to the point of intoxi-
cating, inebriating; mvu éwá
tŏrŏlŏ-rö he drank beer until he
became drunk; ɛ'dɛ́ tŏrŏlŏ sǐ he
fell from drunkenness.

trà = apí, vn. to be satiated, full,
tight; kànì é trà 'bə, ɛ́n̨á mà
èsá-nï 'ǐ li (= ko, atsɛ) tsí when
you are full, a bit of polenta is left
over; á trà (= ma apí) gbaran̨a-
n̨a I am full/well rounded off.

trà = sàrà, T., av. àŋgŏ trà (sǐ),
(at) daybreak, dawn.

tràa(ò), av. with noise; mï àsǐ
mà bɔ̀ŋgɔ́ tràao 'dínï à'do sǐ
yà? why have you torn my cloth
noisily in this way?

tra, vt. (1) to collect, pull/put together; èri tî tra (= əko) àŋgŏ
àlŏ́á he is driving the cattle together into one place; (2) = agbɔ́
to fold; to draw/pull in; èi bɔ̀ŋgɔ́
ətrá-ətrá they fold the cloths;
é tra mǐ pá tràtra! pull in your
legs (at sitting)! é tra mǐ drí
ŋgŏlŏ! draw in your (out-
stretched) hands! (3) to wind,
coil; é tra báká pätǐ rùá! wind
over the stick (wood) with rope

(cf. andzu wind string around
once) (i.e. repeatedly)! (4) to connect (tie into a) knot; 'bá èi əmbɛ̂
(or aísé) tra káríá⸴rö they col-
lect/join grass into a circle (inside the roof of the hut); èi òtù
(= òndù) tra (= pa), èi ǹdrí
'ǐ òtù sía they tie grass (-tops) to
a knot and fasten goats (sheep)
(with their ropes) to it (for
feeding); (5) to invent, conceive,
to make up; á tra (= òmì) ɛ'yɔ́
mà ásía I concocted malicious
plans (or uttered words of sus-
picion or the like) in my mind/
heart; tra ɛ'yɔ́ mà drìá èndzɔ̀
bɛ èndzɔ̀ bɛ he suspects/or in-
vents discreditable or fictitious
stories against me.

trátrá = táa, q.v., tǎn̨í, o'dú
trá = o'dú zù, zùzù, av. always,
constantly, daily, everyday; èmï
emú t—! come every day!

trátrá = érékèrè, av. into countless pieces (cf. òsǐ split).

trátrá = trǐtrˇá, n. a warbler
(? Accentor modularis).

tràí, av. directly, straight towards…; mǐ emú tràí má vŏ!
come straight to me!

tràí-tràí = tékètékè, àl(átát)â-
rö, av. to perfection; (1) snow-
white; cf. tékètékè (2); (2) well
ready (-cooked); ɔ́sŏ́ a'dí t—t—
(= kpírìkpírì) beans are deli-
ciously well (soft) cooked.

trɛ (= ətré), vn. to speak aloud,
strongly; é trɛ! aloud! cry!

tré = tsŏkùtsŏkù, mbóoi, zŏrŏ́,
av. (1) full; brim-full; mǐ əko ǐi
émvóa (émvó sǐ) tré! take up a
full pot of water! tò ǐi tsúpàá tré
he filled up the bottle with water
completely; (2) numerous; mǎ
dzɔ́ tré my households (with respective wives) are numerous.

trèí=kpɛrɛ...vǒ sì, pstp. as far as; up to; é mu t— (or kpɛrɛ) Peter vǒ (àkúa) sì or t— èri vǒ (= vǒ-nï-á) sì! go as far as Peter's village: right up to his abode! mòtòkárì mu t— mâ águì mà rùá sì the motor-car went up close to my friend's side.

trètrèkó = àdzèlìkó, tíiá, n. kind of (smaller) blowing horn, flute; t— 'dì 'bá-nì vö-lé 'dáanïrì'ï a horn people blow at (entertainment) will.

trriì[1], vt. (1) to rub with; t— èlmà rùá éráká sì, ðdo sì they rubbed themselves with ochre and oil; (2) to scrub; cure; águ 'dà èri kàbìlð mà énï(rïkð) tri óní sì that man cures a sheep-skin with a stone; (3) to polish, furbish, smooth; èri sàndú rùâ trri he is polishing the case.

tri[2] = alú, vt. to bewitch; mbàzà tri 'bá ðlè sì; Àdrð ɛri mbàzà mà ti rá old men bewitch people with charm (their angry temper does it!); God gives ear to old men's requests!

trìkítrìkí[1]= ndzìzàrö, a. heavy; á 'bì àfa 'dì 'du tì, èri trìkítrìkî-rö I tried in vain to lift this thing because it is very heavy (opp. hwɛrɛ).

trìkí-trìkí[2], av. coarsely; mì etri mà ŋgókó t—t—! rub/massage my back thoroughly!

trí(-trí) = tìtí, kiki, kírikíri, av. firmly, tightly; é bì trí! catch it firmly!

trð, vt. (1) to take (or get, pull) off ... (cloth over one's head); é trð-trð! take off your shirt (or other garment)! èri bðŋgó trð he takes off his cloth; (2) to take, pull off (rope from peg, &c.); èri

tí (-báká) trðtrð (= ðtrð) he pulls off ropes (from pegs, setting animals free for pasture); é trð tí (or ndrí) trðtrð! set the cows (goats) free! ma kápà trð I am taking off the belt; (3) to heap (or the like); èri àŋá ðtrð (or ŋaa) pírïnï, ŋga àzí kö/or zð ànï kö he eats heaps of polenta to no purpose, he did not work for/or he would not grow.

trö, vt. to take/scrape the hair off; èri énï(rïkð) mà 'bíkð trö (or trri) óní sì he removes the skin's hair with a stone; èì a'ú mà rùâ trö ìì àtsí sì they scald a fowl with boiling water.

trð, vt. to (be) smear, daub over (with paint or ...); èì orété trð drìá tsàandí sì they smear their heads with mud for grief; mvá èri e'dí trð 'ïmà rùá the small child smears himself with gruel (on eating).

troa = kpɛrɛ, pstp. as far as, up to; ma atsí t— Térégòá I journeyed as far as Tɛrɛgo.

trðndzìlì = ndzð rö t—, av. slippery; àŋgð ndzðndzð or àŋgð 'dì trðnzdìlì-rö the ground is slippery.

trótrð = ðsì-rö-ðsì, av. equal, identical; pírí t— they are all the same.

trú or trùu, av. numerous, in quantity; sí sì ðndó mà éfí trùu hailstones knocked out a great quantity of durra grains; di mâ sí trú he knocked out my teeth (a number); mòémbè ɛ'dé vàá trú ðlì sì—lù trùu numberless mangoes fell to the ground by the storm.

trúì, av. with slight hissing; ndzɛ rö t— (feathers or the like) come off/detach with light noise.

trúĕtrúĕ = òdíkía, T., n. a small common river fish.

tsàa¹, vt. to twist, braid, make (basket); èì áɲûba (or tŏŏrŏ́, tǐkò) tsàá they make beer-sifters (bee-hives, wicker hurdle); èì ásé tsàá rá, èì dǐ emú ànï èrò́-átsî 'bŏ (= mŏ) they interlace grass and dress the granary roof with it.

tsàa² = g̱bï, vt. to shoot (with bow, gun); 'bá èì àɲàpá tsàá ŏsu (or 'yé) sǐ they shoot animals with a bow (or arrow).

tsàa³, vt. to gnaw; édrò́-nï enï tsàátsà mice gnaw skins.

tsàa⁴, vt. drì tsàá to induce, persuade; àmbó tsà 'bá 'dàǐ mà drì rá the elder has induced those people (they were unwilling).

tsà, vn. tsàzà = tsókóló, a. (1) to be too watery, thin; éɲá 'dǐrï tsátsà, èri sì rö e'dí lé this polenta is thin (g̱a ǐïrö) it is like gruel; (2) = aká weak, drowsy (from disease, hunger, fear, &c.); 'bá mà rúá tsátsà/tsàzàrö a p. feels weak.

tsáǎ, tsátsà-rö, a. still thin, undeveloped (fruit); àɲá tsátsà or àɲá tsátsàrù undeveloped corn.

tsa¹ (etsá), vn. (1) to arrive, reach; tsa àkúa rá he has arrived home; (2) tsa...zŏ́ to be able to, can; á tsa àfa 'dǐ 'du-zŏ́ kö I am unable to lift this thing; (3) tsa ... 'bá-nǐ to suffice, be sufficient for, to be fit for; fúnò tsa mánǐ kö the ground-nuts were not sufficient for me; àfa 'dǐ tsa 'yέεkὲ (Ac. man òròmò kàkàrὲ) this is quite sufficient; àfa tsápi mánǐ-rǐ é nì kö what suffices for me you do not know; (4) to be a match for; mvá 'dà tsaa mánǐ

àfúa sǐ kö that boy is no match for me in wrestling.

tsa², vt. to winnow, sift (kóbi sǐ with basket); èmï tsa 'dínï àsǐa? mà mu àɲá milê tsa, milé-nï-á àɲá drílékó tsǐ why are you winnowing like this? the corn ought to be winnowed as there is chaff in it; èì òndó pi tsa ósŏ́ bε ndóndó they separate durra from beans.

tsa-g̱à = tsa kö (cf. tsa¹); dǐ tsa g̱à this is not sufficient.

tságòá = ádròá, ág̱òá, n. adze.

tságòà, n. loofah.

tsàkâ, n. a free, bare place (in the open country; cattle, birds, even men like to collect in); t— èri pàrí/àŋg̱ò tí-nï ávâ lï (= kə, tra rö) zŏ́ rǐ'ï; tí èì t— tö rá, 'tsaka' is the place where cattle rest in/collect; cattle trample the place down.

tsàkù = tsàpà, tsàɲù, tsùɲà, kpòlò, a./av. wet; àŋg̱ò àndzù fàa, tsàpà ozóó sǐ the ground is soaked, is wet from rainwater.

tsàandí = èmvò, n. trouble, affliction, grief; ma t— 'bǎ I am in trouble, grief.

tsànóà, T., n. comb (= sànóà).

tsáɲíkǐ, see tsíɲá.

tsàràkàlà, n. a kind of red durra with the species: trótró (alu tò delicious) and ndakà (dràdra bitter).

tsâtsâ, n. a grasshopper.

tsé, av. truly, in accordance with the true facts; á 'yə tsé mínǐ rá; mǐ bílé yə; é 'bì àŋg̱à dǐ 'dé ká (i.e. mǐ εsú àŋg̱à tsàandí mǐdrírǐ 'dǐá ká) I did tell you the truth, but you did not heed; you have now tried it yourself (finding trouble); ε'yó 'dǐrï té mŏ́ké káàsìa, ma εri tsé (kpɛrɛ) the words were quite correct, I heard it well; **mvá 'dàrï tsé 'bá ádarï**; **èri 'bá àzà kə-zà bɛ 'bá àzï mà rùá** that boy is truly a real man, taking pity on other people.

tsɛ¹, vt. **drì tsɛ** to lead; to be or march at the head; **é tsɛ drì, mà ŋgà 'dɛ mï vútiá** go ahead, I shall follow you; **á tsɛ mïnï drì ma 'ï** I was myself at the head of you; **á tê dï mïnï drì tsɛ ma'ï, andralí tê dï ànï mà tsə 'ï** I had marched at the head of you and dew has fallen on me; (**ga drì tsɛ kə sï** he refused to lead); **drìtsépi** leader, guide; **'dï 'bá drìtsépi** this is the guide.

tsɛ², vt. (1) to surround, encircle; **èi ŋgúrú tsɛɛ (ágá) 'dï'di** they are surrounding a wild beast to kill it; (2) to define, mark limits of; **èi àŋǧ tsɛɛ** they are marking out the limits of the area.

tsɛɛ³, vt. to pull out forcibly; to break, tear off; **èi ásé ìi-á-rï tsɛ 'ï** they pull out grass from the river(-side); **èri bákǎ t—** he pulls off the string; **tsɛ rö**, vn. to break, tear, pull off; **báká t— rö rá** the rope broke off; **ɛtsé 'ï ɛtsé-ɛtsé ètrȍ 'ï vàá** it tore and fell off to the ground.

tsèbèó, T. = **tsùlú, q.v. 'bá 'bà 'dàrï tsèbèó⁻rö** they put it on as addition.

tsélétsélé, n. a choice little meal (prepared secretly, out of special affection—especially in first period of marriage) for husband; **ȍkó ɛ́ŋá əva ágúpí drì a'dúlɛ sï (wɛrɛ)**: **èri t— 'bà ágúpí nï** a woman prepares polenta (with choice savoury!) only for her husband.

tsɛndzɛ, n. sharply pointed sticks fixed in the ground on paths frequented by thieves, &c. **èi t— sȍ gìrìá (ȍgù sï) ȍgúo nï.**

tsénï = **àkà sï, tȍəkó, 'dáanï, àmbò sï,** av. of one's own accord, voluntarily, spontaneously; at random; **ɛ'dɛ́ vàá tsénï** it fell down by itself (alone); **ga emú-kə àmbò sï** he refused to come for no reason.

tsèrè, av. far, at a distance; **é tö pá t—!** stand at some distance!

tsérè = **kérè, T.,** n. the shrill calls, or communications (in the falsetto voice typical of Logbara); **èi t— 'bɛ** they make far calls; **'bá tȍrȍ-lȍrö èri atsí tsérè bɛ; lè vínï əmbà 'bá tsə-zȍ** a drunken person goes along crying; is apt also to start quarrelling/fighting.

tsï¹, vn. to exist, be present; **ȍkó 'dï mà mvá tsí** a child of this woman exists/this woman has a child; **ma bəŋgó sàndúkù-á tsí** I have a cloth in the trunk; **Àdrȍnï əvö-zȍ tsí-rï sï 'bá èi drǎ rá a'do ɛ'yɔ́ sï?** while God exists, why do people die?

tsï², av. properly, seemly, fitly; tightly, firmly; **mï èga (or əsé) àfadzó 'dïrï tsí!** do mend the basket properly! **é zi mï ('délé) tsí yȍ?** how are you? (lit. ask yourself well!); answer: **é zi mï èndì!** and how are you (lit. ask yourself also)! common greeting: **é zi mï tsítsí! é sö ɛ'bó (àbé sía) tsí!** fix the hoe to its handle tightly! (construction!) **o'dú kə (= bï, 'bɛ) èri tsí** sleep caught him/he fell asleep/soundly.

tsï¹ = **nyï,** vn. to smile; **èri tsï èri nï tsï-tsï** he smiles at him.

tsï², vn. to make or be ready to swarm (termites); **ȍzí èri tsï ȍtókó mà əmbɛtiá** the 'ozi' bees are ready at their hillside to swarm.

tsï-zà³ = **àtsí**, a. **milé t—** the eyes are restless, eager to see, observe; impatient to report a piece of news to everybody...; keen of sight.

tsï⁴, vt. (1) to bite; **mvá 'dïrï mà drî tsï** the babe bites my hand; (2) **ívî tsï** to lick/munch alkaline earth; **ǹdrí èri ívî tsï** the goat licks alkaline earth; (3) to sew; **ma bòŋgô tsï** (= **sò**) I am sewing a cloth.

tsï⁵, vn. (1) to be sharp (knife) (= **sí bɛ** with good edge); **ëlï 'dï tsï tò** this knife is very sharp; or **ma ëlï mà sí tsï tò** my knife's edge is very sharp; (2) to be keen, sharp sighted; **milé-nï tsïtsï** or **tsï-zà-rö** he has keen eyes; fig. forward, meddlesome; (3) to have an untiring, unflagging tongue; **ágú 'dà mà ti tsïtsï** or **tsï tò**; ti-nï əri kö, èri òlòlòá'rö that man's tongue is untiring; his tongue would not stop, he is extremely talkative.

tsi, drì tsi, vn. to be/feel inconvenienced; (1) to be embarrassed, perplexed, puzzled, confused, at a loss; **kànì séntè mídrí yə, é tsi drì bòŋgó sï kö yà?** if you have no money, are you not embarrassed for cloths?! **kànì mï àlíó'rö, mï ɛsú àfa àzíni kö: mï drì tsi** if you are penniless/indigent, you cannot get anything, you are hard up; (2) distressed, in calamity, misfortune; **kànì àŋgò à'wí'rö, ï̀ 'a-nï-á yə, mï drì tsi ï̀ kòrɛ sï rá** when the country is parched with no water in it you are distressed for thirst; (3) to be grieved, afflicted, troubled; **kànì drà** (or **àzó**) **ndè mï rá, mï drì tsitsi**

when illness overwhelms you, you are in great distress/afflicted; **ágúpí 'à máni ámvú kö, mà dï ànï drì tsi tò** (my) husband has not tilled the field for me, I am now troubled, i.e. **ma àŋá ndǎndà** I am looking for corn; (4) to grow tired, sick of...; to have enough of...; **ma drì tsi mï drí tò** I have grown utterly tired of you.

tsï, see **ga³** (3).

tsíkí, n. a kind of basket.

tsíkíndà = **kɛtɛkɛtɛ**, n. castanet (from emptied shell of **lómŋgbóró** fruit); **ɛzó-andzi èì t—** tsə girls shake/chink the castenets (two connected with string).

tsíkírí, n. **ósǒ t—** (any kind of) beans planted at the end of rainy season (in hollows); **ósǒ 'bá-nï fǎ mbá órómì sï, èì əmvɛ t—** beans people plant about September/October are called 'late beans'.

tsíkətsíkə, av. cautiously, hobbling, limping; **mvá 'dïrï mu t— pá àzó sï** this child walks hobbling from a sore foot.

tsìmvà-tsìmvà-rö, a. brownish-white...

tsíŋá = **tsíŋákí**, **tsáŋíkí**, n. sand; **àŋgò tsíŋá'rö** the ground is sandy.

tsïŋàa, av. with open smiling face; **mïnï tsï-zǒ t—** when you smile all over your face.

tsìŋí-tsïŋí = **kòrí-kòrí**, a. variegated, motley, piebald.

tsipa = **lipa** (**sò pá**), a. stagnant; **ï̀ tsipa-rï̀** stagnant water, i.e. a lake; i.e. **ï̀ lěpi rápi kö** water that would not run; **ï̀ pá sǒpi tsïrï** water standing still.

tsïrr, av. at a pull; **mà rùâ 'yɛ t—** I suffered a sudden shock.

tsiri, av. straight, upright; **á sò**

pá t— I am standing upright;
é 'bà pätí t—! fix the pole straight
upright!

tsírí, av. silently, in silence;
mysteriously; secretly; àvĕ t—
(= ndi) he disappeared mysteriously; ŏvù t— he keeps perfectly
silent; è mu mání t— à'do ɛ'yɔ́
sǐ yà? why have you gone
silently (without telling me)? mǐ
adri tsírí! keep silent!

tsə, vt. to strike, beat; ágú 'dà
tsə èri rá that individual has
beaten him; ɛmbápi-nï mvá
àzǐ əmvɛ tsə-zà-rö the teacher
called a boy to be beaten (punished); tsŏ rö 'bá àzǐ bɛ they
fought with each other; special
uses: (a) à'dî tsə to ring a bell;
ò'dî tsə to play a harp...; (b) èsélé/
= àsálâ tsə to separate; to break
up relations; àdzè-nï àsálâ tsə
to undo/cancel a bargain; ɔ̀kó mà
àdzè-nï àsálâ tsə to break an
engagement (returning bride-
wealth); ɔ̀kó pi tsə àsálá mvá
bɛ 'bə (= tǐ 'bə) the woman was
delivered of a baby (lit. woman
and baby separated); mǎ dî ŋga
ɛ́ŋá àsálâ tsə (= awa, ɔ̀tǐ) ìrrǐ
I will make two portions of
polenta; (c) bbílê tsə to hear attentively; èmǐ etsɔ́ bbílé 'dálé! pay
attention here! (d) ɔ́ŋà̀ tsə to
beat ground of termites (to entice
them out) with a stick (drum-like);
(e) to turn round (lying or standing); tsə 'ïmà ti vélé he turned
and came back; é tsə mǐ̂ ti
(ògù)! turn round! (f) to mention
(or drag in) sby.'s name 'bá àzǐ
mà rû tsə (or ndzɛ); (g) to make,
construct; èi èrŏ tsə bǎbǎlì sǐ
they make a granary with 'babali'
sticks; èi dzɔ̂ tsə wárá sǐ they
make a hut ('s wall) with stakes.

tsɔ̀ = zɔ̀, mba, vn. to grow up;
mvá 'dà tsúrú'dɔ̀ tsɔ̀ àmbó
that child has now grown up (well).

tsóoà, n. (1) = èrïïá, lɔ̀kíà, a
weaver bird (? pirol); (2) = ndzǐ-
ïrò a disapproving tut-tut sound
(in one's mouth); ma mǐnǐ t—
'yɛ ɔ̀mbà sǐ I make (such a
sound) at you out of anger.

tsóéĕ = àkàlàfé, n. a pole; pätí
èinǐ sö ɔ̀gó mà tálárǐ a pole they
push through the holes of posts
(of cattle pen); 'bá ànï tí mà
lítsó tilé 'bǎ they block with it
the cattle-pen opening.

tsòká, T. = ɔ́ŋɔ́fí, n. fingernail.

tsɔ́kɔ́rɔ́ = tsà-zà, q.v.

tsŏkɔ̀tsŏkɔ̀ = tsɔ̀rɔ̀tsɔ̀rɔ̀, av.
fried with oil and onion; ádzê á
ŋa ɛ́ŋá ɔ́sŏ sǐ t— (i.e. ɔ̀do pi
mbásàlà bɛ tsǐ); yesterday I ate
polenta with (oil and onion) fried
beans.

tsŏkùtsŏkù = tré, q.v., av.
(crammed) full; àŋá ga èrɔ́a
(= èrɔ́ sǐ) t—, 'bá òmǐ tǐ the
granary is crammed full of grain,
they press it in vain; òmǐ èi
t—/= tríkítríkí they packed
them to overflowing.

tsolí, T. (cf. Moyo tsowǐ), =ádàrö,
av. right, truly; T. é dzo mání
tsolí=é 'yə mání mŏké/ádàrö!
tell me frankly!

tsómbì-sí, n. head of hip (femur).

tsɔ̀ndzɔ̀lɔ̀, a. /av. large/heavy over-
hanging; à'bŏà ka t— the
banana hangs heavily.

tsɔ́rɔ́kɔ̀lɔ́ = tsúrúkùlú, tsɔ́kɔ́lɔ́,
a. /av. (1) containing (relatively)
too much water = watery; kàni
e'dí (or ɛ́ŋá) bĕ ïǐ 'aléníá àmbôrö, èri adri tsǎ-tsà or t—
when they pour too much water
into the gruel (or polenta), it
becomes watery (weak, insipid);

(2) = tsəkpótsəkpó water showing up (on the ground—from rain); àŋgŏ èrì tsórókɔlɔ̀-rö ìí bɛ, ərété⊥rö the ground is watery/soaked, muddy.

tsootí = òbɛlɛ, av. quickly, instantly; əzɔ́ɔ́ àtĭ t— the rain ceased instantaneously; é mu t—t— é sɔ̀ pá gĭrĭá kö! go quickly and do not stop on the way!

tsùlá (Looi?) = m̀bĭ, n. island.

tsulu, n. heart (physical).

tsulú, in ɛ́n̠á t—, n. special small round lump of polenta added on top of the common portion; èì 'bǎ ágúpí-nĭ wife puts it (only) for husband (and this may keep it for later or next morning).

tsùlùtsùlù, a./av. agitated; unreservedly; mĭ ásí t— tŏ you are quite upset (being unable to keep your temper and wait quietly).

tsumà, S. Lgb. aya, n. iron and any kind of iron tool or machinery.

tsùn̠à = tsǎkù, q.v.

tsúpá, A.S., n. bottle.

tsúrú, tsútsúrù, tsútsúrù ŋgà-dɔ̀, av. now, just now; this moment; immediately; àmà fu rö mĭ bɛ tsútsúrúá 'dɔ̀! I'll fight with you this instant (a sulky challenge)! ma emú tsú-tsúrù ŋgà 'dɔ̀ I have only just arrived now.

tsurù-tsurù = tsərətsərə, av. (of rainwater) remaining visible on surface; əzɔ́ɔ́ 'di 'dálé kö, əzɔ́ɔ́ 'di àma vélé t—t— it did not rain yonder, it rained to overflowing in our area.

tsùrútsùrú = èzèdìzè, n. loofah.

tsútsú = tsúkutsúku, bĭlĭbĭlĭ, a./av. ɛ̀nĭ t— pitch-dark.

tsùtsù-gbĭ, n. children's game; 'bâ ŋga àfa-nĭ gbĭ-gbĭ-rĭ'ĭ làá lĭ-rö they shoot (with play-

arrows, quickly) at sth.: counting the shots is the test.

tú = pĭrĭ, a./av. all; á lɛ̀ andzĭ tú-rĭ mà emú má vŏ 'dĭá I want all the children to come here to me.

tu¹, vn. (1) to mount, rise; to ascend (tree, mountain); to climb up; mà tu èrɔ́á àn̠á e'dú (= èndĭ) I climb and enter the granary to take corn; tu-zà, a. steep, precipitous; ónĭ 'dà tuzàrö that mountain is steep; (2) tu ... drì-á to come upon suddenly; to take unawares, surprise; ɛ'yó tu 'ïmà drìá 'bə trouble/a blow came suddenly upon him.

tu² = pì, vn. to be satiated, full, swollen; mvá 'dà mà 'alé tǔtu that child's belly is swollen/is satiated: has eaten well; tí drà-zà mà 'alé tǔtu/=pĭpì the dead cow's belly has swollen.

tùu = tàa, av. hissing (releasing wind on explosion or the like); əpìrà mà ává fĭ tùu the air went out of the football hissing.

tukú-tukú, n. puppy.

tululúa = goké, n. big horn as blowing instrument.

tùlútúlú'ru, a. uneven, rough; àŋgŏ tùlútúlú'ru the ground is rough (opp. èníkìnì, àlátárá).

túurù, T., n. (1) = Plu. lìŋgɔ̀ elevated clay—ground (side of hut for sleeping); èì mǔ di túurùrö (lìŋgɔ̀rö) laa-zŏ they go to batter down the earth for the 'tuuru' to sleep on; (2)=ŋgɔ̀rǒ elevated, hilly (without rocks) ground.

tùsú, n. spittle; t— (ɔ̀)wĭ to spit; èì t— wĭ (or tsə) rúa-nĭ, drà rúa-nĭ-á-rĭ mà àtĭ ànĭ! they (old men) spit on him (= bless him), that his disease may cease!

tùúti (? cf. túurù), n. waste-heap (at back of hut or village); èì ókŏrŏη̣à dǎ tùúti-á they throw away sweepings on the waste-heap.

tútúǎ, n. motor-cycle (pikipiki).

tútùá, n. small round calabash bowl (kérɛ) with small opening on top, especially for áη̣ú—simsim oil.

U

ùú = wǐ, n. (more particularly upper part of) arm; ùú 'bǎ to offer one's arm as head-support (pillow) to counterpart (wooing); ùú 'bílé(kə̀)/ètǐ = ùú 'bílé-ǹdú, ùú-gbélékù-ètǐ, ùú-lú-ètǐ, ùú-lúló(kə̀)-ètǐ, n. armpit; ùú-mbǐlímbǐ, n. elbow; ùú-sí (-fà), n. shoulder-blade; ùú-ti, n. arm joint.

'ǔǎ-'ǔǎ, n. (1) wild dog (Lycaon Pictus lupinus); (2)= ò'úη̣gù, n. hornbill; 'ǔǎ-'ǔǎ əsɛ'rö the hornbill is fat; drìnï kúlúη̣á'rö it has a thick-knobbly head.

ùwù (èùwù hitherwards), vt. to transfer, transplant, transport; ùwù 'ïmà dzó 'dálé they transplanted his house yonder; kànì 'bá ùwù dzó (i.e. 'ïmà àfa wóró) pärï àzínï-á rá, èì dzǐ mu 'bǎ aŋgŏ àzínǐá; pärí-nï ko 'dàárǐ 'bá əmvɛ 'ándró' nï when a man transports his hut (and everything) elsewhere, they take it and go and plant it elsewhere; that abandoned place they call 'andro'; á lè ma àkú èuwǔ 'dòá I want to transfer my village here; ɛ́dzá ə̀uwǔ to go, collect, and bring firewood; ɛ́dzá de 'ï 'bə ; é mu mánǐ ɛ́dzá ə̀uwǔ! the firewood is finished; go to bring me firewood! (cf. wu-).

V

vǎ or vàá, (=vùrú, T.) av. on the ground; of the country/place we are in; àŋgŏ vǎ 'dǐrï ndrǐzàrö present-day conditions of the place (country, world) are pleasant/or life is pleasant at present; é rï vàá! sit down (or on the ground)! vàá-lé sǐ on (or from) the ground.

và (= nì), vt. (1) to reflect, revolve, turn over in one's mind; to try to remember or conjecture; á và ɛ'yó 'dǐ mà ètǐ tǐ I tried in vain to recall the meaning of this word/or to resolve the implications of this matter; á rï ɛ'yó vǎvà (= ndǎndà, ə̀rə̀ərà), I sat down (or continued) thinking about the matter; (2) to conjecture, guess, discover; recognize; và lə̌kìrì (mà ètǐ) rá he found out/discovered the trick; á và ɛ'yó rá I have solved it; và mǐ tsé he recognized you (well); èri 'ï vǎvà (ògùtáa sǐ) he suggests himself (by some suspicious expression).

va[1], vt. to allure, attract; (often = fu) əŋgô tö-zà (= kə̀rɛ, àvá) va Bìànò rá (the desire of) dancing allured (proved attractive to) Biano; gárì kə̀rɛ va mǎ vǎva, á lè té əndzó ànǐ a bicycle appeals to me, I should like to run with it.

va[2], əvá, vt. to dig, excavate (with claws); ɛ́dró va 'bílé rá a mouse dug a hole; àrǐá va go rá the bird made a hole (in a tree); cf. ma gbándà əvǎ ɖrí sǐ I dig up manioc roots with the hands.

vɛ, ɛvé (1) vt. to burn down, destroy by fire; àtsǐ vɛ ásɛ́ (dzó) rá fire has burned down the grass (the hut); N.B. cf. that man burned down my hut **ágú 'dà 'bà mâ dzó ti rá**; (2) vn. to burn down; **ásέ-nï vέvɛ** the grass is burning; **asì dzi ókŏrŏɳà ɛvé kö yà?** is the rubbish no more taken for burning? **ásέ vɛzà** or **ɛvéréká** (place of) burned grass, kind of stubble-field; (3) fig. to be irritated, angry; **ma ásí vέvɛ mï rùá àákó sì/ɛ'yó mïnï 'yɔ-rï sì** I feel indignant, irritated against you out of anger/at your speech.

véllé or **vélé** (1) pstp. (*a*) of genitive/ possessive; **'dï ńdrí ɛ̀ri-vélé (-rì)**, or **'dï ɛ̀ri-vélé ńdrí (-rì)** this is his goat; **ɛ̀i-vélé-rï** theirs; (*b*) = **vŏ** one's own place; **etsá àma vélé** he arrived at our village; (2) av. behind, afterwards; **ɛ̀ri etsá vélé** he arrived afterwards; **ɛ̀ri dzó vélé 'dàá** he is in that hut behind (some other); **ɛ̀i fúnò** (or **mààkò) vélé ndǎ** he is searching after the ground-nut (or potato) harvest (what escaped collecting); (3) **vélléa**, pstp. (*a*) behind sth.; **ɛ̀ri dzó 'dà mà véléa** he is (found) behind that hut; (*b*) in the absence of, after one's leaving; **ma etsá ma ágúi véléa** I arrived in the absence of my friend (he had left or died); **emú mâ véléa** he came in my absence; (4) **vélé-rï sì**, av. after that, afterwards, in the end; **v— mâ ɳgâ mu rá** afterwards I shall go.

vì, vt. (1) to scratch; **bŏrà vì ma** the cat has scratched me; **ɛ̀ri áɳú vï** she is picking out simsim from pod; (2) = **kà** to pinch off by bits; **ɛ̀ri zá vï** he is pinching off meat (**tíbí** savoury at meal).

vì = **ɛ̀vì**, n. pus; **vì a'yálu mà 'aléa tsí** there is pus in the knee-swelling.

vï = **zɔ̀, tsɔ̀, gbï**, vn. to grow up; **pätí vïvï** the tree is growing; **é 'bà óɳɔfí 'dï vïvï!** let the finger-nail grow! **vï** = **zŏpi ɛ̀zŏ** that grows tall.

vi, vt. to fling, hurl, toss, throw (with a sling); **óní vi-zŏ báká sì** to hurl a stone with a string-sling; (cf. **'bɛ** to throw with hand); **ɔzɔ́ɔ́-nï vïvi** rain is hurled along (by wind).

vï = **ɛ̀vï, wí**, n. gad- or bot-fly.

vï = **vítsó, àvá, kɔ̀rɛ**, n. strong desire, craving, longing, passion (after food, drink); **ií** (or **zá, ɛ́wá, ɛɳá...) ví fu ma kái** yearning for water (meat, beer, polenta...) fills/consumes me.

vínï, vïnï ɛ̀ndì, av. also, likewise; **ɛ̀ri emú vïnï ɛ̀ndì** or **ɛ̀ri vïnï emú ɛ̀ndì** he is coming also (in the end).

vítsó = **vï**, q.v.

vŏ, pstp. (1) to, at; **é mu mï ándríí** (=**àyià) vŏ!** go to your mother! **ɛ̀ri ɳaa 'ïmà ándré vŏ** he eats at his mother's; (2) to; **dzi tí vŏ-nï-á** he brought a cow to him; **Dzuv- fɛ̀ sìlíɳgì kàlí tääwí Gas- nï Dem- vŏ Dzuv-** consigned 50s. for Gas- to Dem-; **Zakaria fɛ̀ tí mání ópí-nï vŏ Z—** gave a cow to his chief for me; **mï ɛ̀fɛ̀ mání ńdrí àmbó vŏ sì!** give me a goat through the headman! (3) **vŏ sì**: (*a*) up to; **ɡa tré tinï vŏ sì** it was full to the brim; (*b*) **mà vŏ sì** on account of; **bï lŏ má ɛ'yó 'dà mà vŏ sì** they caught only me on account of that question; **ma emú ɛmï vŏ (lŏ) ɛ'yó ádzê-rï (mà vŏ) sì** I came to you (only) on account of the discussion of yesterday.

vo, vt. to despise, hold in contempt; **ɛ̀ri 'bâ vo àɳàpá** (or máali) sĭ he despises a man on account of his cattle (wealth); 'bá àfa berĭ èri 'bá àlĭio 'dĭ̈ vo (i.e. àfó sĭ) one provided with goods/a rich man despises the destitute/the poor ones (haughtiness); fàrìséò èri pùblìkánò vo the pharisee despises the publican.

vö, vt. (1) to blow; ma èdzèlèkô vö I am blowing a flute; ma àtsĭ ̣əvö ásé sĭ; mà ŋga àtsĭ èdô, ĭ̈ drĭ-zó I blow (glowing coal) into a flame by means of grass, then I kindle a (proper) fire to boil water; (2) órĭ vö (? 'bâ vö) to bless (with reference to the ancestors); èi órĭ vö 'bâ rùá a'ú sĭ they appeal to the ancestor-spirits for a man with a fowl (held by legs and swung round above the sick).

vò, vt. to cut (hew, strike, knock, bite) off; 'bá èi ámvú (or áisé) vô ŋgòlé (= pèrè) sĭ people cut the grass (of field, &c.) with a scythe; édró nĭ̈ ásé vô sí sĭ a mouse bites off grass (for its movements) with the teeth.

vɔ, vt. (1) to excavate—widen, enlarge space (from inside); èi 'bílê vɔ (= ndrɔ) àvò sa-ző they dig/widen the grave (at side of bottom of ordinary grave-chamber protected against earth falling in) to bury corpse in; but cf. èi 'bílé vă àvò sa-ző they dig (vertically only) a grave to bury a corpse; (2) to form a convex, exterior curvature; èi èrò (or dzó) mà 'alê vɔ they bulge the middle of wall of granary (of hut); əvə-zà see vəŋgərɔ.

vö, vösĭ = pálé, q.v. time or moment of reckoning; vö (-sĭ) sí? or vö sí yà? how many times? vö ssu or vösĭ ssu four times.

vəŋgərɔ = əvə-zà, a. convex or with exterior curvature; pá-nĭ̈ vəŋgərô-rö (= agó-zàrö) his legs form an O (cf. pá-nĭ̈ ədà-zàrö forming an X).

vù, vt. (1) to scrape, brush against; to graze over (with something hurting); élélu èri 'bá vŭ otsí sĭ the 'elelu' caterpillar brushes against a p. with its thorn-like hairs; (2) to strip a thing off; to strip off; èri pätí mà bbí vŭ drí sĭ he is stripping the leaves off a branch; kànì 'dő àróᵖrö, èi vŭ sí sĭ when eleusine is still tender/green, they strip a spike of its grains with the teeth (in mouth); (3) to scrape off; èi àŋgŏ drì vŭ ε'bó sĭ, èi àzínï ko tsĭ they scrape off the surface (of ground) with (longer pulls of) the hoe, leaving parts untouched (cf. əfă to scratch with simple cuts); (4) = əmì to massage, knead, rub; 'bá rùá (or àn̩ə̀, ərə̀) vŭ to knead fitly a p.'s body (fracture, stiffness); èi əkpərəvò vŭ drí sĭ, ədo sĭ (osi-ző) they massage a woman in labour with oil and hands (to assist birth).

vùrù-rö = ólĭ̈ŋgóló̂-rö, a. round.

vúti (1) n. the next; kànì àma èri bε yàá àlö, èri mà v—, ma əkɔ̀ if we two have one mother, he is the next, I the first; or (using the postpositional terms vúti-á, &c.) èri ma vúti-á, ma èri-drìléa he is after me, I before him; N.B. to follow a p.; 'bâ v— bĭ = mu or 'dε 'bá mà vúti-á (= -sĭ); (2)...mà vúti-á/v— sĭ (= véllé-á, véllé sĭ) postp. after, behind; in the absence of...; əzóó mà v—, i.e. əzóó-nĭ̈ àtĭ̈-ző 'bə rĭ sĭ after the rain, i.e. when the rain has ceased; etsá àkúa mà vútiá (= vélléá) he reached home in my absence; ǹdrí èri dzó mà vútiá (= ètíléa) the goat is behind (at the back of) the hut.

W

wàa¹= sàa, wè, vt./vn. to swim; èri wàá rö wàwà he is swimming; èri ǐí wǎ or èri 'ǐ wǎ ǐí-á he is swimming; mvá mu ǐí wǎ/or mu 'ǐ wǎ ǐí-á the boy went to swim.

wàa²= wàŋgì, ɛlí, n. year; wàa 'dǐ sǐ àŋá ka mádrí kö this year the corn did not do well for me.

waa¹, vn. (1) to be clean, smooth, glossy; 'ǐ drí waa àlá³rö his hands are very clean; aráǔ mà drí lè waa kö the Red Hussar monkey's hands would not become clean (fable); (2) to be fresh, sweet (milk); lésú wǎ, ŋgà zɔɔ ó'dí³rö rǐ the milk is fresh, it is freshly milked.

waa² = mba, vn. (fruits) to be fully developed (almost ripe); atsɛ were èrì dǐ 'yɛ nǐnï (=kàka)); à'bóà 'dǐ waa ŋgà kö... waa 'bə this banana bunch is not yet developed...is developed full-grown; waa-zà, a. full-grown; fully developed; mǐ egá à'bóà waa-zàrǐ'ǐ you have cut well-formed bananas; waa (= mba) rá, nï (= ka) ŋgà kö it is fully grown but not yet ripe.

waa³ = mbo, vn. (1) to jump (over sth.; àfa mà drìá (= drìlé) sǐ); é waa ǐí 'dǐ mà drìa sǐ! jump away over this river! (2) to run (jumping) off; vǐ tsï tí nǐ, èri ànï waa (= ndzo) the gad-fly has bitten the cow and it (cow) runs off.

waa⁴ = àtǐ, vn. to stop, cease; əzóó waa 'bə the rain has stopped.

wàa'dí, n. relations by marriage (beginning from one's wife or husband); mâ mu wàa'dí-á! let me go to my relations (by marriage) for a visit!

wáadzó = lésú-ǐí, n. buttermilk; 'bá lésú mà 'alê tsə wáadzó-rö 'ǐ; or lésú-ǐí: ədo-nï fó-zó 'aléníá 'bərǐ'ǐ they churn milk obtaining buttermilk; buttermilk: from which the butter has been taken; lésú-ǐí mà míró yə buttermilk is without cream.

waaka (cf. waa¹), a. smooth, polished.

wàakà-wàakà = wàndrò-wàndrò, a. hazily/vaguely reddish-brown; àdro-òrì èri w—w— the 'adro-ori' ochre is vaguely brownish; àŋgǒ 'dà ɛná wàakà that place there is misty-bright.

wàalà, a. ample, spacious; wide, large; dzó 'dà mà 'alé wàalà-rö that hut (-room) is spacious.

wàalá, n. side course moving in a circle; èì w— ndzo (or drə)/ =w— tǐ they (mostly a couple at a time) dance/jump aside (of the main group) describing a circle or ellipse.

wáláká, n. red soil ŋaakú ɛkarǐ.

wáalàkà = wàalàkà, n. small pot with wide opening; w— tíbí ŋaa-zórǐ'ǐ pot/plate for savoury.

wálàwálà = kàlákàlá = òré (2) q.v., watery.

wànoka, T. = lóòdè, n. stale cow urine (in bowl kéréa); tí kà ədré sǒ, èri mu kéré 'bǎ ədré-nï a'í-zó when a cow makes water, one places a bowl to collect the urine; 'bâ dí əmvɛ lóòdrè they call (such collected urine) lóòdrè or (elsewhere) w—.

'wàŋgàràkà (≈ əsɛ-əsɛ), a. extraordinarily voluminous, enormous, stout.

wàŋgì, n., see wàa², n.

'wàarà or 'wàarà-'wàarà, a. of great age, old; 'bá 'w— or mbàazà or also mbàazà 'w— much respected influential old persons of a community; 'bá (àkúa) 'w—'w— èì ɔmvɛ àmbónï the old people (of a village) are called elders, authorities; 'bá-nï ɔmvɛ mbàazàrö 'dïï drì-bbí ɔzɔfɔrɔ-rö whom they call mbàazà or 'w— have grey hair.

wàarà, n. cotton; èì w— mà ètï ɔfố ɛ'bó sï they dig/clean under the cotton (plants); w— 'du to take up/collect cotton.

wárà, n. tí wárà = tí wɔrɔ́tɔ cowdung.

wárá, T., same as bàbàlì, q.v., èì dzɔ́ tsɔ w— sï they make a hut ('s wall) with 'wara' sticks.

wàrà-wàrà = wàakà-wàakà, q.v.

wárágà, A.S. (Lgb. ɛbbíkɔ leaf), n. paper, copybook, &c.; cf. silíŋgì ɛbbíkɔ'rörï bank note.

wàri, n. the poisonous sap of Euphorbia media (ɔ́yá); ɔ́yá or kɛlɛdzuku: sú-nï mà rú wàri the sap/juice of E. media is called 'wari'; sú-nï 'bá ɛdé wàri'rö: èì w— tri 'yɛ́ mà rùá its sap they use as 'wari'; they rub 'wari' on arrows.

wárígï, árégè, ŋgúlì, n. foreign names for native brandy.

wàáta = àwatá, àwabà, àwaa, T., a. (cf. waa²) acid, sour, unripe; mòɛmbɛ̀ wàátá'rö, ɛri 'bâ sí erí-erí (= T. aɳú-aɳú) the mango is green, it sets one's teeth on edge.

wátsákàlá'rö, a. watery.

wè = sà, wà, vt./vn. to swim; cf. wà¹.

wɛ, vt. (1) to sweep; é wɛ àŋgò yɔ́fɛ́ (or ówɛrɛ) sï! sweep the ground with a broom; (2) to brush, wipe off.

wɛ́ = kpɛrɛ, av. as far as; ɛ̀gɔrɔ́kɔ̀ ɛri 'bílɛ̂ và wɛ́ ìí 'aléa the crab excavates a hole as far as the water; é nɛ̀ ma wɛ́ ŋgɔ́ yà? at what distance did you see me? (provocative question asked by pygmies; it has become their name).

wɛbɛlɛ, a. = ga ìí rö = ɔrɛ́, tsɔ́-rɔ́kɔlɔ́, q.v., watery.

wɛ́ɛkɛ̀ = wɛ́kɛ́á, tɛɛó, n. gourd-rattle of diviner; èì w— ya o'dúkó ezí-zố they shake the rattle to consult the voice (of spirits of deceased).

wɛrɛ, dim. wɛrɛ́á, a. small, little; few; in small quantity.

wï¹ = wu, q.v.

wï², T. = fï, vn. to grow/develop and 'ripen' (of tubers); 'bá kà gbándà saa, èì dï wï/= fï 'bílíalé when they plant manioc (or potato) twigs, these grow up; wï 'bɔ = wï ɔ'(w)íŋgíríkï(rö) it is fully developed.

wí = vï, n. tî wí gad-fly.

'wï = 'wu, 'ï, T., vn. (1) to dry; zâ 'wï ètú sï the flesh dried in the sun; mï òmvu-sï 'wï òrò (-òrò) the mucus in your nose dried; àŋgò 'wï-zàrö the ground is dry, parched; (cf. à'wï'rö); (2) to ripen (by hardening, as corn); àɳâ 'wï 'bɔ the corn is ripe; àɳâ 'wïpi 'wï'wï ripe corn (cf. nï, ka).

wì = wù (= wï, T.), vt. to spit (out, forth); á wì tùsú I spit; ɛ́dzíríkó èì ɳaakú wù/wì ti sï, ɛri ɛmvî ànï ɔ́tɔ́kɔ́'rö the termites spit earth with their mouth and build their hill with it; á wì tábà mà àtsíkà lɔ̈ɔ̈ I eject/blow out tobacco smoke in clouds.

wïa = kókórófà, órókófà, n. shinbone or tibia.

wïa-wïa = ndzɔa-ndzóa, óká (ŋgáliká), drazà, a. sharp, bitter; à'ï 'dòrï wïa-wïá²rö, alu kö; àdzí-nï ɘvi ŋgù (= ɡa) mà drìá kö; mà ŋaa wɛrɛá this salt is bitter, not pleasant; it does not suit my taste; I therefore take little.

wïkɘlí = wïkilí, ò'dúti-àrïïá, see ò'díti-àrïïá.

wïlékò-ètí, n. armpit.

wïlì = wïlïká, n. an arrow without barbs; 'yɛ w— só-nï yɘ the 'wili' w— (arrow) has no barbs.

wïlï (? preceding), n. 'yɛ w— arrow with long iron part, on shaft.

wïlíwïlí²rö, a. well distinct or visible although far down; ɛ'dá w—w—, i e èri ku-zàrö: ku vàálé ndrii it appears distinctly, while it is deep down (in hole, precipice).

wïò-rö, a. bent, inclined; (1) milénï w— he is squint-eyed; (2) èri mà ɘmbɛlɛkò wïòrö/= ɘmbɛlɛkò-nï atsó-atsó his neck/head is bent/inclined

wïïrï, av. in great abundance; ka w— it produced abundantly.

'wïrï, av. gulpingly; kï 'w— he swallowed a large mouthful; èri éwâ mvu 'wïrí'wïrí he drinks beer gulpingly.

wïtsí, wïtsïá, n. yellow wagtail; w— èri fɘrɘfɘrò the yellow wagtail is yellow (-greyish); etsá áŋú-fò-á it arrived at the time of blooming of the sesame; èri a'á tí páléa/èri kùlû ŋaa tí páléa it likes to follow cattle and eat grasshoppers.

wɘdɘ-wɘdò = òkáŋgáliká, a. ugly, repellent (of smell); bitter,

sour (taste) (of rotten, stale food, &c.).

wóɘkò = òóɘkò, n. (1) side, flank; mà w— drí edzía or drí ádàá on my left-hand or right-hand side; (2) ? part, piece of sth.

wóló (cf. ólù), n. croton plant; èi lítsó 'bɛ wóló sï they make a cattle pen (enclosure) by means of (growing) croton plants.

wóró = drïïá, tú, pïrï, indf. prn. all; everybody; everything.

wóróló = wóròló, a. transparent; threadbare; tíbí áŋú kókò-rö— èri wóròló²rö (thin) savoury without simsim oil is transparent.

wórótò = wárá, n. (cow)-dung; èi dzó rùá e'borà (or ɛdɛ̀) w— sï they plaster/(whitewash) the wall of a hut with cow-dung.

wù, ɘwù, vt. to collect; èi fúnò ɘwù dzi dà dzóa they collect (= ɘmvó) pignuts to bring and pour in the hut (cf. ùwù?).

wù = wì, q.v. to spit.

'wu = 'wï, q.v. to dry.

wu = wï, vt. (1) to skin, strip one's skin; flay; èri ndri enïrïkò wùwu he is stripping a goat's skin; (2) to (remove) bark; to shell, husk; ma pätí ógbórókò wu I skin a tree/ remove bark; ma kàïkó (ógbórókɘ) ɘwù I skin beans or also I remove beans from pods; wu rö to come off, to detach.

wùùlébè or ùwulébè (= àlí), n. agreement, concert; wùùlébè-rö in concert; to work in concert; é 'bà àfa 'dï ùwulébèrö yà? are you doing/starting this in agreement (with others; when everybody combines to beat, rob, or the like—somebody)? ma drà ùwulébè-rö ɛ'yó ma átíí véllérï mà ti-á I am sick/dying as a result/on account of my late father's actions.

wúrá, n. colour; **bə̀ŋgɔ́ mà wúránï 'bá milɛ́ àzà-àzà** the (bright) colour of the cloth dazzles one.

wúra-wúra, n. swift or black martin.

Y

ya,[1] vt. to move; (1) to shake; **ɔ́ədzɔ́ ɛ̀ri kə̀yə̀ ya** the sorcerer shakes the gourd-rattle; (2) to (give a) push, knock; **ya 'bá pá** (or **drí**) **sï** he pushed/knocked a p. with his foot (or fist); (3) to shake—rinse; **ɛ̀ri zú 'alɛ̂ ya lɔ̂dè sï** he shakes/rinses the inside of a calabash with cow urine; (4) to besprinkle, bespatter; **é ya ïf mà rùá à'do sï?** why do you spatter water on me? (5) vn. to shiver, tremble; **mà rùá-nï ya ɛ̀gbè sï** I am trembling from cold.

ya², vt. to select, pick out; **èi andzi mòpírà nï 'dïŕ yaa** (= **ə̀pɛ̌**) they pick out boys for football (game).

'ya = 'a, vt. ávâ 'ya to take breath; **ɛ̀ri ávâ 'ya** he takes breath.

'yà¹= 'à (q.v.), **vt.** to till, cultivate; **èi ámvú 'yǎ** they are cultivating the field.

'yà² = ɛ̀'yɛrɛ, av. slowly; **é ŋga àzí 'yà!** work slowly!

yàá = ài̇̀(y)íá, n. mother (intimate); **ma yàá (ài̇̀a, màmàá)!** my mother/mamma!

yàbbí, n. graminia; a good thatching grass (large long leaves, white bushy-woolly flower/often used like cotton); **èi dzɔ̂ tï y— sï** they thatch huts with 'yabbi' grass (cf. Ac. **òbía**).

yàkáni, n. name of a spirit (who takes possession of a p. shaking him and causing disease ...); **y—**

ɛ̀ri 'bá eya-eya; 'bá tí (or **a'úátá**) **li ànï** the 'yakani' shakes a p.; they sacrifice an ox (or cock) at it; **y— dzɔ́** shrine of the 'yakani' spirit; **'bá si ə̀drí sï ɛ̀rɔ́ ètía; èi y— ə̀wï ànï** they build a 'yakani' shrine with clay under a granary; they sacrifice to him.

yámákà, n. stomach (man, animal).

yávíɔ́à, n. a small kind of lizard.

'yɛ́ = 'ɛ́, T., n. arrow; **'yɛ́ mà òbïí: àrípá, bàlàmò?, gə̀əndɛ̀, òmí'yɛ́, ə̀'bariká, wïlí** various kinds of arrows; **ɛ̀ri 'yê gbï** he shoots an arrow. (N.B. Bow and arrow is the characteristic weapon of the Ma'di race; the use of spear and shield is unknown.)

'yɛ = 'ə, T., vt. (1) to do, make; **é 'yɛ mɔ́ké!** do it well! (or you have done it properly); **andzi 'yɛ́ àfa 'dï ə̀ndzí** the boys have done this badly; (2) = **ɛdé** to inflict, affect ...; **'yɛ mvá 'dà rùá ə̀ndzí** he harmed that child; **'yɛ kàlí sï** he beat him with a stick; **'yɛ ma sɔ̀ 'yɛ́ sï** he (evil-) pricked me with an arrow; (3) auxiliary verb of future (see Grammar, § 365).

'yɛ́ɛkè, av. well, all right; **é 'yə 'y—** you have spoken well.

yɛ́kiá = yákiá, n. large, brown, warlike ant; **ɛ̀ri 'bá tsïtsï** it bites one (painfully); going out looting (mostly on termites) in large processions they may attack fowls, a sheep ... leaving only the bones (ə̀tsi) behind.

yëla = ə̀rí, ɔ́lá, drì'báti, n. offspring, descendant; **ko 'ïmà y— rá yà?** has he (dying) left descendants? **èi Drìbbídu mà y—** they are descendants of Dribbidu (people of Tɛrɛgo origin); **Àríïá mà yïïlá** of Ariia descendants ... (Oluko).

yéndéyéndé=ndrindri, a. eka
y— dark red (àrí-lɛ́ like blood.)
yéndú commonly pálá, n. grown
plant with good fibre, its leaves
used as vegetable; èi y— (better
pálá) rï báká'rö, vínî ŋaa
tíbí'rö.
yéŋgèrékè = hàóhàó, a. of coarse,
rough surface (as a file, body with
itch).
yɛrɛ, n. waterbuck.
'yɛrɛ-'yɛrɛ = è'yɛrɛ, av. slowly,
calmly; mí atsí è'y—! walk
slowly!
yɛrɛo, n. the white counterpart of
black mànîà similar (this latter)
to black áníkắní.
yɨ̀, vt. (1) = 'bɛ to throw away; é
yɨ̀ àfa 'dɨ̀! throw this away! èi
bòrósó yɨ̀i a'ú nɨ́ they strew
about bòrósó beans for fowls;
(2) to kick; yɨ̀ ma pá sɨ̀ he kicked
me with his foot.
yɨ̀ríkáá, n. a kind of tiny finch
bird; ti-nï ɛka'rö, rúa-nï ɔ̀m-
ŋgbà-kɔ̀mŋgbà-rö it has a rose-
coloured beak (and breast?) and a
brownish body; èi a'ă óvérékó mà
'aléa éli sɨ̀; èi tra rö kárákàràrö
they prefer burned-down (grass)
places, during the dry season;
they collect in great numbers.
yɨ̀ìàrɨ̀, yɨ̀ìɔ̀rɨ̀, a. in first place;
ɔ̀kɔ̀ y— or kà y— the first; ma
'bá ɔ̀kɔ̀ y— I am the first; má
etsá mɨ́nɨ́ ɔ̀kɔ̀ I came/arrived
first/before you; 'bá etsápi má
vó ɔ̀kɔ̀rɨ̀ ŋgâ ŋaa nɨ̀ who arrives
first at my side, will eat/i.e. have
it.
yɨ̂yɨ́á, n. mosquito; yɨ̂yɨ́á-nï 'bá
tsɨ̀tsɨ̀ the mosquito bites man;
or y— 'bá ŋaápi éní sɨ̀ the gnats
which 'eat' people at night.
yɔ, def. v./av. there is/are not; no.
'yɔ = lö̀, vt. to speak, tell, say;

ɛ'yɔ̂ 'yɔ to speak, inform, tell
about; 'yɔ ɛ'yɔ́ ópí nɨ́ he told, informed, reported to the chief;
ɛ'yɔ́ word; discussion, speech;
question, cause; à'do ɛ'yɔ́ sɨ̀
(yà)? why? for what reason?
ɔ'yɔ́, vn. to talk much; discuss;
chatter.
'yò = dzò, T., n. snake poison;
gala'bá èri 'yò bɛ the 'gala'ba'
snake is poisonous.
yö¹ ≗ ɛmi, vn. to bask; warm oneself at...; àma ètû (or àtsî)
yö/= àma àma ɛmi ètúa (or
àtsɨ́a)(note the different constructions!) we are basking in the sun
(at the fire); à fɔ̌ à'iiɔ̀ yö! let us
go out to bask in the morning
sun!
yö² = zàa, mɔ̀ɔ, vt. to ease, allay,
assuage (pain); 'bá yö (= mɔ̀ɔ́) ii
àtsí sɨ̀ they ease pain (of any part
of body) by applying hot water
(directly or by means of leaves or
a cloth...); èri 'ïmà pâ yö pätí
kápi àtsɨ́árɨ̀ sɨ̀ he assuages his
(paining) leg with a piece of wood
warmed at fire (cf. ɔ̀mì).
yö³, vt. ... àfa mà tɨ̌ yö to lightly
roast (before grinding); èi ósó
(or kàíkɔ,àŋá, fúnò ...)mà tɨ̌ yö
àtsí sɨ̀ (òtáka mà 'aléa)/i.e. èi
osí rá ká/; èi àwǎ, èi 'bǎ a'dɨ̌
ndɔ̀; èi ɔ̀mvɛ àŋgàràbà (áŋú
nɔ̀sɨ̀ fúnò bɛ) they first roast
beans (grain, &c.) lightly on fire
(in a pot); then they crush/grind
it, and cook it (with water; simsim
or ground-nuts are often added);
it is called (in some parts) 'aga-ŋ
raba'; àŋá-nï ti ɔyö wɛrɛ (èri-
nï osí-zö wɛrɛ àtsɨ́a òtáka mà
'aléa) corn is lightly roasted.
yɔ̀ɔ́fɛ́ = yɔ́fɛ́, T., n. (1) a particular kind of delicate stemmed
mid-size grass; (2) better brooms

from the said grass; **andzi ɛkɔ́ àŋgɔ̀ y— sì** the children sweep the ground (hut) with a broom (Ac. **àléenê**).

yǒkö = àdǎti, amuti (q.v.), n. turn; **y— etsá mǐ drì-á** the turn has come upon you; **èi àzî ŋga y— sì** they do work by turns/ alternately.

yɔ̀kɔ̀-yɔ̀kɔ̀ (cf. **kɔ̀yɔ̀kɔ̀yɔ̀**), av. loosely (tied), shaky, not firmly/ tightly.

yòmà = òmɔ̀kɔ́, n. ill-feeling, hatred, enmity; **àma mǐ bɛ yòmà-á** I have/harbour a grudge against you.

yòmàlà, (A.S.=yom Alla God's day), n. Sunday, feast-day; **mǐ emú yòmàlàá yà?** are you coming to the Sunday service?

yɔ̀ɔpi = àmbó, áŋgírí, av. of (comparatively) great quantity; **ndǐ y— ko máńí wɛrɛ** he (eating) pinched off large bits, leaving little for me; **mvá 'dà ŋaa ɛ́ŋá y—, ko 'ïmà ádríí nǐ wɛrɛ** that boy ate polenta by large bits and left little for his brother.

yùu, av. lukewarm; **ïi tə (= drï, dù) yùu** the water is slightly warmed up; **àtsí kà drï 'alénǐá wɛrɛ, ïi tə yùu** if the fire burns only a little under it, the water is lukewarm.

yúdù, n. the tuft of feathers on head of **yúkúdù** is called **y—**: **yúkúdù mà 'bíkə èi əmvɛ y—**.

yúkú, n. milvus or kite (Ac. **abiba**); **y— 'du/bǐ a'ú** the milvus carried off a fowl.

yúkúdù, n. the caucal bird; **yúkú-dùdù**, n. its characteristic cry; **yúkúdù mà èlo**, i.e. **yúdù** the tuft of feathers on head of caucal.

Z

zá = èzá, T., n. flesh; meat; **zá-kálán̪á**, i. e. **zá fàlá-kɔ́kɔ̀ʾrö** boneless meat.

záa = záa-mvá, záa-ŋgá, zǎäpi, zéepi, zíipi, pl. **ézó, ézó-andzi, ɔ̀kó-andzi,** n. daughter; girl; **mǎ zǎ̀ä** or **mǎ zíi** my daughter.

za, T. = zə, q.v., vt. to milk.

zà, vt. (1) = **dɔ̀** to sting, prick; **àn̪ú-nï 'bá zǎzà** bees sting man; (2) = **ɛvé** to burn, bake (earthenware); **èi ɛ́mvó zǎ/ɛvé àtsí sì** they bake pots in fire; (3) to iron (cloth); **ma bɔ̀ŋgɔ́ zǎ pásì sì** I am ironing the cloth with a pressing-iron.

-zà (-rö) formative suffix of verbal adjectives; **ïi ambí-zàrï** cold water; **àfa ŋaa-zà-rï** something to eat, i.e. food (cf. Grammar, § 596).

zàarà, T. = zɔ̀ɔrà, q.v.

zè = dàaká, wárà, n. dirt, filth, excrements; **zè zɛ** to void, evacuate; **mu ásé-á zè zɛ** he went aside/into the grass to evacuate; **é zɛ zè dzóa kö!** do not defecate in the hut! **zè tɛ** to break wind; **zèlé, T. (= ǹdú, ètï)** anus, posterior; lower part of....

zɛ, vt. (1) to push, shove; **é zɛ ma à'do sì yà?** why did you push me? **ma dzótilé òpǐ, òlǐ kà mu-zǒ ɛzé kö** I am shutting the door, lest the wind slams/bangs it; **kànì kǎmì lè mu tî tsï, èri 'bíkɔ̌ zɛ 'ǐ drìá 'dálé** when a lion is about to attack a cow, it raises its (head-) hair; (2) **zɛ** in **zè zɛ** to void (see above).

zèmbùrúkú = òzúmŋgbúrúkú, q.v.

zètoma, n. **pá mà zètoma** sole of the foot.

zì,¹ vt. (1) = ndzì to open; é zì dzɔ́tilé rá! do open the door! ma kàáti zìzì I am opening the door; (2) to lay open, extend, take/break asunder; 'bá kà 'aléni̇̀ zì pätí-á sì̇̀ èri àtsí mà 'alé zì—yɵ̂yö when they lay out the pieces of wood, they spread the fire for basking at it; (3) to till roughly; èì ámvú zì ɛ'bó sì̇̀ they rough-dig (or break) the ground (in preparation for cultivation).

zì², vt. (1) to hide (away), conceal; é zì àfa mádrí mùu à'do sì̇̀ yà? why have you hidden my things so thoroughly? à zì àma drì-ndzá sì̇̀ we hid out of shame; (2) to cover over; to put into; èri màäkò zì (= sö) àtsí-á he pushes potatoes into (under) the fire (for roasting).

zì³ = ga/gä, vt. to startle; zì/gä sí wääli he showed up his full teeth startlingly; ɔ̀vï̀ zì/gä nɛɛ/or wääli it lightened frightningly.

zì, vt. (1) to ask; á zì ɛ'yɔ́ 'bá mà tii-á I asked/consulted a p. about sth.; emú ɛ'yɔ̂ zi mà̇̀ ti-á he came to consult me; (2) to petition; é zi mání silíŋgì ɔ́pí vɵ̌! /or é zi mání ɔ́pí-ni̇̀ mà èfè mání silíŋgì! ask/solicit the chief to give me shillings!/ask for shillings for me at the chief's; é zi mì̇̀ ándríi ní ɛ̀ŋá sì̇̀ ask your mother for polenta! (3) to greet; é zi mì̇̀ tsìtsí! lit. ask yourself fitly! (= how are you?); é sì̇̀ mì̇̀ ádríi mà zi 'ï tsìtsí! write to greet your brother/lit. write that your brother may himself ask properly!

zzìrì = rrè, av. far, distant; àŋgɵ̀ zzìrì it is far.

zɔ̀¹, vn. to grow up (man, animal); mu zɔ̀ 'bá àzí-ni̇̀-rí (or 'ï díi-rí) àmbó²rö he went to be brought up at sby.'s (or at his grandmother's); ɔ̀líïá tsa zɔ̀-zɵ̌ 'bù-á 'dálé kö the 'ɔliia' shrub cannot grow up very high; mvá zɔ̀ 'bɔ the boy has grown up well; ɔ̀fífíá zɔ̀ mï̀ milé-ti-á àmbó²rö (or èzɵ̂rö) large pimples have come out on your face.

zɔ̀², vn. to attack, assail fiercely/suddenly; to pounce upon (drìá); ɔ̀'dó zɔ̀ 'bá drìá a leopard suddenly attacked a man; ɔ̀bálákɵ́ zɔ̀ a'ú drìá a jackal pounced suddenly upon a fowl.

zö, vn. (1) to suffer labour pains (human, animal); ɔ̀kó-ni̇̀ zɵ̂zö (or mvâ zö) èri mu osi rá the woman is down with labour pains, she will give birth; (2) to groan, moan; sigh; 'bá zö àzɔ́ sì̇̀ sby. groans from illness; (3) vt. àyìkɔ̀ zö (= 'bä) to rejoice.

zo = ndè, vt. to bewilder, disconcert, confuse, perplex; ɛ'yɔ́ 'dì̇̀ zo ma rá this matter bewilders me.

zə¹ = za, T., vt. (1) to milk; mu tí lésû zə /seldom mu tî zə he went to milk a cow; lésû zəlɛ̀ zə-rì̇̀ (= lésû zɵ́ 'bə-rì̇̀) kɵ̌ nì̇̀ the milk they have milked (recently) is coagulating; (2) to strain (beer); èri éwâ zə áŋû-ba sì̇̀ she is straining beer with a strainer (special basket).

zə², vt. (1) to wade across; ford; mà mù zə kìdzíá sì̇̀ I shall go to wade across the river at the landing place (port); èrì zə ìí-ti 'áá 'dá sì̇̀ he is wading yonder on the riverside; zə ìí pá (or ɔ́'bə) sì̇̀ he crossed the river on foot (with boat); (2) to go over (crossing a vale or the likè); zə (or atsí) Árúwá he went over to Arua; zə 'áá lɔ̀ he passed over there.

zǒ, cj. for, for the purpose of; to (cf. Grammar, §§. 481 ff.).

zòzò = rèrè, av. far, distant; **àŋgǒ àmadrí-rǐ zòzò** (= rè 'dálέ) our home country/district is far.

zölöŋgö, a. of rough, lumpy surface; **'bá kà έ ἀ drì òmǐ kö, èri adri zölöŋgö²rö** if they do not smooth (duely) the surface of the polenta (with hands, for serving), it(-s surface) will look rough.

zòŋgòrökò = búlàí, n. a large beetle (feedimg on bean flower petals); **z— èri kàíkɔ fǒ ἀáápi-rǐ, nò bǒrǒsǒ fǒ òlǔpi-rǐ** the beetle 'zoŋgoroko' eats bean flowers or causes lentils' flowers to fall off.

zǒrà, av. in great quantity; **mǐ έ ἀ tǐ zǒrà** you pinch off (at meal) (relatively) too large bits of polenta.

zòɔrà, av. divergent (**sí sǐ nòsì ɔ'yó sǐ** said of teeth or horns); **èwá mà sí z—** the elephant's teeth point/go off sideways; **'bá àzǐ mà sí fǒpi z—** some p.s' teeth stick out prominently.

zǒrǒ = trέ (q.v.), av. crammed full (of receptacle); **à ἀ ga èró sǐ z—** the corn fills the granary fully.

zù, zùu, av. always, constantly; regularly, every day; **àma ɔ'á 'dòá zùuu ... (o'dú pǐrǐ)** we are (come) here regularly/every day; **andzi èi emú mǐ vέllέ (or vǒ) zùuu** the boys come every day to you.

zú = kέrɛ, n. a kind of gourd-bottle; **zú ìí ɛbɛ-zǒ (ìí-á)** a gourd-bottle for drawing water (in the river).

zúkùlú, T. = **zú(ǎ), kέrɛ,** n. same as above.